Modern China

MODERN CHINA

Xiaobing Li

Understanding Modern Nations

An Imprint of ABC-CLIO, LLC
Santa Barbara, California • Denver, Colorado

Copyright © 2016 by ABC-CLIO, LLC

Library of Congress Cataloging-in-Publication Data

Names: Li, Xiaobing, 1954-
Title: Modern China / Xiaobing Li.
Description: Santa Barbara, California : ABC-CLIO, 2015. | Series:
    Understanding modern nations
Identifiers: LCCN 2015023735| ISBN 9781610696258 (hardback) |
ISBN 9781610696265 (ebook)
Subjects: LCSH: China. | BISAC: SOCIAL SCIENCE / Ethnic Studies /
    Asian American Studies.
Classification: LCC DS706 .L4843 2015 | DDC 951—dc23 LC record available at
http://lccn.loc.gov/2015023735

ISBN: 978-1-61069-625-8
EISBN: 978-1-61069-626-5

20 19 18 17 16   2 3 4 5

This book is also available on the World Wide Web as an eBook.
Visit www.abc-clio.com for details.

ABC-CLIO
An Imprint of ABC-CLIO, LLC

ABC-CLIO, LLC
130 Cremona Drive, P.O. Box 1911
Santa Barbara, California 93116-1911

This book is printed on acid-free paper ∞
Manufactured in the United States of America

CONTENTS

SERIES FOREWORD

We live in an evolving world, a world that is becoming increasingly globalized by the minute. Cultures collide and blend, leading to new customs and practices that exist alongside long-standing traditions. Advancing technologies connect lives across the globe, affecting everyone, from those in densely populated urban areas to those who dwell in the most remote locations in the world. Governments are changing, leading to war and violence but also to new opportunities for those who have been oppressed. The *Understanding Modern Nations* series seeks to answer questions about cultures, societies, and customs in various countries around the world.

Understanding Modern Nations is geared toward readers wanting to expand their knowledge of the world, ideal for high school students researching specific countries, undergraduates preparing for studies abroad, and general readers interested in learning more about the world around them. Each volume in the series focuses on a single country, with coverage on Africa, the Americas, Asia and the Pacific, and Europe.

Each country volume contains 16 chapters focusing on various aspects of culture and society in each country. The chapters begin with an Overview, which is followed by short entries on key topics, concepts, ideas, and biographies pertaining to the chapter's theme. In a way, these volumes serve as "thematic encyclopedias," with entries organized for the reader's benefit. Following a general Preface and Introduction, each volume contains chapters on the following themes:

- Geography;
- History;
- Government and Politics;
- Economy;
- Religion and Thought;
- Social Classes and Ethnicity;
- Gender, Marriage, and Sexuality;
- Education;
- Language;
- Etiquette;
- Literature and Drama;

- Art and Architecture;
- Music and Dance;
- Food;
- Leisure and Sports; and
- Media and Popular Culture.

Each entry concludes with a list of cross references and Further Readings, pointing readers to additional print and electronic resources that might prove useful.

Following the chapters are appendices, including "A Day in the Life" feature, which depicts "typical" days in the lives of people living in that country, from students to farmers to factory workers to stay-at-home and working mothers. A Glossary, Facts and Figures section, and Holidays chart round out the appendices. Volumes include a Selected Bibliography, as well as sidebars that are scattered throughout the text.

The volumes in the *Understanding Modern Nations* series are not intended to be comprehensive compendiums about every nation of the world, but instead are meant to serve as introductory texts for readers, examining key topics from major countries studied in the high school curriculum as well as important transitioning countries that make headlines daily. It is our hope that readers will gain an understanding and appreciation for cultures and histories outside of their own.

NOTE ON TRANSLITERATION

The *hanyu pinyin* Romanization system is applied to Chinese names of persons, places, and terms. A person's name is written in the Chinese way, surname first, such as Mao Zedong. Some popular names have traditional Wade-Giles spellings appearing in parentheses after the first use of the *hanyu pinyin* in the entry, such as Mao Zedong (Mao Tse-tung), as do popular names of places like the Yangzi (Yangtze) River, Huang (Yellow) River, and Guangzhou (Canton). Exceptions are made for a few figures, whose names are widely known in reverse order like Sun Yat-sen (Sun Zhongshan, or Sun Yixian), and Chiang Kai-shek (Jiang Jieshi); and a few places and institutional names, such as Tibet (Xizang) and Peking (Beijing) University.

ABBREVIATIONS

ABC	Agricultural Bank of China
ACFTU	All-China Federation of Trade Unions
BNU	Beijing Normal University
BOC	Bank of China
CASS	Chinese Academy of Social Sciences
CBA	Chinese Basketball Association
CBC	China's Bank of Communication
CBRC	China Banking Regulatory Commission
CCB	China's Construction Bank
CCP	Chinese Communist Party
CCTV	China Central Television
CCYL	Chinese Communist Youth League
CDB	China Development Bank
CDC	Center for Disease Control
CECC	Congressional Executive Commission on China (U.S. Congress)
CFA	Chinese Football Association
CIB	China Investment Bank
CIEB	China Import and Export Bank
CIRC	China Insurance Regulatory Commission
CJV	Cooperative Joint Venture
CMC	Central Military Commission (CCP)
CMP	Commune Medical Program
CNOOC	China National Offshore Oil Corporation
CNPC	China National Petroleum Corporation
CPBS	Central People's Broadcasting Station
CPG	Central People's Government
CPPCC	Chinese People's Political Consultative Conference
CRI	China Radio International
CSRC	China Securities Regulatory Commission
EJV	Equity Joint Venture
FCCC	Foreign Correspondents' Club of China
FDI	Foreign Direct Investment

FICLBS	Foreign Investment Companies Limited by Shares
FIE	Foreign-Invested Enterprise
GAPP	General Administration of Press and Publications
GATT	General Agreement on Trade and Tariff
GDP	Gross Domestic Production
GI	*Global Insight*
GIP	Government Insurance Program
GMD	Guomindang (Chinese Nationalist Party, or Kuomintang, KMT)
GNP	Gross National Product
GSD	General Staff Department (PLA)
GVIO	Gross Value of Industrial Output
GZAR	Guangxi Zhuang Autonomous Region
HPRS	Household Production Responsibility System
HQ	Headquarters
IAU	Immediate Action Unit
ICBC	Industrial and Commercial Bank of China
ICBM	Intercontinental Ballistic Missile
ICFI	Investment Companies through Foreign Investors
ICPS	Independent Chinese Pen Society
IMAR	Inner Mongolia Autonomous Region
IMF	International Monetary Fund
IMPP	Inner Mongolian People's Party
IPR	Intellectual Property Rights
ISO	International Standardization Organization
KMT	Kuomintang (Chinese Nationalist Party, or Guomindang, GMD)
LAC	Line of Actual Control
LIP	Labor Insurance Program
MFN	Most Favored Nation
MIA	Ministry of Internal Affairs
MII	Ministry of Information Industry
MNC	Multinational Corporation
MOE	Ministry of Education
MOH	Ministry of Health
MPS	Ministry of Public Security
NCEE	National College Entrance Examination
NGO	Nongovernmental Organization
NHAR	Ningxia Hui Autonomous Region
NPC	National People's Congress
PAP	People's Armed Police
PBC	People's Bank of China
PKU	Peking University
PLA	People's Liberation Army
PLAAF	PLA Air Force
PLAN	PLA Navy

POE	Privately Owned Enterprise
PPP	Purchasing Power Parity
PRC	People's Republic of China
RFA	Radio Free Asia
RMB	*Renminbi* (Chinese currency)
ROC	Republic of China
RTL	Reeducation Through Labor
SAC	Second Artillery Corps (PLA's strategic force)
SAR	Special Administrative Region
SARS	Severe Acute Respiratory Syndrome
SEZ	Special Economic Zone
SinoPEC	Sino Petroleum Chemical Corporation
SIPO	State Intellectual Property Office
SOE	State-Owned Enterprise
SSE	Shanghai Stock Exchange
STD	Sexually Transmitted Disease
SWAT	Special Weapons and Tactics
SZSE	Shenzhen Stock Exchange
TAR	Tibet Autonomous Region
UN	United Nations
UNESCO	United Nations Educational, Scientific, and Cultural Organization
UNHRC	United Nations Human Rights Commission
USIA	U.S. Information Agency
WFOE	Wholly Foreign Owned Enterprise
WFTU	World Federation of Trade Union
WHO	World Health Organization
WIPO	World Intellectual Property Organization
WTO	World Trade Organization
WWII	World War II
XUAR	Xinjiang Uyghur Autonomous Region

PREFACE

China represents one of the oldest civilizations in the world with a recorded history of 5,000 years. Based on its unique geographic setting, demographic characteristics, and political structure, Chinese culture evolved gradually from its prehistory and ancient age, through the classic period, Middle Age, and modern times. China has evolved, becoming a modernized country in the late 20th and early 21st centuries. China is rising, and in 2011 it became a world superpower with the second largest economy in the world, following only the United States.

Modern China examines this tremendous transformation and recent experience by detailing the most important and influential people, events, cultural phenomena, and international relations behind the country's modernization. It demonstrates how this third-world country developed into a world superpower in less than 30 years, and explains crucial factors, sources, and conditions for the modernization of a nation like China. This book adopts a general format consisting of overviews on 16 topics, including geography, economy, government, religion and thought, society and ethnicity, education, literature, arts, gender, sexuality, leisure, sports, food, media and popular culture, and days in the life of different Chinese people, followed by nearly 200 entries related to these topics. It provides an overview of civilization, institution, tradition, and international relations that have shaped today's China. The book covers Chinese politics, business, military, culture, and laws that have contemporary relevance. A multidisciplinary work such as this addresses a variety of current issues such as political control, human rights, corruption, the one-child policy, pollution, and civil liberties.

This volume offers a comprehensive resource on modern China, including complete coverage of ideologies from classic Confucianism in 2500 BCE to current communism and nationalism; balanced views of progress and major issues such as poverty, the one-child policy, and the death penalty; and comparison of Chinese standards with Western and American values. Each entry provides a brief history of the topic with a solid, up-to-date foundation for learning about the Chinese system in an accessible, engaging manner. Readers can quickly grasp China's past and will understand the ongoing problems and costs of the modernization of the most populous, as well as one of the largest, country in the modern world. This volume includes a one-of-a-kind "A Day in the Life" feature, which looks into inner circles of Chinese citizens, including farmers, soldiers, workers, students, and housewives, who have defined Chinese characteristics and changed personalities from, for instance, a traditional Chinese man to a modern global citizen throughout its history. The facts and figures, a glossary of key terms, and selected bibliography also provide useful reference tools and available resources for further reading and research.

Modern China expands conventional encyclopedias that are focused on factual information. It provides not only a broad, chronological account of China's modernization, but also addresses Chinese values, concepts, and attitudes regarding social transition and economic growth. All entries are placed within a broad sociopolitical and socioeconomic contextual framework, indicating the Chinese approach to modernization. All the entries are written by one author who lived in China for 30 years. The consistency through the book reflects a Chinese perspective, and an insider's view, offering a better understanding of complicated policies and identifying several general patterns according to China's own logic in its modernization. The book provides enlightening information for those who study Modern China, or are interested in the general topic of Asian Studies.

The completion of this volume on such an important subject requires not only strong support from American universities, but also close cooperation with academic institutes in China. I am grateful to Niu Jun, Zhang Pengfei, Yang Kuisong, Yang Dongyu, Yu Qun, Liu Yue, and Chinese scholars at the China Academy of Social Sciences (CASS), China Society for Strategy and Management (CSSM), Peking (Beijing) University, East China Normal University, Northeast China Normal University, and Shaanxi Normal University, for their help and advice on my research in China. This volume is also supported by "Fundamental Research Funds for the Central Universities" (Project #15JNYH006), under Professor Zhang Weizhen at Ji'nan University, Guangzhou, Guangdong.

Many people at the University of Central Oklahoma (UCO) have contributed to this volume and deserve recognition. First, I thank President Don Betz, Provost John F. Barthell, Associate Vice President Gary Steward, Assistant Dean of the College of Liberal Arts Jessica Sheetz-Nguyen, and Chairperson of the Department of History and Geography Patricia Loughlin. They have been very supportive of the project over the past three years. The UCO faculty merit-credit program sponsored by the Office of Academic Affairs, as well as travel funds from the College of Liberal Arts, provided funding for our research and trips to conferences. The UCO Student Research, Creative, and Scholarly Activities (RCSA) grants sponsored by the Office of High-Impact Practices, made student research assistants available for the project during the past years. Special thanks go to author Beverly Rorem, who edited all entries. Annamaria Martucci provided secretarial assistance. Several graduate and undergraduate students at UCO contributed to the book, including Yatian Gan, Yue Guo, Jacob Jeffery, Xiao Xiao, Lingling You, and Bruce Hanqing Zhang.

I also wish to thank Kaitlin Ciarmiello, Senior Acquisitions Editor at ABC-CLIO, who patiently guided this project for the past three years. Any remaining errors of facts, language usage, and interpretation are my own.

Xiaobing Li

INTRODUCTION

China has become a global superpower, the second largest economy in the world, following only the United States. By 2010, the People's Republic of China (PRC) also became the world's biggest energy consumer and the world's largest consumer market in 2014, surpassing the United States for the first time. IMF (International Monetary Fund), *GI (Global Insight)*, and *Oxford Economics* project the annual economic growth rates of the PRC to be about 6.2 percent in 2014, 6.5 percent in 2015, and 6.8 to 7.4 percent in 2016. The leaders of these two economic powers agree that the United States-China relationship is the most important international relationship in the 21st century. Xi Jinping, president of China in 2012–2022, signaled "a new type of great-power relationship" when he met President Barack Obama in the United States in June 2013. In 2014 President Obama called for a better understanding of China and promised that the U.S. government and American schools are dedicating more resources to understanding China.

Few research cases on national modernization pose more difficulties than the PRC, primarily because the Chinese Communist Party (CCP) is still the state's dominant political party and still controls the mass media. The contrasting institution and unique experience developed during recent years stand out among the factors that differentiate China from other modern nations in East Asia, such as Japan and South Korea. How can we hope to understand the modernization of a communist state? What is the difference between traditional China and the new China as a superpower? What are some key factors behind China's rapid evolution or transformation in the 1980s through the 2010s? What does all this mean to the United States? The goal of this book is to find answers to these puzzling and perhaps seemingly incomprehensible questions, and to map out China's modernization. Those who have these crucial questions will find this book informative and an excellent resource as a handbook to provide the answers. Readers will learn important facts that have never before been presented in one volume. Other titles on the same topic have overlooked the complex nature of the tremendous changes in China during the past 30 years. Using comprehensive coverage to create a broad and solid foundation of knowledge, this volume presents a practical approach and a Chinese perspective of their values, interests, attitudes, and concerns for a better understanding of modern China.

First, the book examines China's industrialization, modernization, and social transition by moving away from conventional frameworks, such as historical experiences of Western countries or of Eastern countries such as Japan and South Korea as a frame of reference, or a traditional analysis of changes in a linear fashion with two opposing ends, such as reformers vs. conservatives, or communists vs. liberals. Instead, this book adopts an objective analysis approach and challenges classical as well as established interpretations. Basing its narrative and explanations entirely on the various realities in China during the reform era, it provides new interpretations of reality rather than attempting to press reality into the established analytical mode or to wait for future developments to fit into the current interpretative framework, which may in fact be out of date. It shows China's development differently, as well as deviant from mainstream world trends and international standards. Few countries in history have successfully achieved such tumultuous transformation while under the uncertain circumstances that China has faced.

Second, it describes the economic and political changes as a significant and permanent evolution of Chinese institutions, or modernization with Chinese characteristics. It means that the current abnormalities are not merely aberrations, nor are they temporary and transitional in nature, as some scholars have said, opining that they were bound to give way to the "normal" patterns of progress and Western-style modernization. Unlike Japan's Meiji transformation in the mid-19th century, China is being forced to undergo wholesale reforms that are, to a great extent, led by the elite and by citizens who have become knowledgeable about the world community and are vocal in their wishes and desires. Clearly, the new interpretation in this volume indicates a unique experience of China's modernization, which certainly does not mean all the changes are positive or the entire transformation was successful. The volume attempts to be value-free, leaving it to readers to make their own judgment.

Third, the book identifies three key elements behind China's modernization in the 1980s–2000s. The first element is human resources available for new economic growth, social transition, and political changes, including the changes in the CCP membership. The CCP, no longer a poor people's party, is willing to recruit professionals and the middle class into the party. The emergence of new social groups demands a major social transition by increasing the membership of the party while making significant changes. The CCP has become more flexible and able to adapt to economic and social changes and to respond to rising demands and expectations of society in the 21st century. The second element indicates there is social pressure outside the party on political reform, including lagging technology, poor living standards, lack of education, and an authoritarian government within society. To create a modern nation, it must build a confident and democratic society, and this will not be possible without drastically improving China's political system. The third necessary element is the way the government compromised for difficult changes while shaping both Chinese attitude and an international view toward China. These elements are crucial for economic growth, social stability, national interests, security concerns, and international relations.

All three elements—Chinese resources, social problem solving, and adaptation and flexible policy—describe unique characteristics of the Chinese experience in modernization. Their continuous efforts in economic globalization and domestic urbanization contradict the standard image in the West concerning Chinese reform at the turn of the century as a period of reactive behavior, anxiety, and self-doubt. Chinese leaders did not appear to feel the need to make an either/or choice between traditional Chinese ideas and modern Western ones. Reports on current leaders who found themselves swept away by a hegemonic "nationalist discourse" were exaggerated, as the conventional accounts that the reform period often suggested. These assumptions seem misleading, as to some extent 19th-century expansionism, including that of the Russians and the Japanese, helped engender variations of reform movements and "nationalism," causing some Chinese leaders to question inherited values as well as leading to avocation of rapid "modernization."

This volume provides a different interpretation in which a balanced examination between social and political history defines unique characteristics of modern China, from its top leaders to ordinary people. These characteristics, not the same as Eastern traditional ones, or as Western modern ones, are unique Chinese characteristics that balance between tradition and modernization. In the near future, Chinese leaders will continue to act effectively as the CCP, so that they can maintain their domination and independence and have an impact when their concerns and interest converge with those in the system. Whether or not political leaders of the new generation will eventually be accepted by the government and people as leading actors, they will shape or reshape domestic and foreign policies.

Nevertheless, Xi Jinping and his party have some limits. Since his new leadership will not abandon one-party politics or the deliberate approach that previous generations of the CCP leaderships had employed for economic reform, the PRC may forever lag behind Western societies in terms of democracy and civil liberties, and may keep its modernization totally dependent on economic success and military support. Any economic recession or financial crisis will slow down or stop China's social transition and political modernization. Chinese analysts worry about the country's macro-economic instability and problems such as unemployment, limited natural resources, energy costs and price hikes, a weak financial system, state-owned enterprises (SOEs), and a decline of foreign investment. Even though these serious challenges will not occur simultaneously, occurrence of some of the problems is certain and may cause serious problems in the country's economy. Some Western analysts are concerned that these problems may lead to a more aggressive foreign policy or even to military expansionism.

To keep the CCP in power, a continuing coalition between the People's Liberation Army (PLA) and the CCP seems necessary for Beijing. President Xi Jinping's vision for a "strong military" may become government policy for China's further development in 2013–2022. To achieve a modern military in a new time, it is important to build on the PLA's long and rich traditions and to preserve them in innovative ways. The PLA needs to follow the fundamental principle and system of absolute Party leadership over the armed forces. In other words, the PLA should support the Xi administration by showing loyalty to the Party Center. The ranks and files should accept Party authority, as well as value social harmony, sharing ideas, and living with them as social norms. The PLA still belongs to the Party, since the latter controls the resources and personnel management for military budgets and professional careers under current leadership. The Party Center can channel the military elite interests and individual consciousness, prejudice, and conflict of the rank and file through the existing strong political institution. These activities are still within the boundaries of the Party Center's preference and control. In the meantime, the PLA should also provide new military capabilities for this policy since there are serious disharmonious factors and unstable elements in China, as well as in the rest of the world. As we know, in the past two decades, disparity in wealth, unsettled social political infrastructure, and international conflicts has resulted in a new set of uncertainties and challenges for China's sustained development.

Perhaps the most important factor, and most effective for the long term, is the significant improvement in China's international standing related primarily, but not exclusively, to a reduction in global and regional threats of conflict. Chinese strategic analysts and military experts hold an optimistic view of current national security and opportunities in the near future. While factors of insecurity and instability remain, they enjoy a favorable surrounding security environment, something seldom seen since the founding of the PRC. It seems possible for the PLA to avoid a major war for a fairly long period of time. The relaxation is still the general trend in the international security situation. If present trends continue, there will be more opportunities and challenges, as well as more hopes and difficulties, for the PLA.

Yet the new leadership will seek a growing role on the global political stage while assuring the international community that China does not pursue a policy of military and political hegemony in a conventional sense. The world community may be willing to accept China as a counterbalance to the United States or Japan. However, while China is repositioning itself by creating new gravity and critical mass in the Asia-Pacific region, there are potential problems for its new demands and needs. A possible source of crisis may come from highly sensitive and increasingly dangerous issues such as Taiwan's independence, the disputed territory between China and Japan, and the islands in the South China Sea. In a broader, historical perspective, China's foreign policy will be driven or directed not necessarily by communist ideology, but by a Chinese nationalism that has been in the making since 1949. The PLA must develop its own theory and tactics of modern warfare to deal with a possible national crisis. New theories and tactics should be based on a new international environment and on China's need for ongoing development. China, for certain, will continue its reforms and will face new challenges under the new CCP leadership in the 21st century. Whatever happens in the coming years, we feel certain, will have a tremendous impact on the future of the Chinese Communist Party, and on the country of China, as well as the whole world.

Xiaobing Li

CHINA

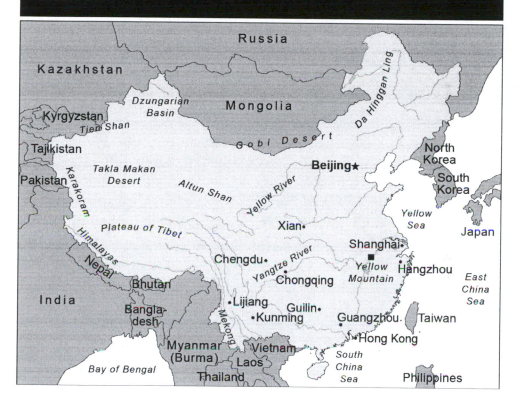

Russia

Kazakhstan

Mongolia

Dzungarian Basin

Da Hinggan Ling

Gobi Desert

Kyrgyzstan

Tien Shan

Tajikistan

Takla Makan Desert

Altun Shan

Yellow River

Beijing★

North Korea

South Korea

Pakistan

Karakoram

Yellow Sea

Japan

Plateau of Tibet

Xian•

Himalayas

Shanghai•

Nepal

Chengdu•

Yangtze River

Yellow Mountain

Hangzhou

East China Sea

Bhutan

Chongqing

India

Bangla-desh

•Lijiang

Guilin•

Guangzhou•

Taiwan

•Kunming

Mekong

•Hong Kong

Myanmar (Burma)

Vietnam

Laos

South China Sea

Philippines

Bay of Bengal

Thailand

CHAPTER 1

GEOGRAPHY

OVERVIEW

Located on the eastern part of the continent of Asia and bordered by the Pacific Ocean on the west, China is the fourth largest country in the world with a total area of 3.69 million square miles, slightly smaller than the United States. It has a land boundary of 12,000 miles, bordering with 14 countries, including North Korea to the east; Russia, Mongolia, Kazakhstan, Kyrgyzstan, and Tajikistan to the north, northeast, and northwest; Afghanistan, Pakistan, India, Nepal, and Bhutan to the west and southwest; and Vietnam, Laos, and Myanmar (Burma) to the south. Its southeastern coast faces the Yellow Sea, East China Sea, and South China Sea with a coastline of 10,800 miles and 5,000 islands off the coast. Influenced by geographic position and atmospheric circulation, China's climate is extremely diverse. The major natural disasters are typhoons along the coasts, damaging floods and droughts, and earthquakes.

China has a varied topography, including low and flat plains in the east, high plateaus and deserts in the west, north and northeast plains, southern hills, and mountainous areas making up 33 percent of the country. It shares with Nepal the Himalaya Mountains, the highest in the world, with Mt. Everest reaching 29,029 feet. Among the other major mountain ranges are the Tianshan (Tien Shan) Mountains in the northwest, with a total length of 1,500 miles; the Kunlun Mountains, over 1,500 miles long in the west; the Qinling Mountains spanning about 900 miles in the central area; and the Changbai Mountains in the northeast. Among its high plateaus (about 26 percent of the country's land) are the Qinghai-Tibet Plateau (or the Tibetan Plateau), known as the "roof of the world" with a total area of 889,000 square miles in the west; the Inner Mongolian Plateau of 386,000 square miles in the north; the Loess Plateau of 154,000 square miles in the northwest; and the Yunnan-Guizhou Plateau of 150,000 square miles in the southwest. Its hills comprise 10 percent of the land surface, and basins and deserts about 19 percent. Less than 12 percent of its terrain is suitable for agriculture on its fertile plains, such as the Northeast Plain, famous for its black soil, containing many organic substances and with a total area of 135,000 square miles; the North China Plain of 120,000 square miles and a well-known grain and cotton producing region; and the Middle and Lower Yangzi Valley Plain of 77,000 square miles, known as the country's "rice bowl."

China has numerous rivers, most of them flowing from west to east and draining into the Pacific Ocean. Among all the rivers, the Yangzi (Yangtze) River (3,988 miles) and Huang (Yellow) River (3,395 miles) are the two longest rivers crossing the country.

Among the other major rivers are the Heilong (Amur) River in Manchuria, over 1,775 miles long; the Zhu (Pearl) River in the south, about 1,317 miles; the Tarim River in the northwest, about 1,305 miles; and the Yarlung Zangbo (Brahmaputra) River flowing from the Himalayas, the highest river in the country, and about 1,232 miles long. China's hydropower potential is the largest in the world. The man-made Beijing (Peking)-Hangzhou Canal (historically known as the Grand Canal) is over 1,067 miles long and flows through six provinces, providing transportation and communication between the north and south and for agricultural irrigation along the canal. China's natural resources include coal, oil, gas, lead, uranium, vanadium, and many minerals. The country is also rich in bauxite, magnetite, mercury, natural graphite, tin, vanadium, and zinc.

China has the largest population in the world, exceeding 1.4 billion in 2015 and accounting for approximately 23 percent of the world's total. The population is not evenly distributed across the country: the east part has more residents than the west, while more than 700 million, over 54 percent of the total, live in urban areas. China is a multiethnic country with 56 nationalities. The Han people comprise the largest population, making up 91.5 percent of the country's total population.

With Beijing as its capital, the People's Republic of China (PRC) was founded on October 1, 1949, under the leadership of the Chinese Communist Party (CCP). During his tenure from 2013 to 2022, Xi Jinping, chairman of the CCP, serves as president of the PRC. The CCP dominates the central and local governments by controlling legislative, executive, and judicial branches. The PRC has 22 provinces, 5 autonomous (provincial) regions, 4 municipalities, and 2 special administrative regions (Hong Kong and Macao). There are 2,862 counties under the provincial and municipal governments.

China is rising in the 21st century and by 2011 became the second largest economy in the world, following only the United States, and for the first time in its history exceeded Japan. Its GDP increased from $1 trillion in 1999 to $8.2 trillion in 2008 with an average annual growth rate over 13 percent; then $9 trillion in 2009 to $10 trillion in 2010 with a growth rate of 10.4 percent; and from $11.3 trillion in 2011 to $12.6 trillion in 2012 with 7.8 percent growth. Its GDP consists of 10.1 percent agriculture, 45.3 percent industry, and 44.6 percent services. Its GDP per capita increased from $2,172 in 1999 to $6,201 in 2008 with an average annual growth rate over 9 percent; then $6,798 in 2009 to $7,571 in 2010 with a growth rate of 9.9 percent; and from $8,411 in 2011 to $9,185 in 2012 with 7.2 percent growth. The Chinese labor force totals 798.5 million, the largest labor force in the world. All China's progress was achieved by an enormous consumption of energy resources as well as costs to the natural environment. In 2010, China's total energy consumption surpassed the United States for the first time ever, making it the world's largest energy consumer, something which has drawn attention worldwide. China also faces serious environmental issues in the 21st century: 16 of the world's 20 most polluted cities are located in China.

Further Reading

Economy, Elizabeth, and Michael Levi. *By All Means Necessary: How China's Resource Quest Is Changing the World*. New York: Oxford University Press, 2014.

Marks, Robert. *China: Its Environment and History.* Boulder, CO: Rowman & Littlefield, 2011.

Ping, Zheng. *China's Geography.* Singapore: Cengage Learning Asia, 2010.

Shambaugh, David. *China Goes Global: The Partial Power.* New York: Oxford University Press, 2013.

Tuan, Yi-fu. *A Historical Geography of China.* Piscataway, NJ: Aldine Transaction, 2008.

Veeck, Gregory et al. *China's Geography: Globalization and the Dynamics of Political, Economic, and Social Change.* 2nd ed. Boulder, CO: Rowman & Littlefield, 2011.

Climate

Influenced by geographic position and monsoonal circulation, China's climate is extremely diverse with five major climatic zones: southern tropical zone; southeast subtropical zone; eastern warm temperature zone; northwest and northeast dry and subarctic cold zone; and the western Tibetan high plateau cold zone. Monsoonal winds blow from the Pacific and Indian Oceans, affecting 70 percent of the country, including the southeast subtropical zone and the east warm-temperate and temperate zones, each with cold and dry winters and hot and rainy summers. In May–July, southeast wind prevails in most regions, and in December–February, northwest wind is prevalent through the country.

Each winter, from October through March, frigid winds sweep down across the country from Mongolia and Siberia. The coldest region covered with snow and ice is located in the Hailar District in Inner Mongolia, where the average temperature is 18 degrees below zero Fahrenheit and the lowest temperature recorded was about 61 degrees below zero. Heilongjiang Province (northern Manchuria) and Hulun Beir of Inner Mongolia are entirely without summer. The wintertime variation between northern and southern China is significant. While citizens in Harbin, a city in Heilongjiang, are visiting the local ice lantern park in severe coldness, those in Guangzhou, in southern Guangdong, are enjoying a blossoming spring.

In the Huai River basin, the four seasons are clearly differentiated. In the city of Kunming, southwestern Yunnan Province, the weather is spring-like all year round. In summer, however, the temperature variation between north and south is only 3 to 6 degrees Fahrenheit. The high temperatures and plentiful rain are very common across the country and benefit agriculture. Hainan Province has a long summer and is virtually without winter. The hottest area is the Turpan District in Xinjiang. Topographically, Xinjiang is the lowest point in China, with Aydingkol Lake at 154 meters below sea level. The average temperature in Turpan in July is 92 degrees Fahrenheit, while the average daytime temperature during the same month exceeds 104 degrees. The highest temperature ever recorded was 119 degrees.

The annual precipitation is unevenly distributed across China, and it decreases gradually from southeast to northwest. In the humid southeast coast, precipitation averages 186 inches annually, while in the arid northwest, the annual figure is 2–3 inches. Every year from June to July, the drainage areas of the Yangzi (Yangtze) River are badgered by incessant rains. These rains are called "mold rain" because of the mold that grows during this rainy season.

The major natural disasters are typhoons along the southern coasts, along with damaging floods and droughts, as well as earthquakes. The 1887 flood of the Huang (Yellow) River killed between 900,000 and 2 million people, and its worst flood, in 1931, killed 2–4 million Chinese. During the Great Tangshan earthquake in northern Hebei Province on July 28, 1976, 242,000 people were killed and 164,000 injured; it was the largest earthquake of the 20th century, judging by number of deaths. During the Wenshan earthquake in southwestern Sichuan Province on May 12, 2008, 69,227 people were killed, 374,643 injured, and 17,923 missing.

See also: Chapter 1: Overview; Huang River; Manchuria; Pollution and the Environment; Taiwan; Tibetan Plateau; Xinjiang; Yangzi River.

Further Reading

Harris, Paul. *China's Responsibility for Climate Change: Ethics, Fairness and Environmental Policy*. Bristol, UK: University of Bristol Policy Press, 2011.

Marks, Robert. *China: Its Environment and History*. Boulder, CO: Rowman & Littlefield, 2011.

Wang, Weiguang, Guoquang Zheng, and Jiahua Pan. *China's Climate Change Policies*. London: Routledge, 2012.

Disputed Islands and Territories

Since the founding of the People's Republic of China (PRC) on October 1, 1949, the government of the Chinese Communist Party (CCP) has disputed territories with Russia and Mongolia along its northern border, with India in the west, and with Vietnam in the south. It also disputed islands with the Philippines, Brunei, Indonesia, Malaysia, and Vietnam in the South China Sea, and with Japan over Senkaku Island in the East China Sea. Some of these tensions and crises have led to border wars between the PRC and some of its neighboring countries between 1962 and 1988 (not including the conflicts between China and Taiwan, the Republic of China, or ROC).

The Sino-Indian War arose over border disputes along the Himalayan Mountains in Ladakh and Aksai Chin, and in the North East Frontier Agency. Britain drew the McMahon Line in 1914 with Tibet, which has served as a buffer between the PRC and India since 1951. In 1962, the PRC declared the McMahon Line "illegal." On October 20, 1962, the PLA crossed the disputed border in the west and attacked Indian garrisons. The war continued until November 21, when a cease-fire became effective, with casualties of 8,700 Indians and 2,400 Chinese troops. In 1993, China and India signed an agreement to maintain peace and tranquility along the Line of Actual Control

(LAC). In 2011, both agreed to formulate some mechanism to handle different situations at the LAC.

Border disputes between China and Russia have a long history, dating back to the 18th century. As the communist allies in the 1950s, the PRC and the Soviet Union agreed on the territorial status quo of their land borders of about 4,150 miles. After the Sino-Soviet split in the 1960s, the border issue resurfaced. Beginning in March 1969, small-scale border skirmishes erupted at the Damansky (*Zhenbao*) and Bacha Islands in the Heilong (Amur) River, in northeast China (Manchuria), and at Taskti and Tieliekti in Xinjiang, northwest China. These border clashes continued until the late 1970s, but never escalated into a total war between the two communist countries. After the collapse of the Soviet Union in 1991, Russia and China agreed to withdraw their armies from the border areas. In 1994, the Agreement on the Sino-Russian Border Management System was signed. In 1997, a settlement was reached for the demarcation of the disputed 2,575-mile eastern sector of the border. The Complementary Agreement was signed in 2004, requiring Russia to transfer some of the islands in the Heilongjiang River to China. The remaining disputed islands are still in Russian possession.

After American troops withdrew from Vietnam in 1973, tension mounted over disputed islands in the South China Sea between China and South Vietnam (Republic of Vietnam, or ROV, 1955–1975). In January 1974, a naval battle occurred between the Chinese and Vietnamese navies at the Paracel (*Xisha*) Islands. After four Chinese submarines sank one Vietnamese destroyer and damaged the other two, the Chinese army landed and began occupying the Paracel Islands with casualties of 85 Chinese and 149 Vietnamese troops. The Paracel Islands, as the second largest group in the South China Sea, includes about 15 to 30 small islands. Although most of these are rocky, small, and uninhabited, the competing claims reflect the interests in oil and gas reserves beneath them by the PRC, Vietnam (then Socialist Republic of Vietnam), and the ROC. The Spratly Islands, the largest group in the South China Sea, covers a water area of 61,775 square miles, and includes approximately 100 small islands. The PRC, Vietnam, the

SINO-VIETNAMESE WAR (1979–1990)

On February 17, 1979, China sent 200,000 troops of the People's Liberation Army (PLA) to invade Vietnam. By the 26th, Chinese troops had taken Lang Son, Lao Cai, Dong Dang, Cao Bang, and other places in northern Vietnam. In early March, the Vietnamese army launched a counterattack and forced the Chinese out of Lang Son. Fierce fighting did not end until March 4 when Chinese retook Lang Son, the most strategic place among all the cities taken by PLA troops. The Chinese began their withdrawal on March 6, and the war was over by March 16. The border conflicts continued after 1979 with large-scale battles in April–May 1984 and in April 1987, and by the end of the 1980s, Beijing and Hanoi had normalized their relationship. In 1992, all Chinese troops withdrew from the Lao Son and Yen Son areas and returned to China.

Philippines, the ROC, Malaysia, and Brunei all claim the Spratly Islands. In 2012, Vietnam passed a law placing both island groups under its jurisdiction.

In 1974, crises also occurred along the disputed land border between China and North Vietnam (Democratic Republic of Vietnam, DRV, 1945–1976). At least 100 border skirmishes occurred that year, and they increased to 1,100 in 1978. On February 17, 1979, two hundred thousand PLA troops launched an all-front attack along the Sino-Vietnamese border. In less than 20 days, the Chinese army took over the northern cities of Caobang, Lao Cai, Cam Duong, and Lang Son, about 80 miles from Hanoi. However, the Chinese suffered very heavy casualties, about 1,350 per day, totaling 26,000 in the first 19 days. By March 16, all Chinese troops withdrew from Vietnam, but not until 37,300 Vietnamese troops were killed and 2,300 were captured. The Chinese withdrawal from Vietnam did not end the border conflicts, which continued until 1990. The largest battle took place in April–May 1984 when the PLA overran Vietnamese positions in the mountains near Lao Son. During this five-week offensive, 1,003 Chinese were killed, and about 2,000 Vietnamese. Artillery played a major role in the 1984–1987 conflicts. In 1991, each normalized their relations, and in 2000 they resolved long-standing disputes over their border.

See also: Chapter 1: Overview; Himalayas; Manchuria; Natural Resources; South China Sea; Taiwan; Tibetan Plateau; Xinjiang. Chapter 3: Chinese Communist Party; People's Liberation Army. Chapter 5: Dalai Lama.

Further Reading

Baker, John, and David Wiencek, eds. *Cooperative Monitoring in the South China Sea: Satellite Imagery, Confidence-Building Measures, and the Spratly Islands Disputes.* New York: Praeger, 2002.

Elleman, Bruce, Stephen Kotkin, and Clive Scholfield, eds. *Beijing's Power and China's Borders: Twenty Neighbors in Asia.* Armonk, NY: M. E. Sharpe, 2012.

Khoo, Nicholas. *Collateral Damage: Sino-Soviet Rivalry and the Termination of the Sino-Vietnamese Alliance.* New York: Columbia University Press, 2011.

Lamb, Alastair. *The China-India Border: The Origins of the Disputed Bounders.* Oxford, UK: Oxford University Press, 1964.

Himalayas

Meaning "land of snow" in the Tibetan language, this is the highest mountain range in the world. The vast Himalayan complex extends about 1,500 miles, in an arc from the Indus River in the west to Tibet in the east and crossing five countries, including Bhutan, India, Nepal, Pakistan, and China, and covering an area of approximately 229,500 square miles in South Asia. It consists of a group of mountain ranges, with more than 30 peaks higher than 25,000 feet. Among other high peaks, Mt. Everest in both Nepal and China, rising to 29,029 feet, is the world's highest mountain. Emerging only several hundred thousand years ago, the Himalayas are the youngest mountains on earth.

SINO-INDIAN WAR (1962)

Chinese troops of the People's Liberation Army (PLA) launched large-scale attacks on October 20, 1962, against the Indian garrisons in Ladakh and Aksai Chin and the North East Frontier Agency, in response to border disputes along the Himalayan Mountains. By October 28, the PLA had wiped out 43 strongholds on the Indian side of the McMahon Line. The Indian troops, ill prepared and poorly supplied, fell back under the PLA assaults. On November 22, the Chinese government announced a cease-fire along the Chinese-Indian border. After December 1, Chinese forces began pulling out of Indian territories and returning to the old boundary, the "traditional" border. According to Chinese reports, between October 20 and November 21, India lost 8,700 troops, including 4,800 killed and 3,900 captured. Total PLA casualties were 2,400 dead and wounded.

The Tibetan Himalaya (or Trans-Himalayas) is the northeastern part of the mountain system in China. It consists of more complex ranges and plateaus, about 600 miles long and 140 miles wide in the center, narrowing to a 20-mile width at the eastern end. Unlike the Great Himalaya, the Tibetan Himalaya ranges are not divided by deep river gorges, and they lack a definite alignment. The Yarlung Zangbo (or Brahmaputra) River, which

A view of the Himalayan Mountains in Chinese-controlled Tibet (Xizang). The Indus River originates in the Himalayas, which are part of the dramatic geographic variety of South Asia. Mt. Everest in both China and Nepal, rising to 29,029 feet, is the world's highest mountain. (Corel)

originated from its northern part, has gentle streams in the upper reaches and flows to the lower reaches, bypassing high mountains in its eastern part and then turning south, forming the largest canyon in the world—the Yarlung Zangbo Canyon. The north slopes are cold, semiarid or arid, and less influenced by the monsoon season than the southern slopes. The altitude also affects their temperature ranges, and the line of permanent snow lies at about 16,500 feet. The high altitude areas have very low temperatures and strong winds with less vegetation. At elevations up to 2,000 feet, a zone of grass and forest can be found in the east. The eastern areas have warm temperatures and plentiful rainfalls with more lush vegetation and large animals such as buffalo and rhinoceros. The Himalayan black bear, languor monkey, goat antelope, and yak are widespread in the forest. The yak has been domesticated by the Tibetans and is used as a beast of burden.

Most of the approximately 3 million Tibetans practice Buddhism and live in the Tibetan Himalaya and Plateau, which has been under the Tibetan Autonomous Regional (TAR) Government of the People's Republic of China (PRC) since 1965. A residence of the Buddhist spiritual leader, the Dalai Lama, is also situated in the Himalayas. He has been in exile since 1959 when he was accused by the PRC government of organizing a separatist movement in Tibet. In 1962, the Sino-Indian War broke out along the Tibetan border. Chinese and Indian governments still dispute their border along the Ladakh and Aksai Chin areas in the Himalayas.

See also: Chapter 1: Overview; Disputed Islands and Territories; Tibetan Plateau. Chapter 5: Buddhism; Dalai Lama. Chapter 6: Major Ethnic Groups.

Further Reading

Bernstein, Jeremy. *In the Himalayas: Journeys through Nepal, Tibet, and Bhutan.* Guilford, CT: Lyons, 1996.

Crossette, Barbara. *So Close to Heaven: The Vanishing Buddhist Kingdoms of the Himalayas.* New York: Vintage, 1996.

Searle, Mike. *Colliding Continents: A Geological Exploration of the Himalaya, Karakoram, and Tibet.* New York: Oxford University Press, 2013.

Hong Kong

Officially the Special Administrative Region-Hong Kong (SAR-HK), this southern peninsula is connected to Guangdong province of the People's Republic of China (PRC) in the north and surrounded by the South China Sea on three sides. It consists of many islands, a portion of the mainland, and a considerable expanse of water surface. With a total area of 403 square miles, Hong Kong can be divided into three main regions: Hong Kong Island and a couple of hundred small islands; the Kowloon (*Jiulong*) Peninsula; and the mainland New Territories, which comprise 42.2 percent of the land area. Both the mainland and the islands are hilly, with steep slopes and a long coastline of 440 miles. Its deep-water harbors have made Hong Kong the shipping hub of Southeast Asia. In the southern subtropical weather zone, the seasonal monsoon winds bring cool humid winters and hot rainy summers. Hong Kong has a total population of 7 million, 95 percent of whom are Chinese. One of the most crowded areas in the world, its overall population density is 15,000 persons per square mile. Both Chinese and English are official languages in Hong Kong.

After the Qing dynasty (1644–1911) lost the First Opium War (1839–1841) to Great Britain, the Chinese government ceded Hong Kong to the British in perpetuity, in the Treaty of Nanjing (1842). After the Second Opium War in the 1850s, the British acquired Kowloon in 1860 and the New Territories in 1898, as part of a 99-year lease. In 1941–1945, Japan occupied Hong Kong. After World War II, Britain resumed its colonial administration of Hong Kong by appointing a British governor as civil and military authority to represent the Crown. In the 1970s, Hong Kong's economy took off with an annual growth rate between 6 and 8 percent. In the 1980s, its exports reached $73 billion. Its GDP per capita totaled $19,000 in 1993, increased to $23,000 in 1996, and then to $42,000 in 2007. Hong Kong's GDP per capita reached $50,900 in 2012, comparing to $9,100 in China, $35,900 in Japan, and $51,700 in the United States that year. Its GDP totaled $365.6 billion 2012.

The PRC government began negotiations with the United Kingdom in the early 1980s for the return of Hong Kong to China. Deng Xiaoping developed a theory of "one country, two systems" to apply the territories under European colonial administrations. In 1984, the PRC and UK governments signed an agreement for China to resume the sovereignty of Hong Kong. On July 1, 1997, Britain returned Hong Kong to China and Beijing established an autonomic government of the SAR-HK. Chee-hwa Tung was elected as the first Hong Kong chief executive in July 1997. Since 2012, the current head of the SAR-HK government is C. Y. Leung.

See also: Chapter 1: Overview; South China Sea. Chapter 2: Timeline; Deng Xiaoping; Lin Zexu and the Opium War. Chapter 4: Foreign Investment. Chapter 5: Falun Gong. Chapter 9: Overview. Chapter 14: Cantonese Dim Sum.

Further Reading

Abbas, Ackbar. *Hong Kong: Culture and the Politics of Disappearance*. Minneapolis: University of Minnesota Press, 1997.

Carroll, John. *A Concise History of Hong Kong*. Boulder, CO: Rowman & Littlefield, 2007.

Studwell, Joe. *Asian Godfathers: Money and Power in Hong Kong and Southeast Asia*. New York: Grove, 2008.

Tsang, Steve. *A Modern History of Hong Kong*. London: Tauris, 2007.

Huang (Yellow) River

The Huang (Yellow) River is the second longest in China after the Yangzi (Yangtze) River, and the sixth-longest in the world, with a total length of 3,395 miles. Originating at the northern foot of the Bayan Har Mountains in Qinghai Province in the west, the Huang (Yellow River) first flows east through deep gorges in its upper reaches on the Tibetan Plateau. It then turns northeast at the city of Lanzhou in Gansu Province, from which point it flows many hundreds of miles through the Ordos Desert in the eastern part of the Gobi Desert. Most of China's hydroelectric power dams and stations are built on its upper reaches. The river then turns east and travels about 200 miles through the Loess Plateau, and in its middle reaches the "Ordos Loop," where its swiftness through a young valley slices into deposits of loamy soil known as loess, between Shaanxi and Shanxi Provinces. The river picks up and carries in suspension yellow silt, revealing a yellow color which gives the river its name.

At Kaifeng, central Henan Province, the river enters its lower reaches. Its middle and lower reaches are one of the origins of China's agriculture, and this area is called China's "Mother River" or the "cradle of Chinese civilization," as it is the birthplace of ancient civilizations. Among the earliest rulers was the Yellow Emperor (Huang-di) (2300–2250 BCE), who led many tribal groups along the western Yellow River about the 2200s BCE. Its basin areas created the most prosperous regions in early history.

At its lower reaches, where the river broadens and its current slows, the huge amount of sand and mud accumulates at the bottom of the riverbed. The buildup over the years has increased the level of the Huang and formed a "suspended river," about 70 feet above the surrounding land. Although dikes have been constructed higher and higher, disastrous floods occur frequently. The 1887 flood killed between 900,000 to 2 million people, and the worst flood, in 1931, killed 2–4 million Chinese.

The river continues to flow eastward through 17 provinces and major cities, draining a total basin area of 290,000 square miles and providing water and irrigation for 140 million people. Its delta area totals 3,100 square miles. It empties into the Yellow Sea carrying a large amount of silt, about 1.6 billion tons annually, from the Loess Plateau. Comparing it with other rivers in the world, the Yellow River carries 34 kg of mud and sand per cubic meter of water, as opposed to 10 kg for the Colorado River in the United States and 1 kg for the Nile River in Egypt. Moreover, in an official report of 2007, the Chinese government agency warned that 33.8 percent of the river system had been polluted worse than "level five" (unfit for drinking, agriculture, industry, and aquaculture), according to the criteria of the UN Environment Program.

See also: Chapter 1: Overview; Pollution and the Environment; Tibetan Plateau; Transportation and Water Conservancy. Chapter 2: Timeline.

Further Reading

Cao, Jinqing. *China along the Yellow River: Reflections on Rural Society*. London: Routledge, 2005.

Sinclair, Kevin. *The Yellow River: A 5,000 Year Journey through China*. Los Angeles, CA: Knapp, 1987.

Tetsuya, Kusuda. *The Yellow River: Water and Life*. Singapore: World Scientific, 2009.

Major Cities

China became urbanized in 2006, when Chinese cities increased from 223 to 695, and more than 30 cities had a population over 1.5 million. Among the major cities according to China's 2010 census are Chongqing with 28.8 million residents; Shanghai, 23 million; Beijing (Peking), 19.6 million; Tianjin, 12.9 million; Shenzhen, 9 million; and Guangzhou (Canton), 8.8 million. Four of them, Beijing, Shanghai, Tianjin, and Chongqing, belong to the municipalities which are directly under the central government rather than a provincial government. Each municipality governs a dozen of metropolitan districts and a couple of counties. Currently, about 700 million Chinese, over 54 percent of the total population, live in cities. With its economic takeoff after 1978, China has generated a substantial portion of capital for the urbanization. The rapid expansion of free enterprise opened up a free labor market in the 1980s. During the 1990s, as many as 100 million rural laborers migrated to the cities seeking work. In less than two decades, hundreds of millions of Chinese people have moved from rural areas into the cities.

As the capital of the People's Republic of China (PRC), Beijing is the political, cultural, and educational center of the state. Its municipality includes 16 metropolitan districts and two counties with a total area of 6,600 square miles. Located in north China and surrounded by the mountains in three sides, it has become a world-renowned city of history. The Liao dynasty (907–1125 CE) made Beijing its capital since 938. Later, Beijing became the capital of the Jin (1115–1234), Yuan (1279–1368), Ming (1368–1644), and Qing (1644–1911) dynasties. The Palace Museum, also called the Forbidden City, was the royal palace of the Ming and Qing, and the world's largest royal palace complex with more than 9,999 rooms inside. The most popular tourist attraction in the city is Beijing's section of the Great Wall, regarded as one of the seven world wonders. Peking Opera is a national treasure with a history of 200 years. Beijing successfully hosted the Summer Olympic Games in 2008.

Shanghai is like New York, the Chinese center of trade, transportation, and international exchange. Located on the estuary of the Yangzi (Yangtze) River and along the coast of East China Sea, its municipality includes 18 metropolitan districts and one county with a total area of 2,450 square miles. Founded in 1927, the city has become the biggest economic center and most important industrial base in the country. Its exports comprise more than 20 percent of China's total, about $2 trillion in 2012, and its transportation lines extend in all directions. With Pudong as the renowned special economic zone, Shanghai has been developing steadily in finance and become the largest center of commerce and finance in China. As a tourist city, it also attracts tens of millions of visitors every year from both home and abroad by its commercial activities and scenic beauty.

Located in southwest China along the upper reaches of the Yangzi River, Chongqing is the most populous city in China with 28.8 million residents. Founded in 1929, the city served as the wartime capital of the ROC under President Chiang Kai-shek (Jiang Jieshi) (1887–1975) in 1938–1945. Its current municipality includes 15 metropolitan districts, 4 townships, 17 counties, and 4 autonomous counties with a total area of 31,780 square miles. Chongqing became the fourth municipality of the PRC in 1997 after Beijing, Shanghai, and Tianjin. It is the center of the Chinese defense industry and the transportation hub in southwest China, since two rivers and four railways meet here. In the subtropical climate zone, Chongqing is one of China's three notorious "ovens" with hot and humid weather.

Located along the Zhu (Pearl) River, Guangzhou is the capital of Guangdong Province and an important cultural and economic center of southern China. Founded in 1925, it was the first city established by the ROC government. The current municipality includes 10 metropolitan districts and 2 townships. Close to the South China Sea, Guangzhou has become the largest transportation hub in south China. It has also become one of the textile and automobile industry centers and the center for international exchange in China. Since 1957, an international export-import commodities fair is held twice in the city every year. It is also the hometown of hundreds of thousands of Chinese (Cantonese) living overseas in the United States, Europe, Latin America, and Southeast Asia.

While the Chinese urban movement has successfully transferred the surplus labor from the countryside to the urban industries that desperately demand free and cheap labors, numerous problems have arisen as a result of this unprecedented large-scale process, such as overcrowding and substandard housing, public transportation, water and air pollution, lack of social services, corruption, and power abuse, often at crisis levels. Recently, housing-related issues became the focus of an anguished national conversation about the future of the country. Those problems are associated with increased concerns by residents over urban improvement, public safety, legal protection, and political transparency.

See also: Chapter 1: Overview; Pollution and the Environment; Population; South China Sea; Transportation and Water Conservancy. Chapter 2: Timeline; Chiang Kai-shek. Chapter 4: Migrant Laborers. Chapter 6: Middle Class; Rural-Urban Conflicts; Urban Poor. Chapter 11: Peking Opera. Chapter 12: The Great Wall; Palaces, Pagodas, and Temples. Chapter 14: Cantonese Dim Sum. Chapter 15: 2008 Beijing Olympics.

Further Reading

Bergere, Marie-Claire. *Shanghai: China's Gateway to Modernity*. Stanford, CA: Stanford University Press, 2009.

Campanella, Thomas. *The Concrete Dragon: China's Urban Revolution and What It Means for the World*. Princeton, NJ: Princeton University Press, 2011.

Chen, Nancy, et al., eds. *China Urban: Ethnographies of Contemporary Culture*. Durham, NC: Duke University Press, 2001.

Li, Lillian, Alison Dray-Novey, and Haili Kong. *Beijing: From Imperial Capital to Olympic City*. London: Palgrave Macmillan, 2008.

Rolandsen, Unn Malfrid. *Leisure and Power in Urban China: Everyday Life in a Chinese City*. London: Routledge, 2011.

Wu, Weiping, and Piper Gaubatz. *The Chinese City*. London: Routledge, 2012.

Manchuria

Manchuria is an area in northeast China of approximately 300,000 square miles, which includes the Heilongjiang, Jilin, and Liaoning Provinces of the People's Republic of China (PRC). The historic name of the region is derived from that of the Manchus, an ethnic group who lived outside the Great Wall until 1644, when they established the Qing dynasty and ruled China until 1911. To protect their home base, the Manchu emperors forbade the Chinese to immigrate into Manchuria and refused to permit development of the region until the late 18th century.

In September 1931, Japanese troops stationed in Manchuria defeated the Chinese forces and occupied the region by establishing a new, pro-Tokyo state, "Manchukuo" beginning in 1932 and ending at the end of World War II in 1945. After the founding of the PRC in 1949, the number of Manchurian provinces was reduced from six to four in 1954, and from four to the present three in 1956. Between 1969 and 1972, Chinese and Soviet troops often clashed along the northern border of Manchuria. After the collapse of the Soviet Union in 1991, Russia and China agreed to withdraw their armies from the Manchurian border areas. In 1994, the Agreement on the Sino-Russian Border Management System was signed. In 1997, a settlement was reached for the demarcation of the disputed 2,575-mile border of Manchuria. The Complementary Agreement was signed in 2004 for Russia to transfer some of the islands in the Heilong (Amur) River to China. The remaining disputed islands are still in Russian possession.

Manchuria is not only strategically important, but is also a major source base for China. Its natural resources include coal, crude oil, natural gas, and other mineral resources. The Daqing Oil Field in Heilongjiang Province remains the highest production oil field in the country since the early 1960s. With an annual crude oil production of 50 million tons (or 1 million barrels per day) from 1976 to 2003, about 40 percent of China's total oil production, and then 40 million tons per year (or 800,000 barrels per

---

SINO-RUSSO BORDER CONFLICT (1969–1972)

The border war between the Soviet Union and China broke out on March 2, 1969, when 40 Chinese soldiers patrolled at Zhenbao (Damansky) Island, one of the disputed uninhabited islands in the Ussuri River. The Soviets dispatched 70 border troops to the island, but the Chinese refused to leave. Each side blamed the other for opening fire. With 200 reinforcements, the Chinese attacked and killed 30 Russian soldiers, losing only six of their own. On March 15, more than 100 Soviet troops and six tanks counterattacked. Heavy artillery pieces shelled both shores. About 40 Chinese were killed and the Soviets lost eight men and one T-62 tank. For the rest of the year, sporadic fighting continued in many places along the border in Heilongjiang in northeast China and at Taskti and Tieliekti in Xinjiang, northwest China. The border conflicts continued until the late 1970s, but they did not escalate into total war between the two communist countries.

day in 2004–2014) thereafter, approximately 20 percent of the annual national total. According to statistics provided by the Ministry of Land and Resources of the PRC, Heilongjiang and Tibet are the regions with the largest oil reserves, altogether having 149.6 trillion tons of oil, accounting for about 47.15 percent of China's total. Manchuria has been the heavy base for steel and iron, automobile manufacturing, mechanics, and petro-chemical industries. The region is also famous for its black soil, a large area of organic substance for commercial farming (roughly 120,000 square miles) over the Northeast China Plains. This area is the largest producer of wheat, soy beans, and corn in China. It is also an important base for husbandry.

Manchuria has a total population of 100 million, including Han Chinese, Manchus, Mongols, Hui, Koreans, and others. Among the major cities are Harbin, provincial capital of Heilongjiang, with 5 million people; Changchun, the capital of Jilin, 4 million; Shenyang, the capital of Liaoning, 5 million; and Dalian, Liaoning Province, 4 million. The region is in a semi-continental zone with long, cold winters and short, warm, and rainy summers.

See also: Chapter 1: Overview; Disputed Islands and Territories; Natural Resources; Population. Chapter 2: Timeline. Chapter 4: Overview; Agriculture; Energy Industry.

Further Reading

Kuramoto, Kazuko. *Manchurian Legacy: Memoirs of a Japanese Colonist*. Ann Arbor: Michigan State University Press, 2004.

Matsusaka, Yoshihisa. *The Making of Japanese Manchuria, 1904–1932*. Cambridge, MA: Harvard University Press, 2003.

Meyer, Michael. *In Manchuria: A Village Called Wasteland and the Transformation of Rural China*. New York: Bloomsbury, 2015.

Tamanoi, Mariko. *Crossed Histories: Manchuria in the Age of Empire*. Honolulu: University of Hawaii Press, 2005.

Natural Resources

China, with its vast territory and diversity of landscapes, is rich in natural resources. By 2013, more than 157 confirmed minerals have been discovered in China, including antimony, coal, oil, gas, lead, uranium, vanadium, and many other minerals. It also holds reserves of magnetite, molybdenum, mercury, and manganese. Minerals deposits are distributed widely through the country; the principal mining regions are Manchuria and the uplands of South China. The country is particularly well endowed with energy resources. Coal reserves of up to 11 trillion tons are claimed, most of it in Manchuria and North China. Compared with its Asian-Pacific counterparts, it has the largest crude oil reserves. Out of the total 41.3 billion barrels of proved oil reserves in the Asia-Pacific, its 14.7 billion barrels in 2013 took up a major portion, with 35.59

percent of the region, and ranking 14th in the world. Its natural gas reserves in 2011 were 3.1 trillion cubic meters, ranking as the second largest natural gas reserves among its Asia-Pacific neighbors, following Australia, and ranking ninth compared with other countries worldwide. Among the total 16.8 trillion cubic meters of gas reserves in the region, its 3.1 trillion cubic meters took up 18.45 percent, second only to Australia's 22.61 percent. Oilfields on land are mainly distributed in northeast, north, and northwest China, and the largest in China is Daqing Oilfield.

Offshore areas of the Yellow Sea, East China Sea, and South China Sea also abound in crude oil and natural gas. The South China Sea has proven crude oil reserves of 7.7 billion barrels in 2013, about 19 percent of the total (41.3 billion barrels) in the Asian-Pacific region. It is expected in the future to have a total of 28 billion barrels of oil reserves to be proven. As oil and gas shift to deep water explorations, international tensions have risen among some of the surrounding countries over the sovereignty of the islands that have been claimed by the People's Republic of China (PRC), the Republic of China (ROC, or Taiwan), the Philippines, Malaysia, Brunei, Indonesia, Singapore, and Vietnam. In terms of total reserves, even though China is rich in mineral resources and takes third place in the world resource reservoir, the reserve per capita ranks only 53rd in the world, owing to its large population.

Although China is a country with one of the longest histories of agriculture development in the world, its land resources are limited, with less than 12 percent of its terrain suitable for agriculture. China must feed 22 percent of the world's population with less than 7 percent of the world's cultivated land. Its fertile plains include the Northeast Plain, famous for its black soil, containing many organic substances, and with a total area of 135,000 square miles, which is growing dry crops like wheat, corn, sorghum, and soybeans. The North China Plain of 120,000 square miles is a well-known grain and cotton-producing region. The Middle and Lower Yangzi River Valley Plain of 77,000 square miles is known as the country's "rice bowl," growing crops year round. The staple crop is rice, which can be harvested two or three times in a year.

The total volume of water resources in China leads the world, but water per capita is only a quarter of the world average. The major rivers are the Yangzi (Yangtze) River, Huang (Yellow) River, Heilong (Amur) River (1,775 miles), Zhu (Pearl) (1,317 miles), Tarim (1,305 miles), and Yarlung Zangbo (Brahmaputra) (1,232 miles). China's hydropower potential is the largest in the world.

China has a great diversity of animals and plants. The species in China, accounting for 10 percent of the world's total, include more than 1,000 types of birds, over 400 kinds of beasts, nearly 200 species of amphibians, and about 2,000 species of fish. Some species extinct elsewhere survive in China. Among these are the great paddlefish of the Yangzi River, the giant panda (found only in Southwest China), and Chinese water deer. As a result of the wide range of climates and topography, China is rich in plant species. Most of the original vegetation has been removed, however, during centuries of settlement and intensive cultivation. Natural forests are generally preserved only in the more remote mountain areas. Environmental protection becomes a hot topic for China, since air, water, and industrial pollutions have reached crisis levels in many parts of the country.

See also: Chapter 1: Overview; Disputed Islands and Territories; Huang River; Manchuria; Population; South China Sea; Taiwan; The Three Gorges Project; Tibetan Plateau; Transportation and Water Conservancy; Xinjiang; Yangzi River. Chapter 4: Overview; Agriculture; Energy Industry.

Further Reading

Collins, Gabriel, et al., eds. *China's Energy Strategy: The Impact on Beijing's Maritime Policies*. Annapolis, MD: Naval Institute Press, 2008.

Kynge, James. *China Shakes the World: A Titan's Rise and Troubled Future—and the Challenge for America*. New York: Houghton Mifflin, 2006.

Lanza, Alessandro. *Resources Accounting in China: Economics, Energy and Environment*. New York: Springer, 2013.

Moyo, Dambisa. *Winner Take All: China's Race for Resources and What It Means for the World*. New York: Basic Books, 2012.

Valencia, Mark, Jon Van Dyke, and Noel Ludwig. *Sharing the Resources of the South China Sea*. Honolulu: University of Hawaii Press, 1999.

Pollution and the Environment

China faces serious environmental issues in the 21st century when 16 of the world's 20 most polluted cities are located in China, according to recent World Bank statistics. In 2011, air pollution in Beijing and other cities across the country reached "crisis" levels. Many air pollutants from the oil and manufacturing industries include nitrous oxides, sulfur oxides, carbon monoxide, hydrogen sulfide, benzene, toluene, and xylenes. Polluted air causes many harmful effects for the environment and for citizens. Reduced visibility, damage to crops and livestock, and serious illness in humans can all result. When nitrous oxide and sulfur dioxide combine with water in the atmosphere, acid rain is produced. Acid rain pollutes anything it comes into contact with, including vegetation and bodies of water. Polluted environments from acid rain can eventually kill local wildlife. These environmental issues have become increasingly problematic, especially in newly rapidly industrializing and urbanizing areas. In 2013, the pollution levels of Beijing, China's capital city with 20 million residents, reached 40 times higher than international safety standards. Automobile emissions, construction projects, and coal burning remain key factors in China's decreasing air quality, and government officials continue to try and tackle this problem.

Some cities in China became "death towns," while some of the rivers are known as "cancer rivers," such as the Huai River, which runs north-south between the Huang (Yellow) River and Yangzi (Yangtze) River. The river basin of the Huai extends to more than 30 cities and 180 counties, totaling a population of 165 million people. Many industrial factories, including petrochemical refineries, steel and iron factories, textile factories, leather manufacturers, and paper producers, are businesses built along the

The skyline of Beijing, China, with the ever-present haze of air pollution. The city government promised the International Olympic Committee (IOC) that it would improve its environment when the city was selected on July 31, 2015, as the host for the 2022 Winter Olympic Games. Beijing will become the first city in the world to have hosted both the Summer and Winter Games. (iStockPhoto.com)

Huai, and badly polluted the river. In 2005, the Chinese Center for Disease Control and Prevention (CDC) conducted research sponsored by the Ministry of Health (MOH) of the People's Republic of China (PRC) on the correlation between water pollution and the region's high cancer rates along the banks of the Huai. The results of the research indicate that both mortality and prevalence of digestive cancers were much higher in the study areas, about 277.8 per 10,000 persons, three to four times higher than the recorded rate in control areas.

China is expanding in the 21st century. It has achieved an average annual economic growth rate of 7–8.5 percent in the past 35 years (1978–2013). It became the second-largest economy in the world by 2011, only behind the United States. However, all this progress has been achieved at the sake of an enormous consumption of energy resources as well as costs to the natural environment. In 2010, China's total energy consumption surpassed the United States for the first time, making it the world's biggest energy consumer, something that has drawn worldwide attention. China consumed 10.2 million barrels of crude oil daily in 2011, accounting for 11.8 percent of the world total with an increase of 6.24 percent over 2010. China's petrochemical industry, ever since its inception, has produced many pollutants and has impacted the environment of various ecosystems across the world. Through oil spills, increased toxicity of natural habitats, and contributions to greenhouse gas emissions and climate change, its petroleum industry has oftentimes had a negative effect on the environment. Its breakneck economic development and industrialization of the past three decades have also turned the country into one of the major polluters in the world.

The government of China took some measures to strengthen environmental improvement in the 2010s, such as issuing a Law on Environmental Protection and by educating businesses and the public. Although environmental protection has become a hot topic and has received more attention inside and outside the government, the GDP-based development policy only serves the purpose of economic growth rather than environmental protection. Unless issues like air and water pollution are solved, China's ever-expanding cities could quickly become uninhabitable.

See also: Chapter 1: Overview; Climate; Hong Kong; Huanghe River; Major Cities; Natural Resources; Population; The Three Gorges Project; Yangzi River. Chapter 4: Overview; Energy Industry.

Further Reading

Chen, Shiyi. *Energy, Environment and Economic Transformation in China*. London: Routledge, 2013.

Economy, Elizabeth. *The River Runs Black: The Environmental Challenge to China's Future*. 2nd ed. Ithaca, NY: Cornell University Press, 2010.

Elvin, Mark. *The Retreat of the Elephants: An Environmental History of China*. Ithaca, NY: Yale University Press, 2006.

Gallagher, Kelly. *China Shifts Gears: Automakers, Oil, Pollution, and Development*. Cambridge, MA: MIT Press, 2006.

Marks, Robert. *China: Its Environment and History*. Boulder, CO: Rowman & Littlefield, 2011.

Nielsen, Chris, and Mun Ho, eds. *Clearer Skies over China: Reconciling Air Quality, Climate, and Economic Goals*. Cambridge, MA: MIT Press, 2013.

Simons, Craig. *The Devouring Dragon: How China's Rise Threatens Our Natural World*. New York: St. Martin's Griffin, 2014.

Stern, Rachel. *Environmental Litigation in China: A Study in Political Ambivalence*. New York: Cambridge University Press, 2013.

Population

The People's Republic of China (PRC) has the largest population in the world, exceeding 1.36 billion in 2013 and accounting for approximately 22 percent of the world's total. Among Chinese age groups are 17.2 percent under 14 years of age, 15.4 percent between 15 and 24 years, 46.7 percent between 25 and 54, 11.3 percent between 55 and 64, and 9.4 percent 65 years and over. The country's median age in 2013 was 36.3 years. Its annual population growth rate was 0.46 percent, ranking 155th in the world; and the birth rate was 12.25 births per thousand, ranking 162nd. The death rate was 7.31 deaths per thousand, and infant death rate was 1.51 deaths per 100 live births, ranking 110th in the world. The average Chinese life expectancy in 2013 was 74.99 years, 72.96 for males and 77.27 for females.

According to the PCR's 2010 census, China's population density is 348.9 persons per square mile. This density is not evenly distributed across the country, but is concentrated southeast along the coast, and south of the northern steppe. The east part of the country, including 11 provinces and special municipalities, has more residents than the west with a high density of 830.4 persons per square mile. The most populated areas are the Yangzi (Yangtze) River Valley, of which the delta region was the most populous; Sichuan Basin; North China Plain, and Zuh (Pearl) River Delta. The five western provinces and autonomous regions, comprising 55 percent of the country's land, have a low density of 39.3 persons per square mile or 5.7 percent of the total population. Meanwhile, more than 700 million, over 54 percent, live in urban areas. The large cities include Shanghai with 23 million residents; Beijing, 19.6 million; Tianjin, 12.9 million; Chongqing, 28.8 million; Shenzhen, 9 million; and Guangzhou, 8.8 million. Guangdong has the largest city population among the 25 provinces and autonomous regions, totaling 104 million. The official, or standard language, is Mandarin (*Putonghua*), based on the Beijing and northern dialects.

The Han Chinese comprise the largest population, making up 91.5 percent of the country's total population. Among the 55 minorities in 2012 are 17 million Zhuang nationals, 11 million Hui, 10 million Manchus, 10 million Uygur, 9 million Miao, 6 million Tibetans, and 4 million Mongols, totaling 110.5 million, or about 8.5 percent of the total population. Some minorities live in certain provinces under an autonomous government; for instance, most Uygur are living in the Xinjiang Uygur Autonomous Region (XUAR), and Tibetans live in the Tibet Autonomous Region, among the five autonomous regions set aside for ethnic minorities. Some religions form large minorities like the Hui and Uygur, which is primarily Muslims. The population below the poverty line (about $1 a day) is approximately 13.4 percent of the total in 2013.

After the founding of the PRC in 1949, Mao Zedong (1893–1976) as its first president considered the population to be an asset of the country. China's population doubled from 540 million in 1949 to 1,130 million in 1990, with an annual growth rate of 2 percent in 1952, 2.32 percent in 1957, and 2.85 percent in 1965. The government realized the rapid population growth was a burden to its development and began making birth control efforts in the late 1960s. But the upheaval of the Cultural Revolution (1966–1976) brought the program to a halt.

After the end of the Cultural Revolution and the death of Mao in 1976, China's family planning and birth control policy, known as the "one-child" policy, began in 1979 in an attempt by the government to solve overpopulation issues. After 1979, having more than one child was punishable by fines and jail time. This policy has become one of the most prominent ways in which the state intrudes into family life. It is illegal in almost all provinces for a single woman to have a baby. Implementation of its "one-child" family planning policy seems to be effective, since the average fertility rate dropped from six children per family in the 1970s, to two per family in 2000, and to just 1.44 per family in 2002.

China had a population growth rate of 0.47 percent in 2009 and 0.46 percent in 2013. It had a birth rate of 12.17 births per thousand in 2010 and 11.93 per thousand in 2013. The reduction in the number of births is largely attributable to the prevalence of contraceptive use and the large number of induced abortions that have occurred, since long-term birth control has been made both more widely available and even compulsory. The United Nations estimates that China's population growth will continue, and that it may stop by 2030, if the Chinese government can solve the problems caused by the "one-child" policy. Rapid fertility reduction faces new demographic and social problems as a result of the "only-child" society. The single-child policy results in selective abortions and even female infanticide. Other challenges include care of the elderly since they will not be able to depend on their children as they had in the past, leaving the state to assume the expense. According to UN statistics, 25 percent of Chinese will be age 65 or older by 2040.

See also: Chapter 1: Overview; Pollution and the Environment; Xinjiang; Yangzi River. Chapter 2: Mao Zedong. Chapter 3: Chinese Communist Party; Human Rights. Chapter 5: Buddhism; Catholicism; Islam. Chapter 6: Overview; Aging Population; Major Ethnic Groups; Mongols; Muslims; Poverty; Retirement and Social Welfare; Rural-Urban Conflicts; Uyghur. Chapter 7: Family Planning Law; Gender Imbalance; Gender Inequality; One-Child Policy; Selective Abortions. Chapter 9: Mandarin.

Further Reading

Chang, Chiung-fang, et al., eds. *Fertility, Family Planning and Population Policy in China.* London: Routledge, 2006.

Greenhalgh, Susan. *Cultivating Global Citizens: Population in the Rise of China.* Cambridge, MA: Harvard University Press, 2010.

Greenhalgh, Susan, and Edwin Winckler. *Governing China's Population: From Leninist to Neoliberal Biopolitics.* Stanford, CA: Stanford University Press, 2005.

Watts, Franklin. *Population 1.3 Billion: China Becomes a Super Superpower.* New York: Scholastic, 2009.

South China Sea

The South China Sea, or simply the China Sea, part of the Pacific Ocean, is located south of mainland China; west of the Philippines; north of Indonesia, Malaysia, and Brunei; and east of Singapore and Vietnam. It covers an oval area from the Taiwan Strait in the northeast to the Malacca Strait in the southwest; from the Gulf of Tonkin in the west to the Philippine islands in the east, totaling 1.4 million square miles. It increases in depth from the south, where much of it is less than 1,000 feet deep, to the north where soundings of more than 13,000 feet have been made off Luzon, the Philippines.

The South China Sea is strategically important because it is the second most used sealane in the world, with one-third of the world's shipping transit passing through its waters and 50 percent of the world's annual merchant fleet tonnage passing through its Strait of Malacca, the Sunda Strait, and the Lombok Strait. The chief ports on or near the sea include Manila, Singapore, Bangkok, Ho Chi Minh City, Hong Kong, and Macau. More than 10 million barrels of crude oil per day are shipped through the Strait of Malacca. The South China Sea is also vital for the global ecosystem since its water holds one-third of the entire world's marine biodiversity.

The South China Sea, beneath its seabed, is rich in crude oil and natural gas deposits. It has proven crude oil reserves of 7.7 billion barrels in 2013, about 19 percent of the total (41.3 billion barrels) in the Asia-Pacific region. The South China Sea is expected to have a total of 28 billion barrels of oil reserves to be proven in the future. It has estimated natural gas reserves of 266 trillion cubic feet, about 45 percent of the total (592.5 trillion cubic feet) in the Asia-Pacific region. As oil and gas shifted to deep water explorations, international tensions have risen among some of the surrounding countries over the sovereignty of the islands in the South China Sea. Several states and territories have borders on the sea: the People's Republic of China (PRC), the Republic of China (ROC, or Taiwan), the Philippines, Malaysia, Brunei, Indonesia, Singapore, and Vietnam.

The South China Sea has more than 250 islands, shoals, reefs, and sandbars, which are grouped into several archipelagos. The Spratly Islands, as the largest group, covers a water area of 61,775 square miles, including about 100 small islands. The Taiping Island is the largest one, with a land area of just over 0.65 square mile. The Paracel Islands as the second largest group includes about 15 to 30 small islands. Although most of these islands are rocky, small, and uninhabited, the competing claims reflect the interests in oil and gas reserves beneath them by bordering countries. The PRC, Vietnam, the Philippines, the ROC, Malaysia, and Brunei claim the Spratly Islands; while the PRC, Vietnam, and the ROC dispute over the Paracel Islands. Different names are also used for these islands; the Spratly Islands are called Nansha in Chinese by both the PRC and the ROC, Quan Dao Truong Sa in Vietnamese, and Kalayaan by the Filipinos; while the Paracel Islands are called Xisha in Chinese by both the PRC and the ROC and Quan Dao Hoang Sa in Vietnamese. In 1974, the Chinese and Vietnamese navies engaged in battles over these islands. Those conflicts have slowed down exploration and production of oil and gas in the South China Sea.

See also: Chapter 1: Overview; Disputed Islands and Territories; Hong Kong; Natural Resources; Taiwan. Chapter 3: People's Liberation Army. Chapter 4: Energy Industry.

Further Reading

Cole, Bernard. *Asian Maritime Strategies: Navigating Troubled Waters*. Annapolis, MD: Naval Institute Press, 2013.

Daniels, Christopher. *South China Sea: Energy and Security Conflicts*. Lanham, MD: Scarecrow, 2013.

Kaplan, Robert. *Asia's Cauldron: The South China Sea and the End of a Stable Pacific*. New York: Random House, 2014.

Raine, Sarah, and Christian Miere. *Regional Disorder: The South China Sea Disputes*. London: Routledge, 2013.

Taiwan

The largest island off the Chinese mainland has a total area of 13,900 square miles, slightly smaller than Maryland and Delaware combined. Off the southeastern coast of China, it is surrounded by the East China Sea in the north, the Pacific Ocean in the east, South China Sea in the south, and the Taiwan Strait (about 120 miles) in the west, separating it from the mainland. As a long, oval island, its length is 225 miles from north to south with a coastline of 979 miles and a mountain range running through the middle, which rises to a peak of 13,110 feet at Yu Shan. The eastern side of the mountain chain is hilly, while to the west is a broad, fertile plain sloping down to the shallow Taiwan Strait. Its tropical weather is warm in winter, and hot and humid in summer. Typhoons occur between June and October during the southwest monsoon season. The island is rich in rice, but its main industrial crops are sugarcane and tea. It produces precious woods and has abundant resources of waterpower, forestry, and fisheries. Its natural resources include small deposits of coal, silver, copper, marble, crude oil, and natural gas.

Taiwanese have lived on the island long before the Sui dynasty (581–618) launched the first recorded expedition from mainland China in 603. In 1590, the Portuguese were the first Europeans to arrive at Taiwan. Later, the Dutch established themselves in 1621 and called the island "Formosa" (beautiful one). The Dutch maintained their settlement until 1658 when Chinese troops landed, driving the Dutch from the island. Thereafter, immigration from the mainland increased during the Qing dynasty (1644–1911). In 1894, Qing lost the first Sino-Japanese War and signed the Treaty of Shimonoseki in 1895, which included ceding Taiwan to Japan. At the end of World War II, Taiwan was returned to the government of the Republic of China (ROC) under President Chiang Kai-shek (Jiang Jieshi) (1887–1975).

A full-scale Chinese civil war broke out in 1946–1949 between Chiang's army and armed forces of the Chinese Communist Party (CCP) under the leadership of Mao Zedong (1893–1976). On October 1, 1949, Mao proclaimed the founding of the People's Republic of China (PRC) after CCP forces defeated Chiang's army on the mainland. Later that year, Chiang had to remove the seat of the ROC government to Taiwan from the mainland. Taiwan then officially became the ROC, and it also controls several smaller islands like Jinmen (Quemoy), Mazu (Matsu), and Penghu (Pescadores). It consists of 16 counties and 2 special municipalities with Taipei as its capital. In 2015 Taiwan's total population was 24 million.

The United States began providing economic and military aid to Taiwan in 1950. As a result, Taiwan had a high 12 percent growth rate of its annual GDP from 1953 to 1964 and an average annual export growth rate of 31 percent in 1961–1964. In the 1980s, Taiwan's annual gross product reached $100 billion ($4,500 per capita). In the 1990s, the economy was growing at an annual rate of 7 percent. In 1996, Taiwan held its first presidential election and entered a new era of multiparty democracy. In 2010, Taiwan's GDP grew 10.7 percent, but its growth slowed to 4 percent in 2011, and fell to 1.3 percent in 2012 when its GDP totaled $918.3 billion and per capita GDP was $39,400. Its exports and natural resources become more dependent on China, its largest trading partner, with 27.1 percent of Taiwan's total exports in 2012, while their political differences and territorial conflicts continue.

See also: Chapter 1: Overview; Disputed Islands and Territories; South China Sea. Chapter 2: Timeline; Chiang Kai-shek; Mao Zedong. Chapter 3: Chinese Communist Party. Chapter 4: Foreign Investment; Joint Ventures.

Further Reading

Brown, Melissa. *Is Taiwan Chinese? The Impact of Culture, Power, and Migration on Changing Identities.* Berkeley: University of California Press, 2004.

Li, Xiaobing, and Zuohong Pan, eds. *Taiwan in the 21st Century.* New York: University Press of America, 2003.

Rigger, Shelley. *Why Taiwan Matters: Small Island, Global Powerhouse.* Boulder, CO: Rowman & Littlefield, 2011.

Roy, Denny. *Taiwan: A Political History.* Ithaca, NY: Cornell University Press, 2002.

Teng, Emma Jinhua. *Taiwan's Imaged Geography.* Cambridge, MA: Harvard University Press, 2006.

The Three Gorges Project

The Three Gorges Dam, 555 feet high and 6,927 feet long, the largest dam in the world, is part of a hydroelectric project over the middle reaches of the Yangzi (Yangtze) River in the city of Yichang, central Hubei Province. The project started in 1994 and was completed in 2006 with a total cost of $25 billion. Its underground hydropower stations became fully operational in 2012. The current annual electric capacity totals 22,500 MW, generated by its 32 main water turbines with a capacity of 700 MW for each. The Three Gorges Dam is designed to raise the water level in the reservoir to 574 feet above sea level and 361 feet higher than river level downstream, with the largest installed electric generating capacity in the world. It provides electric power to central and east China, about 10 percent of the nation's total, and eases the power shortage of these regions.

Its dam reservoir is about 410 miles long with a surface area of 403 square miles, and contains 5 trillion gallons of water. According to official statistics, the Three Gorges Project reduces coal consumption for electric power by 31 million tons annually. The project, the largest key water conservancy project in the country, has improved the navigation condition of the upper Yangzi and has relieved flood threats on the lower reaches of the river.

The project has been a controversial topic because the reservoir flooded a large area, 244 square miles of land, destroying archaeological and cultural sites, and displacing more than 1.3 million people. As a result, the reservoir has submerged 13 cities, 150 towns, and 1,410 villages. Most of the people were relocated to the neighboring Sichuan Province. However many villagers who refused to leave their homes faced forced evictions, legal charges, and punishments. More than 12,000 farmers did not receive the promised compensations, as the funds disappeared due to corruption and mismanagement of the local governments.

As an environmental disaster, the forestation in the Three Gorges area has been reduced from 25 percent coverage before the construction of the dam to less than 10 percent thereafter. The reduction of the forested areas has threatened wildlife in the region, where hundreds of terrestrial animal species and freshwater fish were habitants, and many were already endangered species. The government agrees that the dam construction has caused the extinction of some species. The critiques also believe that the dam has caused significant ecological changes, including water pollution, an increase of landslides, mudslides, and earthquakes.

See also: Chapter 1: Overview; Natural Resources; Pollution and the Environment; Transportation and Water Conservancy; Yangzi River.

Further Reading

Bonavia, Judy, and Richard Hayman. *Yangzi River: The Yangtze and the Three Gorges.* 7th ed. Sidney, Australia: Odyssey, 2004.

Chethan, Deirdre. *Before the Deluge: The Vanishing World of the Yangtze's Three Gorges.* London: Palgrave Macmillan, 2004.

Dai Qing. *The River Dragon Has Come! The Three Gorges Dam and the Fate of China's Yangtze River and Its People.* Armonk, NY: M. E. Sharpe, 1998.

Tibetan Plateau

Also known as the Qinghai-Tibet (Qing-zang) Plateau, the largest plateau in China covers an area of 889,000 square miles (out of 970,000 square miles) in the southwest of China, or approximately 20 percent of the country's total land surface. It begins in the west at Karakoram of the Trans-Himalaya mountain chain and slopes to the Kunlun Mountains in the northeast. This vast, oval tableland stretches about 1,600 miles east to west and 620 miles north to south, with part of Ladakh (about 81,000 square miles), located in Kashmir, in the State of India. As a typical mountainous plateau, it is surrounded by the Kunlun Mountains, Tanggula Mountains, Gandise Mountains, and the Himalayas. The Tibetan Plateau is the highest plateau on earth, with an average elevation exceeding 14,800 feet. It is sometimes called "the Roof of the World."

Because of its high altitude, the Tibetan Plateau has a very low temperature with strong winds. An arid or semiarid climate dominates the plateau, which has an average precipitation of about 15–18 inches per year and is considerably less in many areas. The plateau includes some snow mountains and a large area of glaciers, known as "water towers," which store water and maintain flow. As the principal watershed in Asia, it is also called a solid water reservoir or the "Third Pole." The melted ice and snow become headwaters, and they are the source of many major rivers in South, Southeast, and East Asia. As the most important river in Tibet, the Brahmaputra begins in the plateau and moves westward through India and Bangladesh into the Bay of Bengal of the Indian Ocean. The Indus and Ganges Rivers flow out glaciers in the western Tibetan Plateau, and move southwest across the Indian subcontinent. Rising in central Tibet, the Salween (Nujiang) runs down southward through Myanmar (Burma) and Thailand into the Andaman Sea. The Mekong (Lancangjiang) flows out of the Tibetan Plateau and runs southeast through Thailand, Laos, Cambodia, and Vietnam into the South China Sea. The Yangzi (Yangtze) and Huang (Yellow), the two longest rivers in Asia, originate in the northern plateau and run eastward through China.

Among the largest lakes in the plateau, Ngangla Ringco, Zhari Namco, Nam Co, and Siling Co Lakes are the important irrigating sources of inland China. They also provide water resources for important natural pasture of the northwestern region. Every summer and fall, herds of cows, sheep, and horses graze there. In addition, there are many wild animals on the natural pasture of the plateau.

More than 8 million people live on the Tibetan Plateau in two of China's provinces. Under the government of the Tibetan Autonomous Region (TAR), there are 71 counties and 2 cities with Lhasa as its capital. Its population totals 2.8 million, mostly Tibetans (96 percent of the total), with other ethnic groups like Moinba, Lhoba, and Naxi. The Qinghai Province has 37 counties and 7 cities, with Xi'ning as its capital, and has a total population of 5.8 million, including Han, Tibetan, Hui (Muslims), Mongols, and other ethnic groups. The plateau economy is dominated by subsistence agriculture and raising livestock, such as sheep, cattle, goats, camels, yaks, and horses. In the 21st century, tourism has become an increasingly important sector in the regional economy due to an increased interest in Tibetan Buddhism.

See also: Chapter 1: Overview; Himalayas; Huanghe River; Yangzi River. Chapter 3: Provincial and County Governments. Chapter 5: Buddhism. Chapter 6: Major Ethnic Groups; Mongols; Muslims.

Further Reading

Fleming, Robert, Dorje Tsering, and Liu Wulin. *Across the Tibetan Plateau: Ecosystems, Wildlife, and Conservation.* New York: Norton, 2006.

Gloaquen, R., and L. Ratschbacher. *Growth and Collapse of the Tibetan Plateau.* London: Geological Society, 2011.

Tuttle, Gray, and Kurtis Schaeffer, eds. *The Tibetan History Reader.* New York: Columbia University Press, 2013.

Wang, Luolin, and Ling Zhu, eds. *Breaking Out of the Poverty Trap: Case Studies from the Tibetan Plateau.* Hackensack, NJ: World Century, 2013.

Zheng, Du, Qingsong Zhang, and Shaohong Wu, eds. *Mountain Geo-ecology and Sustainable Development of the Tibetan Plateau*. New York: Springer, 2011.

Transportation and Water Conservancy

Since the 1980s, transportation in the People's Republic of China (PRC) has experienced rapid growth and expansion in terms of railway, airports, roads, and waterways. The railroad is the most important mode of transportation in China, moving about 1 trillion passenger-km per year and 3 trillion ton-km annually, more than half the nation's total freight traffic. Both are the highest in the world. The national rail system, the third largest network in the world, totals more than 60,000 miles of railroads, and about 47 percent of them are electrified. It has 20,800 locomotives, 650,000 cargo cars, and 58,000 passenger coaches. The new railways through Xinjiang in northwest China establish the second Eurasia Continental Land Bridge, passing the Tanggula Mountain, about 15,200 feet above sea level, and making it the highest railway in the world. The world's first commercial high-speed maglev (magnetic levitation) train service was built near the Shanghai Airport in 2003 with German technology. A year later, the first Chinese-made maglev train became operational in Dalian, northeastern Liaoning Province. By 2014, China now has 7,000 miles of high-speed railway passenger services between the major cities, capable of running at 180 miles per hour.

Chinese roads and highways have also grown rapidly in recent decades, extending into rural areas, making most localities accessible, and carrying 769 trillion passenger-km and 11.6 billion tons of freight in 2003. The country had 23.8 million vehicles used for business, 14.8 million passenger cars, and 8.5 million privately owned trucks that year. In 2004 in Beijing, there were about 1.3 million privately owned cars. The total public road network totaled 2.39 million miles by the end of 2010, including 60,273 miles of highway, making China's the longest highway network in the world (ahead of the United States) in 2012. The expressway systems connect all the major cities and carry 49 percent of the passengers. Also, 880,000 miles of this network are classified as local roads, and 478,620 miles are paved roads, or village roads. Public transportation, including bus transit, trolley system, and town tramway, are well developed in urban centers, and the bicycle is still widely used for traveling short distances. China also had 14,000 miles of natural gas pipelines and 9,480 miles of oil pipelines in 2006, carrying about 220 million tons of oil and gas annually.

Among the 27 commercial airlines are Air China, China Eastern, China Southern, Shanghai, Hainan, and Xiamen Airlines, which combined had 860 planes in 2006 and 1,600 planes in 2011. The total is estimated to be 4,000 by 2025. The airlines handled 138 million passengers and 22.2 million tons of cargo in 2005. The Beijing Daxing International Airport, which becomes operational in 2015, will be the country's largest airport with nine runways, and will be the busiest airport in the world. Among the other 500 commercial airports are the Beijing Capital Airport (PEK), Hong Kong

International Airport (HKG), Shanghai Pudong Airport (PVG), Shanghai Hongqiao Airport (SHA), Guangzhou Baiyun Airport (CAN), Chengdu, Chongqing, Dalian, Shenyang, Tianjin, Xiamen, and Xi'an Airports.

China's long coastline and the location of some of the most important industrial cities on the coast have long made coastal shipping an important mode of transportation. It has more than 2,000 ports, and 130 of them are open to foreign ships. Its commercial fleet had more than 3,500 ships by 2004, and its own shipping capacity totals about 3 trillion tons, carrying 35 percent of the world's shipping in 2010. Among its 17 major shipping ports are Dalian, Guangzhou, Nanjing, Ningbo, Qingdao, Qinhuangdao, Hong Kong, and Shanghai. In 2005, its Shanghai Port became the largest cargo port in the world by handling 443 million tons of cargo and surpassing the Singapore Port. China has more than 106,000 miles of navigable inland waterways, accounting for one-fifth of the goods shipped within the country and carrying about 6.3 trillion passenger/km and 1.6 trillion tons of freight to more than 5,100 inland ports in 2003. They also serve as an irrigation system to provide an important water resource for agriculture in China.

Since its water resources are unevenly distributed, in recent decades the country has invested heavily in the extension of water conservancy facilities. China's north lacks water, and the west is always dry. The country built channels and water pumping stations to bring water from the Yangzi River northward to irrigate the North China Plain. Its eastern line of water diversion is about 720 miles from the southeastern lower reaches of the Yangzi (Yangtze) River northward through the Grand Canal, diverting 30 billion cubic meters of water to the North Plain each year. Its western water diversion line is about 625 miles from the middle of the Yangzi and the Han River to the west of North China, annually diverting 30 billion cubic meters of water.

See also: Chapter 1: Overview; Hong Kong; Major Cities; Natural Resources; Population; Yangzi River. Chapter 4: Overview; Agriculture; Energy Industry.

Further Reading

Fallows, James. *China Airborne*. New York: Vintage, 2013.

Guo Songyi. *A Brief History of Water Conservancy in China*. Beijing: China Academy of Social Sciences Press, 2011.

Harwit, Eric. *China's Automobile Industry: Policies, Problems, and Prospects*. Armonk, NY: M. E. Sharpe, 1994.

Lustgarten, Abrahm. *China's Great Train: Beijing's Drive West and the Campaign to Remake Tibet*. New York: St. Martin's Griffin, 2009.

Xinjiang

Largest in area of all the province-level administrative regions of the People's Republic of China (PRC), Xinjiang covers one-sixth of the Chinese territory with a total area of

641,000 square miles. As the borderland in the northwest, it shares borders with Mongolia, Russia, and Kazakhstan in the north, and with Kyrgyzstan, Tajikistan, Afghanistan, Pakistan, and India in the west, with a land border of 3,200 miles. North of Tibet and west of Gansu and Qinghai Provinces, Xinjiang is the hinterland of the Eurasian continent. Historically, Arabic and Chinese merchants traveled through Xinjiang for trade and established the well-known Silk Road connecting the Middle East and China during the Han dynasty (207 BCE–220 CE). Marco Polo and European merchants followed the Silk Road and traveled to China during the Song and Yuan dynasties (1279–1368). In the 20th century, the new railways cross Xinjiang and establish the second Eurasia Continental Land Bridge. Natural resources in Xinjiang include crude oil, natural gas, coal, and farming land, but it lacks natural water resources.

With the Altay Mountains in the north and the Kunlun Mountains in the south, the Tianshan Mountains stretch across central Xinjiang east to west, dividing it into a southern and a northern region. There is a striking difference between the north and the south mountains in temperature, vegetation, and animals. The melted snow and glacier water from these mountains create the nation's largest distribution areas of water supplies and major source of many rivers in the region, including the Tarim River, which flows 1,305 miles as the longest inland river in the country. The grandiose Tianshan area is one of the bases of animal husbandry in Xinjiang.

The Tianshan Mountains separate the Tarim Basin in the south from the Junggar (Dzungarian) Basin in the north of Xinjiang. The Tarim Basin is the largest inland basin in the world with an area of 205,000 square miles. Because of a ring structure of the surrounding mountains, the center of Xinjiang is very dry. From its exterior to the interior are gravel Gobi, oases, and deserts, respectively. The Taklimakan (Takla Makan) Desert is located in the Tarim Basin as the largest desert in the country. It is about 600 miles long from east to west and about 240 miles wide from north to south, covering an area of 138,000 square miles. The Junggar Basin in northern Xinjiang has an area of 147,000 square miles and is the second largest basin in China. In the center of the basin is China's second largest desert—the Gurbantunggut Desert—which holds rich crude oil deposits, coal, and other metal mines within its basin. In the early 1950s, the famous Karamay Oil Field was explored here. Topographically, Xinjiang is the lowest point in China, with Aydingkol Lake at 154 meters below sea level. It has a continental climate, hot in the summer and with little precipitation. The hottest area is the Turpan District where an average temperature in July is 92 degrees Fahrenheit, while the average daytime temperature during the same month exceeds 104 degrees. The highest temperature ever recorded was 119 degrees (in 1941).

The Xinjiang Uygur Autonomous Region (XUAR) was founded in October 1955 as another of China's five autonomous regions for ethnic minorities. The XUAR governs 7 regional districts, 5 autonomous prefectures, 19 cities, 62 counties, and 6 autonomous counties. The city of Urumqi as the provincial capital has 11 metropolitan districts. The XUAR has a population of over 20 million, including 12 million people from 47 different minorities, such as the Uyghur, Kazak, Hui, Mongolian, Tajik, and Tartar peoples. The Uyghur comprise 18 percent of its population, and 99 percent of the Chinese Uyghur live in Xinjiang. Ten minority groups are primarily

Muslim, including the Hui and Uyghur. Most believers follow a faith along ethnic lines; for example, the Uyghur, Kazaks, and Hui believe in Islam.

See also: Chapter 1: Overview; Natural Resources; Population. Chapter 2: Timeline. Chapter 5: Islam. Chapter 6: Overview; Mongols; Muslims; Uyghur.

Further Reading

Bovingdon, Gardner. *The Uyghurs: Strangers in Their Own Land*. New York: Columbia University Press, 2010.

Clarke, Michael E. *Xinjiang and China's Rise in Central Asia*. London: Routledge, 2013.

Mackerras, Colin, and Michael Clarke, eds. *China, Xinjiang and Central Asia: History, Transition and Crossborder Interaction into the 21st Century*. London: Routledge, 2011.

Millward, James. *Eurasian Crossroads: A History of Xinjiang*. New York: Columbia University Press, 2009.

Starr, Frederick. *Xinjiang: China's Muslim Borderland*. Armonk, NY: M. E. Sharpe, 2004.

Tyler, Christian. *Wild West China: The Taming of Xinjiang*. New Brunswick, NJ: Rutgers University Press, 2004.

Yangzi (Yangtze) River

Also called the Changjiang (Long River) in China, the Yangzi (Yangtze) is the longest river in Asia. It flows out of glaciers in the west, crosses the Tibetan Plateau in Qinghai, moving eastward, and crossing the country for 3,988 miles. It is the third longest river in the world, after the Amazon (4,345 miles) and the Nile (4,258 miles), and it finally empties into the East China Sea at Shanghai.

Its source is the Tuotuo River, which originates on the southwestern slopes of snowy Mount Geladandong, the main peak of the Tanggula Mountain in the Himalayas. The Tuotuo joins with the Tongtian and the Jinsha Rivers to form the Yangzi. It runs down from the Kunlun Mountain in Qinghai and Tibet; flows generally south through Sichuan and Yunnan; then turns east, moving across central China through Hubei, Hunan, Jiangxi, Anhui, and Jiangsu through a total of 9 provinces and 18 major cities in China.

On its upper reaches (about 1,377 miles), the river falls from an altitude of 16,000 feet through Qinghai to 1,000 feet at Yibin, and to 630 feet at Chongqing. Between Chongqing and Yichang, two cities in Sichuan Province, at 130 feet and a distance of about 200 miles, the river passes through many gorges flanked by towering mountains, such as the Tiger-Leaping Gorge. The major hydroelectric power dams and stations are built on the upper reaches.

After the Three Gorges, it arrives at the plain area in the middle reaches of the river. From Yichang to the Dongting Lake, Hunan Province, the Yangzi becomes a meandering stream with a broad channel and provides the best navigation for river steamers. By connecting the interior with the coast, the river is the busiest waterway in China. It transports passengers and tourists, and still ships 800 million tons of cargo each year. The middle reaches are characterized with many crooked streams, branches, and lakes. Lake Poyang, the largest freshwater lake in China, merges into the river in Jiangxi Province. Most freshwater lakes in China are scattered over the middle and lower reaches of the Yangzi.

After Wuhan, Hubei Province, a distance of roughly 600 miles from the sea, ocean-going vessels can navigate the Yangzi since it becomes much deeper and wider as it gains water from the lakes and branches along its way. From its mouth, or about 200 miles inland, the Yangzi is virtually at sea level. Recognized as a fertile land of fish and rice, the lower reaches are low and flat, and the water is broad and deep. At the spot where the Yangzi River enters the sea, the river is between 48 and 54 miles wide.

It has a total drainage area of more than 698,266 square miles, which creates an abundance of water power resources. For thousands of years people have used this river for water, irrigation, sanitation, transportation, industry, electric power, boundary-marking, and for war. Hydraulic power plants are constructed at the Gezhou Dam, Three Gorges Dam, and so on. The drainage area of the Yangzi is rich in products, and the economy is well developed. The prosperous Yangzi Delta produces as much as 20 percent of China's GDP. Despite these benefits, floods caused by the river have destroyed much life and property in 1905, 1931, 1954, 1980, 1991, and 1998. About 145,000 people were killed in the 1931 floods.

See also: Chapter 1: Overview; Himalayas; Major Cities; Pollution and the Environment; Population; The Three Gorges Project; Tibetan Plateau; Transportation and Water Conservancy. Chapter 4: Overview; Agriculture.

Further Reading

Butler, Linda. *Yangtze Remembered: The River beneath the Lake.* Stanford, CA: Stanford University Press, 2004.

Lynn, Madeleine. *Yangtze River: The Wildest, Wickedest River on Earth.* New York: Oxford University Press, 1997.

Maloney, Tracy, and Boyce Hutchins. *Yangtze River: Geography, Pollution and Environmental Implications.* Hauppauge, NY: Nova Science, 2013.

Wilkinson, Philip. *Yangtze.* London: BBC Books, 2007.

CHAPTER 2

HISTORY

OVERVIEW

China represents one of the oldest civilizations in the world with a recorded history of at least 5,000 years. These records include rich historical documents and ancient relics as well as folklore. Based on its unique geographic setting, demographic characteristics, and political structure, Chinese culture emerged from an adaptation to the natural environment to productive technological development, society building, and military experience.

During the pre-history (pre-2500 BCE) period, the Chinese gradually progressed from living in groups to living as members of a clan (or tribe). Relics depicting how primitive Chinese people lived in gens communes have been found in many parts of Central China along the Huang (Yellow) River, the cradle of Chinese civilization. Warmer weather, improved tools, and domestication of some animals in 12000–8000 BCE led to agricultural development and an expanding population. In approximately 3000 BCE, many clans along the Yellow River developed into a patriarchal society.

The ancient time (2500–771 BCE) featured conflicts over arable land, slaves, and water resources, which evolved into large-scale warfare among the five major tribal groups. Among the five emperors (*wudi*) (2600–2200 BCE) was the Yellow Emperor (*Huang-di*) (2300–2250 BCE), who led many tribes in the Huaxia (Hua-Hsia) group along the western Yellow River and unified the country in 2250 BCE. The Huaxia shaped Chinese civilization with the Yellow River remaining central to China's historical development. From 2205–1766 BCE, the Xia (Hsia) dynasty was established by the Great Yu (*Dayu*) (2205–?). Although stone was still the major material for making tools and weapons, copper weapons began appearing. Chinese rice productivity along the Yellow and the Yangzi (Yangtze) Rivers generated enough wealth and food to support a large population. The Shang dynasty (1766–1027 BCE) established its capital first in Bo (modern Shangqiu, Henan), and then moved to Yin (Anyang). Inscriptions are found on some early bronzes, but most Shang writing was incised on "dragon bones," which are actually the under-shells of tortoises, the scapulae or shoulder blades of cattle, and other flat bones. After Shang, the Zhou (Chou) dynasty (1027–221 BCE) is historically divided into two periods: the Western Zhou (1027–771 BCE) with the capital of Hao (Xi'an, Shaanxi), and the Eastern Zhou (771–256 BCE) with the capital of Luoyi (Luoyang, Henan).

The classic age (771–206 BCE) began during the Eastern Zhou, which is divided into two historical periods: the Spring and Autumn Period (722–481 BCE) and the Warring

31

States Period (403–221 BCE). Continuing social disorder and endless warfare spurred philosophical and strategic debate. Many schools of philosophy and strategy flourished, and altogether they created "a hundred schools contended," including Confucianism, Daoism (Taoism), Legalism, and Sunzi's (Sun-tzu) (535 BCE–) military classic. During the Warring States Period, among the seven states, the King of Qin (Chin) embarked upon a dramatic conquest of ancient China's separate kingdoms. In 221 BCE, China was unified under Qin (or Chin, from which emerged the nation's Westernized name: China). The Qin dynasty (221–206 BCE) established a highly centralized regime, the first of its kind in Chinese history.

The imperial period (206 BCE–1840 CE) began with the Han dynasty (206 BCE–220 CE), a cycle of dynasties in China that would continue for the next 2,000 years. The Han emperors began conquering territories outside the Great Wall. Successful military expeditions to the west, along with territorial expansion into Korea and Vietnam, convinced the Han emperors and the Chinese people of their superiority in a civilized society. The Han became the first glorious dynasty in Chinese history. The Chinese people began calling themselves the "Han people" (*Hanzu*, or Han nationals, the majority, or 90 percent, of the current population), and their Chinese language was called the "Han language" (*Hanyu*). The Han emperors believed that China (*Zhongguo*) was the "Central Kingdom," superior to all other people and nations under the heavens, and that it occupied a central position in the known universe. After the collapse of the Han dynasty, China had two long periods of division and civil wars. These were the Three Kingdoms, 220–280 and Northern and Southern dynasties, 317–582.

Although the Sui dynasty (581–618) reunified the country again, the emperors squandered public treasure by building palaces for their own comfort and vanity. In 617, an aristocrat, Li Yuan (as Gaozu reigned 618–626), and his son Li Shimin (Li Ch'i-min) (as Taizong reigned 627–649), attacked and occupied Chang'an, the Sui capital. The following year, Li Yuan assumed the imperial title at Chang'an and called his new regime the Tang dynasty (618–907), which became one of the most successful dynasties, making China once again central to Asian affairs. After Tang, the Song dynasty (960–1279) took several measures to prevent the re-emergence of separatist local regimes, and concentrated all power in the central government. The domination of a civilian bureaucracy in military affairs contributed to the Song army's defeats against invading Mongol troops. In 1279, the Mongols destroyed the Chinese army, thus ending the Song dynasty.

The Mongols based their powerful medieval military system on a cavalry whose speed and mobility made them formidable. The Mongol rulers founded the Yuan dynasty (1279–1368) in China, and controlled Xinjiang and Tibet (Xizang) for the first time in Chinese history.

Cruel oppression by the Mongols precipitated a series of revolts. In 1351, the Red Turban Army rose in Yingzhou, Anhui Province, and peasants from many other places joined them. Peasant forces captured Dadu (Beijing), the Yuan capital and overthrew the Mongol regime, establishing the Ming dynasty (1368–1644). In 1627, northern Shaanxi experienced a severe drought, and not a single kernel of grain was harvested that year. As thousands of peasants starved, the survivors raised the standard of revolt.

From Shaanxi and Gansu, peasant leaders emerged, such as Li Zicheng (Li Tzu-ch'eng) (1605–1645), as well as others who jointly commanded dozens of insurgent armies. Not only the Han, but also the Mongolians and the Hui (Muslim) peasants, supported this rebellion. Wherever they went, Li and his men were welcomed by crowds of citizens. The insurgent army quickly snowballed into hundreds of thousands in number. In 1644, Li led the grand army into Beijing, thus ending the Ming dynasty.

In June 1644, however, Manchu troops entered the Great Wall from the north, defeating the peasant army and establishing the Qing (Ch'ing) dynasty (1644–1912). The Manchu state, which occupied northeast China (Manchuria), had been fighting the Ming army for the territory along the Great Wall for decades. The Manchu leaders saw the collapse of the Ming, which weakened Li's military leadership, and decided to take the opportunity to attempt to rule China. At the time of the Qing, capitalism and industrialization rose dynamically in the Western world, and many countries expanded their empires by encroaching upon Chinese territory. Owing to the Manchu rulers' closed-door policy, China's policies, on the whole, became more and more passive.

Chinese modern history (1840) begins with its humiliating defeats in the Opium War. In the late 19th century, frequent peasant rebellions, foreign invasions, and anti-Manchu movements undermined the power of the Qing dynasty. In 1895 China was defeated by Japan, thus losing its central position in Asia. The anti-Manchu movement founded its revolutionary center in Japan, where Sun Yat-sen (1866–1925) became the leader. On October 10, 1911, amid an anti-Qing plot in Wuchang, the provincial capital of Hubei, some New Army officers revolted (October 10, or "Double Tens," became the National Day for the Republic of China). The success of the Wuchang uprising led many officers to join the revolution.

The provisional government elected Sun, who was inaugurated as provisional president of the Republic of China (ROC) on January 1, 1912, at Nanjing. As a great breakthrough in Chinese history, this ended 2,000 years of monarchy and built the first republic in Asian history. Although the Chinese Revolution of 1911 had ended Qing, it failed to turn China into a truly independent and democratic country. From 1916 to 1927, the country entered the "Warlord Period of 1916–1927," in which military commanders of different armies controlled a province or a region. After his successful Northern Expedition in 1926–1927 against the warlords, Chiang Kai-shek (Jiang Jieshi) (1887–1975) established his new government of the ROC under Nationalist Party (Guomindang, GMD; or Kuomintang, KMT) control in Nanjing in April 1927, launching China's Republic Period of 1927–1937.

In the early 20th century, as Soviet ideology and reports of the Bolshevik revolution circulated, the time arrived for the founding of the Chinese Communist Party (CCP). In July 1921, the CCP was founded by 13 delegates, including Mao Zedong (Mao Tse-tung) (1893–1976), representing approximately 50 CCP members across the country. The party mobilized the peasants, established and trained its army, and received instructions and aid from the Soviet Union. The army protected the communist-based areas. Mao described this relationship as the "Political power grows out of the barrel of a gun." On July 7, 1937, the Japanese Imperial Army attacked the GMD troops at the Marco Polo Bridge (*Lugouqiao*) southwest of Beijing. On August 13, Japanese troops

Mao Zedong, chairman of the Chinese Communist Party (CCP), proclaims the founding of the People's Republic of China (PRC) at the Tiananmen Square Gate in Beijing, ushering in a new era of communist rule on October 1, 1949. This proclaimation followed the defeat of Chiang Kai-shek's army in the Chinese Civil War (1946–1949) on the mainland and the retreat of the Nationalists to Taiwan. (AP Photo)

attacked Shanghai and threatened Nanjing. The GMD government came to an agreement with the CCP to jointly resist the Japanese invasion of China (1937–1945). The CCP's regular army had grown from 56,000 in 1937 to 1.27 million in 1945, supported by militias numbering another 2.68 million. China's full-scale civil war resumed between the GMD and the CCP in June 1946. By September 1949, the CCP forces, or the People's Liberation Army (PLA) occupied most of the country except for Tibet, Taiwan, and various offshore islands. Chiang removed the seat of his GMD government from the mainland to Taiwan.

On October 1, 1949, Mao declared the birth of the People's Republic of China (PRC) and of the new republic's alliance with Moscow. China began to move into center stage of the global Cold War between the Soviet Union and the United States, two contending camps headed by two superpowers. The PRC's alliance with the Soviet Union and North Korea pulled China into a foreign war in Korea (1950–1953). The first generation (1949–1976) of CCP leaders developed its political institutions based on the totalitarian model originated by the Soviets. To preserve party unity and to face the tremendous difficulties ahead, Mao established his "permanent revolution" idea and his own personality cult, as Josef Stalin (1878–1953) had. He then launched one political campaign after another, similar to the Cultural Revolution (1966–1976), in an effort to eliminate political rivals.

After Mao's death in 1976, Deng Xiaoping (Deng Hsiao-ping) (1904–1997) became the leading figure of the second generation (1976–1990) leadership and launched a wave of tremendous change, particularly in creating a free-market system, seeking global inclusion, and meeting popular demand for modernization of the country, along with improvements in the standard living. Deng adapted to changing circumstances and prevented the CCP and PRC from bankruptcy. The economic reforms in the 1980s have successfully transformed China from an agricultural economy to one of booming industry, which in turn has brought transformation from a communistic totalitarian government to a socialist authoritarian one.

When Deng retired, the CCP faced the consequence of the bloody showdown at Tiananmen Square in June 1989, which convinced both reformers and conservatives that neither could win without a national disaster. They agreed to a continuation of reform as long as it proceeded more slowly and was approved by Deng's choice of successor, Jiang Zemin (1926–), who shared power and provided moderate leadership of the third generation (1991–2002). When Jiang gradually shifted the party's ideology and political goal from radical communism to moderate nationalism, he faced new challenges, such as increasing demands for improvement of the country's human rights, civil liberties, and relations with Tibet and Taiwan.

After Jiang retired in 2002, Hu Jintao (1942–) became the new leader of the CCP fourth generation (2002–2012). The growing diversity within CCP leadership and the dynamic interdependence among competing factions was emerging at this time. Their increasing factional struggles have constrained Hu from making new domestic and foreign policy initiatives. After Hu retired in 2012, Xi Jinping (1953–) became the new leader of the CCP and the PRC from 2012–2022, and he faces new political struggles, government scandals, and more crises. It appears that the new leadership in Beijing will maintain economic growth at home while seeking a growing role on the global political stage. Power-sharing through checks and balances among competing political camps may entail a more dynamic and institutionalized decision-making process.

Further Reading

Fairbank, John, and Merle Goldman. *China: A New History*. 2nd ed. Cambridge, MA: Harvard University Press, 2006.

Gifford, Rob. *China Road: A Journey into the Future of a Rising Power*. New York: Random House, 2008.

Li, Xiaobing, and Xiansheng Tian, eds. *Evolution of Power: China's Struggle, Survival, and Success*. Lanham, MD: Lexington, 2013.

Spence, Jonathan. *The Search for Modern China*. 3rd ed. New York: Norton, 2012.

Tanner, Harold. *China: A History: From Neolithic Culture through the Great Qing Empire (10,000 BCE-1799 CE)*. Indianapolis, IN: Hackett, 2010.

Wasserstrom, Jeffrey. *China in the 21st Century: What Everyone Needs to Know*. New York: Oxford University Press, 2010.

TIMELINE

3000 BCE	Three Sovereigns (*Sanhuang*) begin.
2600 BCE	Three Sovereigns ends.
	Five-Emperor (*Wudi*) Period begins.
2205 BCE	Great Yu (*Dayu*) establishes Xia dynasty.
1766 BCE	Xia ends.
	Shang dynasty begins.

1027 BCE	Shang ends.
	Zhou or Western Zhou dynasty begins.
771 BCE	Western Zhou ends.
770 BCE	Eastern Zhou dynasty begins.
	Spring and Autumn Period begins.
551 BCE	Confucius is born in Shandong.
535 BCE	Sunzi is born in Zhejiang.
500 BCE	*The Art of War* is written by Sunzi.
	Laozi is born.
475 BCE	Spring and Autumn Period ends.
	Warring States Period begins.
221 BCE	Warring States Period ends.
	Zhou ends.
	Qin dynasty is established by Qin Shi Huangdi.
220 BCE	The Great Wall is under construction.
206 BCE	Qin ends.
	Han or Western Han dynasty begins.
111 BCE	Han Wudi annexes Vietnam.
108 BCE	Han Wudi conquers Korea.
8 CE	Wang Meng topples Western Han.
23	Western Han ends.
25	Liu Xiu restores the Han by establishing Eastern Han (or Later Han) dynasty.
184	Yellow Turban Rebellion begins.
220	Han ends.
	Three Kingdoms Period begins.
	Wei is founded.
221	Shu is founded.
229	Wu is founded.
265	Jin or Western Jin dynasty begins.
280	Three Kingdoms Period ends.
316	Western Jin ends.
317	Eastern Jin dynasty begins.
386	Northern-Southern dynasties begin.
	Northern Wei dynasty begins.
420	Eastern Jin ends.
	Southern Song dynasty begins.
479	Southern Song ends.
502	Liang dynasty begins.
534	Eastern Wei dynasty begins.
535	Northern Wei ends.
	Western Wei dynasty begins.
550	Eastern Wei ends.
	Fubing system begins.
	Northern Qi (Ch'i) dynasty begins.

557	Chen dynasty begins.
	Liang ends.
	Northern Zhou (Chou) dynasty begins.
	Western Wei ends.
577	Northern Qi ends.
581	Northern Zhou ends.
	Sui dynasty begins.
589	Chen ends.
618	Sui ends.
	Tang dynasty begins.
631	Tang Taizong fights Turkic nomads.
645	Tang invades Korea.
655	Tang conquers Korea.
684	Empress Wu seizes power.
705	Empress Wu dies.
755	An-Shi Rebellion begins.
874	Huang Zhao Rebellion begins.
884	Huang Zhao Rebellion ends.
907	Tang ends.
960	Song or Northern Song dynasty begins.
1123	Song fights the Jurchen invading troops in the north.
1125	The Jurchens takes over Kaifeng and establishes the Jin dynasty.
1127	North Song ends.
	Southern Song dynasty begins with Lin'an as the capital in the south.
1234	Song-Mongol War begins.
1271	Yuan dynasty begins.
1279	Southern Song ends.
	Kublai Khan conquers Tibet.
1351	Red Turban Army launches rebellion.
1368	Yuan ends.
	Ming dynasty begins.
1404	Zheng He leads seven expeditions to Persia, Arabia, and Africa.
1593	Ming army defeats Japanese invading army in Korea.
1632	Li Zicheng leads a peasant rebellion.
1644	Li's army takes over Beijing.
	Ming ends.
	Manchus enter the Great Wall and establish the Qing (Ch'ing) dynasty.
1681	Three feudal princes' rebellion begins.
1689	Treaty of Nerchinsk is signed between China and Russia.
1723	Emperor Yongzheng's Banner reforms begin.
1727	Treaty of Kiakhta is signed between China and Russia.
1813	Eight Trigrams Rebellion begins.
1839	First Opium War begins between China and Great Britain.
1841	Hong Kong is ceded to Great Britain by the Qing.

1842	First Opium War ends with a British victory.
	Treaty of Nanjing is signed.
1844	Treaty of Wangxia is signed between China and the United States.
1850	Taiping Rebellion begins.
1851	Nian Rebellion begins.
1853	Taiping army takes over Nanjing.
	Small Sword Society is founded in Shanghai.
1856	Second Opium War begins.
1857	Second Opium War ends with British and French victory.
	Treaty of Tianjin is signed.
1860	Ever-Victorious Army is founded in Shanghai.
	Second Opium War ends.
1861	The Self-Strengthening Movement begins.
1864	Qing army takes over Nanjing.
	Taiping Rebellion ends.
1866	Sun Yat-sen is born.
1868	Nian Rebellion ends.
1884	French-Chinese War begins.
1885	French-Chinese War ends with a French victory.
	Treaty of Tianjin is signed between China and France.
1894	Sino-Japanese War occurs and China is defeated.
	The New Army is founded.
1895	Treaty of Shimonoseki is signed between China and Japan.
1897	Boxer Rebellion begins.
1899	Open Door Policy is initiated by the United States.
1900	Eight foreign armies invade China and defeat the Boxers.
1901	Boxer Protocol is signed between China and eight powers.
1903	Sun publishes the "Three Principles of the People."
1904	Russo-Japanese War begins over Manchuria.
1905	Russian army and navy are defeated by Japan.
	Russo-Japanese War ends.
1906	Beiyang Army and Navy are formed by the Qing.
1911	October 10: New Army officer launches uprising in Wuchang.
	Chinese Revolution begins against the Qing.
1912	January 1: Republic of China (ROC) is founded with Sun as its president.
	February 12: the last emperor abdicates and Qing ends.
	March: Marshal Yuan Shikai becomes ROC president.
	August: Sun reorganizes the Tongmenghui into the Guomindang (GMD).
1916	President Yuan dies.
	Warlord Period begins.
1921	Chinese Communist Party (CCP) is founded.
1924	January: The CCP-GMD coalition begins.
	June 16: Whampoa Military Academy is founded with Chiang Kai-shek as its commandant.

1925	March 12: Sun dies.
	August 26: The National Revolutionary Army is founded with Chiang as its commander.
1926	Northern Expedition begins under the command of Chiang.
1927	Chiang defeats warlords and establishes new ROC government in Nanjing.
	Warlord Period ends.
	April 12: Chiang terminates the CCP-GMD coalition.
	August 1: the CCP launches the Nanchang Uprising.
	September: Mao Zedong leads the Autumn Harvest Uprising.
	December: the CCP launches the Guangzhou Uprising.
1928	CCP Red Army is founded.
	Jinggangshan revolutionary base area set up.
	Mao begins guerrilla warfare against the GMD.
1930	The CCP launches the Changsha Uprising.
	Mao establishes the Jiangxi Soviet.
	Chiang organized four Encirclement Campaigns against the CCP base areas.
1931	September 18: Japan invades Manchuria.
1934	Chiang's Fifth Encirclement Campaigns drives the Red Army out of its base.
	Jiangxi Soviet ends.
	The Red Army's Long March begins.
1935	The Long March ends.
	Yan'an becomes the capital for the CCP for the next 13 years.
1936	Anti-Japanese Military and Political College is founded at Yan'an.
	Xi'an Incident occurs and Chiang is arrested by his generals.
1937	January: The United Front in China is established though a CCP-GMD coalition.
	July 7: Marco Polo Bridge Incident occurs.
	August: CCP Red Army merges as GMD Eighth Route Army and New Fourth Army.
	September: Battle of Pingxingguan occurs.
	December: Japanese seizes Nanjing, the capital of ROC.
	Anti-Japanese War begins.
1938	March-April: Battle of Taierzhuang occurs.
	March-June: Battle of Xuzhou occurs.
1940	The Eighth Route Army's Hundred Regiments Campaign begins.
1941	Japanese "Three-Alls" operations begins.
	American Volunteer Group is formed.
	New Fourth Army Incident occurs.
1942	U.S. General Joseph Stilwell begins to serve as Chiang's military adviser.
	Chiang sends GMD armies to the China-Burma-India Theater.
1943	Sino-American Cooperative Organization (SACO) is created.
1944	Japanese launch "Operation ICHI-GO" in China.
	America's Dixie Mission arrives at Yan'an.
1945	August 6: U.S. forces drop the first atomic bomb on Japan.

August 8: The Soviet Red Army attacks Japanese in China.

August 9: U.S. forces drop the second atomic bomb on Japan.

August 15: Japan surrenders unconditionally.

October: Mao-Chiang negotiation fails at Chongqing.

December: U.S. President Harry Truman sends George Marshall to China for further mediation.

1946 U.S. Secretary of State George Marshall's Mission failed.

Chinese Civil War begins between the CCP and GMD.

Chiang launches an all-out offensive campaign against CCP-held regions.

1947 Marshall returns to the United States.

Chiang's strategy changes from broad assaults to attacking key targets.

The CCP creates field armies as mobile force.

Lin Biao's Northeast Field Army begins offensive campaigns.

1948 The CCP's offensive campaigns begin.

October–November: Liaoning-Shenyang (Liao-Shen) Campaign occurs.

November–January 1949: Pin-Jin (Beiping-Tianjin) Campaign occurs.

November–January 1949: Huai-Hai Campaign occurs.

November: The CCP creates the People's Liberation Army (PLA).

1949 April: The PLA crosses the Yangzi River.

April 23: The PLA seizes Nanjing.

October 1: Mao proclaims the founding of the People's Republic of China (PRC).

Chiang removes the seat of his ROC government from the mainland to Taiwan.

December: Mao visits the Soviet Union and meets Josef Stalin.

1950 February: Sino-Soviet Treaty of Friendship and Alliance is signed.

May: Campaign against Counter-Revolutionaries begins.

June: The PLA begins the Bandit Extermination Campaign.

June 25: The Korean War breaks out.

August: Chinese Military Advisory Group is sent to Vietnam.

October: China intervenes in the Korean War by sending the PLA troops.

November: Chinese launch two offensive campaigns against the UN force.

1951 January: Chinese Third Offensive Campaign in Korea.

February–March: Chinese Fourth Offensive Campaign in Korea.

April–May: Chinese Fifth Offensive Campaign in Korea.

July 10: Truce negotiations begin in Korea.

China launches the Three Antis and Five Antis movements.

1952 Mao calls for a national movement to learn from the Soviet Union.

China continues fighting the Korean War while negotiating for peace.

1953 June: Chinese Summer Offensives begin in Korea.

July 23: Korean Armistice is signed and the Korean War ends.

Campaign against Counter-Revolutionaries ends.

1954 July 20: Geneva Agreement is signed and French troops withdraw from Vietnam.

August–September: The First Taiwan Strait Crisis begins.

September 20: The First National People's Congress (NPC) convenes.

September: The NPC creates new Ministry of Defense with Peng as the minister.

December 2: U.S.-ROC Mutual Defense Treaty is signed for Taiwan's safety.

1955 January 15: China starts its first nuclear weapons program: Project 02.

January 17–19: Battle of Yijiangshan occurs.

July 30: The Second NPC Plenary issues the Military Service Law.

November 4: China makes its first plan for nuclear weapons development.

1956 September 15–27: The Eighth CCP National Congress convenes.

Mao calls for the "Blooming of the Hundred Flowers" movement.

1957 Mao launches the Anti-Rightist Movement.

November: Mao visits Moscow and meets Nikita Khrushchev.

December: A Soviet-made P-2 surface-to-surface missile arrives in Beijing.

1958 The Sino-Soviet split emerges.

The Great Leap Forward movement begins.

The second Five-Year Plan (1958–1962) begins.

August 23: Second Taiwan Strait Crisis occurs.

1959 March: The PLA suppresses the Tibetan rebellion and Dalai Lama flees to India.

April: The Second NPC elects Liu Shaoqi as the PRC's president.

July 2–August 16: The CCP Eighth Plenum purges Peng.

1960 The great Sino-Soviet polemic debate begins and lasts for three years.

Mao criticizes Khrushchev as a "revisionist."

August 13: All 12,000 Russian experts leave China and all Soviet aid stops.

1961 A serious economic depression known as the Three Hard Years begins and claims more than 20 million lives.

1962 September 24–27: CCP Tenth Plenum of the Eighth Central Committee is held.

October 20: Sino-Indian Border War breaks out.

November 22: China announces a cease-fire along the Chinese-Indian border.

1963 April 12-May 16: President Liu visits Indonesia, Burma, Vietnam, and Cambodia.

May: Mao starts the socialist education, also known as the Four Cleanups.

1964 October 16: China carries out its first nuclear bomb test.

December 20: The Third NPC opens and re-elects Liu as president.

Movement to Resist America and Aid Vietnam begins.

1965 May 14: China conducts its second nuclear test.

July: China begins to send troops to Vietnam.

1966 May 16: Mao launches the Great Proletarian Cultural Revolution.

June: The Red Guards are organized as the driving force for the movement.

August: Mao meets millions of the Red Guards in Beijing.

October: Liu, Deng, and many officials are publicly criticized and purged.

The PLA establishes the Second Artillery Corps (Strategic missile force).

1967   January: The mass organizations begin to overtake Shanghai; other cities follow.

March: Armed clashes take place between different mass organizations.

July: An armed clash occurs in Hubei, and more than 180,000 are killed.

To prevent civil war, 2.8 million officers and soldiers of the PLA are employed to restore the order through military administrative committees.

1968   October 13–31: The Twelfth Plenum of the Eighth Central Committee holds and officially purges Liu and many leaders from the party, government, and the PLA.

December: China has sent 23 divisions, totaling 320,000 troops, to Vietnam.

1969   March: Border skirmishes between PRC and USSR occur.

April 1–24: CCP Ninth Congress recognizes Lin Biao as Mao's successor.

November 12: President Liu dies after two years of detention.

1970   The Sino-Soviet border conflicts continues.

U.S. Secretary Henry Kissinger and Le Duc Tho begin secret talks to end Vietnam War.

China withdraws its troops from Vietnam.

April: China launches its first satellite.

1971   Five Seven One (571) Plan is formed.

September 13: Lin Biao and his family are killed in a plane crash in Mongolia. Mao begins a purge in the military and appoints Ye as defense minister.

October: China is admitted to the United Nations.

1972   February 21–28: U.S. President Richard Nixon visits China, where he signs the joint Shanghai Communiqué.

1973   United States and China announce to establish liaison offices in their capitals.

China ends its Movement to Resist America and Aid Vietnam.

August 24–28: CCP Tenth Congress holds and re-elects Mao as the chairman.

1974   January: The PLA's Xisha Islands naval campaign occurs in the South China Sea.

October: Mao brings Deng back from the purge as the first vice premier.

1975   January 13: The Fourth NPC promulgates the second constitution.

April 5: Chiang Kai-shek dies.

December: President Gerald Ford visits Beijing and agrees to terminate the U.S.-Taiwan Defense Treaty and withdraw U.S. military forces from the island.

1976   January 8: Zhou Enlai dies.

July 28: An earthquake measuring 7.8 on the Richter scale rocks Tangshan and becomes the largest earthquake of the 20th century by death toll, about 240,000–255,000 people killed, 164,000 severely injured, and 779,000 injured.

September 9: Mao Zedong dies at 82, and the Cultural Revolution ends.

	October: The Maoist leaders, or the Gang of Four, are arrested by Hua Guofeng, Mao's successor.
1977	July 16–21: CCP Tenth Central Committee supports Hua's leadership.
	August 12–18: CCP Eleventh National Congress elects Hua as chairman.
1978	Deng Xiaoping becomes the key leader and begins an unprecedented seismic reform and opening up to the world to modernize China after his historical speech, "Emancipate the Mind," at the Third Plenum of the Eleventh CCP Central Committee.
1979	January 1: The United States normalizes relations with the PRC.
	January: Deng becomes the first PRC leader to visit America, holding talks with President Jimmy Carter and signing the protocols.
	February: China invades Vietnam with 200,000 PLA troops.
	March–May: The "Democracy Walls" become the "Beijing Spring" movement.
1980	November 20–December 29: The Supreme Court holds open trials of the Gang of Four.
1981	The CCP Central Military Commission elects Deng as chairman.
	Hu Yaobang replaces Hua as chairman of the CCP Central Committee.
1982	September 1–October 1: The CCP holds its Twelfth National Congress.
	December 4: The Fifth Plenary Session of the Fifth NPC adopts the new constitution. The 1982 Constitution becomes the current constitution.
1983	The People's Armed Police (PAP) is established.
1984	April 26–May 1: President Ronald Reagan visits China and meets with Deng.
	October: CCP Central Committee decides to reform the economic structure. Fourteen coastal cities and the island of Hainan are opened to foreign investment.
1985	President Li Xiannian visits Washington signing pact allowing sale of non-military technology to China.
	U.S. Vice President George H. Bush visits China.
1986	Sino-Vietnamese border conflicts continue.
	Deng carries out military reform in the PLA.
1987	The CMC reduces the scale of the PLA's operation in Vietnam.
	Deng lays out three stages of achievement for China's modernization.
1988	April: The First Session of the Seventh NPC adopts two constitutional amendments on private property and protection of the ownership.
1989	April–May: Hundreds of thousands of students and citizens hold demonstrations in Beijing, which later spread to 116 cities.
	May 6–16: The students encamp at Tiananmen Square and begin a hunger strike.
	May 19: The government establishes martial law and deploys 22 infantry divisions in the cities.
	June 3–4: The PLA troops open fire at the students and citizens at Tiananmen Square, estimated thousand casualties.
1990	April: President Yang Shangkun promulgates the Basic Law of Hong Kong Special Administrative Region (SAR) adopted by the Seventh NPC.

1991	After the Tiananmen Incident, Jiang Zemin becomes the top leader as the chairman of both the party Central Committee and Central Military Commission.
	December 25: The Soviet Union collapses.
1992	The political negotiation between China and Taiwan begins.
	May: Falun Gong, one of the *qigong*-based exercise groups, established.
1993	March: The First Session of the Eighth NPC made nine important changes as amendments including some changes in the Preamble to the Constitution.
1994	January: The State Council promulgates the Regulations on the Administration of Sites for Religious Activities.
1995	The Third Taiwan Strait Crisis begins.
1996	July: China fires missiles near Taiwan and conducts military exercise in the Taiwan Strait.
	November: Jiang Zemin called for the "two transformations" of the PLA.
1997	February 28: Deng Xiaoping dies at age of 93.
	July 1: British returns Hong Kong to the PRC.
	Jiang Zemin meets U.S. President Bill Clinton in Washington, D.C.
1998	President Clinton meets Jiang in Beijing.
	The PRC begins publishing the National Defense White Paper.
1999	The People's Armed Police increases to 1 million troops.
	July: Jiang outlaws the Falun Gong movement and arrest 90,000 members.
	December: Portugal turns Macao back to China.
2000	February: Jiang states the "Three Represents" which become his legacy.
	July 31: Beijing court sentences Cheng Kejie, former vice chairman of the National People's Congress, to death for his accepting bribes.
	September 22–28: Jiang makes a speech at the UN Millennium Conference.
	October 9–11: The Fifth Plenary Session of the CCP Fifteenth Central Committee is held in Beijing and passes China's tenth Five-Year Plan.
2001	The Law on Population and Birth Planning is promulgated.
	October: U.S. President George W. Bush visits Shanghai.
	November: China joins the World Trade Organization (WTO).
2002	February: President George W. Bush visits Beijing.
	November: The SARS breaks out in southern China.
2003	The Armed Police has 31 armies, including 508 armed police regiments and 42 special regiments, such as helicopter, artillery, chemical, and tank regiments.
	Official records show 4,143 fatalities in coal mining.
	There are 58,000 mass protests this year.
	July 31: There are 5,328 SARS cases and 349 fatalities.
	October 15: China sends the first human flight into space. China becomes the third country in the world to have independent human spaceflight capability.
2004	There are 74,000 mass protests this year.

November: The government launches a new detention campaign targeting writers, journalists, and political commentators.

2005 There are 87,000 mass protests during the year.

Authorities have 32 journalists in jail this year.

The Ministry of Public Security estimates that 10,000 women and children are abducted and sold each year, and between 2 and 4 million women are involved in prostitution.

October 12: China launches its second human spaceflight, *Shenzhou 6*.

2006 More than 80,000 incidents of social unrest and protest take place this year. China has 490,000 police, 150,000 detectives and investigators, and 1.5 million PAP. At least 930 cases of police torture take place. More than 300 police officers have been killed every year since 1993.

Official statistics show that 31 million people are below the poverty line.

2007 China has more than 580,000 police, 150,000 detectives, and 250,000 traffic cops and special police, all of whom are under the control of the Ministry of Public Security.

Authorities have arrested 270 priests of the underground churches this year.

A total of 1.8 million prisoners are in jail.

The FCCC reports 160 incidents of harassment of foreign journalists when they conduct interviews this year.

2008 March 14: Buddhist riots occur in Lhasa. Official state media reports 4,434 persons are arrested.

March 28: The government confirms 28 civilian and one police officer dead, and 325 civilian were injured during the "3–14 Riots." According to the India-based Tibetan Government-in-exile, more than 220 Tibetans are killed and 7,000 Tibetans are arrested.

April 29: The Lhasa Intermediate Court sentence 30 Tibetans to three years to life in prison for their participations in the "3–14 Riots."

May 12: An earthquake measuring 8.0 on the Richter magnitude scale rocks Wenchuan, Sichuan. Official statistics show at least 69,000 killed, 374,000 injured, 18,000 still missing, and 4.8 million people homeless.

August 8–24: China hosts the Olympic Games in Beijing participated by 10,500 athletics in 302 events of 28 sports.

2009 July 5: Tens of thousands Uyghur demonstrators gather in Urumqi, Xinjiang. After confrontations with police, the demonstration escalates into riots with 197 people died and 1,721 others are injured.

July 18: The World Uyghur Congress reports 600 dead during the "7-5 Xinjiang Riots." The official confirms more than 1,500 rioters have been arrested.

November 14–17: President Barack Obama visits China and explains the significance of civil liberties to Chinese students in Shanghai.

December 23: Liu Xiaobo was sentenced to 11 years' imprisonment.

December 29: British citizen Akmal Shaikh is executed by lethal injection by Chinese authorities after he was convicted of drug smuggling in October.

December: 22 Uyghurs are sentenced to death for participating in the "7-5 Riots."

2010   January: Google makes an announcement that the company will no longer cooperate with China's censorship laws.

February 18: President Obama meets Dalai Lama in the White House.

February 22: CCP Politburo holds meeting, chaired by Hu Jintao.

March 5–14: The Third Plenary Session of the Eleventh National People's Congress is held in Beijing.

April 12: President Hu visits President Obama at the White House in Washington.

April 14: An earthquake takes place at Yushu County, Qinghai Province, 2,046 people killed, 12,135 injured, and 193 missing.

May 1: Shanghai World Expo 2010 opens.

October 8: the Nobel Committee awards the 2010 Peace Prize to Liu Xiaobo.

October 31: Shanghai World Expo 2010 ends after having 70 million visitors.

November 1: China begins its sixth national census since 1949.

2011   January 9–12: U.S. Defense Secretary Robert Gates visits China.

January 19–21: President Hu Jintao meets President Obama for a state visit.

March 5–14: The Fourth Plenary Session of the Eleventh National Congress approves the 12th Five-Year Plan and accepts Xi Jinping as the new leader.

April 28: The sixth national census announces the population of 1,370,536,875 (2011).

May 20–26: Invited by President Hu, North Korean leader Kim Jong-Il visits China.

June 16: President Hu visits Ukraine for the first time.

June 30: The first high-speed railway becomes operational between Beijing and Shanghai.

July 2: The oil spills occurs at the Penglai #19-3 oilfield operated by the CNOOC (China National Offshore Oil Corporation) in the Bohai (Yellow Sea).

July 17: Vice President Xi Jinping heads a delegation to Tibet for the 60th anniversary of its peaceful liberation in 1951.

July 23: Two passenger rail trains collide around Wenzhou, 39 killed and 192 injured.

July 27: U.S. Senate unanimously approves Gary Locke as the new U.S. ambassador to China. He is the first Chinese American ambassador.

October 5: Two Chinese commercial boasts are attacked at the Golden Triangle of the Mekong River in Thailand, 12 killed and 1 missing.

October 11–12: Russian Prime Minister Vladimir Putin visits China and meets Chinese Premier Wen Jiabao in Beijing.

October 15–18: the Sixth Plenary Session of the Seventeenth CCP Central Committee is held in Beijing.

October 30–November 4: President Hu visits Austria and presents at the sixth summit of the 20-nation leaders in France.

2012

January 14: GMD wins the presidential election in Taiwan with Ma Ying-jeou as the ROC president (2012–2016) and Wu Den-yih as vice president.

February 13–22: Vice President Xi Jinping visits the United States, Ireland, and Turkey.

March 5–14: The Fifth Plenary Session of the Eleventh CPPCC National Committee is held in Beijing.

March 5–14: The Fifth Plenary Session of the Eleventh National People's Congress is held in Beijing.

March 25: Leung Chun-ying is elected as the fourth chief executive of Hong Kong-SAR.

April 10: The Pilipino naval warships and Chinese fishing vessels encounter in the South China Sea. Beijing announces that the CCP Central Committee will initiate an investigation of the "serious problems" of Bo Xilai, mayor of Chongqing.

May 9: Chinese-made deep-water submarine oil drilling platform, Offshore Oil 981, begins operation at 4,500 feet below the ocean surface.

June 16: *Shenzhou 9* spacecraft is launched successfully.

July 21: Beijing has a heavy rains flood disaster; 79 people are killed.

August 9: Representatives from Beijing and Taiwan held the eighth meetings and sign the cross-strait business cooperation agreements.

September 25: The first Chinese aircraft carrier *Liaoning* is commissioned to the PLA Navy.

September 28: The Politburo of the CCP Central Committee decides to expel Bo Xilai from the party, dismiss him from all official positions, and transfer his case to the criminal investigation.

November 8–14: The Eighteenth National Congress of the CCP is held in Beijing. About 2,200 party representatives attend the conference and elect the new Central Committee.

November 15: The First Plenary Session of the CCP Eighteenth Central Committee elects Xi Jinping as the secretary-general of the Central Committee (2012–2017).

December 1: The official report shows China's grain products total 589.6 million tons in 2012, about 3.2 percent increase from 2011.

2013

February 2–4: Xi Jinping, secretary-general of the CCP, visits the PLA missile testing ground and satellite launching center in the northwest.

February 26–28: The Second Plenary Session of the CCP Eighteenth Central Committee is held in Beijing, making recommendations of the national leadership to the next National People's Congress.

March 5–17: The Twelfth National People's Congress is held in Beijing, and 2,987 representatives attend the congress, which elects Xi Jinping as the president of the PRC, Zhang Dejiang as the chairman of the NPC, and Li Keqiang as the premier.

March 22–30: President Xi visits Russia, South Africa, Tanzania, and Republic of Congo.

March 26: The official reports show that China imports more than 200 million tons of crude oil in 2012, about 57.8 percent of national total consumption; a big increase of 30.2 percent in 2000.

April 20: Lushan County, Sichuan Province, has an earthquake; 193 are killed, 12,211 injured, and 25 missing.

June 3: A fire burns down a food company in Dehui, Jilin Province; 120 workers are killed and 77 injured.

June 11: Shenzhou 10 is launched and sent to the space with three Chinese astronauts.

June 13: President Xi meets GMD delegation from Taiwan and discusses the cross-strait relations.

June 26: Riots break out in Xinjiang; 24 people are killed.

July 5–12: A joint Chinese-Russian naval exercise takes place in the Sea of Japan.

July 8: Liu Zhijun, the former China's transportation minister, is sentenced to death for accepting bribes.

July 27–August 15: A joint Chinese-Russia ground forces exercise takes place in the Chelyabinsk region in the Urals.

September 22: Bo Xilai, former member of the CCP Politburo and party secretary of Chongqing, is sentenced to life for his corruption and power abuse.

October 2–8: President Xi visits Indonesia and Malaysia and attends the APEC conference at Indonesia.

October 28: A driver and his family exploded their car at the Tiananmen, Beijing, 5 killed and 40 injured.

November 9–12: The Third Plenary Session of the CCP Eighteenth Central Committee is held in Beijing, and Secretary-General Xi Jinping makes an important speech.

November 22: The oil pipeline in Qingdao explodes and 62 people are killed.

November 23: China declares the Designated Air Defense Identification Zone in the East China Sea, including the disputed Senkaku Islands between China and Japan.

December 2: China sends a carrier rocket "Chang E III" into space. The lander successfully lands on the surface of the moon on December 14.

December 25: The CCP Central Committee issues its five-year plans to investigate and punish corrupted officials in the party and government.

December 28: The Standing Committee of the Twelfth National People's Congress decides at its sixth meeting to abolish the Reeducation through Labor (RTL), which was adopted in 1957 and has been part of China's Criminal Justice system.

2014   January 7–8: The National Conference on Political and Legal Tasks is held in Beijing. Xi Jinping attends the meeting and make the keynote speech.

January 19: The CCP Central Committee issues its No. 1 document on further rural reform and agricultural modernization.

January 24: The Politburo of the CCP Central Committee meets and decides to establish its Central Commission of the National Security with Xi Jinping as its chairman.

February 7: Invited by Russian President Putin, Xi Jinping attends the Opening Ceremony of the 2014 Winter Olympics at Sochi. Xi visits Putin.

February 11: Premier Li Keqiang holds executive meeting of the State Council and calls for continuing efforts against the corruption in the government.

February 27: The CCP Central Committee establishes the Central Leading Group of Internet Security and Digitalization with Xi Jinping as its chairman and Li Keqiang and Liu Yunshan as its vice chairmen.

March 1: A terrorist attack takes place at the Kunming Train Station in Yunnan Province. A dozen attackers use knives to kill 29 people and wound 130.

March 3–12: The Second Plenary of the Twelfth CPPCC National Conference is held in Beijing.

March 5–13: The Second Plenary of the Twelfth National People's Congress (NPC) is held in Beijing. The plenary proves the 2014 central and local government budgets.

March 22–26: Xi Jinping visits Holland, France, Germany, Belgium, and the NATO after his attendance at the Third Global Nuclear Summit.

April 10–12: A court jails four activists linked to the New Citizens' Movement, which campaigns for government transparency.

May 21: Xi Jinping and Putin attend a natural gas agreement at Shanghai for a 30-year deal worth an estimated $400 billion for gas supplies from Russia's Gazprom.

May 22: Two vehicles run into the crowd at a public park in Urumqi, Xinjiang, killing 31 people and injuring more than 90.

June 4: The Education Ministry announces that 9.39 million students took the 2014 Annual National College Entrance Examination, about 270,000 more than the previous year.

June 9: Chinese Navy sends its fleet for the first time to participate in the "Pan-Pacific, 2014," a joint international naval exercise organized by the U.S. Navy annually.

June 16: Invited by the British prime minister, Premier Li Keqiang visits London.

June 30: The Politburo holds meeting and decides to dismiss General Xu Caihou, vice chairman of the CCP Central Military Commission, from the party for his bribery and corruption scandal.

July 3–4: Xi Jinping visits South Korea and meets President Park Geun-hye at Seoul.

July 15: The sixth meeting of the BRIC countries is held at Fortaleza, Brazil. Xi Jinping attends the meeting and delivers a speech.

July 28: The CCP Central Committee decides to investigate the corruption case of Zhou Yongkang, a former member of the Politburo Standing Committee.

August 2: An explosion at an automotive parts factory in Kunshan, southeastern Jiangsu Province, kills 75 workers and injures over 180 others.

August 3: An earthquake takes place in Zhaotong, southwestern Yunnan province, killing more than 150 people and injuring 1,300.

September 28–29: The State Council holds its sixth national meeting on ethnic and minority administration in Beijing. Xi Jinping makes the keynote speech.

September–October: Hong Kong students and residents protest against Beijing's plans to control candidate nominations for elections in 2017 and occupy the city central.

October 9: The Supreme Court issues new regulations on illegal activities in the Internet.

October 20–23: The Fourth Plenary of the CCP Eighteenth National Congress is held in Beijing and passes new resolutions on ruling the country by law.

October 27: The PLA dismisses General Xu Caihou, vice chairman of the CCP Central Military Commission, from the military for his bribery and corruption scandal.

November 10–12: APEC holds its meeting in Beijing. Xi Jinping chairs the meeting.

November 12: Xi Jinping meets President Obama in Beijing and discusses bilateral relations and major international regional concerns.

November 15–17: The ninth G20 summit is held in Brisbane, Australia. Xi Jinping attends the meeting and visits Australian Prime Minister Tony Abbott in Canberra.

December 11: Liu Tie'nan, deputy chief of National Development and Reform Commission from 2010 to 2013, jailed for life in a multimillion-dollar bribery scandal.

December 29: The Politburo holds its meeting on the anticorruption campaign. Xi Jinping chairs the meeting which makes a new plan for the 2015 campaign.

Cai Lun (50–121) and Four Great Inventions

Cai Lun was a eunuch who served in the government of the Han dynasty (206 BCE–220 CE). He is regarded as the inventor of paper in forms still recognizable in modern times. Even though a crude type of paper was used for writing before Han, it was rough and inconvenient to write on, since it was made from plant fiber. Cai Lun improved the skill of papermaking, and for the first time in history he experimented with tree bark, odds and ends of hemp, cloth rags, and discarded fishing nets as raw materials to produce a less expensive, more convenient type of paper. This paper, which used hemp as a main material, greatly popularized and promoted writing, and by the third century paper had replaced bamboo slips and silk as the main materials for writing on. The invention of paper became one of the Four Great Inventions in ancient China.

The second great invention was gunpowder, when the Chinese found that a mixture of sulfur, saltpeter, and charcoal would cause an explosion. A book in the mid-Tang dynasty (618–907) recorded the method of making gunpowder, and at the end of Tang, gunpowder was applied for military use. In the Song dynasty (960–1279), gunpowder was also widely used in daily life for construction, mining, road and canal building, hunting, and fireworks. The gunpowder weapons made in the Northern Song dynasty (960–1127) included fire arrows, pili burning balls, and explosives. In the Southern Song dynasty (1127–1279), the Chinese army invented a kind of "fire gun" used against the Mongolian army. A soldier would put the gunpowder into bamboo canisters, and then would add "zike" to them. Zike resembled bullets in character, but was made of stone and iron block. These were the earliest crude muskets in the world.

Another invention in ancient China was the compass, which was made in the Northern Song dynasty. Natural magnets were ground into crude compasses called "*Sinan*" (a device pointing south) as early as the Warring States Period (475–221 BCE), and these were the earliest compasses in the world, 2,000 years ago. The magnetic effect of *Sinan* was weak, as was its ability to guide south. By the Song dynasty, artificial magnets had been invented, whose magnetism was more stable than that of natural magnets. The equipment of the compass had been improved, and Song people invented several guiding tools such as the floating compass.

The fourth great invention was the technique of printing by Bi Sheng of the Northern Song dynasty. Woodblock printing was in use during the Sui dynasty (581–618), but was a laborious and expensive process. Bi Sheng invented the moveable type of printing by carving characters in reverse on blocks of clay. When a group was finished, the blocks were baked in a kiln. The slugs of type were pressed onto a coasting of rosin, wax, and paper ash spread on an iron tray, which was then heated and cooled to fix the slugs in place. If there was a wrong character, it could easily be replaced, and the tray, slugs, and coating could be used over and over again. Bi Sheng laid the foundation for improving the technique of printing. There was a wooden type in West Xia (1032–1227), and in the Ming dynasty (1368–1644) a bronze type was invented, and later, lead type was used.

See also: Chapter 2: Overview; Timeline; Genghis Khan and Kublai Khan; Tang Taizong.

Further Reading

Needham, Joseph. *Science in Traditional China*. Cambridge, MA: Harvard University Press, 1981.

Ronan, Colin. *The Shorter Science and Civilization in China*. Cambridge, UK: Cambridge University Press, 1985.

Temple, Robert, and Joseph Needham. *The Genius of China: 3,000 Years of Science, Discovery, and Invention*. Rochester, NY: Inner Traditions, 2007.

Wells, Allison. *Four Great Inventions of Ancient China, East Asia, and Asia.* New York: Houghton Mifflin, 2006.

Chiang Kai-shek (1887–1975)

He was the most important political and military leader of the Guomindang (GMD, or Kuomintang, KMT; the Chinese Nationalist Party) in the 20th century, founder of the Nanjing government of the Republic of China (ROC) in 1927 and the GMD government in Taiwan (Formosa) in 1949. Chiang Kai-shek (Jiang Jieshi) was born in October 1887 to a salt merchant family in the coastal province of Zhejiang, just as the Qing dynasty (1644–1911) was crumbling. In 1908, young Chiang went to Japan to study at a military college. In 1911, after an uprising in Wuchang, Jiang left Japan to become a regimental commander of the army that was revolting in Shanghai.

During the 1911 Revolution, Chiang allied himself early on with Nationalist leader Sun Yat-sen (1866–1925), first president of the new ROC, created after the Qing emperor's abdication in 1912. Sun sent Chiang to Moscow in 1924 to train with the Soviet Red Army, and he returned to play a critical role in the formation of a new GMD military. The first major project was the creation of a military academy. The Whampoa (Huangpu) Military Academy (the West Point of China) was founded on June 16, 1924, and Chiang was appointed its first commandant. After Sun died on March 12, 1925, of cancer, Chiang began his rise in the GMD, independent of Sun's patronage.

General Chiang scored a round of victories with his new army in what is known as the Northern Expedition in 1926–1927. In just a few months, Chiang defeated two northern warlord armies and enticed other warlords to join him, and soon half of China was in GMD hands. Chiang entered Shanghai in March 1927, and the next month Chiang re-established the ROC under GMD control in nearby Nanjing, with himself as president. Throughout this period, the Chinese Communist Party (CCP) had enjoyed a privileged place within the GMD. However, with Chiang's victory in the Northern Expedition, the CCP became a political and ideological threat to his authority. On April 12, 1927, Chiang unleashed the "White Terror." In GMD-controlled areas, communists were purged and killed, and the CCP was outlawed.

As the CCP and GMD civil war continued through the 1930s, Japan increased its territorial expansion onto Mainland China. After the July 7, 1937, Marco Polo Bridge (*Lugouqiao*) Incident, in which Japanese forces attacked ROC troops, both Nationalist and Communist forces united to fight a war with Japan that lasted until its defeat in 1945 by the United States at the conclusion of World War II. President Chiang suffered heavy losses during those years. Jiang instituted a policy of international diplomacy that had as its cornerstone an alliance with the United States, following Pearl Harbor, against Japan.

The Chinese Civil War broke out in 1946, as Communist and Nationalist armies clashed, and slowly Chiang's grip on control of China slipped away. Chiang moved from offensive operations to defensive retreats by the fall of 1948. In late 1949, Chiang

TAIWAN STRAIT CRISES

The People's Liberation Army (PLA) had attacked the Nationalist (or Guomindang, GMD)-held offshore islands in the Taiwan Straits since the GMD removed the seat of its government of the Republic of China (ROC) from the mainland to Taiwan in 1949. Among the major crises, on September 2, 1954, the PLA artillery on the Fujian coast began a heavy bombardment of Jinmen (Quemoy) and Mazu (Matsu) islands. From November 1, the PLA air force raided the Dachen Islands. On January 18, 1955, the PLA troops landed at Yijiangshan, and GMD lost the island with 1,086 casualties, while the PLA suffered 1,592 casualties. To stop the further PLA attack, U.S. President Dwight Eisenhower requested authorization from Congress for the United States to participate in the defense of Taiwan and some of the offshore islands in the Taiwan Strait. On January 29, Congress passed the Formosa Resolution, which authorized Eisenhower to employ U.S. armed forces to protect Taiwan from a possible PLA invasion. On August 23, 1958, the PLA artillery heavily shelled Jinmen. On September 7, American warships escorted GMD ships to Jinmen. By October 5, the tension in the Taiwan Straits began to ease. From July 21–26, 1995, the PLA conducted a missile test in an area 36 miles north of Taiwan. In mid-August, the PLA conducted another set of missile firings, accompanied by live ammunition exercises. During the crisis, the United States sent an aircraft carrier battle group to the Taiwan Straits in January-February 1996. On March 8, 1996, the PLA conducted its third set of missiles tests, firing three M-9 surface-to-surface missiles just 12 miles from Taiwan's major seaport cities Kao-hsiung and Keelung. On March 11, the United States deployed the *Nimitz* carrier battle group to the Taiwan Straits to join the *Independence* group to monitor Chinese actions. This was the largest U.S. naval movement in the Asia-Pacific region since the Vietnam War.

removed the seat of his government from Nanjing to Taiwan, after losing the Civil War to the CCP. Over the next two decades, Chiang focused on increasing his hold on Taiwan and improving the faltering economy. With U.S. help, Taiwan shifted to a manufacturing economy. Through 1972, Taiwan significantly grew both its GDP and its per capita GDP significantly. Although Taiwan lagged behind Japan, Chiang ensured a faster growth rate than his counterparts in Beijing. Political dissent and the growth of democratic institutions were discouraged throughout Chiang's rule and the GMD maintained a dictatorial power over Taiwan and its offshore island holdings. Jiang held on to power until his death on April 5, 1975.

See also: Chapter 1: Taiwan. Chapter 2: Overview; Timeline; Mao Zedong; Sun Yat-sen. Chapter 3: Chinese Communist Party.

Further Reading

Pepper, Suzanne. *Civil War in China: The Political Struggle, 1945–1949*. Boulder, CO: Rowman & Littlefield, 1999.

Taylor, Jay. *The Generalissimo: Chiang Kai-shek and the Struggle for Modern China*. Cambridge, MA: Harvard University Press, 2009.

Tucker, Nancy Bernkopf. *Strait Talk: United States-Taiwan Relations and the Crisis with China*. Cambridge, MA: Harvard University Press, 2009.

Cixi (1835–1908) and the Boxer Rebellion

Dowager Cixi (Tzu-hsi) was a powerful empress who controlled the Qing dynasty (1644–1911) in China from 1861 to 1908. She was selected as a concubine for Xianfeng (Hsian-feng) emperor (reigned 1851–1862), and gave birth to a son in 1856. After the emperor died in 1861, her son became the Tongzhi (T'ung-chih) emperor (reigned 1862–1875), and Cixi became the empress dowager. She established her personal network to control the Manchu government and the imperial succession. After the Tongzhi emperor died in 1875, she installed her nephew as the Guangxu (Kwang-hsu) emperor (reigned 1875–1908) at the age of four. Empress Dowager Cixi adapted a closed-door policy against Western influence and foreign trade. The Qing military lost the Sino-French War in 1884–1885 and the Sino-Japanese War in 1894–1895. And worst of all, the Chinese people were disillusioned by the Cixi government's corruption, mismanagement, and failure against European, American, and Japanese forces during the Boxer Rebellion.

The 1900 Boxer Rebellion was a mass movement against foreign missionaries and establishments in North China. The "Boxer" (or *Yihetuan*, Society of Righteousness and Harmony) was originally a secret organization whereby peasants in Shandong and Chili (Hebei) resorted to religion in their anti-Qing struggle. It used the means of martial arts and the training it provided to organize the masses for armed struggle against Qing officials. As Western influence, especially Christianity, intensified its expansion into North China, it quickly became the target of *Yihetuan*'s resentment. Toward the end of the 19th century, the number of Western missionaries in China was more than 3,300 and the number of Chinese converts exceeded 800,000. In 1899, the once secret society, the Boxers, went public in Shandong. Its members burned churches, killed missionaries, and chased out the converts. In 1900, the main forces of the Boxers were shifted to Zhili where they joined forces with local groups. The growing strength of the Boxers encouraged Cixi both to deploy them as a force to expel Western powers from China and to stop the domestic reform movement. The Imperial Court issued edicts in January 1900 defending the Boxers. This move drew vociferous complaints from foreign diplomats.

As the Boxers struck against the Westerners without mercy in Beijing and Tianjin, eight powers—Russia, Britain, Germany, France, the United States, Japan, Italy, and Austria—formed an alliance to launch a war against the Boxers as well as the Qing regime, which decided to use the movement's anti-missionary policy to seize popular leadership. On June 10, 1900, more than 2,100 of the allied forces landed on Dagukou and moved toward Tianjin and Beijing. On July 14, the allied forces captured Tianjin. On August 14, with nearly 55,000 men, they occupied Beijing. Cixi and the Guangxu emperor fled to Xi'an, and the Boxer Rebellion ended. On September 7, 1901, the Qing government signed a treaty of peace with 11 countries whereby China agreed to pay an indemnity of 450 million taels of silver over 39 years. The treaty also provided that an area in Beijing be designated a "legation quarter" where foreign troops would be allowed to station permanently for the protection of foreign embassies; and that the allied nations be allowed to station troops in 12 strategic points along the railway between Beijing and Shanhaiguan, Hebei. Empress Dowager Cixi died in 1908, and the Qing ended three years later.

See also: Chapter 2: Overview; Timeline. Chapter 5: Overview. Chapter 15: *Wushu*: Martial Arts.

Further Reading

Harrington, Peter. *China, 1900: The Eyewitnesses Speak; The Boxer Rebellion as Described by Participants in Letters, Diaries and Photographs.* London: Greenhill, 2000.

Preston, Diana. *The Boxer Rebellion: The Dramatic Story of China's War on Foreigners that Shook the World in the Summer of 1900.* New York: Bloomsburg, 2000.

Seagrave, Sterling. *Dragon Lady: The Life and Legend of the Last Empress of China.* New York: Vintage, 1992.

Chinese troops stand with their artillery during the Boxer Rebellion of 1898–1901. After the Imperial Court of the Qing (1644–1911) regime issued edicts in January 1900 supporting the mass rebellion of the Boxers, many Qing troops in North China joined the Boxers' attacks on the foreign missionaries and establishment in the spring, and defended the Boxers against the eight foreign powers' coalition force in the summer. (Library of Congress)

Confucius (551–479 BCE)

One of the greatest teachers and philosophers in China and East Asia, and one of the 10 internationally recognized thinkers, was surnamed Kong, and his given name was Qiu (Chiu). He was born in Zouyi in the State of Lu (present Qufu, Shandong) in the late Spring and Autumn Period (722–481 BCE) during the Zhou dynasty (1027–221 BCE). He was the founder of Confucianism.

Confucius put forth the ideology of benevolence (*ren*) on the part of rulers toward their people, stressing that political rule should be based on virtue and not on force. He emphasized moral conduct, including inner integrity (*zhi*), righteousness (*yi*), loyalty (*zhong*), proper behavior (*li*), and filial piety (*xiao*) as necessary qualities of a gentleman or a man of nobility. As an ideology, Confucianism believes in a man's position in his society, his relations with others, as well as his duties and responsibilities. It explains human nature or the natural laws of human beings through an ethical approach, whereas the Greek philosophers espoused the same through logic, mathematics, physics, or religious approaches. Confucianism as a school of philosophy focuses on individual moral conduct, family relations, and moral government, all in the context of the society. His philosophy became classical, since it provided ideas in how to overcome the civil wars and social disorders that all Chinese rulers had to face.

Confucianism justified an authoritarian family pattern as a basis for social order in political as well as in domestic life. Social or political harmony can be achieved if people follow five important relationships: ruler-minister, father-son, husband-wife, elder brother-younger brother, and friend-friend. The role of emperor and his officials was merely that of the father writ large. It reflects a notion that "mandate of heaven" is the moral law that constitutes the fabric of the universe. A district magistrate, who represented the emperor, was called the "father and mother" of the people (*fumuguan*, parent-official). Confucian and Daoist thoughts blended, along with Buddhist thinking, into Chinese worldview.

His Six Classics, considered central to the Confucian canon, include *The Book of Changes* (*Yijing*), *The Book of Songs* (*Shijing*), *The Book of Rites* (*Li*), *The Book of Music* (*Yue*), *The Book of History* (*Shu*), and *The Spring and Autumn Annals* (*Chunqiu*). They are all important contributions that Confucius made to the development of ancient Chinese civilization.

As a great educator, he advocated that everyone should be equal in achieving education, and he established private schools, breaking the government's monopoly over education. He taught as many as 3,000 disciples, among whom 72 became very famous. Confucius' theories formed the orthodox ruling ideology in China for over 2,500 years.

See also: Chapter 2: Overview; Timeline. Chapter 5: Buddhism; Confucianism; Daoism.

Further Reading

Confucius with Raymond Dawson, trans. *The Analects*. New York: Oxford University Press, 2008.

Fingarette, Herbert. *Confucius: The Secular as Sacred*. Long Grove, IL: Waveland Press, 1998.

Reid, T. R. *Confucius Lives Next Door: What Living in the East Teaches Us about Living in the West*. New York: Vintage, 2000.

Zhang, Dainian, and Edmund Ryden. *Key Concepts in Chinese Philosophy*. New Haven, CT: Yale University Press, 2000.

Deng Xiaoping (1904–1997)

He was secretary-general of the Chinese Communist Party (CCP) and vice premier of the People's Republic of China (PRC) in 1954–1966, chief of staff of the People's Liberation Army (PLA) in 1975–1987, and one of the greatest influences on modern China. Returning to the party center for the third time, Deng Xiaoping (Deng Hsiao-ping) helped to usher in badly needed reforms that would transform the economy of China from centrally planned to market oriented, paving the way for China's ascendancy into the global power it is today.

Deng was born in Guang'an, Sichuan, on August 22, 1904. In 1920 he traveled to France and was exposed to communist ideology. Deng joined the Chinese Communist Youth League (CCYL) in Europe, and in 1926 made his way to Moscow to study Marxist theory. He returned to China by 1927 and became a local leader of the CCP as well as the Red Army. During the Anti-Japanese War (1937–1945), he was appointed secretary of the CCP Central China Bureau. Acting as political commissar of the Second Field Army of the PLA during the Chinese Civil War (1946–1949), he aided the victory of Mao Zedong (Mao Tse-tung) (1893–1976) over the Guomindang (GMD, or Kuomintang, KMT; the Chinese Nationalist Party) armies by capturing some key Nationalist held cities.

After establishment of the PRC in October 1949, Deng was appointed chairman of the Financial and Economic Affairs Committee in 1952. He became vice premier and general secretary of the CCP's Central Committee in 1954 and was appointed to the Politburo in the 1960s. During the Cultural Revolution (1966–1976), Deng was purged by Mao for being too "Bourgeoisie" and in 1966 was forced to retire all his positions. He faced rehabilitation by first being placed under house arrest. Deng was then sent to a tractor repair factory in Jiangxi to work as a regular laborer.

By 1973 Deng was deemed fit to return to his leadership duties as deputy premier and member of the CCP Central Committee. He became vice chairman of the Central Military Commission (CMC) and chief of the General Staff of the PLA in 1975, and was elected vice chairman of the Central Committee and member of the Politburo Standing Committee. Accusations surfaced of Deng disparaging Jiang Qing (Chiang Ch'ing) (1914–1991), Mao's wife, and in 1976 he was again dismissed from his positions. It was not until Mao died and the Gang of Four expunged, later in the year, that Deng was allowed to return into the party fold for the third time.

Deng began consolidating his power and became the top leader in China by 1977. Getting rid of the remaining Maoists, in 1978 Deng delivered a speech, "Emancipate the Mind," at the Plenary Session of the Party Central Committee. With this new mandate in mind, Deng began shifting Chinese policy to be more reform oriented, moving farther away from the ill-fated policies that Mao had spearheaded earlier. Given that these reforms were such a tremendous shift in policy for Communist China, Deng dubbed them as the "second revolution."

As the country adopted more reform policies, China began opening up to the world. Deng pursued an even closer relationship with the United States, paying the first ever PRC state visit to that country. Meeting with President Jimmy Carter (1924–), Deng

---

HUA GUOFENG (1921–2008)

Hua Guofeng was the supreme Chinese leader following the death of Mao Zedong, chief of the first generation of the Chinese Communist Party (CCP) leadership, and before Deng Xiaoping took over as the top leader of the second generation of the CCP leadership. Hua became premier of the People's Republic of China (PRC) in January 1976 after Zhou Enlai died, and later became chairman of the CCP Central Committee and the Central Military Committee (CMC) in September 1976, after Mao's death. One month later, Hua announced the end of the Cultural Revolution (1966–1976) and arrested the Gang of Four, including Mao's wife Jiang Qing, in Beijing. However, Hua attempted to extend Mao's policies, asserting the rightness of Maoist ideologies. Deng, a realistic reformer, together with his supporters, overcame Hua in December 1978 by pushing Deng's reform agenda through the party center. In September 1980, Hua lost the premiership and was replaced by Zhao Ziyang. In June 1981, Hua lost the chair position in the CCP Central Committee and was replaced by Hu Yaobang. Deng took charge of the military by controlling the CMC after Hua's retirement.

---

underlined cooperation as he signed the Carter-Deng normalization agreements. Deng approached the British government in 1982 over the issue of Chinese sovereignty over Hong Kong. He similarly approached the Portuguese with respect to Macau returning back to PRC control. China and Britain finally reached an agreement in 1984 called the Sino-British Joint Declaration on Hong Kong, paving the way for Hong Kong to return to PRC control by 1997.

A significant challenge to the successes of Deng occurred in the spring of 1989. In April, students gathered in Beijing, using the death of Hu Yaobang (1915–1989) to voice their desire for democratic reforms and an end to corruption. By the end of May a crowd of over 100,000 presented a serious dilemma to Deng, and he ordered action to be taken against the demonstrators. On June 4, PLA troops moved into Tiananmen Square by force and killed some students and residents of Beijing. Deng later spoke out against the demonstrations, calling it a "counterrevolutionary rebellion." In reaction to Deng's actions the West responded with outrage and economic sanctions. By the mid-1990s, failing health forced Deng into retirement. Suffering from Parkinson's disease, Deng died on February 28, 1997, in Beijing.

See also: Chapter 1: Hong Kong. Chapter 2: Overview; Timeline; Mao Zedong. Chapter 3: Chinese Communist Party; People's Liberation Army.

Further Reading

Goldman, Merle. *Sowing the Seeds of Democracy in China: Political Reform in the Deng Xiaoping Era*. Cambridge, MA: Harvard University Press, 1994.

Goodman, David. *Deng Xiaoping and the Chinese Revolution: A Political Biography*. London: Routledge, 1994.

Marti, Michael E. *China and the Legacy of Deng Xiaoping: From Communist Revolution to Capitalist Evolution*. New York: Brassey's, 2001.

Yang, Benjamin. *Deng, a Political Biography*. Armonk, NY: M. E. Sharpe, 1998.

Genghis Khan (1162–1227) and Kublai Khan (1215–1294)

One of the greatest and most notorious conquerors in Asia, Genghis Khan (Chinggis Khan or Chengiz Khan; reigned 1206–1227) was able to unite various Mongolian clans into an army that not only defeated everyone in its path but also helped him create an empire that eventually stretched from Beijing (Peking) to the Caspian Sea. The expansion of the Mongols' power affected not only inner Asia, China, and Korea but Russia and Hungary as well, and in each place the legacy of their terror was long remembered.

Temujin, the man who would later become Genghis Khan, was born in 1162 to a powerful Mongolian family in Deluun Boldog near Burkhan Khaldun mountain in northern Mongolia. Genghis had managed to establish himself as ruler of the Mongols, and by 1206, he was acknowledged as Genghis Khan, or "universal ruler." In fighting other Mongol tribes and their neighbors, Genghis created not only an experienced, highly mobile army but also a very large one. As the Mongol military moved away from the clan system, so did Mongol society, and both became more feudalistic.

On August 18, 1227, Genghis died from wounds probably sustained either in battle or while hunting. Genghis's descendants went on to conquer Russia, India, China, Turkey, Iran, Pakistan, and Korea, and threatened Austria, Japan, Persia, and Poland. Though Genghis spelled out directions for succession, which his children followed with little trouble, his grandchildren divided the empire beyond the hope of reunification. In particular, Kublai (Khubilai) Khan (reigned 1260–1294), his grandson, capitalized on Genghis's ideas to create one of the greatest empires in Asian history.

Born in September 1215, Kublai was the fourth son of Tolui, the youngest son of Genghis Khan and his wife, Sorghaghtani. By all accounts, he was Genghis's favorite grandson. As a youth, Kublai participated in campaigns with his father until his death, when Kublai was 17; however, Kublai didn't figure in Mongol leadership until he was in his thirties. As a statesman and military leader, in 1260 he inherited an empire that stretched from the Adriatic Sea to northern China. In 1264, Kublai Khan decided on Dadu (today's Beijing) as his capital. After consolidating his rule over the north, by 1279 his empire extended to southern China. Kublai Khan defeated Southern Song dynasty of China and firmly established the Mongol Yuan dynasty (1279–1368) of China.

Kublai Khan was not, however, without failings. He maintained a large military, the cost of which was a severe burden on the taxpayers. He also sponsored two disastrous invasions of Japan, in 1274 and 1281, which cost a tremendous amount of money and thousands of Mongol and Chinese lives. In order to maintain the splendor of his palaces, he collected vast sums of silver for his treasury, but he introduced printed money to the Chinese economy and overprinted it to the point of high inflation. Kublai died in February 1294. No other ruler of Mongol China ever rose to his stature.

See also: Chapter 2: Overview; Timeline. Chapter 6: Mongols. Chapter 12: Chinese Silk and the Silk Road; The Great Wall; Pagodas, Palaces, and Temples.

Further Reading

Man, John. *Genghis Khan: Life, Death, and Resurrection*. New York: St. Martin's Griffin, 2007.

Marshall, Robert. *Storm from the East: From Genghis Khan to Khubilai Khan*. Berkeley: University of California Press, 1993.

Robinson, David M. *Empire's Twilight: Northeast Asia under the Mongols*. Cambridge, MA: Harvard University Press, 2009.

Saunders, J. J. *The History of the Mongol Conquests*. Philadelphia: University of Pennsylvania Press, 2001.

Han Wudi (Martial Emperor) (156–87 BCE)

Reigning from 140 to 87 BCE, Liu Che was known as Emperor Wudi (Wu-ti) (Martial Emperor) of the sixth emperor of the Han dynasty (206 BCE-220 CE). He had great talent, bold vision, outstanding statecraft, and brilliant military exploits, which helped China enter into a time of great prosperity and become one of the most powerful empires in the world. He became one of China's most famous emperors. Under his rule, China expanded its borders, repelling threats from the north and introducing the Silk Road, a trade route that became an international highway of commerce and cultural transmission. Wudi was also responsible for establishing Confucianism as China's state religion.

Liu Che was born in 156 BCE, youngest son of the Han Emperor Jingdi (Han Ching-ti) (156-141 BCE). His relatives and teachers apparently exposed him to two competing schools of thought: Daoism (Taoism) and Confucianism. When his father died in 141 BCE, Liu Che succeeded him as emperor. He spent his reign engaged in military conquests and the expansion of China's territory, earning him the name "Wu," meaning "martial."

Many of his policies were aimed at creating unity among the various cultures and nationalities that made up the Chinese empire. The Xiongnu, an ancient nomadic tribe in northern China, threatened the northern border regions, and Wudi appointed two generals to lead expeditions against them. They fought against the Xiongnu several times and finally forced them north of the Gobi Desert, ensuring the security of the Hexi Corridor, a crucial passageway on the northern border of China that became an important part of the Silk Road.

Wudi's wars against the northern nomads indirectly resulted in opening up trade between China and the West. In 138 BCE, he sent a group of representatives led by

Zhang Qian to Central Asia in an attempt to secure allies in his fight against the Xiongnu. They did not make any alliances, but they returned to the Han court with tales of foreign cultures and goods. Wudi became very interested in those foreign lands and eventually opened the Silk Road, which became a highway of commercial and cultural exchange between East and West.

To increase northern China's security from nomadic invaders from Mongolia, Wudi had the Great Wall of China renovated. To make alliances firmer, he married his children and allies to the leaders of other nations. He also increased China's territory, conquering some small kingdoms in the south and annexing Hainan Island and the islands of the South China Sea.

The Han Empire rivaled its contemporary, the Roman Empire, for size and glory. Wudi destroyed and annexed the semi-sinicized state of Nan-yueh (Vietnam), and started a thousand years of Chinese rule over northern Vietnam. He conquered Korea in 108 BCE, and a Chinese command remained at Pyongyang until 313 CE. Wudi's military enterprises were expensive; to fund his campaigns, he raised taxes and confiscated property owned by nobles. He also had the state take over many private businesses. Nevertheless, China prospered during his reign.

Successful military expeditions and territorial expansion convinced Wudi and his people that they were superior in civilization and institution. The Han dynasty became the first glorious dynasty in Chinese history. The Han emperors believed that China, or *Zhongguo* in Chinese, was the "Central Kingdom." This perception, combined with a moral cosmology, elevated the Chinese emperor as the "Son of the Heaven," who possessed supreme power and heavenly missions, or the "Mandate of Heaven." It justified Han Wudi's military invasions that incorporated the "barbarian" people into Chinese civilizations through a continuous process of acculturation. Wudi died on March 29, 87 BCE.

See also: Chapter 1: South China Sea. Chapter 2: Overview; Timeline. Chapter 5: Confucianism; Daoism. Chapter 12: Chinese Silk and the Silk Road; The Great Wall.

Further Reading

Fairbank, John. *China: A New History*. Cambridge, MA: Harvard University Press, 1992.

Greenblatt, Miram. *Han Wu Di and Ancient China (Rulers and Their Times)*. Salt Lake City, UT: Benchmark, 2005.

Hardy, Grant, and Anne Kinney. *The Establishment of the Han Empire and Imperial China*. Westport, CT: Greenwood, 2005.

Hu Jintao (1942–)

The top Chinese leader of the fourth generation of the Chinese Communist Party (CCP), Hu Jintao, was president of the People's Republic of China (PRC) from 2003 to 2012, secretary general of the CCP in 2002–2012, and chairman of the CCP Central

Military Commission in 2004–2012. Hu emerged through a protracted service within the government and the party. As his precedent Jiang Zemin, Hu and his cabinet members belonged to the technocrats.

Born in 1942 in Jixi, Anhui, Hu Jintao studied hydroelectric engineering at Qinghua (Tsinghua) University, where he joined the CCP in 1964. He planned to be an expert on hydropower, and once said that he originally had no intention of going into politics. After his graduation in 1965, Hu stayed at Qinghua as a researcher until the beginning of the Cultural Revolution. In 1968 he was sent to work in Gansu, where he served consecutively as technician, office secretary, and deputy party secretary in an engineering bureau. In 1974, he was transferred to the Gansu Provincial Construction Committee and served as party secretary. He was deputy chief of the committee's designing management division from 1975 to 1980, when he was promoted to deputy director of the committee and later became secretary of the Gansu Provincial Committee of CCYL (Chinese Communist Youth League). During the Eleventh CCYL National Congress in 1982, Hu was elected member of the Secretariat of the CCYL Central Committee, and then the first secretary of the Secretariat of the CCYL. In 1985, at 43, Hu was appointed CCP secretary of Guizhou, youngest of his rank across the country. In 1988, he became party secretary of Tibet.

Hu entered the Standing Committee of the Politburo of the Fourteenth CCP Central Committee in 1992, and was the youngest member in this top decision-making body. He was re-elected to the Standing Committee of the Politburo and a member of the Central Committee's Secretariat in 1997. In November 2002, when Jiang Zemin (1925–) retired, Hu became chairman of the CCP at the Sixteenth CCP National Congress. In March 2003, Hu was elected president of the PRC at the Sixth National People's Congress (NPC).

Hu had to face tremendous difficulties with China's economic and political reforms in the midst of continuous social transition. Even though Hu and Jiang had many disputes over specific issues, they reached a consensus on the key objective: China's economic growth and social stability. Hu designed his "scientific development" concept, entrenching it in the party's constitution as an official guiding ideology. Hu emphasized political and social harmony by nurturing good relations with central and local governments as well as supporting the growing professionalism and interest groups inside and outside the government. To deal with the problems left behind by Jiang, Hu made certain important changes in China's economic, military, social, and political policies. He strategically shifted China's economic development from a global-oriented policy to a more regionally balanced one. Hu and Wen Jiabao (1942–), new premier of the PRC, employed the macroeconomic control policies over the rapidly growing economy.

The growing diversity within the CCP leadership and the dynamic interdependence among competing factions was emerging at this time. Their increasing factional struggles have constrained Hu and Wen from making new domestic and foreign policy initiatives. Hu fought back the "Shanghai Gang" first in 2006–2008 by arresting and sentencing Chen Liangyu, mayor and party committee secretary of Shanghai and CCP Politburo member, to 18 years in jail. Then, Hu arrested Bo Xilai, mayor and party committee secretary of Chongqing and CCP Politburo member, in 2012. Hu's victories over Chen and Bo protected his power base through his tenure. After retiring, Xi Jinping became the party chairman and the country's president in 2012.

See also: Chapter 1: Major Cities. Chapter 2: Overview; Timeline; Jiang Zemin and Sino-U.S. Relations. Chapter 3: Chinese Communist Party; Civil Rights; National People's Congress; People's Liberation Army; Xi Jinping. Chapter 4: Overview. Chapter 5: Buddhism. Chapter 8: Qinghua University.

Further Reading

Brown, Kerry. *Hu Jintao: China's Silent Ruler*. Singapore: World Scientific, 2012.

Fewsmith, Joseph. *China since Tiananmen: From Deng Xiaoping to Hu Jintao*. 2nd ed. Cambridge, UK: Cambridge University Press, 2008.

Lam, Willy. *Chinese Politics in the Hu Jintao Era: New Leaders, New Challenges*. Armonk, NY: M. E. Sharpe, 2006.

Li, Xiaobing, and Xiansheng Tian, eds. *Evolution of Power: China's Struggle, Survival, and Success*. Lanham, MD: Lexington Books, 2014.

Shambaugh, David. *China's Communist Party: Atrophy and Adaptation*. Washington, DC: Wilson Center Press, 2008.

Jiang Zemin (1926–) and Sino-U.S. Relations

As the secretary general of the Chinese Communist Party (CCP) in 1989–2002, president of the People's Republic of China (PRC) in 1993–2003, and chairman of the Central Military Commission (CMC) in 1989–2004, Jiang was the most important political and military leader of China at the turn of the century. He was leader of the third generation of the Chinese Communist leadership, after the PRC's founder Mao Zedong (Mao Tse-tung) (1893–1976) from 1949 to 1976, and after the reforming architect Deng Xiaoping (Deng Hsiao-ping) (1904–1997) from 1978 to 1989.

Jiang was born on August 17, 1926, in Yangzhou, Jiangsu. He earned an electrical engineering degree at the prestigious Shanghai Jiaotong University in 1947. During his college years, Jiang participated in the CCP-led student movements and joined the CCP in 1946. After the founding of the PRC in 1949, he served as an associate engineer and deputy director of a factory. In 1955, he was sent to the Soviet Union and worked at the Stalin Automobile Factory as a trainee for one year. After his return home in 1956, he served as a deputy division head, deputy chief power engineer, director of a branch factory, and deputy director and director of factories and research institutes in Changchun, Shanghai, and Wuhan. Speaking some English and Russian, he served as deputy director and then director of the Foreign Affairs Department of the First Ministry of Machine-Building Industry in Beijing. Later, Jiang became minister of the Electronics Industry.

After Deng Xiaoping launched the reform movement of 1978, Jiang became the first city planner of Shenzhen, Guangdong, China's first Special Economic Zone (SEZ). His successful experience won him election as a member of the Twelfth CCP Central Committee in 1982 and mayor of Shanghai, China's largest city, in 1985. Two years later, he became a member of the Politburo at the Thirteenth CCP Central Committee. In June 1989, Jiang was elected a member of the Standing Committee of the Politburo and general secretary of the CCP Central Committee. In November, he became chairman of the Central Military Commission (CMC).

In the early 1990s, Jiang gradually shifted the party's ideology and political goals from radical communism to moderate nationalism as an ideology to unite China, resulting in one more source of legitimacy for the CCP as the country's ruling party. Jiang developed his own theoretical principles as the "Three Represents," that the CCP should represent "the development of China's advanced productive forces, the orientation of the development of China's advanced culture, and the fundamental interests of the broadest masses of the Chinese people." The "Three Represents" became the most essential requirements for officials and officers to fulfill their obligations and duties during Jiang's era from 1990 to 2004 as his legacy.

As the PLA's first civilian commander-in-chief, Jiang developed an institutionalized authority that enabled him to assume the top post as CCP and CMC chairman and the country's president. With military support, Jiang took tougher positions on Tibet (Xizang), human rights issues, and Taiwan, even ordering Chinese forces to fire missiles near the island in 1995–1996, creating another serious international crisis with the United States. The tension also mounted in the Taiwan Strait in July 1995 when the PLA conducted its first missile test in an area only 36 miles north of a ROC-held island. In March 1996, the PLA conducted its third set of missile tests by firing three M-9 surface-to-surface missiles just 12 miles off Taiwan's major seaport cities, Keelung (Jilong) and Kaohsiung (Gaoxiong). Over 70 percent of commercial shipping passes through the targeted ports, which were disrupted by the proximity of the missile test. The Bill Clinton administration sent two U.S. aircraft

STRATEGIC WEAPONS

China's strategic force, or the Second Artillery Corps (SAC), of the People's Liberation Army (PLA) has more than 300 nuclear warheads with 20 intercontinental ballistic missiles (ICBMs) and one ballistic missile submarine (SSBN). SAC has also completed a transformation in its mobility, to ensure deterrence. Before 2000, the force relied upon a vulnerable liquid model. It has now developed a new solid-fuel and road-mobile Dong Feng 31A ICBM system in order to increase the survivability of its nuclear deterrent. The new ICBMs will be combat-ready faster than the liquid-fueled missile, more quickly launched, and easier to hide. Moreover, SAC has more than 1,300 Dong Feng 11 and 15 short-range ballistic missiles along the coastal areas. It is expected to continue to expand its ICBM capabilities and improve upon its land attack cruise missile and anti-ship missile arsenals.

carrier battle groups to the Taiwan Strait to show U.S. readiness to fight over Taiwan. Through the rest of his tenure, Jiang tried to maintain a working relationship with Washington.

By 1997, Jiang had established an unprecedented institutionalized authority that enabled him to preside over a vast central bureaucracy encompassing the party, state, and military. He traveled widely, both domestic and overseas. After Jiang retired, Hu Jintao became the party chairman and the country's president in 2003, and the chairman of the CMC in 2004.

See also: Chapter 1: Major Cities; Taiwan. Chapter 2: Overview; Timeline; Deng Xiaoping; Hu Jintao; Mao Zedong. Chapter 3: Chinese Communist Party; Civil Rights; Human Rights; People's Liberation Army. Chapter 5: Falun Gong.

Further Reading

Gilley, Bruce. *Tiger on the Brink: Jiang Zemin and China's New Elite*. Berkeley: University of California Press, 1998.

Kuhn, Robert. *The Man Who Changed China: The Life and Legacy of Jiang Zemin*. New York: Random House, 2005.

Lam, Willy. *The Era of Jiang Zemin*. Singapore: Prentice Hall, 1999.

Lampton, David. *Following the Leader: Ruling China, from Deng Xiaoping to Xi Jinping*. Berkeley: University of California Press, 2014.

Kangxi (1654–1722)

The second emperor of Qing dynasty (1644–1911), Kangxi (K'ang-hsi), reigned from 1661 to 1722 and was one of China's most powerful emperors. He expelled the last of the anti-Manchu forces from South China, gained control of Taiwan, and increased China's territory in the north. Economically, China blossomed during his reign and became an Asian power for most of the 18th century.

Kangxi was born on May 4, 1654, in Beijing, the third son of the Shunzhi (Shun-ch'ih) (reigned 1644–1661) emperor, who died of smallpox at age 23 in 1661. Kangxi ascended the throne above his five brothers, whose mothers were of lower birth. Because he was only seven years old, the Qing government in the beginning was administered by four conservative attendants. The Kangxi emperor first married at age 11, and he eventually had three wives and more than 30 consorts, who gave birth to his 56 children.

The Kangxi emperor began his reign at the age of 15. His first task was to consolidate China under Manchu control. The resulting war, known as the War of the Three Feudatories, ended in 1681, and all of China was brought under Kangxi's rule. New governors were sent to the rebellious provinces to assimilate them into the Qing realm, and taxes began to flow from those areas into Beijing.

Kangxi next turned his attention to Taiwan and Russia. With little naval power, the emperor was prevented from attacking Taiwan until July 1683, when he had assembled a fleet of 300 war vessels. His fleet delivered a crushing victory, and Taiwan surrendered three months later. The island became a prefecture of the Fujian Province and was placed under the jurisdiction of the Qing. Having secured Taiwan and South China, the Kangxi emperor then attempted to drive the Russians out of the north in 1685. Qing armies began a protracted siege on Albazin in 1686, and in 1689 Kangxi and Russia's Peter I signed the Treaty of Nerchinsk, giving the Amur Valley, as well as Manchuria, to China. Kangxi also gained Outer Mongolia through an attack on the Dzungars (Junggars) at Dzuunmod, which became an important part of the Qing Empire.

Culturally, China blossomed during the Kangxi emperor's reign. He continued the examination system put in place by his father, which brought only the most promising men into civil service, and assembled groups of scholars to write dictionaries and encyclopedias. An avid reader, Kangxi was interested in new developments from Europe, leading him in the late 17th century to employ many Jesuit missionaries in his court. In addition, he allowed them to practice their religion in Beijing and other provinces, though he issued an edict insisting that the Chinese rituals of ancestor worship and homage to Confucius were civil ones and thus could be practiced by Christian converts.

Kangxi faced problems within his own household. Anxious to end the practice of regency government until young emperors came of age, he declared his first-born son, Yinreng, his successor soon after the child's birth in 1674. However, Kangxi withdrew Yinreng's heir-apparent status in 1708 and put him under house arrest, only to release him in 1709. The emperor rearrested his son in 1712, after learning that Yinreng planned to assassinate him. Thereafter, the Kangxi emperor's other 19 sons jostled for the throne.

In 1720, the emperor made his last major stand in foreign affairs, expelling the Dzungars from Lhasa, Tibet, after they invaded the city in 1717. Tibet was incorporated into the Qing Empire, and a new Dalai Lama (Kelzang Gyatso), one loyal to the Qing, was installed. After a celebration of his long reign during the Chinese New Year of 1722, he fell ill. Neglecting to name an heir, the Kangxi emperor died on December 20, 1722, and his son Yongzheng became emperor after Kangxi's death.

See also: Chapter 1: Taiwan. Chapter 2: Overview; Timeline. Chapter 5: Confucianism; Dalai Lama; Chapter 6: Overview.

Further Reading

Crossley, Pamela Kyle. *The Manchus*. Hoboken, NJ: Wiley-Blackwell, 2002.

Rowe, William T. *China's Last Empire: The Great Qing*. Cambridge, MA: Harvard University Press, 2009.

Spence, Jonathan D. *Emperor of China: Self Portrait of K'ang-Hsi*. New York: Vintage, 1988.

Laozi (Lao-tsu) (400 BCE–?)

As founder of Daoism (Taoism), Laozi (Lao-Tzu, "old fellow") was born around 400 BCE. Disappointed by civil wars and social disorder during the Warring States Period (403–221 BCE) of the late Zhou (Chou) dynasty (1027–221 BCE), he fled from his hometown to a remote mountainous area, choosing to live alone and study nature. He wrote *Dao De Jing* (*Tao Te Ching, The Classic of the Way and Virtue*), denouncing political and military struggles as unnatural, and calling for a return to nature, to primitive, agrarian life. His book became the foundation of Daoism, a classic philosophy, religion, and system of magic in China and East Asia. Zhuangzi (Chuang-Tzu) (369–286 BCE), as Laozi's most famous follower, also made great contributions to Daoism.

Daoism challenges the various rules laid down by Confucius, since Laozi believed that, since the Dao was the essence of all, it cannot be named or captured, that there are natural rules beyond the human world, and that it was important for people or their rulers not to merely act or react. The Dao, as the source and ideal of all existence, is immensely powerful but remains unseen. Daoism urged that people should ignore the dictates of society and seek only to conform with the underlying pattern of the universe, the Dao (the "way"). All things and lives have their own way, described by Laozi as Yin-Yang: the harmony of opposites through their interdependency and interaction.

The symbol of Yin-Yang sums up all of life's basic oppositions: good and evil, strong and weak, life and death, positive and negative, are all pairs of opposite aspects of a unity, and these can be transformed into one another. Though principles are in tension, they are never strictly opposed. Instead, they complement and counterbalance one another. Ultimately, apparent opposites penetrate one another (the element in the center of each) and are encompassed by a circle, symbolizing a final unity. Because all oppositions are ultimately subsumed in Daoism, all values are relative.

Laozi also believed that there were correlations of five basic elements (*wuxing*) in the universe, including wood, fire, earth, metal, and water. Like Yin-Yang, the five-element correlations were used in his thought processes to indicate both cosmic activities and conceptual categories. In either case, the pattern of movement was one of ceaseless alteration and cyclical change. In that case, people's desires, wills, and acts may be unnatural and will thus upset the natural balance of the Dao. Alongside the philosophical and mystical approach, Daoism developed on a popular level as a cult, in which immortality was sought through magic and the use of various elixirs. It also became more practical in China and Japan, when martial art masters followed the Daoist ideology to develop "*Qi gong*" (body energy control), "*Tai-chi quan*," and many other exercises. Astrologists developed the "*Feng-shui*" horoscope for people's everyday life.

About 100 CE, the popular Daoist religion emerged by worshiping Laozi, adopting an extensive pantheon, and establishing institutional monasticism. Daoism was recognized as the official religion of China for several periods through its imperial history.

See also: Chapter 2: Overview; Timeline; Confucius. Chapter 5: Buddhism; Daoism; Falun Gong; Feng-Shui. Chapter 10: Heavenly Stems and Earthly Branches. Chapter 15: Qu-Gong; Tai-Chi Quan.

Further Reading

Chan, Wing-Tsit, trans. *A Source Book in Chinese Philosophy*. Princeton, NJ: Princeton University Press, 1969.

Heider, John. *The Tao of Leadership: Lao Tzu's Tao Te Ching Adapted for a New Age*. Palm Beach, FL: Green Dragon, 2005.

Simons, Raphael. *Feng Shui; Step by Step*. New York: Crown Trade Paperbacks, 1996.

Lin Zexu (1785–1850) and the Opium War

As an official of the Qing dynasty (1644–1911) and a Chinese military and political leader, Lin Zexu fought against Great Britain in the First Opium War (1840–1842) by expelling from Guangzhou (Canton) the British merchants, some of whom had been smuggling opium into China. This action was one of imperial China's last victories against European expansionism, even though it contributed to the Opium War, which would constitute the Qing dynasty's first major defeat.

Lin was born on August 30, 1785, in Fuzhou, Fujian. He succeeded in the lowest civil examination at the age of 12, passed the provincial examination six years later, and by the age of 25 had passed the metropolitan and palace examinations in Beijing. After holding a number of increasingly important governmental positions, Lin was named governor-general of Hubei and Hunan Provinces in 1837.

During his tenure in these centrally located provinces, Lin initiated a campaign against the sale and use of opium, part of a national effort to stem the flow of silver out of China. So remarkable were Lin's successes in combating opium consumption, the destruction of drug paraphernalia, and the pursuit of dealers, that he was summoned to Beijing in late 1838 for an extraordinary series of eight audiences with the Daoguang emperor (reigned 1821–1850). Not only did the emperor authorize all the opium-fighting measures advocated by Lin, but he promptly assigned him the most crucial and sensitive role in the crusade: he made him high commissioner, with plenipotentiary powers, and directed him to travel promptly to Guangzhou to suppress the opium trade at its source.

After arriving at Guangzhou on March 10, 1839, Commissioner Lin launched an aggressive campaign against opium smoking and smuggling. Within several weeks, many of the Chinese dealers and addicts were jailed, and some were executed. The Western merchants, however, ignored Lin's order of handing over their opium holdings, and Lin detained the Western community of about 350 men, including British officials, in foreign factories on March 24, in order to force the foreigners to surrender their opium supplies.

These foreigners spent six weeks in detention until Charles Elliot, British superintendent of trade, promised the Western merchants that the British government would compensate for their loss. After the British merchants delivered 21,306 chests of their opium stock by May 18, Lin released the foreigners. In June, Lin destroyed publicly all the British opium at Humen, Guangzhou. Lin became a major Chinese hero in the country's first effort to resist Western aggression.

To protect its merchants and to expand trading rights to the Chinese market, the British government declared war on China on January 31, 1840. In February the British dispatched 16 warships mounting 540 guns, 28 transports, and more than 4,000 troops to China under the command of Rear Admiral George Elliot. Thus, the First Opium War began. In June, British troops arrived at Guangzhou and noticed that Lin and his garrison were well prepared for a strong defense. On June 30, Elliot ordered his troops to sail north along the coast and bombard the Qing army's positions at Xiamen, Fujian. The British troops continued to move north along the coast. On July 6, the British attacked Dinghai, Zhejiang, and took over the city. On July 28, eight British warships sailed farther north and on August 9 arrived at Dagu (Tagu), near Tianjin (Tientsin), less than 80 miles from Beijing. Under the threat of big guns, the Qing government began to waver. It relieved Lin of his duties and ordered him to be investigated and punished. Lin, after being exiled for three years to Yili, died on November 22, 1850.

To gain a better position in the peace negotiation, the British attacked Humen, Guangzhou, with 1,461 men on January 7, 1841. After several hours of fierce fighting, the Qing army lost two fire positions at Humen and suffered 600 casualties in its first formal defense. The British had more than 100 casualties. Later that year, China also lost Zhenhai and Ningbo, Zhejiang. In June 1842, the British attacked Wusong at the mouth of the Yangzi (Yangtze) River, and then captured Shanghai. In August, British warships appeared on the Yangzi outside Nanjing. On August 29, 1842, the Qing government sent an imperial commissioner to a British warship to sign the Sino-British Treaty. The First Opium War was over. The Treaty of Nanjing, which became the first treaty signed by China with Western powers, stipulated that China open five seaports for trade, would cede Hong Kong to the British, and would pay an indemnity of 21 million silver dollars.

See also: Chapter 1: Hong Kong; Major Cities; Xinjiang; Yangzi River. Chapter 2: Overview.

Further Reading

Bello, David A. *Opium and the Limits of Empire: Drug Prohibition in the Chinese Interior, 1729–1850*. Cambridge, MA: Harvard University Press, 2005.

Brook, Timothy, and Bob Tadashi Wakabayashi. *Opium Regimes: China, Britain, and Japan, 1839–1952*. Berkeley: University of California Press, 2000.

Fay, Peter Ward. *Opium War, 1840–1842: Barbarians in the Celestial Empire in the Early Part of the Nineteenth Century and the War by Which They Forced Her Gates*. Chapel Hill: University of North Carolina Press, 1997.

Hanes, III, Travis W., and Frank Sanello. *The Opium Wars*. Naperville, IL: Sourcebooks, 2002.

Melancon, Glenn. *Britain's China Policy and the Opium Crisis*. Burlington, VT: Ashgate, 2003.

Parker, Edward Harper, and Yuan Wei. *Chinese Account of the Opium War*. Charleston, SC: Biblio Life, 2009.

Mao Zedong (1893–1976)

Mao Zedong was the most important Chinese Communist leader in the 20th century as cofounder and chairman of the Chinese Communist Party (CCP), as well as founder and first president of the People's Republic of China (PRC). Born in the village of Shaoshan, Hunan, on December 26, 1893, Mao Zedong (Mao Tse-tung) grew up in a better-off peasant family. Taught by Confucian teachers in the village, he studied classic literature and ancient philosophy.

After his graduation from Changsha First Normal School in 1918, Mao took a job at Beijing University as a library assistant under the head librarian, Li Dazhao (Li Tachao) (1888–1927), who became one of the founding members of the CCP. During the May Fourth Movement of 1919, Mao, as a radical liberalist, was drawn to Marxism-Leninism and the Russian experience. In July 1921, the CCP was founded and 13 delegates attended, including Mao, representing approximately 50 CCP members across the country. In 1924, Sun Yat-sen (1866–1925) convened the First National Congress of the Guomindang (GMD; or Kuomintang, KMT; the Chinese Nationalist Party) and accepted CCP members into the GMD. CCP leaders, such as Li and Mao, participated in the GMD leadership. The CCP membership increased from 994 in 1925 to 57,900 in 1927. On April 12, Chiang Kai-shek (Jiang Jieshi) (1887–1975) began to purge CCP members in order to contain an increasing Soviet influence and left wing activities in the GMD party and the Nationalist Army.

In late 1927, Mao led his small troop into a remote, mountainous area and reorganized them into the Red Army, in order to create a military center. In 1931, Mao made his base region a Soviet government foundation for the CCP. Mao's rural-centered strategy and his guerrilla tactics became CCP revolutionary doctrines. By 1936, the Red Army maintained a contingency of approximately 45,000 troops, after the Long March (1934–1935) when Mao became the unquestionable top leader of the CCP. In 1937, the GMD government came to an agreement with Mao to jointly resist the Japanese invasion of China (1937–1945). The CCP's regular army had grown from 56,000 in 1937 to 1.27 million in 1945, supported by militias numbering another 2.68 million. China's full-scale civil war resumed between the GMD and the CCP in June 1946. By September 1949, the CCP forces or the People's Liberation Army (PLA) occupied most of the country except for Tibet, Taiwan, and various offshore islands. Chiang removed the seat of his GMD government from the mainland to Taiwan later that year.

On October 1, 1949, Mao declared the birth of the PRC and of the new republic's alliance with Moscow. China began to move into center stage of the global Cold War between the Soviet Union and the United States, two contending camps headed by two superpowers. Mao's alliance with the Soviet Union and North Korea pulled China into a foreign war in Korea. During the Korean War, Mao developed the new republic's political institutions based on the totalitarian model originated by the Soviets.

Mao believed that he needed charismatic authority and absolute power to achieve his idealistic goals. He then launched one political campaign after another in an effort to eliminate political rivals and "bad elements" in the society. His first effort to suppress counterrevolutionaries in 1950–1951 became a brutal struggle against former officials and supporters of the GMD government. Then, he launched the Three Antis and Five Antis movements from 1951 to 1954 to target private manufacturing, businesses, and real estate sectors in urban areas. In 1957, Mao launched another political movement, the Anti-Rightist campaign, targeting those who were not interested in communist politics. A large number were exiled to labor camps or remote villages for re-education, and numerous others were jailed or executed.

The Cultural Revolution began in 1966 and lasted for 10 years as a nationwide political movement against Mao's rivalry in the CCP leadership, such as Liu Shaoqi, president of the PRC, and Deng Xiaoping, the secretary-general of the CCP. Mao died in Beijing on September 9, 1976. Shortly after his death, the Maoist leaders, including his wife, Jiang Qing (Chiang Ch'ing) (1914–1991), were jailed and the Cultural Revolution was over.

See also: Chapter 1: Taiwan. Chapter 2: Overview; Chiang Kai-shek; Sun Yat-sen. Chapter 3: Chinese Communist Party; National People's Congress; People's Liberation Army.

Further Reading

Chang Jung, and Jon Halliday. *Mao: The Unknown Story*. New York: Knopf, 2005.

Chen, Jian. *Mao's China and the Cold War*. Chapel Hill: University of North Carolina Press, 2001.

Li, Zhisui. *The Private Life of Chairman Mao*. New York: Random House, 1994.

Short, Philip. *Mao: A Life*. New York: Henry Holt, 1999.

Marco Polo (1254–1324)

An Italian merchant, traveler, and author who wrote *Description of the World* (1299, or *The Travels of Marco Polo* published in French in 1298) as the first connected exposition of the geography, economy, and government of China to be laid before the European public. Many Europeans reached China, but few left with accounts of their travels. For a long time Polo's book was the only existing European source for information on life and customs in the Far East. The book became the basis for some of the first accurate maps of Asia made in Europe. It helped to arouse in Christopher Columbus an interest in the Orient that culminated in his exploration of America in 1492 while attempting to reach the Far East of Polo's description by sailing due west from Europe.

Marco Polo was born on September 16, 1254, in Venice and began his travels in 1271 with his father and uncle, who were Venetian merchants and business partners, and who were making their second journey to China. They made an overland trip to Acre (now in Israel), through Iran, crossed the Oxus River to the Pamir, which led them to

Xinjiang. During that time, most of these routes were under Mongol control, as the Mongol conquest of Eastern Europe, Central Asia, and East Asian had greatly facilitated Eurasian trade and travel. After entering China, the Polos crossed the Gobi Desert to Shangdu in 1275 and reached the court of Kublai (Khubilai) Khan (1215–1294), who established the Yuan dynasty (1279–1368) in China. Mongols differed from the Chinese in terms of culture and were few in number. The new emperor founded a racially based political hierarchy, with Mongols in the highest positions, followed by other Central Asians such as the Turks, Uighur, and even included some Europeans in his government. The Polos knew four languages and had a great deal of Eurasian trading experience. They took the opportunities offered and served as administrative, military, and diplomatic advisers to Kublai Khan.

Marco spent 17 years in Kublai Khan's service, from 1275 to 1292. In the beginning, he entered the Yuan government's diplomatic service as Kublai's agent on missions to many parts of the empire and surrounding states such as Myanmar (Burma). He was impressed by the economic and urban life of Chinese cities such as Hangzhou, which had a population of more than a million (Venice had about 50,000 at the Polos' time). He then served as governor of the city of Yangzhou, Jiangsu Province, for three years. He detailed in his book descriptions of the Yuan's currency circulation with paper money, land and property tax collection, and the civil service examination system. After leaving his post as governor, Marco served as military adviser, along with his father and uncle, to the Yuan Army. During these years, the Polos had asked Kublai Khan for permission to leave China. But the emperor declined their requests. In 1292, an opportunity came when they were asked to escort a Mongol princess traveling from China to Iran. The Polos took sea routes with 14 ships and 600 officials and servants (not including the crew) and sailed through Indian Ocean and Persian Gulf to Iran. After their mission, the Polos traveled overland back home.

In 1295, the Polos returned to their home city of Venice, which was at war with Genoa. Marco served as captain of a Venetian galley, and was taken prisoner in a battle of 1296. During his imprisonment, Marco told his journey to a fellow prisoner. They cooperated in writing the manuscript and soon, in 1298, the book had spread throughout Europe. In 1299, Marco Polo was released from prison and returned to Venice. He married in 1300 and became a wealthy merchant with three daughters. He became very ill in 1323 and died on January 8, 1324. After his death, some skeptics have wondered if Marco Polo actually went to China.

See also: Chapter 1: Overview. Chapter 2: Overview; Timeline; Genghis Khan and Kublai Khan. Chapter 12: Chinese Silk and the Silk Road.

Further Reading

Bergreen, Laurence. *Marco Polo: From Venice to Xanadu*. New York: Vintage, 2008.

Polo, Marco. *The Travels of Marco Polo*. New York: Penguin, 1958.

Wood, Frances. *Did Marco Polo Go to China?* Boulder, CO: Westview, 1998.

Qin Shihuang (The First Emperor) (259–210 BCE)

Qin Shihuang was the first emperor (reigned 221–210 BCE) of the Qin (Ch'in) dynasty (221–206 BCE), the leader who established the first unified government and ended the Warring State Period (475–221 BCE). He was born in 259 BCE in the State of Qin and named Ying Zheng. The State of Qin existed almost as early as 897 BCE. However, half a millennium passed before it really began its march toward universal rule against the other six states during the middle of the fourth century BCE. In 246 BCE, Ying Zheng succeeded the throne at 13 and became King Zheng of Qin when his father died after a reign of only three years.

In 238 BCE, King Zheng grasped all the power in his hand, smashing his political opponents and beginning his ambitious unification wars. The key strategy of the unification wars was to conquer each of the remaining states. King Zheng continued his predecessors' policy of "befriend the far and attack the near (*yuanjiao jingong*)" by pacifying his ally—State Qi—on the one hand and attacking states adjacent to Qin, such as Han, Wei, and Zhao, on the other. Having drafted a massive infantry army, he soon had an efficient military machine under strong commanders. Instead of using chariots, his army possessed cavalry, superior iron weapons, and crossbows, all relatively new developments. His attacks on other kingdoms, especially siege battles, were forceful and merciless.

In 221 BCE, his effort was crowned with success when China was unified under Qin (or Chin, where China got its name in the West: *Chin-a*). The unification of China was followed by the establishment of a highly centralized regime, Qin dynasty, the first of its kind in Chinese history. Ancient China was ended, and imperial China began. Having concentrated all power in his own hands, King Zheng of Qin changed his title to Qin Shihuang (the first emperor) and proceeded with the establishment of a huge bureaucracy. This central monarch system, or imperial system, lasted in China for more than 2,000 years, without significant change.

The empire was based on two main social groups: tax-paying peasants and rich landowners. Qin terminated the separate city-state system and completed a transformation of landownership from dynastic families, relatives, and lords to private owners. The peasants paid onerous corvee and taxation. Regular taxes alone constituted two-thirds of the harvest. If a peasant failed to pay the tax, he had to extend his service in the army. The total number of peasants Qin Shihuang recruited to build the Efang Palace and the Great Wall, as well as those recruited as soldiers for the defense of the frontier, exceeded 2 million. Qin Shihuang did not have difficulty in mobilizing sizable manpower, as China's population reached 54 million by the end of the Qin, and at that time the population of the Roman Empire was no more than 46 million. The Qin, however, did not last long, ending in 206 BCE, only four years after Qin Shihuang died in 210 BCE.

See also: Chapter 2: Overview; Timeline; Terra-Cotta Army. Chapter 12: The Great Wall; Pagodas, Palaces, and Temples.

Further Reading

Lewis, Mark. *The Early Chinese Empires: Qin and Han*. Cambridge, MA: Harvard University Press, 2007.

Rodzinski, Witold. *The Walled Kingdom: A History of China from Antiquity to the Present*. New York: Free Press, 1984.

Sima, Qian. *The First Emperor: Selections from the Historical Records*. Oxford, UK: Oxford University Press, 2009.

Sun Yat-sen (1866–1925)

As the founder of modern China, Sun Yat-sen (Sun Zhongshan) was the most important revolutionary leader, a man who ended the Qing dynasty (1644–1911) and founded the Republic of China (ROC). He was born on November 12, 1866, into a poor peasant family in Guangdong, and he was schooled by an uncle who had fought for the cause of the Taiping Rebellion. At 13, Sun joined his elder brother in Honolulu, Hawaii, where he stayed three years and studied an English curriculum in a Church of England boarding school. From 1886 to 1892, he studied medicine and surgery for his medical degree from a British mission hospital in Hong Kong. After his graduation, Dr. Sun began practicing in Macao.

Sun had been concerned over problems of the Qing regime. He submitted some reforming proposals and petitions to the government, but he received no reply. In 1894, he began his revolutionary career by participating in the local anti-Qing activities. In 1895, a plot to seize the government office was discovered and several of his fellows were executed. Sun escaped and soon made Japan his revolutionary base.

In 1905, Sun organized the "*Tongmenghui*" (the United League) in Japan. Among the 1,000 early members were liberal students, Christian merchants, and patriotic young officers trained in Japan. Sun and his secret society spread their revolutionary ideas and details of their organization from Japan to the world by establishing offices in San Francisco, Honolulu, Brussels, Singapore, and in many branches in 17 of the 24 provinces of China. Thousands and thousands of Chinese, including many New Army officers, joined the league by participating in multiple anti-Manchu activities and accepting Sun's "*Sanmin zhuyi*" (Three Principles of the People), including "nationalism" (both anti-Manchu and anti-imperialism), "democracy" (a constitution with people's rights), and "people's livelihood" (a classic term for social equality). Sun became the leader of the anti-Qing movement at home and overseas.

On October 10, 1911, amid an anti-Qing plot in Wuchang, the capital of Hubei, some New Army officers revolted (October 10, or "Double Tens," celebrated as the National Day for the ROC at Taiwan). The success of the Wuchang uprising led many more officers to join the revolution. In the next two months, 15 provinces proclaimed their independence from the Qing Empire. The rebellious provinces and *Tongmenghui* joined forces, setting up a provisional government at Nanjing. The provisional government elected Sun president, and he was inaugurated in Nanjing on January 1, 1912. As a great breakthrough in Chinese history, it ended 2,000 years of monarchy and built the first republic in Asian history.

Sun and his revolutionary leaders never controlled the New Army or any armed force. In an attempt to avoid civil war, he negotiated with Marshal Yuan Shikai (Yuan Shih-k'ai) (1859–1916), commander of the New Army, and offered him the presidency of the new republic. On February 12, 1912, Yuan forced the last emperor, only six years old at the time, to step down, thus ending the Qing dynasty. Sun then resigned as president. On February 14, Yuan became ROC president. Yuan, however, until his death in 1916, tried to establish his own dictatorship and monarchy against the revolutionaries. Thereafter, the central government collapsed completely. From 1916 to 1927, the country entered the Warlord Period, in which military commanders of different armies controlled a province or a region. Sun's struggles for democracy, or his "second revolution," against the warlords failed each and every time. While most Western powers rejected or ignored his idea, the Soviet Union was willing to help him to build a revolutionary army. In 1923, Sun made major policy changes in favor of the Soviet Union and the Chinese Communist Party (CCP). In January 1924, he convened in Guangzhou the First National Congress of the Guomindang (GMD; or Kuomintang, KMT, Chinese Nationalist Party). The party congress enacted a new constitution and agreed that Communists might join the GMD as individuals. Sun died in Beijing on March 12, 1925.

See also: Chapter 1: Hong Kong. Chapter 2: Overview; Timeline. Chapter 3: Chinese Communist Party.

Further Reading

Amman, Gustav. *The Legacy of Sun Yat-sen: A History of the Chinese Revolution*. Whitefish, MT: Kessinger Publishing, 2004.

Bergère, Marie-Claire, and Janet Lloyd. *Sun Yat-sen*. Stanford, CA: Stanford University Press, 1998.

Sharman, Lyon. *Sun Yat-sen; His Life and Its Meaning; A Critical Biography*. Stanford, CA: Stanford University, 1968.

Sunzi (Sun-tsu) (535–496 BCE)

Sunzi (Sun-Tzu) was an ancient Chinese military strategist and author of *The Art of War* (*Sunzi bingfa*), which became the best and most influential military classic in Chinese history. Sunzi was born as Sun Wu in the State of Qi (southeast China) during the Spring and Autumn Period (770–476 BCE), and then he lived through the Warring States Period (475–221 BCE). The period had many years of ferocious warfare aimed at expansion and annexation among the seven states. Sunzi read military classics during his young age and learned from the war experiences of previous dynasties.

In 517 BCE, Sunzi left Qi and went to the southern state of Wu, present day Suzhou, Jiangsu, where he farmed and wrote the famous military classic *The Art of War*. In 515

BCE, the new king, Heliu, was crowned in the State of Wu. Supporting the king's plan to reunify the country, Sunzi presented King Heliu his newly finished book. Although the king was amazed by Sunzi's strategy, warfighting tactics, military organization, and civil-military relations in his book, he wanted to test Sunzi's theories by commanding him to train the palace guards in 512 BCE. According to historical sources, Sunzi became a heroic general for the king of Wu. He rescued the neighboring state by defeating the invading troops from the State of Chu in 506 BCE.

Years later, after his retirement, Sunzi revised and improved his short book, *The Art of War* (*Sunzi Bingfa*), with his war experiences and tested expertise. His strategies dominate all 13 chapters, and his goal of winning the battle underlies the entire book. It covers the following subjects: laying plans, waging war, attacking by stratagem, tactical dispositions, energy, weak points and strong, maneuvering, variation of tactics, the army on the march, terrain, the nine situations, the attack by fire, and the use of spies. *The Art of War* is the first important work on strategy and theory in world military history. The book, which is considered a product of Daoist (Taoist) thinking, has had a significant impact on Chinese and Asian history and culture. After his death, his son, Sun Ming, was granted the title Lord of Fuchun. His descendant, Sun Bin, also became a military strategist and wrote a treatise on military tactics.

See also: Chapter 2: Overview; Timeline. Chapter 5: Daoism.

Further Reading

McNeilly, Mark. *Sun Tzu and the Art of Business: Six Strategic Principles for Managers.* New York: Oxford University Press, 2011.

Sawyer, Ralph. *The Essence of War: Leadership and Strategy from the Chinese Military Classics.* Boulder, CO: Westview, 2004.

Sun-Tzu. *The Art of War: Translation, Essays, and Commentary by the Denma Translation Group.* Boston, MA: Shambhala, 2009.

Tao, Hanzhang. *Sun Tzu's Art of War: The Modern Chinese Interpretation.* New York: Sterling, 2007.

Tang Taizong (626–649)

Li Shimin (Li Ch'i-min) became known by the royal name Taizong (T'ai-Tsung) as the second emperor of the Tang dynasty (618–907). Li was born in January 598 in Wugong (Xianyang, Shaanxi). His father, Li Yuan, was a general of the Sui dynasty (581–618). Although the Sui emperors reunified the country, they squandered public treasure in building palaces for their own comfort and vanity. The amount of wasted manpower and financial resources was enormous. They attempted to reconquer Korea three times, and several million peasants were drafted as soldiers and laborers for the military expeditions. As a result, peasant population was exhausted and the Sui treasury nearly empty. While the flame of peasant uprisings was burning across the country, in 617 Li Yuan and his son Li Shimin raised the revolt and quickly occupied Chang'an, the Sui capital. Li Shimin went on to establish control over eastern China and to pacify north and south. After Li Shimin killed his brothers, Gaozu (Li Yuan reigned 618–626) abdicated in 626 so that Li Shimin could rule.

After taking the throne from his father, Li Shimin became Tang Taizong (626–649) and was regarded as one of the finest of all Chinese emperors. He expanded China's borders far westward. He fought Turkic nomads in the west and defeated those in the east. In addition, Taizong cultivated Chinese relations with Tibet ca. 634. After initiating talks, the Tibetan head of state requested a Chinese bride to seal their relationship, and the Tibetans began adopting Chinese culture. The emperor also began establishing sovereignty over Western kingdoms along the Silk Road.

Taizong carried out many enlightened policies and measures beneficial to the country and the people by lowering taxes, instituting a fair civil service, and setting the example for his government to follow. As a Confucian, he believed that it was necessary for a leader to promote the harmony of his people by personal excellence. His efforts consolidated the state power of the Tang dynasty and restored social stability.

During the Tang dynasty, the economy of China prospered, exchanges with the outside world were frequent, and impressive scientific and cultural achievements appeared. Calligraphy, painting, and sculpture flourished during the Tang dynasty. In particular, Tang poetry is regarded as the acme of this genre. Chang'an, the capital of Tang, was not only the political center of China, but also one of the centers for economic and cultural exchanges for the whole Asian region. Chinese people were called the "People of Tang" by their neighbors. Even today, worldwide, the place where there is a Chinese community in a foreign land is still called "*Tangren jie*" (Tang People's town, or Chinatown).

See also: Chapter 2: Overview; Timeline. Chapter 5: Confucianism. Chapter 11: Tang-Song Poetry. Chapter 12: Chinese Silk and the Silk Road; Pagodas, Palaces, and Temples; Tang Pottery and Song Porcelain; Traditional Chinese Painting.

Further Reading

Benn, Charles. *China's Golden Age: Everyday Life in the Tang Dynasty.* New York: Oxford University Press, 2002.

Gascoigne, Bamber. *The Dynasties of China: A History.* New York: Caroll and Graf, 2003.

Lorge, Peter. *War, Politics and Society in Early Modern China, 900–1795.* London: Routledge, 2005.

Terra-Cotta Army

The emperor who commissioned the building of the Terra-Cotta Army was Qin Shihuang, the first emperor (reigned 221–210 BCE) of the Qin dynasty (221–206 BCE), to defend the emperor in his afterlife. The discovery of the Terra-Cotta Army in 1974 in a field outside of the village Xiyang, Lintong county, near Xi'an, in northwestern Shaanxi Province, remains one of the greatest finds of the century. The discovery came when a group of six farmers started digging a water well 1.6 kilometers east of the first emperor Qin's burial mound. After more excavation, the archaeologist noted that the warriors had differing hairstyles, costumes, and facial features.

The construction of the figures gave an impression that each figure appears to be hand sculpted. In actuality, the artists took a small repertoire of body parts such as arms, legs, and torsos that they attached to other parts in different combinations, and afterward the finer details of the facial region and the armor were done by hand. Although each warrior was different, they do not appear to be actual portraits of individual warriors. On most of the warriors there have been inscriptions found that appear to have a "unit" or an overseer of a work group's name stamped on it. This is an early form of quality control to track which groups were making certain statues. In addition, this allows for the number of figures in production to be traceable as well, and lets the overseers of the project know if one group was doing poor work. The figures then would have been painted and placed in their spot in the pit. The method was repeated until the project was complete, over an estimated 36-year period. The pit containing the warriors is 25,000 square meters. This pit not only contained foot soldiers but also chariots, horses, and commanders of the army. Current estimates for the total army size are around 8,000 sculptures including 400 chariot-pulling horses and 300 cavalry horses.

This was not the only pit near the burial complex that contained terra-cotta figures. Acrobats, musicians, and birds are in surrounding pits as well. In addition, supplemental buildings are beneath the ground; such as, for example, the stable pit found to the southeast of the mound. The damage to some of the statues occurred soon after the burial of the emperor. Archaeologists believe that raids on the pits for weapons by marauders caused some destruction, while the biggest destroyer of the statues was fire, which had roared through some of the pits. The fire left behind evidence of itself by charring one of the pit walls as well as burning the wood supports holding the roof up. The first excavation of the site lasted six years, from 1978 to 1984. The excavation exposed over 1,000 statues in the largest of the three pits. The second excavation took place over the span of just a year in 1985, but failed, due to technological issues. The third excavation began 24 years later in June 2009. As of 1987, UNESCO has declared the site a World Heritage Site.

See also: Chapter 2: Overview; Timeline; Qin Shihuangdi. Chapter 12: The Great Wall.

Further Reading

Capek, Michael. *Emperor Qin's Terra Cotta Army*. Minneapolis, MN: Twenty-First Century Books, 2008.

Portal, Jane. *The First Emperor: China's Terracotta Army*. London: British Museum, 2007.

Zhang, Wenli. *The Qin Terracotta Army: Treasures of Lintong*. New York: Scala, 1996.

Zheng He (Cheng Ho) (1371–1435)

Between 1405 and 1433, an imperial official, naval admiral, diplomat, and eunuch of the Ming dynasty (1368–1644) who made seven voyages to the Western seas. Eunuchs were males who had survived having their scrotums and penises removed and performed a variety of palace roles. Zheng He was ranked the Grand Eunuch as international relations adviser to the Ming Yongle Emperor (reigned 1402–1424).

Zheng He was born as Ma He into a Muslim family in southwestern Yunnan Province. At age 10, he was castrated by the Ming Army after being captured in his hometown. He was then sent north to serve Prince Zhu Di. When Zhu Di launched a large-scale military offensive campaign against the Mongols on the northern frontier in 1390, Zheng He made contributions to winning the battles. After that, Zheng He became known as the "Eunuch Sanbao." After Hongwu (the first Ming emperor, 1368–1398) died in 1398, a power struggle occurred between Prince Zhu Di and his nephew, who succeeded Hongwu as the Jianwen Emperor (1399–1402). Zheng He became one of the commanders of Zhu Di's rebellion army against the Jianwen emperor. In 1402, Zhu Di defeated the Jianwen's Imperial Army at Nanjing, the capital city, and took over the imperial throne as the Yongle Emperor. As a favorite of the new emperor, Zheng He was promoted to grand director of the Directorate of Palace Servants, the highest position of all eunuchs. In 1404, Emperor Yongle conferred the surname "Zheng" to him.

That year Zheng was appointed as the admiral in charge of a huge fleet, armed forces, and shipyards near Nanjing for undertaking the emperor's overseas expeditions. Over 2,000 vessels were built under Zheng's command in 1404–1419, including a hundred big "treasure ships," approximately 370 to 440 feet in length and 150 to 180 feet abeam. The average loading capacity is estimated to have been about 3,000 tons each. With four to nine masts up to 90 feet high, a dozen watertight compartments, and stern-post rudders, they might have had as many as 50 cabins and been capable of carrying 450 to 500 men each.

In June 1405, Admiral Zheng He embarked on his first voyage with over 200 vessels, of which 62 were treasure ships, carrying silk, porcelain, gold, and 26,800 men. His fleet sailed west to Vietnam, Java, Bengal, and India. Zheng visited many port cities. He also exchanged with the countries for local products. His fleet returned to Nanjing in the fall of 1407. Between 1407 and 1411, Zheng He made two more voyages to Central and West Asian countries. As one major function, he carried tribute envoys to China and back home again. He conducted some trade, but he mainly engaged in extensive diplomatic relations with foreign governments. Though seldom violently aggressive, he fought some battles during his first three voyages.

His fourth voyage from 1413 to 1415 reached many ports on the east coast of Africa, as far south as Malindi (near Mombasa). Detachments of the fleet made special side trips, one of them to Mecca. The new exchanges enrolled tributaries and brought back geographic information and scientific curiosities such as giraffes, which were touted as auspicious unicorns. From 1417 to 1422, Zheng He made two more voyages, visiting and revisiting 30 countries in East Africa, the Persian Gulf, Arabia, and the Red Sea. After the Yongle Emperor died in 1424, his son the Hongxi Emperor discontinued the oversea voyages in 1425. Emperor Xuande (1426–1435) then resumed the expedition by ordering Zheng He to his seventh voyage into the "Western Ocean" (Indian Ocean). In 1431–1433, he made his final voyage. Zheng He died in 1435 shortly after the seventh voyage.

See also: Chapter 2: Overview; Timeline. Chapter 5: Islam. Chapter 6: Muslims. Chapter 12: Chinese Silk and the Silk Road; Tang Pottery and Song Porcelain.

Further Reading

Dreyer, Edward. *Zheng He: China and the Oceans in the Early Ming, 1405–1433*. New York: Longman, 2007.

Levathes, Louise. *When China Ruled the Seas: The Treasure Fleet of the Dragon Throne, 1405–1433*. New York: Oxford University Press, 1996.

Wang, Jienan. *Zheng He's Voyages to the Western Oceans*. Beijing: China Intercontinental, 2010.

Yamashita, Michael. *Zheng He*. Vercelli, Italy: White Star, 2006.

CHAPTER 3

GOVERNMENT AND POLITICS

OVERVIEW

China is a communist party-state, where the Chinese Communist Party (CCP) controls the executive, legislative, and judicial branches of the People's Republic of China (PRC), and where CCP members hold most offices in the central and local governments. Chinese society has been centered as a unitary party-state in which one party, the CCP, maintains control of most economic and social sources, mass media, and non-government organizations (NGOs). The other seven political parties are small and cooperative with the CCP because their survival depends on their political support to the CCP. There is no political challenge, major opposition, or election campaign at the national level. The military, or the People's Liberation Army (PLA), belongs to the party rather than the state, since the CCP controls resources and personnel management for the military budget and for professional careers. The party used the government, including the military, to serve its political agenda as a totalitarian authority from 1949 to 1990 and as an authoritarian regime after the 1990s.

In preparation for the emergence of the new communist state in 1949, the CCP leadership named the new country the "People's Republic of China" to differentiate it from the old Nationalist state, the Republic of China (ROC, established in 1911). During its early years, the new China followed the Soviet authoritarian model and limited the people's rights by expanding state power through political campaigns and class struggle. In September 1949, the First Chinese People's Political Consultative Conference (CPPCC) passed the Common Program in Beijing and established the Central People's Government under the leadership of the CCP, with Mao Zedong (Mao Tse-tung) (1893–1976), the CCP chairman, as the first PRC president. Mao appointed CCP elites for government offices, military posts, and judicial positions. Next, they selected CCP members to serve in their administrations.

During the early 1950s, the CCP government established a new socioeconomic system based on Soviet Marxism-Leninism, modified to fit the Chinese situation, resulting in Mao Zedong Thought. In 1952, Mao called for a national movement to learn from the Soviet Union under the leadership of Josef Stalin (1878–1953), and China became the most Soviet-influenced country to maintain its identity within the communist camp through the 1950s.

On September 20, 1954, the First National People's Congress (NPC) passed the first formal constitution by secret ballot and promulgated the Chinese Constitution. This document was much like the Soviet Union's constitution of 1936, and Russian legal experts assisted in rewriting the code to better fit conditions in China. Thereafter, in 1975, 1978, and 1982, China has promulgated three state constitutions. The current constitution was adopted by the Fifth NPC on December 4, 1982. Even though the 1982 Constitution has had some changes and revisions in 1988, 1993, 1999, and 2004, the political institution established in 1954 has remained the same with few modifications.

According to the Constitution, the NPC is the highest state body and the only legislative house (a unicameral parliament) in China. In almost all cases, the NPC's representatives have been determined by the CCP, which maintains effective control over the composition of the body at various levels. From the bottom up, each of the 700,000 villages elects its own representative, with no restriction on the number of candidates, as the lowest level in the electoral system. Only this representative can enter the next level as a candidate, in order to become the town or city congressional representative. After the approval of the party committee of each town or city, each elected representative can then enter the county-level election. Following the approval of the county's party committee, each elected representative can serve a five-year term in the county people's congress and enter as a candidate at the district election. The next level after the district is the provincial election. The provincial representatives who serve in the provincial people's congress can enter the race to be elected to the National People's Congress.

The NPC exercises most of its power on a day-to-day basis through the Standing Committee in Beijing. Due to its overwhelming majority in the Congress, the CCP has had total control over the composition of this committee, which follows the policy of the CCP Politburo Standing Committee, in order to make NPC polices and legislatures. After the 1990s, the NPC and congresses at local levels began to play a new role, discussing their own issues and making their own decisions. But there is still a long way to go before the NPC can play a separate role as an independent legislature in the Chinese government.

The Constitution includes the president as the chief executive, the State Council as the executive body, and the courts and procurates as the judicial branch. Nevertheless, the members of the Standing Committee of the CCP Politburo, the *de facto* highest decision-making body of the country, such as Mao, Zhou Enlai, Zhu De, and Liu Shaoqi, took over national leadership positions.

The NPC also elects the president, whose term of office is the same as the term of the NPC (five years), and the president and vice-president are both limited to two consecutive terms. On September 27, 1954, the NPC elected Mao as PRC president with Zhu De (Chu Teh) (1886–1976) as vice president. Mao then nominated Zhou Enlai (Chou En-lai) (1898–1976) as premier and foreign minister, and the congress elected Liu Shaoqi (Liu Shao-ch'i) (1898–1969) as chairman of the First NPC Standing Committee. In April 1959, Mao stepped down as head of state, and Liu was elected as the PRC's second president, where he remained in office until he fell victim to the pressures of the Cultural Revolution (1966–1976) and died in jail in 1969. Thereafter, two acting presidents served until 1975 when the new constitution abolished the position. The 1982

ZHOU ENLAI (1898–1976)

Zhou Enlai was the premier of the People's Republic of China (PRC) in 1949–1976, foreign minister of the PRC in 1949–1958, vice chairman of the Chinese Communist Party (CCP) in 1935–1976, and chief of general staff of the People's Liberation Army (PLA) in 1949–1955. He became the second only to Mao Zedong (1893–1976) in CCP rank as early as 1935. After the founding of the PRC in 1949, Zhou's most notable achievements were in the diplomatic realm. In his capacity as premier, he spent much of his time aboard, boosting the PRC's international standing. His diplomatic approach was flexible and pragmatic. Zhou survived the Cultural Revolution in 1966–1976, when most of the old leaders were purged. Exploiting his undisputed role as the chief administrator, he tried to make compromises between radical idealists and conservative pragmatists. Zhou could not stop the revolutionary fever, however, and had to accept the injustices and impracticalities of Mao Zedong's measures to disrupt the party apparatus and government bureaucracy. His death on January 8, 1976, triggered mourning demonstrations that contributed to the overthrow of the radical Gang of Four, who succeeded Mao following his death later that year, and their replacement by the more pragmatic Deng Xiaoping.

Constitution reinstalled the presidency, and Li Xiannian (1909–1992) served from 1983 to 1988 and Yang Shangkun (1907–1998) in 1988–1993. Both were vice chairman of the CCP. The CCP Central Committee now reserves the post of president for its current secretary general. Jiang Zemin (1926–) served from 1994 to 2002 and Hu Jintao (1942–) in from 2002 to 2012; both were secretary-general of the CCP.

From November 8–14, 2012, the CCP held its Eighteenth National Congress in Beijing and elected Xi Jinping (1953–) as the new secretary-general of the Central Committee and the first ranked member of the Politburo. From February 26–28, 2013, the Eighteenth Central Committee held its Second Plenary Session in Beijing, making decisions on the new national executive leadership for the next NPC. From March 5–17, the Twelfth NPC was held in Beijing and 2,987 representatives attended. On March 14, the Congress elected party secretary-general Xi as president on a one-name ballot.

According to the Constitution, President Xi's most important political power is to nominate the premier of the PRC for the executive branch, or the State Council. On March 15, President Xi nominated Li Keqiang (1955–) to the congress as new premier, head of the government in China, who is the second ranked member of the CCP Politburo Standing Committee. Li was elected as the most important political appointment in the Chinese government the same day from a one-name ballot.

In April, 2013, Premier Li Keqiang appointed the entire State Council, including one executive vice premier, 3 vice premiers, 5 state councilors, and 25 ministers for all the ministries and national commissions. In his current cabinet there are ministers of Finance, Foreign Affairs, National Defense, State Security, Public Security, Justice, and Human Resources and Social Security; as well as chairmen of National Development and Reform Commission, Central Bank, and National Audit Office. More than

20 national agencies are also under the State Council, including the General Administration of Customs, State Administration of Taxation, and National Bureau of Corruption Prevention.

The CCP also dominates local governments by controlling their legislative, executive, and judicial branches. The PRC has 22 provinces, 4 municipalities, and 2 special administrative regions (Hong Kong and Macao). There are 2,862 counties under the provincial and municipal governments. The party employs similar methods to have political control of the provincial, district, metropolitan, and county governments by appointing CCP members to the local posts and approving or disapproving the nominations. Most of the provincial governors, lieutenant governors, city mayors, district executives, county heads, and local congressional leaders are CCP members.

As a result of party control, the legal system is also highly centralized in China. The Constitution authorizes the NPC Standing Committee to select, appoint, and dismiss Supreme Court justices and procurators at the national level. In 1955, the Ministry of Public Security granted local party committees authority to manage the public security and police force at its level. The standing committees of the local congresses can appoint and dismiss local judicial personnel. Moreover, all the local judges, court clerks, police, detectives, and public attorneys are hired as civil service staff of the national government, and many are CCP members.

In the late 1990s, China began its legal reform, even though the judicial branch is not yet depoliticized. China's law enforcement personnel, one of the largest police forces in the world, play an important role in maintaining political control and social order under CCP leadership. Among other forces, Chinese law enforcement includes the People's Armed Police (PAP), similar to police SWAT (Special Weapons and Tactics) in the United States. In recent years, the Chinese government has spent more money on domestic security than on its national defense.

Further Reading

Dreyer, June Teufel. *China's Political System*. 8th ed. New York: Pearson, 2011.

Gries, Peter, and Stanley Rosen, eds. *Chinese Politics: State, Society and the Market*. London: Routledge, 2010.

Guo, Sujian. *Chinese Politics and Government: Power, Ideology, and Organization*. London: Routledge, 2013.

Joseph, William, ed. *Politics in China: An Introduction*. New York: Oxford University Press, 2010.

Li, Xiaobing, and Qiang Fang, eds. *Modern Chinese Legal Reform: New Perspectives*. Lexington: University Press of Kentucky, 2013.

Lieberthal, Kenneth. *Governing China: From Revolution to Reform*. 2nd ed. New York: Norton, 2003.

MacFarquhar, Roderick, ed. *The Politics of China: Sixty Years of the People's Republic of China*. Cambridge, UK: Cambridge University Press, 2011.

Chinese Communist Party (CCP)

As one of the few communist parties that survived the Cold War (1946–1991), the Chinese Communist Party (CCP) is the world's largest communist party with 88 million members, and it still maintains control of the government, economic and social resources, armed forces, and mass media of the People's Republic of China (PRC). Among current party members, 31 percent are farmers, 23 percent professionals, 18 percent retirees, 9 percent workers, 8 percent officials and government staff, 3 percent students, and 8 percent others. Males make up 77 percent of party membership, while females make up 23 percent. Those who accept the CCP Constitution and are willing to fight for the party's mission can apply for membership.

In the late 1910s, Soviet ideology and reports of the Bolshevik revolution were circulating in China. In July 1921, the CCP was founded by 13 delegates, including Mao Zedong (Mao Tse-tung) (1893–1976), representing approximately 50 CCP members across the country against the Guomindang (GMD, or Kuomintang, KMT: Nationalist Party) government of the Republic of China (ROC). By 1928, when the CCP held the Sixth National Congress in Moscow, it had 130,000 members. In 1937, the GMD government came to an agreement with the CCP to jointly resist the Japanese invasion of China. By 1945, the CCP's regular army had grown from 56,000 in 1937 to 1.27 million in 1945, and its membership was 1.21 million. China's full-scale civil war resumed between the GMD and the CCP in June 1946. By September 1949, the CCP forces, or the People's Liberation Army (PLA), occupied most of the country except for Tibet, Taiwan, and various offshore islands.

After the founding of the People's Republic in October 1949, the Central Government was established under the leadership of the CCP, with Mao, CCP chairman, as the first PRC president, and with other top CCP leaders as his premier, ministers, and Supreme Court justices. Mao also appointed CCP elites for government offices, military posts, and judicial positions. On September 20, 1954, the First National People's Congress (NPC) passed and promulgated the Chinese Constitution, which emphasized that

---

HU YAOBANG (1915–1989)

Hu Yaobang was the chairman and then secretary-general of the Chinese Communist Party (CCP) from 1981 to 1987. After Deng Xiaoping's return to power, Hu was promoted to a series of high political positions in the CCP, pushing economic, social, and political reforms in the 1980s. His reform efforts upset some powerful party elders, who opposed political reforms and accused Hu of "bourgeois liberalism" undermining party authorities. Hu was forced to resign as secretary-general and was replaced by Zhao Ziyang in 1987. On April 15, 1989, Hu died of a heart attack during a Politburo meeting. A day later, a small-scale demonstration commemorated him and demanded that the government reassess his legacy. A week later, 100,000 students marched on Tiananmen Square, leading to the Tiananmen Square protests of May–June, and the Tiananmen Square Massacre on June 4, 1989.

the PRC was "under the leadership" of the CCP. In 1956 the Eighth CCP National Congress convened with a total of 10.7 million party members. The current constitution, adopted by the Fifth NPC on December 4, 1982, keeps the same law of the land, and provides that China is under CCP leadership. By 1982, when the CCP held its Twelfth National Congress in Beijing, it had 39 million members.

The CCP held its Eighteenth National Congress (once every five years) in Beijing on November 8–14, 2012. At the Congress, 2,270 party delegates from 40 constituencies elected the new Central Committee. The First Plenary Session of the Eighteenth Central Committee was held on November 15, and Xi Jinping (1953–) was elected new secretary-general of the Central Committee for 2012–2017 and the first ranked member of the CCP Political Bureau, which is the top executive body of the party. When the plenum of the Central Committee is not in session, the Politburo exercises the functions and powers of the Central Committee. The Central Committee's First Plenary Session also elected 25 members for the new CCP Politburo, and seven members for the Standing Committee of the Politburo, the *de facto* highest decision-making body of the country.

The Central Committee held its Second Plenary Session in Beijing on February 26–28, 2013, making decisions on new national executive leadership for the next NPC. The Twelfth NPC was held in Beijing March 5–17 and 2,987 representatives attended. On March 14, the Congress elected party secretary-general Xi as president on a one-name ballot. According to the Constitution, President Xi's most important political power is to nominate the premier for the executive branch, or the State Council. On March 15, Xi nominated Li Keqiang to the congress as new premier, who is the second ranked member of the Politburo Standing Committee. In April, Premier Li appointed the entire State Council, including an executive vice premier, 3 vice premiers, 5 state councilors, and 25 ministers for all the ministries and national commissions. Zhang Dejiang, the third ranked member of the Politburo, was then elected chairman of the Standing Committee of the Twelfth NPC as head of the legislative branch. Yu Zhengsheng, the fourth ranked member of the Politburo, was elected chairman of the National Committee of the Chinese People's Political Consultative Conference (CPPCC).

Under the CCP Central Committee are the local party committees, which dominate local legislative, executive, and judicial branches. The leaders of local party committees of various provinces, regions, municipalities, and counties are appointed or elected as governors, lieutenant governors, mayors, regional executives, county chiefs, local congressional chairmen, and judges. They employ similar methods to have political appointments in the governments of 22 provinces, 5 autonomous regions, 4 municipalities, and 2,862 counties. CCP members are appointed to the government offices, official agencies, administrative posts, and management. They support and promote the party members during their tenures in office. Provincial and municipal party congresses are held once every five years. Members and alternate members of these party committees are elected for a term of five years at the local party congresses. Only two special administrative regions (Hong Kong and Macao) have their own elections for the executives.

Under the local party committees are grass-roots party committees in townships, districts, and neighborhoods; in business enterprises, commercial companies, manufacturing factories, and retail stores; in all universities, public school districts, and research institutes; and in all military army, divisional, regimental, and battalion commands. Each grass-roots party committee has a secretary, deputy secretaries, and committee members, who are elected at the grass-roots level and approved by the next higher level. These committees supervise the general party branches and party branches in the villages, departments, offices, and PLA companies. Each party branch elects a secretary, a deputy secretary, and a committee, and leads the party teams, which as the most basic unit in the CCP organization have 3 to 10 party members. One of the important tasks of the party teams is to recruit new party members.

See also: Chapter 1: Major Cities; Taiwan. Chapter 2: Overview; Timeline; Chiang Kai-shek; Mao Zedong. Chapter 3: Overview; Constitution; First Chinese People's Political Consultative Conference; Li Keqiang; National People's Congress; People's Liberation Army; Provincial and County Governments; Xi Jinping.

Further Reading

Callick, Rowan. *The Party Forever: Inside China's Modern Communist Elite*. London: Palgrave Macmillan, 2013.

McGregor, Richard. *The Party: The Secret World of China's Communist Rulers*. New York: Harper Perennial, 2012.

Shambaugh, David. *China's Communist Party: Atrophy and Adaptation*. Berkeley: University of California Press, 2008.

Sharp, Jonathan ed. *The China Renaissance: The Rise of Xi Jinping and the 18th Communist Party Congress*. Singapore: World Scientific, 2014.

Zheng, Yongnian. *The Chinese Communist Party as Organizational Emperor: Culture, Reproduction, and Transformation*. London: Routledge, 2010.

Civil Rights

The Constitution of the People's Republic of China (PRC) lists protected civil rights, but the limits and problems of China's rights protection can be better identified in legislative, executive, and judicial procedures. The constitution stresses in its preamble that any expression of rights or freedoms is unlawful if they violate the Four Basic Principles; namely, to keep the country on the socialist road, to uphold the people's democratic dictatorship, to promote the leadership of the Chinese Communist Party (CCP), and to follow Marxism-Leninism and Mao Zedong's (Mao Tse-tung, 1893–1976) Thought. Moreover, a citizen's exercise of his or her rights and freedoms cannot conflict with the state's interests or with other citizens' rights.

Overriding the constitution, existing laws put restrictions on freedom of speech and set up punishment for violations such as antirevolutionary propaganda. The Chinese government continues to issue even more regulations in order to limit citizens' rights. No youth programs are permitted in churches, temples, and mosques; and minors are not allowed to participate in worship activities. Chinese judicial procedures allow the legislature and the legal system to restrain freedom of speech and freedom of the press.

Chinese journalists, lawyers, intellectuals, and activists who raise issues of official corruption, public health, and environmental crises face persecution, prosecution, harassment, detention, torture, and imprisonment. Gao Yaojie (1927–), an 82-year-old physician was fighting the spread of AIDS in China's countryside when she was named to receive a Human Rights Award from an international women's organization in the United States in 2006. At the award ceremony, Gao criticized Chinese policies and the lack of health care in rural areas. After her return to China, she was arrested for "violating the rights of other citizens." Liu Xiaobo (1955–) was arrested in 2008 after he coauthored the *Charter 08*, calling for increased political freedoms and human rights in China. He was sentenced to 11 years of imprisonment in 2009 for "the crime of inciting subversion of state power." In 2010, Liu was awarded the Nobel Peace Prize.

Although the constitution recognizes that worship is part of a citizen's rights, it requires respect for those who do not have a religious belief. Since the ruling that CCP is an atheistic party, it maintains control of religious exercises through a registration process. All theistic groups must be registered with the authorities, and all religious publications, personnel appointments, and seminary programs must go through a continuous official review and approval process. The church or temple can conduct only government-approved worship and activities. The growth of religious groups in China is tempered by state control and persecution. Reprisals against unregistered groups have primarily focused on Christians who, for various reasons, choose to attend "house churches" or "underground churches." Some Catholics remain loyal to the pope and the Vatican rather than to the Chinese Catholic Patriotic Association. Officially, there are about 5 million Catholics in China; according to the Vatican and other Catholic sources, the number is closer to 10 million, with half of them worshipping outside the state-managed churches. The official number of Protestants is 18–20 million, but unofficial estimates indicate that there are more than 30 million Protestants in China today.

The Chinese government dislikes having religious groups and activities outside the system, especially with connections to foreign religious groups. In 2004, Xu Shuangfu,

1989 TIANANMEN SQUARE MASSACRE

On June 4, the troops of the 22 infantry divisions of the People's Liberation Army (PLA) clashed with students and citizens at the Tiananmen Square, Beijing's equivalent of the Mall in Washington, D.C., or Red Square in Moscow. Hundreds of thousands of students and citizens had joined together and held demonstrations since April, protesting corruption and power abuse of the government. As a result of the massive use of armed forces, including tanks and machine guns, an estimated 1,300 students and city residents were killed that early June morning. After the Tiananmen Square massacre, Western countries, including the United States, joined in all-out condemnation of China's military suppression of the student-led pro-democracy movement.

leader of an underground church known as the Three Grades of Servant, was arrested. Some Westerners consider it to be an orthodox Christian house church network, an unofficial church based in China's northeast that claims millions of followers. In July 2006, the Heilongjiang Provincial Court sentenced Xu to death and executed him immediately. The court also gave death sentences to three other church leaders. Eleven church members received various sentences from 3 to 15 years in prison. Yao Liang, a Catholic bishop of an underground church, was arrested in 2006 in Hebei and was sentenced to seven years in prison. In December 2009, Yao died in jail. In 2007, authorities arrested 270 priests of the underground Christian churches. Many of them received prison sentences. The government continues to suppress larger and most popular religious groups such as Falun Gong, one of the Buddhist groups. The organization estimated that nearly 90,000 members were arrested, 60,000 of whom were tortured in prison, and 3,000 who died during or after their incarceration or forced labor.

In Tibet, authorities continue to control Buddhist activities, and repression of religious freedom remains commonplace. In March 2008, a Buddhist demonstration took place and turned violent on the 14th. By March 28, the government confirmed that 28 civilians and one police officer were dead; 325 civilians were injured, 58 of them

Falun Gong followers protest by practicing outside of the Immigration Tower in Wanchai, Hong Kong. Falun Gong started as a Buddhist exercise group in the early 1990s, and gained popularity in the mid-1990s with tens of millions of members. In 1999, the Chinese government banned Falun Gong and declared it unlawful as an "evil cult." The organization estimated that thereafter nearly 90,000 members were arrested, 60,000 of whom were tortured in prison, and 3,000 of whom died during or after their incarceration or forced labor. (AFP/Getty Images)

critically, along with 241 police officers. The India-based Tibetan government-in-exile reported more than 220 Tibetans were killed in the crackdown. After March 14, the Chinese government arrested 7,000 Tibetans from various parts of Tibet.

Most of the 8 million Uyghurs are Muslims, who face harsh religious policies. In June 2007, for example, during the traditional period for a pilgrimage to visit Mecca, Xinjiang authorities collected the passports of all Muslims to prevent any non-state-approved pilgrimage. In early July 2009, tens of thousands of Uyghur demonstrators gathered at Urumqi, the capital city of Xinjiang, protesting the government's handling of the deaths of two Uyghur workers and demanding a full investigation of the killings. After confrontations with police, the peaceful demonstration escalated into riots on July 5–7. The government reported that 197 people were killed and 1,721 others were injured during the two-day riot. The World Uyghur Congress reported a much higher tally, at approximately 600 deaths. Officials also confirmed on July 18 that more than 1,500 Uyghurs were arrested. By December 2009, authorities had sentenced 22 Uyghurs to death for their participation in the July 5 religious and ethnic rioting.

The Chinese government realizes the importance of a civil society and a country governed by the rule of law. However, little structural change has been made within the constitution. Chinese citizens have few rights to a fair trial, a lawyer, or appellate review, and little freedom from unfair interrogation, torture, and cruel and unusual punishment. In 2006, only 30 percent of all prisoners had a lawyer or legal consultant on their case. Among 933,156 defendants tried that year, only 1,147 were found not guilty. The conviction rate was and still is over 99 percent.

The Criminal Law increased the number of crimes punishable by death to 68, including robbery, rape, and economic crimes. China leads the world in the number of its executions, accounting for over 70 percent of all criminals executed in the world each year, and in 2005 put 1,770 criminals to death. Some international human rights groups believe that the official count is much lower than the actual number. Amnesty International concluded that the number of executions in 2005 was closer to 3,000. In 2014, the U.S. Department of State issued its annual report on Chinese people's rights and stated that the condition of human and civil rights in China "remained poor."

See also: Chapter 1: Xinjiang. Chapter 2: Mao Zedong. Chapter 3: Chinese Communist Party; Constitution; Criminal Law; Death Penalty; Human Rights; Law Enforcement; Liu Xiaobo; People's Armed Police; Political Dissents. Chapter 5: Buddhism; Catholicism; Christianity; Falun Gong; Islam; Underground Churches. Chapter 6: Muslims. Chapter 16: Censor System; Freedom of Speech.

Further Reading

Foot, Rosemary. *Rights Beyond Borders: The Global Community and the Struggle over Human Rights in China*. Oxford, UK: Oxford University Press, 2001.

Li, Xiaobing, and Qiang Fang eds. *Modern Chinese Legal Reform: New Perspectives*. Lexington: University Press of Kentucky, 2013.

Rossabi, Morris. *Governing China's Multiethnic Frontiers*. Seattle: University of Washington Press, 2004.

Svensson, Marina. *Debating Human Rights in China: A Conceptual and Political History.* Boulder, CO: Rowman & Littlefield, 2002.

Constitution

Since the founding of the People's Republic of China (PRC) in 1949, China has approved four state constitutions: in 1954, 1975, 1978, and 1982. In the past 60 years, the Chinese constitution has gone through several periods of importation, acceptance, rejection, and rewriting.

On September 20, 1954, the First National People's Congress (NPC) passed the first formal constitution by secret ballot, promulgating the Chinese Constitution. This document included a preamble and was divided into 106 articles in four chapters, much like the Soviet Union's constitution of 1936. Many Soviet legal codes were translated into Chinese, and Russian legal experts helped rewrite it to suit Chinese conditions.

The 1954 Constitution named the president as the chief executive, the NPC as the main legislative body (a unicameral parliament), the State Council as the executive body, and the courts and procurates as the judicial branch. On September 27, the NPC elected Mao Zedong (Mao Tse-tung) (1893–1976), chairman of the Chinese Communist Party (CCP), as the PRC's president.

The second PRC Constitution was adopted by the Fourth NPC at the First Plenary Session on January 13, 1975. It contained only 30 articles, in stark contrast to the hundreds included in the 1954 Constitution. It had a completely rewritten preamble consistent with the times, and ended with a slogan to struggle for new successes. Article 2 stated that the CCP was the leading force of the Chinese people. It also integrated the state constitution with the party by stating that the People's Liberation Army (PLA) was under the command of the Central Committee of the CCP. Radical terms such as "dictatorship of the proletariat," "social imperialism," and "proletarian internationalism" can be found in many places in this second constitution.

NATIONAL EMBLEM

On June 28, 1950, the Central People's Government (CPG) of China adopted a design for the national emblem, which was submitted by the CPPCC (Chinese People's Political Consultative Conference). In 1954, the Constitution of the People's Republic of China (PRC) states: "The national emblem of the PRC depicts Tiananmen in the center, illuminated by five stars and encircled by ears of wheat and a cogwheel." The Tiananmen Square stands as the center of the capital city. The cogwheel and ears of wheat stand respectively for the working class and peasantry, while the five stars represent the alliance of the Chinese people under the leadership of the Chinese Communist Party (CCP).

The 1975 document minimized or completely eliminated the courts and procurators. It did not retain individual rights such as freedom of speech and of the press. As in the first constitution, these rights were only for those loyal to Mao and the CCP. After Mao died in 1976, the human rights and civil liberty conditions in China began to improve.

In order to start his reform movement, Deng Xiaoping (Deng Hsiao-ping) (1904–1997), supreme leader of the second generation of the CCP leadership, urged the NPC to work on a new constitution. At the Plenary Session of the Fifth NPC on March 5, 1978, the third PRC constitution was disseminated. It doubled the number of articles from 30 to 60 and contained a new preamble. Two years after the downfall of the Maoists, including the "Gang of Four," the new constitution restored the courts and procurators. It also reinstated some citizens' rights, such as the right to strike.

For the first time, the new constitution stated that Taiwan was part of China and that it must be liberated by the PRC, thus finishing the great task of reunifying the motherland. In 1979, the government added an amendment dropping the liberation stance, instead opting for peaceful reunification.

To prepare a new constitution, a Committee to Amend the Constitution was established on September 10, 1980. It completed a draft version in February 1982, which was then submitted to the NPC Standing Committee for national discussion. On December 4, 1982, the Fifth Plenary Session of the Fifth NPC adopted the new document by secret ballot. The 1982 Constitution was the longest document in PRC history, and included 138 articles. It was a mix of continuity and change over previous versions.

Many sections of the current document were adapted directly from the 1978 Constitution, while new concepts and articles were added. For example, the 1982 Constitution stated that class struggle was no longer the top priority for the country and its people. Instead, it placed economic development and an improvement in people's living standard as its top priority. It also affirmed the idea of legality and other related concepts, expressly stating that the party must operate within the scope of the constitution and of the law.

The current constitution was adopted by the Fifth NPC in 1982. It has four chapters, including "The Fundamental Rights and Duties of Citizens." Some of the new provisions in the latest version were specifically designed to avoid civil and human rights violations of the Great Cultural Revolution in the 1960s. This section also listed several fundamental rights and duties of citizens which were enacted after the constitution was ratified. After 1982, the constitution has had important changes and revisions in 1988, 1993, 1999, and 2004. Even though some civil rights and legal codes were provided by the constitution, many have not been enacted until recent years.

See also: Chapter 1: Taiwan. Chapter 2: Overview; Deng Xiaoping; Mao Zedong. Chapter 3: Overview; Chinese Communist Party; Civil Rights; Human Rights; National People's Congress; People's Liberation Army.

Further Reading

Lubman, Stanley. *Bird in a Cage: Legal Reform in China after Mao*. Stanford, CA: Stanford University Press, 2002.

Muhlhahn, Klaus. *Criminal Justice in China: A History*. Cambridge, MA: Harvard University Press, 2009.

Peerenboom, Randall, ed. *Judicial Independence in China: Lessons for Global Rule of Law*. Cambridge, UK: Cambridge University Press, 2009.

Standing Committee of NPC. *The Constitution of the People's Republic of China*. Beijing: People's Publishing House, 2004.

Zhang, Qianfan. *The Constitution of China: A Contextual Analysis*. Oxford, UK: Hart, 2012.

Corruption and Punishment

In spite of tough policy and punishment by the government of the People's Republic of China (PRC), official corruption, abuses of power, and theft of public property are rampant. The reform movement since the 1980s has not yet contributed significantly to the country's democratic transformation or to its social stability. The new leaders in the 1990s focused on liberal economic reform while discouraging and even stifling political reform. As a result, economic interest groups successfully established an alliance with Chinese Communist Party (CCP) officials to effectively control economic policy-making and to share political governance. More and more CCP members have increased the private enterprise sector from 12 percent of the total party membership in 1993, to 17 percent in 1997, and more than 20 percent in 2002. The entrenchment of the power-capital establishment institutionalizes corruption as a logical consequence of China's economic development. In the 2000s, corruption has become one of the key elements of the power-capital institution with three ways of connecting politics and business: making money through abusing power; seeking power through paying bribery; and pursuing power and/or money by pawning intellectual capital.

The officials who control the resources, public land management, limited quotas of materials, and other valuable assets constitute one of the major power-interest groups. Benefiting from the monopolization of land, resources, and bank notes, their way of transferring their power to capital is to take bribery and rent-seeking. For instance, in 2000, due to bribery and embezzlement, China lost as much as 3.7 billion yuan *Renminbi* (RMB) (about $610 million) in revenue. Consequently, the power-interest groups have gradually spread from the upper class to middle class, demonstrated by the exceptionally gray income of 6.2 trillion yuan RMB (about $1 trillion), which was 12 percent of the GDP in 2011. The growth of gray income represents the extensive scope of corruption in China. Instead of reinvesting profits in domestic enterprises, assets under the power-capital economy are usually transferred overseas. The transferred resources are seldom invested in overseas enterprises but rather, they have been placed in an individual's savings accounts, or used for the purpose of facilitating immigration of family members, education of their children or relatives, purchase of houses, and so on, because owners of these assets know that most of their income is illegally obtained. In 2000, the amount of cash that flew overseas from China totaled $48 billion. By 2011, that number reached $65 billion, and China had become the fourth largest country in the world to witness massive outflow of capital, after Venezuela, Mexico, and Argentina. Reported by the People's Bank of China (China's central bank) in 2008, more than 18,000 government officials and state-owned enterprise CEOs escaped from China, taking 800 billion yuan RMB (about $133 billion) in cash to foreign countries since the mid-1990s.

In the 2000s, Chinese leaders have paid special attention to political scandals, corruption, and mismanagement in the government and in the party. In 2005–2006, more than 6,000 officials were investigated, detailed, and sentenced by prosecutors. One of the major cases was the arrest and sentencing of the CCP Politburo member and Shanghai Party Committee Secretary Chen Liangyu (1946–) in 2006. Chen was charged with corruption and misuse of the city's pension fund. He was responsible for 3.45 billion yuan RMB ($439.4 million) from funds that had been siphoned off from the Shanghai Social Security Pension Fund for illicit loans and investments. In November 2008, Chen was convicted and sentenced to 18 years in prison by the Tianjin Court.

The years of 2012–2014 witnessed one of the greatest challenges the CCP had ever experienced. Bo Xilai (1949–), party chief and mayor of Chongqing and a member of the Politburo, was reported to have been deeply involved in huge illegal financial transactions, retaliation against his opponents, and even murder (and cover-up). On September 28, 2012, Bo Xilai was officially expelled from the CCP. In November, he was stripped of all his positions in the party, the government, and the National People's Congress (NPC). On July 25, 2013, the Municipal Court of Ji'nan, Shandong, sued Bo for corruption, bribery, and power abuse. On September 22, the Ji'nan Court decided

BO XILAI (1949–)

Bo Xilai was the mayor and party committee secretary of Chongqing, one of the four municipalities which are directly under the central government rather than a provincial government, and member of the Politburo of the Chinese Communist Party (CCP) in 2007–2012. As a member of China's princelings power group, his father Bo Yibo served as vice premier and the minister of Finance of the People's Republic of China (PRC) and a member of the Politburo. After his graduation with a master's degree in 1982, Bo Xilai was on the fast track in his political career. He became the northeastern city of Dalian's vice mayor in 1990 and mayor in 1993. He was promoted to acting governor of Liaoning Province in 2001 and governor in 2003. Then, he served as China's minister of Commerce in 2004–2007. After becoming the mayor of Chongqing in 2007, Bo became popular in the city after he launched mass movements, such as "Singing the Red and Smashing the Black" (*Changhong dahei*), targeting organized crime. But in 2012 he was charged with retaliation against his opponents, illegal financial transactions, bribery, and even murder (and cover-up of it), of Neil Heywood, a British businessman who died in Chongqing in 2011. Bo was dismissed from all positions in 2012, and was convicted of corruption and sentenced to life imprisonment on September 22, 2013.

its verdict, convicted him, and sentenced Bo to life in jail for his crimes. The Chinese government continues its anti-corruption campaign under Xi Jinping's (1953–) leadership, which has emphasized tough penalties against corruption, including the death penalty.

See also: Chapter 3: Overview; Chinese Communist Party; Criminal Law; Death Penalty; National People's Congress; Provincial and County Governments; Supreme People's Court; Xi Jinping.

Further Reading

Brown, Kerry. *The New Emperors: Power and the Princelings in China*. London: Tauris, 2014.

Callick, Rowan. *The Party Forever: Inside China's Modern Communist Elite*. London: Palgrave Macmillan, 2013.

Kwong, Julia. *The Political Economy of Corruption in China*. Armonk, NY: M. E. Sharpe, 1997.

Schell, Orville, and John Delury. *Wealth and Power: China's Long March to the Twenty-first Century*. New York: Random House, 2013.

Wedeman, Andrew. *Double Paradox: Rapid Growth and Rising Corruption in China*. Ithaca, NY: Cornell University Press, 2012.

Criminal Law

After the Constitution of the People's Republic of China (PRC) was passed in September 1954, the Standing Committee of the National People's Congress (NPC) established a state law codification commission which created the first criminal code to describe liability in detail, for social control, criminal justice, and public security. In 1954–1957, the commission published a series of criminal codes for law enforcement, judicial institutions, and an assessor system. It was a copy of Soviet criminal code, which had some functional resemblance to the legal practice from the Western common legal tradition. This body of legal provisions provided "principal punishments," including criminal detention, fixed-term imprisonment, life imprisonment, and the death penalty.

The Criminal Code was issued in November 1976, laying the foundation for China's new legal system. Among more than 300 laws there are 26 crimes, including rape and robbery, which are punishable by the death penalty. The NPC Standing Committee then adapted the Criminal Law in 1979 with the emphasis that only "a national law passed by the NPC can criminalize behavior." Over the past 35 years, the NPC and its Standing Committee amended the Criminal Law on 10 different times, from 1995 to 2011, by adding more punishable acts, due to an increase of crime in the country. The current PRC Criminal Law has 10 chapters and 452 articles and has increased publishable crimes by the death penalty from 26 in 1976, to 60 in 1995, and to 68 in 1997. Capital punishment for some crimes, including tax fraud, passing fake negotiable notes, and the illegal "pooling" of funds, is unique to the Chinese judicial system. The government claims that this level of punishment is necessary to combat increasing corruption. The 1997 legislation also further decentralized the appeals process, giving final authority to the provincial courts rather than the Supreme Court. Both of these measures have increased the number of executions in recent years. Executions are often carried out on the same day as the sentencing.

Under some criticism, the criminal code includes a category of "counterrevolutionary offenses," such as anti-government propaganda, speech, assembly, or other acts that "endanger the PRC" and are "committed to the goal of overthrowing the political power of the dictatorship of the proletariat and the socialist system." Additionally, because legal provisions for the freedom and civil liberties were incomplete, the rights of citizens can be restricted administratively. There are extralegal restrictions, which include those enacted by government agencies, party leaders, local officials, and various policies, none of which are legally binding.

The authorities continue to employ law enforcement and related organizations charged with duties, such as monitoring speeches and religious activities, to reach this end. A censorship system also has been adopted for news of great importance, which must be issued only by appointed authoritative bodies and not by private media outlets. If news or a speech that includes controversial material is made public, or is disseminated to overseas audiences, those involved are often punished. Chinese journalists, lawyers, intellectuals, and activists who raise issues of official corruption, public health, and environmental crises face persecution, prosecution, harassment, detention, torture, and imprisonment.

All local and special courts have a two-hearing system, except for the two special regions of Hong Kong and Macau, which have their own judicial systems and are not under the jurisdiction of the Supreme People's Court in Beijing. Chinese citizens have few rights to a fair trial or a lawyer or an appellate review, and little freedom from unfair interrogation, torture, and cruel and unusual punishment. Defendants' rights have only recently become an indispensable part of the criminal justice system. In 2006, only 30 percent of all prisoners had a lawyer or legal consultant for their case. Defense

CHEN LIANGYU (1946–)

Chen Liangyu was mayor and party committee secretary of Shanghai, and member of the Politburo of the Central Committee of the Chinese Communist Party (CCP) in 2002–2007. Chen was charged in 2006 with corruption and misuse of the city's pension fund. The Shanghai party committee and city government put pressure on the prosecution and procurement of Chen's case, including a threat to remove the chief prosecutor from his office. The court had to agree with the prosecutor to relocate the case from Shanghai to the northern city of Tianjin. Then, the prosecutor won the case, and Chen was dismissed from all of his positions in the party and city government in 2007. In November 2008, Chen was convicted and sentenced to 18 years in prison by the Tianjin Court.

attorneys often face chronic difficulties in accessing information for clients. Among 933,156 defendants tried that year, only 1,147 were found not guilty. The conviction rate was, and still is, more than 99 percent. The extreme emphasis on punishment by Criminal Law reflects China's legal tradition that the core purpose of law is to enforce punitive measures rather than to protect rights.

See also: Chapter 3: Civil Rights; Constitution; Death Penalty; Human Rights; Law Enforcement; National People's Congress; People's Armed Police; Political Dissents; Supreme People's Court.

Further Reading

He, Weifang. *In the Name of Justice: Striving for the Rule of Law in China.* Washington, DC: Brookings Institution Press, 2012.

Hsu, Stephen, ed. *Understanding China's Legal System.* New York: New York University Press, 2003.

Lubman, Stanley. *Bird in a Cage: Legal Reforms in China after Mao.* Stanford, CA: Stanford University Press, 2002.

McConville, Mike. *Criminal Justice in China: An Empirical Inquiry.* London: Edward Elgar, 2012.

Mühlhahn, Klaus. *Criminal Justice in China: A History.* Cambridge, MA: Harvard University Press, 2009.

Death Penalty

At the First National People's Congress (NPC) of the People's Republic of China (PRC) in 1954, the NPC Standing Committee authorized a state law codification commission to create the criminal code for the country's social control, criminal justice, and public security. In 1954–1957, the commission published a series of criminal codes for law enforcement, judicial institutions, and an assessor system, including criminal detention, fixed-term imprisonment, life imprisonment, and the death penalty. In November 1976, the Criminal Law was issued with 22 crimes, including rape and robbery, punishable by the death penalty.

Regarding the most serious legal punishment, the death sentence, relevant provisions have increased. In 1979, the Criminal Code included 26 crimes punishable by death. By 1995, an amendment raised this number to 60. The 1997 Criminal Law increased the number of "absolute" cases of the death penalty to 68, and included bombings and economic crimes. Capital punishment for these latter crimes, including tax fraud, passing fake negotiable notes, and the illegal "pooling" of funds, is unique to the Chinese judicial system. This move, however, is justified by the government, which claims that the punishment is necessary to combat increasing corruption.

The 1997 legislation further decentralized the appeals process, giving final authority to the provincial supreme courts rather than the national Supreme Court. Executions are often carried out the same day as the sentencing. Both of these measures have increased the number of executions in recent years.

Authorities' attempts to expand the scale of capital punishment reflect the government's concerns over the increasing crime rate. This is inconsistent with the global trend of seeking to reduce or eliminate the death sentence altogether, despite China signing two key international human rights treaties in the 2000s that included articles against the sentence. The country leads the world in executions, and in 2005 topped the list with 1,770. Amnesty International claims that official figures are much lower than the actual number and states that in China, statistics are considered state secrets. Amnesty International concluded the number of executions was closer to 3,400. In March of the same year, however, a senior member of the NPC announced that China executes approximately 10,000 people per year. China accounts for over 70 percent of criminals executed in the world per year, and some international human rights organizations put the number at between 10,000 and 15,000 a year, or around 20 to 30 per day, more than the rest of the world combined. The Supreme Court only regained the right to review all death penalty decisions on January 1, 2007.

Defendants in criminal proceedings have been executed following convictions that sometimes involved major lack of due process, as well as inadequate channels for appeal. In 2004, Xu Shuangfu, leader of an underground church known as the Three Grades of Servant, was arrested. Some Westerners consider it to be an orthodox Christian house church network, an unofficial church based in China's northeast that claims millions of followers. In July 2006, the Heilongjiang Provincial High Court sentenced Xu to death and immediately executed him. The court also gave death sentences to three other church leaders.

Wu Weihan was arrested in Beijing in 2005, and charged with conducting espionage for Taiwan. At the time of his arrest, he had received his PhD in Germany in the 1990s and worked in an Austrian biomedical company as a researcher. Wu was sentenced to death in May 2007 by Beijing's court. No appeal and no family visits were allowed by the court during his entire prison time. One day before his execution, the court gave special permission for his daughter's visit. On November 28, 2008, Wu was executed by gunshot. In early July 2009, tens of thousands of Uyghur demonstrators gathered at Urumqi, the capital city of Xinjiang, protesting the government's handling of the deaths of two Uyghur workers and demanding a full investigation of the killings. After confrontations with police, the peaceful demonstration escalated into riots from July 5–7. The official confirmed that on July 18 more than 1,500 Uyghurs were arrested. By December 2009, authorities had sentenced 22 Uyghurs to death for their participation in the July 5 religious and ethnic rioting.

In October 2009, British Prime Minister Gordon Brown condemned the Chinese government decision to execute a British citizen in Xinjiang. Despite his request and the British family's appeals for clemency on the grounds of mental illness, Chinese authorities executed the British man by lethal injection on December 29. In 2014, the U.S. Department of State issued its annual report on Chinese people's rights and stated that the condition of civil rights in China "remained poor."

See also: Chapter 1: Xinjiang. Chapter 3: Civil Rights; Criminal Law; Human Rights; Law Enforcement; National People's Congress; Supreme People's Court. Chapter 5: Underground Churches. Chapter 6: Uyghur.

Further Reading

Hood, Roger, and Carolyn Hoyle. *The Death Penalty: A Worldwide Perspective.* 4th ed. Oxford, UK: Oxford University Press, 2008.

Lu, Hong, and Terance Miethe. *China's Death Penalty: History, Law and Contemporary Practices.* London: Routledge, 2007.

Trevaskes, Susan. *The Death Penalty in Contemporary China.* London: Palgrave Macmillan, 2012.

First Chinese People's Political Consultative Conference (CPPCC)

The First Chinese People's Political Consultative Conference (CPPCC) was held in September 1949 under the leadership of the Chinese Communist Party (CCP). It served as a national coalition, including the democratic parties, noncommunist associations, religious groups, industrial and commercial chambers, various political organizations such as the Revolutionary Committee of the Guomindang (Kuomintang), Democratic League, Democratic National Construction Association, Association for Promoting Democracy, and Chinese Peasants' and Workers' Democratic Party. Due to the overwhelming majority of the CCP representatives, the First CPPCC supported the CCP to found the People's Republic of China (PRC) in October 1949.

Thereafter, the CPPCC became part of the national government of the PRC by serving as a consultative and advisory organ to the ruling party. The CPPCC elected its representatives at county and provincial levels, organized local and national committees, and established a standing committee. The national committee elected the standing committee members, a chairman, and multiple vice chairmen. Mao Zedong (Mao Tse-tung) (1893–1976), CCP leader, was elected the First CPPCC chairman in 1949;

NATIONAL ANTHEM

Before the founding of the People's Republic of China (PRC), the Preparatory Committee for the CPPCC (Chinese People's Political Consultative Conference) decided to solicit "The March of the Volunteers" as the national anthem on September 27, 1949. During the Cultural Revolution in 1966–1976, "The East Is Red" was used as a substitute national anthem. In 1978, the National People's Congress (NPC) brought back the "The March of the Volunteers," making some changes in its lyrics. In 1982, the Fifth NPC restored the original 1935 version of the song as the official national anthem.

Zhou Enlai (Chou En-lai) (1898–1976) was elected second, third, and fourth in 1954, 1959, and 1965; and Deng Xiaoping (Deng Hsiao-ping) (1904–1997) was the fifth in 1978. The current chairman is Yu Zhengsheng (1945–) who was elected at the Twelfth CPPCC in 2013.

Since 1949, the CPPCC exercised the functions and powers of the legislative branch, as the national congress was not convened until 1954. The CPPCC delegates passed the Common Program at the First Plenary Session in Beijing. The Common Program served as China's provisional constitution from 1949 to 1954 and established the Central People's Government (CPG) under the leadership of the CCP, with Mao as the first PRC president until 1954. The First Plenary Session of the CPPCC created the Supreme People's Court. Nevertheless, the CCP leadership followed the Soviet model and established communist control over the country through class struggle.

In 1952, to deal with increasing complaints, the CPPCC Standing Committee decided to create a national people's congress through general elections. At its Forty-Third session, held on December 24, 1952, this body agreed to commence the drafting of a constitution. On January 13, 1953, a committee for this purpose was established, a draft was unanimously approved on June 14, 1954, at the Thirtieth CPG Plenary Session, and a revised version was discussed and approved by the Thirty-Fourth CPG Plenary Session.

On September 20, 1954, the First National People's Congress (NPC) passed the first formal constitution by secret ballot and promulgated the Chinese Constitution, much like the Soviet Union's constitution of 1936, which can be regarded as a civil law system. Much of the Soviet legal code was translated into Chinese, and Russian legal experts helped rewrite it to suit Chinese conditions. The First NPC elected Mao as the PRC's president on September 27, 1954.

The CPPCC's political function was then significantly reduced. Until the 1980s, the CPPCC and its Standing Committee played only a symbolic role as a powerless rubber-stamp governmental body. Nonetheless, it protected some of the non-communist political parties, democratic organizations, and liberal individuals through the massive political movements launched by Mao, such as the Cultural Revolution (1966–1976). Although these parties were never able to challenge the CCP authorities, they coexisted and survived in the communist state.

During the 1980s, the CPPCC and its Standing Committee began to engage more and more in shaping national policies and offering opinions and advice on major issues. In 1983, over 64 percent of the Standing Committee members were not communists. Its local committees paid more attention to petitions from ordinary people and organized social investigations. In the meantime, the CPPCC has also actively participated in policy debates and social survey, in order to play an increased supervisory role in the government.

See also: Chapter 2: Overview; Timeline; Deng Xiaoping; Mao Zedong; Chapter 3: Overview; Chinese Communist Party; Civil Rights; Constitution; National People's Congress; Political Dissents; Supreme People's Court.

Further Reading

General Affairs Office, CPPCC National Committee. *The Chinese People's Political Consulta-tive Conference*. Beijing: Foreign Languages Press, 2004.

Lieberthal, Kenneth. *Governing China: From Revolution to Reform*. 2nd ed. New York: Nor-ton, 2003.

MacFarquhar, Roderick. *The Politics of China: Sixty Years of the People's Republic of China*. Cambridge, UK: Cambridge University Press, 2011.

Saich, Tony. *Governance and Politics of China*. 3rd ed. London: Palgrave Macmillan, 2011.

Human Rights

As China became more cooperative in business and diplomacy, it began participating in international human rights organizations. The country has increasingly been active in the UN Human Rights Commission, Human Rights Council, and other interna-tional nongovernmental organizations (NGOs). In March 2004, the Second Session of the Tenth National People's Congress (NPC) adopted and published 14 important amendments to the PRC Constitution. Among the most important amendments is the phrase added to Article 33: "The state respects and guarantees human rights." This marks the first time the Constitution mentions human rights.

However, the constitutional amendment has not yet improved the condition of hu-man rights in the PRC. Pragmatic nationalism is dictated by the government to pursue China's unity, strength, prosperity, and dignity rather than choosing civil and human rights as its core. Oftentimes the government has even called on individuals to sacrifice personal rights for the national interest. The country has its own normative principles, which have been described as the "Chinese characteristics."

China's economic growth is based on low production cost. The problems of Chinese labor have become serious in terms of low wages, poor working conditions, and human rights. By 2006, more than 120 million peasants had left their farms and sought work in cities, resulting in problems related to employment, housing, public health, transporta-tion, and law enforcement. About 74 percent of migrant laborers, working 10–12 hours a day, earn only $80–200 a month, about 12–30 percent of the average urban salary. Full-time workers continue to confront many problems, such as safety in the work-place. Coal mining is still the most dangerous profession in China. Official statistics show that the number of mineworker fatalities increased from 3,082 in 2000, to 3,790 in 2002, to 4,143 in 2003; and in 2004 and 2005, fatalities reached a horrendous high of more than 6,000 miners each year. According to a report by the World Federation of Trade Union in 2006, some Chinese manufacturing companies hire child laborers, be-tween the ages of 12 and 15, during the summer and winter breaks for full-time work-ers. These child laborers are paid much less than the minimum wage and are required to work as many hours a day as adult workers.

Child labor, human trafficking, prostitution, drug addiction, as well as domestic vio-lence and abuse are entrenched and very resistant to change. The Ministry of Public

Security (MPS) has estimated that 20,000 women and children are abducted and sold each year, and some NGOs estimate that between 30,000 and 50,000 have been trafficked annually. The estimated number of sex workers ranges from 4 million to as many as 10 million. Subsequent to the first HIV case being diagnosed in 1985, the official number of infected people reached 22,517 in 2000, 40,560 in 2002, and 840,000 in 2003. By 2005, AIDS had become the third largest killer (after tuberculosis and rabies) among all contagious diseases in China. Intravenous drug use reportedly accounted for between 60 and 70 percent of these cases. Before 1985, there were very few female drug users, but the figure escalated quickly in the 1990s and 2000s. The number of registered female drug users reached 118,000 in 1999, climbed to 138,000 in 2000, and was estimated to represent roughly 16 percent of all drug users (more than 1.1 million) nationwide, in both 2002 and 2003. By 2006, more than 30.7 million Chinese people were living below the poverty line ($1 a day), without sufficient food and clothing. Nearly 20 million urban residents were dependent on government and social welfare.

The population control program continues to negatively affect Chinese women. Aggressive actions, such as forced abortions and sterilization, have been taken against many women who failed to follow the government's one-child policy. The single-child policy results in selective abortions and even female infanticide. Some women attempted to terminate their pregnancy if they knew they were having a female baby. This is a significant contribution to the gender imbalance in China, where, in 2012 there was a ratio of 135 male to 100 female infants. Activists who asked for more protection of women's rights have been attacked by officials or arrested by the police. There are only limited rights for the criminally accused, and torture, abuse, and insulting behavior toward prisoners are frequently reported in China. The U.S. Department of State reported in 2014 that the condition of human rights in China "remains poor."

See also: Chapter 3: Chinese Communist Party; Civil Rights; Constitution; National People's Congress. Chapter 4: Migrant Laborers; Workplace Safety. Chapter 6: Poverty; Urban Poor. Chapter 7: Child Labor; Domestic Violence; Family Planning Law; Gender Imbalance; Gender Inequality; Human Trafficking; One-Child Policy; Selective Abortions; Sex Trade.

Further Reading

Angle, Stephen C. *Human Rights in Chinese Thought: A Cross-Cultural Inquiry*. Cambridge, UK: Cambridge University Press, 2002.

Angle, Stephen C., and Marina Svensson, eds. *The Chinese Human Rights Reader: Documents and Commentary, 1900–2000*. Armonk, NY: M. E. Sharpe, 2002.

Foot, Rosemary. *Rights beyond Borders: The Global Community and the Struggle over Human Rights in China*. Oxford, UK: Oxford University Press, 2001.

Nielsen, Gert Holmgaard. *Walking a Tightrope: Defending Human Rights in China*. Copenhagen, Denmark: Nordic Institute of Asian Studies, 2014.

Svensson, Marina. *Debating Human Rights in China: A Conceptual and Political History*. Boulder, CO: Rowman & Littlefield, 2002.

Law Enforcement

China has one of the largest law enforcement bodies in the world. According to official statistics from 2010, the People's Republic of China (PRC) has more than 1.5 million armed police, 640,000 police, and 250,000 detectives and investigators, all under the control of the Ministry of Public Security (MPS) in Beijing. This ministry has a bureau of public security in each province and county, a metropolitan police department in each city, and precinct offices in each district. In 2008, this top-down centralized police system had 31 provincial bureaus of public security; 356 metropolitan police departments; 2,972 county police headquarters; and 41,941 local police stations. There are also more than 350,000 traffic police, street patrollers, special police, and some cities even have anti-riot units. Estimates of the total of China's law enforcement forces may vary, but are usually in the vicinity of 2.4 million and rising. All the law enforcement personnel are hired and paid as the "cadres of the national government."

As a general rule, police officers in China do not perform static guard duty, but are tasked with controlling the population, fighting crime, and maintaining safety. Police officers patrol on foot, in vehicles, and often operate out of small, interconnected command boxes on city streets. Some urban centers have anti-riot units equipped with a few armored cars. Previously, those involved in law enforcement went unarmed, but since late 1994, circumstances have required them to carry sidearms more often. The official Chinese newspaper reported that more than 500 police officers have been killed each year since 1993. In January 1996, new rules were issued concerning the use of batons, tear gas, handcuffs, water cannons, firearms, and explosives. These regulations updated the 1980 guidelines and were a response to the rise in crime. Despite these new adjustments, police forces are not considered part of the armed forces of China as defined by the National Security Law. Police officers have a system of ranks composed of triangles, diamonds, and gold leaves.

As part of the recent legal reforms, China strengthened the People's Armed Police (PAP) in the 1990s. This national organization was established in 1983 and has regular troops, somewhat like a combination of the National Guard with SWAT (Special Weapons and Tactics) teams in the United States. In 2000, PAP was comprised of 1 million members.

Aside from the state police force, private and collective security guards assist in law enforcement, particularly at the entrances to many factories, construction sites, residential areas, hotels, sports arenas, and civilian businesses. They are usually hired by a private company and receive a limited amount of specialized training. These personnel, estimated in 1993 to number around 200,000, are often demobilized soldiers of the People's Liberation Army (PLA) as well as itinerant workers from the countryside and cities.

The Chinese government often launches "strike hard" campaigns against crime. During these times, the police force vigorously combats crime, including organized and gang-related offenses, murder, rape, kidnapping, and other serious violent actions. These campaigns result in severe punishments and mass executions. In 2009, for example, the Chinese police cracked 3.1 million criminal cases. Law enforcement officials continue to conduct illegal searches and to utilize extended detention, torture, and forced confessions. The rights of a defendant continue to be sharply limited and can be violated by law enforcement agencies. In China, police can arrest and detain suspects with their administrative detention powers and without warrants from a court. Under the law, police can detain persons up to 37 days before formally placing them under arrest or releasing them. The criminal law also allows police and prosecutors to detain persons up to seven months before the conclusion of investigating their cases. In routine criminal cases, police often detain individuals without notification to their family members. During detention, especially in the pretrial period, torture remains prevalent as policemen, detectives, and armed police continue to make use of the practice. In China, 99 percent of defendants admitted to the charges brought against them.

See also: Chapter 3: Constitution; Criminal Law; Death Penalty; Human Rights; People's Armed Police; People's Liberation Army; Political Dissents.

Further Reading

Bakken, Borge, ed. *Crime, Punishment, and Policing in China*. Boulder, CO: Rowman & Littlefield, 2007.

Biddulph, Sarah. *Legal Reform and Administrative Detention Powers in China*. Cambridge, UK: Cambridge University Press, 2008.

Li, Xiaobing. *Civil Liberties in China*. Santa Barbara, CA: ABC-CLIO, 2010.

Xiang, Wan E. *Explore the Socialist Judicial Law and Improve the Civil and Commercial Legal System*. Beijing: China Press, 2000.

Li Keqiang (1955–)

One of China's top leaders in 2012–2022, Li is premier of the People's Republic of China (PRC), secretary of the Chinese Communist Party (CCP) Committee of the State Council, and Standing Committee member of the CCP Politburo. He is described as a technocrat who emerged through protracted service within the party and the government.

Born in Dingyuan, Anhui, Li was sent to the countryside, farming at Fengyang, Anhui, in 1974, after finishing his secondary education. He joined the CCP in 1976 and soon became party secretary of the village production brigade. After China resumed higher education, Li enrolled in Peking (Beijing) University in 1978, studying law. He was elected president of the university student council in 1981.

His political career began in 1982 when he was appointed secretary of the Chinese Communist Youth League (CCYL) at Peking University, after graduating with an LLB degree. In 1983 he was elected secretary-general of the National University Student Association, head of the Education Department of the CCYL Central Committee, and a standing committee member of the Central Committee. In 1985, he became a member of the CCYL Central Secretariat and worked closely with Hu Jintao (1942–), then the first secretary of the CCYL

Central Secretariat. From 1988 to 1994, he enrolled at the College of Economics of Peking University and received his MA and PhD degrees in economics. He was elected first secretary of the CCYL Central Secretariat in 1993, and a member of the CCP Fifteenth Central Committee in 1997. Li was promoted to the office of lieutenant governor of Henan in 1998, governor in 1999, and party chief of Henan in 2002. He was re-elected as a Central Committee member at the CCP Sixteenth National Congress in 2002. He was appointed party chief of Liaoning in 2004, and chairman of the Provincial People's Congress in 2005.

In 2007, Li was elected as one of the seven members of the Standing Committee of the Politburo of the CCP Seventeenth Central Committee under Hu's leadership. From 2008 to 2013, Li served as the first vice premier, director of the State Council's Three Gorges Project, and chief of the national medical reform commission under Premier Wen Jiabao (1942–). He soon became one of the leading economic policymakers. In November 2012, he was re-elected as a Standing Committee member of the Politburo at the CCP Eighteenth National Congress. In March 2013, when Wen retired, Li became premier at the Twelfth National People's Congress (NPC) under the leadership of Xi (1953–); who is PRC president and CCP secretary-general in 2012–2022. In 2014, Li was appointed the first vice chairman of the National Security Commission. Li has continued to work on economic reform by establishing a domestic consumption-based economy rather than an export-oriented one. He calls for frugality in government, a more fair distribution of wealth in the country, and diverse foreign policy. He traveled to Asian, African, and European countries during his first few years as China's premier. Li was ranked the 14th among the World's Most Powerful People by *Forbes* magazine in 2013.

See also: Chapter 1: The Three Gorges Project. Chapter 2: Hu Jintao. Chapter 3: Overview; Chinese Communist Party; National People's Congress; Xi Jinping. Chapter 8: Peking University.

Further Reading

Callick, Rowan. *The Party Forever: Inside China's Modern Communist Elite*. London: Palgrave Macmillan, 2013.

Li, Cheng, ed. *China's Changing Political Landscape: Prospects for Democracy*. Washington, DC: Brookings Institution Press, 2008.

McGregor, Richard. *The Party: The Secret World of China's Communist Party*. New York: Harper Perennial, 2012.

Liu Xiaobo (1955–)

A Nobel Peace Prize Laureate, human rights activist, and political prisoner, born on December 28, 1955, in Changchun, Jilin, Liu grew up in an intellectual family. During the Cultural Revolution (1966–1976), his father lost his job in the city and in 1969 was sent to the countryside of Inner Mongolia for re-education. Xiaobo began farming in Jilin after he completed his secondary education in 1974. After higher education resumed, he enrolled in Jilin University in 1977, majoring in Chinese literature. He graduated in 1982 with a bachelor's degree in literature and later that year was admitted as a graduate student at the Department of Chinese Literature of Beijing Normal University (BNU). He graduated with a master's degree in literature in 1984 and accepted a teaching position at the same department. Liu married Tao Li in 1984, and in 1985 the couple had a son, Liu Tao. Liu enrolled in a doctoral program at BNU in 1986.

While teaching at BNU, Liu began writing critical literary reviews for various professional journals as well as popular magazines. Since his articles contained sharp comments and radical opinions against official doctrine and institutions, he soon became well known as a "dark horse" in the literary circle. Liu called for multi-party elections and separation of powers, while urging the government to be accountable for its wrongdoings. In 1987, he published his first book, *Criticism of the Choice*, which challenged the basic ideology of the Chinese Communist Party (CCP) and soon became a national nonfiction bestseller. His strong influence on intellectuals in China was called "Liu Xiaobo Shock" or the "Liu Xiaobo Phenomenon." He received his PhD in literature in 1988, and his dissertation, *Aesthetic and Human Freedom*, was published as his second book. In 1989, he traveled to the United States and Europe as a visiting scholar. During his trip, Liu developed a pro-West stance and published his third book, *The Fog of Metaphysics*, a review on Western philosophies.

During the Tiananmen Square pro-democracy protests in the summer of 1989, Liu actively supported the student rallies, participated in the hunger strike, and became committed to the human rights movement. On June 6, two days after the Tiananmen Square massacre on June 4, he was arrested and subsequently fired by BNU in September. All his publications were banned, including his upcoming fourth book, *Going Naked toward God*, and in 1990 some of his books were published in Taiwan. In January 1991, he was released from jail, although he had been convicted for "counter-revolutionary propaganda and incitement." Liu was divorced that year, and in 1992 he published his fifth book, *The Monologues of a Doomsday's Survivor*, in Taiwan. In 1993, he was invited to visit the United States and Australia while continuing his efforts in demanding that the Chinese government respect the basic rights of its people.

Liu was again arrested in May 1995 and released in February 1996. However, that October he was again arrested, after the publication of his coauthored "October Tenth Declaration," which suggested a peaceful reunification with Taiwan by opposing the CCP's military threats toward the island. He was sentenced to three years in a labor camp, and his name became censored online. In 1996 in the labor camp, he married Liu Xia. After his release in 1999, he continued his freelance writing and published more books, including *A Nation That Lies to Conscience* in Taiwan in 2000, *Selection of Poems* in Hong Kong in 2001, and *The Beauty Offers Me Drug* in China in 2003. He began writing the annual Human Rights Report of China. He established the Independent Chinese Pen Society (ICPS) in November 2003 and was elected to its board of directors and its president. In 2004, Liu was awarded the Foundation de France Prize by "Reporters Without Borders" as a defender of press freedom. That year Liu published two books in the United States, *The Future of Free China Exists in Civil Society* and *Single-Blade Poisonous Sword: Criticism of Chinese Nationalism*.

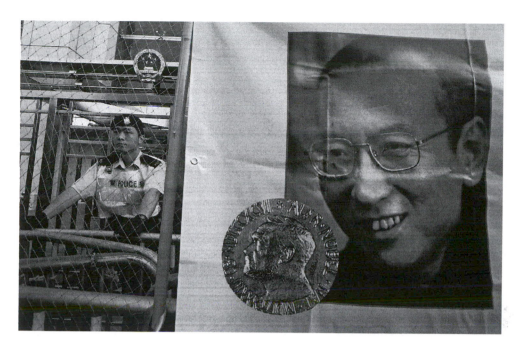

A police officer stands guard beside the picture of jailed Chinese dissident Liu Xiaobo outside of the Chinese government liaison office in Hong Kong on December 5, 2010. Protesters rallied in Hong Kong for the release of the jailed Nobel Peace Prize winner, who has been sentenced to remain in jail in China until 2020. (AP Photo/Kin Cheung)

In 2008, he co-authored the *Charter 08* manifesto, calling for increased political freedoms and human rights in China and posted it online on December 10. By the following September, the Charter had collected over 10,000 signatures. Liu was arrested in December 2008 and on December 23, 2009, was sentenced to 11 years of imprisonment for "the crime of inciting subversion of state power." Due to the nature of the charges, Liu is described as a political prisoner.

In March 2009, Liu was given the Homo Homini Award at the One World Film Festival for promoting freedom of speech and human rights. In December, the European Union issued an official appeal calling for the unconditional release of Liu. In January 2010, the European Association for Chinese Studies sent Chinese President Hu Jintao an open letter, signed by over 800 scholars from 36 countries, calling for his release.

In October 2010, Liu was awarded the Nobel Peace Prize for his "long and non-violent struggle for fundamental human rights in China." However, the Nobel Committee is still waiting for him to collect his medal, pick up his prize money, and give his Nobel lecture. Liu, however, has been sentenced to remain in jail until 2020.

See also: Chapter 1: Taiwan. Chapter 2: Hu Jintao. Chapter 3: Chinese Communist Party; Civil Rights; Human Rights; Political Dissents. Chapter 16: Censor System; Freedom of Speech; Internet and Social Media.

Further Reading

Beja, Jean-Philippe, and Eva Pils. *Liu Xiaobo, Charter 08 and the Challenges of Political Reform in China*. Hong Kong: Hong Kong University Press, 2012.

He, Rowena. *Tiananmen Exiles: Voices of the Struggle for Democracy in China*. London: Palgrave Macmillan, 2014.

Link, Perry, and Liu Xia, eds. *No Enemies, No Hatred: Selected Essays and Poems of Liu Xiaobo*. New York: Belknap, 2012.

Liu Xiaobo. *June Fourth Elegies: Poems*. Boston, MA: Graywolf, 2012.

National People's Congress (NPC)

According to the Constitution of the People's Republic of China (PRC), the National People's Congress (NPC) is the highest state body and the only legislative house (a unicameral parliament) in China. The Constitution states that "The National People's Congress and the local people's congresses at various levels are the organs through which the people exercise state power." The NPC passes laws, elects the president and vice president, and approves nominations for premier, vice premier, ministers, and other state hierarchies.

On March 5–17, 2013, the most recent NPC, or the Twelfth NPC, was held in Beijing. On March 14, the Congress elected Xi Jinping (1953–), secretary-general of the Chinese Communist Party (CCP), as president of the PRC on a one-name ballot. On March 15, President Xi nominated Li Keqiang (1955–) to the Congress as new premier for the executive branch, or the State Council, head of the government in China, who is the second ranked member of the CCP Politburo Standing Committee. On the same day, Li was elected by the Congress. Premier Li then gave his first major speech to all 2,987 congressional representatives on March 17, at the conclusion of the NPC assembly.

The elections of congressional representatives take place from bottom up, progressively, advancing gradually in due order from one level to the next higher level. Each village may elect its own representatives, as the lowest level in the electoral system, with no restriction on the number of candidates. Only one of these representatives can enter

---

NATIONAL FLAG

The national flag of the People's Republic of China (PRC) is the five-star red flag. The face of the flag is red, the color of revolution, and its shape is rectangular, with the length of its sides in 3:2 proportion. In the upper left hand corner are five yellow stars: one large star which stands for the Chinese Communist Party (CCP) and four smaller stars in an arc. The diameter of the large star measures three-tenths of the height of the flag, while the diameter of the smaller stars is precisely one-tenth of the height. Collectively, the five stars symbolize the great unity of the Chinese people under the CCP. On October 1, 1949, Mao Zedong personally raised the first five-star red flag in Tiananmen Square in Beijing.

the next level as a candidate to become the township congressional representative. Each elected township representative can then enter the county level election. At this level, the party exercises control over the process by limiting the number of candidates in proportion to the number of seats available. At the election of the county's people's congress (about 2,862 counties and county-level administrations in 2014), a maximum of 130 candidates are allowed per 100 seats. Following the approval of the county's party committee, each elected representative can serve a five-year term and enter as a candidate at the district election. After the district level, the next one is the provincial election. At this level, the ratio is 120 candidates per 100 seats. Delegates who are re-elected by the provincial people's congresses can then enter the election for the National Congress. At this highest level, the ratio decreases again to only 110 candidates per 100 seats. This tiered electoral structure makes it impossible for a candidate to become a member of a higher legislative body without party approval.

The NPC exercises most of its power on a day-to-day basis through the Standing Committee in Beijing. In March 2013, Zhang Dejiang (1946–), the third ranked member of the CCP Politburo Standing Committee, was elected chairman of the Standing Committee of the Twelfth NPC as head of the legislative branch. The Constitution also authorizes the Standing Committee to select, appoint, and dismiss Supreme Court justices and procurators at the national level. The standing committees of the local congresses can appoint and dismiss local judicial personnel.

Due to its overwhelming majority in the Congress, the CCP has total control over the composition of this committee. Seven other political parties are small, and they are cooperative with the CCP because their survival depends on their political support to the CCP. There is no political challenge, major opposition, or election campaign at the national level. Until the late 1980s, the NPC and its Standing Committee played only a symbolic role as a powerless rubber-stamp legislature. During the 1990s, the NPC and local congresses began playing a new role, discussing their issues, making their decisions, and sometimes departing from the party's political agenda. But there is still a long road to travel before the People's Congress will play a separate role as an independent legislature in the Chinese government.

See also: Chapter 2: Overview. Chapter 3: Overview; Chinese Communist Party; Constitution; Li Keqiang; Provincial and County Governments; Supreme People's Court; Xi Jinping.

Further Reading

Jiang, Jinsong. *The National People's Congress of China.* Beijing: Foreign Languages Press, 2003.

MacFarquhar, Roderick, ed. *The Politics of China: Sixty Years of the People's Republic of China.* Cambridge, UK: Cambridge University Press, 2011.

O'Brien, Kevin. *Reform without Liberation: China's National People's Congress and the Politics of Institutional Change.* Cambridge, UK: Cambridge University Press, 2008.

Saich, Tony. *Governance and Politics of China.* 3rd ed. London, UK: Palgrave Macmillan, 2011.

People's Armed Police (PAP)

As part of the national law enforcement, the PAP or CPAPF (officially Chinese People's Armed Police Force) was established in 1982 as a paramilitary force, similar to a combination of the National Guards with SWAT (Special Weapons and Tactics) teams in the United States. Although it is not clear how the force may be ordered into action, the PAP's primary duties are domestic security, civilian policing, anti-terrorism, rescue operation, and lending support to the People's Liberation Army (PLA) during wartime.

By 1986, the PAP totaled 600,000 troops under the Ministry of Public Security (MPS) of the State Council. The PAP Command then took over the regular troops of the border control, internal security (ports and airports), and immediate action units (IAU) of the PLA. In 1996, the Central Military Commission (CMC) transferred 14 more infantry divisions of the PLA regular troops, totaling 150,000 men, to the PAP force. In 2000, the PAP was comprised of 1 million men in 31 armies, including 508 armed police regiments and 42 special regiments, such as helicopter, artillery, tank, chemical, and engineering regiments. The PAP also had 32 command academies and 29 hospitals across the country. As part of recent legal reform, China strengthened the PAP in the 2010s, and it has totaled 1.5 million troops under the current command of General Wu Shuangzhan and General Meng Jianzhu as its political commissar at the PAP General Headquarters in Beijing. Both are members of the Central Committee of the Chinese Communist Party (CCP).

The PAP General HQ (*Zongbu*) currently commands its 34 army (*zongdui*, army corps) headquarters at provincial, municipal, and special region levels. Each PAP army has 35,000–50,000 troops, and commands its 18–23 regimental (*zhidui*, column) headquarters at municipal and district levels. Each regiment commands three to seven battalions (*dadui*, brigade) at county levels, and each battalion has three or four companies (*zhongdui*). The PAP troops have military-style uniforms and insignia that look very similar to those of the PLA. The PAP ranking system, established in 1988, is also similar to that of the PLA army ranks, including lieutenant general, major general, senior colonel, colonel, lieutenant colonel, major, captain, lieutenants, and sergeants. The PAP commander in chief and political commissar are always transferred from the PLA high command, with the rank of general.

The duties performed by the PAP in the routine maintenance of internal security differ considerably from those of the police. In addition to guarding their own facilities, the branch's troopers perform several standard public security missions; static guard at important bridges, government and party buildings, safeguarding foreign diplomatic areas and ensuring senior leadership protection. Additionally, they participate in street patrols, ceremonial duties, and, as mentioned previously, to back up the police forces. PAP members are usually conscripted during the same recruiting period observed by the PLA, and which branch a new recruit enters many be nothing more than luck of the draw. The PAP uses many of the same regulations and manuals as the army. Advanced techniques for each branch, however, are considerably different. By maintaining a strict differentiation between the missions of the two forces, both are better able to concentrate on their primary roles.

In many cities, the PAP and police jointly patrol the streets and conduct roadblocks and the accompanying searches. At particularly sensitive times and locations, members of both forces will dress in civilian clothes to lower their profile as they monitor a situation, and, if necessary, swarm to control an incident they deem potentially dangerous. Both have the primary objective of containing any disturbance, no matter how small, before it grows out of control.

See also: Chapter 3: Chinese Communist Party; Civil Rights; Criminal Law; Human Rights; Law Enforcement; People's Liberation Army. Chapter 5: Falun Gong.

Further Reading

Bakken, Borge, ed. *Crime, Punishment, and Policing in China.* Boulder, CO: Rowman & Littlefield, 2007.

Biddulph, Sarah. *Legal Reform and Administrative Detention Powers in China.* Cambridge, UK: Cambridge University Press, 2008.

Li, Nan, ed. *Chinese Civil-Military Relations: The Transformation of the People's Liberation Army.* London, UK: Routledge, 2006.

People's Liberation Army (PLA)

As China's armed forces, the People's Liberation Army (PLA) has 2.3 million active servicemen and women. The PLA's army has 1.7 million men, making it the largest standing ground force in the world, with 800,000 reserve personnel. The main force of the PLA has 35 group armies, comprised of 118 infantry divisions, 13 armored divisions, and 33 artillery and antiaircraft artillery divisions, plus 71 independent regiments. The main force has a 4-4 formation, in which each group army has 46,000 men in four divisions; each infantry division has 10,000 soldiers in up to four regiments; each regiment has 2,000 men in four battalions; each battalion has 500 soldiers in four infantry companies; and each company has 120 soldiers.

The group armies are under seven PLA regional commands named after major cities, such as Beijing, Shenyang, Nanjing, and Guangzhou Military Region. The provincial ground forces include 73 divisions of border defense and garrison troops, plus 140 independent regiments. These local divisions have a 3-3 formation under the PLA provincial commands, such as the Liaoning Provincial Military Command and Tibetan Military Command, which are under the command of the military regions. The PLA army has a total of 8,000 main battle tanks, 1,200 light tanks, 6,300 heavy artillery pieces, 1,700 self-propelled artillery pieces, 1,800 rocket artilleries, and 1,500 surface-to-air missile (SAM) air defense systems.

The PLA Navy (PLAN) has 290,000 troops with more than 600 warships, including an aircraft carrier and nuclear submarines, and is the second largest navy in the world, exceeded only by the U.S. navy. The Chinese navy has five branches in three fleets: North Sea Fleet, East Sea Fleet, and the South Sea Fleet. Its submarine force has 69 submarines, which consist of 13 nuclear subs, including Type-095, Type-093 (Shang class, four in active service), and Type-091 (Han class, three in active service). The naval surface force includes one aircraft carrier (67,500 ton *Liaoning*), as well as 26 destroyers, 45 frigates, 10 corvettes, 5 replenishment oilers, and a large fleet of auxiliary vessels. Its coastal defense force has 25,000 troops with 122 missile boats, 231 patrol vessels, 107 mine countermeasure vessels, 3 amphibious transport docks, and a large coastal artillery force. The primary weapons of the coastal defense troops are the HY-2, YJ-82, and C-602 anti-ship missiles. The PLAN Marine Corps has 12,000 marines in two brigades stationed with the South Sea Fleet. They are considered elite troops and are part of the rapid mobilization forces of the Chinese military. The naval air force includes 35,000 personnel and 450 warplanes, including fighters, bombers, strike aircraft, tankers, reconnaissance, maritime patrol, seaplanes, transports, and helicopters.

The PLA Air Force (PLAAF) totals 330,000 personnel, the largest air force in Asia. It has 36 divisions, including 24 fighter divisions, 4 attacking divisions, 4 bomber divisions, 3 transport divisions, 3 airborne divisions, and 8 independent regiments with 2,800 aircraft over more than 150 air force bases. Its combat fleet mainly consists of Chinese J-10 and J-11 fighters and improved H-6 bombers (Tu-16). The PLAAF also purchased over 100 Russian-made Su-30MKK fighters in the 2000s.

The PLA's strategic force, or the Second Artillery Corps (SAC), totals 120,000 troops in six ballistic missile brigades. Their nuclear arsenal is estimated between 240 and 380 warheads; their long-range ICBM (inter-continental ballistic missiles) between 50 and 75 land and sea-based missiles; and more than 1,300 short-range ballistic missiles along coastal areas. The SAC is under the direct command of the Central Military Commission (CMC) of the Chinese Communist Party (CCP). The PLA still belongs to the party rather than to the state.

The CCP established the army on August 1, 1927 (celebrated as the birthday of the Chinese armed forces), known as the Chinese Red Army of Workers and Peasants (or

---

KOREAN WAR (1950–1953)

On June 25, 1950, more than 90,000 Russian-armed troops of North Korea (officially the Democratic People's Republic of Korea, DPRK) invaded South Korea (Republic of Korea, ROK). The UN Security Council denounced the northern invasion and demanded an immediate withdrawal of all communist troops from the south. On July 7, the UN adopted a resolution calling for all possible means to aid the ROK, and organized the UN forces under the command of General Douglas MacArthur. On September 15, MacArthur landed UN troops in Inchon, rapidly changing the war situation in Korea. On October 1, the UN troops crossed the 38th parallel into North Korea. On October 19, China sent the troops to Korea to rescue the DPRK. Thereafter, the Korean conflict became a war between the United States and the People's Republic of China (PRC). Between 1950 and 1953, more than 3 million Chinese troops entered the Korean War, and their casualties totaled 1 million. On July 27, 1953, a truce agreement was signed by the United States, PRC, ROK, and DPRK, and the war was over.

simply the Red Army), against the Guomindang (GMD, or Kuomintang, KMT; the Nationalist Party) government of the Republic of China (ROC). The party mobilized the peasants and sent in new recruits, while the army protected the communist-based areas and engaged armed rebellion. Mao Zedong (Mao Tse-tung) (1893–1976), the CCP leader, described this relationship as "Political power grows out of the barrel of a gun." After the GMD government came to an agreement with the CCP to jointly resist the Japanese invasion of China (1937–1945), the CCP's regular army grew to 1.27 million by the end of World War II, supported by militias numbering another 2.68 million. China's full-scale civil war between the GMD and the CCP resumed in June 1946. By September 1949, the CCP forces, renamed the PLA in 1948 and totaling 5.5 million, occupied most of the country except for Tibet, Taiwan, and various off-shore islands. The GMD removed the seat of its ROC government from the mainland to Taiwan.

On October 1, 1949, Mao declared the birth of the People's Republic of China (PRC) and of the new republic's alliance with Moscow. The PRC's alliance with the Soviet Union and North Korea pulled China into a foreign war in Korea. Mao sent 3.1 million PLA troops to the Korean War (1950–1953). The combat experience the Chinese armed forces gained against the United Nations and U.S. forces bolstered PLA modernization in accordance with the Russian military model. From 1951 to 1956, the Soviet Union rearmed 106 Chinese infantry divisions, 17 artillery divisions, 17 anti-aircraft artillery divisions, 9 cavalry divisions, and 4 tank divisions with Soviet weapons and equipment. During the same period, China purchased 5,000 Russian aircraft and 200 Russian vessels. In 1956, the Soviets began providing technology and material assistance to China's nuclear weapons program. Shortly after the Sino-Soviet split, China launched its first missile in 1960; had its first successful nuclear bomb test in 1964; the first hydrogen bomb in 1967; and the first satellite launch in 1970. The PLA established its strategic missile forces, or the Second Artillery Corps, in 1966. In less than 15 years, China became a nuclear power.

ZHU DE (1886–1976)

Zhu De was commander in chief of the People's Liberation Army (PLA) in 1949–1976, chairman of the National People's Congress (NPC) in 1959–1976, first vice president of the People's Republic of China (PRC), and vice chairman of the Central Military Commission (CMC) of the Chinese Communist Party (CCP) in 1949–1976. Second to Mao Zedong (1893–1976) in the CCP in the 1920s, Zhu organized and trained the Red Army, developed guerrilla strategy, and made himself the top military leader in the PLA in the 1940s. He was made the first marshal of the PLA in 1955 and was elected chairman of the National Congress in 1959. During the Cultural Revolution of 1966–1976, Zhu was dismissed from his position on the Standing Committee of the Congress. Zhou Enlai (1898–1976) supported him and prevented him from being harmed or imprisoned. In 1971, Zhu was reinstated as the chairman of the Congress Standing Committee.

After the end of the Cold War in 1991, although the PLA had experienced tremendous changes through military reforms, it remained the CCP party-army. From November 8–14, 2012, the CCP held its Eighteenth National Congress (held once every five years) in Beijing. The First Plenary Session of the Eighteenth Central Committee was held on November 15, electing Xi Jinping (1953–) as the new secretary-general of the Central Committee for 2012–2017 and the new Political Bureau, which is the *de facto* highest decision-making body of the country. Among the elected 25 Politburo members are Air Force General Xu Qiliang (1950–) and Army General Fan Changlong (1947–). The Central Committee then elected Xi as chairman of the CCP Central Military Commission (CMC), with Generals Xu and Fan as vice chairmen. As the highest commanding body of the PLA, the CMC's eight members include the chiefs of the services, heads of the four general departments in the PLA General Headquarters, and the defense minister of the PRC.

The PLA General Headquarters in Beijing has four departments: General Staff, Political, Logistics, and Armaments. The General Staff Department (GSD) carries out the staff and operational functions of the PLA and its implemented modernization plans. Within the defense hierarchy, the GSD conveys policy directives from the CCP Central Committee and commands the Chinese forces on behalf of the CMC. It also has organizational functions in war planning, intelligence collecting and analysis, troop training, routine operations, and foreign military exchanges.

See also: Chapter 1: South China Sea; Taiwan. Chapter 2: Overview; Chiang Kai-shek; Mao Zedong. Chapter 3: Overview; Chinese Communist Party; Xi Jinping. Appendix: A Day in the Life of a PLA Soldier.

Further Reading

Joffe, Ellis. *The Chinese Army after Mao.* Cambridge, MA: Harvard University Press, 1987.

Kondapalli, Srikanth. *China's Military: The PLA in Transition.* New Delhi, India: Knowledge World, 1999.

Li, Xiaobing. *A History of the Modern Chinese Army.* Lexington: University of Kentucky Press, 2007.

Mulvenon, James. *The People's Liberation Army in the Information Age.* Santa Monica, CA: RAND, 1999.

Ryan, Mark, David Finkelstein, and Michael McDevitt, eds. *Chinese Warfighting; The PLA Experience Since 1949.* Armonk, NY: M. E. Sharpe, 2003.

Shambaugh, David. *Modernizing China's Military: Progress, Problems, and Prospects.* Berkeley: University of California Press, 2002.

Political Dissents

Those who criticize the revolutionary policies or organize the masses against the Chinese Communist Party (CCP) are primarily labeled as political dissenters in the

People's Republic of China (PRC). The government has little tolerance for criticism or calls for greater transparency and accountability, and instead emphasizes political control and social stability by employing the law enforcement and legal system to suppress political dissents. The Criminal Law adopted by the National People's Congress (NPC) in 1979, and amended in 1997, provides a category of "counterrevolutionary offenses," such as antigovernment propaganda or other acts that "endanger the PRC" and are "committed to the goal of overthrowing the political power of the dictatorship of the proletariat and the socialist system." Therefore, these political dissenters or the counter-revolutionaries should face punishment, including property seizures, deportation, imprisonment, tortures, and the death penalty. Wei Jingsheng (1950–), a worker at the Beijing Zoo, posted a critique of Deng Xiaoping (Deng Hsiao-ping) (1904–1997), calling for democracy in 1978. He was arrested in 1979 and was sentenced to 15 years in jail. After his release in 1993, Wei was jailed again until 1997.

The freedoms of speech, political expression, the press, association, assembly, and peaceful demonstrations are limited in China. Beijing continues to restrict some of its citizens' fundamental rights by targeting unregistered organizations and unauthorized activities. Liu Xiaobo (1955–), professor of Beijing Normal University with a PhD in literature (1988), served as president (2003–2007) of the Independent Chinese Pen Society. In 2008, he co-authored the *Charter 08* manifesto and posted it online, calling for increased political freedoms and human rights in China. He was arrested in 2009 and sentenced to 11 years of imprisonment on December 23, 2009, for "the crime of inciting subversion of state power." Due to the nature of the charges, Liu is described as a political prisoner. In October 2010, Liu was awarded the Nobel Peace Prize for his "long and non-violent struggle for fundamental human rights in China." The Nobel Committee is still waiting for him to collect his medal, pick up his prize money, and give his Nobel lecture. Liu, however, will likely remain in jail until 2020.

Some Chinese journalists, lawyers, intellectuals, activists, and even artists are arrested and sentenced as political dissenters when they raise issues of official corruption, public health, and environmental crises. In 2010, Tan Zuoren (1954–), an editor of a local journal in Chengdu, Sichuan, and an environmentalist writer, was sentenced to another imprisonment of five years after being released on parole for a three-year imprisonment for "inciting subversion of state power" since he criticized the government environmental policy. In 2011, Ai Weiwei (1957–), a visual artist, was arrested at Beijing International Airport. Ai had led a "citizens' investigation team" to Sichuan after the earthquake on May 12, 2008, in response to the government's lack of release and transparency. In 2014, a local court sentenced four cyber activists for years in jail for organizing the New Citizens movement online. There is no sign of loosening political control in China.

See also: Chapter 2: Deng Xiaoping. Chapter 3: Overview; Chinese Communist Party; Civil Rights; Criminal Law; Human Rights; Law Enforcement; Liu Xiaobo; National People's Congress. Chapter 16: Censor System; Cyber Policing; Freedom of Speech; Internet and Social Media; Netizen and Online Guerrilla.

Further Reading

Chase, Michael, and James Mulvenon. *You've Got Dissent! Chinese Dissident Use of the Internet and Beijing's Counter-Strategies*. Santa Monica, CA: RAND, 2002.

Goldman, Merle. *China's Intellectuals: Advice and Dissent*. Cambridge, MA: Harvard University Press, 1998.

Li, Xiaobing. *Civil Liberties in China*. Santa Barbara, CA: ABC-CLIO, 2010.

Ogden, Suzanne. *Inklings of Democracy in China*. Cambridge, MA: Harvard University Press, 2002.

Provincial and County Governments

According to the Constitution of the People's Republic of China (PRC), "People's congresses and people's governments are established in provinces, municipalities directly under the Central Government, counties, cities, municipal districts, townships, nationality townships, and towns." China has 27 provinces and provincial autonomous regions, four municipalities, two special administrative regions (SAR Hong Kong and Macao), and 2,862 counties and county-level administrations. All local governments (except the two SARs), as well as the central government, set up a tripod of power—party, people's congress, and administration, tied together by the leadership of the Chinese Communist Party (CCP). The CCP continues the Soviet political tradition of the party-state, in which the party leadership manages the governments all the way down to the village and neighborhood levels. The central government includes the CCP Central Committee as the leadership, National People's Congress (NPC) as the legislative branch, State Council as executive branch, and Supreme People's Court as the judicial branch in Beijing.

Under the CCP Central Committee are the provincial party committees. Each party chief is appointed by the Central Committee as first leader of the provincial government. Most of the governors, lieutenant governors, and staff are CCP members and are appointed by party committees at various levels. They employ similar methods in making political appointments to the various governments, supporting and promoting party members during their tenures in office. Under the provincial committees are grass-roots party committees in the counties, townships, and villages. Each county party committee has a secretary, as well as deputy secretaries and standing committee members, who are appointed by the provincial committees as the most important leaders in county governments. These committees supervise the county governments, including administrative, legislative, and judicial branches. CCP provincial, county, and municipal party congresses are held once every five years. Members and alternate members of these party committees are elected for a term of five years at the local party congress. Only the two SARs have their own elections for executives.

The elections of congressional representatives take place from the bottom up, progressively, advancing gradually in due order from one level to the next higher level. Each elected township representative can then enter the county level election. At this level, the party exercises additional control over the process by limiting the number of candidates in proportion to the number of seats available. At the election of the county's people's congress, a maximum of 130 candidates are allowed per 100 seats. Following the approval of the county's party committee, each elected representative can serve a five-year term and enter as a candidate at the district election. After the district level, the next is the provincial election. At this level, the ratio is 120 candidates per 100 seats. Delegates who are reelected by the provincial people's congresses can then enter the election for the NPC. The provincial and county congresses exercise most of their power on a day-to-day basis through the standing committees. The constitution authorizes the standing committees to select, appoint, and dismiss court judges and local judicial personnel at the provincial and county levels. However, all local judges, court clerks, and police are hired and paid as "official staff of the national government."

According to the constitution, all provincial and county governments are state administrative organs under the State Council and are subordinate to it. The governors and county chiefs organize their administrations to supervise local industry, agriculture, electricity and water resources, finance, transportation, commerce, education, and public security. The various administrations appoint or remove local officials, train and evaluate them, and reward or punish them. The administrations also have the power to approve and alter requests or decisions from subordinate departments and the governments at lower levels, audit local finance, and report to the people's congresses on a regular basis.

See also: Chapter 1: Hong Kong; Major Cities. Chapter 3: Overview; Chinese Communist Party; Constitution; Law Enforcement; National People's Congress; Supreme People's Court.

Further Reading

Li, Xiaobing, and Xiansheng Tian, eds. *Evolution of Power: China's Struggle, Survival, and Success.* Lanham, MD: Lexington Books, 2014.

MacFarquhar, Roderick, ed. *The Politics of China: Sixty Years of the People's Republic of China.* Cambridge, UK: Cambridge University Press, 2011.

Saich, Tony. *Governance and Politics of China.* 3rd ed. London: Palgrave Macmillan, 2011.

Xie Chuntao. *Why and How the CCP Works in China.* Beijing: New World, 2012.

Supreme People's Court

The First Plenary Session of the CPPCC created the provisional Supreme Court in September 1949 and appointed Shen Junru as president. On September 20, 1954, the First National People's Congress (NPC) passed the formal constitution which included courts and procurates as the judicial branch. It authorized the Standing Committee of the NPC to select, appoint, and dismiss judges, procurators, and judicial personnel at the national level. The First NPC Plenary Session established the Supreme People's

Court that September and elected Dong Biwu (Tung Pi-wu) (1886–1975) as the first president of this highest judicial organ of the country. The plenary also created the Ministry of Justice and promulgated the Court Organization Law and Procuratorial Law, establishing a general structure for state legal institutions. When Dong became the vice president of the PRC in 1959, Xie Juezai (1884–1971) took his seat until 1965. Then, Yang Xiufeng (in office 1965–1975), Jiang Hua (in office 1975–1983), Zheng Tianxiang (in office 1983–1988), Ren Jianxin (in office 1988–1998), Xiao Yang (in office 1998–2007), and Wang Shengjun (in office 2008–2013) served as its president. The current president and chief grand justice is Zhou Qiang (in office 2013–).

Currently, the Supreme People's Court has 9 vice presidents, 340 judges, and 8 departments and bureaus, including judicial, administrative, office affairs, foreign affairs, general affairs, research, personnel, and education. It works with the Supreme People's Procuratorate which is the highest national agency for prosecution and investigation. The Supreme Court judges meet in small tribunals to decide cases in the criminal, civil, economic, and administrative courts, and they also set up other special courts for actual judicial needs. From November 1980 to January 1981, for example, the Supreme People's Court set up a special court for the trial of the "Gang of Four," including Jiang Qing (Chiang Ch'ing) (1914–1991), the wife of Mao Zedong (Mao Tse-tung) (1893–1976), and the founder of the PRC.

The Supreme People's Court in Beijing also oversees, supervises, and evaluates the administration of all courts at three lower levels in the country. The court system in China has four levels, with the Supreme Court at the top; the high people's courts at the level of the provinces and special municipalities; the intermediate people's courts at the level of counties and municipalities; and the basic people's courts at the level of towns and municipal districts. Each court level has a president and several vice presidents, while each individual court has judges, assistant judges, and members of judicial committees. The Supreme Court also supervises special courts such as military courts, railway transport courts, and maritime courts, each of which has their special jurisdictions. All local and special courts have a two-hearing system, except for the two special regions of Hong Kong and Macau, which have their own judicial systems and are not under the jurisdiction of the Supreme People's Court in Beijing.

In 2003, the high court formulated 20 documents of judicial interpretation of criminal, civil, and administrative law enforcement and regulation on legal aid. The higher court developed a human network for the country's legal service system and defined a scale of citizens' rights to such services. The number of legal aid offices had increased from 2,418 in 2002 to 2,774 in 2003, from serving 129,775 individuals in 2002 to 166,433 cases in 2003. By 2007, China had 12,285 full-time legal aid personnel who provided legal services to 420,000 cases.

In 2005, the Supreme Court created its third five-year plan designed to strengthen the courts. The plan laid out 50 goals, including the improvement of court finances, the appointment of judges, and the reform of procedures for the prosecution of capital cases. The same year, the Supreme Court also instructed all sitting judges below the age of 40 that they must get a college degree within five years or risk losing their jobs; judges at the age of 50 or older could stay at the court without a college education, but they must complete a legal training course. By mid-2005, for the first time, more than 50 percent of Chinese judges had college degrees. This was a substantial increase from the 6 percent in 1995 and 20 percent in 2000.

See also: Chapter 1: Hong Kong. Chapter 2: Mao Zedong. Chapter 3: Constitution; Criminal Law; Death Penalty; First Chinese People's Political Consultative Conference; Law Enforcement; National People's Congress.

Further Reading

Hsu, Stephen, ed. *Understanding China's Legal System.* New York: New York University Press, 2003.

Keith, Ronald, Zhiqiu Lin, and Shumei Hou. *China's Supreme Court.* London: Routledge, 2013.

Li, Xiaobing, and Qiang Fang, eds. *Modern Chinese Legal Reform: New Perspectives.* Lexington: University Press of Kentucky, 2013.

Otto, Jan. *Law-making in the People's Republic of China.* New York: Springer, 2000.

Potter, Pitman. *The Chinese Legal System: Globalization and Local Legal Culture.* London: Routledge, 2001.

Xi Jinping (1953–)

Xi Jinping is the top Chinese leader in 2012–2022, the president of the People's Republic of China (PRC), secretary-general of the Chinese Communist Party (CCP), and chairman of the CCP Central Military Commission (CMC). Some believe that Xi belongs to the technocrats, who emerged through protracted service within the government. But others argue that he is one of the "princelings," children of the first generation of the CCP leaders. His father Xi Zhongxun (1913–2002) was a Communist veteran, serving as vice premier of the State Council, vice chairman of the Standing Committee of the National People's Congress (NPC), and a member of the Politburo and the CCP secretariat.

Xi Jinping was born in June 1953 into a political family in Beijing. Nonetheless, his father experienced the same ups and downs as most Chinese leaders during the Cultural Revolution (1966–1976). He was jailed in 1968 when Jinping was 15. Jinping's secondary education was cut short when he was sent to the rural area in Yanchuan, Shaanxi, in 1969 for his re-education. Xi Jinping joined the Chinese Communist Youth League (CCYL) in 1971 and the CCP in 1974. That year he became the party branch secretary of the village and enrolled in the prestigious Qinghua (Tsinghua) University in 1975, majoring in chemical engineering. After his graduation in 1979, Xi joined the service as secretary to Geng Biao (1909–2000), vice chairman of the CMC in Beijing.

His political career began when he was sent to Zhengding, Hebei, to serve as deputy secretary of the county's party committee in 1982 and its secretary in 1983. He was appointed as vice mayor of the city of Xiamen, Fujian, in 1985–1988. He visited

Muscatine, Iowa, in 1985 with a provincial delegation to study American agriculture. Xi became party chief of the Ningde District, Fujian, in 1988–1990, and party secretary of the Fuzhou Municipal Committee in 1990–1995. He was promoted to the office of lieutenant governor of Fujian in 1995, acting governor in 1999, and governor in 2000. In 1998, Xi enrolled in an "on-the-job" graduate program at Qinghua University and received a doctor of law (LLD) degree in 2002. He was then transferred to Zhejiang, and served as acting governor in 2002, governor in 2003, and provincial party committee secretary in 2003–2007. Xi was appointed as party secretary of the Shanghai Municipal Committee in 2007, one of the most important local positions in the CCP.

Xi became an alternate member of the CCP Fifteenth Central Committee in 1997 and a member of the Sixteenth Central Committee in 2002. He entered the nine-man Standing Committee of the Politburo at the Seventeenth CCP National Congress in 2007, and became a national leader. Xi was in charge of the Hong Kong and Macau affairs and the 2008 Summer Olympics in Beijing. He became president of the CCP Central Party Academy and vice president of the PRC in 2008, a clear indication that he would succeed Hu Jintao (1942–) as the next top leader.

In November 2012, when Hu retired, Xi became the CCP secretary-general and CMC chairman at the party's Eighteenth National Congress. In March 2013, he was elected president of the PRC at the Twelfth NPC in Beijing. Since taking office, Xi has made it clear that China is a superpower, and that it wants to be treated as a global power. The new leader made some important policy changes to fit nationalist ideas and popular social movements. He therefore continues to employ nationalism as an ideology to unite China and to fight for its superpower status, perhaps resulting in one more source of legitimacy for the CCP as the country's ruling party. Xi has been taking tougher positions on political control, the anti-corruption movement, national defense, and military modernization, as well as territorial issues such as the disputed islands in the South China Sea.

See also: Chapter 1: Disputed Islands and Territories; Hong Kong; Major Cities. Chapter 2: Timeline; Hu Jintao. Chapter 3: Overview; Chinese Communist Party; Corruption and Punishment; National People's Congress; Provincial and County Governments. Chapter 8: Qinghua University. Chapter 16: Freedom of Speech.

Further Reading

Brown, Kerry. *Carnival China: China in the Era of Hu Jintao and Xi Jinping*. London: Imperial College Press, 2014.

Lampton, David. *Following the Leader: Ruling China, from Deng Xiaoping to Xi Jinping*. Berkeley: University of California Press, 2014.

Sharp, Jonathan, ed. *The China Renaissance: The Rise of Xi Jinping and the 18th Communist Party Congress*. Singapore: World Scientific, 2013.

Zheng, Yongnian, and Lance Gore, eds. *China Entering the Xi Jinping Era*. London, UK: Routledge, 2014.

CHAPTER 4

ECONOMY

OVERVIEW

The People's Republic of China (PRC) has since 2012 the second largest economy in the world (second only to the United States) due to its rapid growth over the past 20 years. China's GDP was only $559 billion in 1994, but it doubled five years later, reaching $1,083 billion in 1999. It increased to $1.9 trillion in 2004, and doubled again to $4.9 trillion in 2009. By 2013, China's GDP had reached $9.3 trillion according to the exchange rate, or $13.39 trillion as purchasing power parity (the U.S. GDP-PPP was $16 trillion; and Japan's was $5 trillion). China's GDP had an annual growth rate of 7 to 12 percent between 1994 and 2014. Its GDP per capita was only $469 in 1994, but it almost doubled, reaching $865 in 1999. Increasing to $1,490 in 2004, it doubled again in 2009 to $3,749. By 2013 it reached $9,185 as purchasing power parity (the U.S. GDP-PPP per capita was $52,800; and Japan's was $37,100). China's GDP per capita had an annual growth rate of 6 to 12 percent between 1994 and 2014. China's foreign exchange reserves reached $470.6 billion in 2004, continued to increase to $941.1 billion in 2006, and was $1,808.8 billion by June 2008, making it the highest foreign reserve in the world. Its foreign reserves continued to increase to $2.13 trillion in 2009, $3.2 trillion in 2011, and $3.99 trillion in 2014. Among the total reserves, 70 percent are U.S. dollar assets, including $447.5 billion U.S. government bonds and debt; 10 percent are Japanese yen assets; and the euro and the British pound account for some of the remaining portion.

The leading industrial outputs are manufacturing, energy industry, transportation, telecommunication, and digital products. It can also be divided into heavy industry such as steel, machinery, automobile, and shipbuilding, and light industry such as electronics, instrument, tools, and consumer products. During the late 1990s and early 2000s, the country has become a global manufacturing center, due to its cost of production and participation in international trade organizations such as the WTO (World Trade Organization). In 2010, China had 19.8 percent of the world's total manufacturing output, becoming the largest manufacturer in the world. Its manufacturing accounted for 31.6 percent of China's GDP in 2013, an increase of 7.6 percent from 2012, and it is the largest GDP contributor in the world. It hires more than 400 million manufacturing workers, about 52.3 percent of the labor force in the industries. As the largest steel supplier in the world, China was producing 45 percent of the world's steel in 2011. Low labor costs have made China one of the major sources for low-priced manufactured products in the world, in general, and in the United States, in particular, during the 1980s. China's exports to the United States and other countries significantly increased in the 1990s.

Since 2000, the PRC government expanded its exports and moved far beyond producing cheap manufacturing such as toys, games, shoes, and textiles. It accomplished this by adding petrochemicals, fertilizers, polymers, machine tools, shipping, and electric appliances in its exports. By 2005, China replaced the United States as Japan's main trading partner. In the following year, China's total trade reached $1.4 trillion, of which $762 billion was with the United States. China imported electrical machinery, optical and medical equipment, organic chemicals, and telecommunications and sound equipment, as well as oil and mineral fuels. China's total foreign trade rose from $1.15 trillion in 2004, to $2.17 trillion in 2007, to $3.64 trillion in 2011, and to $4.16 trillion in 2013, more than tripling in less than 10 years.

Automobiles, locomotives, shipbuilding, and aircraft industries also play a pivotal role in China's economy. Automobile manufacturing increased from 443,400 vehicles in 1985, to 1.1 million in 1992, to 2.3 million in 2001, 4.44 million in 2003, and to 5.71 million in 2005. China ranked the third largest automotive manufacturer and had the second largest vehicle market in the world by 2006. In 2006, a total of 7.22 million automobiles were sold in China. Automobile production continues to grow, from 8.88 million in 2007, to 9.35 million in 2008, and to 13.83 million in 2009, when China became the largest automaker in the world. In 2010, China became the largest vehicle consumer in the world when 18 million new cars were sold that year. After 2000, China began exporting cars and auto parts. Its vehicle and component export reached $70 billion in 2010.

Accounting for about 25–28 percent of the country's industrial value, China's energy industry, including crude oil, natural gas, coal, electricity, and nuclear energy, has become one of the fastest-growing sectors in the past 25 years. Energy production and consumption, taken together, can be regarded as a sign of how the national economy operates. In 2010, China's total energy consumption surpassed the United States for the first time, making it the world's largest energy consumer. China ranks fifth in world oil production and produced 4.1 million barrels a day in 2011, an increase of 23.56 percent from 2001. Saudi Arabia, Russia, the United States, and Iran were the only countries producing more oil that year than China. China's domestic oil production increased from 202.876 million tons in 2011 to 207.478 million tons in 2012, an annual increase of 2.2 percent. China ranks sixth in world natural gas production, producing 102.5 billion cubic meters in 2011, accounting for 3.1 percent of the world's total, and an 8.1 percent increase in production from 2010. China is rich in coal reserves, and since the 1990s its coal output has totaled more than 1 billion tons annually. The state has made a long-term commitment to adopt new washing and dressing technologies, coal liquefaction, and underground gasification abilities; to construct more large-scale opencast mines; and to improve workplace safety for miners. In 2014–2016, the Chinese government entered a period of reforming its energy economy and is trying to reduce its energy dependency.

As a traditionally agrarian country, agriculture has played a crucial role in China's economy and its social stability. Its current agriculture must meet the food needs of 1.3

billion people, over 20 percent of the world's total population. The country has more than 300 million farm workers today, and agriculture consists of 13 percent of China's GDP in 2014. The country's agricultural production covers five areas: crop farming, forestry, husbandry, fishery, and village sideline products. The grain crops include wheat, corn (maize), soybean, millet, and tubers. Other main cash crops include cotton, oil-bearing crops, sugarcane, sugar beets, tea, and fruit. The total year-end amount of livestock on hand increased from 60 million head in 1949 to 95.2 million in 1980, including cattle, pigs, sheep, horses, and donkeys. Their individual head counts were 71.7 million head, 305.4 million head, 187.3 million head, 11 million head, and 7.7 million head, respectively. Total meat outputs increased from 2.2 million tons in 1949 to 8.6 million tons in 1978, and 59.6 million tons in 1999. China is the world's leading producer of pigs, chickens, and eggs. The country's total aquatic products increased from 450,000 tons in 1949, to 4.7 million tons in 1978, and to 41.2 million tons in 1999.

The service industry, or tertiary industries, such as real estate, financial, insurance, accounting, legal service, tourism, entertainment, public transportation, post, commerce, and telecom services, has seen significant growth in China since the 1980s. Market-oriented economic reform, which began in 1978, focused on an open-trade and consumer-oriented growth strategy that encouraged service sectors with favorable policy support. As a result, the service industry grew much faster than the whole economy from 1979 to 2001, when the GDP grew 7 to 9.4 percent annually, and the service sectors grew in double digits, per annum. By 2010, China established the third largest service industry in the world (after only the United States and Japan). The service industry produced 43 percent of the country's annual GDP, second only to manufacturing.

Among the service sectors, telecom service has shown a rapid development by establishing numerous communications systems that link all parts of the country by Internet, telephone, telegraph, radio, and television. Approximately 100 million cell phones were sold in 2006, and in 2007 190 million were sold, an increase of 74 percent. In 2007, more than 600 million mobile phones were manufactured in China, more than 50 percent of the world's total production. Internet users grew to 137 million in 2006, 162 million in 2007, and 618 million in 2014. The tourism industry, one of China's fastest-growing service sectors, today contributes more than $250 billion annually to China's economy, about 2.6 percent of the total GDP. New hotels, resorts, restaurant chains, shopping malls, and luxury-goods retail shops have been constructed all over the country. In 2002, domestic tourists totaled 878 million and spent $49 billion. In 2003, more than 20 million Chinese tourists traveled out of the country, overtaking Japan for the first time. In 2011, 58 million international tourists arrived in China and spent more than $48 billion. In 2012, total business-travel spending reached $135 billion. By 2014, Chinese business-travel spending was the highest in the world, overtaking the United States.

After China joined the WTO in 2001, the World Bank, United Nations, and some countries and areas, such as Taiwan, Hong Kong, and Japan, began to provide loans to China's state and local banks. In 2002, China became the world's top recipient of foreign direct investment (FDI). In 2005 China received $80 billion FDI and $69.5 billion FDI in 2006. Foreign banks are allowed to purchase minority stakes in local banks. By 2004, foreign financial assets in China reached $47 billion. Sixty-two foreign banks from 19 countries set up 191 business institutions in China, and 211 foreign bank branches operated in China. In 2007, the Shanghai Stock Exchange (SSE) had 904 stock listings with a market value of $4.5 trillion, and annual turnover value of $5.08 trillion. The total market value of the mainland's stock exchanges in 2007 made China the third largest stock market in Asia, after Japan and Hong Kong. By December 2011, SSE became the sixth largest stock market in the world by market capitalization of $2.3 trillion. The Shenzhen Stock Exchange (SZSE) had an annual turnover value of $2.7 trillion in 2009, and market capitalization of $1 trillion by 2011. In September 2013, China established the Shanghai Free Trade Zone as new effort for more foreign investment, which now has access to almost all financial sectors in the metropolitan economy. It is predicted that China will be the third largest stock market in the world by 2016.

The rapid growth of China's economy has left many problems unsolved. Environmental issues have become increasingly problematic, especially in the new rapidly industrializing coastal and urban areas. Pollutants from manufacturing industries include nitrous oxides, sulfur oxides, carbon monoxide, hydrogen sulfide, benzene, toluene, and xylenes. Polluted air has numerous harmful effects for the environment and for its citizens. In addition, while the government failed to protect intellectual property rights (IPR), Chinese companies continued to manufacture, distribute, and even export counterfeit products, especially brand names, including electronic appliances, medicine and medical devices, auto parts, sporting goods, designer apparel, toys, and consumer products. The U.S. Commerce Department estimated that over 20 percent of all consumer products in the Chinese import market were counterfeit. China had the highest rate (over 90 percent) in counterfeits and piracy, and U.S. companies have lost billions of dollars in legitimate businesses each year to piracy. Both foreign and domestic companies were targets and victims of the counterfeiters and pirates. The Chinese government agency estimated that nearly 200,000 people were killed in 2001 in China as a result of taking counterfeit medicines. Moreover, in recent years, as prosperity has raised China's cost production, some manufacturing factories, previously concentrated in China, began outsourcing work to neighboring countries such as Vietnam, the Philippines, and India, in order to take advantage of cheap labor in maintaining competitive prices, as it continued to expand exports to international and U.S. markets.

Further Reading

Haley, Usha, and George Haley. *Subsidies to Chinese Industry: State Capitalism, Business Strategy, and Trade Policy*. Oxford, UK: Oxford University Press, 2013.

Hsueh, Roselyn. *China's Regulatory State: A New Strategy for Globalization*. Ithaca, NY: Cornell University Press, 2011.

Lin, Justin Yifu. *Demystifying the Chinese Economy*. Cambridge, UK: Cambridge University Press, 2011.

Naughton, Barry. *The Chinese Economy: Transitions and Growth*. Cambridge, MA: MIT Press, 2006.

Rein, Shaun. *The End of Cheap China: Economic and Cultural Trends That Will Disrupt the World*. Hoboken, NJ: Wiley-Blackwell, 2014.

Schell, Orville, and John Delury. *Wealth and Power: China's Long March to the Twenty-first Century.* New York: Random House, 2013.

Shambaugh, David. *China Goes Global: The Partial Power.* Oxford, UK: Oxford University Press, 2013.

Agriculture

A traditionally agrarian country since ancient times, China requires agriculture to meet the food needs of 1.3 billion people, more than 20 percent of the world's total population. To complicate matters, less than 12 percent of China's terrain is suitable for agriculture. The per capita amount of farm land is about 1.6 acres per household, for approximately 200 million households in today's countryside. China's fertile land includes the Northeast Plain, famous for its black soil, and containing many organic substances, with a total area of 135,000 square miles; the North China Plain encompasses 120,000 square miles, a well-known grain and cotton-producing region; and the Middle and Lower Yangzi Valley Plain of 77,000 square miles is known as the country's "rice bowl." Among its 540,541 square miles of arable land, only 37.6 percent, or 203,012 square miles, are irrigated, and only 8 percent, or 45,012 square miles, can permanently support crops. The country consists of more than 300 million farm workers today, and agricultural products consist of only 13 percent of China's GDP in 2014.

The country's agricultural production covers five areas: crop farming, forestry, husbandry, fishery, and village sideline products. Crops had 87.5 percent of total farming acreage in 1949, but only 80 percent in 1978. The total grain outputs increased from 113.2 million tons in 1949, to 304.8 million tons in 1978, and to 508.4 million tons in 1999. They were about 83 percent of the gross value of the total agricultural outputs in 1949, 64 percent in 1978, and 51 percent in 1999. China's most important grain is rice, about 20 percent of total crop farming acreage in 1949 and 23.8 percent in 1978. The total outputs of rice were 48.6 million tons in 1949 and 135 million tons in 1978; about 43 percent of the total grain outputs in 1949 and 45 percent in 1978. Over the millennia, rice cultivation has dramatically transformed landscapes throughout central and southern China as well as in Taiwan. In these areas, rainfall is sufficient to sustain wet rice cultivation, which is capable of being highly productive.

The grain crops also include wheat, corn (maize), soybean, millet, and tubers. The total outputs of each crop were 54.2 million tons, 61.7 million tons, 7.9 million tons, and 27.8 million tons in 1980. The other main cash crops include cotton, oil-bearing crops, sugarcane, sugar beets, tea, and fruit. The total outputs of each crop were 3.8 million tons, 26 million tons, 74.7 million tons, 8.6 million tons, 0.7 million tons, and 62.4 million tons, respectively, in 1999.

Among its forest resources, China is the world's leading bamboo grower. Its timber output increased from 6.6 million cubic meters in 1949, to 53.6 million cubic meters in 1980. The total year-end amount of livestock on hand increased from 60 million head in 1949 to 95.2 million head in 1980, including cattle, pigs, sheep, horses, and donkeys. Their individual head counts were 71.7 million head, 305.4 million head, 187.3 million

Farmers tend to the rice harvest in southern China. Rice is the most important grain of China's agriculture, totaling 135 million tons in production in 1978, about 45 percent of the total grain outputs in that year. Over the centuries, rice cultivation has dramatically transformed landscapes through central and southern China. In these areas, rainfall is sufficient to sustain wet rice cultivation, which is capable of being highly productive with at least two harvests a year. (Corel)

head, 11 million head, and 7.7 million head, respectively. The total meat outputs increased from 2.2 million tons in 1949, to 8.6 million tons in 1978, and to 59.6 million tons in 1999. China is the leading country for producing pigs, chickens, and eggs. The country's total aquatic products increased from 450,000 tons in 1949, to 4.7 million tons in 1978, and to 41.2 million tons in 1999. Rural sideline products account for 4.3 percent of total agricultural output value in 1949, and increased to 17.1 percent in 1980. Over 1.48 million rural sideline enterprises hired more than 30 million workers in 1980.

China's agriculture has lost its workforce, young and new farming laborers, to factory jobs during industrialization. In the 1950s, 84.2 percent of China's total workforce was in agriculture, since the majority of the population, 560 million out of the total of 680 million, lived in the countryside. In 1978, this workforce composition was reduced to 67.4 percent. It continued to drop to 55.8 percent in 1988, 44 percent in 1999, 40.3 percent in 2004, and an estimated 36 percent in 2015. During this period, the per capita annual net income of urban households was 6 to 10 times higher than that of rural households. Labor migration from rural to urban areas emerged as a nationwide phenomenon in the late 1980s. By the early 1990s, an estimated 36 million individuals had made this move. The number of migrant workers totaled 120 million in 2005, 136 million in 2007, and 151 million in 2010. More than 46 percent of urban employment is of rural migrant laborers. Official estimates suggest that as of 2014, more than 169 million peasants may have fled the countryside.

See also: Chapter 1: Overview; Huanghe River; Natural Resources; Pollution and the Environment; Population; Yangzi River. Chapter 4: Overview; Land and Household Policy; Migrant Laborers. Chapter 6: Rural-Urban Conflicts. Chapter 15: Chinese Tea. Appendix: A Day in the Life of a Farmer.

Further Reading

Naughton, Barry. *The Chinese Economy: Transitions and Growth*. Cambridge, MA: MIT Press, 2006.

Oi, Jean. *Rural China Takes Off: Institutional Foundations of Economic Reform*. Berkeley: University of California Press, 1999.

Whiting, Susan. *Power and Wealth in Rural China: The Political Economy of Institutional Change*. Cambridge, UK: Cambridge University Press, 2006.

Wittwer, Sylvan, Yu Youtai, Sun Han, and Wang Lianzheng. *Feeding a Billion: Frontiers of Chinese Agriculture*. East Lansing: Michigan State University Press, 1987.

Cost Production

The economic growth in the 1980s and the new industrial mode of production in the 1990s have changed China forever. China's industrialization, however, has been partly based on low production cost, including low wages paid to workers and minimum workplace safety. Low labor costs have made China one of the major sources for low-priced manufactured products in the world in general, and in the United States in particular. China's export-oriented manufacturing has included miscellaneous manufactured articles such as toys, games, clothing and apparel, footwear, and plastic products in the 1990s. China's entry to the World Trade Organization (WTO) in 2001 further promoted its international trade and its exports to the world. By 2002, China's exports to the United States exceeded those of Japan.

Many workers were paid below the minimum wage, worked seven days a week, and often 12–13 hours a day. Some workers did not have even one day off during the entire month. Both full-time and part-time workers continue to confront dangerous working conditions, toxic environments, a lack of protection and training, employer violations of minimum wage rules, unpaid pensions and wages, child labor, and forced and uncompensated overtime, especially among migrant workers and female workers.

Labor migration from rural to urban areas emerged as a nationwide phenomenon in the late 1980s. The number of migrant workers totaled 151 million in 2010. More than 46 percent of urban employment is of rural migrant laborers. Official estimates suggest that as of 2014, more than 169 million peasants may have left the countryside. Some of these migrant workers are treated unfairly and many are underpaid. Approximately 74 percent of migrant laborers earn 580–1,400 yuan *Renminbi* or RMB (between $80 and $200) a month. Many of them have no legal rights to housing, school, and health care in the cities.

Since the 2000s, China's industry has expanded and moved far beyond cheap manufacturing by including petrochemicals, fertilizers, polymers, machine tools, and electric appliances as exports. By 2005, China replaced the United States as Japan's main trading partner. In the following year, China's total international trade reached $1.4 trillion, of which $762 billion was with the United States. In recent years, as prosperity raised China's cost production, some manufacturing factories, previously concentrated in China, began outsourcing to neighboring countries such as Vietnam, the Philippines, or India, for cheap labor to maintain competitive prices, continuing to expand exports to international markets in general and to U.S. markets in particular.

See also: Chapter 4: Overview; Exports; Manufacturing; Migrant Laborers; Sino-U.S. Trade and Other Trading Partners; Trade Union and Labor Movement; Workplace Safety; WTO and Stock Exchanges. Chapter 7: Child Labor; Gender Inequality. Appendix: A Day in the Life of a Factory Worker.

Further Reading

Gallagher, Mary. *Contagious Capitalism: Globalization and the Politics of Labor in China*. Princeton, NJ: Princeton University Press, 2007.

Harney, Alexandra. *The China Price: The True Cost of Chinese Competitive Advantage*. New York: Penguin, 2009.

Hurst, William. *The Chinese Workers after Socialism*. Cambridge, UK: Cambridge University Press, 2012.

Zeng, Ming, and Peter Williamson. *Dragons at Your Door: How Chinese Cost Innovation Is Disrupting Global Competition*. Cambridge, MA: Harvard Business Review Press, 2007.

Energy Industry

Accounting for about 25 to 28 percent of the country's industrial value, China's energy industry, including crude oil, natural gas, coal, electricity, and nuclear energy, has become one of the fastest-growing sectors in the past 25 years. Energy production and consumption taken together can be regarded as a sign of how the national economy operates. In 2010, China's total energy consumption surpassed the United States for the first time ever, making it the world's biggest energy consumer. In 2014–2016, the Chinese government carried out a full range of energy diplomacy, aiming at promoting cooperation between China and many countries in Asia, Africa, and the Americas. Significant progress has also been made between China and Iran, Australia, Indonesia, Venezuela, and Canada.

China ranks fifth in world oil production and produced 4.1 million barrels a day in 2011, accounting for 5.1 percent of that year's world total and an increase of 23.56 percent from 2001. Saudi Arabia, Russia, the United States, and Iran were the only countries which produced more oil than China that year. China took up 50.74 percent of the Asia-Pacific total oil production and its domestic oil production increased from 202.9 million tons in 2011 to 207.5 million tons in 2012, an annual increase of 2.2 percent. Since the 2000s, Beijing has encouraged and emphasized the importance of major Chinese state-owned oil companies going abroad to seek development and cooperation opportunities. SinoPEC (Sino Petroleum Chemical Corporation), CNPC (China National Petroleum Corporation), CNOOC (China National Offshore Oil Corporation), and the other most important state-owned oil companies have gained a share of the oil from Saudi Arabia, Brazil, Sudan, Angola, and 50 other countries and regions.

China ranks sixth in world natural gas production. China produced 102.5 billion cubic meters in 2011 and 106.73 billion cubic meters in 2012, an annual increase of 4.1 percent. The United States, Russia, Canada, Iran, and Qatar were the only countries that produced more gas than China. However, looking at the growth rate compared with the 2001, China came second with 238.28 percent, with Qatar ranking first with a growth rate reaching 443 percent. China ranks first in the Asia-Pacific region for natural gas production.

China is rich in coal reserves and its coal output has totaled more than 1 billion tons annually since the 1990s. The state has made a long-term commitment to adopt new washing and dressing technologies, coal liquefaction, and underground gasification abilities; construct more large-scale opencast mines; and improve the workplace safety for the miners. Coal mining is still the most dangerous profession in China with an average of 6,000 fatalities each year. Electricity power industry has also entered its fastest growing period in the 2000s with main power grids covering all the cities and most rural areas. The electricity produced in 2013 totaled 5.4 trillion kilowatt hours, the top electricity power producer in the world. The power system development focuses on large power plant construction, large generating units, inter-provincial power grids, and ultra-high voltage and automation. About 30 percent of the electricity was generated by hydroelectric power plants, other renewable sources, and nuclear fuels. China has a total nuclear power generation capacity of 8.7 million kilowatts in use and generated 50 billion kilowatt hours of electricity in 2004, breaking the country's record. More nuclear power facilities are under construction, and will reach 36 million kilowatt generation capacities by 2020. To relieve the energy supply shortage, China is developing renewable energy sources such as solar, wind, geothermal, and tidal power.

See also: Chapter 1: Natural Resources; Pollution and the Environment; The Three Gorges Project. Chapter 4: Overview; Joint Ventures; Sino-U.S. Trade and Other Trading Partners; State-Owned Enterprises; Workplace Safety.

Further Reading

Andrews-Speed, Philip. *The Governance of Energy in China: Transition to a Low-Carbon Economy*. London: Palgrave Macmillan, 2012.

Collins, Gabriel et al., eds. *China's Energy Strategy: The Impact on Beijing's Maritime Policies.* Annapolis, MD: Naval Institute Press, 2008.

Economy, Elizabeth. *By All Means Necessary: How China's Resource Quest Is Changing the World.* Oxford, UK: Oxford University Press, 2014.

Kong, Bo. *China's International Petroleum Policy.* Santa Barbara, CA: ABC-CLIO, 2010.

Moyo, Dambisa. *Winner Take All: China's Race for Resources and What It Means for the World.* New York: Basic Books, 2012.

Wright, Tim. *The Political Economy of the Chinese Coal Industry: Black Gold and Blood-Stained Coal.* London: Routledge, 2011.

Exports

During his economic reforms from 1978 to 1989, Deng Xiaoping (Deng Hsiao-ping) (1904–1997), China's leader in 1978–1989, believed there were necessary strategies for entering world markets, and he established an export-oriented manufacturing in many areas. Low labor costs have made China one of the major sources for low-priced manufactured products in the world, in general, and in the United States in particular, during the 1980s. China's exports to the United States and other countries significantly increased in the 1990s, and included miscellaneous manufactured articles such as toys, games, clothing and apparel, as well as footwear and plastic products. After Hong Kong became part of China, and Taiwan had developed extensive trade relations with the mainland, China's entry to the World Trade Organization (WTO) in 2001 further promoted its international trade and its exports to the world. By 2002, China's export to the United States exceeded that of Japan.

In 2002–2012, the government, under the new leadership of President Hu Jintao (1942–) and Premier Wen Jiabao (1942–), expanded the exports and moved far beyond cheap manufacturing by including petrochemicals, fertilizers, polymers, machine tools, shipping, and electric appliances in their exports. By 2005, China replaced the United States as Japan's main trading partner. In the following year, China's total trade reached $1.4 trillion, of which $762 billion was with the United States. The leading export partners currently are the United States (20 percent), Hong Kong (12 percent), Japan (9 percent), South Korea (8 percent), and Germany (5 percent).

Since the 1980s, the U.S.-China trade has become imbalanced in favor of China. Among the total U.S.-China trade of $20 billion in 1990, Chinese exports to the United States increased to $15.2 billion, about four times more than the $3.8 billion in 1985; while during the same time period American exports to China totaled $4.8 billion, a small increase from $3.8 billion in 1985. China enjoyed a trade surplus of $10.4 billion that year. China's exports to the United States continued to rise to $100 billion in 2000 and $321.5 billion in 2007, while American exports to China were $16.2 billion in 2000 and $65.2 billion in 2007. The United States suffered a trade deficit of $83.8 billion in 2000 and $256.3 billion in 2007. According to the U.S. Census Bureau, this trade imbalance has continued in recent years when the U.S. trade deficits with China increased from $226.9

billion in 2009, to $273 billion in 2010, $295.2 billion in 2011, $315.1 billion in 2012, and $318.7 billion in 2013. The increasing U.S. trade deficit with China has become a major issue between the two countries.

See also: Chapter 1: Hong Kong; Taiwan. Chapter 2: Deng Xiaoping; Hu Jintao. Chapter 4: Overview; Cost Production; Foreign Investment; International Trade Policies; Joint Ventures; Manufacturing; Sino-U.S. Trade and Other Trading Partners; WTO and Stock Exchanges.

Further Reading

Hufbauer, Gary. *U.S.-China Trade Disputes: Rising Tide, Rising Stakes.* London: Institute for International Economics, 2006.

Lord, James. *The Essential Guide for Buying from China's Manufacturers: The 10 Steps to Success.* Charleston, SC: Book Surge Publishing, 2007.

Roach, Stephen. *Unbalanced: The Codependency of America and China.* New Haven, CT: Yale University Press, 2014.

Zeng, Ming, and Peter Williamson. *Dragons at Your Door: How Chinese Cost Innovation Is Disrupting Global Competition.* Cambridge, MA: Harvard Business Review Press, 2007.

Financial Institutions

On December 1, 1948, the Chinese Communist Party (CCP) created the People's Bank of China (PBC), which began issuing *Renminbi* (RMB) in the liberated areas during the Chinese Civil War (1946–1949). After the People's Republic of China (PRC) was founded in 1949, its Central Government published the "Provisional Regulations on the State Budget and Final Accounts" in July 1951, which defined the function of the financial institutions and business enterprises. PBC played a central role in issuing the currency, controlling circulation, and disbursing budgetary expenditures. In September 1954, the PRC Constitution was promulgated and created the State Council as the executive body, which established the Ministry of Finance, State General Administration of Exchange Control, and the State Capital Construction Commission. These agencies participated in preparing the state budget and in revenue planning; collecting industrial, commercial, customs duties, and salt taxes; allocating funds and supervising all financial accounts; as well as investigating and correcting any illegal practices and violations in the 1950s to 1980s. PBC administered the accounts, payments, and receipts of government offices, agencies, and organizations.

While the PBC continued to function as the central bank, the State Council also created other banks in 1954–1956, including People's Construction Bank of China (or China Construction Bank, CCB), Agricultural Bank of China (ABC), China's Bank of Communications (CBC), and Industrial and Commercial Bank of China (ICBC). To meet new financial needs for its economic reform which began in 1978, the PRC government created several more new banks, including the Bank of China (BOC), China Development Bank (CDB), China Import and Export Bank (CIEB), and China Investment Bank (CIB) in 1979–1983. The state owns 98 percent of all banking assets and governs their administrations and practices, while more than 75 percent of bank loans are allocated to state-owned enterprises (SOEs) and 20 percent to governments at all levels.

In 1983, the centralized, state-owned and operated financial institutions began their reforms by moving to exercise monetary control though setting reserve requirements, managing credit funds, and granting more loans to the private sector, such as Western mechanisms. The banks were also decentralized by separating from PBC and specializing in their particular spheres of influence, much as ABC handles financial needs in agriculture; CCB and CBC focus on domestic transactions; ICBC, CDB, and CIB work with loans and lending activities; and BOC specializes in international transactions, having numerous branch officers in many countries. Since the mid-1980s, a secondary financial market gradually developed for government bonds. In August 1986, the Shenyang Trust and Investment Company first began with over-the-counter trading, then the Shanghai Stock Exchange (SSE) opened in December 1990, and the Shenzhen Stock Exchange (SZSE) opened in July 1991, creating a bond market to generate new financial resources from the society.

In 1994, a new state budget law separated the banking system from the government by establishing bank autonomy, prohibiting government offices from borrowing from the banks. The major banks are responsible for their own profits and losses. In 1995, the government issued the Commercial Bank Law, allowing state-owned banks to be commercialized, and commercial banks were established. Many much smaller, local banks had been established, and stock-market trading was booming. More private-sector firms had access to commercial loans and to domestic stock markets. In 1997, the CCP Fifteenth National Congress announced an initiative that provided for the sale of most of the SOEs. Two years later, several national financial asset management companies were established to purchase and manage bad loans from the state banks.

After China joined the World Trade Organization (WTO) in 2001, the World Bank, United Nations programs, and some countries and areas such as Taiwan, Hong Kong, and Japan provided loans to China's state and local banks, including the Bank of Shanghai and Bank of Shenzhen. In 2002, China became the top recipient of foreign direct investment (FDI) in the world. In 2003, the Chinese government founded the China Banking Regulatory Commission (CBRC), which was followed by the establishments of China Securities Regulatory Commission (CSRC) and China Insurance Regulatory Commission (CIRC), as a new financial regulatory system. In 2005 China received $80 billion FDI and received $69.5 billion FDI in 2006. Foreign banks are allowed to purchase minority stakes in local banks. By 2004, foreign financial assets in China reached $47 billion. There were 62 foreign banks from 19 countries, set up in 191 business institutions in China, and 211 foreign bank branches operating in China.

In 2007, SSE had 904 stock listings with a market value of 27 trillion yuan ($4.5 trillion) with an annual turnover value of 30.5 trillion yuan ($5.08 trillion). The total market value of the mainland's stock exchanges made China the third largest stock market in Asia by 2007, after Japan and Hong Kong. By December 2011, SSE has become the sixth largest stock market in the world by market capitalization of $2.3 trillion. SZSE had an annual turnover value of $2.7 trillion in 2009, and market capitalization of $1 trillion by 2011. In September 2013, China established the Shanghai Free Trade Zone as a new effort for more foreign investment, which now has access to almost all financial sectors in the metropolitan economy. China is predicted to be the third largest stock market in the world by 2016.

See also: Chapter 3: Chinese Communist Party. Chapter 4: Overview; Foreign Investment; *Renminbi* and Currency Exchange; Service Industry; State-Owned Enterprises; WTO and Stock Exchanges.

Further Reading

Bell, Stephen, and Hui Feng. *The Rise of the People's Bank of China: The Politics of Institutional Change*. Cambridge, MA: Harvard University Press, 2013.

Cousin, Violaine. *Banking in China*. 2nd ed. London: Palgrave and Macmillan, 2011.

Howie, Fraser, and Carl Walter. *Privatizing China: Inside China's Stock Markets*. Hoboken, NJ: Wiley-Blackwell, 2006.

Koepp, Robert. *Betting on China: Chinese Stocks, American Stock Markets, and the Wagers on a New Dynamic in Global Capitalism*. Hoboken, NJ: Wiley-Blackwell, 2012.

Sanderson, Henry, and Michael Forsythe. *China's Superbank: Debt, Oil and Influence—How China Development Bank Is Rewriting the Rules of Finance*. New York: Bloomberg, 2013.

Walter, Carl, and Fraser Howie. *Red Capitalism: The Fragile Financial Foundation of China's Extraordinary Rise*. Hoboken, NJ: Wiley-Blackwell, 2012.

Foreign Investment

As a developing country, China needed foreign capital and technology when it began economic reform in 1978. Beijing established a diplomatic relationship with Washington, D.C., on January 1, 1979, while improving economic relations with Japan, France, Taiwan, and Hong Kong. That year the People's Republic of China (PRC) promulgated a foreign investment law. From 1980 to 1985, restrictions on the type, size, and operations of foreign investment were progressively relaxed. Permissible forms of foreign investment eventually included compensatory trade, processing of materials, assembly, joint ventures, and complete foreign ownership. The cheap labor force, low-cost facilities, and huge domestic markets became attractive to foreign investors. They began their investment in processing manufacturing, by processing imported materials or components into exports. The share of processing exports in total exports rose from 18 percent in 1986 to 55 percent in 2000. China's export-oriented manufacturing strategy encouraged foreign-invested enterprises (FIEs) to engage in processing trade. In the early 1990s, the FIEs (mainly from Hong Kong and Taiwan) manufactured more than 58 percent of China's exported goods.

After 1992, China further intensified its effort to attract foreign investment, especially the foreign direct investment (FDI). Beijing paid greater attention to foreign concerns, and in particular, to ways of improving the local investment climate. Under such conditions, Chinese leaders had little choice but to undertake a liberalization of prevailing commercial norms and practices. In 1997, the government approved 21,046 foreign investment projects and received over $45 billion in FDI. In the 1990s, China was second only to the United States in direct foreign investment received. The annual total was $39 billion FDI in 1999 and $41 billion FDI in 2000. More than 300 enterprises belonging to the Fortune Global 500 invested in China by 2000.

Foreign investment accelerated industrialization in the 1990s by establishing various industries that absorbed a large proportion of the low-wage rural labor force. Foreign investors also contributed to the urbanization in the 2000s by getting directly involved in the development of the real estate sector and urban infrastructure. After China joined the World Trade Organization (WTO) in 2001, the government reduced certain investment measures and opened up more sectors that had previously been closed to FDI. In the first decade of the 21st century, while countries around the world entered hard economic times, China still prospered. In 2002–2014, the GDP rose between 7 and 9.4 percent each year. Foreign investment was a central component of China's continuing economic growth. In 2002, China became the top recipient of foreign investment in the world. It received $80 billion FDI in 2005 and $69.5 billion FDI in 2006. In September 2013, China established the Shanghai Free Trade Zone as a new effort to attract more foreign investment, which now has access to almost all sectors in the metropolitan economy.

See also: Chapter 1: Hong Kong; Taiwan. Chapter 4: Cost Production; Exports; International Trade Policies; Joint Ventures; Sino-U.S. Trade and Other Trading Partners; WTO and Stock Exchanges.

Further Reading

Behrman, Jack et al. *Direct Investment and Joint Ventures in China*. New York: Praeger, 1991.

Huang, Yasheng. *Selling China: Foreign Direct Investment during the Reform Era*. Cambridge, UK: Cambridge University Press, 2005.

Santoro, Michael. *China 2020: How Western Business Can—and Should—Influence Social and Political Change in the Coming Decade*. Ithaca, NY: Cornell University Press, 2009.

Thun, Eric. *Changing Lanes in China: Foreign Direct Investment, Local Governments, and Auto Sector Development*. Cambridge, UK: Cambridge University Press, 2006.

International Trade Policies

During his economic reform movement, beginning in 1978, Deng Xiaoping (Deng Hsiao-ping) (1904–1997) gave greater play to market forces and encouraged foreign trade with, and investment in, China. The open door foreign economic policy reflected

SINO-SOVIET ALLIANCE (1950–1959)

After the founding of the People's Republic of China (PRC) in October 1949, Mao Zedong declared the "lean-to-one-side" policy and that the new republic would favor the Soviet Union and join the socialist and communist camp in the post-WWII world. Mao Zedong (1893–1976) visited Moscow in December 1949, and signed, with Josef Stalin, the Sino-Soviet Treaty of Friendship, Alliance, and Mutual Assistance in February 1950. The agreement between Beijing and Moscow was the cornerstone of the communist international alliance system in the 1950s. China began establishing a Stalin-style government based on the Soviet model and moved to center stage of the Cold War between the Soviet Union and the United States, and their respective camps.

a fundamental change in China's developmental strategy from the isolationist policy of previous Chinese leaders such as Mao Zedong (Mao Tse-tung) (1893–1976). In the early 1980s, four Special Economic Zones (SEZs) were set up, including Shenzhen across the border from Hong Kong. Fourteen coastal cities were soon open for international trade and for investment with special tax breaks and incentives to promote China's exports and to lure foreign capital and technology. In 1987, China resumed its status as a member of the General Agreement on Trade and Tariff (GATT). China's total foreign trade had risen from $21 billion in 1978 to over to $80 billion in 1988, a fourfold increase within 10 years.

After Deng's retirement, Jiang Zemin (1926–), the new leader in 1990–2002, expanded China's foreign trade by adopting new policies to promote international economic relations such as the Maritime Commerce Law enacted in 1993, Anti-Subsidy Rules issued in 1997, and revised the Foreign Investment Law in 2001. Hong Kong then became part of China, and Taiwan had developed extensive trade relations with the mainland. China's total foreign trade had risen from $80 billion in 1988 to $300 billion by 1997, a more then threefold increase in less than 10 years. China's entry to the World Trade Organization (WTO) in 2001 further promoted its international trade. By 2002, China's exports to the United States exceeded that of Japan. China's total foreign trade rose from $300 million in 1997 to $620 billion in 2002, more than doubling in five years. In 2002 the ranking of China in the world's trading nations jumped from 36th to 60th.

During 2002–2012, the government, under the new leadership of President Hu Jintao (1942–) and Premier Wen Jiabao (1942–), expanded the exports and moved far beyond cheap manufacturing such as toys, games, shoes, and cloth by adding petrochemicals, fertilizers, polymers, machine tools, shipping, and electric appliances in their exports. By 2005, China replaced the United States as Japan's main trading partner. In the following year, China's total trade reached $1.4 trillion, of which $762 billion was with the United States, about 20 percent. China imported electrical machinery, optical and medical equipment, organic chemicals, telecommunications and sound equipment, as well as oil and mineral fuels. Currently, the leading import partners are Japan (16 percent), Hong Kong (12 percent), South Korea (12 percent), the United

States (9 percent), Taiwan (8 percent), and Germany (7 percent). China's total foreign trade rose from $1.15 trillion in 2004, to $2.17 trillion in 2007, to $3.64 trillion in 2011, and to $4.16 trillion in 2013, more than tripled in less than 10 years.

The power transition from Hu to Xi Jinping (1953–) and its international trade policy changes indicate that China has entered a new era, which differs from previous generations. Xi, as the new leader (2012–2022), has made some important policy changes in the international trade such as food safety, medical inspection, transportation facilities, contract laborers, and financial cooperation. China has also developed new trade partnerships with more countries in Africa, Southeast Asia, and Latin America.

See also: Chapter 1: Hong Kong; Taiwan. Chapter 2: Deng Xiaoping; Hu Jintao; Jiang Zemin and Sino-U.S. Relations; Mao Zedong. Chapter 3: Xi Jinping. Chapter 4: Overview; Exports; Foreign Investment; Joint Ventures; Sino-U.S. Trade and Other Trading Partners; WTO and Stock Exchanges.

Further Reading

Hsueh, Roselyn. *China's Regulatory State: A New Strategy for Globalization.* Ithaca, NY: Cornell University Press, 2011.

Hufbauer, Gary. *U.S.-China Trade Disputes: Rising Tide, Rising Stakes.* London: Institute for International Economics, 2006.

Kynge, James. *China Shakes the World: A Titan's Rise and Troubled Future—and the Challenge for America.* New York: Houghton Mifflin Harcourt, 2006.

Shambaugh, David. *China Goes Global: The Partial Power.* Oxford, UK: Oxford University Press, 2013.

Joint Ventures

After his economic reform began in 1978, Deng Xiaoping (Deng Hsiao-ping) (1904–1997) brought China back into the international community in order to seek maximum opportunities for its growing economic and technological development. He signed numerous trade treaties with Western governments and joined many international organizations. From 1979 to 1982, Deng established four Special Economic Zones (SEZ), including Shenzhen across the border from Hong Kong, Zhuhai opposite Macao, and Xiamen across from Taiwan, as "open cities" in order to lure foreign capital. The joint ventures soon became practical for foreign investors in the SEZs, looking for a Chinese partner, setting up a joint company or a project through agreements, and then carrying out operations by both parties. Cheap labor, low-cost facilities, and huge domestic markets were attractive for foreign investors. In Shenzhen, the manufacturing factories increased from 26 in 1980 to 500 in 1984. In that year, this previously underdeveloped Chinese town had fulfilled over 3,000 business agreements with foreign investors from 50 countries, with a total value of $2.3 billion. In 1991, the four SEZ cities accounted for 14.32 percent of the national export value.

In the 1980s, Deng opened 14 more cities along China's coast for foreign investments and joint ventures. After Deng's retirement, Jiang Zemin (1926–), the new Chinese leader in 1990–2002, continued to offer the joint-venture enterprises in SEZs with import and export rights not available to Chinese companies, with special tax breaks, regulation exemptions, and some protective policies as business incentives. In the 1990s, China ranked with the United States as one of the two largest recipients of foreign direct investment.

After China joined the World Trade Organization (WTO) in 2001, the Western multinational corporations (MNCs) increased their share through joint ventures in China. Among the five major categories of these joint ventures, three belong to industry and services, including equity joint ventures (EJVs), co-operative joint ventures (CJVs), and wholly foreign-owned enterprises (WFOEs). The proportions of the three joint ventures, WFOEs, EJVs, and CJVs changed from 46.9 percent, 35.8 percent, and 17.3 percent in 2000, to 60.2 percent, 20.4 percent, and 11.4 percent in 2002, and to 66.8 percent, 26.9 percent, and 6.3 percent, respectively, in 2004. Large Western MNCs have great bargaining power relative to developing countries, including China. The other two joint ventures serve as financial vehicles for foreign investment, including foreign investment companies limited by shares (FICLBS) and investment companies through foreign investors (ICFI). In 2002, China became the top recipient of foreign direct investment in the world.

After Jiang, although the Hu Jintao (1942–) and Wen Jiabao (1942–) administration in 2002–2012 strategically shifted China's economic development from a global-oriented policy to a more regionally balanced one, they continued to support the joint ventures and to encourage foreign investment. By 2003, the government had approved establishment of 500,000 joint ventures. In 2004, the United States had 45,000 joint ventures in China with a total investment of $48 billion. Among the major American companies in China are Boeing, General Motors, ExxonMobil, Chevron, Conoco-Phillips, IBM, and General Electricity. The Chinese government, under the new leadership of Xi Jinping (1953–), works with the joint ventures to more effectively use domestic markets and resources, strives to open more international markets, and takes an active part in regional economic cooperation and multilateral trade systems in 2012–2022.

See also: Chapter 1: Hong Kong. Chapter 2: Deng Xiaoping; Hu Jintao; Jiang Zemin and Sino-U.S. Relations. Chapter 3: Xi Jinping. Chapter 4: Overview; Cost Production; Exports; Foreign Investment; International Trade Policies; Sino-U.S. Trade and Other Trading Partners; WTO and Stock Exchanges.

Further Reading

Behrman, Jack et al. *Direct Investment and Joint Ventures in China*. New York: Praeger, 1991.

Devonshire-Ellis, Chris, Andy Scott, and Sam Woollard, eds. *Setting up Joint Ventures in China*. New York: Springer, 2011.

Pearson, Margaret. *Joint Ventures in the People's Republic of China: The Control of Foreign Direct Investment under Socialism*. Princeton, NJ: Princeton University Press, 1991.

Tian, Xiaowen. *Managing International Business in China*. Cambridge, UK: Cambridge University Press, 2007.

Zhang, Kevin H., ed. *China as the World Factory?* London: Routledge, 2005.

Land and Household Policy

According to the Constitution of the People's Republic of China (PRC), land in the urban areas is owned by the state, and "land in the rural and suburban areas is owned by collectives except for those portions which belong to the State as prescribed by law." From the 1950s to 1970s, the government under the leadership of Mao Zedong (Mao Tse-tung) (1893–1976) created the rural people's communes, and private land ownership and independent farming were nonexistent. By 1975, 52,615 people's communes had been established, managing 677,000 production brigades, including 4.83 million production teams and 164.48 million households. Deng Xiaoping (Deng Hsiao-ping) (1904–1997) as the new leader carried out the "household production responsibility system" (HPRS) in 1979 after a short pioneer experiment in some areas. The HPRS contracts a land allotment to each individual rural household. Long-dissatisfied peasants started to redistribute the land to households on the condition that each household would submit a certain amount of output to the government.

In 1985, each HPRS contract specified a quota output to sell to the government, but the rest of the output belonged to the individual farmer, who could sell it to a free market, the first free market established during Deng's reform. His commercialization of farming motivated individual farmers who could manage their productivity and make profits. The state retreated substantially from grass-roots rural society. The production contracting system simply gave villagers control rights to production. Small farmers were determined to improve their living standard, and they succeeded, leading directly to the collapse of the entire commune system in the 1980s. With a sizable land and able hands, some of the peasants in the southern provinces got rich quick and became "*wanyuanhu*" (10,000 yuan *Renminbi*, or RMB, family) with an annual income about U.S. $3,000, compared to a national peasant average income of 200 yuan ($60) a year in the 1960s. The redistribution or the fear of redistribution prevented peasants from leaving their village. A peasant family needed as many household members as possible in order to receive a larger piece of land.

The land reform, however, is incomplete since land is not a commodity in China, and it still belongs to the state. People only have the rights to use the land, but don't own the land. Many young farmers, especially those hard-working with ambition, decided to build their own small business or move to the cities for a manufacturing job. Their parents will pass on merely a household production responsibility contract rather than a family farm or a piece of private land to them. And, very often, provincial, municipal, county, town, and village officials recollect the land by terminating the contracts "in the public interest."

See also: Chapter 2: Deng Xiaoping; Mao Zedong. Chapter 3: Constitution. Chapter 4: Overview; Agriculture; Migrant Laborers. Chapter 6: Rural-Urban Conflicts. Appendix: A Day in the Life of a Farmer.

Further Reading

Chen, Jean Jinghan, and David Wills, eds. *The Impact of China's Economic Reforms upon Land, Property and Construction.* London: Ashgate, 1999.

Ho, Peter. *Developmental Dilemmas: Land Reform and Institutional Change in China.* London: Routledge, 2005.

Zhao, Yongjun. *China's Disappearing Countryside: Towards Sustainable Land Governance for the Poor.* London: Ashgate, 2013.

Zweig, David. *Freeing China's Farmers: Rural Restructuring in the Reform Era.* Armonk, NY: M. E. Sharpe, 1997.

Manufacturing

China's manufacturing includes metallurgical, machinery, transportation, petrochemical, defense, electronics, and textile industries. It also can be divided into heavy industry such as steel, machinery, automobile, and shipbuilding, and light industry such as electronics, instrument, tools, and consumer products. From the 1950s to 1970s, the output proportion between heavy and light industries has changed from 35.5 percent versus 64.5 percent, to 56.9 percent versus 43.1 percent. During the late 1990s and early 2000s, the country has become a global manufacturing center, due to its cost of production and participation in international trade organizations such as the WTO (World Trade Organization). In 2010, China had 19.8 percent of the world's total manufacturing output and became the largest manufacturer in the world. Its manufacturing accounted for 31.6 percent of China's GDP in 2013, an increase of 7.6 percent from 2012, and it is the largest GDP contributor in the country. It hires more than 400 million manufacturing workers, about 52.3 percent of the labor force in the industries.

The metallurgical industry has first priority in China's manufacturing since its industrialization requires steel, iron, copper, aluminum, tin, and other metal outputs. Its steel outputs increased from 64.3 million tons in 1980 to 140 million tons in 2000, 419 million tons in 2006, and to 683 million tons in 2011, which was an increase of 9 percent from 2010. As the largest steel supplier in the world, China was producing 45 percent of the world's steel in 2011. Its iron ore production increased from 38 million tons in 1980 to 100 million tons annually in the 1990s. As the top exporter of steel in the world, China exported 59.2 million tons of steel in 2008, an increase of 5.5 percent from the previous year.

China's transportation includes automobile, locomotives, shipbuilding, and aircraft industries. Its automobile manufacturing increased from 140,000 in 1975 to 222,000 in 1980, 443,400 in 1985, 1.1 million in 1992, 2.3 million in 2001, 4.44 million in 2003, and 5.71 million in 2005. China ranked as the third largest automaker in the world after the United States and Japan in 2006. That year, a total of 7.22 million automobiles were sold in China, making it the second largest auto consumer in the world only after the United States. Automobile production continues to grow, from 8.88 million in 2007, to 9.35 million in 2008, and to 13.83 million in 2009, when China became the largest automaker in the world. By 2010, China had also become the largest vehicle consumer in the world when 18 million new cars were sold that year. After 2000, China began exporting cars and auto parts. Its vehicle and component export reached $70 billion in 2010.

China's petrochemical industry supplies refined oil products and major petrochemical products, including synthetic resin, synthetic fiber monomers and polymers, synthetic fiber, synthetic rubber, chemical fertilizer, and petrochemical intermediates. Throughout 2012, it processed 2.2 percent more crude oil than the previous year, and its oil processing volume in a single month broke 20 million tons for the first time. The operation rate of refining units was 91.3 percent, and the load factor was 98.4 percent. The light chemical feedstock totaled 37.38 million tons in 2011, increasing 6.8 percent from 2010. The output of ethylene amounted to 9,894 million tons in 2011, up by 9.2 percent from the previous year, and the total sales volume of chemical products reached 50.80 million tons.

The defense industry plays an important role not only in manufacturing, but also in technology research and development. Out of the annual military spending of $189 billion in 2013, an increase of 14 percent from 2012, an estimated 37.5 percent went to the defense industry for manufacturing weapons, ammunition, military vehicles, and communication equipment. China has also begun to export weapon systems, including missiles, to foreign countries.

The environmental issues have become increasingly problematic, especially in new, rapidly industrializing coastal and urban areas. Many pollutants from the manufacturing industries include nitrous oxides, sulfur oxides, carbon monoxide, hydrogen sulfide, benzene, toluene, and xylenes.

See also: Chapter 1: Pollution and the Environment; Transportation and Water Conservancy. Chapter 4: Overview; Agriculture; Cost Production; Energy Industry; Joint Ventures; Sino-U.S. Trade and Other Trading Partners; State-Owned Enterprises; WTO and Stock Exchanges.

Further Reading

Chang, Leslie. *Factory Girls: From Village to City in a Changing China*. New York: Spiegel & Grau, 2009.

Hurst, William. *The Chinese Workers after Socialism*. Cambridge, UK: Cambridge University Press, 2012.

Midler, Paul. *Poorly Made in China: An Insider's Account of the China Production Game*. Hoboken, NJ: Wiley-Blackwell, 2011.

Mitchell, Bruce. *13 Steps to Manufacturing in China*. London: Palgrave Macmillan, 2012.

Migrant Laborers

While China has established a socialist market economy, rural areas are typically less well off than urban areas. In the 1980s, the per capita annual net income of urban households was 6 to 10 times higher than that of rural households. Labor migration from rural to urban areas emerged as a nationwide phenomenon in the late 1980s. By the early 1990s, the estimation of the number of individuals who had made this move was approximately 36 million. In the early 2000s, as many as 100 million rural laborers were estimated to be on the move and seeking work in cities and coastal areas. The number of migrant workers totaled 120 million in 2005, 136 million in 2007, and 151 million in 2010. Official estimates suggest that as of 2014, more than 169 million peasants may have left the countryside, leaving behind an equal number of peasants who are underemployed in their home rural communities. These resulting problems, related to employment, housing, public education, health care, transportation, and law enforcement, are most prevalent in the cities.

Since it takes time for many peasants to find full-time employment, they have become part of the mobile or "floating" population, those who have no rights to housing, school, and health care. In the large cities, such as Beijing, Shanghai, and Tianjin, between 2 and 4 million transients are camped in train and bus stations, as well as other public places. Neither city nor rural governments have any control over them since the central government has no viable regulations relating to labor issues. The city governments continue to deny permanent residency to these formerly rural residents. This urban-rural segregation is creating serious concerns and has generated hostility between the government and the migrants. Rural workers are required to have six passes to work in cities or provinces other than their own, and are often considered second-class citizens. Although rural migration had urbanized the country by 2005, the problems of China's migrant laborers have become serious in terms of their living conditions and their rights.

China's industrialization is partly based on low wages paid to its workers, especially migrant workers, who consist of 46 percent of all the urban employment in 2007. Some of these migrant workers are treated unfairly and many are underpaid. Approximately 74 percent of migrant laborers earn 580–1,400 yuan *Renminbi* or RMB (between $80 and $200) a month. Aside from these issues, Chinese laborers do not have a unified voice for their own rights and interests. Ethnic, social, gender, and religious diversity has divided Chinese migrant workers in troubling ways. Females comprise more than 30 percent of all migrant workers in the country. They face numerous challenges in the workplace, including longer working hours and lower wages, and do not have access to a safe and sanitary work environment. The children of migrant workers lack sufficient parenting and face serious family problems. There are more than 150,000 urban "street children" according to state-run media. Many of them are the children of the migrant workers who spend their days on the street. In 2008, state media reported that the number of children in rural areas left behind by their migrant worker parents totaled 5.8 million.

See also: Chapter 4: Overview; Cost Production; Trade Union and Labor Movement; Workplace Safety. Chapter 6: Poverty; Rural-Urban Conflicts; Urban Poor. Chapter 7: Child Labor; Gender Inequality; One-Child Policy.

Further Reading

Chang, Leslie. *Factory Girls: From Village to City in a Changing China*. New York: Spiegel & Grau, 2009.

Hurst, William. *The Chinese Workers after Socialism*. Cambridge, UK: Cambridge University Press, 2012.

Loyalka, Michelle. *Eating Bitterness: Stories from the Front Lines of China's Great Urban Migration*. Berkeley: University of California Press, 2013.

Miller, Tom. *China's Urban Billion: The Story behind the Biggest Migration in Human History*. London: Zed Books, 2012.

Pirating and Copyright Issues

Intellectual property rights (IPR) were not protected in the People's Republic of China (PRC) until the 1980s. After joining the World Intellectual Property Organization (WIPO) in 1980, the PRC adopted its Trademark Law in 1982, issued its first Patent Law in 1984, created the State Intellectual Property Office (SIPO) for patent applications and IPR enforcement in 1988, and published the Copyright Law in 1990. However, pirating intellectual property and violations of copyright continued during the 1990s.

Chinese companies continued to manufacture, distribute, and even export their counterfeit products, especially brand names, including electronic appliances, medicine, medical devices, auto parts, sporting goods, designer apparel, toys, and various consumer products. The U.S. Commerce Department estimated that over 20 percent of all consumer products in the market were counterfeit. China had the highest rate (over 90 percent) in counterfeits and piracy, and U.S. companies lost billions of dollars in legitimate business each year to piracy. Both foreign and domestic companies were targets and victims of the counterfeiters and pirates. The Chinese governmental agency estimated that nearly 200,000 people died in 2001 in China due to use of counterfeit medicines.

After its entry to the World Trade Organization (WTO) in 2001, under international obligations and pressure, the Chinese government combined its domestic laws with the WTO rules and international practices on IPR. Still, China continues to remain a major risk for IPR. In 2007, U.S. trade representatives announced that the United States would begin WTO dispute settlement consultations with the PRC over deficiencies in China's protection and enforcement of copyrights and trademarks on a wide range of products. The Office of the U.S. Trade Representative in 2014 has put China on its Priority Watch List for a 10th consecutive year.

Some experts believe that a possible solution of pirating and copyright issues may result from an increasing demand of IPR protection by Chinese citizens themselves. The more companies and individuals become patent holders, the more the Chinese will take the IPR issues seriously. The patent applications increased from 171,000 in 2006 to 314,000 in 2010. The number of inventions granted by SIPO reached 217,000 patents in 2012, an increase of 26.1 percent from 2011. Also, Chinese courts had received 87,420 civil lawsuits of IPR violations in 2012, an increase of 46 percent from 2011; and handled 83,850 cases during that year, an increase of 44 percent from the previous year. About 60,000 suspects were arrested, and 29,852 of them were convicted for crimes of IPR infringement and producing and selling substandard commodities that year, with a total value of $1.83 billion. China has 2,731 IPR judges sitting in 420 courts. The country owns the world's largest number of trademarks with a total of 6.4 million effective registered trademarks in 2013. The number of patent applications is estimated to reach 500,000 by 2015, higher than the estimated 400,000 in the United States and 300,000 in Japan.

See also: Chapter 4: Cost Production; Exports; International Trade Policies; Joint Ventures; Manufacturing; Sino-U.S. Trade and Other Trading Partners; WTO and Stock Exchanges.

Further Reading

Cheung, Gordon. *Intellectual Property Rights in China: Politics of Piracy, Trade and Protection*. London: Routledge, 2011.

Devonshire-Ellis, Chris, Andy Scott, and Sam Woollard, eds. *Intellectual Property Rights in China*. New York: Springer, 2011.

Dimitrov, Martin. *Piracy and the State: The Politics of Intellectual Property Rights in China*. New York: Cambridge University Press, 2012.

Hannas, William, James Mulvenon, and Anna Puglisi. *Chinese Industrial Espionage: Technology Acquisition and Military Modernization*. London: Routledge, 2013.

Pang, Laikwan. *Creativity and Its Discontents: China's Creative Industries and Intellectual Property Rights Offenses*. Durham, NC: Duke University Press, 2012.

Renminbi and Currency Exchange

As the official currency of the People's Republic of China (PRC), *renminbi* literally means "people's currency" with its abbreviation as RMB. The code issued by ISO (International Organization for Standardization) for RMB is CNY (meaning "Chinese *yuan*") or CN¥. The basic unit of RMB is *yuan* with a sign of ¥. One yuan is divided into 10 *jiao*; and one jiao is subdivided into 10 *fen*. In current circulation, the RMB notes have 10 denominations, including ¥0.10 yuan (1 jiao), ¥0.20 yuan (2 jiao), ¥0.50 yuan (5 jiao), ¥1, ¥2, ¥5, ¥10, ¥20, ¥50, and ¥100 yuan. The RMB coins are available in seven denominations, including ¥0.01 yuan (1 fen), ¥0.02 yuan (2 fen), ¥0.05 yuan (5 fen), ¥0.10 yuan (1 jiao), ¥0.20 yuan (2 jiao), ¥0.50 yuan (5 jiao), and ¥1.00 yuan (1 yuan). The state-owned and operated People's Bank of China (PBC) issues RMB and regulates its circulation in line with state regulations.

After it was founded in 1948, the PBC issued RMB first in areas controlled by the Chinese Communist Party (CCP) during the civil war. After the founding of the PRC in 1949, the CCP government made the PBC a centralized national bank, or the monetary authority of the PRC, which continued to issue *renminbi* as the unified currency for the new state with 12 denominations from 1 yuan to 50,000 yuan. In 1955, the PRC adjusted the currency value with ratio of 1: 10,000 and issued new notes from 0.01 to 10 yuan. In 1957, the PBC issued new aluminum coins of 0.01, 0.02, and 0.05 yuan. By 2014, the PBC had issued five series of RMB banknotes with different commemorative designs. The RMB notes are printed in both the Chinese and the native languages when they were issued in the ethnic regions such as Tibet or Inner Mongolia. RMB is not legal tender in Hong Kong and Macau since 1997 and 1999, when China took back these territories from British and Portuguese governments, even though RMB has been accepted in the streets and by the local banks.

In 1949, the PBC decided on exchange rates between RMB and foreign currencies. There are two exchange rates of the RMB—the buying price and the selling price, and the intermediate price is the average of the two. From 1949 to 1979, RMB remained a fairly stable currency, approximately 2.46 yuan per U.S. dollar. In 1979, the PRC State Council established the State General Administration of Exchange Control in Beijing, which serves as a state agency to supervise the PBC and the Bank of China (BOC), and to implement foreign exchange control.

Since the 1980s, the RMB was devalued to improve the competitiveness of Chinese manufactured goods for exports. The exchange rates between the RMB yuan and the U.S. dollar declined from 1.53 yuan to the dollar in 1980, but then increased to 2.8 yuan to the dollar in 1985, to 3.71 yuan in 1987, 7.2 yuan in 1989, and 8.62 yuan in 1994. Therefore China's exports to the United States increased 22 percent annually during this period. China's exports to the United States increased from $100 billion in 2000 to $321.5 billion in 2007, while the United States suffered a huge annual trade deficit of $256.3 billion in 2007. One of the critiques against China for its unfair trade practices has been artificial currency devaluation. In 2007–2009, China began to internationalize the RMB with some success. It became the eighth most widely traded currency in the world by 2013.

The U.S. government had asked the PRC to stop its RMB devaluation, stating that it should allow its currency to fluctuate freely in international markets. China argues that it must control its currency because it's important for the stability of Chinese markets and trade. In 2005–2010, the RMB appreciated to 1:6.83; and from 2010 to 2015, it has held steady at 6.2 yuan per dollar.

See also: Chapter 3: Chinese Communist Party. Chapter 4: Overview; Exports; Financial Institutions; Reserve and Foreign Debts; Sino-U.S. Trade and Other Trading Partners; WTO and Stock Exchanges.

Further Reading

Chen, Yulu. *Chinese Currency and the Global Economy: The Rise of the Renminbi*. New York: McGraw-Hill, 2014.

China Development Research Foundation. *China's Exchange Rate Regime*. London: Routledge, 2014.

Eichengreen, Barry, and Masahiro Kawai, eds. *Renminbi Internationalization: Achievements, Prospects, and Challenges.* Washington, DC: Brookings Institution, 2015.

Fung, Hung-Gay, Glenn Chi-Wo Ko, and Jot Yau. *Dim Sum Bonds: The Offshore Renminbi-Denominated Bonds.* Hoboken, NJ: Wiley-Blackwell, 2014.

Zhang, Peter. *The Chinese Yuan: Internationalization and Financial Products in China.* Hoboken, NJ: Wiley-Blackwell, 2011.

Reserve and Foreign Debts

The ratio of foreign reserves, or exchange reserves, to foreign debt is important to each country that has been deeply involved in global economy. Many countries have borrowed much more than they have saved, so that their risk indicators are very high. Between the 1980s and 2000s, China has experienced a historic transformation from foreign debtor to the largest reserve-saving country in the world.

In the early 1980s China began borrowing heavily from abroad for reconstruction and new technology. Its annual borrowing was $4.3 billion in 1981 and increased to $6.2 billion in 1993. Its total accumulated foreign debts was $15.8 billion in 1985, more than tripled to $52.45 billion in 1990, doubled to $106.59 billion in 1995, increased to $151.83 billion in 1999, and to $182.6 billion in 2003, when China became the fourth-largest debtor among developing countries (after Brazil, Russia, and Mexico). China

SINO-SOVIET SPLIT (1960–1989)

After Josef Stalin died in 1953, the new leaders in Moscow held differing versions of the communist movement. In 1956, Nikita Khrushchev, supreme leader of the Soviet Union in 1954–1964, issued an international communist conference secret report, denouncing Stalin as a dictator and calling for peaceful coexistence with Western imperialist countries. In 1957, when he attended an international communist conference at Moscow, Mao disagreed with Khrushchev's policy. The great Sino-Soviet polemic debate thereafter further undermined the ideological foundation of the Sino-Soviet alliance. The conflicts between the two communist parties extended to strategic and security issues. On July 16, 1959, the Soviet government informed the Chinese government that it would withdraw all of its nuclear scientists and experts from China. In 1960, Moscow unilaterally ended 500 bilateral contracts and withdrew all 12,000 Soviet experts from China, along with their blueprints and designs. In 1961, the Soviets canceled all projects of scientific and technical cooperation, including the joint nuclear programs. In 1962, Soviet agents instigated the migration of tens of thousands of Chinese citizens from Yili prefecture to the Soviet Union. In 1966, the Soviet government ordered all Chinese students to leave the country within one week. As tension mounted, both Soviet and Chinese armies deployed a large number of troops along the Russo-Chinese border where the armed conflicts occurred in 1969–1972. The Sino-Soviet relationship was eventually normalized at the end of the 1980s.

had a high risk indicator in 1981, since its debt totaled $4.3 billion while its foreign exchange reserves were only $0.9 billion. Japan became the largest creditor of China with $2.4 billion in 1996 when the World Bank ranked second with $1.9 billion and the United States was third with $1.16 billion.

After 2000, however, China's foreign exchange reserves increased significantly from $0.8 billion in 1979 to $165.6 billion in 2000, and reached $346.5 billion by 2003, when its reserves were higher than its outstanding debt ($182.6 billion). Its surplus on trade had significantly contributed to the increase of its foreign exchange reserves. Thus, China's risk exposure of foreign debt is low because most of its foreign debts are long term and its foreign reserves are much larger than its outstanding foreign debt. China invests its reserves, mostly U.S. dollars, in U.S. Treasury debt. Outward investment is a way to avoid these foreign exchange losses. Another purpose for Chinese government to encourage outflows of money from China is to reduce pressure on the *renminbi* (RMB) and inflation in China.

China's foreign exchange reserves reached $470.6 billion in mid-2004, and continued to increase to $711 billion in 2005, $941.1 billion in 2006, $1,332.6 billion in 2007, and $1,808.8 billion by June 2008, making it the highest foreign exchange reserve in the world. It was equal to nearly $1,500 per person for the entire Chinese population of 1.3 billion. China's foreign reserves continued to increase to $2.13 trillion in mid-2009, $2.45 trillion in 2010, $3.2 trillion in 2011, $3.82 trillion in 2013, and $3.99 trillion in 2014. Among the total reserves, 70 percent are U.S. dollar assets, including $447.5 billion U.S. government bonds and debt; 10 percent are Japanese yen assets; and the euro and the British pound account for some of the remaining portion.

See also: Chapter 4: Overview; Exports; Financial Institutions; Foreign Investment; International Trade Policies; *Renminbi* and Currency Exchange.

Further Reading

Gao, Jian. *Debt Capital Markets in China*. Hoboken, NJ: Wiley-Blackwell, 2007.

Hong, Tu. *Foreign Exchange Control in China*. Leiden, Netherlands: Kluwer Law International, 2005.

Labonte, Marc, and Wayne Morrison. *China's Holdings of U.S. Securities: Implications for the U.S. Economy*. Washington, DC: Congressional Research Service, 2012.

Sheng, Shuangqing. *Questions and Answers Concerning China's Control of Foreign Exchange, Foreign Debts and Guarantees*. Beijing: Foreign Languages Press, 2000.

Zhang, Peter. *The Chinese Yuan: Internationalization and Financial Products in China*. Hoboken, NJ: Wiley-Blackwell, 2011.

Service Industry

The service industry, or tertiary industries, such as real estate, finance, insurance, accounting, legal services, tourism, entertainment, public transportation, post, commerce, and telecom services, has had a significant growth in China since the 1980s. The market-oriented economic reform which started in 1978 focused on an open-trade and consumer-oriented growth strategy that encouraged service sectors with favorable policy support. From 1989 to 2001, a total of 6,251.6 billion yuan RMB ($781.5 billion) was invested in urban development, an increase of more than 10 times compared with the previous decade. Of the amount, 37 percent went into the transport, post, and telecom sector, 35 percent into the energy supply facilities, and 12 percent into public utilities.

As a result, the service industry grew much faster than the whole economy from 1979 to 2001, when the GDP grew 7 to 9.4 percent annually, as the service sectors grew in double digits per annum. By 2010, China has established the third largest service industry in the world (only after the United States and Japan). The service industry produced 43 percent of the country's annual GDP, only after manufacturing. The tertiary industry also increased its shared value with primary and secondary industries. The shares of value among the three industries have changed from 28.1 percent, 48.2 percent, 23.7 percent in 1978, to 15.2 percent, 51.1 percent, and 33.7 percent in 2001, and to 12.6 percent, 35.5 percent, and 51.9 percent, respectively, in 2013. The service industry has become the largest industry in today's China. The shares of employment among the three industries have also changed from 70.5 percent, 17.3 percent, 12.2 percent in 1978, to 50.1 percent, 22.3 percent, and 27.7 percent in 2001, and to 21.6 percent, 26.4 percent, and 52 percent in 2012. The growth of the service industry interacted with China's urbanization during the 2000s. In the meantime, among the 300 million jobs created in the cities, 70 million went to primary industry, 94.5 million to secondary industry, and 140 million jobs to the tertiary industry.

Among the service sectors, telecom service has shown rapid development by establishing numerous communication systems that link all parts of the country by Internet, telephone, telegraph, radio, and television. About 100 million cell phones were sold in 2006, and 190 million were sold in 2007, increasing by 74 percent. In 2007, more than 600 million mobile phones were made in China, over 50 percent of the world's total production. In 2003, more than 80 million households logged in to the Internet. By 2009, the number of domestic Web sites grew to 3.23 million, an annual increase rate of 12.3 percent. Internet users grew to 137 million in 2006, 162 million in 2007, and 618 million in 2014.

The tourism industry, as one of the fastest-growing service sectors, contributes more than $250 billion annually to China's economy today, about 2.6 percent of the total GDP. Many new hotels, resorts, restaurant chains, shopping malls, and luxury goods retail shops were constructed throughout the country. In 2002, domestic tourists totaled 878 million and spent $49 billion. In 2003, more than 20 million Chinese tourists traveled overseas, overtaking Japan for the first time. In 2011, 58 million international tourists arrived and spent more than $48 billion in China. In 2012, total business-travel spending reached $135 billion. Chinese business-travel spending was the highest in the world by 2014, overtaking the United States.

See also: Chapter 1: Transportation and Water Conservancy. Chapter 4: Overview; Financial Institutions. Chapter 16: Internet and Social Media.

Further Reading

Chinoy, Mike. *China Live: People Power and the Television Revolution*. Boulder, CO: Rowman & Littlefield, 2013.

Keane, Michael. *China's New Creative Clusters: Governance, Human Capital and Investment*. London: Routledge, 2011.

Li, Li. *Within the Tertiary Industry Structure: Optimization and Countermeasures*. Beijing: China Press, 2000.

Nyiri, Pal. *Scenic Spots: Chinese Tourism, the State, and Cultural Authority*. Seattle: University of Washington Press, 2007.

Otis, Eileen. *Markets and Bodies: Women, Service Work, and the Making of Inequality in China*. Stanford, CA: Stanford University Press, 2011.

Pettis, Michael. *Avoiding the Fall: China's Economic Restructuring*. New York: Carnegie Endowment, 2013.

Sino-U.S. Trade and Other Trading Partners

Since the founding of the People's Republic of China (PRC) in 1949, the PRC had traded only with the Soviet Union and other communist countries. After the Sino-Soviet split in the 1960s, China was isolated from both the Soviet bloc and the free world. International problems paved the way for U.S. President Richard Nixon's historic visit to Beijing in February 1972, when the absolute confrontation between the United States and China ended after more than 20 years. In September 1972, China and Japan established a formal diplomatic relationship. Japan was the first, among all major industrial/capitalist countries, to provide China with substantial technological and financial support.

In 1978 Deng Xiaoping (Deng Hsiao-ping) (1904–1997) emerged as the new paramount Chinese leader. He launched new reform policies and opened up China to the outside world. The normalization of Sino-U.S. relations, beginning on January 1, 1979, led to the rapid creation of an institutional and legal framework for expanded economic cooperation. On July 7, the Sino-U.S. Trade Relations Agreement was signed with mutual MFN on a reciprocal basis. The total trade between the two countries reached $2.4 billion that year. In 1980, more agreements were signed between Beijing and Washington, including textile trade, civil aviation and sea transportation, as well as tariff. After 1981, China was given access to higher levels of U.S. technology than the Soviet Union.

These efforts allowed the United States to gradually loosen trade restrictions, shifting the PRC to the category of "friendly, non-allied" country in May 1983. By 1985, the U.S.-China trade totaled $7.6 billion a year, which was nearly doubled from $4 billion in 1980. China then replaced the Soviet Union as the United States' largest communist trading partner. The total of China's international trade increased to $80 billion in 1988, and its trade with the United States increased to $20 billion in 1990s, about 25 percent of its world total.

Low labor costs have made China a major source for low-priced manufactured products in the world in general and in the United States in particular. China's exports

---

SINO-U.S. RAPPROCHEMENT (1972)

The threat from the Soviet Union in the late 1960s motivated the Chinese leaders to pursue rapprochement with the United States. President Richard Nixon saw an improvement in the relationship with China as beneficial to the United States as it would, in the short run, help America get out of the Vietnam War, and, in the long term, would dramatically enhance the strategic position of the United States in a global confrontation against the Soviet Union. A period known as Rapprochement began, with both sides considering the possibilities of establishing bilateral relations with one another, including the "ping pong diplomacy." On February 21, 1972, Nixon, accompanied by Henry Kissinger and several other advisers, made his way to Beijing, the first U.S. president who had ever visited the communist state since 1949. He met Mao Zedong (1893–1976) and Zhou Enlai (1898–1976) and released the Shanghai Communique on February 28. Taking the "Soviet threat" as an overriding concern, Beijing and Washington thereafter established a strategic working relationship. The diplomatic relationship between the two countries was finalized on January 1, 1979.

---

to the United States and other countries significantly increased in the 1990s, and the Bill Clinton administration referenced China as a "strategic partner" in the late 1990s.

Since the 1980s, U.S.-China trade has become imbalanced in favor of China. Among the total of $20 billion in 1990, Chinese exports to the United States increased to $15.2 billion about four times the 1985 $3.8 billion; while American exports to China totaled $4.8 billion, a small increase from $3.8 billion in 1985. China enjoyed a trade surplus of $10.4 billion that year. When the United States supported PRC's application to join the World Trade Organization (WTO), the imbalance of trade got even worse. China's exports to the United States continued to rise to $100 billion in 2000 and $321.5 billion in 2007, while American exports to China were $16.2 billion in 2000 and $65.2 billion in 2007. The United States suffered a trade deficit of $83.8 billion in 2000 and $256.3 billion in 2007. According to the U.S. Census Bureau, this trade imbalance has continued in recent years while U.S. trade deficits with China increased from $226.9 billion in 2009, to $273 billion in 2010, $295.2 billion in 2011, $315.1 billion in 2012, and $318.7 billion in 2013. The growth of the U.S. trade deficit with China has become a major issue between the two countries.

See also: Chapter 2: Deng Xiaoping. Chapter 4: Cost Production; Exports; Foreign Investment; International Trade Policies; Joint Ventures; Manufacturing; WTO and Stock Exchanges.

Further Reading

Bergsten, Fred et al. *Bridging the Pacific: Toward Free Trade and Investment between China and the United States*. New York: Peterson Institute, 2014.

Hufbauer, Gary. *U.S.-China Trade Disputes: Rising Tide, Rising Stakes*. London: Institute for International Economics, 2006.

Roach, Stephen. *Unbalanced: The Codependency of America and China.* New Haven, CT: Yale University Press, 2014.

Santoni, Arthur, ed. *China and the U.S.: Trade and Commitment Issues.* Hauppauge, NY: Nova Science, 2014.

Steinberg, James, and Michael O'Hanlon. *Strategic Reassurance and Resolve: U.S.-China Relations in the Twenty-first Century.* Princeton, NJ: Princeton University Press, 2014.

State-Owned Enterprises (SOEs)

After the founding of the People's Republic of China (PRC) in 1949, Mao Zedong (Mao Tse-tung) (1893–1976) followed the Soviet model and launched a collective movement of "proprietors toward socialism" against the bourgeoisie, the business owners, and private entrepreneurs. His movements had successfully transferred more than 68 percent of China's industry, commerce, finance, and service to either state or collective ownership by the end of the 1950s. The state owned many key national enterprises of leading industries such as energy, steel and iron, defense, automobiles, high tech, and transportation. Other SOEs were medium-sized enterprises such as machinery, manufacturing, textile, construction, retails, medicine, mass media, entertainment, and service under the provincial, municipal, and county-level governments. The collectively or publicly owned enterprises included local factories and small businesses such as hotels, restaurants, and stores. By the mid-1960s, the state and the public owned 94 to 96 percent of business, and privately owned enterprises (POE) were almost nonexistent. By 1966, SOEs produced 77.6 percent of China's gross value of industrial output (GVIO), the collectively owned enterprises 22.4 percent, and POEs zero.

After Mao died in 1976, Deng Xiaoping (Deng Hsiao-ping) (1904–1997) began economic reform by establishing a socialist market economy. To increase SOE productivity, Deng terminated the central planning in the early 1980s by giving autonomy to SOEs and by experimenting with remuneration to performance. He then instituted a "two-track system" in which SOEs first fulfilled the production quota and could then produce beyond the quota and sell at market (usually higher) prices.

After Deng's retirement, Jiang Zemin (1926–) began to privatize SOEs in the 1990s, especially the medium and small enterprises. The government terminated its ownership with more than 80 percent of the small and medium-size enterprises by 2000. The state ownership rights were transferred through leasing or contracting them out to the private sector, merging or reconstructing them with collectively owned enterprises, and bankrupting or selling them to joint companies by foreign investors. To clear the entanglement of poorly performing SOEs and inefficient debt-ridden state banks, Jiang in 1999 set up four state asset management agencies to purchase, manage, and dispose of the bad loans of state banks. Instead of paying banks interest, the debtor SOEs paid dividends to the asset agency. Those loans were then sold as initial public offerings or transfers of ownership. By 2000, POEs accounted for roughly 40 percent of the economy. A direct outcome of this change is that POEs pushed SOEs to become more competitive. SOEs could either shake off inertia or disintegrate into POEs.

As the result, the share of GVIO produced by SOEs has decreased from 77.6 percent in 1966 to 17.5 percent in 2010, while the number of large-sized SOEs declined from 118,000 in 1995 to 46,800 in 2010. In the 2000s, SOEs faced even greater challenges to their survival because of fierce competition from both domestic POEs and from foreign firms. Many entry barriers to previously state-monopolized industries such as telecommunication, banking, automobiles, insurance, and public utilities have been broken following China's entry into the WTO (World Trade Organization).

See also: Chapter 2: Deng Xiaoping; Mao Zedong. Chapter 4: Cost Production; Energy Industry; Financial Institutions; Manufacturing; WTO and Stock Exchanges. Appendix: A Day in the Life of a Factory Worker.

Further Reading

Haley, Usha, and George Haley. *Subsidies to Chinese Industry: State Capitalism, Business Strategy, and Trade Policy*. Oxford, UK: Oxford University Press, 2013.

Lin, Justin Yifu. *State-Owned Enterprise Reform in China*. Hong Kong: Chinese University Press, 2002.

Mazzucato, Mariana. *The Entrepreneurial State: Debunking Public vs. Private Sector Myths*. London: Anthem Press, 2013.

Sheng, Hong, and Nong Zhao. *China's State-Owned Enterprises: Nature, Performance and Reform*. Singapore: World Scientific, 2012.

Yusuf, Shahid, Dwight Perkins, and Kaoru Nabeshima. *Under New Ownership: Privatizing China's State-Owned Enterprises*. Stanford, CA: Stanford University Press, 2005.

Trade Union and Labor Movement

After the founding of the People's Republic of China (PRC) in 1949, the government promulgated the Trade Union Law in 1950 to regulate the labor movement. According to the trade union law, the Chinese Communist Party (CCP), as the ruling party of the country, effectively established several state organizations at the grass-roots level to "represent" the masses and to curb complaints about the lack of people's liberties and basic rights. Among these organizations was the All-China Federation of Trade Unions (ACFTU). The ACFTU is the largest trade union in the world and currently has 134 million union members in 1.7 million primary trade union organizations. It is divided into 31 provincial federations and 10 national industrial unions. The party-controlled ACFTU facilitates government policy, not necessarily the protection of workers' rights. ACFTU has a monopoly on trade unionizing in China and any creation of competing unions is illegal. This restriction on labor activism, coupled with increasingly intense labor disputes, has contributed to an increasing number of workers taking to the streets and the courts to press claims related to their problems.

Chinese laborers do not have a unified voice for their own rights and interests. Ethnic, social, gender, and religious diversity has divided Chinese migrant workers in troubling ways. Chinese workers are still forbidden to form independent trade unions. The law does not protect the workers' right to strike. Many full-time, part-time, and rural migrant workers continue to confront dangerous working conditions, toxic environments, the lack of protection and training, employer violations of minimum wage rules, unpaid pensions and wages, child labor, and forced and uncompensated overtime. The rights of some Chinese manufacturing workers have been violated by their employers. These workers were paid below the minimum wage and had to work seven days a week, and often 12–13 hours a day. Some of these workers did not have one day off during the entire month.

The Human Rights Watch organization reported that "This restriction on legally-sanctioned labor activism, coupled with increasingly intense labor disputes, in which protesting workers have few realistic routes for redress, has contributed to an increasing number of workers taking to the streets and the courts to press claims related to unpaid pensions and wagers, child labor, and dangerous working conditions." According to some social surveys, the current concerns of Chinese workers are: (1) health care, (2) government corruption, and (3) housing. Workers who seek the rectification of their situation have organized rallies, strikes, and demonstrations. In 2013, an estimated 90,000 incidents of social unrest and protest took place across the country.

See also: Chapter 3: Chinese Communist Party; Civil Rights. Chapter 4: Cost Production; Migrant Laborers; Workplace Safety. Chapter 6: Health Care; Retirement and Social Welfare. Chapter 7: Child Labor; Gender Inequality. Appendix: A Day in the Life of a Factory Worker.

Further Reading

Brown, Andrew, and Jane Hutchison, eds. *Organizing Labor in Globalizing Asia*. London: Routledge, 2002.

Friedman, Eli. *Insurgency Trap: Labor Politics in Post-socialist China*. Ithaca, NY: ILR Press, 2014.

Pringle, Tim. *Trade Unions in China: The Challenge of Labor Unrest*. London: Routledge, 2011.

Sheehan, Jackie. *Chinese Workers: A New History*. London: Routledge, 2002.

Workplace Safety

China's industrialization in the 1980s and 1990s was based partly on low-cost production, including low wages paid to workers and minimum workplace safety. Many full-time, part-time, and rural migrant workers continue to confront safety problems such as a dangerous working condition, toxic environments, lack of protection and safety education, as well as forced and uncompensated overtime. Many workers labor under extremely dangerous conditions. In August 2014, an explosion at an automotive parts factory in Kunshan, Jiangsu, killed 75 workers and injured over 180 others.

The official statistics show that the number of fatalities in coal mining increased from 3,082 in 2000, to 3,790 in 2002, and to 4,143 in 2003. Then, in 2004 and 2005, the fatalities reached a horrendous high of approximately 6,000 miners each year. The majority of workers who take this type of high-risk job are migrant laborers. They make up 90 percent of the mining jobs, 80 percent of construction workers, and almost 100 percent of firework manufacturers.

Females comprise more than 30 percent of all workers in the country. According to official statistics from 2002, approximately 335.5 million women were employed, or 45.5 percent of the total female population. Many female workers face numerous challenges in the workplace, and do not have access to a safe and sanitary work environment. Moreover, although Chinese law prohibits the employment of children under the age of 16, the United Nations reports point out that child labor remains a "persistent problem." According to the report of the World Federation of Trade Unions (WFTU) in June 2006, some manufacturing companies hire child laborers during summer and winter breaks. One such company employed more than 20 children between the ages of 12 and 15 for full-time jobs.

Chinese laborers do not have a unified voice for their own rights and interests. Ethnic, social, gender, and religious diversity has divided Chinese migrant workers in troubling ways. Chinese workers are still forbidden to form independent trade unions, and the law does not protect the workers' right to strike. Nonetheless, workers who seek the rectification of their situation have organized rallies, strikes, and demonstrations. In 2006, an estimated 80,000 incidents of social unrest and protest took place across the country. The government has begun to realize the problems plaguing the workplace, including labor relations, the abuse of migrant laborers, discrimination against women, and unsafe working conditions.

See also: Chapter 1: Pollution and the Environment. Chapter 3: Human Rights. Chapter 4: Cost Production; Energy Industry; Manufacturing; Migrant Laborers; Trade Union and Labor Movement. Chapter 7: Child Labor; Gender Inequality.

Further Reading

Friedman, Eli. *Insurgency Trap: Labor Politics in Post-socialist China.* Ithaca, NY: ILR Press, 2014.

Pringle, Tim. *Trade Unions in China: The Challenge of Labor Unrest.* London: Routledge, 2011.

Sheehan, Jackie. *Chinese Workers: A New History.* London: Routledge, 2002.

WTO and Stock Exchanges

On November 10, 2001, the Fourth Ministerial Conference of the World Trade Conference (WTO) adopted a decision on China's accession to the WTO. As of December 11, China officially became the 143rd member of the WTO, which marked the fact that

China's "opening-to-outside world" policy had entered a new era. The WTO globalizes free trade among its member countries, and each should have an open market for foreign enterprises without government intervention. This has a strong impact on China's financial institutions and its stock markets.

China has transformed its financial sector from a centralized banking system to a fractional-reserve system under the supervision of national commissions of the State Council. Banking assets have expanded approximately 35 percent annually and have become the major source of business finance. By mid-2002, there were 167 foreign commercial financial institutions (excluding insurers) in China. The World Bank, United Nations, and some countries and areas such as Taiwan, Hong Kong, and Japan provided loans to China's state and local banks. In 2002, China became the top recipient of the foreign direct investment (FDI) in the world. Beginning in December 2003, foreign banks have been allowed to conduct transactions with the local corporate sector in *renminbi* (RMB) and to purchase minority stakes in local banks.

Since China joined the WTO, its capital market has developed rapidly. The PRC's first stock was issued in 1985. In August 1986, the Shenyang Trust and Investment Company began over-the-counter trading as its first public exchange. The national stock market was established after the Shanghai Stock Exchange (SSE), opened in December 1990 and the Shenzhen Stock Exchange (SZSE) opened in July 1991. Nonetheless, the government divided the stock market into two submarkets: A shares and B shares. A shares denominated in RMB can be held and traded by domestic institutional as well as individual investors. B shares denominated in the United States and Hong Kong dollars used to be legally held and traded by foreign investors only.

In 2001, the Chinese government allowed local investors with foreign currency deposits to purchase B shares. The policy change has significantly reduced the price differentials between A and B shares. According to its commitments to WTO, from the beginning of 2005 China also allows joint ventures to underwrite A shares and to underwrite and trade B shares, and these joint ventures with up to 33 percent foreign ownership were allowed to engage in fund management businesses upon accession with the ownership ceiling rising to 49 percent.

In 2007, SSE had 904 stock listings with a market value of 27 trillion yuan RMB ($4.5 trillion) and annual turnover value of 30.5 trillion yuan ($5.08 trillion). The total market value of the mainland's stock exchanges made China the third largest stock market in Asia by 2007, after Japan and Hong Kong. Since December 2011, SSE has become the sixth largest stock market in the world by market capitalization of $2.3 trillion. SZSE had an annual turnover value of $2.7 trillion in 2009, and market capitalization of $1 trillion by 2011. In September 2013, China established the Shanghai Free Trade Zone as a new effort for more foreign investment, which now has access to almost all financial sectors in the metropolitan economy. By 2016, China is expected to be the third largest stock market in the world.

See also: Chapter 1: Hong Kong; Taiwan. Chapter 4: Overview; Financial Institutions; Foreign Investment; Joint Ventures; *Renminbi* and Currency Exchange.

Further Reading

Bhattasali, Deepak, Shantong Li, and William Martin, eds. *China and WTO: Accession, Policy Reform, and Poverty Reduction Strategies.* Washington, DC: World Bank, 2004.

Howie, Fraser, and Carl Walter. *Privatizing China: Inside China's Stock Markets.* Hoboken, NJ: Wiley-Blackwell, 2006.

Koepp, Robert. *Betting on China: Chinese Stocks, American Stock Markets, and the Wagers on a New Dynamic in Global Capitalism.* Hoboken, NJ: Wiley-Blackwell, 2012.

Lo, Vai Lo, and Xiaowen Tian. *Law and Investment in China: The Legal and Business Environment after China's WTO Accession.* London: Routledge, 2005.

Panitchpakdi, Supachai, and Mark Clifford. *China and the WTO: Changing China, Changing World Trade.* Hoboken, NJ: Wiley-Blackwell, 2002.

Walter, Carl E. *Privatizing China: The Stock Markets and Their Role in Corporate Reform.* Hoboken, NJ: Wiley-Blackwell, 2003.

CHAPTER 5

RELIGION AND THOUGHT

OVERVIEW

China represents one of the oldest civilizations in the world with a recorded history of 4,500 years, which includes various philosophical theories and religious ideologies. Based on its unique geographical setting, demographic characteristics, and political structure, Chinese ancient religions and classic philosophies such as Confucianism, Daoism (Taoism), and Legalism emerged from its economic growth, historical experience, social changes, intellectual interaction, education, and technological development. As the largest country in Asia in both population and territory, China has frequently been engaged in trade, exchanges, and wars with neighboring countries. Many foreign religions and philosophies were introduced to China and accepted by the Chinese government and its people, including Buddhism, Islam, Christianity, and communism. Each imperial dynasty and modern government came to power with its own ruling ideology. The Chinese Communist Party (CCP) established the People's Republic of China (PRC) in 1949 and continues to rule China in the 21st century.

Early Chinese religious and philosophical traditions evolved gradually through its prehistory, ancient, and classical periods. Numerous contrasting ideas and theories developed during these past ages still stand out among the factors that differentiate China from other early civilizations, including those of Rome, Egypt, and India. Chinese intellectuals thought according to their own experience and consistent inner logic in their society, and responded to the problems of their times by interpreting the issues, providing some solutions, and predicting the future. Relics showing how primitive Chinese people lived in gens communes have been discovered in many parts of central China along the Huang (Yellow) River, the cradle of Chinese civilization from around 12000–8000 BCE. The principal religious faiths were based on ancestor and nature worship, with many sects and different denominations. In approximately 3000 BCE, many clans along the river developed a patriarchal society and tribal coalition to protect their land, population, and water resources. Chinese leaders, who began calling themselves the "emperors" after 2600 BCE and their regime the "dynasty" after 2205 BCE, believed that they occupied a central position in the known universe. This perception, combined with a moral cosmology, elevated the Chinese emperor as the "Son of the Heaven," who possessed supreme power and a heavenly mission: the "Mandate of Heaven."

During the Shang dynasty (1766–1027 BCE), inscriptions occurred on some early bronzes, but most writing has been found incised on "dragon bones," actually the under-shells of tortoises, the scapulae or shoulder blades of cattle, and other flat bones. Relics discovered in the Yin ruins indicate large religious ceremonies and official participation in the worship of the heaven. The Zhou (Chou) dynasty (1027–221 BCE) is historically divided into two periods: the Western Zhou (1927–771 BCE) and the Eastern Zhou (771–221 BCE). The latter is subdivided into two historical periods: the Spring-Autumn Period (771–476 BCE) and the Warring States Period (475–221 BCE), times when philosophy and literature flourished and many great thinkers, such as Laozi (Lao-tzu) (400 BCE–?), Zhuangzi (Chuang-tzu) (369–286 BCE), Confucius (551–479 BCE), Xunzi (Hsun-tzu) (310–215 BCE), Mencius (Mengzi or Meng-tzu) (370–300 BCE), and Hanfeizi (Han Fei-tzu) (233 BCE–?) appeared. They offered different ideas, and together created "a hundred schools contended."

Confucius's philosophy became classical, since it provided ideas on how to overcome the civil wars and social disorders that all Chinese rulers constantly faced. It explains human nature or the natural laws of human beings through an ethical approach, whereas the Greek philosophers did so through logic, mathematics, physics, or religious approaches. The emperors of the Han dynasty (206 BCE–220 CE) adopted Confucianism as the ruling ideology, and the Confucius philosophy of his "Four Books and Five Classics" became the guideline of behavior. The Han became the first glorious dynasty in Chinese history. The Han's success has been a benchmark for future leaders in terms of geopolitics and cultural assimilation. When more and more Chinese began worshiping Confucius and Laozi, the Confucianism and Daoism became religions during the Han.

A statue of the Chinese philosopher Confucius. Confucianism has had a profound impact on Chinese thought and ethics. It has become the core of the Chinese civilization as a ruling ideology, educational doctrine, social value, and religion. Confucianism is also popular in the eastern Asian countries like Korea, Vietnam, and Singapore. (Espion/Dreamstime.com)

Buddhism was introduced to China by Indian merchants during the Han, and became popular in the Sui (581–618) and Tang (618–907) dynasties. Confucian and Daoist thoughts blended with Buddhism into the Chinese worldview. In imperial China, Chinese thoughts emphasized man as a social and political being, highlighting his duty within an agrarian society, according to Confucianism, Buddhism, and Daoism. This was in sharp contrast to the emphasis that Indian and Mediterranean civilizations placed on the holy world of man as God's servant. The founder of the Sui dynasty was Yang Jian or Sui Wendi (Wen-ti) (reigned 581–604), who had been raised by a Buddhist nun and later married a pious Buddhist wife. During the succeeding Tang dynasty, one of the most prosperous dynasties in Chinese history, several emperors, including Wu Zhao, also known as Empress Wuzetian (Wu Tse-tien) (reigned 684–704), the only female emperor in Chinese history, claimed themselves as Buddhists. Among other Tang monks was Xuanzang (602–664) who traveled to India, studied Buddhism there for 15 years, and brought back 657 Buddhist scriptures.

Confucianism was revived during the Song dynasty (960–1279) by Zhu Xi (Chu Hsi) (1130–1200) and other philosophers, who extended traditional ideas in many directions and made them practical and easy to follow. Neo-Confucianism suppresses individualism in favor of familism. The affluent extended family stressed the Confucian ethics of filial piety and social relations. The Mongol rulers defeated the Song and established the Yuan (1279–1368) dynasty in China and a Eurasian empire in the world, when many Muslims, Christians, and Jews traveled to China.

Islam was introduced to China through the Silk Road by Arab and Persian merchants around 616–618. During Yuan, hundreds of thousands of Muslim immigrants were relocated from Central and Western Asia by Mongols to help with control and administration of China. After Great Britain defeated the Qing dynasty (1644–1911) during the 1840 Opium War, Chinese society was further affected by the influence of Western ideas and institutions. In the late 19th century, China, for the first time, was significantly exposed to Western democratic ideas. Scholars and intellectuals began to translate and introduce the concepts of "citizenship," "constitution," and "democracy" to the Manchu emperors. Since strong conservative forces in Qing opposed Western ideas, many movements such as the 1898 Hundred Day Reform and 1905 Constitutional Movement failed.

In October 1911, the republican revolution led by Sun Yat-sen (1866–1925) ended the Qing dynasty and established the Republic of China (ROC). Sun mobilized the masses for the revolution by his "Three Principles of the People": nationalism (both anti-Manchu and anti-imperialist), democracy (a constitution with people's rights), and people's livelihood (a classic term for social equality). These three principles included many of the key concepts contained in updated Western ideas. Even though the revolution was incomplete, the struggle for democracy and modernization continued. New ideas from Western civilizations persisted in inspiring Chinese intellectuals and students, who launched the New Cultural movement in the 1910s and the May 4 Movement of 1919. During those years, Western democracy and liberalism began to take root in China.

Most Chinese Communist leaders also studied Western philosophy and ideas. Mao Zedong (Mao Tse-tung) (1893–1976), founding member of the CCP and the founder of the PRC, read Western liberal works by Montesquieu, Thomas Carlyle, and John Stuart Mill. As a result, he changed from a Confucian reformer to a radical liberalist in the late 1910s. Among Western ideologies, Karl Marx, a German philosopher of the 19th century, used communism to criticize the predominant Western capitalist and economic systems. The Russian October Revolution of 1917, under the leadership of Vladimir Lenin, provided a model for the Chinese to follow. Lenin attempted to turn Marx's ideas into a reality through a bloody revolution, establishing the first communist state, the Soviet Union. Mao was drawn to Marxism-Leninism and the Russian experience and became a revolutionary, joining with 50 others to found the CCP in 1921. Mao's successful strategy of cooperating with Jiang Jieshi (Chiang Kai-shek) (1887–1975), leader of the Guomindang (GMD, or Kuomintang, KMT, the Chinese Nationalist Party) and mobilizing guerrilla warfare behind Japanese lines in the Anti-Japanese War increased CCP members from 40,000 in 1937 to 1.2 million with more than 1 million regular troops and 2 million militia by 1945 at the end of World War II. Their successful experience convinced Chinese communist leaders such as Mao that a new China would follow the Soviet model after the CCP took over the country in 1949.

During the early 1950s, Mao carried out Soviet-style social and economic reforms. The Chinese Communist revolution established a new socioeconomic system based on Soviet Marxism-Leninism and modified it to fit the Chinese situation, resulting in Mao Zedong Thought. Between 1949 and 1979, the Communist government, following Marxist concepts, declared religion to be deceptive, monstrous, and perverse. This definition was based on two arguments: first, that religion was a man-made illusion, or, to use Marx's phrase, the opium of the people; second, it served as a tool through which Western imperialists and other dominating classes could gain spiritual control over Old China. After 1949, religious practice was condemned, and, in most cases, prohibited. In the 1950s, many churches and temples were shut down and congregations dismantled, as the government followed policies of persecution. Naturally, religion became a major target of the Cultural Revolution (1966–1976), and during the Destruction of Four Olds campaign in the late 1960s and early 1970s, the Red Guards burned Bibles, tortured monks and nuns, and destroyed many religious institutes.

By 1976, when Mao died in Beijing, China was a totalitarian state captivated by his cult of personality. In 1977, Deng Xiaoping (Deng Hsiao-ping) (1904–1997) staged his third comeback as head of the CCP in a new generation of leadership. Firmly in control of Beijing and having removed the Maoists, Deng made a historical speech, "Emancipate the Mind," at the Third Plenary Session of the CCP Eleventh Central Committee in 1978—a declaration of unprecedented seismic reform and an opening to the world to bring about the Four Modernizations to China. After Deng's retirement, Jiang Zemin (1926–) gradually shifted the party's ideology and political goals from radical communism to moderate nationalism. The leaders began to emphasize national interests, traditions, and patriotism in order to mobilize popular support for their reform efforts. The Chinese nationalism, which was deeply rooted in the hearts of several generations, has risen significantly since the 1990s as a result of explosive growth during the previous 20 years.

China today has little in common with the Cold War China of 1949–1978. Official scholars have brought back Confucianism and nationalism as ruling philosophies and ideologies, subjects that had been destroyed during the CCP's revolutions in the 1960s. Nevertheless, this pragmatic nationalism has not yet improved the condition of civil and human rights in the PRC. This ideology is dictated by the government to pursue China's unity, strength, prosperity, and dignity rather than to value human rights and democracy at its core.

In past decades, China has seen a surge in the number of people turning to religions such as Buddhism, Islam, Protestantism, Catholicism, and Daoism. As a result of rapid economic growth and sweeping social, ideological and political change, more and more Chinese people are searching for meaning and emotional stability in their lives. According to official statistics in 2008, there were more than 250 million followers of various religious faiths. The Chinese government has become more tolerant of officially recognized churches, temples, and religious groups by pursuing a more flexible policy. There are now more than 85,000 sites for religious activities, 300,000 clergy, and more than 3,000 religious organizations. In addition, there are 74 religious schools and colleges run by ecumenical organizations for training clerical personnel. The government still maintains control of religious exercises through a registration process and national organizations. All theistic groups must be registered with the authorities, and the worship and services must be held in a government-controlled church, mosques, or temple. All religious activities, publications, personnel hiring and promotion, and social events must get official approval. Oversight is also empowered by top-down national organizations. Among the five officially recognized religions are the Buddhist Association of China, Daoist Association of China, Islamic Association of China, Chinese Patriotic Catholic Association, Chinese Catholic Bishop's College, Three-Self Patriotic Movement Committee of the Protestant Churches of China, and the China Christian Council. All local groups must incorporate themselves into these national institutions. Additionally, teachings in these associations are monitored and sometimes modified by the government. It further scrutinizes their membership, financial records, and employees. The national organizations retain the right to approve or deny applications for any sub-group activities. Those who fail to register are considered illegal and may be subject to criminal prosecution, fines, and closure.

The ruling party has its own political considerations, since the CCP is still an atheistic party and must protect its own political base. The party's members, approximately 88 million in the 2015, have not been allowed to practice any religion and are required to commit themselves to the atheistic revolutionary cause. Some members privately violate this rule, as doing so openly can limit their political career and professional development.

Further Reading

Bays, Daniel. *A New History of Christianity in China*. Hoboken, NJ: Wiley-Blackwell, 2011.

Chan, Alan. *Philosophy and Religion in Early Medieval China*. Albany: State University of New York Press, 2011.

Israeli, Raphael. *Islam in China: Religion, Ethnicity, Culture, and Politics*. Lanham, MD: Lexington Books, 2007.

Lopez, Donald. *Religions of China in Practice*. Princeton, NJ: Princeton University Press, 1996.

Reid, T. R. *Confucius Lives Next Door: What Living in the East Teaches Us about Living in the West*. New York: Vintage, 2000.

Yan, Xuetong. *Ancient Chinese Thought, Modern Chinese Power*. Princeton, NJ: Princeton University Press, 2013.

Yang, Fenggang. *Religion in China: Survival and Revival under Communist Rule*. Oxford, UK: Oxford University Press, 2011.

Zhang, Dainian, and Edmund Ryden. *Key Concepts in Chinese Philosophy*. New Haven, CT: Yale University Press, 2000.

Buddhism

As the major religion in China, Buddhism was founded by Buddha, known as Shakyamuni or Prince Siddhartha Gautama, around 500 BCE in today's Nepal. His Dharma teachings were introduced by the Indian Buddhist monks along the Silk Road to China during the Han dynasty (206 BCE–220 CE). The essence of Buddhism, which was expressed in the Fourth Noble Truths and Eightfold Path, offers the "middle way" between extremes of self-indulgence and self-mortification. The end goal was Nirvana, the breaking of the chain of existence through the ending of all desires. As an organized universal faith, its personalized modification, tolerance for other religious concepts, and peaceful lifestyle soon gained popularity in China. The fourth to eighth centuries were called the Buddhist Age of both Chinese and East Asian history. The founder of the Sui dynasty (581–618) was Yang Jian or Sui Wendi (reigned 581–604) who was raised by a Buddhist nun and later married a pious Buddhist wife. During the succeeding Tang dynasty (618–907), one of the most prosperous dynasties in Chinese history, several emperors, including Wu Zhao, also known as Empress Wuzetian (reigned 684–704), the only female emperor in Chinese history, claimed themselves as Buddhists. Among other Tang monks was Xuanzang (602–664), who traveled to India, studied Buddhism for 15 years, and brought back 657 Buddhist scriptures. Among the traditional religions, Buddhism is not only popular in China, but also represents different ways of life and many minority groups, such as the Tibetans, with a total population of 3 million.

There are more than 80 million Buddhist followers in today's People's Republic of China (PRC). Buddhism has a total of 13,000 temples, including 3,000 Tibetan and 1,600 Pali structures. These structures house approximately 200,000 Buddhist monks and nuns, including 120,000 lamas and more than 10,000 Bhiksu and senior monks. Nevertheless, the Chinese government maintains control of religious exercises through a registration process and through national organizations. All theistic groups must be registered with the authorities, and, while China recognizes the right to believe, there is limited worship in a state-controlled system of registered and controlled churches, congregations, mosques, monasteries, and temples. Oversight is also empowered by top-down national organizations. Among the five officially recognized religions is the Buddhist Association of China. All local groups must incorporate themselves into these national institutions. Additionally, teachings in these associations are monitored and sometimes modified by the government.

The government also maintains control through leadership choices. The Chinese authorities, for example, have the power to ensure that no new Living Buddha can be identified. After the Panchen Lama died in 1989, the search began in Tibet to locate a soul boy as the reincarnation of the Panchen Lama and as a new Living Buddha for Tibetan Buddhism. The Dalai Lama followed Tibetan Buddhist tradition and completed the search in May 1995. The spiritual leader of Tibetan Buddhism announced that the search had identified the 11th reincarnation of the Panchen Lama. The Chinese government denied the recommendation by the Dalai Lama (1935–) in America. The government continues to exercise political control over Buddhist exercises in Tibet by restricting religious study before age 18, removing unapproved monks from monasteries, implementing quotas on the total number of monks in an attempt to reduce the spiritual population, and forcing recitation of patriotic scripts in support of the Chinese government.

Beijing continues to force denunciation of the Dalai Lama as a spiritual leader, a human rights fighter, and a peace envoy. Regionalism remains high, and some Tibetan Buddhists have been arrested, detained without public trial, and tortured, for expressing their views or for organizing activities without government permission. On September 30, 2006, Chinese border patrol troops opened fire on 70 Tibetans who tried to cross the border into Nepal. A 17-year-old Buddhist nun died and several others were wounded. In March 2008, a large-scale Buddhist demonstration began in Tibet and several surrounding provinces on the anniversary of the 1959 uprising in Tibet against the PRC Central government. On March 14, the protest in Lhasa turned violent between Tibetans and non-Tibetan groups and between protesters and police. On March 28, the government confirmed that 28 civilians and one police officer were dead, and 325 civilians were injured, 58 of whom were critically wounded. According to the India-based Tibetan government-in-exile, more than 220 Tibetans were killed in the crackdown after March 14, and the Chinese government arrested over 7,000 Tibetans from various parts of Tibet.

See also: Chapter 3: Civil Rights; Human Rights. Chapter 5: Overview; Dalai Lama. Chapter 6: Major Ethnic Groups. Chapter 11: *Journey to the West*. Chapter 12: Chinese Silk and the Silk Road.

Further Reading

Gernet, Jacques. *Buddhism in Chinese Society*. New York: Columbia University Press, 1998.

Kieschnick, John. *The Impact of Buddhism on Chinese Material Culture*. Princeton, NJ: Princeton University Press, 2003.

Marcello, Patricia Cronin. *The Dalai Lama: A Biography*. Westport, CT: Greenwood, 2003.

Shakya, Tsering. *The Dragon in the Land of Snows: A History of Modern Tibet since 1947*. New York: Penguin, 2000.

Catholicism

Roman Catholicism was introduced to China by the Italian priest John of Montecorvino, who built a church at Beijing, China's capital, in 1299 during the Yuan dynasty (1271–1368). By 1300 there were approximately 6,000 to 30,000 Chinese converts. Another Franciscan priest, the Venerable Gabriele Allegra, completed the first translation of the Catholic Bible into the Chinese language in 1368. After the Catholic Reformation, Matteo Ricci established the permanent mission of the Catholic Church in 1601, during the Ming dynasty (1368–1644). The first emperor of the Qing dynasty (1644–1911) appointed a German Jesuit, Adam Schall von Bell, as director of the Board of Astronomy in 1644. The Benedictines of St. Vincent Archabbey established the Catholic University of Peking in 1925. After World War II ended in 1945, there were more than 4 million Chinese Catholics in 3,080 missions, served by 2,557 Chinese priests. China presently has 5 million Catholics, 4,000 clergy, and more than 4,600 churches and meeting houses. According to official reports, each church has 700 believers. According to the Vatican and other Catholic sources, it is suggested that the number of converts is closer to 10 million, and that half of them worship outside the state-managed churches.

The government of the People's Republic of China (PRC) maintains control of religious exercises through a registration process and national organizations. All Catholic churches must be registered with the authorities, and, while China recognizes the right to believe, worship is limited to a state-controlled system of registered and controlled churches. The official registration process requires government vetting and continuing scrutiny of publications, seminary applications, and personnel. Oversight is also empowered by top-down national organizations. Among the five officially recognized religions is the Chinese Patriotic Catholic Association, along with the Chinese Catholic Bishop's College, Three-Self Patriotic Movement Committee of the Protestant Churches of China, and the China Christian Council. All local groups are required to incorporate themselves into these national institutions. Additionally, teachings in these associations are monitored and sometimes modified by the government, which further scrutinizes membership, financial records, and employees. The national organizations retain the right to approve or deny applications for any sub-group activities. Those who fail to register are considered illegal and may be subject to criminal prosecution, fines, and closure.

The government also maintains control through leadership choices and an activity approval system. In 1998, for example, the government barred the outspoken Hong Kong Catholic bishop Joseph Zen from traveling to mainland China following a speech he gave in the Vatican that attacked the communist country's lack of religious freedom. He repeated demands that Beijing release detained underground Catholic bishops and to provide religious freedom to all to worship outside of state-backed "patriotic" organizations. In April 2005, after Pope John Paul II died in the Vatican, China permitted officially sponsored prayers for the deceased, but refused to send an envoy to his funeral. In Beijing alone, nearly 10,000 Catholics attended masses held in five major Catholic churches. Officially sanctioned ceremonies were also held in Shanghai, Tianjin, and other major cities. Many religious activists have asserted that the government of the PRC is unlikely to ever allow direct ties between Chinese Catholics and the Vatican.

The growth of religious groups in China is tempered by state control and persecution. The state-approval system prevents the rise of groups or sources of authority, outside the control of the government. Reprisals against non-registered groups have primarily focused on Christians who, for various reasons, attend "house churches" or "underground churches." Some Catholics remain loyal to the pope in the Vatican rather than the Chinese Patriotic Catholic Association. The Vatican insists that it has ultimate authority over doctrine and the appointment of Catholic church officials. What has made Beijing even angrier is that the Vatican still maintains its diplomatic relations with the government of the Republic of China (ROC) on Taiwan.

See also: Chapter 1: Hong Kong; Taiwan. Chapter 3: Civil Rights. Chapter 5: Overview; Christianity; Underground Churches.

Further Reading

Chu, Cindy Yik-yi. *The Catholic Church in China: 1978 to the Present*. London: Palgrave Macmillan, 2014.

Clark, Anthony. *China's Saints: Catholic Martyrdom during the Qing (1644–1911)*. Bethlehem, PA: Lehigh University Press, 2013.

Madsen, Richard. *China's Catholics: Tragedy and Hope in an Emerging Civil Society*. Berkeley: University of California Press, 1998.

Yan, Kejia. *Catholic Church in China*. Beijing: China Intercontinental, 2004.

Christianity

As the third largest religious doctrine in China, Christianity includes Catholicism, Protestantism, and Eastern Orthodoxy. Christianity was introduced to China in approximately 635 during the Tang dynasty (618–906). The first emperor of the Qing dynasty (1644–1911) appointed a German Jesuit, Adam Schall von Bell, as director of the Board of Astronomy in 1644. Protestant Christianity was introduced to southern China after the Opium War of 1840. The Taiping Rebellion in 1850–1864, a major uprising that came close to overthrowing the Qing dynasty, was influenced by Protestant teaching. The millenarian Christian leader Hong Xiuquan (Hung Hsiu-ch'uan) (1814–1864) told his followers that he was the younger brother of Jesus Christ. Christianity became popular after the 1911 Revolution since some Chinese leaders, including Sun Yat-sen (1866–1925), the first president of the Republic of China (ROC), were converts to Christianity and influenced by its teachings. Chiang Kai-shek (Jiang Jieshi) (1887–1975), ROC president in 1928–1931 and 1943–1975 and premier in 1931–1943, was also converted from Buddhism to Christianity in the 1930s.

More than 1 million Christians are in today's Taiwan (ROC); one half are Catholic and the other half Protestants. Protestants total 20 million in the People's Republic of

China (PRC), including 18,000 clergy, 12,000 churches, and 25,000 meeting places. In an apparent attempt to contain the flood of new Christian converts, authorities in Beijing have built two new churches in the capital, each of which accommodates approximately 1,000 congregants. The city's Religious Affairs Office stated that the city government will continue to endorse the officially recognized Beijing Municipal Christian Association.

Nestorian Christianity was introduced to China during the Tang dynasty and its missionary built Daqin Pagoda in Xi'an, Tang's capital city. During the Qing dynasty, Russian Orthodox missionaries arrived in Manchuria in 1685 when Russians settled in the captured territory along the Heilongjiang (Amur River). An Orthodox Archimandrite, Hilarion, established a mission in Beijing, the Qing's capital in 1715. The church was nearly destroyed, and more than 220 Chinese Orthodox Christians were killed during the Boxer Rebellion in June 1900. China had 106 Orthodox churches by 1949, serving more than 10,000 converts. Many of these churches were destroyed during the Cultural Revolution (1966–1976).

The PRC government maintains control of religious exercises through a registration process and national organizations. All Christian groups are required to be registered with the authorities, and, while China recognizes the right to believe, worship is limited to a state-controlled system of registered and controlled churches and congregations. All religious activities, publications, personnel hiring and promotion, and social events must get official approval. Oversight is also empowered by top-down national organizations. Among the five officially recognized religions are the Chinese Patriotic Catholic Association, Chinese Catholic Bishop's College, Three-Self Patriotic Movement Committee of the Protestant Churches of China, and the China Christian Council. All local groups must incorporate themselves into these national institutions. Additionally, teachings in these associations are monitored and sometimes modified by the government, which further scrutinizes membership, financial records, and employees. The national organizations retain the right to approve or deny applications for any subgroup activities. Those who fail to register are considered illegal and may be subject to criminal prosecution, fines, and closure.

The growth of religious groups in China is tempered by state control and by persecution. The state-approval system prevents the rise of groups or sources of authority outside the control of the government. Reprisals against non-registered groups have primarily focused on the Christians who attend, for various reasons, "house churches" or "underground churches." Many new Christians choose to worship outside of state-run churches. The official number of Protestants is 20 million, and church statistics estimate that there are more than 40 million Protestants in China today. Some of the "underground" Christian churches receive financial and biblical assistance from overseas, and it is also true that foreign religious groups may support Catholic and Protestant "underground" congregations.

See also: Chapter 1: Taiwan. Chapter 2: Chiang Kai-shek; Lin Zexu and the Opium War; Sun Yat-sen. Chapter 3: Civil Rights. Chapter 5: Overview; Catholicism; Underground Churches.

Further Reading

Aikman, David. *Jesus in Beijing: How Christianity Is Transforming China and Changing the Global Balance of Power*. New York: Regnery Publishing, 2006.

Bays, Daniel. *Christianity in China: From the Eighteenth Century to the Present*. Stanford, CA: Stanford University Press, 1999.

Bays, Daniel. *A New History of Christianity in China*. Hoboken, NJ: Wiley-Blackwell, 2011.

Clark, Anthony, ed. *A Voluntary Exile: Chinese Christianity and Cultural Confluence since 1552*. Bethlehem, PA: Lehigh University Press, 2013.

Yang, Huilin. *China, Christianity, and the Question of Culture*. Waco, TX: Baylor University Press, 2014.

Confucianism

A combination of several ancient thoughts, Confucianism is a humanistic philosophy that emphasizes the close ties between humans and nature. The founder of Confucianism, Confucius (551–479 BCE) was born in Zouyi in the State of Lu (present Qufu, Shandong) in the late Spring-Autumn Period (722–481 BCE) and Warring States Period (475–221 BCE) during the Eastern Zhou dynasty (771–221 BCE). Confucius emphasized moral conduct, including inner integrity (*zhi*), righteousness (*yi*), loyalty (*zhong*), proper behavior (*li*), and filial piety (*xiao*) as necessary qualities of a gentleman or a man of nobility. Confucianism upholds a man's position in his society, his relations with others, as well as his duties and responsibilities. It explains human nature or the natural laws of human beings through an ethical approach, whereas the Greek philosophers espoused the same through logic, mathematics, physics, or religious approaches.

Confucianism emphasizes a social order that includes good family relationships and a moral government. It justified a paternalistic family pattern, emphasizing the father's rule as the family authority, or the emperor in the political power center, and family members and the people were under an absolute obligation to obey. As children of the emperor, the Chinese people observed traditional ideas, ethical codes, suitable relations, and a mutual obligation between the emperor and themselves to serve the empire for their own welfare and protection. An individual might receive some limited freedoms through his/her loyalty to the emperor, being trusted by authority, and by working hard for the government. Paternalistic rule was dependent on Confucian ethics and was not secured by a system of formal legal and institutional safeguards.

Among other scholars who joined Confucius was Mencius (Men-tzu) (372–289 BCE), one of the principal interpreters of Confucianism and the most famous Confucian after Confucius himself. Mencius's paradigm idea of meritocracy is in part inspired by the introduction of the imperial examination system into traditional China. This system was well established by the Song dynasty (960–1279), and continued until 1905.

Confucian teaching emphasizes that moral conduct, inner integrity, righteousness, and kind heartedness should be used to create a harmonious society. In Chinese life, one's virtues of decency, loyalty, sincerity, and benevolence, which are taught by parents, grandparents, and relatives, provide the norms for social conduct. Confucian basic political conservatism makes it a controlling ideology used by most subsequent governments in China, Taiwan, and Hong Kong. The Chinese government currently uses this idealized philosophy of the past as a social and political ethos. The balanced nature of Confucianism may help explain its popularity and success in China and Asian countries such as Korea, Japan, Vietnam, and Singapore. The works of Confucius were translated into European languages by Jesuit scholars stationed in China in the 1600s. Since it became popular, Confucianism faced a number of critiques, especially in modern times. Some critics claim Confucius has a negative view of women because he stated that women should have no dignity and fewer rights than men. Some scholars argue that Confucianism has heavily shaped the Chinese people in the past 2,000 years, limiting their rights and their freedom.

See also: Chapter 2: Overview; Timeline; Confucius. Chapter 5: Overview. Chapter 7: Gender Inequality.

Further Reading

Bell, Daniel, and Hahm Chaibong, eds. *Confucianism for the Modern World.* Cambridge, UK: Cambridge University Press, 2003.

Gardner, Daniel. *Confucianism: A Very Short Introduction.* Oxford, UK: Oxford University Press, 2014.

Gardner, Daniel. *The Four Books: The Basic Teachings of the Later Confucian Tradition.* Indianapolis, IN: Hackett, 2007.

Goldin, Paul R. *Confucianism.* Berkeley: University of California Press, 2011.

Sun, Anna. *Confucianism as a World Religion: Contested Histories and Contemporary Realities.* Princeton, NJ: Princeton University Press, 2013.

Yao, Xinzhong. *An Introduction to Confucianism.* Cambridge, UK: Cambridge University Press, 2000.

Dalai Lama (1935–)

Buddhist spiritual leader and Tibetan in exile since 1959, His Holiness the Dalai Lama was born Lhamo Dhondrub on July 6, 1935, in Taktser, Tibet (Xizang), to a peasant family. In 1937 he was recognized by Tibetan Buddhist authorities as the reincarnation of the 13th Buddhist Lord of Compassion. On February 22, 1940, he was enthroned as the 14th Dalai Lama, beginning his reign in the Potala, a 1,000-room palace in Lhasa, the capital city of Tibet. The Dalai Lama's education began when he was six years old, directed by Buddhist monks. It ended in 1959 when he was awarded the Geshe Lharampa degree (doctorate of Buddhist philosophy).

After the People's Republic of China (PRC) was founded in 1949, the government of the Chinese Communist Party (CCP) called upon the Dalai Lama to assume the role of the Tibetan leader on November 17, 1950. The following year, Beijing and Tibet signed the Agreement on Measures for the Peaceful Liberation of Tibet. The People's Liberation Army (PLA) then entered Tibet. During the 1950s, the Dalai Lama engaged in a policy aimed at preserving Tibetan traditional religious and political structures while attempting to negotiate with PRC leaders. In March 1959, Lhasa erupted in violence after a huge anti-CCP demonstration was savagely crushed by the PLA. Beijing accused the Dalai Lama of backing a separatist movement. Fearing for his safety, his advisers counseled the Dalai Lama to flee Tibet. He escaped into India and took up residence in Dharamshala, the official seat of the Tibetan government-in-exile.

Since his forced exile, the Dalai Lama has constantly sought to focus the world's attention on the plight of the Tibetan people, even appealing to the United Nations for support. He has also encouraged Tibetans to engage in nonviolent civil disobedience against CCP rule. He displayed considerable diplomatic and political skill in presenting Tibet's case on the

The exiled spiritual leader of Tibetan Buddhism, Tenzin Gyatso, the 14th Dalai Lama, has maintained a vigilant effort to focus international attention on the plight of his people, whom he left behind after his exile in 1959. Gyatso received the Nobel Peace Prize in 1989 for his efforts. (Shutterstock.com)

international stage, winning widespread respect. In 1989 the Dalai Lama was awarded the Nobel Peace Prize for his nonviolent opposition to Tibetan occupation. The PRC continues to denounce the Dalai Lama's "interference" and "sabotage" against China. In 1995, the Chinese government issued a document titled "State Administration for Religious Affairs," which includes 14 regulations designed to limit the influence of the Dalai Lama. Most notably, it declares that no "Living Buddha [may be reincarnated] without government approval."

The numerous publications of the Dalai Lama—both political and spiritual in nature—as well as constant traveling to make personal appeals for support, along with his non-confrontational approach, began bearing fruit in 2002. That year he again undertook negotiations with the Chinese government for Tibetan autonomy, which are still ongoing. In 2014, U.S. President Barack Obama again met the Dalai Lama in the White House, after similar meetings in 2010 and 2011. The Dalai Lama hinted in 2015 that he might not be reincarnated, if Beijing continues its control of Buddhist succession in Tibet.

See also: Chapter 3: Chinese Communist Party; Civil Rights; Human Rights; People's Liberation Army. Chapter 5: Buddhism. Chapter 6: Major Ethnic Groups.

Further Reading

Dalai Lama. *Freedom in Exile: The Autobiography of the Dalai Lama*. New York: Harper Perennial, 2008.

Laird, Thomas. *The Story of Tibet: Conversations with the Dalai Lama*. New York: Grove, 2007.

Marcello, Patricia Cronin. *The Dalai Lama: A Biography*. Westport, CT: Greenwood, 2003.

Piburn, Sidney. *The Dalai Lama: A Policy of Kindness*. Ithaca, NY: Snow Lion, 1990.

Strober, Deborah, and Gerald Strober. *His Holiness the Dalai Lama: An Oral Biography*. Hoboken, NJ: Wiley, 2005.

Daoism (Taoism)

A classic philosophy and an ancient religion explain the natural world and the human race as existing through natural law. The founder of Daoism, Laozi (Lao-Tzu, "old fellow") was born around 400 BCE. Disappointed by civil wars and social disorder during the Warring States Period (403–221 BCE) of the Eastern Zhou (Chou) dynasty (1027–221 BCE), he fled from his hometown to a remote mountainous area, choosing to live alone while studying nature. He wrote *Dao De Jing* (*Tao Te Ching, The Classic of the Way and Virtue*), denouncing political and military struggles as unnatural, and calling for a return to nature, to primitive, agrarian life. His book became the foundation of Daoism, a philosophy, religion, and system of magic in China and East Asia. Zhuangzi (Chuang-tzu, 369–286 BCE), Laozi's most famous follower, also made great contributions to Daoism.

Laozi believed that, since the Dao was the essence of all, it cannot be named or captured, that there are natural rules beyond the human world, and that it was important for people or their rulers to not merely act or react. The Dao, as the source and ideal of all existence, is immensely powerful but remains unseen. While Confucianism commands people to conform to the standards of an ideal social system, Daoism urged that people should ignore the dictates of society and seek only to conform to the underlying pattern of the universe, the Dao (the "way"). All things and lives have their own way, described by Laozi as Yin-Yang: the harmony of opposites through their interdependency and interaction.

The symbol of Yin-Yang sums up all of life's basic oppositions: good and evil, strong and weak, life and death, positive and negative, high and low, cold and hot, light and dark, male and female, are all pairs of opposite aspects of a unity, and these can be transformed into one another. Though principles are in tension, they are never strictly opposed. Instead, they complement and counterbalance one other. Ultimately, apparent opposites penetrate one another (the element in the center of each) and are encompassed by a circle, symbolizing a final unity. Because all oppositions are ultimately subsumed in Daoism, all values are relative.

Laozi also believed that there were correlations of five basic elements (*wuxing*) in the universe, including wood, fire, earth, metal, and water. Like Yin-Yang, the five-element correlations were used in his thought processes to indicate both cosmic activities and conceptual categories. In either case, the pattern of movement was one of ceaseless alteration and cyclical change. The order of the elements and the process by which one displaced another varied according to different schemes. In such cases, people's desires, wills, and acts may be unnatural and thus upset the natural balance of the Dao. Alongside the philosophical and mystical approach, Daoism developed on a popular level as a cult, in which immortality was sought through magic and the use of various elixirs. It also became more practical in China and Japan, when martial art masters followed the Daoist ideology to develop "Qi-gong" (body energy control), "Tai-chi quan," and many other exercises. Astrologists developed the "Feng-shui" horoscope for people's everyday life.

In about 100 CE, the popular Daoist religion emerged by worshiping Laozi, adopting an extensive pantheon, and establishing institutional monasticism. Daoism was recognized as the official religion of China for several periods through its imperial history. In the People's Republic of China (PRC) today, Daoism is the second largest religion, after Buddhism. Among the five officially recognized religions are the Daoist Association of China, which has 45 million followers, with a total of more than 1,500 temples and more than 25,000 priests and nuns. Daoist religion is also popular in Hong Kong, Taiwan, Korea, and Japan.

See also: Chapter 1: Taiwan. Chapter 2: Laozi. Chapter 5: Overview; Feng-Shui. Chapter 10: Chinese Zodiac; Heavenly Stems and Earthly Branches; Symbols of Auspice in Tradition. Chapter 15: Qi-Gong; Tai-Chi Quan.

Further Reading

Bokenkamp, Stephen. *Early Daoist Scriptures*. Berkeley: University of California Press, 1999.

Heider, John. *The Tao of Leadership: Lao Tzu's Tao Te Ching Adapted for a New Age*. Palm Beach, FL: Green Dragon, 2005.

Pregadio, Fabrizio. *Great Clarity: Daoism and Alchemy in Early Medieval China*. Stanford, CA: Stanford University Press, 2006.

Zhang, Dainian, and Edmund Ryden. *Key Concepts in Chinese Philosophy*. New Haven, CT: Yale University Press, 2000.

Falun Gong

This is one of the "Qi-gong" (body energy control) based exercise groups established in China in May 1992. As founder of the Falun Gong, Li Hongzhi (1951–) explained the group's name as meaning "Dharma Wheel Practice," or "Falun Dafa." Li called it "Dafa," meaning "the Great Law," or the "Great Law of the Dharma Wheel." The group's practices include five sets of simple slow motion breathing "Qi-gong" exercises meant to increase health and spirit. Regular practice will put a "dharma wheel" into the lower abdomen, which believers can rotate to release energy for their needs. The ultimate objective of practicing Falun Gong is to "attain the Dao" (way of the Buddha). According to Li, Falun Gong, as one of the Buddhist laws, could help those who truly seek salvation through a lifetime of commitment to the practice, and eventually lead to their "consummation." In an interview in early 1999, before the government purged his group, Li told *Time* magazine that the group's practices "are primarily aimed at healing illnesses or keeping fit and maintaining good health. I am teaching a higher level of qigong."

In the mid-1990s, the group spread into almost every province of China. It evolved into a religious cult with characteristics attractive to many Chinese, including the middle class, elderly women, and weak elements of society. In 1997, Falun Gong claimed to have 100 million members, while the government has put estimates at 10 million. Problems began when more and more CCP (Chinese Communist Party) members participated in its daily practices and large assemblies, which were often held at city centers. The local party committees and governments tried to stop party members from participating and limited their exercise grounds. In 1997–1998, practitioners presented a number of appeals and petitions, but achieved negligible results. On April 25, 1999, 10,000 members of Falun Gong gathered at Zhongnanhai, the residential compound of the country's top leaders, an action that finally led Jiang Zemin (1926–), president of the People's Republic of China (PRC), to persecute the group.

On July 20, 1999, the government banned Falun Gong and declared it unlawful as an "evil cult." On July 29, the authorities ordered the arrest of the group's founder and leader, Li Hongzhi. The party leadership then began a nationwide crackdown by mobilizing every aspect of society to become involved in the persecution, including the police, army, media, workplaces, educational system, and families. The campaign was driven by large-scale propaganda through television, newspaper, radio, and Internet announcements. The organization estimated that nearly 90,000 members were arrested, 60,000 of whom were tortured in prison, and 3,000 died during or after their incarceration or forced labor.

Following the 1999 edict, protests in the cities were frequent, but have now been largely eradicated. From January to July 2008, for example, 586 Falun Gong members were arrested in the Beijing area alone. Many Falun Gong practitioners fled the country. Many of them have regrouped in Hong Kong and Taiwan. They are also active in appealing to foreign governments, Western media, and people of their respective countries, in order to protest the situation in China.

See also: Chapter 1: Hong Kong; Taiwan. Chapter 2: Jiang Zemin and Sino-U.S. Relations. Chapter 3: Chinese Communist Party; Civil Rights; Human Rights. Chapter 5: Buddhism; Daoism. Chapter 15: Qi-Gong; Tai-Chi Quan.

Further Reading

Chang, Maria Hsia. *Falun Gong: The End of Days*. New Haven, CT: Yale University Press, 2004.

Ownby, David. *Falun Gong and the Future of China*. Oxford, UK: Oxford University Press, 2008.

Penny, Benjamin. *The Religion of Falun Gong*. Chicago: University of Chicago Press, 2012.

Schechter, Danny. *Falun Gong's Challenge to China: Spiritual Practice or Evil Cult*. New York: Akashic Books, 2001.

Feng-Shui

The authentic school of Feng-shui (or *Fengshui*) is the classic Daoist (Taoist) conception behind the mandate of heaven. In ancient China, Feng-shui was originally the branch of philosophic knowledge in which Daoist scholars studied astronomy and geography and expressed their view of the universe and the environment, and their priorities and interactions. It brought together the three elements of time, place, and Man in a system for distinguishing good and ill fortune.

After the Han dynasty (206 BCE–220 CE) Feng-shui became popular when some Daoist practitioners consistently found ways to make direct connections between personal circumstances and movements of the stars and earth. This enhanced the practical usefulness of Feng-shui, and its sphere of application gradually became restricted to the divination of individual fortunes. Practitioners continually injected such ingredients as the eight trigrams, the five elements, and finally the principles of fortune-telling, so the factors on which judgments were to be based became more and more complex. Furthermore, the Song (960–1279) Confucian philosopher Zhu Xi (Chu Hsi) (1130–1200) had high praise for Feng-shui, so that in later times, with this classic authority to back them up, scholars, officials, and the rich and powerful felt no qualms about openly and confidently supporting Feng-shui.

Today Feng-shui and fortune-telling books have their own special section in bookstores in Taiwan, Hong Kong, and China, and they sell well. Chinese newspapers also have their special sections for Feng-shui advertisements. Some construction companies hire their own Feng-shui consultants to satisfy their customers' desire for auspicious housing. Many colleges in America and Europe offer Feng-shui classes, and they fill up quickly.

Many of the new generation of Feng-shui specialists have received higher education or even studied in Daoist temples, are well versed in logic, and can fluently draw on a wide range of evidence from physiology, psychology, biology, and even cosmology. They apply their training in academic logic to the study and practice of Feng-shui, marshalling individual cases, drawing inferences and analyzing, and are quite able to expound their own pet theories.

Most Feng-shui specialists use two of Chinese astrological systems: *bazi* (*ba tzu*), or "eight words," also called "the four pillars," and *jiuxing* (*jyo hsing*), or "nine stars," also called "the study of qi" (*chi*). *Bazi* requires the ability to work with the Chinese lunar calendar and with a large number of Chinese characters. *Jiuxing* is the Heavenly Stems and Earthly Branches system, the oldest known horoscope system. Heaven, earth, and man are the three coordinate powers. Heaven corresponds to time, earth corresponds to space, and man corresponds to the mind. Each individual associates herself or himself with certain outer and inner elements. The inner relations are between body and mind, feeling and thinking, and emotion and action. The outer relations are between human and earth and heaven, and between our world and the universe, which embraces Chinese astrology and divining theories; and one's relationship to earth can be found by using compass and form methods, based on horoscope principles and techniques.

See also: Chapter 1: Hong Kong; Taiwan. Chapter 5: Overview; Confucianism; Daoism; Chapter 10: Heavenly Stems and Earthly Branches; Lunar-Solar Calendar.

Further Reading

Brown, Simon. *The Feng Shui Bible: The Definitive Guide to Improving Your Life, Home, Health, and Finances*. New York: Sterling, 2005.

Carter, Karen Rauch. *Move Your Stuff, Change Your Life: How to Use Feng Shui to Get Love, Money, Respect, and Happiness*. New York: Simon & Schuster, 2000.

Sang, Larry. *The Principles of Feng Shui*. San Gabriel, CA: American Feng Shui Institute, 1995.

Wong, Eva. *A Master Course in Feng-shui*. Boston, MA: Shambhala, 2001.

Wu, Baolin, and Jessica Eckstein. *Lighting the Eye of the Dragon: Inner Secrets of Taoist Feng Shui*. New York: St. Martin's Press, 2000.

Islam

Rising as a religious movement in approximately 610 CE in today's Saudi Arabia, Islam was introduced to China through Arab and Persian merchants, travelers on the Silk Road. Chinese Muslims who mixed with the Hans and Mongols formed the Hui minority in the Song dynasty (960–1271). During the Yuan dynasty (1271–1368), hundreds of thousands of Muslim immigrants were relocated from Central and Western Asia by Mongols in an effort to help control the administration of China. The Ming dynasty (1368–1644) became the golden age of Islam in China when the Muslim population grew to more than 3 million. Many mosques were built, and some Muslims served in the hierarchy for Ming emperors such as Admiral Zheng He (Cheng Ho) (1399–1402). By the end of the Qing dynasty (1644–1911), there were 6–8 million Muslims in China, approximately 2 percent of the total population.

According to official reports from the People's Republic of China (PRC), Islam currently has a total population of 35 million in China. Their 30,000 mosques are served by 40,000 Imams and Akhunds, each mosque for about 1,170 Muslims. The government maintains control of religious exercises through a registration process and national organizations. All Islamic groups must be registered with the authorities, and worship is limited to a state-controlled system of registered and controlled mosques, monasteries, and temples. Among the five officially recognized religions is the Islamic Association of China. All local groups must incorporate themselves into the national institution. Additionally, teachings in these associations are monitored and sometimes modified by the government. Those who fail to register are considered illegal and may be subject to criminal prosecution, fines, and closure.

Among the traditional religions, Islam is not only popular, but also represents different ways of life and forms many of the minority groups in China. With a total population of 35 million, Islam has 10 minority groups among its adherents, including the Hui and Uygur in the northwestern Xinjiang Uyghur Autonomous Region (XUAR). Xinjiang's population is more than 20 million, including 12 million people from different minorities, such as Uygur, Kazak, Hui, and Mongolian. The region is primarily composed of Muslims, Buddhists (including Tibetan Buddhists), Protestants, Catholics, and Daoists. Most believers follow a faith along ethnic lines.

In November 2004, top Chinese officials in the XUAR government called for an intensification of "ideological work" among the ethnic Uyghur university students. Local officials were ordered to report anyone fasting during the month of Ramadan. In most Islamic countries, restaurants remain closed from dawn to dusk during Ramadan, when the majority of the adult population is fasting. This is not, however, the case in Xinjiang. City officials ensure that restaurants stay open, and college administrators must report anyone who appears to participate. In many grade schools, before the children leave school they receive free candy to eat. In June 2007, Xinjiang authorities began collecting Muslim passports in order to prevent them from making non-state-approved pilgrimages to Mecca. The XUAR government also indoctrinates clerics, civil servants, and teachers against the "three evil forces"—separatism, religious extremism, and terrorism.

In 2008, tensions mounted between the Uyghurs and the Han Chinese people. On July 5, 2009, more than 1,000 Uyghur demonstrators gathered in the commercial center of Urumqi, the capital city of XUAR, protesting the government's handling of the death of two Uyghur workers and demanding a full investigation of the killings. After confrontations with police, the peaceful demonstration escalated into riots from July 5–7. PAP (People's Armed Police) and city police attempted to quell the rioters with tear gas, water hoses, armored vehicles, and roadblocks, while the XUAR government imposed a curfew in Urumqi. According to government reports, 197 people died and 1,721 others were injured during the two-day riot.

See also: Chapter 1: Xinjiang. Chapter 2: Zheng He. Chapter 3: People's Armed Police. Chapter 5: Overview. Chapter 6: Major Ethnic Groups; Muslims; Uyghur. Chapter 12: Chinese Silk and the Silk Road.

Further Reading

Gladney, Dru. *Muslim Chinese: Ethnic Nationalism in the People's Republic.* 2nd ed. Cambridge, MA: Harvard University Press, 1996.

Israeli, Raphael. *Islam in China: Religion, Ethnicity, Culture, and Politics.* Lanham, MD: Lexington Books, 2007.

Lipman, Jonathan. *Familiar Strangers: A History of Muslims in Northwest China.* Seattle: University of Washington Press, 1998.

Mi, Shoujiang, and You Jia. *Islam in China.* Beijing: Chinese Intercontinental, 2004.

Starr, Frederick. *Xinjiang: China's Muslim Borderland.* Armonk, NY: M. E. Sharpe, 2004.

Zang, Xiaowei. *Islam, Family Life, and Gender Inequality in Urban China.* London: Routledge, 2014.

Underground Churches

The government of the People's Republic of China (PRC) maintains control of religious gatherings through a registration process and by monitoring national organizations. All Christian groups must be registered with the authorities, and, while China officially recognizes the right to believe, worship is limited to a state-controlled system of registered and controlled churches and congregations. The official registration process requires government vetting and continued scrutiny of publications, seminary applications, and personnel. Oversight is also empowered by top-down national organizations. Among the five officially recognized religions are the Chinese Patriotic Catholic Association, Chinese Catholic Bishop's College, Three-Self Patriotic Movement Committee of the Protestant Churches of China, and the China Christian Council. All local groups must incorporate themselves into one of these national institutions. Additionally, teachings in these associations are monitored and sometimes modified by the government, which scrutinizes membership, financial records, and employees. The national organizations retain the right to approve or deny applications for any subgroup activities. Those who fail to register are considered illegal and may be subject to criminal prosecution, fines, and closure.

The growth of religious groups in China is tempered by state control and persecution. The state-approval system prevents the rise of groups or sources of authority outside the control of the government. Reprisals against non-registered groups have primarily focused on Christians who, for various reasons, attend "house churches" or "underground churches." Some Catholics remain loyal to the pope in the Vatican rather than the Chinese Catholic Patriotic Association. The Vatican insists that it has ultimate authority over doctrine and the appointment of Catholic Church officials. The Chinese government believes that this is interference in China's internal affairs. What has made Beijing even angrier is that the Vatican still maintains its diplomatic relations with the government of the Republic of China (ROC) on Taiwan. For these reasons, many Catholics choose to worship outside the state-controlled congregations. Officially, there are about 5 million Catholics in China. The Vatican and other Catholic sources suggest that the number is closer to 10 million, and that half of them worship outside state-managed churches. Many of the new converts, especially among Christians, choose to worship outside state-run churches. The official number of Protestants is 20 million; however, church statistics estimate there are more than 40 million Protestants in China today. Some of the "underground" Christian churches receive financial and biblical assistance from overseas. It is also true that many foreign religious groups support Catholic and Protestant "underground" congregations.

The Chinese government dislikes religious groups and activities outside the system, and especially connections with foreign religious groups, which they see as reminiscent of missionary work of past Western imperialist aggression against China. On January 13, 1994, the State Council promulgated "The Administrative Regulations on Religious Sites," placing severe restrictions on family churches and citizens' faith-based activities. Since house churches operate outside state regulations and restrictions, their members are sometimes harassed by local government officials. Heavy fines are common and often result in the confiscation of personal effects in lieu of a payment that is ignored or unavailable. Sometimes this persecution takes the form of a prison sentence or re-education through manual labor.

In early April 2004, for example, Xu Shuangfu (or Xu Shengguang), leader of the group known as the "Three Grades of Servant," was abducted, along with another prominent house-church leader, by unidentified individuals driving a police jeep. The "Three Grades of Servant," or Church of Truth, is an unofficial religious group claiming millions of followers, based in northeast China. Some Westerners consider it an orthodox Christian house church network. On April 27, police in Heilongjiang raided some house churches of the "Three Grades of Servant," and arrested dozens of people. On July 7, 2006, the provincial court sentenced Xu to death and executed him immediately. The court also gave death sentences to 3 other church leaders with a two-year reprieve, which usually leads to a life sentence. Eleven church members received various sentences from 3 to 15 years in prison.

See also: Chapter 3: Civil Rights; Death Penalty; Law Enforcement. Chapter 5: Overview; Catholicism; Christianity.

Further Reading

Lian, Xi. *Redeemed by Fire: The Rise of Popular Christianity in Modern China*. New Haven, CT: Yale University Press, 2010.

Liao, Yiwu. *God Is Red: The Secret Story of How Christianity Survived and Flourished in Communist China*. New York: HarperOne, 2011.

Madsen, Richard. *China's Catholics: Tragedy and Hope in an Emerging Civil Society*. Berkeley: University of California Press, 1998.

Xin, Yalin. *Inside China's House Church Network*. Lexington, KY: Emeth, 2009.

Yang, Fenggang. *Religion in China: Survival and Revival under Communist Rule*. Oxford, UK: Oxford University Press, 2011

CHAPTER 6

SOCIAL CLASS AND ETHNICITY

OVERVIEW

In 1949–1985, Chinese society was fragmented into four major groups: farmers, consisting of 68 percent of workforce; workers, approximately 23 percent; professionals, 4–5 percent; and cadres, 2–3 percent. Disparities in political prestige, income, and education were obvious, and the ability of farmers and workers to "narrow the gap" in these areas was severely limited. After the mid-1980s, Chinese social strata have been in the process of restructuring in response to the rapid economic reform since 1978. The boundaries were diminished between different social statuses and between rural and urban residents that had been clearly and rigidly marked in the past. In the 1980s, the per capita annual net income of urban households was 6 to 10 times higher than that of rural households. Partly because of this inequality, agricultural laborers are also the most mobile. Understandably, they make constant efforts to squeeze into other social strata. Labor migration from rural to urban areas emerged as a nationwide phenomenon in the late 1980s.

The loosening of government control over people's mobility further allowed farmers to take up occupations originally only available to urban residents. By the early 1990s, the approximately 36 million individuals had made this move. By 1999, the composition of the social groups changed when farmers decreased to 46 percent; workers increased to 28 percent; professionals to 17 percent; administrators, approximately 3–5 percent. Since the turn of the century, the rapid change in China's traditional social strata has largely been perceived as beneficial to the healthy growth of its society. It increases opportunities for the general public and helps bring the social mechanisms of choice and reward to the general populace, a norm that did not exist in the past. In the early 2000s, as many as 100 million rural laborers were estimated to be on the move, seeking work in cities and coastal areas.

Government policies and the market economy function as the two major forces in bringing about the emergence of new social structures at the turn of the century. Among the new social classes are increased urban poor, a booming middle class, and wealthy entrepreneurs. The number of migrant workers totaled 120 million in 2005, 136 million in 2007, and 151 million in 2010. Official estimates suggest that as of 2014, more than 169 million peasants may have left the countryside. Since it takes time for many peasants to find full-time employment, they have become part of a mobile or "floating" urban population; that is, those who have no rights to housing, school, and health care. In large cities such as Beijing, Shanghai, Guangzhou, and Tianjin, about 2–4 million transients camped in train and bus stations as well as other public places. Rural workers are required to have six passes to work in cities or provinces other than their own and are often considered second-class citizens. Although rural migration urbanized the country by 2005, the problems of China's migrant laborers have become serious in terms of living conditions and their rights. China's industrialization is partly based on low wages paid to its workers, especially migrant workers, who consist of 46 percent of all urban employment in 2007. Some of these migrant workers are treated unfairly and many are underpaid. Approximately 74 percent of migrant laborers earn 580–1,400 yuan *renminbi* or RMB ($80–200) a month. Females comprise more than 30 percent of all migrant workers in the country.

Continued reform of the state-owned enterprises (SOEs) has resulted in increasingly more urban workers losing their jobs. Many workers have lost their "iron rice bowls," or secured incomes. It is estimated at least 35 million workers have lost their jobs at former SOEs, and many of them have joined the unemployed and urban poor. In the cities, more than 20 million residents are urban poor, depending on government and social welfare because they are not able to find a full-time job to support their families. According to official statistics, more than 31 million Chinese people were living below the poverty line by 2006. The poverty line in China is set at 2 yuan RMB ($0.33) a day, or 683 yuan ($113.83) a year, and at that rate a person does not have enough food to meet his or her basic needs. It is well below the international standard of poverty of $1 (6 yuan) a day or $365 (2,190 yuan) a year.

After 30 years of economic reform, more and more Chinese have improved their standard of living and moved into the middle class. The developing middle class includes managers, specialists, professional technicians, legal service staff, business administrators, and private business owners. The estimated number of the middle class increased from 13.8 percent of China's workforce in 1988, to 19 percent in 1999, and to 26.3 percent in 2010. Another striking feature of China's social classes in the 2010s is the rapid social stratification or polarization of wealth. In 2000, the combined estimated wealth of the top 50 richest entrepreneurs in China was $10 billion. The wealthiest was worth $2 billion and the number 50 slot was worth $42 million. For China's farmers, who account for more than one-third of the total population, the average annual wage was well below $500 the same year. According to *Forbes*, the top 100 richest Chinese were worth $376 billion in 2014, up 19 percent from 2013. The top three were Jack Ma worth $19.5 billion, Robin Li $14.7 billion, and Ma Huateng $14.4 billion.

The gap between rich and poor has widened. In 2003, the National Bureau of Statistics issued an official calculation of 0.375 as its Gini coefficient; by 2004, the Gini coefficient increased to 0.4725; and by 2014, it continued to increase to 0.474. For China's agricultural workers, who account for one-third of the total population, the average annual wage was $500 for 2004 and below $850 for 2014. The distribution of wealth is even more uneven for ethnic minorities.

China's minority population totals 112 million in 2014, about 8.5 percent of the national total, from 55 officially recognized ethnic groups. The minority population has increased from 67 million, about 6.7 percent of the national total in 1982, to 108.5 million, about 8 percent in 1995, according to the national census. The Han Chinese comprise the largest population, making up 91.5 percent of the country's total population. Among the 55 minorities in 2012 are 17 million Zhuang nationals, 11 million Hui, 10 million Manchus, 10 million Uygur, 9 million Miao, 6 million Tibetans, and 4 million Mongols, totaling 110.5 million, or about 8.5 percent of the total population. Among the 55 national minorities, excepting the Hui and Manchu who use the Chinese language, 53 have their own languages. Their spoken and written languages are used in judicial, administrative, and education fields, as well as in political activities and social life. Among the 55 ethnic groups, 44 live in certain provinces and counties under an autonomous government.

The five autonomous regions (provinces) where most minority ethnic groups live accommodate a large proportion of agricultural workers and other lower-income social groups. The five autonomous (provincial) regions are the Xinjiang Uygur Autonomous Region (XUAR), Tibet (Xizang) Autonomous Region (TAR), Inner Mongolia Autonomous Region (IMAR), Guangxi Zhuang Autonomous Region (GZAR), and Ningxia Hui Autonomous Region (NHAR), set aside for ethnic minorities. The five autonomous regions govern 30 autonomous prefectures (districts), 120 autonomous counties (or banners in IMAR), and 1,256 ethnic townships. About 44 of 55 ethnic groups live in their own autonomous areas, with a population of 75 percent of total minorities and a territory of 64 percent of the whole country.

Even though the minorities are the "majority" in these autonomous regions, they do not have a dominant influence in government. Local policies result from the support and concern of the Han Chinese-controlled regional and central governments, which have neglected minorities' basic needs, and have also used their land and resources without consultation. TAR and NHAR are among the three lowest GDP provinces in the country.

Many ethnic groups live on plains, hillsides, and remote mountainous areas with limited transportation and communication resources, while the Han Chinese live in cities and towns. Isolated from the outside world, these minority communities maintain economic backwardness and have limited resources to improve living conditions. Within each autonomous region, counties with concentrations of ethnic minorities are at a greater disadvantage. For instance, out of 104 poverty-stricken villages in the Yili County in the XUAR, 102 are national minority villages. In Guizhou, another relatively low-income province, 21 of 31 poverty-stricken counties are in minority regions, accounting for half the total minority population in the province. In 1994, when the state identified 592 counties (out of a total of 2,862 counties) as poverty alleviation counties, 257 were ethnic minority counties, making up 43.4 percent.

Xinjiang is a border region in northwest China and has a total population in excess of 20 million, including 12 million from different minorities such as the Uyghur, Kazak, Hui, and Mongolian peoples. The Uyghur comprise 43 percent of its population, and 99 percent of the Chinese Uyghur live in Xinjiang. Xinjiang is the only province in the country where the ethnic population outnumbers the Han Chinese. Even though the minorities are the "majority" in the region, they do not have a dominant influence in government and policy-making. Any change or improvement of social and political status depends on the support and concern of the Han Chinese-controlled government.

Uighur (Uyghur) students listen to their teacher read Arabic in Urumqi, Xinjiang Uyghur Autonomous Region (XUAR), China. In 2004, the Chinese government earmarked $9 million to improve Chinese language skills among teachers in Xinjiang Province in hopes of making the Muslim-dominated region more Chinese. (Goh Chai Hin/AFP/Getty Images)

Tibetans live in the Tibet (Xizang) Autonomous Region (TAR), founded in 1959. It is another of China's five autonomous regions for ethnic minorities. The total population of 3 million includes Tibetans, Moinba, Lhoba, and Naxi ethnic groups. All these minority groups practice Buddhism and live in Tibet. Most believers follow a faith along ethnic lines. While the constitution promises freedom of religious belief, the government has placed many restrictions on this liberty, maintaining control of religious exercises through a registration process and national organization. For example, the government continues to exercise control over Buddhist activities in Tibet, using policies including the restriction of religious study before age 18, the expulsion of unapproved monks from monasteries, the implementation of quotas on the number of monks in an attempt to reduce the spiritual population, and the forced recitation of patriotic scripts in support of the Chinese government.

Nationalistic and integrationist strategies threaten to erase religious preference, ethnic identity, and minority languages. These policies have caused growing social unrest and even mass riots among minorities living in autonomous regions. In March 2008, for example, a large-scale Buddhist demonstration began in Tibet, and the protest turned violent between protesters and police. Approximately 220 Tibetans were killed in the crackdown and at least 7,000 Tibetans were arrested. In July 2009, a bloody riot took place in Xinjiang, and 260 were killed, 1,700 injured, and 2,500 rioters arrested.

Ethnic problems in China are worsening, and religious tension continues. In May 2014, an attack at a vegetable market in Urumqi, capital of Xinjiang, killed 43 people and injured more than 90. This is just one of the more than 260 fatal mass attacks that have taken place in China early this year, an increase of approximately 32 percent from the previous year.

Further Reading

Gladney, Dru. *Dislocating China: Muslims, Minorities, and Other Subaltern Subjects*. Chicago: University of Chicago Press, 2004.

Jacka, Tamara, Andrew Kipnis, and Sally Sargeson. *Contemporary China: Society and Social Change*. Cambridge, UK: Cambridge University Press, 2013.

Li, Cheng, ed. *China's Emerging Middle Class: Beyond Economic Transformation*. Washington, DC: Brookings Institution, 2010.

Li, Xiaobing, and Fuliang Shan, eds. *Ethnic China: State, Society, and Minority*. Lanham, MD: Lexington Books, 2015.

Lu, Xueyi. *Social Structure of Contemporary China*. Singapore: World Scientific, 2012.

McCarthy, Susan. *Communist Multiculturalism: Ethnic Revival in Southwest China*. Seattle: University of Washington Press, 2009.

Mullaney, Thomas. *Coming to Terms with the Nation: Ethnic Classification in Modern China*. Berkeley: University of California Press, 2011.

Xu, Ying, and Baoqin Wang. *Ethnic Minorities of China*. Beijing: China Intercontinental, 2008.

Aging Population

The one-child policy, which began in 1979, has affected China's overall societal structure in significant ways. One of the results is the considerable aging of today's population. Estimates of the percentage of citizens over 65 years of age suggest a rise from 6.3 percent in 2000, to 10.9 percent in 2014, with a prediction of 17.4 percent in 2024, and 22.7 percent in 2050. The United Nation reports that the aged population in China will increase 111 percent between 2000 and 2015. According to Chinese official statistics, the number of the eldest (those over 80 years of age) also increased from 11.5 million in the year 2000, to 27 million in 2014, and is predicted to be 99 million by 2050. This group, which comprised 13 percent of the elderly population (age 65 and older) in 2000, will comprise 30 percent of the elderly population in 2050. During the same period, the number of Chinese children (0–14 years of age) has dropped from 40.4 percent of the total population in 1964 (before the one-child policy) to 23.9 percent in 1998, and is estimated to be 19.3 percent by 2020. Overall, the average age of China's population will increase by 13.8 years during the first half of the 21st century, as opposed to the average age of the U.S. population increasing by 3.6 years in the same time period. China will become the first major country to grow older before it becomes wealthy.

The aging situation has become particularly severe in the cities, when China became urbanized in the 2010s. Shanghai, for example, was one of the youngest cities in the world at the time the Chinese Communist Party (CCP) founded the People's Republic of China (PRC) in 1949. Shanghai, in the 2010s, has now become one of the oldest cities in the world. The proportion of people living in Shanghai over age 60 was only 3.6 percent in the 1950s, but it had increased to 9 percent in the 1970s, 18 percent in 1999, and is estimated to be 32 percent by 2030. Those over age 80 totaled 11.3 percent of the elderly population in 1999 and will peak at 16.3 percent of the total population of Shanghai. In 1983, Chinese cities had 38.8 retirees. This number increased to 129.2 million in 2000.

The aging population creates serious issues for the state in terms of meeting dependency ratios and pension obligations. In 1990, there were 13.74 elderly for each 100 people at work. This number increased to 15.6 in 2000, to 19.46 in 2014; it is estimated at 29.64 in 2025 and 48.49 by 2050. The ratio of the working to nonworking population is also quickly dropping: in 1991 it was 6:1; but is anticipated to be 2:1 by 2020. Also, Shanghai had the highest elderly dependency ratio at 17.72 percent in 2002. Due to the absence of an economic protection system, the existing elderly support system will be increasingly insufficient to satisfy the financial and physical needs of the elderly, especially the vast number of rural elderly.

In rural areas, the household, rather than the government, carries the main financial burden for the elderly. In today's China, family members such as children and spouses are still seen as primary sources of economic support to the elderly. The urban elderly are less financially dependent on their adult children than those in rural areas. About 81 percent of rural elderly reported having low or no income, compared to 36 percent for urban elderly. Only 18 percent of rural elderly had a low monthly income between 45 and 100 yuan RMB ($7.50–$16.70), compared to 37 percent for urbanites. And only 1 percent of the rural elderly reported a higher income (more than 100 yuan per month), compared to 27 percent of their urban counterparts.

See also: Chapter 1: Major Cities; Population. Chapter 3: Chinese Communist Party. Chapter 6: Health Care; Poverty; Retirement and Social Welfare; Rural-Urban Conflicts; Urban Poor. Chapter 7: One-Child Policy.

Further Reading

Chen, Sheying, and Jason Powell, eds. *Aging in China: Implications to Social Policy of a Changing Economic State*. New York: Springer, 2011.

Dorfman, Mark, et al. *China's Pension System: A Vision*. New York: World Bank, 2013.

England, Robert. *Aging China: The Demographic Challenge to China' Economic Prospects*. New York: Praeger, 2005.

Wacker, Robbyn. *Aging Social Policies: An International Perspective*. Thousand Oaks, CA: Sage, 2010.

Health Care

In the 1950s China introduced health care through two major publicly funded insurance programs: the Labor Insurance Program (LIP) and the Government Insurance Program (GIP). LIP was a mandated employment-based program sponsored by state-owned enterprises (SOEs) for most of their employees, covering about 78 percent of the urban workforce or 10 percent of the total population. GIP was a government sponsored program serving people who worked at various administrative levels in local and central governments, covering 5 percent of the total population. For the rural population, approximately 75 to 80 percent of the national total, heath care was paid either out of patients' own pockets or through the cooperative medical plans (CMP), operated through voluntary contributions of local residents at the village or township level.

After China launched its economic reform in 1978, access to health services was still widely available in the 1980s. However, health care became more dependent on income in the 1990s. The number of hospitals has increased from 42,711 in 1965, to 59,614 in 1985, and to 65,424 in 2001. The number of hospital beds has increased from 766,000 in 1965 to 2.2 million in 1985, and to 3.2 million by 2001. The hospital bed density was about 3.8 beds per 1,000 people in 2010. The number of physicians has increased from 762,800 in 1965 to 1.4 million in 1985, and to 2.1 million by 2001. In 2010, the physician density was about 1.46 doctors per 1,000.

In the 1990s, however, the village-based CMP plans collapsed massively since the rural collective economy gave way to a market economy, centered on individual household responsibility rather than collective farming in the people's communes. Combined with rising income inequality, the unequal distribution of resources, as well as incentives for spending priorities during the 1990s, accounted for large variation in the provision of public goods and services.

In the late 1990s, the government launched health care reform by socializing health care finance to integrate the GIP and LIP to form a citywide insurance pool across all enterprises, schools, or government agencies. The new plan included the three-tier payment system with patient cost-sharing policies, some predetermined payment schedules to providers, and rationing policies such as drug formulary and coverage lists for other medical services. In the late 2000s, the reform extended from health care financing to health care organization, including hospital institutional reform and the pharmaceutical market. It now faces tremendous difficulties since China's health care institutions are dominated by state-run hospitals. Moreover, pharmacies are predominately run by hospitals, and sales of drugs have long been the major source of revenue for hospitals in China, where pharmaceutical costs account for more than 50 percent of total health care expenditures. This health care institution contrasts sharply with that in many Western nations, including the United States, where drug expenditures are often below 10 percent of total health care spending.

The ongoing health care reform has been largely concentrated on the demand side of the market and has lacked emphasis on the supply side, a more difficult and complicated sector to reform. The current urban insurance plans are for the employed, which leaves more than half the total urban population uninsured. As a result, according to an official survey in 2003, 25.1 percent of Chinese who should have sought medical help did not because of the lack of health insurance and its high cost. Moreover, 17.2 percent of those who should have stayed in the hospital after surgery or a serious illness did not do so. And the most challenging health care issue in China is the urban-rural inequality in both health care financing and health outcomes.

See also: Chapter 4: State-Owned Enterprises. Chapter 6: Overview; Poverty; Retirement and Social Welfare; Rural-Urban Conflicts; Urban Poor.

Further Reading

Huang, Yanzhong. *Governing Health in Contemporary China*. London: Routledge, 2014.

Unschuld, Paul. *Medicine in China: A History of Ideas*. Berkeley: University of California Press, 2010.

Wong, Chack-kie, Yai Lo Lo, and Kwong-leung Tang. *China's Urban Health Care Reform: From State Protection to Individual Responsibility*. Lanham, MD: Lexington, 2005.

Major Ethnic Groups

China's minority population totals 112 million in 2014, about 8.5 percent of the national total, from 55 officially recognized ethnic groups. The minority population has increased from 67 million, about 6.7 percent of the national total in 1982, to 108.5 million, about 8 percent in 1995, according to the national census. There are 15 ethnic groups that have populations in excess of 1 million, including Zhuang nationals as the largest, with a total population of 17 million, then 12 million Hui, 10 million Manchus, 10 million Uyghur, 8 million Miao, 7 million Yi, 5 million Tibetans, 5 million Mongols, 4 million Tujia, 3 million Bouyei, 3 million Koreans, 2 million Dong, 2 million Yao, 2 million Bai, and 1 million Hani.

The major ethnic groups live in specified regions under an autonomous provincial government. The People's Republic of China (PRC) has set aside five autonomous (provincial) regions for ethnic minorities: the Guangxi Zhuang Autonomous Region (GZAR), Xinjiang Uygur Autonomous Region (XUAR), Tibet Autonomous Region (TAR), Inner Mongolia Autonomous Region (IMAR), and Ningxia Hui Autonomous Region (NHAR). All these regions are highlands, or hilly pastoral or forest regions, and situated in the frontier areas. Government policies, such as forced migrations into frontier regions, militarization of the border areas, and reclamation projects, have combined to bring about the present situation in which the various minorities live both together in mixed groups as well as in their own compact communities. Even though the minorities are the "majority" in these autonomous regions, they do not have a dominant influence in government.

Guangxi is a southwestern frontier province bordering with Vietnam, and it became the Zhuang Autonomous Region, or GZAR, in 1958. Zhuang nationalities make up one-third of the total provincial population of 49 million. Most of the Zhuang people as well as other minorities such as the Miao, Yao, Dai, and Bai live on plains, hillsides, and remote mountainous areas with limited transportation and communication resources, while the Han Chinese live in cities and towns. Isolated from the outside world, these minority communities maintain their own festivals and customs so that the GZAR has become a tremendous place for folk customs tours or anthropological and genealogical research.

Xinjiang is a border region in northwest China and the hinterland of the Eurasian continent. It became XUAR in 1955 for the Uyghur nationalities. Among its total population of 20 million people are 12 million minorities, including the Uyghur, Kazak, Hui, Mongolian, Kirgiz, Tajik, Uzbek, and Tartar peoples. The Uyghur comprise 43 percent of its population, and 99 percent of the Chinese Uyghur live in Xinjiang. Religions in China form large minorities based on religious groups, such as the Uygur in Xinjiang, which is primarily Muslim.

Tibet (Xizang) became TAR for Tibetans in 1959. The total population of 3 million includes Tibetans, Moinba, Lhoba, and Naxi ethnic groups. All of these minority groups practice Buddhism and live in Tibet. While the constitution allows freedom of religious belief, the government has placed many restrictions on this liberty, maintaining control of religious exercises through a registration process and national organization. For example, the government continues to exercise control over Buddhist activities in Tibet, using policies such as the restriction of religious study before age 18, the expulsion of unapproved monks from monasteries, the implementation of quotas on the number of monks in an attempt to reduce the spiritual population, and the forced recitation of patriotic scripts in support of the Chinese government. While most minority people live in their concentrated communities in one or several autonomous regions, other members are scattered in other parts of the country, intermingling with the Han Chinese.

See also: Chapter 1: Xinjiang. Chapter 3: Civil Rights; Constitution; Provincial and County Governments. Chapter 5: Buddhism; Islam. Chapter 6: Overview; Mongols; Muslims; Uyghur. Chapter 13: Folk Dance.

Further Reading

Hansen, Mette Halskov. *Lessons in Being Chinese: Minority Education and Ethnic Identity in Southwest China*. Seattle: University of Washington Press, 1999.

Harrell, Stevan, ed. *Cultural Encounters on China's Ethnic Frontiers*. Seattle: University of Washington Press, 1996.

Lee, Joseph Tse-Hei, Lida Nedilsky, and Sui-Keung Cheung, eds. *Marginalization in China: Recasting Minority Politics*. London: Palgrave Macmillan, 2009.

Li, Xiaobing, and Fuliang Shan, eds. *Ethnic China: State, Society, and Minority*. Lanham, MD: Lexington, 2015.

McCarthy, Susan K. *Communist Multiculturalism: Ethnic Revival in Southwest China*. Seattle: University of Washington Press, 2009.

Mullaney, Thomas. *Coming to Terms with the Nation: Ethnic Classification in Modern China*. Berkeley: University of California Press, 2011.

Middle Class

Since the 1980s, China has experienced unprecedented social transition with the establishment and growth of its middle class. After 30 years of economic reform, increasingly more Chinese have improved their standard of living and moved up to the social middle. The developing middle class includes managers, specialists, professional technicians, legal service staff, business administrators, and private business owners. The estimated number of the middle class increased from 13.8 percent of China's workforce in 1988, to 19 percent in 1999, and to 26.3 percent in 2014.

Chinese society was fragmented from 1949 to 1985 into four major groups: farmers, consisting of 68 percent of workforce; workers, about 23 percent; professionals, 4–5 percent; and cadres, 2–3 percent. Disparities in political prestige, income, and education were obvious, and the ability of farmers and workers to "narrow the gap" in these areas was severely limited. Since the mid-1980s, Chinese social strata have been in the process of restructuring, in response to the rapid economic reform since 1978. The boundaries were diminished between different social statuses and between rural and urban residents that had been clearly and rigidly marked in the past. In the late 1980s, the loosening of government control over people's mobility further allowed farmers to take up occupations previously only available to urban residents. By 1999, the composition of social groups had changed when the number of farmers decreased to 46 percent; workers increased to 28 percent; professionals to 17 percent; and administrators about 3–5 percent.

All these changes helped move many technicians, foremen, seasoned workers, and specialists up to the professional and administrative levels, where they have become the "career persons." They have higher-than-average income, higher social prestige, and are engaged in more stable and respected professions. Since the 1990s they have joined managers, doctors, lawyers, and private business owners to create the "social middles" when the Chinese society had become stratified between rich and poor. With the resumption and improvement of China's higher education, holders of a college degree also joined the group since they have a middle-class income and have managed to maintain the middle position in the new social structure. Socially highly respected, the intellectual stratum, including artists, educators, and writers, does not necessarily have higher incomes. Of the social middles, private enterprise owners gained wealth faster than others in this process of redistribution of wealth and power.

In the 2000s, the urbanization is eventually establishing a middle class in China by concentrating a large number of social middles in the urban areas and providing a stable income and a new life style. A typical middle class family has two incomes, owns a house or an apartment and a car, and has enough for leisure, entertainment, and travel. Nevertheless, income, occupation, and education are not the only things that count in regard to the middle class status in China. The officials of the Chinese Communist Party (CCP), middle-level officers in the People's Liberation Army (PLA), and government office-holders also have what might be considered a middle-class lifestyle, and their political power remains. While Western countries, especially the United States, hope that the Chinese middle class will promote political reform in China, Xi Jinping

(1953–), president of the People's Republic of China, encourages the middle class to play a larger role in the society. The middle class seems to be a new and important factor for either the CCP's survival or China's democratization in the future.

See also: Chapter 3: Chinese Communist Party; People's Liberation Army; Xi Jinping. Chapter 6: Overview; Rural-Urban Conflicts. Chapter 8: Overview.

Further Reading

Chen, Jie. *A Middle Class without Democracy: Economic Growth and the Prospects for Democratization in China*. Oxford, UK: Oxford University Press, 2014.

Hsiao, Hsin-Huang Michael. *Chinese Middle Classes: Taiwan, Hong Kong, Macao, and China*. London: Routledge, 2013.

Li, Cheng, ed. *China's Emerging Middle Class: Beyond Economic Transformation*. Washington, DC: Brookings Institution, 2010.

Osburg, John. *Anxious Wealth: Money and Morality among China's New Rich*. Stanford, CA: Stanford University Press, 2013.

Ren, Hai. *The Middle Class in Neoliberal China: Governing Risk, Life-building, and Themed Spaces*. London: Routledge, 2012.

Tsang, Eileen Yuk-Ha. *The New Middle Class in China: Consumption, Politics and the Market Economy*. London: Palgrave Macmillan, 2014.

Zhang, Li. *In Search of Paradise: Middle-class Living in a Chinese Metropolis*. Ithaca, NY: Cornell University Press, 2010.

Mongols

The Mongol minority is one of the 55 ethnic groups in the People's Republic of China (PRC). They have a different appearance than most Chinese people and use unique names. Their population increased from 3.41 million in 1982 to an estimated 4,806,850 in 2012. About 88 percent of Mongol minorities live in the northern province of Inner Mongolia. Others live in frontier provinces such as the northwestern provinces of Xinjiang, Qinghai, and Gansu, as well as the northeastern provinces of Heilongjiang, Liaoning, and Jilin. Even though they maintain the Mongolian languages, only about 80 percent of Mongols can speak their own language and only 50 percent of them can read and write in Mongolian.

Inner Mongolia is a border region in north China, bordering the Republic of Mongolia and Russia and covering approximately 455,600 square miles, about 12 percent of China's total territory. The term of "Inner Mongolia" (Nei Mongol) is used to differentiate from "Outer Mongolia" (Wai Mongol), or the Republic of Mongolia. As one of the five autonomous regions set aside for ethnic minorities, the Inner Mongolia Autonomous Region (IMAR) was founded in 1947–1948 with Hohhot as the capital. IMAR has a total population of 24 million, including 19 million Han Chinese and 4.22 million Mongols, about 17.1 percent of the IMAR population. With a more lenient childbirth policy than that of the Han Chinese, a Mongol family may have two or three children.

The Mongolian language is used officially by both central and local autonomous governments. The National People's Congress (NPC), for example, issues its documents in Mongolian and other ethnic languages as well as the Chinese language. Simultaneous interpretation is provided for the Mongolian and other minority representatives at congress sessions. Most local government documents, school textbooks, newspapers, radio and TV stations, as well as advertisements in IMAR, are bilingual (Chinese/Mongolian). Grade schools and colleges in areas inhabited by Mongols teach most classes in Mongolian.

Even when living in their autonomous region, the Mongols do not have a dominant influence in government. Local policies result from the support and concern of the Han Chinese-controlled regional and central governments. Neither Mongols nor other minorities are able to exercise significant legislative or administrative power to carry out self-governance in their own communities. During the Cultural Revolution of 1966–1976, for example, the Mongol administration of IMAR collapsed, and Ulanhu, founder of IMAR and its governor in 1947–1967, was purged. The Han Chinese in the region launched a wave of repressions against the Mongols.

The government maintains control of religious exercises through a registration process and national organizations. About 80 percent of Mongols declare to worship *Tian* and *aobao* (meaning the soil and stone that serve as altars of sacrifice). Both Mongolian religions represent Chinese folk religion and Mongolian shamanism. Other Mongols belong to Buddhism, Daoism (Taoism), or Islam. All religious groups must be registered with the authorities, and, while China recognizes the right to believe, worship is limited to a state-controlled system of registered and controlled mosques, monasteries, churches, and temples.

See also: Chapter 3: National People's Congress. Chapter 5: Buddhism; Daoism; Islam. Chapter 6: Major Ethnic Groups. Chapter 7: Family Planning Law; One-Child Policy. Chapter 9: Overview.

Further Reading

Atwood, Christopher. *Young Mongols and Vigilantes in Inner Mongolia's Interregnum Decades*. Leiden: Brill, 2002.

Bulag, Uradyn. *Collaborative Nationalism: The Politics of Friendship on China's Mongolian Frontier*. Boulder, CO: Rowman & Littlefield, 2010.

Buyandelger, Manduhai. *Tragic Spirits: Shamanism, Memory, and Gender in Contemporary Mongolia*. Chicago: University of Chicago Press, 2013.

Muslims

According to the national census, the Muslim population in China increased from 14 million in 1982, to 21 million in 2000, and to an estimated 32 million in 2014. Most are Sunni Muslim, worshiping in 30,000 mosques and served by 40,000 Imams and

Akhunds, each mosque serving approximately 1,160 Muslims. Among the traditional religions, Islam is not only popular, but also represents the different ways of life and forms of some major ethnic groups in China. Islam has 10 minority groups among its adherents. The Hui and Uygur are the two major nationalities with populations of 7.2 million Hui and 6 million Uygur in 1982, 10 million Hui and 8.5 million Uygur in 2000, and an estimated 14 million Hui and 12 million Uygur in 2014.

The majority of the Hui population looks much like the Han Chinese; they speak Chinese and use similar Chinese names, the exception being that they practice Islam. It is unique that the Hui nationality is the only ethnic minority in China that does not have a non-Sinitic language. They follow Islamic dietary laws and do not consume pork. Hui males wear white caps and females have headscarves or veils as is the case in many Islamic cultures. Many Hui people live in northwestern China, including Ningxia, Gansu, Qinghai, Xinjiang, and Shaanxi. Ningxia is a northwestern province with a total territory of 25,500 square miles and a population of 6.3 million in 2010. The Ningxia Hui Autonomous Region (NHAR) was founded in October 1958 with Yinchuan as its capital, set aside for the Hui people. Other Hui communities have also been established across the country as well as in major cities such as Beijing and Tianjin.

The Uyghur, as a Turkic ethnic group, has a different appearance from the Chinese, they maintain their own speaking and written languages, and use their unique names. The modern Uyghur languages are part of the Turkic language family, and they use Arabic script. The Uyghur people consider Islam to be part of their identity. About 90 percent of Uyghur minorities live in Xinjiang, or the Xinjiang Uygur Autonomous Region (XUAR), founded in October 1955. It has a total population of more than 20 million, including 12 million from the minorities such as the Uyghur, Hui, and Kazak peoples. The Uyghur comprise 43 percent of its population. However, the Uyghur and Hui Muslims in XUAR normally worship in separate mosques. Even though the Muslims are the "majority" in XUAR, they do not have a dominant influence in government.

The government maintains control of religious exercises through a registration process and national organizations. All Islamic groups must be registered with the authorities, which, while recognizing the right to believe, limit worship to a state-controlled system of registered and controlled mosques, monasteries, and temples. Among the five officially recognized religions is the Islamic Association of China. All local groups must incorporate themselves into the national institution. Additionally, teachings in these associations are monitored and sometimes modified by the government, which scrutinizes their membership, financial records, and employees. The national organization retains the right to approve or deny applications for any sub-group activities. Those who fail to register are considered illegal and may be subject to criminal prosecution, fines, and closure.

In most Islamic countries, restaurants remain closed from dawn to dusk during Ramadan, when the majority of the adult population is fasting. This is not, however, the case in Xinjiang. City officials ensure that restaurants stay open, and college administrators must report anyone who participates. In many grade schools, before the children leave school, they receive free candy to eat. In June 2007, Xinjiang authorities began collecting Muslim passports, in order to prevent them from making non-state-approved pilgrimages to Mecca. The XUAR government also indoctrinates clerics, civil servants, and teachers against the "three evil forces"—separatism, religious extremism, and terrorism. In 2008, tensions mounted between the Uyghurs and Han Chinese people. On July 5, 2009, more than 1,000 Uyghur demonstrators gathered in the commercial center of Urumqi, the capital city of XUAR, protesting the government's handling of the death of two Uyghur workers and demanding a full investigation of the killings. After confrontations with police, the peaceful demonstration escalated into riots from July 5–7. According to government reports, 197 people died and 1,721 others were injured during the two-day riot.

See also: Chapter 1: Xinjiang. Chapter 5: Islam. Chapter 6: Overview; Major Ethnic Groups; Uyghur. Chapter 9: Overview.

Further Reading

Dillon, Michael. *China's Muslim Hui Community: Migration, Settlement and Sects.* London: Routledge, 1999.

Gladney, Dru. *Muslim Chinese: Ethnic Nationalism in the People's Republic.* 2nd ed. Cambridge, MA: Harvard University Press, 1996.

Israeli, Raphael. *Islam in China: Religion, Ethnicity, Culture, and Politics.* Lanham, MD: Lexington, 2007.

Lipman, Jonathan. *Familiar Strangers: A History of Muslims in Northwest China.* Seattle: University of Washington Press, 1998.

Mi Shoujiang, and You Jia. *Islam in China.* Beijing: Chinese Intercontinental, 2004.

Poverty

According to the official statistics, by 2007 more than 31 million Chinese people were living below the poverty line. The number had declined from 250 million in 1977 and 42 million in 1998. The poverty line in China is set at 2 yuan *renminbi* or RMB ($0.33) a day, or 683 yuan RMB ($113.83) a year, and at that rate a person, does not have enough food and clothing to meet his or her basic needs. It is well below the international standard of poverty of $1 (6 yuan) a day or $365 (2,190 yuan) a year. The Asian Development Bank, using the norm of $1 per day, suggested that China should have about 230 million poor residents in 2007, some 18.5 percent of the total population.

After 30 years of economic reform, many Chinese have improved their standard of living and moved into the middle class. However, the gap between the rich and the poor has widened. A large number of less fortunate individuals, particularly the less educated, unemployed, urban poor, and many minorities, have experienced great injustice as the gap continues to grow. In 2003, the National Bureau of Statistics issued an official calculation of 0.375 as its Gini coefficient; by 2004, the Gini coefficient increased to 0.4725; and by 2014, it continued to increase to 0.474. For China's agricultural workers, who account for one-third of the total population, the average annual wage was around $500 for 2004 and below $850 for 2014.

The distribution of wealth is even more uneven for ethnic minorities. The five autonomous regions where most minority ethnic groups live accommodate a large proportion of agricultural workers and other lower-income social groups. Within each region, counties with concentrations of ethnic minorities are at a greater disadvantage. For instance, in Guizhou, another relatively low-income province, 21 of 31 poverty-stricken counties are in minority regions, accounting for half the total minority population in the province.

In the 1980s, the per capita annual net income of urban households was 6 to 10 times higher than that of rural households. Labor migration from rural to urban areas emerged as a nationwide phenomenon in the late 1980s. The number of migrant workers totaled 120 million in 2005, 136 million in 2007, and 151 million in 2010. Official estimates suggest that as of 2014, more than 169 million peasants may have left the countryside. Since it takes time for most peasants to find full-time employment, they have become part of the mobile or "floating" urban population, with no rights to housing, school, and health care. Rural workers are required to have six passes to work in cities or provinces other than their own, and are often considered second-class citizens. Although rural migration urbanized the country by 2005, the problems of China's migrant laborers have become serious in terms of their living conditions and their rights.

Continued reform of state-owned enterprises (SOEs) has resulted in many more urban workers losing their jobs. Many workers lost their "iron rice bowls," or secured incomes. It is estimated that at least 35 million workers have lost their jobs at the former SOEs, and many of them have joined the unemployment and the urban poor. In the cities, more than 20 million residents are urban poor and depending on government and social welfare because they are not able to find a full-time job to support their families.

See also: Chapter 1: Xinjiang. Chapter 3: Human Rights. Chapter 4: Migrant Laborers; State-Owned Enterprises. Chapter 6: Overview; Major Ethnic Groups; Rural-Urban Conflicts; Urban Poor.

Further Reading

Cho, Mun Young. *The Specter of "the People": Urban Poverty in Northeast China*. Ithaca, NY: Cornell University Press, 2013.

Davis, Deborah, and Feng Wang, eds. *Creating Wealth and Poverty in Post-socialist China*. Stanford, CA: Stanford University Press, 2008.

Donaldson, John. *Small Works: Poverty and Economic Development in Southwestern China*. Ithaca, NY: Cornell University Press, 2011.

Wang, Xiaolin, Limin Wang, and Yan Wang. *The Quality of Growth and Poverty Reduction in China*. New York: Springer, 2014.

Retirement and Social Welfare

China introduced social welfare in 1951. Since the Chinese wage system is built upon seniority, by the time a worker is ready to retire, he/she has reached one of the higher wages on the pay scale. Retirement ages are 60 for male workers and 55 for females. His/her company bore the sole responsibilities for providing pension benefits and other social welfare services. Yet this social welfare is only for state sectors, namely, only for workers who are employed by the state and entitled to this pension after retirement. By 1966, the state-owned enterprise (SOEs) produced 77.6 percent of China's gross value of industrial output (GVIO), while in urban areas approximately 71 percent of retirees were from the SOE sector.

Since the economic reform began in 1978, the share of GVIO produced by SOEs has decreased from 77.6 percent in 1966 to 17.5 percent in 2010. While the urban employment share of SOEs decreased from 78 percent in 1978 to 38 percent in 2000, the employment share of the collective, private-owned, foreign-funded, and joint-venture enterprises has increased significantly. Therefore, the lack of social welfare for an increasingly diversified workforce has caused social problems and urban protests. In 1983, China had 38.8 million retirees, while the number increased to 129.2 million in 2000.

China began to change its old-age insurance in the 1980s with pension-pooling programs in some cities. In this system, participating enterprises put a portion of total wages into a pension fund pool managed by a local old-age insurance bureau. A key objective of this reform was to relieve individual enterprises of full responsibility for their workers' retirement pensions by establishing funds that pool resources and share risks among enterprises. Since 1997, the government tried to implement a new pension scheme to solve the problems associated with a large retiree population and to avoid urban protests. The system covered employees in all urban sectors as well as the urban self-employed. Responsibilities for the operation of the pension scheme were transferred from enterprises to social insurance agencies. After the adoption of this system, employees participating in the old-age insurance program increased from 86.7 million in late 1997 to 94.3 million in 1999 and 106.3 million by the end of 2001. The number of retirees who enjoyed the basic old-age pension also increased from 25.3 million to 29 million and 33.5 million, respectively. In 2003, the financial minister announced a 38.6 percent increase in the social security budget to help those in difficult circumstances and to head off social unrest. However, strong competing budgetary demands make such increases difficult to maintain over the long term.

In the 2010s, the government adopted a new long-term social welfare strategy by moving away from centralized pension pool administration and opening the pension funds to a market-driven approach. The traditional intergenerational support approach is gradually being replaced by an investment approach. The nature of the new program for the elderly is shifting from welfare to self-protection, where the aged are entitled to receive benefits based on their own contributions. Some private pension arrangements are being developed. Other annuity-like old-age insurance policies have also appeared in recent years, although most peasants have little confidence in them.

In rural areas, only a very small portion (about 8 million) of retired workers and staff members collect their pensions. Six percent of the rural elderly are included in the state-sponsored "Five Guarantees Program." With the implementation in 1978 of the "Responsibility System," the elderly often depend on their children and other relatives. About 80 percent of the Chinese living in rural areas are not covered by the retirement system that provides services for the urban elderly. Rural households usually carry the main financial burden.

See also: Chapter 4: Land and Household Policy; State-Owned Enterprises. Chapter 6: Aging Population; Health Care; Poverty; Rural-Urban Conflicts; Urban Poor. Chapter 7: One-Child Policy.

Further Reading

Chen, Aimin, Gordon Liu, and Kevin Zhang, eds. *Urbanization and Social Welfare in China.* London: Ashgate, 2003.

Frazier, Mark. *Socialist Insecurity: Pensions and the Politics of Uneven Development in China.* Ithaca, NY: Cornell University Press, 2010.

Yin, Jason, Shuanglin Lin, and David Gates, eds. *Social Security Reform: Options for China.* Singapore: World Scientific, 2000.

Rural-Urban Conflicts

As the result of its economic reform and industrialization in the 1980s and 1990s, China became urbanized in the 2000s. After the founding of the People's Republic of China (PRC) in 1949, 560 million out of the total of 680 million Chinese people lived in the countryside. In the 1950s and 1960s, its urban population totaled 150 million. This number had increased from 223 million in 2002 to 695 million in 2012. More than 700 million Chinese, over 54 percent of the total population, live in cities in 2015. The rapid urbanization has benefited cities at the cost of China's countryside, where the peasants lost land, population, and political power to the urban-centered economic reforms.

Since 1949, China has lost one-fifth of its agricultural land due to urban and industrial expansion, which created soil erosion and desertification. Although China is a country with one of the longest histories of agricultural development in the world, its land resources are limited, with less than 12 percent of its terrain suitable for agriculture. China must feed 22 percent of the world's population with less than 7 percent of the world's cultivated land. From the 1980s, the physical setting in rural areas had begun to change. Factories were built in rural areas to take advantage of cheaper labor costs. Farming also became an enterprise for profit, not for subsistence.

During industrialization, China's agriculture has also lost much of its workforce, young and new farming laborers, to factory jobs. In the 1950s, 84.2 percent of China's total workforce was in agriculture, since the majority of the population lived in the countryside. In 1978, this workforce composition was reduced to 67.4 percent. It

A man pushes his bike at a market in Huairou, Beijing's northeastern rural outskirts in China, on December 11, 2008. December 18 marks the 30th anniversary of when the country began its economic reforms. The capitalistic changes transformed the lives of many of the country's 1.3 billion people. Hundreds of millions have been lifted out of poverty but many parts of the Chinese countryside have not seen the same breakneck development as urban centers. (AP Photo/Alexander F. Yuan)

continued to drop to 55.8 percent in 1988, 44 percent in 1999, 40.3 percent in 2004, and an estimated 36 percent in 2014. During this period, the per capita annual net income of urban households was 6 to 10 times higher than that of rural households. Partly because of this inequality, agricultural laborers are also the most mobile citizens. Labor migration from rural to urban areas emerged as a nationwide phenomenon in the late 1980s. By the early 1990s, an estimate of the number of individuals who had made this move was approximately 36 million. In the early 2000s, as many as 100 million rural laborers were estimated to be on the move, seeking work in cities and coastal areas. The number of migrant workers totaled 120 million in 2005, 136 million in 2007, and 151 million in 2010. More than 46 percent of urban employment is of rural migrant laborers. Official estimates suggest that as of 2014, more than 169 million peasants may have fled the countryside.

Environmental protection and industrial pollutions have reached crisis level in some parts of the country. Many industrial factories, including petrochemical refineries, steel and iron factories, textile factories, leather manufacturers, and paper producers, are businesses built along the major rivers like Yangzi (Yangtze), Huang (Yellow), and Huai, and they have badly polluted these rivers. The Huai is known as a "cancer river," running north-south between the Huang and Yangzi Rivers. The river basin of the Huai extends to more than 180 counties, totaling a population of 165 million people. Polluted air has many harmful effects for the environment and for peasants. Reduced visibility, damage to crops and livestock, and serious illness in humans can all result. When nitrous oxide and sulfur dioxide combine with water in the atmosphere, acid rain is produced. Acid rain pollutes anything it comes in contact with, including vegetation and bodies of water. Polluted environments from acid rain can eventually kill local wildlife.

See also: Chapter 1: Huanghe River; Natural Resources; Pollution and the Environment; Yangzi River. Chapter 4: Agriculture; Cost Production; Land and Household Policy; Manufacturing; Migrant Laborers. Chapter 6: Overview; Urban Poor.

Further Reading

Economy, Elizabeth. *The River Runs Black: The Environmental Challenge to China's Future*. 2nd ed. Ithaca, NY: Cornell University Press, 2010.

Oi, Jean. *Rural China Takes Off: Institutional Foundations of Economic Reform*. Berkeley: University of California Press, 1999.

Whiting, Susan. *Power and Wealth in Rural China: The Political Economy of Institutional Change*. Cambridge, UK: Cambridge University Press, 2006.

Wittwer, Sylvan, Yu Youtai, Sun Han, and Wang Lianzheng. *Feeding a Billion: Frontiers of Chinese Agriculture*. East Lansing: Michigan State University Press, 1987.

Urban Poor

China became urbanized in 2006, when the number of Chinese cities increased from 223 to 695, and more than 30 cities had a population higher than 1.5 million. Among the major cities, according to China's 2010 census, are Chongqing with 28.8 million residents; Shanghai, 23 million; Beijing, 19.6 million; Tianjin, 12.9 million; Shenzhen, 9 million; and Guangzhou (Canton), 8.8 million. Currently, about 700 million Chinese, over 54 percent of the total population, live in cities. While many urban residents have improved their standard of living, the gap between the rich and the poor has widened. A large number of less fortunate individuals, particularly the less educated and unemployed rural migrants, have become the urban poor, who have experienced great injustices as the gap continues to grow.

Before the 1990s, poverty had been a rural problem, since the majority of the 42 million Chinese people who lived below the poverty line were in the countryside. After 2000, the population of the urban poor has increased significantly, according to the Asian Development Bank. The number of China's urban poor increased from 14.8 million in 2001 to 19.63 in 2007, 21.4 million in 2010, and to 24 million in 2014. More than half of the destitute Chinese are in the cities, about 2.8 to 3.1 percent of the total urban population, and are dependent on government and social welfare because they are unable to support their families. Poverty lines are different between cities. Beijing and Shanghai, for example, set up their poverty (benefit) lines at 2,400–3,828 yuan *renminbi* or RMB (about $400–638) per person a year, while Chongqing at 1,680–2,400 yuan (about $280–400). Beijing is one of the cities with a low urban poor rate, less than 2 percent, and northwestern cities in the provinces of Shaanxi, Ningxia, and Tibet have the highest urban poor rates, above 8 percent.

In the 1980s, the per capita annual net income of urban households was 6 to 10 times higher than that of rural households. Labor migration from rural to urban areas emerged as a nationwide phenomenon in the late 1980s. The number of migrant workers totaled

120 million in 2005, 136 million in 2007, and 151 million in 2010. Official estimates suggest that as of 2014, more than 169 million peasants may have fled the countryside. Since it takes time for most peasants to find full-time employment, they have become part of the mobile or "floating" urban population, those who have no rights to subsidized housing, school, and health care. In large cities, such as Beijing, Shanghai, Guangzhou, and Tianjin, between 2 and 4 million homeless transients are camped in train and bus stations, as well as other public places. Rural workers are required to have six passes to work in cities or provinces other than their own and are often considered second-class citizens. Although rural migration had urbanized the country by 2005, the problems of China's urban poor have become serious in terms of their living conditions and their rights as citizens.

Moreover, continued reform of the state-owned enterprises (SOEs) has resulted in an increased number of urban workers losing their jobs. In 1995–2000, at least 35 million workers have lost jobs at the former SOEs, about 28 percent of the jobs in the SOEs. Since the non-state sector has not been able to offer an increased number of jobs to these unemployed workers, many of them have become urban poor. The unemployment rate has been approximately 7.6 percent in urban areas. Aside from these issues, Chinese laborers do not have a unified voice for their own rights and interests. Ethnic, social, gender, and religious diversity has divided Chinese migrant workers in troubling ways. In the 2010s, urban poverty has come to be seen as a problem that potentially threatens a substantial percentage of China's entire urban population.

See also: Chapter 1: Major Cities. Chapter 4: Migrant Laborers; State-Owned Enterprises. Chapter 6: Overview; Poverty; Retirement and Social Welfare; Rural-Urban Conflicts.

Further Reading

Cho, Mun Young. *The Specter of "the People": Urban Poverty in Northeast China*. Ithaca, NY: Cornell University Press, 2013.

Davis, Deborah, and Feng Wang, eds. *Creating Wealth and Poverty in Post-socialist China*. Stanford, CA: Stanford University Press, 2008.

Zhang, Li. *Strangers in the City: Reconfigurations of Space, Power, and Social Networks within China's Floating Population*. Stanford, CA: Stanford University Press, 2002.

Uyghur

The Uyghur (or Uighur), as a Turkic ethnic group, has a different appearance from the Chinese, maintains its own spoken and written languages, and uses its own unique names. The modern Uyghur languages are part of the Turkic language family and use Arabic script. The Uyghur people consider Islam to be part of their identity. Their population increased from 6 million in 1982, to 8.5 million in 2000, and an estimated 12 million in 2014. Approximately 90 percent of Uyghur minorities live in Xinjiang.

Xinjiang is one of the five autonomous regions set aside for ethnic minorities. The Xinjiang Uygur Autonomous Region (XUAR) was founded in October 1955 with Urumqi as its capital. It has a total population of more than 20 million, including 12 million from the minorities such as the Uyghur, Hui, and Kazak peoples. The Uyghur comprise 43 percent of its population. It contains more than 24,000 venues for religious activities, of which 23,753 are Islamic mosques. Even though the Muslims are the "majority" in XUAR, they do not have a dominant influence in government. Local policies result from the support and concern of the Han Chinese-controlled regional and central governments. Neither Hui nor Uyghur are able to exercise significant legislative or administrative power to carry out self-governance in their own communities.

In November 2004, top Chinese officials in the XUAR government called for an intensification of "ideological work" among ethnic Uyghur university students. Local officials were ordered to report anyone fasting during the month of Ramadan. According to the Five Pillars of Islam, there are five practices every Muslim must follow: witness, pray, give alms, fast during the month of Ramadan, and make a pilgrimage to Mecca, the city of the prophet, where certain rituals must be completed by the believer at specific times. In most Islamic countries, restaurants remain closed from dawn to dusk during Ramadan, when the majority of the adult population is fasting. This is not, however, the case in Xinjiang. City officials ensure that restaurants stay open, and college administrators must report anyone who participates in any of the five practices of Islam. In many grade schools, before the children leave school, they receive free candy to eat. In June 2007, Xinjiang authorities began collecting Muslims' passports in order to prevent them from making non-state-approved pilgrimages to Mecca. The XUAR government also indoctrinates clerics, civil servants, and teachers against the "three evil forces"—separatism, religious extremism, and terrorism.

Tensions mounted between the Uyghurs and the Han Chinese people, about 40 percent of the XUAR population, in 2008. On July 5, 2009, more than a thousand Uyghur demonstrators gathered in the commercial center of Urumqi, the capital city of XUAR, protesting the government's handling of the death of two Uyghur workers and demanding a full investigation of the killings. After confrontations with police, the peaceful demonstration escalated into riots from July 5–7. PAP (People's Armed Police) crashed the rioters with armored vehicles and automatic weapons, and the authorities imposed a curfew in Urumqi. The riots continued when hundreds of Han people clashed with both police and Uyghurs. According to government reports, 197 people died and 1,721 others were injured during the two-day riot.

See also: Chapter 1: Xinjiang. Chapter 3: People's Armed Police. Chapter 5: Islam. Chapter 6: Overview; Major Ethnic Groups; Poverty.

Further Reading

Bovingdon, Gardner. *The Uyghurs: Strangers in Their Own Land*. New York: Columbia University Press, 2010.

Chen, Yangbin. *Muslim Uyghur Students in a Chinese Boarding School: Social Recapitalization as a Response to Ethnic Integration*. Lanham, MD: Lexington, 2008.

Chen, Yu-Wen. *The Uyghur Lobby: Global Networks, Coalitions and Strategies of the World Uyghur Congress*. London: Routledge, 2014.

Dautcher, Jay. *Down a Narrow Road: Identity and Masculinity in a Uyghur Community in Xinjiang China*. Cambridge, MA: Harvard University Press, 2009.

Rudelson, Justin. *Oasis Identities: Uyghur Nationalism along China's Silk Road*. New York: Columbia University Press, 1998.

Thum, Rian. *The Sacred Routes of Uyghur History*. Cambridge, MA: Harvard University Press, 2014.

CHAPTER 7

GENDER, MARRIAGE, AND SEXUALITY

OVERVIEW

After the founding of the People's Republic of China (PRC) in 1949, the abolition of arranged marriages became a priority for the government. The legal marriage age is 22 for men and 20 for women. The mean age at first marriage for men in rural areas had increased from 18 in the 1950s to 21 in the 1980s, and to 22 in the 1990s. In the 1980s, the average female age at first marriage rose to 20. In rural areas, however, the practice, typically, is more a continuation of tradition. In the mid-1990s, about a third of all marriages involved at least one partner who was below the legal minimum age.

Nearly all girls receive some primary education. In 2002, 98.6 percent of all school-age children were enrolled in primary schools, including 98.5 percent of all girls. Females made up 46.7 percent of the high school population and 46.7 percent of four-year college students.

Since 2001, the government has enacted or revised numerous laws and regulations, including the Marriage Law, Law on Population and Family Planning, Implementation Procedures for the Law on Healthcare for Mothers and Infants, and Regulations for Premarital Healthcare. In 2001, the Chinese government promulgated and put into effect the "Outline for the Development of Chinese Women 2001–2010" and the "Outline for the Development of Chinese Children 2001–2010." In 2002, the PRC State Council revised and implemented the "Regulations on Prohibiting the Use of Child Labor." In 2004, the Law on the Protection of Women's Rights and Interests was revised. The formulation, revision, and implementation of these laws, regulations, and policies demonstrate that the government has begun to pay attention to women's health care, education, employment, marriage, and family issues. In 2005, the government amended the Law on the Protection of Women's Rights to include a ban on prostitution and sexual harassment.

Although the government has made some efforts to crack down on the sex trade, an estimated several million women have been involved in prostitution in the country. The government has also recognized the problem of human trafficking that is taking place in China. The state began cracking down on the abduction and selling of women and children, as well as other criminal offenses perpetrated against these members of society. As in most societies, human trafficking, prostitution, drug addiction, and domestic violence and abuse are entrenched and very resistant to change. The women were reportedly sold into marriages in rural communities for 20,000 yuan *renminbi* or RMB (approximately $3,000) to 30,000 yuan RMB (approximately $4,400) each.

Gender discrimination, domestic violence, violation of homosexual rights, human trafficking, and the sex trade remain significant problems in China. Critics pointed out that the National People's Congress (NPC) failed to clearly define domestic violence in its 2005 legislation on the protection of women's rights. The Chinese media reported that about 30 percent of Chinese families suffer from domestic violence.

China's family planning and birth control policy, the "one-child policy," began in 1979 in an attempt by the government to alleviate the problem of overpopulation. This policy has become one of the most prominent ways in which the state intrudes into family life. In the 1980s, having more than one child was illegal and punishable by fines and jail time. The first punishment was a heavy fine of about 3,000 yuan ($500), which is equivalent to an average one-year income in rural areas, plus the loss of all benefits. The second consequence for a couple bearing a child outside the plan could lead to the immediate end of their career or professional development. Connecting young people's careers to their family planning provided a powerful control since most young couples did not want to risk their career. The third punishment for those who fail to follow the plan is to face administrative discipline, including demotion, relocation, or even termination of employment. Since employers or officials at all levels are subject to rewards or penalties based on their efforts in reaching population control goals, their promotion and salary raises depend on meeting population targets set up by their superiors. In some cases, employers have fired pregnant female employees before delivering their babies, since the employers did not want a bad record of family planning for their company or school.

In 2001, the NPC passed Legislation on Population and Birth Planning. The document legalized the population policy of controlling population growth and implemented the basic state policy of family planning in a comprehensive way. The legislation suggested late marriage and late childbearing, while advocating the continuing practice of "one child per couple." It continues to be illegal to have a second child in most urban areas, and illegal in almost all provinces for a single woman to have a child. The population control program continues to negatively affect Chinese women. Some forceful methods have been taken against many women who did not follow the government's one-child policy. The one-child policy has also caused gender imbalance since most traditional families prefer a male baby as the only child. Some women tried to terminate their pregnancy if they knew they were having a female baby. Many cities have more than 125 boys for every 100 girls.

Gays and lesbians have had no rights in China since Beijing regarded homosexuality as "hooliganism" and banned homosexuality during the era of Mao Zedong (Mao Tse-tung) (1893–1976). In the 1950s and 1970s, homosexuals were classified as "bad elements," one of the "five black categories" of people who had no rights to education, employment, or political participation, and no defense from anyone's abuse or attack. After Mao died in 1976 and Deng Xiaoping (Deng Hsiao-ping) (1904–1997) launched the reform movement in 1978, the mistreatment of homosexuals continued. In the 1980s, gays and lesbians were routinely harassed in public places, arrested and interrogated by police, and jailed or sentenced by the court. Homosexuality was on the list of mental illnesses publicly issued by the Ministry of Health of the PRC.

Some scholars have stated that lacking political clout or rights protection, gays and lesbians were easy targets for police and authorities, "and became sacrificial lambs to broader goals of government and society." For example, when HIV and AIDS spread in China and reached a crisis level in the 1990s, the government and mass media pointed to gay men as a high-risk group which needed special attention. Beijing established an AIDS hotline by gay rights/AIDS activists in 1992 under the aegis of the China Health Education Institute. The policy effort clearly related gay men to HIV/AIDS. In 2009, about 26,000 people died of AIDS. By 2012, there were an estimated 780,000 people living with HIV/AIDS. Nevertheless, in 1997, the Chinese government legalized adult, consensual, and non-commercial homosexuality in China. The national penal codes against homosexuals were abolished, and homosexuality was removed from the Ministry of Health's list of mental illnesses in 2001 (a step the American Psychiatric Association had taken in 1974). In the 2000s, public awareness of homosexuality began to emerge, and many urban residents knew that certain parks, street corners, restaurants, and public baths were gathering places for small groups of gays in their cities. In the 2010s, the Chinese media began covering symbolic gay and lesbian weddings in a positive way. Also, more films, music, and novels reflecting the life and loves of gays and lesbians have become available.

Further Reading

Barlow, Tani. *The Question of Women in Chinese Feminism*. Durham, NC: Duke University Press, 2004.

Davis, Deborah, and Sara Friedman, eds. *Wives, Husbands, and Lovers: Marriage and Sexuality in Hong Kong, Taiwan, and Urban China*. Stanford, CA: Stanford University Press, 2014.

Farquhar, Judith. *Appetites: Food and Sex in Post-Socialist China*. Durham, NC: Duke University Press, 2002.

Fong, Vanessa. *Only Hope: Coming of Age under China's One-Child Policy*. Stanford, CA: Stanford University Press, 2006.

Greenhalgh, Susan. *Just One Child: Science and Policy in Deng's China*. Berkeley: University of California Press, 2008.

Mann, Susan L. *Gender and Sexuality in Modern Chinese History*. Cambridge, UK: Cambridge University Press, 2011.

White, Tyrene. *China's Longest Campaign: Birth Planning in the People's Republic, 1949–2005*. Ithaca, NY: Cornell University Press, 2006.

Yuen, Sun-Pong, Pui-Lam Law, Yuk-Ying Ho, and Fong-Ying Yu. *Marriage, Gender and Sex in a Contemporary Chinese Village*. London: Routledge, 2004.

All-China Women's Federation (ACWF)

After the founding of the People's Republic of China (PRC), the Chinese Communist Party (CCP) effectively established several state organizations at the grass-roots level to "represent" the masses and curb complaints about the lack of people's liberties and basic rights. Among these national organizations, All-China Democratic Women's Federation (ACDWF) was established in 1949 with its headquarters in Beijing. Its first president was Cai Chang (1900–1990), and first vice president was Deng Yingchao (1904–1992), the wife of Zhou Enlai (Chou En-lai) (1898–1976), premier and foreign minister of the PRC. Both Cai and Deng as senior CCP members were elected at the First ACDWF National Congress in 1949, and re-elected at the Second and Third National Congresses in 1953 and 1957. The ACDWF was renamed the All-China Women's Federation (ACWF) in 1957. In 1978, Kang Keqing (1911–1992), the wife of Marshal Zhu De (Chu Teh) (1886–1976), commander in chief of the People's Liberation Army (PLA), was elected as second president at the Fourth ACWF National Congress. Current president and first vice president, Shen Yueyue (1957–) and Song Xiuyan (1955–), elected at the Tenth ACWF National Congress in 2010, are the CCP members. ACWF is still under leadership of the CCP, even though it was officially labeled as a nationwide non-governmental organization (NGO) in 1995.

ACWF is the largest women's organization in the world, with more than 100 million members in 1.4 million primary organizations at local village, company, school, and factory levels. From the bottom up, it has more than 80,000 administrative committees at county, township, district, and corporate levels to supervise and manage the grassroots organizations. They each report to the next higher level of the ACWF provincial, municipal, and regional committees. At the top are the elected National Executive Committee and Standing Committee. The party-controlled ACWF facilitates government policy, since it has a strong connection to the CCP through women's committees in the government.

Even though there are laws designed to protect women and children, gender discrimination, violence, human trafficking, and the sex trade remain significant problems. Critics pointed out that ACWF failed to clearly define domestic violence in its 2005 campaign on the protection of women's rights. The Chinese media reported that about 30 percent of Chinese families suffered from domestic violence, while 90 percent of the victims are women and children.

Since ACWF has a monopoly on organizing women's movements in China, creating competing organizations is illegal. This restriction on women rights activism, combined with an increasing number of disputed policy issues, such as the "one-child" policy, forced abortion, child labor, gay and lesbian policies, workplace safety, and gender inequalities, means that more and more women are pressing court claims related to their civil and human rights issues.

See also: Chapter 3: Chinese Communist Party; Civil Rights; Human Rights; People's Liberation Army. Chapter 7: Overview; Child Labor; Domestic Violence; Family Planning Law; Gender Inequality; Human Trafficking; One-Child Policy; Sex Trade.

Further Reading

ACWF. *Women of China*. Beijing: China Intercontinental, 2004.

Barlow, Tani. *The Question of Women in Chinese Feminism*. Durham, NC: Duke University Press, 2004.

Ko, Dorothy, and Wang Zheng, eds. *Translating Feminisms in China*. Hoboken, NJ: Wiley-Blackwell, 2007.

Milwertz, Cecelia. *Beijing Women Organizing for Change: A New Wave of the Chinese Women's Movement*. Copenhagen, Denmark: Nordic Institute of Asian Studies, 2003.

Women's Studies Institute of ACWF. *A Review of the Social Status of Women in China*. Beijing: New World, 1995.

Child Labor

The government recognizes the problem of child labor that is taking place in China. In 2002, the State Council of the People's Republic of China (PRC) revised the Regulations on Prohibiting the Use of Child Labor. Although Chinese law prohibits the employment of children under the age of 16, United Nations (UN) reports point out that the Chinese government has not adopted a "comprehensive policy to combat child labor." One UN report concludes that child labor remains a "persistent problem." According to the report by the World Federation of Trade Unions (WFTU) in June 2006, some manufacturing companies hire child laborers during summer and winter breaks. One such company employed more than 20 children between the ages of 12 and 15 for full-time jobs. These underage employees were paid much lower than the minimum wage and were required to work as many hours a day as adult workers.

On May 9, 2007, six parents who had lost their children went to the provincial television station in Henan for help. They believed that their boys, between the ages of 8 and 13, were kidnapped or abducted to sell to owners of illegal coal mines in Shanxi. On June 25, state police from Henan and Shanxi Provinces raided the illegal mines and rescued 532 slave laborers, including 109 children. Most of the children were kidnapped or abducted at bus stops or train stations and then sold for 500 yuan *renminbi* or RMB ($70) per child.

Some international rights groups have suggested that the state should fund a comprehensive social security system for labor protection, and must narrow the gap between the rich and the poor while improving the standard of living for people throughout the country. In order to accomplish this, however, it must first solve the problem of poverty.

See also: Chapter 3: Civil Rights; Human Rights. Chapter 4: Cost Production; Workplace Safety. Chapter 7: Human Trafficking. Chapter 8: Elementary and Secondary Education.

Further Reading

Chang, Leslie. *Factory Girls: From Village to City in a Changing China*. New York: Spiegel & Grau, 2009.

Harney, Alexandra. *The China Price: The True Cost of Chinese Competitive Advantage*. New York: Penguin, 2009.

Schmitz, Cathryne. *Child Labor: A Global View*. Westport, CT: Greenwood, 2004.

Sheehan, Jackie. *Chinese Workers: A New History*. London, UK: Routledge, 2002.

Domestic Violence

Even though there are laws designed to protect women and children in China, domestic violence remains a major problem. Increasing domestic violence has caused major social problems such as broken families, poverty, illness, and suicide. As demonstrated by a joint investigation conducted by the World Bank and the World Health Organization (WHO), China's female population constitutes 21 percent of the world's total, but female suicides in China account for 56.6 percent of the world's female suicides. More tellingly, in almost every country, more men commit suicide than women; in China, however, the reverse is true. The reasons behind domestic violence and female suicide are distinctive from those in Western countries such as the United States.

Deeply-entrenched cultural beliefs and practices, which had institutionalized discrimination against women for thousands of years, continue to govern the lives of Chinese women in the 21st century. The government's movement of "women's liberation" ironically created unprecedented dilemmas and difficulties for the female population in China. On the one hand, women have the opportunity to compete with men outside of their homes as a modern female, and women constitute more than 40 percent of China's workforce. On the other hand, once returning to the home sphere, they are still expected to function as a traditional woman, as her husband, parents-in-law, and others expect. In many cases, when a woman brought home new ideas as well as her salary, or acted non-traditionally, there were arguments, fights, and violence. More and more women no longer accept domestic violence as a way of life, yet they cannot rely on a well-established legal system for protection. Massive and multidimensional changes throw many women into uncertainty and, in some cases, despair. Under these circumstances, some of them opt for divorce or even suicide to end their battle against domestic violence.

The critics pointed out that the National People's Congress (NPC) failed to clearly define domestic violence in its 2005 legislation on the protection of women's rights. Some women's rights activists have asked for more protection of women's rights and more legal and social education against domestic violence for both men and women. One wife committed suicide, leaving a child behind, after being beaten by her husband. Neither the husband nor her parents and relatives could understand the reason for such an "irrational" behavior. The husband, while mourning the loss of his wife and the mother of his young son, did not blame himself for her death. The traditional value is no doubt atrocious, but the fact that the young woman was courageous enough to resist such a deeply-entrenched tradition was itself a sign that some Chinese women have become aware of their own rights.

See also: Chapter 3: Civil Rights; Human Rights; National People's Congress. Chapter 5: Confucianism. Chapter 6: Poverty. Chapter 7: All-China Women's Federation; Family Planning Law; Gender Inequality; One-Child Policy.

Further Reading

Barlow, Tani E. *The Question of Women in Chinese Feminism.* Durham, NC: Duke University Press, 2004.

Milwertz, Cecelia. *Beijing Women Organizing for Change: A New Wave of the Chinese Women's Movement.* Copenhagen, Denmark: Nordic Institute of Asian Studies, 2003.

Wei, Rong, and Yi Deng. *Domestic Violence Research and Intervention Strategies.* Beijing: China Social Sciences, 2003.

Zhang, Lu. *Transnational Feminisms in Translation: The Making of a Women's Anti-Domestic Violence Movement in China.* Saarbrucken, Germany: VDM Verlag, 2009.

Dowry and Bride-Wealth

At a Chinese wedding ceremony, the bride brings her bridal dowry consisting of gifts that she brings to her husband's home. The dowry usually includes electronic appliances, small furniture, clothes and bedding, kitchen supplies, jewelry, and cash. In well-to-do families, it also includes items of substantial value, such as gold, a boat, or a car. Weeks before the wedding takes place, a list of the dowry items is discussed, exchanged, and announced by each of the bride's and groom's families. In southern China, the bride's family delivers the dowry to the groom's family a few days before the wedding. When the bride arrives at her new home, or her in-laws' house, her dowry has already been placed in the living room, bedroom, and kitchen. Her dowry arrangement may help her feel at home in her husband's house rather than a totally strange place.

In traditional China, many marriages were arranged by the parents, or by matchmakers. During negotiations, the bridal dowry became an important bargaining issue for either the bride's parents choosing a better man for their daughter, or the groom's parents asking for more money in dowry. After both families agreed on the list of dowry that the bride would bring, a written agreement, including the wedding date, would be signed and exchanged. The idea was to match families with those of similar status, in order to maintain or even build up family wealth and reputation.

Since ancient times, the dowry has become part of the Chinese wedding tradition because of the family system and property ownership. The family head was usually the senior male, either the father or the grandfather, who decided how to divide the family property, such as land, among his children or grandchildren. Family land was thus only divided among the sons (in many cases passing only to the eldest son), and daughters did not receive a share of the family property. Some more affluent families began providing a daughter with substantial goods as her dowry when she married and moved out of her parents' home. Other families began to prevent a widow from taking her dowry with her when she became remarried and moved out of her in-laws' house. However, they still allowed their daughters-in-law to draw from their dowries in order to help their own daughters, or their husbands' sisters, marry well. Nevertheless, well-off families always practiced the traditional funeral service to bury a married woman with her splendid and costly dowry, including gold and jewelry.

See also: Chapter 7: Gender Inequality; Traditional Wedding. Chapter 14: Holiday Feasts. Appendix: A Day in the Life of a Housewife.

Further Reading

McLaren, Anne. *Performing Grief: Bridal Laments in Rural China*. Honolulu: University of Hawaii Press, 2008.

Ruf, Gregory. *Cadres and Kin: Making a Socialist Village in West China, 1921–1991*. Stanford, CA: Stanford University Press, 2000.

Schneider, Melissa. *The Ugly Wife Is a Treasure at Home: True Stories of Love and Marriage in Communist China*. Washington, DC: Potomac, 2014.

Family Planning Law

Family planning, also called the "one-child policy," became China's national policy in 1979. It became law in 2001 when the National People's Congress (NPC) passed the Legislation on Population and Birth Planning. The document legalized the policy of controlling population growth and implemented the basic state policy of family planning in an all-inclusive way. The legislation called for late marriage and late childbearing, and advocated the continuing practice of "one child per couple." It continues to be illegal to have a second child in most urban areas today, and it is illegal in almost all Chinese provinces for a single woman to have a child.

One explanation for the stabilization of the population is China's one-child policy, which has had strict government enforcement. After 1979, having more than one child was illegal and punishable by fines and jail time. The 2001 legislation lists all the punishments for those who break the official rules of family planning. The first punishment is to pay a heavy fine of approximately 3,000 yuan *renminbi* or RMB ($500), equivalent at that time to an average one-year income in rural areas, plus the loss of all benefits. The second consequence for a couple bearing a child outside the plan may lead to the immediate end of their career or professional development. Connecting the young people's career to their family planning has provided a powerful control, since most young couples do not want to risk their careers. The third punishment for those who fail to follow the plan is to face administrative discipline, including demotion, relocation, or even termination of employment. Since their employers, or officials at all levels, are subject to rewards or penalties based on their efforts in reaching population control goals, their promotion and raises in salary depend on meeting population targets set up by their superiors. The population control program continues to negatively affect

Chinese women. Some forceful methods have been taken against many women who did not follow the government's one-child policy.

Some women's rights activists have been attacked by government officials and the police. In September 2005, Chen Guangcheng, a blind activist in the city of Linyi, Shandong Province, was grabbed and forced into the back of an undercover police vehicle, dragged and beaten, and threatened with charges of spying because she revealed the abuse of rural women in the name of family planning policies.

See also: Chapter 1: Population; Xinjiang. Chapter 3: Civil Rights; Human Rights; Law Enforcement; National People's Congress. Chapter 7: Gender Imbalance; Gender Inequality; Marriage Law; One-Child Policy; Selective Abortions.

Further Reading

Chang, Chiung-Fang, and Che-fu Lee. *Fertility, Family Planning and Population Policy in China*. London: Routledge, 2006.

Goh, Esther. *China's One-Child Policy and Multiple Care-giving: Raising Little Suns in Xiamen*. London: Routledge, 2011.

Scharping, Thomas. *Birth Control in China 1949–2000: Population Policy and Demographic Development*. London: Routledge, 2002.

White, Tyrene. *China's Longest Campaign: Birth Planning in the People's Republic, 1949–2005*. Ithaca, NY: Cornell University Press, 2006.

Gender Imbalance

China's family planning and birth control policy, known as the "one-child policy," began in 1979 in an attempt by the government to alleviate the problem of overpopulation. This policy has become one of the most prominent ways in which the state intrudes in family life. In the 1980s, having more than one child was illegal and punishable by fines and jail time. Violent actions, such as forced abortions and sterilization, have been taken against many women who did not follow the government's one-child policy. While the population control program continues to negatively affect Chinese women, it has also affected the social structure in significant ways, affecting birth rate, population aging, individual dependency, and distortion of male-female ratios.

After the one-child policy was implemented, some women tried to terminate their pregnancy if they knew they were having a daughter. Laws and regulations forbade the termination of pregnancies based on the sex of the fetus, but, given a traditional preference for males, an unintended consequence of the single-child policy has been the selective abortion of female fetuses and even the revival of female infanticide. Son preference has deep cultural roots in China. In actuality, preferential treatment toward males is part of the Confucian value system, and son preference is prevalent among Chinese families. Girls are not welcome in families, and Chinese mothers are usually under great pressure to have a boy.

The Law on the Protection of Juveniles forbids infanticide, but there was evidence that the practice continued. Sex-selective abortions have caused gender imbalance. Many cities have more than 125 boys for every 100 girls. In rural areas, the reported discrepancy between female and male children is alarmingly larger. In southeastern Jiangxi and southern Guangdong Provinces, the male to female ratios are 138.1:100 and 137.8:100, respectively. In the rural areas of Guangdong, however, the ratio is 143.7:100.

The trend of further gender imbalance in the ratio will continue over the next 15 to 25 years. It indicates clearly that more than 1 million men in China every year will not be able to find a marriage partner, and that there could be over 100 million Chinese bachelors by 2020. This causes certain social problems, such as the illegal trade of women, as well as prostitution, divorce, and domestic violence. Homosexuality and relationships outside marriage may provide other alternatives. Large numbers of male peasants who cannot find a bride in their villages are moving into cities and presenting a potential source of unrest.

See also: Chapter 3: Human Rights. Chapter 4: Migrant Laborers. Chapter 5: Confucianism; Chapter 7: Domestic Violence; Gender Inequality; Family Planning Law; Homosexuality; Human Trafficking; Marriage Law; One-Child Policy; Selective Abortions; Sex Trade.

Further Reading

Fong, Vanessa. *Only Hope: Coming of Age under China's One-Child Policy*. Stanford, CA: Stanford University Press, 2006.

Goh, Esther. *China's One-Child Policy and Multiple Care-giving: Raising Little Suns in Xiamen*. London: Routledge, 2011.

Greenhalgh, Susan. *Just One Child: Science and Policy in Deng's China*. Berkeley: University of California Press, 2008.

Nie, Jing-Bao. *Behind the Silence: Chinese Voices on Abortion*. Boulder, CO: Rowman & Littlefield, 2005.

Scharping, Thomas. *Birth Control in China 1949–2000: Population Policy and Demographic Development*. London: Routledge, 2002.

Gender Inequality

Since 2000, the Chinese government has enacted or revised numerous laws and regulations in an attempt to provide gender equality in China. Among these are the Marriage Law, Law on Population and Family Planning, Regulations for the Administration of Family Planning Technology and Service, Implementation Procedures for the Law on Healthcare for Mothers and Infants, and Regulations for Premarital Healthcare. In 2001, the government promulgated and put into effect the "Outline for the Development of Chinese Women 2001–2010." In 2004, the Law on the Protection of Women's Rights and Interests was revised. In 2005, the Third Session of the Tenth National

People's Congress (NPC) amended the Law on the Protection of Women's Rights and Interests by including a ban on sexual harassment, human trafficking, and the sex trade, which remain significant problems.

Unequal pay, mistreatment, domestic violence, and abuse of women also remain serious problems in China. One explanation for gender inequalities is the lack of involvement by women in politics, especially in all levels of leadership. At the national level, the 2005 Tenth NPC is comprised of 20.2 percent women and its Standing Committee only 13.2 percent. According to official reports, among the Chinese Communist Party (CCP) and government leaders, at all levels in 31 provinces, autonomous regions, and municipalities directly under the Central Government, less than 25 percent of the officials are women. Another reason is that traditional views such as Confucianism consider men and women unequal, with different roles and responsibilities, and are still popular in most rural areas. Also, China's family planning and birth control policy, known as the "one-child policy," continues to negatively affect Chinese women. Violent actions, such as forced abortions and sterilization, have been taken against many women who do not follow the government's one-child policy. It continues to be illegal to have a second child in most urban areas, and it is illegal in almost all provinces for a single woman to have a child.

Combined with rising income inequality, unequal opportunities, unfair treatment, gender discrimination, and inadequate distribution of resources across local governments, business, schools, and health care have accounted for a huge variation between men and women in the provision of public goods and services. According to official statistics, by 1996 women constituted 39 percent of the workforce, yet those who lost their jobs accounted for 59 percent of all those who were laid off. In other words, women had to bear the brunt of economic downsizing. Job discrimination is also evident in hiring practices, being blatantly publicized to the extent that some job announcements even declare that no women should bother to apply. Such practices are seldom criticized; in fact, society in general has become accustomed to and acquiescent to them.

China's manufacturing growth is partly based on low wages paid to its workers, especially migrant workers, who consist of 46 percent of all urban employment in 2007. Some of these migrant workers are treated unfairly and many are underpaid. Female workers, more than 30 percent of all migrant workers, have to work longer hours and are paid less. Some of them are fired if they get pregnant or give the birth.

See also: Chapter 3: Chinese Communist Party; National People's Congress. Chapter 4: Cost Production; Migrant Laborers; Trade Union and Labor Movement; Workplace Safety. Chapter 5: Confucianism. Chapter 6: Poverty. Chapter 7: Overview; All-China Women's Federation; Domestic Violence; Family Planning Law; Human Trafficking; Marriage Law; One-Child Policy; Sex Trade.

Further Reading

Chen, Lanyan. *Gender and Chinese Development: Towards an Equitable Society*. London: Routledge, 2008.

Fincher, Leta Hong. *Leftover Women: The Resurgence of Gender Inequality in China*. London: Zed, 2014.

Otis, Eileen. *Markets and Bodies: Women, Service Work, and the Making of Inequality in China*. Stanford, CA: Stanford University Press, 2011.

Watson, Rubie, and Patricia Ebrey, eds. *Marriage and Inequality in Chinese Society*. Berkeley: University of California Press, 1991.

Homosexuality

Homosexuality has been recorded in China since the Zhou dynasty (1122–221 BCE), including many Song (960–1279) and Ming (1368–1644) emperors who had their favorites of both sexes. Much classic and popular literature such as *Outlaws of the Marsh* and *Dream of the Red Chamber* described in detail homosexual activities in ancient China. Although opposition to homosexuality raised in the Tang dynasty (618–907) and the Song outlawed male prostitution, it was still acceptable in these medieval societies, since the dominant philosophies such as Confucianism, as well as popular religions such as Buddhism and Daoism (Taoism), either avoided the issue or maintained neutrality. It was the Qing (1644–1911) government which began to ban homosexuality by issuing penal codes and cracking down on homosexual activities. Some scholars argue that increased influence from the West, especially Christianity and Islam, contributed to an opposition to homosexuality in China.

Since the 1800s, an antihomosexual trend has taken root in China. The Nationalist government of the Republic of China (ROC) continued the antihomosexual policy and considered homosexual behavior a "crime injurious to custom." After the founding of the People's Republic of China (PRC) in 1949, Beijing regarded homosexuality as "hooliganism" and banned homosexual activities during the era of Mao Zedong (Mao Tsetung) (1893–1976). From the 1950s to the 1970s, homosexuals were classified as "bad elements," one of the "five black categories" of people who had no rights to obtain education, employment, or political participation, and no defense from anybody's abuse or attack.

After Mao died in 1976 and Deng Xiaoping (Deng Hsiao-ping) (1904–1997) launched the reform movement in 1978, mistreatment against homosexuals continued. In the 1980s, gays and lesbians were routinely harassed in public places, were arrested and interrogated by police, and jailed or sentenced by the court. Homosexuality was on the list of mental illnesses publicly issued by the Ministry of Health of the PRC. To demand their freedom, in the summer of 1989, gay rights activists publicly participated in the pro-democracy student protesting movement at Tiananmen Square in Beijing and other major cities. Some scholars have stated that lacking political clout or rights protection, gays and lesbians were easy targets for police and the authorities, "and became sacrificial lambs to broader goals of government and society." For example, when HIV and AIDS spread in China and reached a crisis level in the 1980s, the government and mass media pointed to gay men as a high-risk group that needed special attention.

Beijing established an AIDS hotline by gay rights/AIDS activists in 1992 under the aegis of the China Health Education Institute. The policy effort clearly related gay men to HIV/AIDS. In 2009, about 26,000 people died of AIDS. By 2012, there were an estimated 780,000 people living with HIV/AIDS in China.

In 1997, the Chinese government legalized adult, consensual, and non-commercial homosexuality in China. The national penal codes against homosexuals were abolished, and homosexuality was removed from the Ministry of Health's list of mental illnesses in 2001 (a step the American Psychiatric Association had taken in 1974). In the 2000s, public awareness of homosexuals began to emerge, and many urban residents knew that certain parks, street corners, restaurants, and public baths had become gathering places for small groups of gays in their cities. In 2009, *China Daily*, a national newspaper, printed detailed coverage and photos of a male couple holding a symbolic wedding in public and appearing in a photograph in a passionate embrace across its pages. In the 2010s, the Chinese media began to cover these symbolic gay and lesbian weddings in a positive way. And more films, music, and novels reflecting the life and love of gays and lesbians have become more easily available.

Photographers surround a lesbian couple as they kiss during an event to celebrate Valentine's Day organized near a shopping mall in Beijing on February 14, 2011. Beijing's gay and lesbian community celebrated Valentine's Day by calling for extended gay rights in China. (AP Photo/ Andy Wong)

See also: Chapter 2: Timeline; Deng Xiaoping; Mao Zedong. Chapter 3: Human Rights. Chapter 5: Buddhism; Christianity; Confucianism; Daoism; Islam. Chapter 7: Sex Trade. Chapter 11: *A Dream of Red Mansions*; *Outlaws of the Marsh*.

Further Reading

Hinsch, Bret. *Passions of the Cut Sleeve: The Male Homosexual Tradition in China*. Berkeley: University of California Press, 1992.

Ho, Loretta Wing Wah. *Gay and Lesbian Subculture in Urban China*. London: Routledge, 2011.

Kang, Wenqing. *Obsession: Male Same-Sex Relations in China, 1900–1950*. Hong Kong: Hong Kong University Press, 2009.

Kong, Travis. *Chinese Male Homosexualities: Memba, Tongzhi and Golden Boy*. London: Routledge, 2012.

Sang, Tze-Lan. *The Emerging Lesbian: Female Same-Sex Desire in Modern China*. Chicago: University of Chicago Press, 2003.

Human Trafficking

In September 2000, the Chinese government signed the "Optional Protocol to the Convention on the Rights of the Child on the Sale of Children" and "Child Prostitution and Child Pornography." In April 2004, the State Council of the People's Republic of China (PRC) revised the Law on the Protection of Women's Rights and Interests. In March 2005, the Third Session of the Tenth National People's Congress (NPC) amended the Law on the Protection of Women's Rights and Interests by including a ban on sexual harassment, human trafficking, and sex trade, all of which remain significant problems. In June, the Ministry of Public Security (MPS) estimated that 10,000 women and children were abducted and sold each year, and between 2 and 4 million women were involved in prostitution. Some nongovernmental organizations estimated that between 20,000 and 30,000 were trafficked annually.

On May 9, 2007, six parents who had lost their children went to the provincial television station in Henan for help. They believed that their boys, between the ages of 8 and 13, had been kidnapped or abducted to sell to the illegal coal mines in Shanxi, a neighboring province. After the reporters' investigation, the station on June 5 broadcast a program titled "Tragedy of the Child Laborers." Following this, the station received letters from 400 parents who had lost their children. On June 25, the state police from Henan and Shanxi Provinces raided the illegal mines and rescued 532 slave laborers, including 109 children. Most of the children had been kidnapped or abducted at bus stops or train stations and then sold for 500 yuan *renminbi* or RMB ($70) per child. The MPS reported about 2,500 kidnapping and trafficking cases during 2008, although experts claim the number was much higher.

An estimated total of several million women have been involved in prostitution in China. According to official statistics in 2007, 94,687 cases involving prostitution were investigated by police. The government had provided medical treatment and conducted a general survey of gynecological diseases. Recently, it also did a nationwide, systematic health examination of women in pregnancy and confinement. By the end of 2002, 68 percent of unmarried pregnant women and 90.1 percent of those married had undergone prenatal examinations. In 2002, the country hosted 3,067 maternity and childcare facilities. The same year, 97.2 percent of rural areas had adopted modern midwifery techniques. Over a significant number of years, the state has instituted a planned immunity, prevention, and vaccination system, as well as carried out activities to prevent and cure juvenile pneumonia, diarrhea, rickets, and iron-deficiency anemia.

The government has also recognized the problem of human trafficking that is taking place in China. The state began to crack down on the abducting and selling of women and children, as well as other criminal offenses perpetrated against these members of society. The public security officials of Hunam, for example, rescued over 2,000 children and women from human traffickers in 2003. The Fujian law enforcement arrested a group of men who organized a network through which they had trafficked more than 130 women between 2004 and 2006. The provincial court sentenced these men to 13, 8, and 5 years in jail.

See also: Chapter 3: Civil Rights; Human Rights; Law Enforcement; National People's Congress. Chapter 7: Child Labor; Domestic Violence; Gender Imbalance; Gender Inequality; Marriage Law; One-Child Policy; Sex Trade.

Further Reading

Chin, Ko-lin, and James Finckenauer. *Selling Sex Overseas: Chinese Women and the Realities of Prostitution and Global Sex Trafficking.* New York: New York University Press, 2012.

Li, Xiaobing, and Qiang Fang, eds. *Modern Chinese Legal Reform: New Perspective.* Lexington: University Press of Kentucky, 2013.

U.S. Department of State. *China (Tibet, Hong Kong, Macau): Human Rights.* Washington, DC: Government Printing Office, 2014.

Marriage Law

After the founding of the People's Republic of China (PRC) in 1949, the Marriage Law was promulgated by the Central Government on May 1, 1950. In September 1954, the First National People's Congress (NPC) passed the Constitution of the PRC and established the Ministry of Internal Affairs (MIA). On June 1, 1955, the MIA published the Marriage Registration Law which detailed the legal documentation and official approval process for each marriage.

According to the Marriage Law, when two persons of the opposite sex decide to get married, they each require a letter from their workplace confirming that neither is already married. They also undertake a health check including blood testing. They then present the official letters and positive test results to a civil affairs department at a local government, where they fill out a form with both signatures, stating they are not from the same family, nor are they close relatives. This civil registration, without vocally pledging their commitment to each other, and by receiving a marriage certificate, indicates the legal beginning of their married life. During the 1950s–1970s, the mean age at a first marriage for men was 18 in rural areas, and 19 in urban areas.

China's family planning and birth control policy, known as the "one-child policy," began in 1979 in an attempt by the government to alleviate the problem of overpopulation. This policy has become one of the most prominent ways in which the state intrudes into family life. The legislation suggested late marriage and late childbearing. It continues to be illegal to have a second child in most urban areas, and illegal in almost all provinces for a single woman to have a child. In 1980, the Third Plenary Session of the Fifth NPC passed the new Marriage Law. The amendments set the minimum marriage age for women at 20 years of age and for men at 22. Thereafter, the mean age at first marriage for men had increased from 18 in the 1950s to 21 in the 1980s, and to 22 in the 1990s. The average female age at first marriage in urban areas rose to 20 in the 1980s and to 23 in 2001. Since 2001, the government has enacted or revised numerous laws and regulations, including the Marriage Law, Law on Population and Family Planning, Implementation Procedures for the Law on Healthcare for Mothers and Infants, and Regulations for Premarital Healthcare. In 2001, the Chinese government promulgated and put into effect the "Outline for the Development of Chinese Women 2001–2010."

Nevertheless, population control programs continue to negatively affect young people who find it more and more difficult to get married and to maintain their marriage because of gender imbalance, forced abortions, domestic violence, and divorce, often caused by the "one-child policy." According to a government estimate released on February 28, 2008, the male-female sex ratio at birth was 120:100. Many cities have more than 125 boys for every 100 girls. In rural areas, the reported discrepancy between female and male children is alarmingly larger. These statistics indicate clearly that more than 1 million men in China every year will not be able to find a marriage partner, and that there could be over 100 million Chinese bachelors by 2020. This causes social problems, such as illegal trade of women, prostitution, divorce, and domestic violence. Homosexuality and relationships outside marriage may provide other alternatives. Large numbers of male peasants who cannot find a bride in their villages are moving into cities and presenting a potential source of unrest.

See also: Chapter 3: Civil Rights; Constitution; National People's Congress. Chapter 4: Migrant Laborers; Chapter 7: Overview; Domestic Violence; Family Planning Law; Gender Imbalance; Gender Inequality; Homosexuality; Human Trafficking; One-Child Policy; Selective Abortion; Sex Trade; Traditional Wedding.

Further Reading

Davis, Deborah, and Sara Friedman, eds. *Wives, Husbands, and Lovers: Marriage and Sexuality in Hong Kong, Taiwan, and Urban China.* Stanford, CA: Stanford University Press, 2014.

Kuo, Margaret. *Intolerable Cruelty: Marriage, Law, and Society in Early Twentieth-Century China*. Boulder, CO: Rowman & Littlefield, 2012.

Poston, Dudley, Wen Shan Yang, and Nicole Farris, eds. *The Family and Social Change in Chinese Societies*. New York: Springer, 2014.

Yuen, Sun-Pong, Pui-Lam Law, Yuk-Ying Ho, and Fong-Ying Yu. *Marriage, Gender and Sex in a Contemporary Chinese Village*. London: Routledge, 2004.

One-Child Policy

In July 1979, the Fifth National People's Congress (NPC) announced family planning and birth control as a national policy. It was an attempt by the government to alleviate the problem of overpopulation. This policy has become one of the most prominent ways in which the state intrudes in family life. In 2000, the Central Committee of the Chinese Communist Party (CCP) and the State Council of the People's Republic of China (PRC) issued a joint "Decision on Strengthening Population and Family Planning Work." In 2001, the NPC passed the Legislation on Population and Birth Planning. The document legalized the population policy of controlling population growth and implemented the basic state policy of family planning in a comprehensive way. The legislation suggested late marriage and late childbearing, and advocated the continuing practice of "one child per couple." It continues to be illegal to have a second child in most urban areas, and illegal in almost all provinces for a single woman to have a child.

Since the implementation of the "one-child" family planning policy, the average fertility rate has dropped from 6 children per family in the 1970s, to 2 per family in 2000, about 1.44 per family in 2002 and down to 1.27 per family in 2014. The government views this as a success and claims that 250 million births have been prevented. It also asserts that the decline in the growth rate has improved health care among women and children. This is largely attributable to the prevalence of contraceptives and the large number of induced abortions that have occurred as long-term birth control has been made both more widely available and compulsory.

Another explanation for the stabilization of the population is the improvement of public education. Education has a direct effect on the desired family size of Chinese women. Illiterate women desired 3.1 children, those literate with less than a middle school education hoped for 2.6, while middle school educated women wanted, on average, 2.4, and those with a high school education or above desired 2 children. Approximately 58 percent of illiterate women have not discussed family planning with their husbands, while those with less than a middle school education, or a middle school education and high school and above, have percentages of 42, 35, and 29, respectively. Chinese women have begun to reshape their perceived self-interest.

Another explanation for the success of China's one-child policy has been strict government enforcement. After 1979, having more than one child was illegal and punishable by fines and jail time. The 2001 legislation lists all punishments for those who break official rules of family planning. The first punishment is to pay a heavy fine of about 3,000 yuan *renminbi* or RMB ($500) equivalent to an average one-year income in rural areas, plus the loss of all benefits. The second consequence for a couple bearing a child outside the plan may lead to the immediate end of their career or professional development. Connecting young people's careers to family planning provided a powerful control since most young couples did not want to risk their professions. The third punishment for those failing to follow the plan is to face administrative discipline, including demotion, relocation, or even termination of employment. Since employers or officials at all levels are subject to rewards or penalties based on their efforts in reaching the population control goals, their promotions and payraises depend on meeting population targets set up by their superiors. In some cases, the employers fired pregnant female employees before they delivered their babies since the employers did not want to have a bad record of family planning for their company or school.

Critics argue that there have been many forced abortions, female infanticide, abandonment, and sex-selective abortions. The population control program continues to negatively affect Chinese women. Violent actions, such as forced abortions and sterilization, have been taken against many women who did not follow the government's one-child policy.

Since 2002, the government began to adjust its one-child policy with the expectation of achieving both population reduction and social stability. The first Family Planning Law, adopted in September 2002, allows provinces and municipalities to establish local regulations, such as allowing couples meeting special provisions to have a second child. Some local governments had already adopted laws to that effect.

See also: Chapter 1: Population. Chapter 3: Chinese Communist Party; Civil Rights; Human Rights; National People's Congress. Chapter 7: Family Planning Law; Gender Imbalance; Gender Inequality; Marriage Law; Selective Abortions. Chapter 8: Elementary and Secondary Education.

Further Reading

Croll, Elizabeth, and Delia Davin. *China's One-Child Family Policy*. London: Palgrave Macmillan, 1985.

Greenhalgh, Susan. *Just One Child: Science and Policy in Deng's China*. Berkeley: University of California Press, 2008.

Greenhalgh, Susan, and Edwin Winckler. *Governing China's Population: From Leninist to Neoliberal Bio-politics*. Stanford, CA: Stanford University Press, 2005.

Nie, Jing-Bao. *Behind the Silence: Chinese Voices on Abortion*. Boulder, CO: Rowman & Littlefield, 2005.

Scharping, Thomas. *Birth Control in China 1949–2000: Population Policy and Demographic Development*. London: Routledge, 2002.

White, Tyrene. *China's Longest Campaign: Birth Planning in the People's Republic, 1949–2005*. Ithaca, NY: Cornell University Press, 2006.

Selective Abortions

Since China's implementation of the "one-child" family planning policy in 1979, the average fertility rate has dropped from six children per family in the 1970s, to two per family in 2000, about 1.44 per family in 2002, and down to 1.27 per family in 2014. The government views this as a success and claims that 250 million births have been prevented. This is largely attributable to the prevalence of contraceptives and the large number of induced abortions that have occurred as long-term birth control has been made both more widely available and compulsory. Critics argue that violent actions, such as forced abortions and sterilization, have been taken against many women who did not follow the government's one-child policy, and that there have been many female infanticide, abandonment, and sex-selective abortions.

Since the one-child policy was implemented, some women have tried to terminate their pregnancies if they knew they were having a female baby. Laws and regulations also forbid the termination of pregnancies based on the sex of the fetus. But son preference has deep cultural roots in China. Actually, preferential treatment toward males is part of the Confucian value system, and son preference is prevalent among Chinese families. Girls are not welcome in families; Chinese mothers are usually under great pressure to have a boy. As another adverse consequence of the one-child policy, there has been a distortion of male-female ratio.

The Law on the Protection of Juveniles forbids infanticide, but there is evidence that the practice has continued. First, a pregnant woman has to find a doctor who can provide prenatal sex identification, which is not legal in China. If she learns she is having a baby girl, her family may reach a decision, with or without her agreement, to carry out an abortion to terminate her pregnancy. Sex-selective abortions have caused sex imbalance in China. According to a government estimate released on February 28, 2008, the male-female sex ratio at birth was 120:100.

See also: Chapter 1: Population. Chapter 3: Civil Rights; Human Rights. Chapter 5: Confucianism. Chapter 7: Domestic Violence; Family Planning Law; Gender Imbalance; Marriage Law; One-Child Policy.

Further Reading

Garrow, James. *The Pink Pagoda: One Man's Quest to End Gendercide in China*. Washington, DC: WND Books, 2012.

Huang, Hua-lun. *The Missing Girls and Women of China, Hong Kong and Taiwan: A Sociological Study of Infanticide, Forced Prostitution, Political Imprisonment, "Ghost Brides," Runaways and Thrownaways, 1900–2000s*. Jefferson, NC: McFarland, 2012.

Johnson, Kay Ann. *Wanting a Daughter, Needing a Son: Abandonment, Adoption, and Orphanage Care in China*. Seoul, Korea: Yeong & Yeong, 2004.

Nie, Jing-Bao. *Behind the Silence: Chinese Voices on Abortion*. Boulder, CO: Rowman & Littlefield, 2005.

Scharping, Thomas. *Birth Control in China 1949–2000: Population Policy and Demographic Development*. London: Routledge, 2002.

Sex Trade

Prostitution in China has a written record since the Shang dynasty (1523–1028 BCE), lasting for thousands of years and tolerated and regulated as a form of subculture for most of Chinese history. During the Han dynasty (206 BCE–220 CE), brothel keepers were licensed and taxes were collected. During the Tang (618–907) and Song (960–1279) dynasties, the golden age of Chinese literary history, almost every great poet or politician mentioned his visits to prostitutes without any shame. It is not an exaggeration to claim that prostitutes played a role in stimulating some of the best poems in Chinese history. However, the official position toward prostitutes changed in the late Song dynasty since Neo-Confucianism was highly moralistic and reified the hypocritical practice by making elite men's visits to prostitutes a secret activity. From that time on, Confucian ethics prohibited its public expression in the form of written works in the Ming (1368–1644) and Qing (1644–1911) dynasties. The government of the Republic of China (ROC) did not adopt any harsh means to control prostitution, nor of suppressing all traffic related to this activity before removing its seat from mainland China to Taiwan.

After the founding of the People's Republic of China (PRC) in 1949, Mao Zedong (Mao Tse-tung) (1893–1976), chairman of the Chinese Communist Party (CCP), criticized prostitution, drug, and religions as ugly social phenomena of the old society and eliminated sex trade entirely in 1950–1952. After Mao died in 1976, Deng Xiaoping (Deng Hsiao-ping) (1904–1997) launched the reform movement in 1978 by introducing the capitalist market economy to China. In the 1980s, prostitution reemerged once China commenced its economic open-door policy. Prostitutes are easily found in all cities and towns, even though prostitution remains illegal in China. Prostitutes work in entertainment establishments such as nightclubs, dance halls, discos, karaoke, and bars or personal service sectors like hair salons, massage parlors, saunas, and hotels. The estimated number of sex workers ranges from 4 million to as many as 10 million. The use of female sex workers by Chinese men from all social classes and all walks of life is extensive. The late-marriage policy and gender imbalance caused by the one-child policy also contributed to the rapid growth of the sex trade. In addition to anxiety about morality, public concerns about sexually transmitted diseases (STD), HIV/AIDS, public health, and human trafficking were the driving force to push the government to carry out a tougher policy against prostitution.

During the 1980s there was no explicit law against prostitution. Both the Criminal Law and Criminal Procedure Law of 1979 made no reference to the activities of prostitutes and their clients. The control of prostitution was left to local law enforcement and public safety bureaus. In 1991, the National People's Congress (NPC) passed both the Decision on Strictly Forbidding the Selling and Buying of Sex and the Decision on the Severe Punishment of Criminals Who Abduct and Traffic in or Kidnap Women and Children. In 1992, the NPC adopted the Law on Protecting the Rights and Interests of

Women, which defines prostitution as a social practice that abrogates the inherent rights of women to personhood. In 1997, the Criminal Law was revised, including the death penalty for involving serious aggravating factors such as organizing prostitution, forcing underage (younger than 14 years old) girls into prostitution, committing rape, and causing serious bodily injury. The activities of first-party participants (both prostitutes and their clients) continue to be regulated by administrative measures, with the exception of those who have sex with a minor less than 14 years of age. The government has also recognized the problem of human trafficking that is taking place in China. Since the 2000s, the state began to crack down on organized human trafficking in Hunan, Fujian, and Guangxi. The provincial law enforcement had rescued more than 18,000 women and children in 2007–2009. Since the 2010s, the government has also provided medical treatment and conducts a general survey of gynecological diseases. Recently, it did a nationwide, systematic health examination of women in pregnancy and confinement.

See also: Chapter 2: Deng Xiaoping; Mao Zedong. Chapter 3: Chinese Communist Party; Criminal Law; Law Enforcement; National People's Congress. Chapter 5: Confucianism. Chapter 7: Gender Imbalance; Gender Inequality; Homosexuality; Human Trafficking. Chapter 11: Tang-Song Poetry.

Further Reading

Burger, Richard. *Behind the Red Door: Sex in China*. Hong Kong: Earnshaw Books, 2012.

Jeffreys, Elaine. *China, Sex and Prostitution*. London: Routledge, 2004.

Meng, Jinmei. *On the Decriminalization of Sex Work in China: HIV and Patients' Rights*. London: Palgrave Macmillan, 2013.

Zheng, Tiantian. *Ethnographies of Prostitution in Contemporary China: Gender Relations, HIV/AIDS, and Nationalism*. London: Palgrave Macmillan, 2012.

Zheng, Tiantian. *Red Lights: The Lives of Sex Workers in Post-socialist China*. Minneapolis: University of Minnesota Press, 2009.

Traditional Wedding

The wedding, often considered one of the most important events in the life of Chinese people, is symbolic of the joining of two people and their families. Thus, traditionally the parents of the perspective bride and groom become involved in the details of their children's wedding plans, ceremony, and reception. In traditional Chinese society, marriages were arranged by parents and matchmakers, who visited each other's family and made proposals and offers. If the couple was deemed compatible and their offers were acceptable, a marriage arrangement was brokered.

The first step in planning the traditional wedding is the selection of auspicious dates. Some families refer to the lunar calendar or almanac for "good" days. The others ask a monk of the Buddhist temple or a fortune teller of the Taoist (Daoist) school to select a suitable date. The wedding date is announced via invitations about six months prior.

The betrothal is an important part of the Chinese wedding tradition. Moreover, the bride's family receives the bride price, *pinjin*, in red envelopes. The amount varies from region to region. In Southern China, the bride price is much higher than in Northern China. Wedding invitations are distributed to friends and relatives approximately one or two months before the wedding day. Each family makes announcements to their relatives and friends by sending out "Double Happiness Cakes," baked with dragon and phoenix imprints on the styles, with fillings of lotus seed paste and red bean paste.

A traditional wedding is lively, ceremonious, and joyful. In the morning, the bridal sedan, core of the traditional wedding, is accompanied by several bridesmaids. The bride wears a red veil and is led along by the groom, who holds a red silk scarf in his hand as she enters the bridal sedan. The bride sits in the sedan, and is then lifted and carried from her mother's home to her husband's home while relatives and friends, usually numbering from 40 to 60 people, accompany the bride, holding festive gongs,

A Chinese bride and groom are carried in a sedan chair during a traditional wedding ceremony in Guangdong, China, on November 13, 2010. The bridal sedan is the core of the traditional Chinese wedding. Accompanied by several bridesmaids, the bride sits in the sedan, which is led along by the groom and carried by several best men from her mother's home to her husband home while relatives and friends follow with festive gongs and the bridal dowry. The bride's dowry consists of gifts that the bride brings to her husband's home. Once a woman marries in China, she leaves her home and becomes part of her husband's family. The value of the dowry is used to determine a woman's status in her new household. (Yao Shengbo/Dreamstime.com)

umbrellas, and fans. Some well-off families hire a marching band, a lion dance crew, local musicians, and martial arts masters and students, performing along with the bridal group and attracting thousands of residents onto the street, watching and cheering the bridal parade through town.

When the bride arrives, the wedding ceremony, the most important part of a traditional wedding, begins. The newlyweds go to a table that is decorated for heaven and earth, where there is a basketful of grain. Many coins are placed in the four corners of the basket to represent "luck" to the guests. The groom stands on the left, the bride by his side, while a Buddhist monk, a Taoist master, or a village chief, officiates. "First bow to the heaven and the earth; second bow to the parents, and third bow is to each other." At the ceremony, the bride brings her bridal dowry consisting of gifts for her husband's home. The official wedding ceremony is followed by a tea service in the afternoon. At the end of the rituals, the wedding party proceeds in the evening to the banquet venue, or wedding reception.

The reception is hosted by the groom's family and is generally considered a public recognition of the union, since the guests, often several hundred people, may include coworkers, supervisors, associates, schoolteachers, temple friends, and neighbors. In remote mountainous areas, a few separate wedding feasts are given by the parents of bride and groom for their respective communities, companies, and temples at different locations because of the lack of transportation and communication.

See also: Chapter 5: Daoism; Feng-Shui. Chapter 7: Dowry and Bride-Wealth; Gender Imbalance; Marriage Law. Chapter 10: *Ketou*: Bowing; Lunar-Solar Calendar. Chapter 14: Holiday Feasts.

Further Reading

Chai, May-lee, and Winberg Chai. *China A to Z: Everything You Need to Know to Understand Chinese Customs and Culture*. New York: Plume, 2007.

Flower, Kathy. *China—Culture Smart! The Essential Guide to Customs and Culture*. London: Kuperard, 2010.

Lau, Laura, and Theodora Lau. *Wedding Feng Shui: The Chinese Horoscopes Guide to Planning Your Wedding*. New York: William Morrow, 2010.

CHAPTER 8

EDUCATION

OVERVIEW

Classic and traditional education became available in the Zhou dynasty (1066–221 BCE) when government-run academies and private schools were first established. During the Spring and Autumn (770–476 BCE) and Warring States (475–221 BCE) periods of Eastern Zhou, scholars such as Confucius (551–479 BCE), Mencius (Mengzi or Meng-tzu) (370–300 BCE), and Han Fei-tzu (233 BCE–?) gave private lessons to groups of their students. After the Opium War in 1840, China became increasingly exposed to Western educational practices. By the late 19th century, some imperial and traditional curriculum had transformed into a modern system through educational and political reforms. After the 1911 Revolution, China began developing a Western system encompassing all levels of education, from elementary school to college.

When the People's Republic of China (PRC) was founded in 1949, the government seized all public and private schools and established a national education system after the Soviet model, which centralized the national education through a bureaucratic system of the Ministry of Education (MOE). MOE plans and allocates national funds, oversees instruction and curriculum, provides teachers and training, and evaluates the results. Each provincial government has an education bureau, which follows MOE policy and provides leadership in the region. Under the provincial government, each county, metropolis, and district government has an educational department that organizes the local public education programs. China has the largest education system in the world, totaling more than 1 million schools at these levels in 1981 and 242.6 million students enrolled in 2002.

The public education system includes preschool (before the age of six); primary education (six years of elementary school); lower secondary education (or three years of middle school); and higher education, including four years for bachelor's degrees, two to three years for the master's degree, and three to four years for doctorates. The nine-year primary and lower secondary education has already become universal in the country. The PRC Compulsory Education Law states that all children who have reached the age of six should be enrolled and shall remain in a primary school for six years. By the 1980s, primary education had been nearly popularized in areas covering 91 percent of the country's population. By 1995, approximately 131.95 million children had attended 491,300 elementary schools with an enrollment rate of 98.5 percent for children of school age.

Promoted by the popularization of elementary education, middle schools have seen considerable development in recent decades. In 2002, MOE reported that China had 66,000 middle schools with an enrollment of 65.1 million, totaling approximately 88.7 percent of all children between 12 and 15. The enrollment rate increased to 90 percent in 2005. There were 14,900 high schools and 21,800 specialized professional schools with a total enrollment of 29 million students, about 42.8 percent of all teenagers between 15 and 18 years. By 2005, the enrollment rate in the upper secondary education increased to 60 percent. Two-thirds of high school graduates plan to attend college after graduation.

Higher education is very competitive because of limited sources for a huge population. It requires a national entrance examination to select only the best high school graduates. MOE holds the National Higher Education Entrance Examination or National College Entrance Examination (NCEE) every summer for high school seniors who are applying for college and universities in China. The number of students who took the NCEE increased from 1.64 million in 1984 to 2.51 million in 1994, to 3.75 million in 2000, 7.29 million in 2004, and to 10.5 million in 2008. The examination has been very competitive with an acceptance/admission rate of 29 percent in 1984, 36 percent in 1994, 59 percent in 2000, 61 percent in 2004, and 57 percent in 2008. It means that among the 10.5 million college candidates who took the NCEE in June 2008, about 5.9 million (57 percent of the total) passed the examination and were eligible to enroll in colleges and universities in September. The others, about 4.6 million students, had to wait for a year to retake the NCEE in 2009 if they still desired a college education. Some of the candidates have taken the exam two or three times before they are able to pass the entrance examination. Many high school students spend most of their senior year preparing for NCEE.

In the early 1980s, only 4 percent of high school graduates could be admitted to colleges and universities. By 2004, about 16 million students enrolled in 2,236 college and universities in China. By 2005, more than 15 percent of high school graduates could be admitted to colleges and universities, and 5 million students graduated from a university in 2008.

By 1981, China had 704 colleges and universities and 1.6 million students enrolled by 1982, about 4 percent of all high school graduates. By 2004, about 16 million students were enrolled in 2,236 college and universities in China. Among the colleges and universities are more than 700 under the Ministry of Education and other ministries as national universities, and the others are provincial and metropolitan colleges and universities. MOE launched "Project 211" in the late 1990s to establish hundreds of key universities to lead the reform of higher education and to strengthen a number of key disciplinary areas, a national priority for the 21st century. MOE named it Project 211, as it hoped that by the year 2000 it would have 100 participating universities in the project.

A supplementary section to China's educational system includes private colleges and universities, kindergartens, primary, secondary, and training schools. They are funded or sponsored by individuals or social organizations, and are supervised by local education administrations. By 2001, the country had 56,274 private schools and enrolled 9 million students at all levels, with a teaching faculty of 420,000. As of 2006, private colleges and universities accounted for 6 percent of student enrollment, about 1.3 million out of 20 million students enrolled in higher education. Some criticism questions the quality of private colleges since many of their students fail to pass the NCEE and could not get into the public colleges.

Further Reading

Gao, Lan. *Impacts of Cultural Capital on Student College Choice in China*. Lanham, MD: Lexington, 2011.

Morgan, W. John, and Bin Wu, eds. *Higher Education Reform in China: Beyond the Expansion*. London: Routledge, 2011.

Ryan, Janette, ed. *China's Higher Education Reform and Internationalization*. London: Routledge, 2010.

Su, Spring. *Property Ownership and Private Higher Education in China: On What Grounds?* Lanham, MD: Lexington, 2011.

Yang, Ming. *Educational System in China*. Paramus, NJ: Homa & Sekey, 2009.

Zhao, Yong. *Who's Afraid of the Bid Bad Dragon: Why China Has the Best (and Worst) Education System in the World*. San Francisco, CA: Jossey-Bass, 2014.

Elementary and Secondary Education

Chinese children begin attending school at the age of six. Their schooling begins with primary education (six years of elementary school); lower secondary education (or middle school, three years); upper secondary education (or high school, three years). Higher education can include four years for a bachelor's degree, two to three years for a master's degree, and three to four years for doctorates. China has the largest education system in the world, totaling more than 1 million schools at these levels in 1981, and having a total of 242.6 million students enrolled in 2002. Both primary and lower secondary schools belong to a nine-year public compulsory education for Chinese children.

ABACUS AND ABACUS CALCULATION

An abacus is made of a rectangular wooden frame with small rods fixed inside. Designed on the basis of the Counting Rod that Chinese people had used for a long period in the ancient time, the rods are strung with wooden beads, and a girder across the middle separates the abacus into upper and lower parts. Each rod has two beads in the upper part, each bead representing the number five, and five in the lower part, each presenting the number one. By the Ming dynasty (1368–1644), people could use the abacus for addition, subtraction, multiplication, and division. Later, the abacus was introduced and became popular in Japan, Korea, and Vietnam.

Primary school students attend class in Liajiang, China. Nine years of education are compulsory in China today. All children who have reached the age of six should be enrolled and remain in a primary (elementary) school for six years, and then a secondary (middle) school for three years. (Hung Chung Chih/Dreamstime.com)

The nine-year primary and lower secondary education has already become universal in the country. The Compulsory Education Law states that all children who have reached the age of six should be enrolled and shall remain in a primary school for six years, and then attend a lower secondary school for three more years. The central government began public education in the 1950s by establishing the Ministry of Education (MOE) in 1954. The ministry plans and allocates government funds, oversees instruction and curriculum, provides teachers and training, and evaluates outcomes. Under the MOE, each provincial government has an education bureau that carries out MOE policy and provides leadership in the region. Under the auspices of the provincial government, each county, metropolis, and district government has an education department that organizes local public education programs. By 1957, nine years of free education became available for the public after local governments opened elementary and middle schools in many villages, in most towns, and in every city.

By the 1980s, primary education had been nearly popularized in areas covering 91 percent of the country's population. By 1995, approximately 131.95 million children had attended 491,300 elementary schools with an enrollment rate of 98.5 percent for children of school age. In China's elementary schools, 40 weeks a year are devoted to study, including 4 weeks for reviews and examination, 10 weeks for summer and winter vacations, and 2 weeks for extracurricular activities. During busy farm seasons, students in rural areas are given extra time off to provide supplementary labor service to their family farms or productive needs in their villages. Students from the first to sixth grades (ages between 6 and 12) attend 24–27 hours of classes per week, studying ethics, Chinese, mathematics, natural science, geography, history, music, physical culture, and fine arts. The extracurricular activities, including meetings, manual labor, and social events, do not exceed six hours a week. Only 1.5 percent of students have discontinued primary education, and 90.8 percent of elementary school graduates have entered a middle school.

Promoted by the popularization of elementary education, middle schools have seen considerable development in recent decades. For each academic year, middle school students devote 40 weeks to learning, leaving 10 to 11 weeks for summer and winter vacations, holidays, and festivals. In addition, four weeks are set aside for physical labor and technical training. Students attend between 30 and 31 hours of classes per week. The time allotted for extracurricular activities generally does not exceed seven hours. The courses offered during the three years at middle school include Chinese, mathematics, foreign languages, politics, history, geography, biology, physics, chemistry, physiology and physical culture, music, and fine arts. MOE reported in 2002 that China had 66,000 middle schools with an enrollment of 65.1 million, totaling approximately 88.7 percent of all children between 12 and 15 years. The enrollment rate increased to 90 percent in 2005.

The upper secondary education in China is not part of the compulsory system, and it is divided into two separate entities: high schools and specialized professional schools, such as technical, vocational, nursing, and normal schools. High school studies last for three years, but professional schools are for two, three, or even four years depending on subject specialty. Most high schools and professional schools are located in large cities and economically developed areas. The lower secondary (middle school) graduates in these areas may continue their education by passing an entry examination and paying tuition and fees, even though most of these schools are sponsored by the government. By 2001, there were 14,900 high schools and 21,800 specialized professional schools with a total enrollment of 29 million students, about 42.8 percent of all teenagers between 15 and 18 years. By 2005, the enrollment rate in the upper secondary education increased to 60 percent. Two-thirds of high school graduates plan to go to college after graduation.

See also: Chapter 3: Provincial and County Governments. Chapter 6: Rural-Urban Conflicts. Chapter 7: Child Labor. Chapter 8: Overview; Private vs. Public Education. Appendix: A Day in the Life of a High School Student.

Further Reading

Li, Xiaoming, ed. *Education in China: Cultural Influences, Global Perspectives and Social Challenges*. Hauppauge, NY: Nova Science, 2013.

Ma, Liping. *Knowing and Teaching Elementary Mathematics: Teachers' Understanding of Fundamental Mathematics in China and the U.S.* 2nd ed. London: Routledge, 2010.

Maslak, Mary Ann. *Vocational Education of Female Entrepreneurs in China*. London: Routledge, 2014.

Ryan, Janette, ed. *Education Reform in China: Changing Concepts, Contexts and Practices.* London: Routledge, 2011.

Foreign Exchange Programs

During the 1870s, the Qing government (1644–1911) began engaging in educational exchange programs with Western countries for new military technology, medicine, and literature. Through foreign exchange programs, Chinese students were sent overseas to study in the United States, Great Britain, France, Germany, and Japan. Between 1872 and 1881, Qing sent 120 Chinese children to the United States for elementary through higher education as the first government-sponsored group. From 1896 to 1911, Qing sent more than 22,000 Chinese students to Japan to study military, technology, and medicine in Japanese colleges and academies. In 1908, Qing and the U.S. government reached an agreement to establish the Boxer Rebellion (1900) indemnity scholarship, which was allocated by the United States for the education of Chinese students at American institutions from war reparations of $333 million paid by the Chinese government to foreign powers, including $25 million to the United States, according to the Boxer Protocol of 1901. About 1,800 Chinese students studied in the United States on the Boxer indemnity scholarship.

After the founding of the Republic of China (ROC) in 1912, the Chinese government continued foreign exchanges such as Work-Study Programs in France and Germany. From 1911 to 1924, for example, about 1,600 Chinese students studied in France on the Work-Study Program. Chinese academic institutions also hired foreign instructors, imported advanced teaching instruments, and translated Western curriculum. Some of the returning students played important roles in Chinese politics, military, economy, and education.

When the People's Republic of China (PRC) was founded in 1949 by the Chinese Communist Party (CCP), the government of the PRC sent 10,000 students to study in the Soviet Union, an ally of China during the Cold War, until 1960, when Moscow requested that all Chinese students leave Russia subsequent to the Sino-Soviet split. Many CCP leaders and scholars received their education and training overseas, including many founding members of the PRC, top experts in science and technology, and leading scholars in academia and education. In 1960–1976, however, China's international exchange programs were reduced to a minimum, since the PRC had become isolated from the rest of the world.

Since 1978, after China launched its reform movement and opened up to the outside world, its foreign exchange programs in education have grown rapidly. Tens of thousands of students and scholars are sent by the Chinese government annually to study and conduct research in foreign countries in general, and in the United States particularly. Many more scholars study overseas on their own financial support. From 1978 to 2003, about 700,000 Chinese studied overseas, with a large percentage going to the United States. It is estimated that 270,000 Chinese students came to the United

States and studied at American colleges and universities on a student visa in 2013, increasing nearly four times since 2005.

Since the 1980s, most Chinese colleges, universities, research institutes, and professional academies have developed their own educational or academic research exchange programs with foreign institutes such as Peking University (China's Harvard) with Cornell University and Qinghua (Tsing-hua) University with Stanford University and MIT. From 1978 until 2002, China admitted 350,000 foreign students to study in China. In 2002, approximately 445,000 foreign scholars and teachers traveled to China for academic conferences, scholarly research, and other educational exchanges. China's Ministry of Education (MOE) has been hosting 120,000 foreign students annually since 2007. Beginning in the 2000s, China has also established Chinese studies exchange in foreign countries through outreaching programs such as the "Confucius Institute" and "Confucius Classroom" programs under the State Council's *Hanban* and MOE. By 2015, more than 448 Confucius Institutes had been established in 121 countries, including 143 institutes in the United States.

See also: Chapter 2: Chiang Kai-shek; Cixi and Boxer Rebellion. Chapter 3: Chinese Communist Party. Chapter 8: Peking University; Qinghua University; Returning Students.

Further Reading

Kurlantzick, Joshua. *Charm Offensive: How China's Soft Power Is Transforming the World.* New Haven, CT: Yale University Press, 2007.

Li, Hongshan. *U.S.-China Educational Exchange: State, Society, and Intercultural Relations, 1905–1950.* New Brunswick, NJ: Rutgers University Press, 2008.

Li, Mingjiang, ed. *Soft Power: China's Emerging Strategy in International Politics.* Lanham, MD: Lexington, 2009.

Ryan, Janette, ed. *China's Higher Education Reform and Internationalization.* London: Routledge, 2010.

National College Entrance Examination (NCEE)

China's Ministry of Education (MOE) holds the National Higher Education Entrance Examination or National College Entrance Examination (NCEE, called *Gaokao* in Chinese, meaning The Higher Test) every summer for high school seniors who are applying for college and universities in China. The number of students who took the NCEE increased from 1.64 million in 1984 to 2.51 million in 1994, to 3.75 million in 2000, 7.29 million in 2004, and 10.5 million in 2008. The examination has been very competitive with an acceptance/admission rate of 29 percent in 1984, 36 percent in 1994, 59 percent in 2000, 61 percent in 2004, and 57 percent in 2008. It means, among the 10.5 million college candidates who took the NCEE in June 2008, about 5.9 million (57 percent of the total) passed the examination and were eligible to enroll in the colleges and universities in August. The others, about 4.6 million students, had to wait for a year to retake the NCEE in 2009 if they still wanted to get a college education. Some candidates have taken the exam two or three times before they are able to pass the entrance examination. Many high school students spent most of their senior year preparing for NCEE.

The NCEE was established in 1952 by the government of the People's Republic of China (PRC), founded in 1949. Following the Soviet model, the PRC government centralized a high education system and prepared a unified national entrance examination system for college and university admissions. Their scores are used to allocate all students according to their application choices. Those who get the highest scores are admitted to Peking University (China's Harvard) or Qinghua University (China's MIT), and the others may enroll in national or provincial universities according to their scores. Again, more than half of the candidates are not able to attend college since their scores were below the required score based upon the annual higher education budget and the planned total enrollment.

In the late 1950s, the National Matriculation Tests Policies were criticized since many candidates from worker and peasant families were not able to attend college due to their low NCEE scores. In 1966, all colleges and universities stopped their recruitment and enrollment because of the Cultural Revolution, which actually collapsed the higher education program in China from 1966 to 1972. In 1973, some institutes tried to resume their recruitment and enrollment without an entrance examination. These admissions depended upon recommendations by factories, villages, and military units for recruiting their workers, peasants, and soldiers of the People's Liberation Army (PLA). After the Cultural Revolution ended in 1976, China resumed its higher education by holding its first college entrance examination in 1977 after the NCEE had been abolished 20 years earlier. More than 5.7 million took the NCEE in 1977, and only 277,000 were accepted by colleges and universities, about 4.8 percent of the total.

In 2000, NCEE made some student-friendly changes by lifting the registration age limits and offering different tests for different majors, or known as "3+2" and "3+comprehensive" tests. The three common tests include Chinese, mathematics, and foreign language for all majors. The two tests are not the same, either including history and geography for students applying for a liberal arts degree or including physics and chemistry for students intending to study science. The comprehensive test includes general subjects. On June 7–8, 2014, 9.39 million students took NCEE across the country, and 6.98 million were accepted, about a 74.3 percent admission rate.

See also: Chapter 3: People's Liberation Army. Chapter 8: Overview; Elementary and Secondary Education; Peking University; Project 211 and Key Universities; Qinghua University. Appendix: A Day in the Life of a High School Student.

Further Reading

Gong, Yanna. *Gaokao: A Personal Journey behind China's Examination Culture*. Beijing: China Books, 2014.

Morgan, John, and Bin Wu, eds. *Higher Education Reform in China: Beyond the Expansion*. London: Routledge, 2011.

Wang, Xin. *Higher Education as a Field of Study in China: Defining Knowledge and Curriculum Structure.* Lanham, MD: Lexington Books, 2010.

Yang, Ming. *Educational System in China.* Paramus, NJ: Homa & Sekey Books, 2009.

Peking (Beijing) University

Founded in 1898 as the Imperial University of Peking during the Qing dynasty (1644–1911), it was renamed Peking University (PKU, or National Peking University; known as *Beijing Daxue,* or *Beida*) after the founding of the Republic of China (ROC) in 1912. It established the first schools of liberal arts, agriculture, medicine, and law in China's higher education. Located in the former site of the Qing imperial gardens in northern Beijing, it is one of the preeminent universities in the People's Republic of China (PRC). It has more than 35,000 students, including 15,000 graduate students and 2,000 international students. There are 6,441 full-time faculty members in 118 departments of 30 colleges and 12 institutes. Under the Ministry of Education (MOE) of the PRC, PKU offers 225 bachelor's degrees, 199 master's degrees, and 173 doctoral degrees. In 2000, PKU took over Beijing Medical University, creating the University Health Science Campus. In 2001, PKU set up a branch campus in Shenzhen in Guangdong, creating the Peking University Shenzhen Graduate School. In 2004, the university established its second business administration school, Peking University HSBCE Business School. In 2014, the Chinese University Alumni Association and MOE China Education Center again ranked PKU the best university in China. It is sometimes known as the "Harvard of China" to imply its top status in the country.

As part of MOE Project 211, Peking University has become a major Chinese research university as a member of the C9 League and a national center for research and development in sciences, medicine, humanities, education, social sciences, and space technology, with 216 research institutes and research centers, 81 national key disciplines, 12 national laboratories, 8 university hospitals, and 12 medical and health science institutes. The *QS World University Rankings* ranked PKU as the best university in arts and humanities in Asia and 10th in the world in 2006. The *Times Higher Education* ranked it the 4th best comprehensive university in Asia and the 48th in the world in 2014. The *U.S. News and World Reports* rank it the 39th best university in the world in 2015. Asteroid #7072 was named *Beijing-Daxue* after the PKU.

Throughout its past, Peking University has led many national movements in Chinese history, including the New Cultural movement in the 1910s, the May 4 Movement of 1919, the Cultural Revolution of 1966–1967, the Tiananmen Square student pre-democracy protest of 1989, and other national events. The university also hosted and trained many important national leaders of modern China, including the leaders of the Chinese Communist Party (CCP) such as Mao Zedong (Mao Tse-tung) (1893–1976), former library assistant and later the founder and president of the PRC in 1949–1959; Chen Duxiu (Ch'en Tu-hsiu) (1879–1942), professor and dean of letters, one of the CCP founders, and secretary-general of the CCP Central Committee in 1921–1927;

The Beijing (Peking) University quadrangle in 2007. Founded in 1898, the university has 35,000 students, including 15,000 graduate students and 2,000 international students with 6,441 full-time faculty members in 118 departments in 30 colleges and 12 institutes. It offers 225 bachelor's degrees, 199 master's degrees, and 173 doctoral degrees. In 2014, China Education Center of the Ministry of Education and Chinese University Alumni Association ranked Beijing University as the best university in China. It is sometimes known as the "Harvard of China," implying its top status in the country. (Bruce Connolly/Corbis)

and Li Dazhao (Li Ta-chao) (1888–1927), head librarian and one of the CCP founders in 1921. It also educated and produced many prominent modern Chinese thinkers, scholars, and officials such as Hu Shi (Hu Shih) (1891–1962), Lu Xun (Lu Hsun, or Zhou Shuren) (1881–1936), Liu Bannong (or Liu Fu) (1891–1934), and Li Keqiang (1955–), current PRC premier since 2012.

See also: Chapter 2: Mao Zedong. Chapter 3: Chinese Communist Party; Li Keqiang. Chapter 8: Overview; Project 211 and Key Universities; Returning Students.

Further Reading

Lin, Xiaoqing. *Peking University: Chinese Scholarship and Intellectuals, 1898–1937*. Albany: State University of New York Press, 2006.

Morgan, John, and Bin Wu, eds. *Higher Education Reform in China: Beyond the Expansion*. London: Routledge, 2011.

Pattberg, Thorsten. *Inside Peking University*. New York: LOD Press, 2012.

Ping, Hao. *Peking University and the Origins of Higher Education in China*. Los Angeles, CA: Bridge 21 Publications, 2013.

Private vs. Public Education

Most K–12 schools, professional academies and institutes, and colleges and universities in China belong to the public education system, and they are owned and operated at different levels by the government. The Ministry of Education (MOE) plans and allocates national funds, oversees instruction and curriculum, provides teachers and training, and evaluates their outcome. Each provincial government has an education bureau, which carries out MOE policy and provides leadership in the region. Under the provincial government, each county, metropolis, and district government has an education department organizing the local public education programs. China has the largest education system in the world, totaling more than 1 million schools at these levels in 1981, and totaling 242.6 million students enrolled in 2002.

The public education system includes preschool (prior to the age of six); primary education (six years of elementary school); lower secondary education (or middle school, three years); upper secondary education (or high school, three years); and higher education, including four years for bachelor's degrees, two to three years for master's degrees, and three to four years for doctorates. Both primary and lower secondary schools belong to a nine-year public compulsory education for Chinese children. The upper secondary education in China is not part of the compulsory system, and is divided into two separate systems: high schools and specialized professional schools such as technician, vocational, nursing, and normal schools.

Higher education is very competitive because of limited resources for a huge population. It requires a national entry examination to select the best of high school graduates. In the early 1980s, only 4 percent of high school graduates could be admitted to colleges and universities. By 2004, about 16 million students enrolled in 2,236 colleges and universities in China. By 2005, more than 15 percent of high school graduates were allowed to be admitted to colleges and universities, and 5 million students graduated from a university in 2008. There are more than 700 colleges and universities under the MOE and other ministries as national universities and the remainder are provincial and metropolitan colleges and universities. MOE launched "Project 211" in the late 1990s to establish 100 key universities to lead the reform of higher education and to strengthen a number of key disciplinary areas as a national priority for the 21st century.

Corresponding with the increasing demands, the private sector in education has rapidly expanded since the 2000s. As a supplementary section to China's educational system, it includes private colleges and universities, kindergartens, primary, secondary, and training schools. They are funded or sponsored by individuals or social organizations, and supervised by local education administrations. By 2001, the country had 56,274 private schools and had enrolled 9 million students at all levels with a teaching faculty of 420,000. Among these private schools were 44,562 kindergartens that had enrolled 3.4 million children, 16.9 percent of the country's total; 4,846 elementary schools with 1.8 million students, 1.4 percent of the national total; 4,572 middle schools and high schools with 2.3 million students, 3 percent of the national total; 1,040 vocational schools with 377,300 students, 8 percent of the national total; and 1,202 colleges and universities with 1.1 million students. As of 2006, private colleges and universities accounted for 6 percent of student enrollment, about 1.3 million out of 20 million students enrolled in higher education. There is some criticism questioning the quality of private colleges, since many of their students fail to pass the NCEE and are not able to get into public colleges.

See also: Chapter 1: Population. Chapter 8: Overview; Elementary and Secondary Education; National College Entrance Examination; Project 211 and Key Universities.

Further Reading

Lin, Jing. *Social Transformation and Private Education in China*. New York: Praeger, 1999.

Pong, Myra. *Educating the Children of Migrant Workers in Beijing: Migration, Education, and Policy in Urban China*. London: Routledge, 2014.

Ryan, Janette, ed. *Education Reform in China: Changing Concepts, Contexts and Practices*. London: Routledge, 2011.

Su, Spring. *Property Ownership and Private Higher Education in China: On What Grounds?* Lanham, MD: Lexington, 2011.

Project 211 and Key Universities

Since China launched the reform movement in 1978, its higher education has experienced tremendous changes in the past 40 years, including popularizing higher education and strengthening key universities. Some Chinese universities have transformed from the third-world teaching colleges in the 1980s to world-class research universities today, through government-sponsored programs such as "Project 211." The Ministry of Education (MOE) designed the project in 1995 and planned to concentrate national funds on certain top-level universities to raise their research standards, contribute to China's economic and social development, and to compete globally. MOE gave the project its name as it hoped that by the beginning of the 21st century it would have 100 participating universities in the project. From 1996 to 2000, the MOE spent $2.2 billion on key universities during the first phase of Project 211.

By 1982, China had 704 colleges and universities and 1.6 million students enrolled, about 4 percent of all high school graduates. Among these higher educational institutes were comprehensive universities as well as specialized ones in certain fields such as engineering, normal, agriculture, mining, petroleum, arts, business administration and economics, and foreign languages. There were 316 universities (out of 704) offering graduate programs, including both master's and PhD degrees. To promote higher education, in the mid-1990s MOE encouraged provincial and metropolitan governments to establish local colleges. In the early 2000s, the government allowed organizations and individuals to open private higher educational institutes. By the end of the decade, there were 89 private institutions of higher education accredited by MOE to offer degrees and diplomas. By 2004, approximately 16 million students were enrolled in 2,236 colleges and universities in China. By 2005, more than 15 percent of high school graduates could be admitted in colleges and universities, and 5 million students graduated from universities in 2008. There are more than 700 colleges and universities under MOE and other ministries as national universities, while the others are provincial and metropolitan colleges and universities.

By 2014, MOE had selected 118 universities as Project 211 institutes, about 6 percent of the national total. These 211 key universities are either the top-level institutes such as Peking, Qinghua, and Nankai universities, or universities which have certain advanced research programs or degrees matching international standards. They have 96 percent of the state's key laboratories and use 70 percent of state research grants to train four-fifths of doctoral students, two-thirds of all graduate students, and half of all international students from abroad.

See also: Chapter 3: Deng Xiaoping. Chapter 8: Overview; National College Entrance Examination; Peking University; Private vs. Public Education; Qinghua University.

Further Reading

McAloon, Patrick. *Studying in China: A Practical Handbook for Students.* North Clarendon, VT: Tuttle, 2014.

Ryan, Janette, ed. *China's Higher Education Reform and Internationalization.* London, UK: Routledge, 2010.

Wang, Guoqing, and Cheng Qian. *Project 211 of Southwest University of Finance: Planning Materials and Finance.* Beijing: China Books, 2000.

Wang, Xin. *Higher Education as a Field of Study in China: Defining Knowledge and Curriculum Structure.* Lanham, MD: Lexington, 2010.

Qinghua (Tsing-hua) University

Founded in 1911 as the Tsing-hua College, this university's mission was to prepare overseas students on the 1900 Boxer Rebellion scholarships. These had been allocated by the U.S. government for the education of Chinese students at American institutions, funded from war reparations of $333 million paid by the Chinese government to foreign powers. Located on the site of a former Qing royal garden in northern Beijing, the preparatory school was transformed into a university and in 1925 was renamed National Tsing-hua University. During the Chinese Civil War of 1946–1949, then Tsinghua President Mei Yi-qi led part of the faculty to Taiwan, and in 1955 established National Tsing Hua University of Taiwan. After the founding of the People's Republic of China (PRC) on the mainland in 1949, its Beijing campus became Qinghua University. Currently, it has 44,000 students, including 16,000 graduate students and 4,000 international students, with 7,200 faculty and staff in 74 departments of 22 colleges and institutes. Under the Ministry of Education (MOE) of the PRC, Qinghua offers 141 bachelor's degrees, 139 master's degrees, and 107 doctoral degree programs. Along with Peking (Beijing)

University, it has become the best science and technology university in the country and even called the "MIT of China" to imply its specialty in sciences and engineering. As a comprehensive university, Qinghua also has colleges of Social Sciences, Humanities, Economics, Life Sciences, Public Policy and Management, Arts and Design, and Law School.

As part of MOE Project 211, Qinghua University has become a major Chinese science and technological research university as a member of the C9 League and a national center for research and development with an annual research grant total of 20 billion yuan *renminbi* or RMB ($3.3 billion) on 1,400 research projects. With the increase of state investment in science and technology, Qinghua is receiving more financial support from the Chinese government. In 2003, it set up a branch campus in Shenzhen in Guangdong, the Graduate School at Shenzhen, Qinghua University. From 2003 to 2010, the *Chinese University Ranking* considered Qinghua the best university in China, and it has become second, after Peking University, since then. The *Times Higher Education* ranked it the best in China and 36th best in the world in 2014.

The university also educated and trained many important national leaders in modern Chinese history, including the leaders of the Chinese Communist Party (CCP) such as Xi Jinping (1953–), current chairman of the CCP and president of the PRC since 2012; Hu Jintao (1942–), CCP chairman and China's president in 2002–2012; Wu Bangguo (1941–), chairman of the National People's Congress (NPC) in 2003–2013; and Zhu Rongji (1928–), PRC premier and CCP vice chairman in 1998–2003. It also hosted and produced many prominent modern Chinese thinkers, scholars, and Nobel winners such as Liang Qichao (1873–1929), philosophy professor and one of China's most groundbreaking scholars in the 20th century; Tsung-Dao Lee (1926–), physics professor and Nobel winner in 1957; and Chen-ning Franklin Yang (or Chen-Ning Franklin Yang) (1922–), physics professor and also a Nobel winner.

See also: Chapter 1: Taiwan. Chapter 2: Cixi and Boxer Rebellion; Hu Jintao. Chapter 3: Chinese Communist Party; National People's Congress; Xi Jinping. Chapter 8: Peking University; Project 211 and Key Universities.

Further Reading

Li, Hongshan. *U.S.-China Educational Exchange: State, Society, and Intercultural Relations, 1905–1950*. New Brunswick, NJ: Rutgers University Press, 2008.

Ryan, Janette, ed. *China's Higher Education Reform and Internationalization*. London: Routledge, 2010.

Tsinghua University. *Top Chinese Universities Series—Tsinghua University*. Hong Kong: Gale Asia, 2011.

Returning Students

Those who have studied overseas and returned, so-called "returning students" or "*haigui*" (returnees from overseas), have played an important role in China's industrialization, modernization, and democratization. In 1872, the Qing government (1644–1911) sent 120 Chinese children to study in the United States. Among the returnees were Zhan Tianyou (Tien Yow Jeme) (1861–1919), who completed his college program at Yale University and became "the father of China's railways," Liang Tunyen, minister of Foreign Affairs of the Qing government until the 1911 Anti-Qing Revolution, and Tang Shaoyi (1862–1938), first premier of the Republic of China (ROC) after the Qing dynasty collapsed in 1912. Nineteen other returning students became naval admirals or army generals. Between 1896 and 1911 the Qing government also sent 22,000 students to study in Japan, and many returned as revolutionary leaders who ended the Qing regime and reshaped Chinese politics in decades to come, including Chiang Kai-shek (Jiang Jieshi) (1887–1975), president of the ROC in the mainland China in 1927–1948 and in Taiwan from 1950–1975.

During the ROC period approximately 1,800 students were sent to America to study on the Boxer Rebellion (1900) indemnity scholarship. Many received PhD degrees from prestigious universities such as Harvard, Columbia, and MIT, and later served as political leaders, military commanders, leading scientists in their fields, and key university presidents after returning. Among others were Mei Yiqi, who became president of Qinghua (Tsing-hua) University, and Hu Shi (Hu Shih) (1891–1962) and Ma Yinchu, each of whom became president of Peking University. The returnees also established the Western Returned Scholars Association (*Omei Tongxuehui*) in Beijing in 1913.

During the same period, over 2,400 Chinese students went to Europe on the Work-Study Programs in France and Germany, and 800 to the Soviet Union. Having joined the Communist movement overseas, they soon became leaders of the Chinese Communist Party (CCP) in the 1930s and founding members of the People's Republic of China (PRC) in 1949. For instance, Liu Shaoqi (Liu Shao-ch'i) (1898–1969) studied in Russia and served as president of the PRC in 1959–1967; Zhou Enlai (Chou En-lai) (1898–1976) studied in France and Japan and became the PRC premier in 1949–1976; Marshal Zhu De (Chu Teh) (1886–1976) studied in Germany and served as commander in chief of the People's Liberation Army (PLA) from 1949 to 1976; and Deng Xiaoping (Deng Hsiao-ping) (1904–1997) studied in France and became PRC vice premier from 1954 to 1966 and chairman of the CCP Central Military Commission (CMC) in 1980–1990.

In the early 1950s, the PRC government encouraged overseas Chinese students and scholars to return and rebuild "the new China." In the 1950s, approximately 2,500 out of 7,000 Chinese students who were studying or working in Western countries and Japan returned to China. These returning students and experts were critical to the research and development of China's science and technology, including nuclear and space programs. Qian Xuesen (Ch'ien Hsueh-sen) (1911–2009), for example, received his master's degree from MIT in 1936 and his PhD from Caltech in 1939. He then worked with the U.S. intercontinental military ballistic missile (ICBM) program (the Titan) as a designer, and later as a director of the Jet Propulsion Laboratory in Pasadena, California. In 1945–1953, Qian designed an intercontinental space plane. His work would inspire the X-20 Dyna-Soar, which would later influence the development of the American Space Shuttle. In 1955, Qian returned to China and thereafter made important contributions to the Chinese missile program, nuclear weapon development, and space technology. He also served as one of the national leaders of China's strategic weapon programs, defense industry, and international military technology exchanges in charge of theoretical analyses, scientific experiments, research design, and problem solving for the missile programs. He was the founder and first director of the Fifth Academy (China's NASA) from 1957 to 1970 and again from 1982 to 1991. Qian became known as the "Father of Chinese Missiles," or "King of Rocketry."

Through the 1950s the PRC sent more than 10,000 students to the Soviet Union and Eastern European countries, communist allies of China during the Cold War. Among the prominent returnees from the Soviet Union were Jiang Zemin (1926–), who studied engineering and became the CCP chairman and PRC president in 1990–2002; Li Peng (1928–), who was the PRC premier in 1988–1998 and chairman of the National People's Congress (NPC) in 1998–2003; and General Cao Gangchun (1935–), who attended the Leningrad Advanced Military Engineering School to study missile design in 1957–1963, and who later became China's defense minister in 2003–2008.

After China launched the reform movement in 1978, increasingly more students studied abroad in the 1980s, either on governmental scholarships or family financial support. The number of Chinese students who studied overseas increased from 30,000 in 1986 to 96,000 in 1989, 220,000 in 1993, about 300,000 in 1998, and to 700,000 by 2003. Among the total of 125,000 students and scholars who left China to study abroad in 2002, 3,500 (about 2.8 percent) were state-sponsored, 4,500 (3.6 percent) were institution-sponsored, and 117,000 (93.6 percent) were self-funded. The returnees numbered 22,000 in 1989, 75,000 in 1993, more than 100,000 in 1998, and had risen to 172,800 by 2003. Understandably, the self-sponsored students had a lower return rate than the state- or institution-sponsored students.

See also: Chapter 1: Taiwan. Chapter 2: Chiang Kai-shek; Cixi and Boxer Rebellion; Deng Xiaoping; Jiang Zemin and Sino-U.S. Relations. Chapter 3: Chinese Communist Party; National People's Congress; People's Liberation Army. Chapter 8: Foreign Exchange Programs; Peking University; Qinghua University.

Further Reading

Abrami, Regina, William Kirby, and Warren McFarlan. *Can China Lead? Reaching the Limits of Power and Growth.* Cambridge, MA: Harvard Business Review Press, 2014.

Li, Chen, ed. *Bridging Minds across the Pacific: U.S.-China Educational Exchanges, 1978–2003.* Lanham, MD: Lexington, 2005.

Li, Hongshan. *U.S.-China Educational Exchange: State, Society, and Intercultural Relations, 1905–1950.* New Brunswick, NJ: Rutgers University Press, 2008.

Li, Mingjiang, ed. *Soft Power: China's Emerging Strategy in International Politics.* Lanham, MD: Lexington, 2009.

CHAPTER 9

LANGUAGE

OVERVIEW

The Chinese language usually refers to the standard writing and speaking language and its various dialects used by the Chinese people. It is also known as *Hanyu* (or Han language) since it is used by the Han people, more than 1.2 billion Chinese on the mainland of China (about 93.5 percent of the total population in the People's Republic of China, or PRC), and many millions in Taiwan, Hong Kong, and foreign countries such as the United States, Canada, and Australia where 20 million overseas Chinese and foreign citizens of Chinese origin have migrated. It is called *Huayu* (Chinese language) in Singapore and Malaysia. The Chinese language is also one of the five official working languages of the United Nations.

The standard speaking language of Chinese is Mandarin (or *Putonghua*, meaning "common language"), which has the Beijing pronunciation as its standard pronunciation, the northern dialect as its basic dialect, and the typical vernacular Chinese as its grammatical standard. The use of Mandarin is centered between the Huang (Yellow) River valley and the Yangzi (Yangtze) River basin through northern, northeastern, northwestern, southwestern, and central China, and offers convenience for communication between people in different areas. The Mandarin dialect is spoken by more than 70 percent of the Chinese population. It is also called *Guoyu* (national language) in Taiwan. After the founding of the PRC in 1949, the government made Mandarin the official spoken language in China and promoted *Putonghua* through mass media and public education. The nine-year elementary and middle school education has become universal in the country and all classes are taught in Mandarin, including Chinese language and literature classes. High schools, colleges, universities, and professional institutes also offer all classes in Mandarin.

Although the Chinese language is used in China, people speak in different ways in different areas, using local languages or dialects. Various dialects differ in three aspects: pronunciation, vocabulary, and grammar. Among the 230 different dialects in China, there are six major dialects. The *Wu* dialect, represented by the Shanghai dialect, is commonly used in some regions of Jiangsu and Zhejiang. The *Xiang* or Hunan dialect, represented by Changsha dialect, is commonly used in most areas of Hunan Province, while the *Gan* dialect, represented by the Nanchang dialect, is generally used in Jiangxi and Hubei. The *Hakka*, represented by the *Meixian* dialect of Guangdong, is mainly used in Guangdong, western and northern Fujian, and southern Jiangxi. The *Min* dialect is generally used in Fujian, Hainan, and Taiwan. The *Yue* or Guangdong dialect, represented by the Guangzhou dialect, is generally used in central and southwestern Guangdong, eastern and southern Guangxi, Hong Kong, and Macao. Local people use their dialects at home and in the street, even though Mandarin is used in schools, offices, and mass media.

The Chinese language is written in the form of symbols usually known as characters. These characters have an age-old history and complex structure and are extremely rich in variety. Originating approximately 6,000 years ago, they constitute one of the world's earliest written languages. It is estimated that Chinese characters were first systematized in the early Xia dynasty (2205–1766 BCE), but some experts believe that the date was even earlier. The earliest characters are the oracle bone inscriptions of the later Shang dynasty (1766–1027 BCE), which were carved on tortoise shells and animal bones for use in divination, and the later inscriptions are found on bronze ritual vessels. Modern Chinese characters evolved directly from those found on early inscriptions. Pictographs resembling the objects they represent gradually evolved into characters capable of expressing more abstract concepts, and elaborate characters gradually became simplified. This process of evolution culminated in modern logophonetic characters, with one element or group of elements indicating meaning and the other elements indicating sound. At present, each character in the Chinese language represents a single word. The large majority are logophonetic, although some pictographic and ideographic elements have been retained. The *Kangxi Dictionary* (1716) contains more than 40,000 characters, but of these only between 5,000 and 8,000 are commonly used today.

Chinese characters are basically square in shape and are often described as "square characters" in Chinese. The 11 different basic brush strokes used—in various combinations and permutations—to write Chinese characters include dots; horizontal strokes; perpendicular strokes; down-strokes to the left; down-strokes to the right; short rising strokes; horizontal strokes with a short downward hook; perpendicular strokes with an upward hook to the left; oblique downward strokes with an upward hook to the right; horizontal dashes with an abrupt downward stroke; and perpendicular downward strokes with a curve to the right. A study undertaken by the Publications Bureau of the PRC Ministry of Culture revealed that in a sample of 20 million characters selected from contemporary books and magazines, only 6,335 different characters were used. Among these, 2,400 appeared frequently, 1,770 appeared infrequently, and 2,165 were used rarely.

Since they are complex in form and vast in number, it is difficult to master the Chinese characters. Thus it is important for China to reform its written language and to adopt a system of romanization or phoneticization to facilitate international communication. After 1949, the government has followed ineluctable historical trends and been instrumental in popularizing education in China and making the written language faster and easier to learn. Phonetic scripts, or *Hanyu Pinyin* (Chinese Spelling Language, Romanized Characters), of the Chinese language were adopted in 1958. They are now widely used as an aid to beginning students of the language and in international communication. In 1964, the government of the PRC approved the

"Proposal Concerning the Simplification of Chinese Characters" prepared by the Committee on the Reform of the Written Language. The benefits of these new simplified characters became obvious as soon as they were put into circulation. Nevertheless, traditional characters are still used in Taiwan, Hong Kong, Macao, and overseas Chinese communities.

Although the Chinese language is used in government, business, education, mass media, and daily communication in the society, ethnic groups still use their own minority languages. The Mongolian, Koreans, Tibetan, Uyghur, and other minority languages are used officially by central and local government, the ethnic business community, and public schools in minority regions, along with the Chinese language in a bilingual system. The National People's Congress (NPC), for example, issues its documents in the Chinese language and other ethnic languages at the same time. Simultaneous interpretation is provided for minority representatives at congressional sessions. Most local government documents, school textbooks, newspapers, radio and TV stations, as well as advertisements in minority regions, are bilingual. Grade schools and colleges in areas inhabited by minorities teach most classes in Chinese as well as the local ethnic languages.

Further Reading

Dong, Hongyuan. *A History of the Chinese Language*. London: Routledge, 2014.

Harbaugh, Rick. *Chinese Characters: A Genealogy and Dictionary*. New Haven, CT: Yale University Press, 1999.

Li, Charles, and Sandra Thompson. *Mandarin Chinese: A Functional Reference Grammar*. Berkeley: University of California Press, 1989.

Norman, Jerry. *Chinese (Cambridge Language Survey)*. Cambridge, UK: Cambridge University Press, 1988.

Sun, Chaofen. *Chinese: A Linguistic Introduction*. Cambridge, UK: Cambridge University Press, 2006.

Chinese Characters

The Chinese language is written in the form of symbols, usually known as characters, or *Hanzi* (Han characters). These symbols have an age-old history, a complex structure, and are extremely rich in variety. Originating approximately 6,000 years ago, they constitute one of the world's earliest written languages. It is estimated that Chinese characters were first systematized in the early Xia dynasty (2205–1766 BCE), but some experts believe that the date was even earlier. The earliest characters are the oracle bone inscriptions of the later Shang dynasty (1766–1027 BCE), which were carved on tortoise shells and animal bones for use in divination, and the later inscriptions found on bronze ritual vessels. Modern Chinese characters evolved directly from those found on these early inscriptions. Pictographs resembling the objects they represent gradually evolved into characters capable of expressing more abstract concepts, and elaborate characters gradually became simplified. This process of evolution culminated in modern logophonetic characters, with one element or group of elements indicating meaning and the other elements indicating sound. At present, each character in the Chinese language represents a single word. The large majority are logophonetic, although some pictographic and ideographic elements have been retained. The *Kangxi Dictionary* (1716) contains more than 40,000 characters, but of these only between 5,000 and 8,000 are commonly used today.

Chinese characters are basically square in shape, and are often described as "square characters" in Chinese. The 11 different basic brush strokes used—in various combinations and permutations—to write Chinese characters include dots, horizontal strokes, perpendicular strokes, down-strokes to the left, down-strokes to the right, short rising strokes, horizontal strokes with a short downward hook, perpendicular strokes with an upward hook to the left, oblique downward strokes with an upward hook to the right, horizontal dashes with an abrupt downward stroke, and perpendicular downward strokes with a curve to the right. A study undertaken by the Publications Bureau of the Ministry of Culture of the People's Republic of China (PRC) revealed that in a sample of 20 million characters selected from contemporary books and magazines only 6,335 different characters were used. Among these, 2,400 appeared frequently, 1,770 appeared infrequently, and 2,165 were used only rarely.

Since they are complex in form and vast in number, it is difficult to master the Chinese characters. It is important for China to reform its written language and adopt a system of romanization or phoneticization to facilitate international communication. After the founding of the PRC in 1949, the government has followed ineluctable historical trends and been instrumental in popularizing education in China and making the written language faster and easier to learn. Phonetic scripts, or *Hanyu Pinyin* (Chinese Spelling Language, Romanized Characters), of the Chinese language were adopted in 1958. They are now widely used to assist beginning learners of the language and in international communication. In 1964, the government of the PRC approved the "Proposal Concerning the Simplification of Chinese Characters" prepared by the Committee on the Reform of the Written Language. The benefits of these new simplified characters became obvious as soon as they were put into circulation. Nevertheless, traditional characters are still used in Taiwan, Hong Kong, Macao, and overseas Chinese communities.

Although the Chinese language is used in government, business, education, mass media, and daily communication in the society, ethnic groups still use their own minority languages. The Mongolian, Korean, Tibetan, Uyghur, and other minority languages are used officially by central and local governments, ethnic business communities, and public schools in minority regions, along with the Chinese language, in a bilingual system. The National People's Congress (NPC), for example, issues its documents in the Chinese language and other ethnic languages at the same time. Simultaneous interpretation is provided for minority representatives at congress sessions. Most local government documents, school textbooks, newspapers, radio and TV stations, as well as advertisements in minority regions, are bilingual. Grade schools and colleges in areas

A protester wears a headband with the simplified Chinese characters "Citizen disobedience" during a rally in Hong Kong on August 31, 2014. After China took over Hong Kong in 1997, more and more residents learned to use the new simplified Chinese characters from the mainland, rather than the traditional characters they had used before. (AP Photo/ Vincent Yu)

inhabited by minorities teach a majority of classes in Chinese as well as the local ethnic languages.

See also: Chapter 1: Hong Kong; Taiwan. Chapter 2: Timeline; Kangxi. Chapter 3: National People's Congress. Chapter 6: Major Ethnic Groups; Uyghur. Chapter 8: Elementary and Secondary Education. Chapter 9: *Hanyu Pinyin*; Mandarin.

Further Reading

Dong, Hongyuan. *A History of the Chinese Language*. London, UK: Routledge, 2014.

Harbaugh, Rick. *Chinese Characters: A Genealogy and Dictionary*. New Haven, CT: Yale University Press, 1999.

Heisig, James, and Timothy Richardson. *Remembering Traditional Hanzi: How Not to Forget the Meaning and Writing of Chinese Characters*. Honolulu: University of Hawaii Press, 2008.

Sun, Chaofen. *Chinese: A Linguistic Introduction*. Cambridge, UK: Cambridge University Press, 2006.

Wieger, L. *Chinese Characters: Their Origin, Etymology, History, Classification, and Signification: A Thorough Study from Chinese Documents*. 2nd ed. Mineola, NY: Dover, 1965.

Hanyu Pinyin

Hanyu Pinyin is the Chinese name for an official phonetic language system transcribing the Mandarin (or *Putonghua*, meaning "common language") pronunciations of Chinese characters into the Latin spelling alphabet in the People's Republic of China (PRC). *Hanyu* means "Han language," since more than 93 percent of the Chinese are the Han people. *Pinyin* means "spelled-out sounds," and there are several different systems of *pinyin* in China, Taiwan (the Republic of China, or ROC), and Singapore.

The Chinese language is written in the form of symbols usually known as characters. They have an age-old history and a complex structure. Since they are complex in form and vast in number, it is difficult to learn and master the Chinese characters. Some European scholars developed the Wade-Giles system in 1859 to spell Chinese names, places, and terms, such as Peking, Canton, Chiang Kai-shek (1887–1975), and Mao Tse-tung (1893–1976). For more than 120 years, it has become the most common way to transcribe Chinese characters into English.

After the founding of the ROC in 1911, the government organized scholars and educators to reform its written language and look for a system of romanization or phoneticization to facilitate international communication. Among several published books were *Gwoyeu Romatzyh* (National language romanization) in 1928 and *Latinxua Sin Wenz* (New characters in Latin) in 1931. The ROC government also developed the *Zhuyin* system, the diacritic markings for Chinese characters. During the 1930s, the Soviets taught Chinese leaders who had been sent by the Chinese Communist Party (CCP) to receive training in the Soviet Union a phonetic alphabet using roman letters to spell Chinese pronunciations. This system, called *Sin Wenz*, or "New Writing," soon became available in CCP-controlled areas in China during the 1930s and 1940s.

After the founding of the PRC in 1949, the government followed unavoidable historical trends that have been instrumental in making the Chinese written language faster and easier to learn. First, the government made Mandarin the official spoken language in China and promoted *Putonghua* through mass media and public education. The nine-year elementary and middle school studies have already become universal, and all classes are taught in Mandarin, including Chinese language and literature classes. High schools, colleges, universities, and professional institutes also offer all classes in Mandarin.

In 1954, the Ministry of Education (MOE) appointed a Committee for the Reform of the Chinese Written Language to develop the romanization system, headed by Zhou Youguang, known as "the Father of Pinyin." In 1956, Zhou and the committee published their first edition of the Pinyin system of phonetic scripts, or *Hanyu Pinyin* (Chinese spelling language in roman alphabets). It uses Western spelling language as a decoding system to enable non-native speakers to produce sounds close to the Chinese pronunciations. *Pinyin* vowels are pronounced in a similar way to vowels in Roman languages. A native English speaker will find the *Hanyu Pinyin* spellings easy to use for fairly close interpretations of Mandarin, except in the case of certain sounds that are not commonly used by most native English speakers. The *Hanyu Pinyin* system also uses diacritics to make the four different tones of Mandarin. It differs from the traditional Wade-Giles system in several ways, such as changing Peking to Beijing, Canton to Guangzhou, Chiang Kai-shek to Jiang Jieshi, and Mao Tse-tung to Mao Zedong.

In February 1958, at its Fifth Session of the First National Congress, the National People's Congress (NPC) adopted *Hanyu Pinyin* as part of the Chinese language system. Thereafter, all grade schools, colleges, and institutes began using *Hanyu Pinyin* to teach standard Mandarin Chinese in classroom and to improve the literacy rate among adults. In 2001, the PRC government issued the National Common Language Law, requiring the use of *Hanyu Pinyin* in government communications, business practice, mass media, education, and computer technology. It is also used in teaching Chinese as a foreign language. The ISO (International Organization for Standardization) adopted *Hanyu Pinyin* as an international standard in 1982 after the normalization of diplomatic relations between the United States and the PRC. The United Nations adopted *Pinyin* in 1986. Thereafter, Western publications, the global business community, and international government communications began using *Hanyu Pinyin* regarding China instead of the traditional Wade-Giles system. The system was also adopted as the official standard in Singapore in 2000 and Taiwan in 2009.

See also: Chapter 1: Taiwan. Chapter 3: Chinese Communist Party; National People's Congress. Chapter 8: Elementary and Secondary Education. Chapter 9: Overview; Chinese Characters; Mandarin.

Further Reading

Chen, Ping. *Modern Chinese: History and Sociolinguistics.* Cambridge, UK: Cambridge University Press, 1988.

Ross, Claudia. *Chinese Demystified: A Self-Teaching Guide.* New York: McGraw-Hill, 2010.

Shen, Helen H. *Introduction to Standard Chinese Pinyin System.* Beijing: Beijing Language and Culture University Press, 2007.

Local Dialects

Although the standard speaking language of Chinese is Mandarin (or *Putonghua*, meaning "common language"), which has the Beijing pronunciation as its standard pronunciation, people speak in different ways in different areas of China. Local people use their own languages at home and in the street, even though Mandarin is used in schools, offices, and mass media. These local languages are called Chinese dialects, which differ from one another in three aspects: pronunciation, vocabulary, and grammar. Among the 143 different Chinese dialects are seven major dialects.

The first is the Northern Dialect (*Beifanghua*), the most widely spoken dialect in China. Its use is centered in the Huanghe (Yellow) River valley and is spoken through the provinces of the north, northeast, northwest, and central part of the Yangzi (Yangtze) River basin. The northern dialect offers convenience for communication between people in different areas and is spoken by more than 70 percent of the Chinese population. Standard Mandarin uses the northern dialect as its basic dialect.

The second is the *Wu* dialect, spoken in the Shanghai region and commonly used in some regions in southeastern Jiangsu and most of the Zhejiang.

The third is the *Xiang* or Hunan dialect, represented by Changsha dialect, and is commonly used in most areas of Hunan with the exception of the northwestern area.

The fourth dialect is the *Gan* dialect, represented by the Nanchang dialect, which is generally used in southeastern Hubei and Jiangxi, with the exception of the areas bordering the Yangzi and the southern areas.

The fifth dialect is the *Min* family of dialects, which are generally used in Fujian and Hainan, as well as in Taiwan. The dialect is divided into northern and southern *Min* dialects. Northern *Min* dialect is spoken in parts of northern Fujian and Taiwan. Southern *Min* dialect is spoken throughout southern Fujian as well as in the Chaozhou and Shantou areas of Guangdong and in Hainan Island. Southern *Min* dialect is also spoken by many overseas Chinese.

The sixth dialect is the *Hakka* or *Kejia* dialect, represented by the *Meixian* dialect of Guangdong, and is mainly used in Guangdong, western and northern Fujian, and southern Jiangxi.

The last but not least is *Yue* or Guangdong (Cantonese) dialect, represented by the Guangzhou dialect, and is generally spoken through central and southwestern Guangdong, eastern and southern Guangxi, Hong Kong, Macao, and also by many overseas Chinese.

Although the standard Mandarin language is used in government, business, education, mass media, and daily communication, local people still use their own dialect in the street and at home. Many regional TV and radio stations have broadcasting and commercials in local dialects. The Central People's Broadcasting Station in Beijing also broadcasts in Cantonese, Xiamen dialect, *Kejia* dialect, and *Chaozhou* dialect for overseas audiences in Taiwan, Singapore, Australia, Southeast Asia, and North America.

See also: Chapter 1: Hong Kong; Huanghe River; Population; Taiwan; Yangzi River. Chapter 9: Overview; Mandarin.

Further Reading

Ebrey, Patricia Buckley, ed. *Chinese Civilization: A Sourcebook.* 2nd ed. New York: Free Press, 1993.

Hashimoto, Mantaro. *The Hakka Dialect: A Linguistic Study of Its Phonology, Syntax and Lexicon.* Cambridge, UK: Cambridge University Press, 2010.

Hashimoto, Oi-kan. *Studies in Yue Dialects: Phonology of Cantonese.* Cambridge, UK: Cambridge University Press, 2011.

Simmons, Richard Van Ness. *Chinese Dialect Classification: A Comparative Approach to Harngjou, Old Jintarn, and Common Northern Wu.* Amsterdam, Netherlands: John Benjamin, 1999.

Mandarin

The standard speaking language of the Chinese is Mandarin (or *Putonghua*, meaning "common language"), which has the Beijing pronunciation as its standard pronunciation, the northern dialect as its basic dialect, and the typical vernacular Chinese as its grammatical standard. Mandarin is spoken between the Huanghe (Yellow) River valley and the Yangzi (Yangtze) River basin through northern, northeastern, northwestern, southwestern, and central China, and offers convenience for communication between people in those different areas. The Mandarin dialect has been spoken by more than 70 percent of the Chinese population. In 1932, the government of the Republic of China (ROC) approved the proposal submitted by the ROC National Language Unification Commission, deciding on Mandarin (or Beijing dialect) as the standard Chinese language. In Taiwan today, it is also called *Guoyu* (national language).

After the founding of the People's Republic of China (PRC) in 1949, the new government designated Mandarin the official spoken language in mainland China and promoted *Putonghua* through mass media and public education. The nine-year elementary and middle school education has already become universal in the country and all classes are taught in Mandarin, including the Chinese language and literature classes. High schools, colleges, universities, and professional institutes in the PRC offer all classes in Mandarin. It is also used by many millions in Taiwan, Hong Kong, and foreign countries such as the United States, Canada, and Australia where 20 million overseas Chinese and foreign citizens of Chinese origin have migrated. It is called *Huayu* (Chinese language) in Singapore and Malaysia. Mandarin Chinese is also one of the five official working languages of the United Nations.

In 1958, the PRC National People's Congress (NPC) adopted the *Pinyin* system of the phonetic scripts, or *Hanyu Pinyin* (Chinese spelling language in Roman alphabets) at its Fifth Session of the First National Congress. *Hanyu Pinyin* uses Western spelling of language as a decoding system to enable non-native speakers to produce sounds close to the Mandarin Chinese pronunciations. *Pinyin* vowels are pronounced in a similar way to vowels in roman languages. A native English speaker will find the *Hanyu Pinyin* spellings easy to use for fairly close sounds of Mandarin except in the case of certain sounds that are not commonly used by most native English speakers. The *Hanyu Pinyin* system also uses diacritics to make the four different tones of Mandarin. Thereafter, all grade schools, colleges, and institutes began using *Hanyu Pinyin* to teach standard Mandarin Chinese in classrooms and to improve the literacy rate among adults. It is also used in teaching Chinese as a foreign language. Although the standard Mandarin language is used in government, business, education, mass media, and daily communication in society, local people still use their own dialects in the streets and at home. Many regional TV and radio stations have broadcasting and commercials in local dialects.

See also: Chapter 1: Taiwan. Chapter 2: Timeline. Chapter 3: National People's Congress. Chapter 8: Elementary and Secondary Education. Chapter 9: Overview; *Hanyu Pinyin*; Local Dialects.

Further Reading

Berlitz. *Basic Mandarin Chinese*. London: Berlitz Publishing, 2009.

Chen, Ping. *Modern Chinese: History and Sociolinguistics*. Cambridge, UK: Cambridge University Press, 1988.

Fallows, Deborah. *Dreaming in Chinese: Mandarin Lessons in Life, Love, and Language*. New York: Walker, 2011.

CHAPTER 10

ETIQUETTE

OVERVIEW

China is a country of etiquette, attaching importance to rules about many things. Chinese culture observes separate rules of etiquette for public events, business meetings, social gatherings, religious celebration, and daily activities. Expectations regarding good manners, however, differ from region to region and from family to family. Certain ways of behaving, practiced by the Chinese for thousands of years, built a tradition, as well as customs and culture, and reflect their common value, social order, and even national characteristics. Westerners often describe the Chinese as "inscrutable," since stereotypes of description fail to explore the significance of the Chinese way of life, and a foreigner may miss the key links that connect a person to his family and the society.

Chinese names are different from English names and have their own tradition and features. As in the Eastern Asian countries, the Chinese surname (last name) comes first, and is followed by the given name, such as Sun Yat-sen and Xi Jinping, and with the titles before their surnames like Dr. Sun and President Xi. The spelling of Chinese names in English literature has two systems: Wade-Giles traditional spelling (1859), which gives Chiang Kai-shek (1887–1975) and Mao Tse-tung (1893–1976), and the *Hanyu Pinyin* system (1986), which spells these names as Jiang Jieshi and Mao Zedong. Although international organizations have adopted the *Hanyu Pinyin* romanization system since the 1980s, the traditional Wade-Giles system is still popular in Taiwan, Hong Kong, and overseas Chinese communities. When Chinese people travel, live, and migrate to the Western countries such as the United States, they follow the Western ordering of names by officially writing their given name first and surname last. Some also have an English first name like Gary Faye Locke and Elaine Lan Chao.

It is popular in China, when a person is born, that one animal, or *Shuxiang*, also called *Shengxiao* (birth likeness), is used to symbolize the year. The Chinese zodiac has 12 animals in this order: rat, ox, tiger, rabbit, dragon, snake, horse, goat, monkey, rooster, dog, and pig. They are associated with the Heavenly Stems and Earthly Branches system, which has long been used as a revolving cycle to number the years, months, days, and hours since ancient China. Some Daoist (Taoist) Feng-shui masters and fortune tellers have also developed certain traditional details, characteristics, personalities, and compatibilities from different animal signs for them to offer putative guidance in life or for love and marriage.

The Chinese lunar-solar calendar is also based on the Heavenly Stems and Earthly Branches system. The Heavenly or Celestial Stems have 10 stems which are frequently used as symbols to denote numerical order, and appeared in order in a 10-day cycle, providing the names of the days of the week. There are 12 Earthly Branches, which were used to record chronological order. Each of them appeared in order in a cycle, providing the hours of the day in a double-hour system and months of the year in the Chinese lunar calendar. The divisions of the calendar had been based upon the waxing and waning of the moon. The months begin on the day with the dark moon and end on the day before the next dark moon. The summer and winter solar terms were taken into consideration with the Branches system. In the lunar-solar calendar, the length of the year and months is determined by various celestial phenomena. Since the founding of the People's Republic of China (PRC) in 1949, the government has adopted the Gregorian calendar as its official calendar. Nevertheless, the lunar-solar calendar is still used to mark traditional holidays, festivals, and historical events, and also used by peasants to observe farming seasons according to the 24 terms. It still plays an important role in Feng-shui astrological charts and fortune telling.

In ancient China, a number of symbolic animals, birds, and attributes were used at ceremonies, painted and sculptured as decorations, and even built on the roof of palaces and temples. Among the auspicious symbols are four kinds of animals, or Four Deities. They are the Qilin (or *Kylin*), Fenghuang (or Phoenix), Tortoise, and Dragon. The Chinese consider these "Four Lucky Animals" miraculous as good omens. According to Chinese tradition, these four symbolic auspices represent good fortune, serenity, longevity, success, protection, and prosperity, and they are symbolic of the offering made by heaven since, except for the tortoise, they are all legendary animals which were creatures from the divine world. As the number one animal of the Chinese totem, and the most important mascot in the country, the dragon has now become the symbol of the whole Chinese nation. Chinese all over the world call themselves the Dragon's descendants. The rest of the world is also quite familiar with the image of the dragon from popular literature, Disney movies, and video games. The dragon is the most important among the "Four Lucky Animals."

The Chinese show the highest respect by *ketouing* (kowtowing) to their elders, superiors, officials, and spiritual leaders. This act, as the highest sign of reverence, is to kneel down on both knees and bow so low as to have one's head touching the ground. It was also widely adopted for religious worship, military surrendering, and diplomatic events. In modern China and East Asia, *Ketou* is still popular for wedding ceremonies, funeral services, and temple visits. People sometimes also use it for help when desperately begging for their survival. Although *ketou* remains alive today, it has been reduced physically in different ways. At the Chinese dinner table, when an elder or official pours hot tea or refills your wine glass, you can just knock your second finger on the table as a symbolic *ketou* rather than jumping off your seat and knocking your head on the ground.

During dinner time, a Chinese family or a group of friends always sit together around a table and share food from the same commonly served plates and bowls with their chopsticks. This differs from the Western dining custom of doling out food into an individually served plate. Many foreigners are uncomfortable with the Chinese way of food-sharing since other individuals' chopsticks, which touch the communal plates, might carry saliva and food residue. For hygienic concerns, additional serving spoons or chopsticks known as public spoons or public chopsticks are available.

At dinner, a toast can be made to express one's respect to the elders or superiors. Before drinking the wine, the toaster touches his cup to the elders' or superiors' cups to show affection. When the toaster begins to drink, his cup must be lower than the elders and superiors to show respect. The toaster needs to empty his cup of wine first to show sincerity.

Further Reading

Chai, May-lee, and Winberg Chai. *China A to Z: Everything You Need to Know to Understand Chinese Customs and Culture.* New York: Plume, 2007.

De Mente, Boye Lafayette. *Etiquette Guide to China: Know the Rules that Make the Difference.* North Clarendon, VT: Tuttle, 2008.

Eberhard, Wolfram. *Dictionary of Chinese Symbols: Hidden Symbols in Chinese Life and Thought.* London: Routledge, 1986.

Evans, Polly. *Fried Eggs with Chopsticks: One Woman's Hilarious Adventure into a Country and a Culture Not Her Own.* McHenry, IL: Delta, 2006.

Fang, Jing Pei. *Symbols and Rebuses in Chinese Art: Figures, Bugs, Beasts, and Flowers.* New York: Ten Speed, 2004.

Graff, Kristen, and Rio Ramadhana. *Chinese Dining Etiquette.* Austin, TX: Magnolia, 2011.

Ostrowski, Pierre, and Gwen Penner. *It's All Chinese to Me: An Overview of Culture and Etiquette in China.* North Clarendon, VT: Tuttle, 2009.

Seligman, Scott. *Chinese Business Etiquette: A Guide to Protocol, Manners, and Culture in the People's Republic of China.* New York: Grand Central, 1999.

Chinese Names

The people in mainland China, Taiwan, Hong Kong, Macao, and the Chinese diaspora overseas use Chinese language, including both speaking language, or *Hanyu* (Han language), and written language, *Hanzi* (Han characters), for their surnames and given names. A typical Chinese name consists of three syllables. A monosyllabic family name has a particular tone and is written as a single Chinese character. A disyllabic given name has certain meaning or features and is written in two Chinese characters. As in the Eastern Asian countries, the Chinese surname comes first and is followed by the given name, as in Sun Yat-sen (1866–1925) and Xi Jinping (1953–), with the titles before their surnames, like Dr. Sun and President Xi. In some cases, surnames have two or more Chinese characters such as Sima and Ouyang; while some given names have only one character, like Li Bai (Li Po) (701–762) and Zhu De (Chu Teh) (1886–1976). Many ethnic minorities, like Tibetans and Uyghur, have different patterns for their names.

During the ancient age, a long period elapsed before the Chinese gradually progressed from living in groups to living as members of a clan (or tribe) along the Huanghe (Yellow) River. Clans distinguished themselves from one another by using a name. Their surnames often came from creatures worshiped in remote antiquity such as *Ma* (horse), *Niu* (cattle), and *Yang* (sheep); ancient states' names such as Zhao, Song, Qin, and Wu; or official positions, ranks, and nobility titles. Some surnames have origins with locations, residential places, rivers, and mountains. An estimated 4,000 Chinese surnames are in use today, and about 100 of them are commonly used. The three most popular surnames are Li (Lee), Wang (Wong), and Zhang (Chang), used by more than 20 percent of the population, or about 260 million people. A married woman keeps her name unchanged, without adopting her husband's surname. The surname passes down from one generation to the next and a child inherits his or her father's surname, the same as in Western countries. Preferential treatment toward males is part of the Confucian value system, and son preference is prevalent among Chinese families, since male members in the family carry on the surname. Given a traditional preference for males, an unintended consequence of the single-child policy has been the selective abortion of female fetuses.

The Chinese given name has its own tradition and features. Chinese given names usually have a specific meaning, expressing some sort of wish. Some names expect possession of wealth, health, and happiness such as *Youcai* (getting rich), *Changfu* (happiness forever), and *Jian* (health). Some names reflect the natural world as in *Shan* (mountain), *Song* (pine tree), and *Peng* (hawk). Female names often have characters representing kindness and beauty, such as *Yufeng* (jade phoenix), *Cailian* (colorful lotus), and *Wenjing* (nicely quiet).

The spelling of the Chinese names in English literature has two systems: Wade-Giles traditional spelling (1859) as in Chiang Kai-shek (1887–1975), Mao Tse-tung (1893–1976), and Deng Hsiao-ping (1904–1997); and the *Hanyu Pinyin* system (1986) which spells these names as Jiang Jieshi, Mao Zedong, and Deng Xiaoping. Although the international organizations have adopted the *Hanyu Pinyin* romanization system since the 1980s, the traditional Wade-Giles system is still popular in Taiwan, Hong Kong, and overseas Chinese communities. When Chinese people travel, live, and migrate to Western countries such as the United States, they follow the Western ordering of names by officially writing their given name first and surname last. Some also have an English first name, such as Gary Faye Locke and Elaine Lan Chao. They may be called Gary and Elaine, or Governor and Ambassador Locke (Washington State in 1997–2005 and U.S. Ambassador to China in 2011–2014), and Secretary Chao (U.S. Secretary of Labor in 2001–2009).

See also: Chapter 1: Hong Kong; Huanghe River; Taiwan. Chapter 2: Chiang Kai-shek; Deng Xiaoping; Mao Zedong; Sun Yat-Sen. Chapter 3: Xi Jinping. Chapter 6: Major

Ethnic Groups; Uyghur. Chapter 7: Gender Inequality; One-Child Policy; Selective Abortions. Chapter 9: Overview; Chinese Characters; *Hanyu Pinyin*; Mandarin.

Further Reading

Chan, Kwok-bun, ed. *International Handbook of Chinese Families*. New York: Springer, 2012.

Harbaugh, Rick. *Chinese Characters: A Genealogy and Dictionary*. New Haven, CT: Yale University Press, 1999.

Louie, Emma. *Chinese American Names: Tradition and Transition*. Jefferson, NC: McFarland, 1998.

Chinese Zodiac

In China it is popular, when a person is born, that one animal, or *Shuxiang*, also called *Shengxiao* (birth likeness), is used to symbolize the year of birth. The Chinese zodiac has 12 animals in the order of rat, ox, tiger, rabbit, dragon, snake, horse, goat,

An antique Chinese Zodiac Wheel with a Feng-shui compass made of engraved bone and wood. The zodiac has 12 animals in the order of rat, ox, tiger, rabbit, dragon, snake, horse, goat, monkey, rooster, dog, and pig. The year 2016 is the year of the monkey, according to the Chinese zodiac. (Rozenn Leard/Dreamstime.com)

monkey, rooster, dog, and pig. Depending on the translations, the goat is sometimes interchangeable with a sheep or ram; the rabbit with a hare; a snake with a serpent or baby dragon; the rat with a mouse; an ox with a cow; and a pig with a boar. There are many ancient folk stories about the zodiac origin and the 12 different animals. The Japanese, Korean, and Vietnamese zodiacs are almost identical to the Chinese zodiac.

During the Han dynasty (206 BCE–220 CE), the 12 zodiac signs became associated with the Heavenly Stems and Earthly Branches system, which had been used as a revolving cycle to number the years, months, days, and hours in China. The Earthly Branches have 12 signs which were used to record chronological order: *Zi, Chou, Yin, Mao, Chen, Si, Wu, Wei, Shen, You, Xu,* and *Hai.* These symbols matched the Chinese zodiac in the order *Zi* rat, *Chou* ox, *Yin* tiger, *Mao* rabbit, *Chen* dragon, *Si* snake, *Wu* horse, *Wei* ram, *Shen* monkey, *You* rooster, *Xu* dog, and *Hai* pig. Each appeared in order in a cycle, providing a year based upon observations of the orbit of Jupiter (the Year Star) in a 12-year cycle. The Han dynasty used the Stems and Branches system to date official documents, to number the years, and to record a person's age.

Thus, the *Zi* Year is the Year of the Rat, the *Chou* Year is the Year of the Ox, the *Yin* Year is the Year of the Tiger, and so on. Therefore, when a person is born, he or she has an animal as his or her symbolic animal. The year 2015 was a *Wei* Year under the lunar calendar, also the Year of the Ram (or Goat or Sheep), so children born in 2015 are all Ram babies. According to the 12-year cycle, a person who is a Horse is 12, 24, 36, 48, or 60 years old in 2014. He or she was born in 1954, 1966, 1978, 1990, or 2002.

Although the Chinese government now uses the years and their age under the Gregorian calendar, the people still continue to use the zodiac. So you can infer a person's exact age without asking his or her birthday but finding out his or her symbolic animal on an office desk or in the car. Some Daoist (Taoist) Feng-shui masters and fortune tellers have also developed certain traditional details, characteristics, personalities, and compatibilities from different animal signs for them to offer putative guidance in life or for love and marriage. Fir example, the Rat has the best match with Ox, Dragon, and Monkey; an adequate match with Dog, Rat, Goat, Snake, Pig, and Tiger; but should not match with Horse, Rabbit, and Rooster.

See also: Chapter 2: Timeline. Chapter 5: Daoism; Feng-Shui. Chapter 10: Overview; Heavenly Stems and Earthly Branches; Lunar-Solar Calendar.

Further Reading

Lau, Theodora, and Laura Lau. *The Handbook of Chinese Horoscopes.* 7th ed. New York: Harper Perennial, 2010.

Thompson, Gerry. *The Guide to Chinese Horoscopes: The Twelve Animal Signs—Personality and Aptitude Relationships.* London: Watkins, 2012.

Wu, Shelly. *Chinese Astrology: Exploring the Eastern Zodiac.* Pompton Plains, NJ: New Page Books, 2013.

Chopsticks

Chopsticks come in pairs of equal length, usually between 8 and 16 inches, and are in the shape of thin round sticks. They are the eating utensils of China. Subsequently, most dishes of Chinese cuisine are prepared in small pieces, easy to pick up with chopsticks and easy to chew. Chopsticks appeared in China as early as the Shang dynasty (1766–1027 BCE) and became popular during the Han dynasty (206 BCE–220 CE) with its large population growth. Later, through trade and Buddhist missionaries, they were introduced to Korea, Japan, and Vietnam.

In a typical Chinese meal, each individual picks food frequently with his or her chopsticks from the communal dish(s) in the center of the table through the dinner. This differs from the Western diet custom of doling out individual servings of the dishes at the beginning of the meal. Many foreigners are uncomfortable with the Chinese way of food-sharing since other individuals' chopsticks which touch the communal plates might carry saliva and food residue. For hygienic concerns, additional serving spoons or chopsticks, known as public spoons or public chopsticks, are often made available. The serving or public chopsticks are usually longer (about 12 to 16 inches in length) than the table or individual chopsticks (between 8 to 12 inches). The serving chopsticks are also used for cooking.

People use chopsticks as the primary eating utensil in Chinese and Japanese culture for solid foods, while using a wide, flat-bottomed spoon made of ceramic to enjoy soups and other liquids. Most Chinese use their dominant hand to hold the chopsticks between the thumb and fingers to pick up pieces of food from the dish plates and rice bowl. Some keep one of them stationary by tucking it under the thumb and between the ring finger and middle finger. They hold the second chopstick much like a pencil and move it up and down to pull food into the grasp of the chopsticks. When picking up food with chopsticks, one cannot pick up too much at once. One cannot poke his chopsticks vertically into the center of his rice bowl. One should also try not to make sounds with the chopsticks by touching or tapping the bowl or dishes. Young children often have difficulties to grasp the last few pieces of rice with their chopsticks. Some Chinese elementary schools stopped providing chopsticks during school lunch time since the administrators believe that it takes longer for the pupils to finish their lunch with chopsticks than by using spoons and folks.

Chopsticks can be made of gold, silver, ivory, wood, bamboo, plastic, or stainless steel. Wood and bamboo are the most common materials. Recently, disposable chopsticks have replaced reusable ones in many small and take-out restaurants. An estimated 45 billion pairs of disposable chopsticks are used annually in China, using about 25 million fully grown trees every year. Due to recent logging shortfalls in China and other East Asian countries and regions, as well as increasing concerns over the environment, reusable chopsticks have become the first choice in many restaurants.

See also: Chapter 1: Pollution and the Environment. Chapter 2: Timeline. Chapter 4: Agriculture. Chapter 10: Overview; Table Manners. Chapter 14: Overview.

Further Reading

Berkeley, Jon. *Chopsticks*. New York: Random, 2005.

Evans, Polly. *Fried Eggs with Chopsticks: One Woman's Hilarious Adventure into a Country and a Culture Not Her Own.* McHenry, IL: Delta, 2006.

Graff, Kristen, and Rio Ramadhana. *Chinese Dining Etiquette.* Austin, TX: Magnolia, 2011.

Low, Jennie. *Chopsticks, Cleaver, and Wok.* Bloomington, IN: iUniverse Publishing, 2011.

Wang, Q. Edward. *Chopsticks.* Cambridge, UK: Cambridge University Press, 2015.

Heavenly Stems and Earthly Branches

The term "Stems and Branches" refers to the Chinese counting system wherein one character from each of the two series is combined to form a regular sequence composed of 60 paired combinations. The sequence thus formed was used in ancient times as a revolving cycle to number the years, months, days, and hours. The system has been used in Daoism (Taoism), and this sexagenarian cycle played an important role in calendrical systems in China and other parts of Asia such as Japan, Korea, and Vietnam.

Each combination from the Stems and Branches system consists of two Chinese characters, the first from the Heavenly Stems (*Tiangan*), and the second from the Earthly Branches (*Dizhi*). The Heavenly or Celestial Stems have 10 stems which are frequently used as symbols to denote numerical order: *Jia, Yi, Bing, Ding, Wu, Ji, Geng, Xin, Ren,* and *Gui.* Each character represents an original meaning during the Shang dynasty (1766–1027 BCE): *Jia* shell; *Yi* fishguts; *Bing* fishtail; *Ding* nail; *Wu* lance; *Ji* threads on a loom; *Geng* evening star; *Xin* to offend superiors; *Ren* burden; and *Gui* disposed grass. Each appeared in order in a 10-day cycle, providing the names of the days of the week. Historical evidence shows the use of the cycle for days remained popular through the Zhou dynasty (1066–221 BCE).

There are 12 Earthly Branches that were used to record chronological order: *Zi, Chou, Yin, Mao, Chen, Si, Wu, Wei, Shen, You, Xu,* and *Hai.* They matched the Chinese zodiac in ancient times: *Zi* rat, *Chou* ox, *Yin* tiger, *Mao* rabbit, *Chen* dragon, *Si* snake, *Wu* horse, *Wei* goat, *Shen* monkey, *You* rooster, *Xu* dog, and *Hai* pig. Each appeared in order in a cycle, providing the hours of the day in a double-hour system, months of the year in the Chinese lunar calendar, four seasons of each year, and the 12 years of the Jupiter cycle. Each branch is used in the form of double-hours, such as *Zi* from 11 p.m. to 1 a.m., *Chou* from 1 a.m. to 3 a.m., *Yin* from 3 a.m. to 5 a.m., and so on. Each branch represents one month of a year according to the Chinese lunar calendar, such as *Zi,* month 11, *Chou,* month 12, *Yin,* month 1, and so on. The four seasons of the year are each associated with three of the branches: *Hai, Zi,* and *Chou* represent winter; *Yin, Mao,* and *Chen* represent spring, *Si, Wu,* and *Wei* represent summer, and *Shen, You,* and *Xu* represent autumn. In Confucius's classic *Spring and Autumn Annals,* all the events were in chronological order based on the Earthly Branches system. Each branch also represents a year based upon observations of the orbit of Jupiter (the Year Star) in a

12-year cycle. The Han dynasty (206 BCE–220 CE) used the Stems and Branches system to record official documents.

This system has survived in the present-day lunar calendar, which still uses the Heavenly Stems and Earthly Branches to enumerate the years and days. The system still plays an important role in Daoist Feng-shui astrological charts and fortune telling. Traditional Chinese medicine uses the movements of heavenly bodies around the earth to guide acupuncture theory and their clinical applications. The stems and branches are commonly used in articles, documents, and contracts where English speakers would use A, B, C, etc. They are also used to rank sport leagues, students' grades, and approval rates. In teaching history, they refer to events occurring in certain years. For example, the 1894 Sino-Japanese War is officially called the "Jia-Wu War"; and the Revolution of 1911 is known as the "Xin-Hai Revolution" in all Chinese history writings.

See also: Chapter 2: Timeline; Confucius. Chapter 5: Daoism; Feng-Shui. Chapter 9: Chinese Characters. Chapter 10: Chinese Zodiac; Lunar-Solar Calendar. Chapter 15: Acupuncture, Moxibustion, and Narcotherapy.

Further Reading

Cheung, Albert, and Alexandra Harteam. *The Emperor's Stargate—Success on All Levels: A Guide to the Ancient Chinese System of Zi Wei Dou Shu.* Huntsville, AR: Ozark Mountain, 2013.

Golding, Roisin. *The Complete Stems and Branches: Time and Space in Tradition Acupuncture.* London: Churchill Livingstone, 2008.

King, Jerry. *Qi Men Dun Jia: An Ancient Chinese Divination System.* Las Vegas, NV: CreateSpace Independent, 2014.

Lu, Henry. *Chinese Acupuncture of Stems and Branches with Calendars.* Las Vegas, NV: CreateSpace Independent, 2013.

Wu, Zhongxian. *Heavenly Stems and Earthly Branches—Tiangan Dizhi: The Keys to the Sublime.* London: Jessica Kingsley, 2014.

Ketou: Bowing

A traditional Chinese gesture shows deep respect by prostration. It is also spelled as *kowtow* (or *koutou*, literally meaning "knock head") in Cantonese. The act as the highest sign of reverence is to kneel down on both knees and bow so low so as to have one's head touching the ground. *Ketou* was regularly used to show the highest respect for one's elders, superiors, officials, and especially the emperor. It was also widely adopted for religious worship, military surrendering, and diplomatic events. In modern China and East Asia, *ketou* is still popular for wedding ceremonies, funeral services, and temple visits. Sometimes people also use it for desperate help when begging for their survival.

Since the Xia dynasty (2205–1766 BCE), *ketou* had become imperial protocol in the court, and evolved into many different formats and styles depending on the ranking, occasions, and audiences. By the Ming dynasty (1368–1644), governmental officials had to perform the "grand *kotou*" in front of the emperor, including three kneelings and nine *ketous*, which involved kneeling from a standing position three times, and each time lowering their heads to the ground three times while kneeling. In the 19th century, the Qing (1644–1911) government also required foreign emissaries to undertake the ceremony of the "full *ketou*" before the Chinese emperor in royal audiences as a formal acknowledgment of China's cultural and political prestige. The 1911 Revolution ended the Qing regime and most of its court rituals, including *ketou*.

However, *ketou* remains practical and popular as a part of traditional etiquette in China, Taiwan, Hong Kong, and overseas Chinese communities. Confucianism has a strong influence over Chinese society, and it requires great reverence to parents, grandparents, married partners, and teachers. The ideology also emphasizes a natural harmony between one's body and mind, whose actions should be transferred into his or her mind. As *ketou* lowers one's body and head, the gesture should convert the respectful motion to a feeling of respect. *Ketou* continues to play a role in a formal induction ceremony involving commitment, apprenticeship, and discipleship. In a traditional wedding ceremony, for example, the bride and groom stand side by side before a Buddhist monk, a Taoist (Daoist) master, or a village officiate. When he announces, "First *ketou* to the heaven and the earth; second *ketou* to the parents, and third *ketou* is to each other," the couple would perform *ketou* three times in three different directions. According to a folk saying, they will not be a formal couple until *ketouing* to both heaven and earth. In Chinese martial arts schools, students *ketou* to their master first thing every morning.

Two businessmen bow to each other in Beijing, China. Bowing is a traditional component of Chinese etiquette, showing respect by prostration, and has been widely adopted for diplomatic events, business meetings, social ceremonies, religious services, and everyday life at school, workplace, community, and home. It is also popular in other east Asian countries such as Japan, Korea, and Vietnam. (Shannon Fagan/Dreamstime.com)

Although *ketou* remains alive today, it has been reduced physically in different ways. First, some of the *Wushu* (martial arts) Kong Fu schools only require the "half *ketou*," or one-knee down instead of both knees. Second, one can hold both his hands together and raise them up to the front of his face, and then lower the forehead to knock the hands, a symbolic ground, rather than reaching the real ground. Third, bowing has replaced *ketou* in many occasions such as Sumo matches in Japan and Taekwondo tournaments in Korea, where the opponents bow to each other before their fight. Finally, at the Chinese dinner table, when an elder or official pours hot tea or refills your wine glass, you can merely knock your second finger on the table as a symbolic *ketou* rather than jumping off your seat and knocking your head on the ground.

See also: Chapter 2: Timeline. Chapter 5: Confucianism; Daoism. Chapter 7: Traditional Wedding. Chapter 10: Overview; Chapter 15: *Wushu*: Martial Arts.

Further Reading

Kuhn, Dieter. *The Age of Confucian Rule: The Song Transformation of China*. Cambridge, MA: Harvard University Press, 2011.

Loewe, Michael. *Everyday Life in Early Imperial China*. Indianapolis, IN: Hackett, 2005.

Rowe, William. *China's Last Empire: The Great Qing*. Cambridge, MA: Harvard University Press, 2012.

Lunar-Solar Calendar

A Chinese traditional calendar has been used from the Zhou dynasty (1066–221 BCE) to the 21st century. It divides the year into months and days by the Stems and Branches system. The Heavenly or Celestial Stems have 10 stems which are frequently used as symbols to denote numerical order: *Jia, Yi, Bing, Ding, Wu, Ji, Geng, Xin, Ren,* and *Gui.* Each appears in order, in a 10-day cycle, providing the names of the days of the week. Historical evidence shows that the use of the cycle for days remained popular through the Zhou dynasty.

The Earthly Branches have 12 branches, which were used to record chronological order: *Zi, Chou, Yin, Mao, Chen, Si, Wu, Wei, Shen, You, Xu,* and *Hai.* Each appeared in order in a cycle, providing the hours of the day in a double-hour system and months of the year in the Chinese lunar calendar.

During the late Zhou dynasty, the calendar evolved from the lunar system to a lunisolar system. The divisions of the calendar had been based upon the waxing and waning of the moon. The months began on the day with the dark moon and ended on the day before the next dark moon. The summer and winter solar terms were then taken into consideration of the Branches system. In the lunar-solar calendar, the length of the year and the months is determined by various celestial phenomena. Three of the 12 branches identify one of the four seasons of each year, and Hai, Zi, and Chou represent the winter; Yin, Mao, and Chen represent the spring; Si, Wu, and Wei represent the summer; and Shen, You, and Xu represent the autumn. According to this system, each branch represents two portions of the season based on the sun's position on the ecliptic. Beginning with the solar term called the "Small Cold" (*Xiaohan* in Chinese), each 15-degree movement of the sun along the ecliptic represents one solar term. The first day of each solar term is referred to by the name of the term. Thus, the entire year is divided into 24 portions with different terms.

The lunar-solar calendar is superior to the lunar calendar. Each branch also represents a year based upon observations of the orbit of Jupiter (the Year Star) in a 12-year cycle. The Han dynasty (206 BCE–220 CE) used the Stems and Branches system to record official documents. One of its few defects was the large difference between the length of the ordinary years and the leap years. Thereafter, the Chinese calendar has experienced more evolution and many changes. It also has many different versions today.

Since the founding of the People's Republic of China (PRC) in 1949, the government has adopted the Gregorian calendar as its official calendar. Nevertheless, the lunar-solar calendar is still used to mark traditional holidays, festivals, and historical events, as well as by peasants to observe farming seasons according to the 24 terms. Many traditional holidays and festivals follow the lunar calendar rather than the official calendar, so that they are celebrated on different dates each year. The Chinese New Year, or Spring Festival, for example, is the most important and popular holiday of all Chinese holidays in China. People take three to five days off work to celebrate the first day of a new lunar year, but it is usually in late January or early February on the official calendar. All the traditional holidays follow the lunar-solar calendar such as the Lantern Festival, Dragon Boat Festival, and Mid-autumn Festival (or Moon Festival). The lunar-solar calendar still plays an important role in Daoist Feng-shui astrological charts and in fortune telling. In teaching history, it refers to events occurring in certain years. For example, the 1894 Sino-Japanese War is officially called the "Jia-Wu War"; and the Revolution of 1911 is known as the "Xin-Hai Revolution" in all Chinese history writings.

See also: Chapter 2: Timeline. Chapter 5: Daoism; Feng-shui. Chapter 9: Chinese Characters. Chapter 10: Chinese Zodiac; Heavenly Stems and Earthly Branches.

Further Reading

Ben-Dov, Jonathan, Wayne Horowitz, and John Steele, eds. *Living the Lunar Calendar*. Oxford, UK: Oxbow, 2012.

Deng, Ming-dao. *The Lunar Tao: Meditations in Harmony with the Seasons*. New York: HarperOne Books, 2013.

Paungger, Johanna, and Thomas Poppe. *Guided by the Moon: Living in Harmony with the Lunar Cycles*. Jackson, TN: Da Capo, 2002.

Symbols of Auspice in Tradition

In ancient China, a number of symbolic animals, birds, and attributes were used at ceremonies, painted and sculptured as decorations, or even built on the roof of palaces and temples. Among the auspicious symbols are four animals, or Four Deities, which are symbols of luck and peace. They are the Qilin (or *Kylin*), Fenghuang (or Phoenix), Tortoise, and Dragon. The Chinese consider them miraculous and good omens, referring to them as the "Four Lucky Animals." According to Chinese tradition, these four symbolic auspices represent good fortune, serenity, longevity, success, protection, and prosperity, and they are the offering made by heaven since, except for the tortoise, they are all legendary animals, creatures from the divine world.

In legend the Qilin has a body like a deer, with a single nubby horn on its head. It is therefore sometimes translated in English as "Chinese unicorn," although it may also have two horns. Its feet are like the hooves of horses, and the tail is like the oxtail. The *qilin* is regarded as a very kind animal with a moral character, and emperors in past dynasties regarded it as the symbol of peace. In the Forbidden City and the Summer Palace of Beijing and the Drum Tower and Bell Tower of Xi'an, there are many statues of *qilin*. Some are copper-casting, and some are carved in stone. There is another tradition classed "*qilin* brings son," which both symbolizes the success of a new generation and also represents the wish for the birth of a son and continuation of the family tree.

The Fenghuang is a mythological bird that reigns over all other birds and is referred to in the West as the Chinese phoenix. It has a beautiful crista on its head and colorful feathers on its body. It is an imaginary bird of luck that is combined from characters of other birds, including the head of a golden pheasant, the tail of a peacock, the legs of a crane, the mouth of a parrot, and the wings of a swallow. It represents power sent from the heavens to the Empress as the symbol of her power and dignity. When used to decorate a house it symbolizes the loyalty and honesty of the people who live there, and that it only stays when the ruler is without darkness and corruption. The Chinese phoenix became a mascot among the people, and especially in the traditional Chinese wedding, it is the most important decoration on the bridal dress and headwear, signifying luck and happiness.

The Tortoise is an exception in the "Four Lucky Animals," as it exists; it also has the longest life span among animals. The Chinese not only regard it as the symbol of longevity, but also think it has the ability to foresee the future. A Feng-shui master or a fortune teller bakes the shell of a tortoise before significant events and then reads the future according to the cracks in the shell. The emperors' palaces always had statues of tortoises that were made of copper or stone, giving a blessing for the long life of the dynasties.

As the number one animal of the Chinese totem, and the most important mascot in the country, the Dragon has become the symbol of the entire Chinese nation. Chinese all over the world call themselves the dragon's descendants. Most people in the world are quite familiar with the image of the dragon from popular literature, Disney movies, and video games, even though it was born from the imagination of the people. A combination of different species of animals, the imaginary dragon can walk on the land, fly in the sky, and swim under water. Since it has incredible powers, the emperors in China treated it as the symbol of power and wealth, while common citizens believe in its virtue and dignity. One can find the image of the dragon everywhere in China, on the Great Wall, pagodas, imperial palaces, and ancient temples. During the holidays and festivals, people post the picture of the dragon, play the dragon dance, ride on the dragon boat, and light the dragon lanterns. Even when they name their children, the parents are likely to include the word dragon (*long* in Chinese). The Dragon is the most important among the "Four Lucky Animals."

See also: Chapter 5: Daoism; Feng-Shui. Chapter 11: Ancient Mythology. Chapter 12: The Great Wall; Pagodas, Palaces, and Temples; Traditional Chinese Painting.

Further Reading

De Visser, Marinus. *The Dragon in China and Japan*. London: Forgotten Books, 2012.

Eberhard, Wolfram. *Dictionary of Chinese Symbols: Hidden Symbols in Chinese Life and Thought*. London: Routledge, 1986.

Fang, Jing Pei. *Symbols and Rebuses in Chinese Art: Figures, Bugs, Beasts, and Flowers*. New York: Ten Speed, 2004.

Sanders, Tao Tao Liu, and Johnny Pau. *Dragons, Gods, and Spirits from Chinese Mythology*. New York: Peter Bedrick, 1994.

Table Manners

Chinese culture observes several different rules of etiquette for table manners, which are also different among regions, ethnic groups, and families. The host usually sits at the head of the table or faces the door with his wife on the left and the guest of honor on his right. After everyone sits, he offers to pour tea or wine into the cup of the guest and then to the eldest person at the table, as a gesture of respect.

Since Chinese people use chopsticks, most dishes in Chinese cuisine are prepared in small pieces that are easy to pick up and to chew. People use chopsticks as the primary eating utensil in Chinese culture for solid foods, while a wide, flat-bottomed spoon made of ceramic is used to enjoy soups and other liquids. Chopsticks came into use in China as early as the Shang dynasty (1766–1027 BCE) and soon became popular in Korea, Japan, Vietnam, Laos, and Thailand. They might be made of gold, silver, ivory, wood or bamboo, or plastic; however, wood and bamboo are the most common materials. When picking up food with chopsticks, one cannot grasp too much at once. One cannot poke his chopsticks vertically into the center of his rice bowl. One should also try not to make sounds with the chopsticks by touching or tapping the bowl or dishes. Currently, disposable chopsticks have replaced reusable ones in many small and take-out restaurants. Due to recent logging shortfalls in China and other East Asian countries and regions as well as increasing concerns over the environment, reusable chopsticks have again become the first choice in those restaurants.

At a Chinese meal, each individual uses his or her chopsticks to pick up food from communal dishes at the center of the table, differing from the Western custom of doling out individual servings at the beginning of the meal. Many foreigners are uncomfortable with the Chinese way of food-sharing since other individuals' chopsticks, which touch the communal plates, might carry saliva and food residue. For hygienic concerns, additional serving spoons or chopsticks know as public spoons or public chopsticks are sometimes made available. While eating, one should not make noises with the mouth; when having soup, one cannot slurp or be sloppy. When finished with the meal, one should say "I've eaten well" or "I'm full," rather than saying "I'm done."

For a New Year's Eve family dinner in north China, four cold dishes are generally served first, usually containing meat or seafood. Next, hot dishes are served with meat dishes and soup on the right while pasta and rice are at the left. The main entrée, such as a whole crispy fish or other special dish, is placed in the center of the table. Hot entrees are properly served beginning on the left of the seat across from the main guest. Ice water and cold drinks are not traditionally served at meal time. In north China, soup is always served before the end of the meal. At the end of a formal dinner or banquet, a sweet dish is usually served, such as sliced fresh fruits, sesame balls, fried banana, or tapioca sweet soup, which may be served either warm or cold. There are no fortune cookies in China or Taiwan.

Wine and beers are offered and served at dinner tables, and people celebrate their birthdays, holidays, and important events with alcoholic beverages. If you like to express your respect to the elders or superiors, you may make a toast. Before your drinking, you must use your cup to touch the elders' or superiors' cups (*pengbei* in Chinese) to show affection. When you begin to drink, your cup should be lower than the elders and superiors to show respect. It is customary to empty your cup of wine first (*ganbei* in Chinese) to show sincerity.

See also: Chapter 7: Traditional Wedding. Chapter 10: Overview; Chopsticks. Chapter 14: Overview; Holiday Feasts. Chapter 15: Alcoholic Beverages; Chinese Tea.

Further Reading

Dunlop, Fuchsia. *Shark's Fin and Sichuan Pepper: A Sweet-Sour Memoir of Eating in China.* New York: Norton, 2009.

Evans, Polly. *Fried Eggs with Chopsticks: One Woman's Hilarious Adventure into a Country and a Culture Not Her Own.* McHenry, IL: Delta, 2006.

Graff, Kristen, and Rio Ramadhana. *Chinese Dining Etiquette.* Austin, TX: Magnolia, 2011.

CHAPTER 11

LITERATURE AND DRAMA

OVERVIEW

Literature and theater are the most dynamic reflections of Chinese culture throughout its long history. They have made splendid achievements in building Chinese civilization as well as the nation-state, and greatly contributed to cultural evolution over the centuries as well as cultural assimilation between Chinese and ethnic groups. The incorporation of "other peoples," including invading forces and foreign rulers into Chinese culture during its long history was a continuous process of acculturation. For centuries, a succession of diversified literary forms, for example ancient mythologies, vari-drama of the Mongol Yuan dynasty (1279–1368), and fictions of the Ming (1368–1644) and Qing (1644–1911) dynasties, have become part of the mainstream of Chinese literature and theater.

Many great litterateurs of the ancient age, the classic period, and modern times are still read and performed today. The revolutionary culture continues its influence in the government of the People's Republic of China (PRC) since 1949, while contemporary literature and theater began gaining new popularity after the 1980s. China also has one of the longest and richest histories of theater in the world, including more than 1,400 traditional local operas, over 600 kinds of shadow and puppet theater, and 4,600 kinds of modern drama, opera, dance-drama, and ethnic minority theatrical forms. These distinctive forms of Chinese theater, with roots that go deep into mass culture, constitute an important component of the cultural life of the Chinese people and occupy a secured place in world theater.

Ancient literature began in the pre-Xia (2205–1766 BCE) period with mythologies, centrally featuring heroic stories and humanism. From the beginning, ancient Chinese literature was more concerned with great semi-divine cultural heroes than with a theory of beginnings. The earlier a figure is placed in mythological time, the more godlike its attributes. This literary tradition accounts for the origins of the cosmos, the dominant metaphor being that of procreation or of "giving birth," rather than that of fashioning or creating, and seems to be connected with the centrality of ancestor worship and the mentality of humanism. Ancient mythologies were passed on orally through the Xia dynasty and then recorded in written language during the Shang dynasty (1766–1027 BCE). They portray the people's dauntless, hard-bitten spirit in struggles against natural difficulties in the early ages. These mythologies contributed to the foundation of the early literature, and the classic writers and philosophers from the Zhou

(1026–221 BCE) to the Han (206 BCE–220 CE) dynasties constantly looked to them for subjects, inspiration, and new answers.

Among the elaborate literature of Zhou, Qin (221–207 BCE), and Han dynasties are *The Book of Songs* (*Shijing*, or *The Book of Odes*), *Poetry of the State Chu* (*Chu Ci*), and *Yuefu Songs* (*Han Yuefu*, or *Music Bureau Ballads*). *The Book of Songs* is the first collection of poems in Chinese literature history, including 305 poems or lyrics over a period of 500 years (between 1066 and 560 BCE). They were written and composed by officials and were presented to the Zhou emperors. As the root of Chinese poetry, the collection has great impact on Chinese poetry in terms of both ideological and artistic achievements. *The Poetry of the State Chu* was local style poetry in the 300s BCE and was influenced by folk songs and music of the Chu State. As its central figure, Qu Yuan (340–278 BCE) is regarded as the first great poet known by name, and he is held in highest esteem in Chinese literary history. "Li Sao" is his most well-known work, consisting of 373 lines with a strong flavor of romanticism throughout. After Qu Yuan, Song Yu and Tang Le also wrote exquisite works in the same style, making *The Poetry of the State Chu* a typical genre of poetry in the ancient period. "Yuefu" referred to the Music Bureau in the Han State established by Han Emperor Wu (Han Wudi) to collect and write the literati's poems and folk ballads. Folk songs are an essential part of the *Yuefu Songs*, including the best-known poems such as "Jiangnan" (South of the Yangzi River) and "Kongque Dongnan Fei" (Peacocks Flying Southeast). Among other ancient masters are Sima Qian (145–90 BCE), Cao Zhi (192–232), and Tao Yuanming (365–427).

The classic period witnessed a peak in Chinese literature, and made the Tang dynasty (618–907) one of the most glorious in Chinese history. Tang, for example, produced hundreds of thousands of poems, and 48,900 of them were written by famous and popular poets in Chinese literature history such as Li Bai (Li Po) (701–762), Du Fu (Tu Fu) (712–770), and Bai Juyi (Po Chu-i) (772–846). Li Bai's extant work includes more than 900 poems, covering a broad thematic range and touching all aspects of life and society. His influence on the development of Tang and later poetry is considerable. Du Fu inherited the tradition of realism. His approach is objective and serious, and his tone is profound and solemn, touched with melancholy and resolution. His language is concise, trenchant, and powerful, and he excels in introducing popular expressions into his verse. He is regarded as a model by all later poets. In the Song dynasty (960–1279), some progressive writers carried on the reform in poetry led by Ouyang Xiu (1007–1072) and backed by Wang Anshi (1021–1086) and Su Shi. Their call for simple and plain writing won wide support, and Song poetry and prose stayed on the path to the new lyric form. The Chinese lyric is a type of poetry with lines of unequal length, set to music.

After the Mongols defeated the Song dynasty (960–1297) in China, Mongol rulers founded the Yuan dynasty (1297–1368). The Yuan made China, once again, central to Asian economy, politics, and literature. The most notable achievement of Yuan literature is the vari-drama (*Zaju*), or the opera. It consists basically of a single and complete story in four acts or song sequences, and it has the unique characteristic that the songs or arias are sung only by the protagonist, either male or female. This unique dramatic form was created by actors and musicians on the basis of northern folk drama, and the operas touch on all levels of Yuan society. The rise of Yuan vari-drama made the Yuan dynasty the golden age of Chinese drama. Between the 1000s and 1200s, there were more than 200 recorded playwrights and 700 drama and opera scripts. Guan Hanqing (1213–1297) was the greatest and most prolific playwright of Yuan, writing 67 plays such as *Snow in Midsummer, Rescued by a Coquette, The Jade Mirror-Stand, The Wife-Snatcher*, and *Lord Guan Goes to the Feast*. After several hundred years, their appeal is still fresh, both in China and abroad.

Chinese literature in the Ming (1368–1644) and Qing (1644–1911) dynasties achieved great success in the creation of fiction. During this early modern period, political power became concentrated to an unprecedented degree in the hands of the emperor, and class conflict became increasingly acute. The spread of nationalist ideas gave the progressive literature of this period its characteristic anti-imperial flavor. The traditional episodic novel made great progress, and its thematic range is broad, including historical romances, chivalric tales, ghost stories, social satire, and love stories. Although the episodic nature of the traditional novel continued well into Qing, by mid-Ming the role of the author had already become more important in the creation and arrangement of material. Wood-block printing, first used for printing Buddhist scriptures in the Sui and Tang dynasties, flourished in the Ming and Qing, promoting literature and art and populating books and paintings. Illustrations for novels, opera scripts, and tales of the marvelous, and also New Year's pictures by folk artists and albums by professional artists, were all printed from skillfully carved wood-blocks.

The early Ming novel was typically produced on the basis of Song and Yuan historical tales and storytellers' scripts, compiled and polished by one or more authors, as in *Romance of the Three Kingdoms, Outlaws of the Marsh, A Dream of Red Mansions, Journey to the West, Strange Tales of Liaozhai,* and *Jin Ping Mei*. The novel as the creation of an individual writer like *Jin Ping Mei* began appearing during the middle of the Ming. The latter development reached its peak under the Qing, in novels such as *A Dream of Red Mansions* and *The Scholars*. Those works have gained worldwide attention and won international audiences. *Romance of the Three Kingdoms, Outlaws of the Marsh, A Dream of Red Mansions*, and *Journey to the West* have become the Four Great Classic Novels of Chinese literature.

As the most popular and influential opera in China, Peking (Beijing) Opera is a form of opera that began in the capital city in the 1800s during the Qing dynasty (1644–1911). Peking Opera troupes can now be found in most regions of China. Developed from local folk song and balladry, local operas in China were comparatively close to the people. Their subject matter was drawn mostly from historical legends, folk stories, and people's daily lives. Opera music is based on two different types of tune-families, *erhuang* tunes from southeastern Anhui Opera and *xipi* tunes from central Hubei Opera, including *Kunqu*. For the past 200 years, Peking Opera has been the dominant form of theater throughout China. The most famous Peking Operas include *The Empty City Ruse, The Gathering of Heroes, Women Generals of the Yang House, the King Parts from His Favorites, The Universal Sword, The Fisherman's Revenge, The Fork in the Road*, and *Havoc in Heaven*. It has become a national treasure and enjoys a high reputation both inside and outside China.

The formative years of the Republic of China (ROC) in 1912–1927 saw the introduction of Western literature and drama to China. Known in Chinese as "new drama" or "civilized theater," it dispensed with the singing and stylized acting typical of traditional Chinese opera in favor of a realistic acting style and spoken dialogue. Some young performers began new drama by adapting *Uncle Tom's Cabin* in the 1910s. The May 4th Movement of 1919 became a turning point in Chinese literature history. A new literature arose in opposition to the old feudal literature, and many progressive literary societies and periodicals made their appearance. Several hundred new literary magazines and journals were published in 1921–1925, and more than 100 literary societies were funded, including the Literary Research Society established in Beijing in 1921, and the Creation Society, established in Tokyo, Japan, also in 1921. A host of new writers, such as Lu Xun (penname of Zhou Shuren) (1881–1936), Hu Shi (Hu Shih) (1891–1962), Guo Moruo (1892–1978), Mao Dun (also known as Shen Yanbing) (1896–1981), Tian Han (Tien Han) (1898–1968), Ba Jin (Pa Chin) (1904–2005), Lao She (penname of Shu Qingchun) (1899–1966), Bingxin or Xie Bingxin (penname of Xie Wanying) (1900–1999), and Cao Yu (Ts'ao Yu) (1910–1996), reflected ongoing struggles in their works, adding new treasures to the storehouse of Chinese literature. The style itself became known as "May 4th Literature," and it marks the beginning of modern literature in China.

The Chinese Communist Party (CCP) soon turned the literary revolution into the revolutionary literature. Many of the new writers, such as Mao Dun and Guo Moruo, became radicalized, taking part in the CCP movement by organizing the League of the Left-Writers in Shanghai in 1930. The development of the left-wing literary movement encouraged a great upsurge in writing in the 1930s, protesting the Japanese invasion of China and then in the Chinese Civil War (1946–1949) against the ROC government, supportive to the CCP's takeover of the mainland China.

Chinese contemporary literature, beginning in 1949 when the CCP founded the People's Republic of China (PRC), can be divided into two periods: Mao Zedong's era from 1949 to 1976, and the reform era from 1979 to 2012. During the first era, even though the modern literature from the basis of the new literature since the May 4th movement continued to develop, Mao and the CCP launched several political campaigns in the 1950s and 1960s against "bourgeois idealism" and Western ideology, including political democracy, individual freedom, and liberal literature. The Anti-Rights Movement in 1957, for example, targeted those writers, journalists, and educators who might have said something negative about the CCP. More than 550,000 intellectuals were labeled as rightists, and were purged and denied the right to work, teach, or live with their families. A large number were exiled to labor camps or remote villages for reeducation, and numerous others were jailed or executed. Among a few survived socialist writers and their works are Liu Qing's *The Builder* (*Chuangye Shi*), Yang Mo's *The Song of Youth* (*Qingchun Zhi Ge*), Qu Bo's *Tracks in the Snowy Forest* (*Linhai Xueyuan*), Liang Bin's *Keep the Red Flag Flying* (Hongqi Pu), and Wu Qiang's *The Red Sun* (Hongri).

When the Cultural Revolution began in 1966 and became a nationwide political movement with extensive purges, literature and theaters were the first to come under attack from Red Guards, and mass organizations to support Mao's struggle against his political rivalry emerged. From 1966 to 1976, traditional literature was trashed, and classic books were burned as one of the Four Olds (old ideas, old culture, old customs, and old habits). Previously popular novels, films, drama, and opera were banned. Most of the writers, including Guo Moruo, Ba Jin, and Bingxin, were purged, jailed, and denied their rights to practice their professions. Some committed suicide, or were tortured or killed. Their works were proscribed, and all the writers and artist organizations were dissolved. The Cultural Revolution ended after Mao died in 1976.

During China's reform movement after 1978, the reputations of writers and artists who had suffered persecution, and of works which had been wrongly criticized, were restored. The Fourth National Congress of Literature and Arts was convened in Beijing in 1979. It assessed positive and negative experiences in literature and theater over the previous 30 years, and affirmed their tasks in the new reforming era. The second era from 1979 to 2012 was a fruitful time for Chinese literature and theater, since writers became freer to write in unconventional styles and to treat sensitive subject matters. Fiction writers who took advantage of a spirit of literary experimentation in the 1980s were Wang Meng (1934–), Zhang Xinxin (1953–), Zong Pu (1928–), and Gao Xingjian (1940–). Gao was awarded the Nobel Prize for Literature in 2000 and became the first Chinese Nobel Literature Prize winner, even though he had become a French citizen in 1998. Most of those works were rooted in real life, faithfully depicting the features of the age and the people's aspirations in a wide variety of style forms. New literary organizations were established, and many new literary magazines became popular. *People's Literature* and *Monthly Fiction*, for example, both printed over a million copies per issue. National awards were made for many categories, and most of the award-winning works were on new achievements during this period.

In the 1990s, Guo Jingming (1983–), Liu Zhenyun (1958–), Mian Mian (1970–), and Yu Dan (1965–) became popular when the book market was open and a strong commercialization of literature occurred. In 1979–2000, more than 83,000 novels, 450,000 short novels, and 420,000 short stories were published. Substantial developments were also made in journalist literature, poetry, women's literature, children's literature, films, dramas, operas, and minority literature. In the first decade of the 21st century, Chinese literature seemed to have overcome the commercialization of literature and touched major concerns and issues of society. In 2005, according to the official report, China published 128,000 new books. Some translated titles also had a large market in the country. *The Kite Runner*, for example, sold 1.2 million copies after it was translated into Chinese in 2006. Among the realistic writers are Han Han (1982–) and Mo Yan (1955–). Han's novel *His Land* (*Ta De Guo*) was written in a social critical style and opposed the uncritical mainstream literature. Mo Yan was awarded the Nobel Prize in Literature in 2012 for his work as a writer "who with hallucinatory realism merges folk tales, history and the contemporary."

Further Reading

Birch, Cyril, ed. *Anthology of Chinese Literature: From Early Times to the Present Day*. New York: Grove Press, 1994.

Denton, Kirk, ed. *Modern Chinese Literary Thought: Writings on Literature, 1893–1945*. Stanford, CA: Stanford University Press, 1996.

Kinkley, Jeffrey, ed. *After Mao: Chinese Literature and Society, 1978–1981.* Cambridge, MA: Harvard University Press, 1985.

Lau, Joseph S. M., and Howard Goldblatt. *The Columbia Anthology of Modern Chinese Literature.* 2nd ed. New York: Columbia University Press, 2007.

Mackerras, Colin, ed. *Chinese Theater: From Its Origins to the Present Day.* Honolulu: University of Hawaii Press, 1988.

McDougall, Bonnie, and Kam Louie. *The Literature of China in the Twentieth Century.* New York: Columbia University Press, 1999.

Riley, Jo. *Chinese Theatre and the Actor in Performance.* Cambridge, UK: Cambridge University Press, 2006.

Ancient Mythology

Ancient mythologies are an important part of Chinese literature, created collectively by people of the primitive age of the pre-Xia (Hsia) dynasty (2205–1766 BCE). These early stories underwent far-flung years of oral circulation until writing symbols became available and provided a permanent method of recording. The recorded contents of most Chinese mythologies reflect the vivid imagination of people living along the Huanghe (Yellow) River, the cradle of Chinese civilization, when faced with the unknown. Survival depended on better understanding of the living environment, and on improving relations between nature and humans, including natural resources and the advancement of tool making. Their development also depended on a better understanding of the society one lived in, such as learning from others, creating better social relations, and producing good leaders who could save the world.

Therefore, heroic stories dominated Chinese ancient literature, and humanism is central in Chinese literature and philosophies. Creation myths were developed at an early stage to explain the origins of the earth and its peoples. However, from the beginning, ancient Chinese literature was more concerned with great semi-divine cultural heroes than with a theory of beginnings. The earlier a figure is placed in mythological time, the more godlike its attributes. In literacy accounts of the origins of the cosmos, the dominant metaphor is that of procreation or "giving birth," rather than that of fashioning or creating, and has something to do with the centrality of ancestor worship and the mentality of humanism.

Ancient mythologies seemed unable to think of society without an emperor. For them, neither gods nor mystical beings, but rather images of great emperors dominated legends of how universe, life, and civilization began. These ancient myths attributed the creation of the basic elements of universe and civilization as the products of a long historical development. Among the heroic and colorful ancient leaders were Pan Gu (Pangu or P'an-ku), Fu Xi (Hsi), Nu Wa (Nugua or Nu-kua), Gun and Yu, Hou Yi, Kua Fu, Jing Wei, and Shennong Shi.

According to these mythologies, Pan Gu is a creator figure, who was born of a cosmic egg. He continued to grow for 18,000 years within a world with no sky or earth. He is often shown waving an axe, and separating the sky from the earth. When he died, his

Nu Wa, Chinese goddess of creation. This image of Nu Wa is from a 10th-century stone carving in the famous cave complex at Dunhuang in China. The work reflects the influence of Indian art, a result of cultural exchange along the Silk Road, a trade route that linked China with the Mediterranean. (Library of Congress)

eyes became the sun and the moon; his blood, the rivers and oceans; and his hair, the grasses and trees. Humans and animals derived from his body lice. His story became *Pan Gu Separates the Sky from the Earth.*

Fu Xi was believed to have been the founder of animal husbandry, marriage, the calendar, and musical instruments. Fu Xi, his wife, and his sister Nu Wa were depicted in a dynasty with serpentine bodies and human heads. It is said that Nu Wa used clay to create human beings and to fill the sky with stones. During her time, half of the sky suddenly collapsed, and a huge hole appeared, so that the human race was in great danger. Nu Wa came out and mended the sky with five-colored rocks so that the world regained peace and people again lived a happy life. Among the written literature of her stories are *Nu Wa Makes Men*, *Nu Wa Mends the Sky*, and so on.

Among other ancient stories in literature are *Hou Yi Shoots Down Eight Suns*; *Kua Fu Chases the Sun*; *Gun and Yu Harness Water*; and *Shennong Shi Tastes Medicine*. These ancient mythologies passed orally through the Xia dynasty and were recorded in written language during the Shang dynasty (1766–1027 BCE). They represent the people's dauntless, hard-bitten spirit in the struggle against natural difficulties in the early ages. They are also endowed with a deep sense of romanticism, which had a great impact upon the development of classic literature, as the classic writers and philosophers of the Zhou (1026–221 BCE) and Han (206 BCE–220 CE) dynasties continuously looked to mythology for subjects and inspiration.

See also: Chapter 1: Huanghe River. Chapter 2: Timeline. Chapter 4: Agriculture. Chapter 5: Confucianism. Chapter 11: Overview.

Further Reading

Allan, Tony, and Charles Phillips. *Ancient China's Myths and Beliefs*. New York: Rosen, 2011.

Birrell, Anne M. *Chinese Mythology: An Introduction*. Baltimore, MD: Johns Hopkins University Press, 1999.

Roberts, Jeremy. *Chinese Mythology A to Z*. New York: Chelsea, 2009.

Roberts, Moss. *Chinese Fairy Tales and Fantasies*. New York: Pantheon, 1980.

Sanders, Tao Tao Liu, and Johnny Pau. *Dragons, Gods, and Spirits from Chinese Mythology*. New York: Peter Bedrick Books, 1994.

Yang, Lihui, and Deming An. *Handbook of Chinese Mythology*. Oxford, UK: Oxford University Press, 2008.

Ba Jin (1904–2005)

Ba Jin is one of the few leading Chinese writers in the 20th century who survived the Republic period of 1927–1937, the Sino-Japanese War of 1937–1945, the Chinese Communist revolution in the 1940s and 1960s, the Cultural Revolution of 1966–1976, and China's reform movement from 1978 to 2000. He was born on November 25, 1904, as Li Yaotang (also known as Li Feigan), in Chengdu, Sichuan. As a young man he began studying in France in 1927, where he began his literary career and wrote under the penname of Ba Jin (Pa Chin).

In 1928, Ba Jin returned to Shanghai and worked as an editor at various publishing firms and journals for nearly 10 years. Most of his important works date from the late 1920s and early 1930s, including *Destruction, New Life, Love, A Trilogy* (*Fog, Rain, Lightning*), and the short story collections *Revenge, Glory,* and *The General*. His writing was filled with sympathy for the Chinese masses who were suffering from poverty and civil wars, and his writing reflected anger against the corruption and political scandals in the Chinese government. He wrote tirelessly to explore the dark side of China's society. In 1936, he joined the League of Left-Wing Writers, which included Lu Xun, Guo Moruo, Mao Dun, and Ye Shengtao. These writers laid the groundwork for the formation of a literary united front against Japanese aggression against China in the late 1930s. During the Sino-Japanese War of 1937–1945, Ba Jin completed *The Torrent* (*Family, Spring,* and *Autumn*).

The Torrent is his best-known work, especially its first volume, *Family* (*Jia* in Chinese). Through behind-the-scenes description of life in a bureaucratic landlord family, he scathingly criticizes the shameless degradation of the feudal landlord class and the hypocrisy and cruelty of feudal ethics. Based on his own life, *Family* is filled with depictions of realistic incidents and lively, believable characters. Its passionate sincerity has moved the hearts of generations of young people.

The novel *Fire* was written during the Sino-Japanese War and describes how Shanghai youth took part in the national struggle after the outbreak of hostilities. In the 1940s, Ba Jin wrote several more novels, including *The Garden of Rest, Cold Nights,* and *Ward Number Four*. He also completed about 100 short stories.

After the founding of the People's Republic of China (PRC) in 1949, Ba Jin chose to draw away from fiction. He wrote several volumes of essays, travel notes, and reminiscences. He was persecuted as a counterrevolutionary during the Cultural Revolution, in which his wife died. Ba Jin was rehabilitated in 1977 and was elected to several important national literary posts, including chairman of the Chinese Writers' Association in 1984–2005. He received the Fukuoka Asian Culture Prize in 1990. Diagnosed with Parkinson's disease in 1983, he ultimately died of cancer in 2005 in Shanghai. Asteroid 8315 is named *Bajin* in his honor.

See also: Chapter 2: Timeline. Chapter 3: Chinese Communist Party. Chapter 8: Foreign Exchange Programs; Returning Students. Chapter 11: Overview; Guo Moruo.

Further Reading

Ba, Jin. *The Autobiography of Ba Jin.* Indianapolis, IN: University of Indianapolis Press, 2008.

Ba, Jin. *Selected Works of Ba Jin.* Trans. Sidney Shapiro. Beijing: Foreign Languages Press, 1988.

Denton, Kirk, ed. *Modern Chinese Literary Thought: Writings on Literature, 1893–1945.* Stanford, CA: Stanford University Press, 1996.

McDougall, Bonnie, and Kam Louie. *The Literature of China in the Twentieth Century.* New York: Columbia University Press, 1999.

A Dream of Red Mansions

Also known as *Hongluo Meng* (or *Hung Lou Meng*) or *Shitou Ji* in Chinese, and as *Dream of the Red Chamber* or *The Story of a Stone* in English, this is often considered the best classic Chinese novel. It was written in the late 18th century and represents the peak of development in the traditional Chinese realistic novel during the Qing dynasty (1644–1911); it is also a masterpiece of world literature. "Redology" is the field of study in China devoted exclusively to this book.

The author, Cao Xueqin (Tsao Hsueh-chin) (1715–1764), one of the greatest literati of Qing, was born in Nanjing into a wealthy bureaucratic family. In 1727, his father was dismissed from office on a charge of embezzlement, and the family fortunes began declining. The family moved to Beijing, and it was there that Cao spent his last years in poverty, despite his talents as a poet and painter. *A Dream of Red Mansions* is a product of his last years, but it was left incomplete at the time of his early death. An 80-chapter text from his pen first circulated under the title *Shitou Ji* (*The Story of a Stone*), and the novel's present title and form were the contribution of a later writer, Gao E, who added a final 40 chapters along the lines of the author's original intentions. The novel is believed to be an autobiographical history of Cao's own family.

In the 120-chapter novel, a tragedy of romance between Jia Baoyu of a noble clan and Lin Daiyu, a beautiful cousin of Jia, gives an account of the history of a noble clan from its glory days to its final collapse. Through the changing fortunes of the aristocratic Jia family, the novel depicts the corruption of the bureaucratic system and its inevitable collapse. There are more than 400 characters vividly described in the novel, and three main characters are powerfully portrayed: Jia and Lin, two rebels against a feudal society, and Xue Baochai, a loyal upholder of orthodoxy. The author also details the life of women, whose individual characteristics are drawn with meticulous care, and shows how each in their different fate suffered from the oppression of women inherent in the traditional system.

Cao demonstrates extraordinary versatility in various modes of writing: narration, dialogue, poetry, descriptions of natural scenery, and catalog-like descriptions of the luxurious items of daily use in the Jia household. Altogether a model of the classic Chinese novel, it caused an immediate sensation in its appearance, and handwritten copies circulated for over 30 years until 1791 when, for the first time, it was printed. Although it was repeatedly banned by the Qing government, there was no way of preventing its circulation, and its influence on later Chinese literature is inestimable. With its enduring appeal to generations of young and old alike, this masterpiece is one of the best loved works in Chinese literary history. The early English translations began with selected chapters in 1812, and complete translations became available in French in the 1950s and in German in 1958. Eventually, the first complete English translation, in three volumes, was made by David Hawkes in 1973.

See also: Chapter 2: Timeline. Chapter 11: Overview; Fictions of the Ming and Qing Dynasties.

Further Reading

Cao, Xueqin. *The Story of the Stone*. Trans. David Hawkes. New York: Penguin Classics, 1974.

Hegel, Robert. *Novel in Seventeen Century China*. New York: Columbia University Press, 1981.

Hucker, Charles O. *China's Imperial Past: An Introduction to Chinese History and Culture*. Stanford, CA: Stanford University Press, 1975.

Tsao, Hsueh Chin. *A Dream of Red Mansions*. Trans. Yang Hsien Yi. Boston, MA: Cheng & Tsui, 1999.

Fictions of the Ming and Qing Dynasties

Chinese literature in the Ming (1368–1644) and Qing (1644–1911) dynasties achieved great success in the creation of fiction. During this early modern period, political power became concentrated to an unprecedented degree in the hands of the emperor, and class conflict became increasingly acute. The spread of nationalist ideas gave the progressive literature of this period its characteristic anti-imperial flavor. The traditional episodic novel made great progress, and its thematic range is broad, including historical romances, chivalric tales, ghost stories, social satire, and love stories. Although the episodic nature of the traditional novel continued well into the Qing, by mid-Ming the role of the author had already become more important in the creation and arrangement of material.

The early Ming novel was typically produced on the basis of Song and Yuan historical tales and storytellers' scripts, compiled and polished by one or more authors, as in *Romance of the Three Kingdoms, Outlaws of the Marsh, A Dream of Red Mansions, Journey to the West, Strange Tales of Liaozhai,* and *Jin Ping Mei.* The novel as the creation of an individual writer like *Jin Ping Mei* began appearing around the middle of the Ming. The latter development reached its peak under the Qing, in novels such as *A Dream of Red Mansions* and *The Scholars. Romance of the Three Kingdoms, Outlaws of the Marsh, A Dream of Red Mansions,* and *Journey to the West* have become the Four Great Classical Novels of Chinese literature.

Romance of the Three Kingdoms (*Sanguo Yanyi* or *Sanguozhi* in Chinese), authored by Luo Guanzhong (Lo Kuan-chung), was based on existing written and oral accounts of the Three Kingdoms Period (220–280), tracing the rise and fall of three competing states, and reflecting the upheavals of the time in the last years of the Eastern Han dynasty (25–220). He successfully created a cast of over 400 impressive characters with its central figures. His influence in East Asia has been compared to that of the works of Shakespeare's influence on English literature.

Outlaws of Marsh, authored by Shi Nai'an (1296–1372), tells the story of a peasant rebellion at the area of Liangshan, or Mt. Liang (in present Shandong), against the corruption of the Song government. It relates the stories of the 108 men and women civilians who were forced by persecution of officials to flee their hometowns and to gather at Liangshan.

Journey to the West, also known as *Xiyou Ji* in Chinese, or *Monkey* and *Pilgrimage to the West* in English, is a mythological novel by Wu Cheng'en (1500–1582). He wrote this novel in accordance with stories about Tang Seng (Xuanzeng) (602–664), a Buddhist monk of the Tang dynasty (618–907), who traveled to India in the face of many difficulties in search of the original scriptures. In the novel, Tang Seng is accompanied by several mythological figures led by the real hero of the book, Sun Wukong (Monkey King), who escorted and protected the master on his way to the West.

A Dream of Red Mansions, also known as *Hongluo Meng* (or *Hung Lou Meng*) or *Shitou Ji* in Chinese, and as *Dream of the Red Chamber* or *The Story of a Stone* in English, by Cao Xueqin (Tsao Hsueh-chin) (1715–1764), one of the great litterateurs of Qing, can be regarded as the best Chinese classic novel. Cao demonstrates extraordinary versatility in different modes of writing: narration, dialogue, poetry, descriptions of natural scenery, and catalog-like descriptions of the luxurious items of daily use in the Jia household.

See also: Chapter 2: Timeline. Chapter 5: Buddhism. Chapter 11: Overview; *A Dream of Red Mansions*; *Journey to the West*; *Outlaws of the Marsh*; *Romance of the Three Kingdoms*; Vari-Drama of the Yuan Dynasty.

Further Reading

Besio, Kimberly, and Constantine Tung. *Three Kingdoms and Chinese Culture.* Albany: State University of New York Press, 2007.

Hegel, Robert. *Novel in Seventeen Century China*. New York: Columbia University Press, 1981.

Li, Qiancheng. *Fictions of Enlightenment: Journey to the West, Tower of Myriad Mirrors, and Dream of the Red Chamber*. Honolulu: University of Hawaii Press, 2004.

Wu, Cheng-en. *The Monkey and the Monk: An Abridgement of the Journey to the West*. Trans. Anthony Yu. 2nd ed. Chicago: University Press, 2012.

Guo Moruo (1892–1978)

Guo Moruo (Kuo Mo-jo) was a prolific writer and poet; a renowned historian and archaeologist; and a Communist government official in the People's Republic of China (PRC). He served a lifelong term as president of the Chinese Academy of Social Sciences (CASS) from its founding in 1949 until his death in 1978; he was first president of the University of Science and Technology (USTC) and was elected representative in the Ninth National Congress of the Chinese Communist Party (CCP) in 1969–1973.

Guo Moruo was born in November 1892 in Sichuan. In 1914 he went to Japan to study medicine. During his studies abroad he came in contact with a wide range of Western literature. In 1914, he married a Japanese woman from a Christian family. They had five children and stayed together for 20 years, until the war broke out between China and Japan. In Japan, Guo translated numerous Japanese and Western literature works and began writing his own poetry in 1918. His first collection, *The Goddesses*, was published in 1921.

The Goddesses was the first and most important collection of new poetry, and it had an enormous influence in the history of modern Chinese literature. The poems themselves are highly romantic as well as patriotic. He also wrote many poems exalting personal liberation and supporting socialist ideology. Guo's style is grand and heroic, deeply emotional, inventive, and imaginative. His adoption of free verse revolutionized the writing of poetry in China, setting it free from the traditional strict rules of prosody.

In the 1920s, Guo Moruo returned to China. He cofounded the Creation Society in Shanghai and joined the CCP in 1927. After the failure of a CCP-sponsored uprising in Nanchang, he fled to Japan in late 1927. During the next 10 years, Guo published history and anthropology works on inscriptions found on oracle bones and bronze vessels. After the Sino-Japanese War broke out in 1937, he left his wife in Japan and returned to China alone. Guo joined the anti-Japanese resistance, and in 1939, in Shanghai, he embarked on a second marriage with Yu Liqun (1916–1979).

After the founding of the PRC in 1949, Guo continued to support and praise Mao Zedong (Mao Tse-tung) (1893–1976) and the CCP while holding important government offices in the 1950s and 1960s. He was awarded the Stalin Peace Prize in 1951. Nevertheless, he was one of the first targets to be attacked by Red Guards when Mao launched the Cultural Revolution in 1966. Mao spared Guo, but not his family. Two of his sons reportedly committed suicide in 1967 and 1968, following persecution by Red Guards.

Since his scholarship and literary writing provided support and justification to the CCP regime, some critics call him the first of the "Four Contemporary Shameless Writers." He once called himself China's answer to Germany's Goethe, and this title was nationally accepted. A scholar once said, "You are Goethe, but the Socialism New Era Goethe."

See also: Chapter 2: Mao Zedong. Chapter 3: Chinese Communist Party; People's Liberation Army. Chapter 8: Foreign Exchange Programs; Returning Students.

Further Reading

Chen, Xiaoming. *From the May Fourth Movement to Communist Revolution: Guo Moruo and Chinese Path to Communism.* Albany: State University of New York Press, 2008.

Dirlik, Arif. *Snapshots of Intellectual Life in Contemporary People's Republic of China.* Durham, NC: Duke University Press, 2008.

Kinkley, Jeffrey, ed. *After Mao: Chinese Literature and Society, 1978–1981.* Cambridge, MA: Harvard University Press, 1985.

Kuo, Mo-jo. *Five Historical Plays: Selected Works of Guo Moruo.* Beijing: China Books, 1984.

Journey to the West

Also known as *Xiyou Ji* in Chinese, or *Monkey and Pilgrimage to the West* in English, *Journey to the West* is a mythological novel. The author, Wu Cheng'en (1500–1582), lived in the Ming dynasty (1368–1644) and wrote this novel in accordance with stories of Tang Seng (Xuanzeng) (602–664), a Buddhist monk (commonly referred to as Tripitaka) of the Tang dynasty (618–907), who traveled to India in the face of great difficulties, in search of original scriptures between 629 and 646. Wu based his version on existing popular legends and written tales, but his imaginative use of the material and his skill in organizing the vast scale of this work are major contributions. *Journey to the West* was first published in the 16th century and has become one of the Four Great Classical Novels of Chinese literature.

In the 100-chapter novel, Tang Seng is accompanied by several mythological figures led by the real hero of the book, Sun Wukong (Monkey King), who escorted and protected their masters on the way to the West. They subdued many demons during the journey, and survived 81 calamities, to eventually bring back the scriptures. The adventures of Sun Wukong and the others, including Zhu Bajie (Monk Pig, or "Pig of the Eight Prohibitions") and Sha Wujing ("Sand Awakened to Purity," or Sandy), were related in a fluent, lively style, constituting China's most famous comic masterpiece. Monkey was the most important character in the novel, who showed the loyalty, bravery, and powerful fighting skills used to protect the Buddhist master, Tangzeng, and secure his journey.

Some of its chapters, stories, and characters have been further exploited into new novels, Peking Operas, films, comics, TV series, and popular video games in China and abroad. There are 17 stage plays, 26 films, 16 TV series, 34 video games, and 136 comics that have been made from *Journey to the West* in China, Japan, United States, Britain, France, Canada, the Czech Republic, Hong Kong, Taiwan, and Korea. One of the best English translations was offered in 1942 by Arthur Waley, *Monkey: A Folk-Tale of China*. In 1982, William John Francis Jenner published a complete translation in three volumes, titled *Journey to the West*. In 2006, Anthony C. Yu published his translation as *The Monkey and the Monk*, including for the first time, the poems and songs in four volumes.

See also: Chapter 2: Timeline. Chapter 5: Buddhism. Chapter 11: Overview; Fictions of the Ming and Qing Dynasties.

Further Reading

Li, Qiancheng. *Fictions of Enlightenment: Journey to the West, Tower of Myriad Mirrors, and Dream of the Red Chamber*. Honolulu: University of Hawaii Press, 2004.

Wu, Cheng-en. *The Monkey and the Monk: An Abridgement of the Journey to the West*. Trans. Anthony Yu. 2nd ed. Chicago: University Press, 2012.

Outlaws of the Marsh

Also known as *Shui Hu Zhuan* in Chinese, and *Water Margin* or *All Men Are Brothers* in English, it is the first novel about peasant uprisings in imperial China. Its author, Shi Nai'an (1296–1372), lived in the late Yuan (1279–1368) and early Ming (1368–1644) dynasties. He collected material from oral legends, storytellers' scripts, and Yuan operas on popular stories about a peasant rebellion led by Song Jiang in the later years of the Song dynasty (960–1279). His novel provides continuity between unconnected episodes and improves the literary quality. It was printed in 100–120 chapters in the 1580s and later edited into 70 chapters. The book is one of the Four Great Classical Novels of Chinese literature.

Outlaws of the Marsh describes the rise and fall of the peasant rebellion in the area of Liangshan, or Mt. Liang (in present eastern Shandong province), against the corruption of the Song government. It relates the stories of 108 civilian men and women who were forced by persecution of officials to flee their hometowns, and who gathered at Liangshan. Their stories show the inevitable process of peasant revolts from initial occurrence through defeat, reflecting basic contradictions in Chinese traditional society. The novel represents a new advance in the art of fiction by its delineation of character growth and development, presenting the leadership style of Song Jiang and characteristics of his 36 companions. It depicts the heroic rebels' reactions to their changes in fortune in terms of their origins and experiences, and sets forth factors behind their surrendering to the Song government in 1121. The novel successfully created 108 characters, who joined the peasant rebellion and fought together against corrupted government. The language of *Outlaws of the Marsh* is a refinement of northern colloquial speech and is fresh, lively, and humorous. It became not only a source for many later literary works but was also a powerful weapon in creating the resistance of the masses in traditional society.

Some of its chapters, stories, and characters have been further exploited into new novels, Peking Operas, films, comics, TV shows, and popular video games. *Jin Ping Mei*, for example, another Chinese classic novel in 1610, is based on the story of Wu Song, one of the 108 heroes in *Outlaws of the Marsh*. Other versions, including *Wu Song Strikes a Tiger* and *Lu Zhishen Pulls Out a Willow Tree*, remain vivid, even now. *Outlaws of the Marsh* was first translated into Japanese in 1757, along with the first volume of an early version of *Suikoden* (*Shui Hu Zhuan* in Japanese). Later, many other versions were printed, such as *Japanese Water Margin* (*Honcho Suikoden*) in 1773, *Women's Water Margin* (*Onna Suikoden*) in 1783, and *Chushingura Water Margin* (*Chushingura Suikoden*) in 1801. The first English translation from the 70-chapter version, *All Men Are Brothers*, was published in 1933.

See also: Chapter 2: Timeline. Chapter 11: Overview; Fictions of the Ming and Qing Dynasties; Peking Opera.

Further Reading

Kuhn, Dieter. *The Age of Confucian Rule: The Song Transformation of China*. Cambridge, MA: Harvard University Press, 2009.

Shi, Nai'an. *The Water Margin: Outlaws of the Marsh*. Trans. J. H. Jackson. North Clarendon, VT: Tuttle, 2010.

Peking Opera

As the most popular and influential opera in China, Peking (Beijing) Opera is a form that went national from the capital city in the 1800s during the Qing dynasty (1644–1911), and Peking Opera troupes can now be found in most regions of China. Developed from local folk songs and balladry, local operas in China were united with the people. Their subject matter was drawn mostly from historical legends, folk stories, and people's daily lives. Its music is based on two different types of tune-families, *erhuang* tunes from southeastern Anhui Opera and *xipi* tunes from central Hubei Opera including *Kunqu*. It is regarded as one of the "three quintessences of Chinese culture," the other two being traditional Chinese medicine and traditional Chinese painting.

For the past 200 years, Peking Opera has been the dominant form of theater throughout China. Many opera stories are taken from historical novels such as *Outlaws of the Marsh*, *Romance of the Three Kingdoms*, and *A Dream of Red Mansions*, and put together collectively by the performers. Four main roles in the opera are *Sheng* (leading male actors), *Dan* (female roles), *Jing*, and *Chou*. *Sheng* can be divided into three different male roles: *Laosheng*, *Xiaosheng*, and *Wusheng*. *Dan* means "female impersonators," and most

A Beijing Opera artist performs during a show titled "The Revenge of Prince Zidan" which is adapted from William Shakespeare's *Hamlet*, in Shanghai, China, on June 8, 2013. Beijing Opera, Chinese theatrical performance, is a popular entertainment that combines theatrical performance, music, dance, and acrobatics. (AP Photo/Eugene Hoshiko)

are played by male actors. Male actors usually play *Jing*, the face-painted roles representing warriors, heroes, statesmen, adventures, and demons. *Chou* play roles representing wit, alertness, and humor.

The four main roles in the opera combine singing, recital, acting, and acrobatic fighting. Singing follows certain tunes including *erhuang* and *xipi*. Recital refers to monologues by performers and dialogues between them. Acting includes body movement and facial expressions. Acrobatic fighting choreographs martial art. The most famous Peking Operas include *The Empty City Ruse*, *The Gathering of Heroes*, *Women Generals of the Yang House*, the *King Parts from His Favorites*, *The Universal Sword*, *The Fisherman's Revenge*, *The Fork in the Road*, and *Havoc in Heaven*. Peking Opera has become a national opera, and it enjoys a high reputation both inside and outside China.

See also: Chapter 11: Overview; *A Dream of Red Mansions*; *Outlaws of the Marsh*; *Romance of the Three Kingdoms*. Chapter 13: Folk Dance; Traditional Instruments. Chapter 15: *Wushu*: Martial Arts.

Further Reading

Bonds, Alexandra. *Beijing Opera Costumes: The Visual Communication of Character and Culture*. Honolulu: University of Hawaii Press, 2008.

Goldstein, Joshua. *Drama Kings: Players and Publics in the Re-creation of Peking Opera, 1870–1937*. Berkeley: University of California Press, 2007.

Li, Ruru. *The Soul of Beijing Opera: Theatrical Creativity and Continuity in the Changing World*. Hong Kong: Hong Kong University Press, 2010.

Wichmann, Elizabeth. *Listening to Theatre: The Aural Dimension of Beijing Opera*. Honolulu: University of Hawaii Press, 1991.

Xu, Chengbei. *Peking Opera: Introduction to Chinese Culture*. 3rd ed. New York: Columbia University Press, 2012.

Yang, Richard Fusen. *Mei Lanfang and Peking Opera*. Beijing: Foreign Languages Press, 2009.

Romance of Three Kingdoms

Also known as *Sanguo Yanyi* or *Sanguozhi* in Chinese, the first complete historical novel in China was authored by Luo Guanzhong (Lo Kuan-chung), who lived between the 1310s and 1400s, or in the late Yuan (1279–1368) and early Ming (1368–1644) dynasties. He lived in Taiyuan, central Shanxi Province, and Hangzhou, southeastern Zhejiang Province. His book was based on existing written and oral accounts of the Three Kingdoms Period (220–280), tracing the rise and fall of three competing states of Wei (220–265), Shu (221–263), and Wu (229–280), and reflecting the upheavals of the time in the last years of the Eastern Han dynasty (25–220). His original version numbered 20 to 24 volumes and was made between 1522 and 1690. In the 1660s, some Qing scholars edited Lou's text into 120 chapters by reducing 900,000 words to 800,000, today's standard text.

The book begins with events in 169 and ends with the national reunification in 280. It describes the conflicts, relations, warfare, and politics which eventually led to the end of the Han dynasty. The decline and fall of the Han is attributed to a variety of factors, generally deriving from government overspending, heavy taxes, and service drafting. To secure the empire, Han emperors maintained a large army of over 1 million men and continued military expeditions and territorial expansion. As a result, army generals developed their own personally accountable troops and controlled large territories. In 220, the last Han emperor was deposed by such dissenting generals, bringing the dynasty to a close and plunging China into the Three Kingdoms Period. One of the greatest achievements of the book is the extreme complexity of its stories and characters. Its central theme includes the rise and fall of the Shu State with an emphasis on its ideal leader Liu Bei and genius minister Zhuge Liang; the triangular relations among the three kingdoms, especially the conflict between Shu and Wei; political alliance and problems between Shu and Wu; and warfare of the dynastic governments. The book became exceedingly popular not only in China but worldwide, and made the Three Kingdoms Period one of the most romanticized eras in Chinese history.

In the novel, Luo Guanzhong successfully creates more than 400 impressive characters, including Cao Cao, Guan Yu, Zhang Fei, Liu Bei, and Zhuge Liang. Its panoramic scope has captured the imaginations of generations of readers. The author excels in battle scenes, and no two of the many battle scenes are depicted alike. The language, a mixture of the literary and the vernacular, is easy and fluent. Its appearance gave rise to many other historical novels and plays about the Three Kingdoms, and in the repertoire of 19th-century Peking Opera there were more than 100 such works. It is the most widely read novel in China, and some popular video games, TV programs, films, and comics are also derived from its stories. *Romance of the Three Kingdoms* is one of the Four Great Classical Novels of Chinese literature. Its first English translation was published in 1907.

See also: Chapter 2: Timeline. Chapter 11: Overview; Fictions of the Ming and Qing Dynasties; Peking Opera.

Further Reading

Besio, Kimberly, and Constantine Tung. *Three Kingdoms and Chinese Culture*. Albany: State University of New York Press, 2007.

Chen, Wei Dong. *Three Kingdoms: Heroes and Chaos*. Minneapolis, MN: JR Comics, 2013.

Luo Guanzhong. *Three Kingdoms: A Historic Novel*. Trans. Moss Roberts. Berkeley: University of California Press, 2004.

Tang-Song Poetry

Chinese literature experienced a peak development during the Tang (618–907) and Song (960–1279) dynasties, especially for classic poetry. Tang, for example, produced hundreds of thousands of poems, and 48,900 of them remain widely known today. So many works also made more than 2,300 poets famous and popular such as Li Bai (Li Po) (701–762), Du Fu (Tu Fu) (712–770), and Bai Juyi (Po Chu-i) (772–846). *Ci*, or Chinese lyric, is another type of this poetry and can be sung to music. It reached its zenith in the Song, which holds a very important position in the history of Chinese literature. Among the outstanding poets are Su Shi (1037–1101), Li Qingzhao (1084–1151), Xin Qiji (114–1207), and Lu You (1125–1210).

In early Tang poetry, the formalism and ornamentation of previous styles still prevailed. However, a new atmosphere was soon created with the poetry of Wang Bo (648–676) and Luo Binwang (640–?). Two important forms of poetry came to maturity in 712–756: "regulated" poetry, an eight-line verse form with either five or seven characters per line, and strictly regulated in regard to tone patterns, choice of words and so on; and "cut-short" poetry, a four-line version of the regulated form where the central idea is implied rather than openly stated. More than a thousand poets appeared at this time and their poems can be counted by the tens of thousands. Many different schools and styles emerged in this remarkable profusion of literary talent. Landscape poetry is represented by Meng Haoran (689–740) and Wang Wei (701–761). Frontier poetry is represented by Gao Shi (702–765), Cen Shen (716–770), and Wang Changling (698–757).

The twin peaks of high Tang poetry are the romantic poetry of Li Bai and the realistic poetry of Du Fu. The greatest poets of the Tang, they are also the outstanding representatives of realism and romanticism in China's classic poetry.

Li Bai is the first great romantic poet after Qu Yuan, and like Qu, Li's life included exile from court and a long period of wandering. Because he looked with contempt on the powerful families at court and passionately defended his freedom, he repeatedly came under their attack. He died destitute and homeless. His extant work includes more than 900 poems, covering a broad thematic range and touching on all aspects of life and society; for example, poems in praise of resistance to autocracy and support for acts of chivalry, and also poems exposing ruling class corruption and the dark side stories. Although some of his poems were written during the years of frustration and adversity, most are strongly positive, full of contempt for autocracy and a yearning for freedom. His language is extremely beautiful and natural, with many variations in the use of tones and harmony. His influence on the development of Tang and later poetry is considerable.

Du Fu lived at the turning point of the Tang when it began its decline. His own personal misfortunes brought him close to the people at the lower levels of society, and his poems reach a depth never before achieved. Another collection expresses his strong admiration for the hard work and courage of the common people. Du Fu inherited the tradition of realism. His approach is objective and serious, and his tone is profound and solemn, touched with melancholy and resolution. His language is concise, trenchant, and powerful, and he excels in introducing popular expressions into his verse. He is regarded as a model by all later poets—no writer in the history of Chinese literature has had as broad a following as Du Fu.

The late Tang, from 780 to 907, saw new ballads flourish. Among the famous balladeers of the time were Bai Juyi and Yuan Zhen (779–831); and famous poets were Liu Yuxi, Li Shangyin, Han Yu, and Liu Zongyuan (773–819). Bai Juyi left behind 1,914 regulated poems and 170 satirical poems, which are rich in realistic significance. His poems are fresh, moving, and easy to read, standard-bearers for the current school of "popular poetry."

In the Song dynasty, some progressive writers carried on the reform in poetry led by Ouyang Xiu (1007–1072) and backed by Wang Anshi (1021–1086) and Su Shi. Their call for simple and plain writing won wide support, and Song poetry and prose stayed on the path of healthy development. Su Shi (also known as Su Dongbo) subsequently extended the reform in poetry and prose to the new lyric form. As the lyric was broadened and deepened by involvement in the real world, it reached its peak of perfection in Song, and many outstanding works were created as a major achievement of Song literature. The Chinese lyric is a type of poetry with lines of unequal length, set to music. Song lyrics are divided into two groups, one known for grace and the other for vigor. Representative poets of the former type include Liu Yong, Qin Guan, and Li Qingzhao. Their lyrics are mostly confined to two themes, love and sorrow at parting, and are written in a tender and graceful style. The vigor type of lyric is represented in the works of Su Shi and Xin Qiji. The latter left behind 600 lyrics expressing his longing for the recovery of national unity, his frustration at not being able to realize his ambitions, and his criticism of the capitulationist acts of the Southern Song ruling elite, in a bold and resolute style.

See also: Chapter 2: Timeline; Tang Taizong. Chapter 11: Overview.

Further Reading

Cai, Zong-qi, ed. *How to Read Chinese Poetry: A Guided Anthology.* New York: Columbia University Press, 2007.

Hinton, David, ed. and trans. *Classical Chinese Poetry: An Anthology.* New York: Farrar, Straus and Giroux, 2010.

Lin, Shuen-fu, and Stephen Owen, eds. *The Vitality of the Lyric Voice: Shih Poetry from the Late Han to the Tang.* Princeton, NJ: Princeton University Press, 1987.

Pine, Red, trans. *Poems of the Masters: China's Classic Anthology of Tang and Song Dynasty Verse.* Port Townsend, WA: Cooper Canyon, 2003.

Vari-Drama of the Yuan Dynasty

After the Mongols defeated the Song dynasty (960–1294), Mongol rulers founded the Yuan dynasty (1297–1368) in China. The Yuan made China, once again, central to Asian economy, politics, and literature. The most notable achievement of Yuan literature is the vari-drama (*Zaju*), or the opera. It consists basically of a single and complete story in four acts or song sequences, and has the unique characteristic that the songs or arias are sung only by the protagonist, either male or female. Apart from the arias, there are also dialogue, stage action, and dance, performed to musical accompaniment. This comprehensive dramatic form was created jointly by actors, musicians, and playwrights on the basis of northern folk drama, and the operas touch on all levels of Yuan society.

The rise of Yuan opera made the Yuan dynasty the golden age of Chinese drama. Between the 1000s and 1200s, more than 200 recorded playwrights and 700 drama and opera scripts, including masterpieces such as *Snow in Midsummer* (also known as *The Grievance of Dou'e*, or *Dou E Yuan*), *The Western Chamber* (*Xixiang Ji*), and *The Orphan of Zhao* (*Zhaoshi Gu'er*). After several hundred years, their appeal is still fresh, both in China and abroad.

Guan Hanqing (1213–1297) was the greatest and most prolific playwright of Yuan, writing 67 plays such as *Snow in Midsummer*, *Rescued by a Coquette*, *The Jade Mirror-Stand*, *The Wife-Snatcher*, and *Lord Guan Goes to the Feast*. *Snow in Midsummer*, a tragedy about a virtuous young woman from an ordinary family, who is punished for a crime she did not commit, is his best-known work. Her defiant spirit, in Guan's representation, had the power to move heaven and earth to redress her wrongs. The play has been regarded as a classic of Chinese tragedy. Guan's works include comedy, courtroom opera, and historical drama. His characters are rich and varied, creatures of flesh and blood, and he is skilled at presenting character and reflecting social stratification through dramatic conflict.

Wang Shifu (the late 1300s and early 1400s) was another renowned playwright of Yuan, writing 14 plays including *The Western Chamber*, his most successful work and the best of Yuan romantic opera. Through the love story of a beautiful girl, Cui Yingying, and a talented young scholar, Zhang Sheng, this opera eloquently praises courage in the pursuit of free marriage and in opposition to feudal ethics.

Among other well-known playwrights are Bai Pu (1226–1306), who wrote 16 plays; Ma Zhiyuan (1250–1324), having 13 plays; and Ji Junxiang (about the late 1300s), who is known mainly for *The Orphan of Zhao*, one of the first Chinese plays to be translated into a European language and then converted into a play titled *The Orphan of China*, which received global attention. The Yuan operas hold a very high position in the history of Chinese literature. Today many are still performed onstage, and some have been made into films and TV series.

See also: Chapter 2: Timeline; Genghis Khan and Kublai Khan. Chapter 11: Overview; Peking Opera; Tang-Song Poetry.

Further Reading

Crump, J. I. *Chinese Theater in the Days of Kublai Khan.* Tucson, AZ: University of Arizona Press, 1982.

Hsia, C. T., Wai-yee Li, and George Kao, eds. *The Columbia Anthology of Yuan Drama.* New York: Columbia University Press, 2014.

West, Stephen, and Wilt Idema, eds. *The Orphan of Zhao and Other Yuan Plays.* New York: Columbia University Press, 2014.

Zhang, Guangqian. *Selected Plays from the Yuan Dynasty.* San Francisco, CA: Long River, 2012.

CHAPTER 12

ART AND ARCHITECTURE

OVERVIEW

During the Neolithic Age, Chinese pottery vessels were painted with decorative patterns or primitive representations of human faces, animals, and plants. Typical examples are the painted pottery bowls with a pattern of human faces and fish excavated at Banpo near Xi'an, and the pottery basin painted with figures of dancers excavated at Datong, western Qinghai Province.

The characteristic art form of the first stages of recorded history in China, from the Shang (1766–1027 BCE) to the Zhou (1066–221 BCE) dynasties, is represented by bronze ritual vessels and other bronze ware, which were often richly decorated. A bronze mirror unearthed at Ji County, central Henan Province, for example, is engraved with a battle scene on land and water which depicts more than 290 figures in hand-to-hand combat, shooting arrows, rowing, beating drums, awarding prizes, and bidding farewell. Paintings on silk first appeared during the Warring State Period (475–221 BCE). The earliest examples discovered so far are two silk paintings from tombs in the State of Chu, one of human figures, dragons, and phoenixes, and one of human figures riding dragons. They are in the form of line drawings executed with a hair-tipped brush, the basic technique of traditional Chinese painting.

Wall painting was a development of the Qin (221–207 BCE) and Han (206 BCE–220 CE) dynasties. Along with wall paintings in palaces and temples, there were also a great number in tombs of that period. The earliest Chinese mural so far discovered was in the Han tomb of Bu Qianqiu and his wife near Luoyang, Henan Province. It depicts the buried couple ascending to heaven in the company of immortals and mythical beasts. Han tomb murals have also been found in other provinces. Sculpture is represented by the life-size terra-cotta soldiers and horses in the tomb of Qin Shihuangdi, and the stone figures lining the approach to the tomb of General Huo Qubing. Both sets of sculptures are extremely lifelike, and each figure is a distinct creation. Of the large quantity of line engravings and low relief carvings dating from the Han dynasty, the most famous are those in the Wuliang Temple in eastern Shandong Province.

Religious art thrived as never before between the 200s and 500s. The spread of Buddhism in this period led to the practice of making cliff grottoes and furnishing them with sculptures and wall paintings of Buddhist images. The most famous of these, known the world over, are the Kizil Grottoes in Xinjiang; the Mogao Grottoes at Dunhuang, western Gansu Province; the Yungang Grottoes at Datong, Shanxi; and the

Longmen Grottoes at Luoyang. Construction at the grottoes at Dunhuang began in 366 and continued for more than 1,000 years. Today, 492 caves are still in a fairly good condition of preservation and contain 2,500 painted clay sculptures and 45,000 square meters of murals. The Dunhuang sculptures and murals are outstanding in scale and detail.

Chinese art reached a new height during the Sui (581–618), Tang (618–907), and Song (960–1279) dynasties, when the main schools which still dominate traditional Chinese art were formed. China's earliest-known landscape scroll, *The Spring Outing*, dates from the Sui dynasty. Many famous painters emerged during the Tang, such as Wu Daozi and Wang Wei. Wu was called by his contemporaries "the sage of painting"

A female photographer takes photos at the Longmen Caves near Luoyang City, Henan Province, China. Longmen Caves, or Dragon Door Grottoes, are situated in Central China, 17 kilometers southwest of Luoyang, the ancient imperial capital of nine dynasties in Chinese history. These grottoes were created during the fifth to seventh centuries, and most of the figures and the grottoes were financed by the nobility of that time. There are more than 1,300 grottoes and 700 niches, containing 40 pagodas, 2,780 inscriptions, and more than 100,000 statues and images. Many of the most beautiful sculptures were stolen or beheaded in the beginning of the 20th century and can now be found in various museums in the Western world. Just like the Dunhuang Cave Murals in the far north (at the end of the Silk Road), the Longmen Grottoes give a good impression of Buddhist art and show the various styles of the northern Wei-dynasty (386–534) and the Tang-dynasty (618–907). The largest of these statues is 17 meters tall, and the tiniest is less than 2 centimeters. (Trix1428/Dreamstime.com)

for his skill in both figures and landscapes. Wang was the inventor of ink-wash landscape painting, which reached its peak during the early Song dynasty. The most famous example of genre painting in the Song period is Zhang Zeduan's *Riverside Scene at the Qingming Festival*, a vivid portrayal of the bustling social life of Kaifeng, the capital city at that time. During the Ming (1368–1644) and Qing (1644–1911) dynasties, painting developed along two distinct lines: old schools faithfully following the old masters; and the Yangzhou school, emphasizing the expression of personal feelings.

The best-known statuary of this period are the stone figures leading up to the imperial Ming tombs in Nanjing and Beijing. Wood-block printing, first used for printing Buddhist scriptures in the Sui and Tang dynasties, flourished as an art from in the Ming and Qing. Illustrations for novels, opera scripts, and tales of the marvelous, and also New Year's pictures by folk artists and albums by professional artists, were all printed from skillfully carved wood blocks. A further and distinctly Chinese development was ink-wash wood-block printing in several colors. Among the most famous early examples of illustrations made by this method is the Ming *Notepaper from the Ten Bamboo Studio* and the Qing *Mustard Seed Garden Album*.

Twentieth-century Chinese art grew up at a time of wars and revolutions and was inevitably affected by them. Notable achievements were made in the cartoonist's art in this period. The appearance and development of satiric cartoons, in a sense, marked the growth of liberal and democratic thinking in a traditional society. Satiric sketches first made their appearance in the late Qing, and newspaper cartoons developed rapidly in the aftermath of the 1911 Revolution. Foreign cartooning was introduced to China around this time. A cartoonists' association was set up in Shanghai in 1927 and published a weekly called *Shanghai Cartoons*. Many cartoonists expressed their strong sense of responsibility to society by producing cartoons that exposed social injustice. Oil painting was first introduced to China from the West in the late 16th century, but its first main growth was in the 1940s. The creative efforts of Chinese artists before and after the founding of the People's Republic of China (PRC) in 1949 opened up new ground for Chinese art, laid a solid foundation, and prepared waves of artists for the development of fine arts in the 21st century.

In the field of Chinese architecture, China has retained many sites of ancient structures and traditional buildings as national treasures, from the Great Wall to the Underground Palace, from unique pagodas to resplendent imperial palaces, and from diverse religious temples to picturesque pavilions. The Great Wall of China, now more than 2,000 years old, is one of history's most ambitious construction projects. The United Nations recognized the importance of the Great Wall to human history in 1987, when it declared the structure a UNESCO World Heritage Site.

The imperial palaces were the residences of the emperor and his family and were located in ancient capitals like Xi'an, Luoyang, and Beijing. Palace architects have achieved great success in terms of scale, details, and perfection in order to show the supremacy of the emperor along with his authority to rule the country. The best preserved palace structure today is the Beijing Palace Museum, or the Forbidden City. There were 24 emperors of the Ming (1368–1644) and Qing (1644–1911) dynasties who lived in the Forbidden City. Over centuries, millions of temples were built in China by Buddhist, Taoist, Islamic, and Confucian disciples. The ancient pagodas were another Chinese architectural achievement in history, including circular, hexagonal, and octagonal pagodas. The Wooden Pagoda in Ying County of Shanxi, built 1,000 years ago, has nine stories and is 234 feet high.

Further Reading

Andrews, Julia, and Kuiyi Shen. *The Art of Modern China.* Berkeley: University of California Press, 2012.

Cai, Yanxin. *Chinese Architecture: Introduction to Chinese Culture.* 3rd ed. Cambridge, UK: Cambridge University Press, 2011.

Clunas, Craig. *Art in China: Oxford History of Art.* 2nd ed. Oxford, UK: Oxford University Press, 2009.

Cody, Jeffrey, Nancy Steinhardt, and Tony Atkin, eds. *Chinese Architecture and the Beaux-Arts.* Honolulu: University of Hawaii Press, 2011.

Gao, Minglu. *Total Modernity and the Avant-Garde in Twentieth-Century Chinese Art.* Cambridge, MA: MIT Press, 2011.

Wu, Hong, and Peggy Wang, eds. *Contemporary Chinese Art: Primary Documents.* Durham, NC: Duke University Press, 2010.

Chinese Silk and the Silk Road

Chinese silk is known throughout the world for its numerous varieties, which include silk fabric, satin, damask, silk gauze, crepe silk, tough silk, raw silk, georgette crepe, and velvet, as well as embroidered silk and printed silk. China's geography and climate are well suited for the cultivation of mulberry and oak trees (the leaves of these trees being the natural food of two types of silkworms), and China has numerous mulberry and oak sericulture farms. Because of its fine texture and exquisite crafts, Chinese silk has often been singled out among the finest textiles produced in the Far East. At present, facilities for manufacturing silk can be found throughout the country, and exports of raw and finished silk have gained first place in the world.

China was also the first country in the world to manufacture and use silk. Archaeologists have discovered a partially unraveled silk cocoon among the Neolithic Age relics unearthed at a site in Shanxi. The Shang government (1766–1027 BCE) first began sponsoring silk production workshops. By the time of the Zhou dynasty (1066–221 BCE), the production of silk had spread as far as the Han River, Huai River, and Yangzi (Yangtze) River valleys. At that time, the Chinese were producing splendid silks with subtle designs woven into the fabric, as well as silk decorated with colored embroidery. This was soon followed by the invention of silk gauze and brocade silk. Considerable progress was made in weaving and dyeing techniques during the Han dynasty (206 BCE–220 CE).

In 138 and 119 BCE, the Han Emperor Wudi (140–87 BCE) sent his representative, Zhang Qian, plus 300 delegates, to explore the west and establish official relations with countries in central Asia. After Zhang's trips to the western region, commercial activities between China and central Asia, as well as Europe, began to blossom and increase dramatically. Chinese silk became extremely popular in central Asia and Europe, and was soon a precious commodity. Due to the heavy trading of silk products, the route became known as the Silk Road. Along this 4,200-mile route, silk and porcelain products were symbols of the east Asian culture and civilization. The silk was not only a luxury consumer product, but also an effective political tool used by various Chinese dynasties. The kings and noble families in many western countries used Chinese silk dyed with Phoenician red, as well as Chinese porcelain, as interior decor to show their prestige and nobility.

Another important role played by the Silk Road was the dissemination of religions. In 100–200 CE, the Silk Road became famous for helping spread Buddhism from India to China. Many merchants from central Asia were Buddhists, who took Buddhist monks with them on their trading trips to China. During the Han, Buddhism became recognized in China and assimilated into Chinese culture. Buddhism continued to disseminate from China farther east to Korea, Japan, and other Asian countries. During the medieval age, more European merchants traveled along the Silk Road from the west to China because of Mongol domination over eastern Europe and central Asia, which had made such a journey profitable. Over the Silk Road, many Europeans reached China and a few left accounts of their travels. Marco Polo (1254–1324) was only one of many. However, no other European traveler has ever given such great detail as Marco Polo did on geography, economic life, and governments along the Silk Road.

During the Tang dynasty (618–907), further advances were made in silk manufacturing, resulting in even more delicate and exquisite products. By the time of the Qing dynasty (1644–1911), silk production greatly increased, and the silk of Zhejiang enjoyed an especially high reputation. China currently produces several hundred varieties of silk in thousands of colors and designs. These silk products have found ready markets in more than 100 countries in the world.

See also: Chapter 1: Xinjiang; Yangzi River. Chapter 2: Timeline; Genghis Khan and Kublai Khan; Han Wudi; Marco Polo. Chapter 5: Buddhism. Chapter 6: Mongols. Chapter 12: Tang Pottery and Song Porcelain.

Further Reading

Foltz, Richard. *Religions of the Silk Road: Pre-Modern Patterns of Globalization*. London: Palgrave Macmillan, 2010.

Kuhn, Dieter, and James Watt, eds. *Chinese Silk: The Culture and Civilization of China*. New Haven, CT: Yale University Press, 2012.

Liu, Xinru. *The Silk Road in World History*. Oxford, UK: Oxford University Press, 2010.

Millward, James. *The Silk Road: A Very Short Introduction*. Oxford, UK: Oxford University Press, 2013.

Vainker, Shelagh. *Chinese Silk: A Cultural History*. New Brunswick, NJ: Rutgers University Press, 2004.

The Great Wall

The Great Wall of China, now more than 2,000 years old, is one of history's most ambitious construction projects. The Great Wall extends from Shanhai Pass (*Shanhaiguan*) to Jiayu Pass (*Jiayuguan*), for a total length of approximately 4,500 miles. It first began as many disconnected fortifications in the seventh century BCE, and the Great Wall was combined into a single defensive fortification in the third century BCE. Although the wall has suffered considerable damage due to warfare and weather over its long life, and the era of the Great Wall as a functional fortification has now passed, vast sections remain standing today, as one of the most important symbols of China's strength and endurance. The United Nations recognized the importance of the Great Wall to human history in 1987, when it declared the structure a UNESCO (UN Educational, Scientific, and Cultural Organization) World Heritage Site.

When construction of the Great Wall began, ancient China had emerged as a variety of independent states, often at war with one another as well as with raiding tribal groups from Mongolia and Central Asia in the Spring and Autumn Period (770–476 BCE) and the Warring States Period (475–221 BCE) of the Zhou dynasty (1066–221 BCE). In the seventh century BCE, the State of Chu began construction on what would eventually become precursors to the Great Wall of China. The success of the Chu wall inspired many other Chinese states to do the same, and over the next three centuries, a variety of walls were erected in many parts of what is now called China, including the States of Qi and Wei.

Between 214 and 204 BCE, hundreds of thousands of workers from all over China were conscripted and sent to the northern border to build the Great Wall, designed to keep nomadic raiders out. The wall itself was made largely of earth, with tall watchtowers for sentries to observe advancing hordes on the horizon. The notion of the wall remained central to Chinese military and political thought, and the Han dynasty (206 BCE–220 CE) rebuilt and expanded the wall during the second and first centuries BCE, with important ecological and economic results. The Han wall was famous because it protected larger areas of land suitable for agricultural exploitation, and as a result, food production increased significantly, as did the population.

The Great Wall, as it is known today, was largely a creation of the Ming dynasty (1368–1644). The Ming emperors found themselves threatened by the Mongols and suffered greatly at the hands of Mongol chief Esen Taiji when his forces attacked China between 1449 and 1454. A century later, the Mongols again threatened China, this time led by Altan Khan, who besieged the Chinese capital, Beijing, in 1550. As a result, Ming leaders were determined to create a new Great Wall to serve as an impenetrable fortification that would protect China from further invasion.

Learning from the engineering mistakes of their predecessors, the Ming commanded their architects and engineers to create a much stronger wall made of local limestone or granite—or fired bricks mixed with egg whites and sticky rice for extra strength—with elaborate watchtowers, storehouses, and barracks built directly into the wall itself. Between 1560 and 1640, Ming leaders channeled extraordinary amounts of money and manpower into this ambitious project. The new wall was taller, thicker, and

Considered one of the world's greatest manmade structures, The Great Wall of China extends about 4,500 miles, from the Shanhai Pass in the east to the Jiayu Pass in the west. Large parts of the wall date from the seventh through the fourth centuries BC, and much of the wall was built during the Ming dynasty (1368–1644). In 1987, the UNESCO declared the structure a World Heritage Site. On July 7, 2007, China's Great Wall was added to the list of the New Seven Wonders of the World. (Corel)

larger than any of the previous walls, extending over roughly 4,000 miles of northern China, from the Bohai Sea in the east to the Uyghur region in the west. This structure, upon completion, became the longest and most expansive fortification of all time. Moreover, in western China, the wall itself ended at the Jiayu Pass, an important Silk Road oasis on the edge of the Gobi Desert. The Chinese monitored conditions and possible invasions along the Silk Road with a series of watchtowers that communicated using smoke signals. In that way, the defense of the wall was expanded far beyond its physical presence.

The Great Wall continued to protect China through the centuries, with varying degrees of effectiveness, until 1933. In that year, the battle known as the Defense of the Great Wall was fought between China and Japan, after the Japanese invasion of Manchuria in 1931.

In the recent years, the Chinese government has funneled money into restoring and rebuilding large parts of the wall, including the Badaling area near Beijing, today's most visited section of the wall. Moreover, various Chinese municipalities have used the wall as a centerpiece for tourism, including the city of Tianjin, which began an annual Great Wall Marathon in 2000. Despite the fact that it no longer stands as a viable barrier between China and its enemies, the Great Wall continues to merit fame and fascination throughout the world, and the People's Republic of China (PRC) still recognizes the symbolic importance of this ancient marvel.

See also: Chapter 1: Manchuria. Chapter 2: Timeline; Han Wudi; Qin Shihuangdi. Chapter 6: Mongols. Chapter 12: Overview; Chinese Silk and the Silk Road.

Further Reading

Cai, Yanxin. *Chinese Architecture: Introduction to Chinese Culture.* 3rd ed. Cambridge, UK: Cambridge University Press, 2011.

Turnbull, Stephen. *The Great Wall of China, 221 BC–1644 AD.* Essex, UK: Osprey, 2007.

Waldron, Arthur. *The Great Wall of China: From History to Myth.* New York: Cambridge University Press, 2008.

Yamashita, Michael, and William Lindesay. *The Great Wall: From Beginning to End.* New York: Sterling, 2007.

Jade Carving

Jade carving is one of the oldest carving arts in traditional China. Crude jade tools appeared as early as in the late Paleolithic Age. Cave dwellers selected eye-catching jade, pebbles, and other kinds of stones, carefully drilled a hole through them, threaded them together, and hung them around their necks. In the late Neolithic Age, ornaments made from jade, which is much firmer than stone, began appearing as pierced discs, pendants, and beads, which still have an aesthetic appeal today. In the Shang (1766–1027 BCE) and Zhou (1066–221 BCE) dynasties, jade articles were given special social significance as symbols of political authority, ritual objects, or symbols of personal morality and wealth.

As a high quality stone with many variants, raw jade comes in numerous shapes, sizes, and colors such as white, yellow, and green. Jade carving refers to the process of transforming a piece of jade into a fine art object, since in actuality jade is too dense to be carved. Rather, objects are fashioned by chiseling, grinding, crushing, and boring. Typical subjects include artistic articles such as dragons, flowers, birds, animals, and pavilions; household items like incense burners, vases, and containers; human figurines such as beautiful women, figures from history or legend, and religious leaders; decorative objects; and small items such as a brooch, ring, or seal. The Chinese jade industry now uses some 40 types of precious stone including white jade (nephrite), jasper, green jade, black jade, jadeite, agate, coral, crystal, sapphire, turquoise, and malachite.

The carvers' skill is shown in their ability to use the specific character of the raw material to its best advantage, according to its natural colors and shape, by enhancing its beauty and minimizing its flaws. For example, Zhou Shouhai, a master carver at the Shanghai Jade Carving Studio, can carve a jade incense burner hung with chains, standing 20 inches tall, without a break, out of a piece of unpolished jade only 6.3 inches high. Wang Shusen, a famous old master carver in Beijing, is known for his carvings of Bodhi dharma (the Buddhist missionary who came to China in 526), Guanyin (the Goddess of Mercy), immortals, and beauties.

See also: Chapter 2: Timeline. Chapter 5: Buddhism. Chapter 10: Symbols of Auspice in Tradition. Chapter 12: Overview.

Further Reading

Johnson, John and Chan Lai Pik. *5,000 Years of Chinese Jade: Featuring Selections from the National Museum of History, Taiwan, and the Sackler Gallery, Smithsonian Institution.* Seattle: University of Washington Press, 2011.

Li, Hongjuan. *Chinese Jade: The Spiritual and Cultural Significance of Jade in China.* Shanghai: Shanghai Press, 2012.

Nott, Stanley. *Chinese Jade throughout the Ages: A Review of Its Characteristics, Decoration, Folklore, and Symbolism.* 2nd ed. North Clarendon, VT: Tuttle, 2013.

Rawson, Jessica. *Chinese Jade from the Neolithic to the Qing.* Chicago, IL: Art Media Resources, 2002.

Pagodas, Palaces, and Temples

China has retained many traditional buildings and building sites as national treasures, from unique pagodas to resplendent imperial palaces, from diverse religious temples to picturesque pavilions. For centuries, Chinese people have created one architectural wonder after another, including the Forbidden City of the Yuan dynasty (1279–1368), the Underground Palace of the Ming (1368–1644), and the Summer Palace of the Qing (1644–1911).

CLASSICAL GARDENS

Classical gardens are a popular tourist attraction at historical sites throughout the country, offering beautiful scenery, unique structures, and unique architectural styles from the 17th to 19th centuries. Classical gardens can be divided into two categories. The imperial gardens in the north used natural elements in creating clusters of stylish architectural structures in imitation of those that are the best in the country. They evoke a sense of magnificence and grandeur in such places as the Summer Palace in Beijing and the Summer Resort in Chengde. The private gardens in the south are mostly seen in Suzhou, Nanjing, Hangzhou, and Yangzhou, and include the Jichang Garden in Wuxi and the Zhuozheng and Liuyuan Gardens in Suzhou. With ingenious designs, including miniature mountains and rivers, they are natural and tranquil with variable scenery.

The imperial palaces were the residences of the emperor and his family, and they were located in ancient capitals like Xi'an, Luoyang, and Beijing. Palace architects had made great achievement in terms of scale, details, and perfection in order to show the supremacy of the emperor along with his authority to rule the country. The best palace structure surviving today is the Beijing Palace Museum, or the Forbidden City, with 9,999 rooms. This palace has been used by 24 emperors of both the Ming and Qing dynasties.

Over centuries, millions of temples were built in China by Buddhist, Taoist, Islamic, and Confucian disciples. Daoist temples are called *gong* (palace) or *guan* (temple); mosque is the term for Muslim worship buildings; and temple, tope, and grotto are called the "Three Great Structures of Buddhism." Some of the renowned temples were built in remote mountainous areas, especially near the Four Buddhist Holy Mountains, Mt. Wutai, Mt. Emei, Mt. Jiuhua, and Mt. Putuo.

Construction of ancient pagodas also made a contribution to the architectural arts. Chinese pagodas were built in circular, hexagonal, and octagonal shapes with different materials, such as wood, bricks, rocks, iron, and bronze. The Wooden Pagoda in Ying County, built 1,000 years ago, has nine stories and is 234 feet high. It is the oldest and highest existing timber pagoda in the world.

See also: Chapter 5: Buddhism; Daoism; Islam. Chapter 6: Muslims. Chapter 12: Overview.

The Forbidden City in Beijing, China, is the largest palace complex in the world. It had served as the royal palace for the emperors and empresses for more than 600 years from the Yuan dynasty (1271–1368), to the Ming dynasty (1368–1644), and the Qing dynasty (1644–1911). It became the Beijing Palace Museum thereafter, the largest history, arts, and architecture museum in the world. It covers 183 acres and comprises 9,999 buildings. (Chen Lirong/ Dreamstime.com)

Further Reading

Cai, Yanxin. *Chinese Architecture: Introduction to Chinese Culture.* 3rd ed. Cambridge, UK: Cambridge University Press, 2011.

Cody, Jeffrey, Nancy Steinhardt, and Tony Atkin, eds. *Chinese Architecture and the Beaux-Arts.* Honolulu: University of Hawaii Press, 2011.

Kleutghen, Kristina. *Imperial Illusions: Crossing Pictorial Boundaries in the Qing Palace.* Seattle: University of Washington Press, 2014.

Knapp, Ronald, Jonathan Spence, and Chester Ong. *Chinese Houses: The Architectural Heritage of a Nation.* North Clarendon, VT: Tuttle, 2006.

Ringmar, Erik. *Liberal Barbarism: The European Destruction of the Palace of the Emperor of China.* London, UK: Palgrave Macmillan, 2013.

Ward, Adrienne. *Pagodas in Play: China on the Eighteenth-Century Italian Opera Stage.* Lewisburg, PA: Bucknell University Press, 2010.

Tang Pottery and Song Porcelain

Porcelain, or "china," is another of the ancient inventions of China. Porcelain was developed on the basis of pottery. The appearance of pottery began in the Neolithic Age, when the inhabitants of the Huanghe (Yellow) River basin, the cradle of Chinese civilization, began making earthenware pottery from clay. Having mastered these techniques, they proceeded to create painted pottery. The quality of the clay used in ancient earthenware pottery is very fine. Before the vessels were baked, their surfaces were rubbed smooth and color was applied. They were then fired in a kiln at approximately 1,000 degrees Centigrade, which set the colors permanently and gave the surfaces a glossy sheen. By the time of the Shang dynasty (1766–1027 BCE), vitreous glazes had come into use. These glazes were dark in color and were called "black glazes." According to chemical analyses, the black-glazed ceramic products contain characteristics of porcelain and are the forerunner of the green and blue porcelain ware of a later period. Primitive porcelain developed gradually and did not attain a high level of artistic maturity until the Han dynasty (206 BCE–220 CE), when the center of its manufacture was located at Shanyu in Zhejiang.

The Tang (618–907) and Song (960–1279) dynasties were a time of rapid development in pottery and porcelain manufacturing and technology. Tang tricolor pottery had green, blue, and yellow colors and went through the process of firing. Sometimes glazes would drip down and became mingled. Tang tricolor potteries were made in shapes and image of human figurines such as ministers, generals, ladies, boy servants, maids, and artisans. Other images of Tang tricolor potteries included animals and plants.

During the Song dynasty, porcelain manufacturing spread north and west, and production techniques were gradually perfected. There were five major kilns, each producing porcelain of a certain characteristic style: white *ding* ware; powdery blue *ru* ware; the "purple mouth and iron foot" (*zikou tiezu*) ware of the *guan* or official kilns; *ge* ware with a crackled surface, and *jun* ware with color transmutations that took place during baking. After the Song period, celadon wares produced by the Longquan Kiln in Zhejiang began to be exported abroad. The Istanbul Museum in Turkey alone has a collection of more than 1,000 pieces of celadon wares made in the Longquan Kiln in the Song and Yuan (1279–1368) dynasties. After the Yuan dynasty, the porcelain industry rose swiftly in Jingdezhen of Jiangxi, which became known as the Capital of Porcelain. The porcelain ware of Jingdezhen is light and artful in weight, refined, and exquisite in design. The most precious items include blue and white porcelain, colored porcelain, exquisite blue and white porcelain, and eggshell porcelain. The later ceramics in Liling of Hunan, Tangshan of Hebei, Shiwan of Guangdong (Canton), and Zibo of Shandong, are also well known for their respective features. China today continues to create new varieties of precious porcelain wares.

See also: Chapter 1: Huanghe River. Chapter 2: Timeline. Chapter 12: Overview.

Further Reading

Chen, Kelun. *Chinese Porcelain: Art, Elegance and Appreciation*. San Francisco, CA: Long River, 2000.

Li, Zhiyan, Virginia Bower, and Li He, eds. *Chinese Ceramics: From the Paleolithic Period through the Qing Dynasty*. New Haven, CT: Yale University Press, 2010.

Wood, Nigel. *Chinese Glazes: Their Origins, Chemistry, and Recreation*. Philadelphia: University of Pennsylvania Press, 2011.

Traditional Chinese Painting

Traditional Chinese painting is applied to a piece of Xuan paper (thin or rice paper) or silk, with a Chinese brush that has been soaked with black ink or colored pigments. Chinese traditional painting has become a composite artistic style integrating poetry, calligraphy, painting, and seal-engraving, a form of expression entirely unique to China.

Traditional Chinese paintings can be categorized by subject: that is, paintings of figures, landscapes, buildings, flowers, birds, animals, insects, or fish. Different expressive effects are achieved by thinning or thickening the pigment or ink, painting with a dry or moist brush, deliberately leaving blanks, or space, in the composition, and by varying its sparseness and density. Chinese paintings have many formats, such as murals, screens, scrolls, albums, and fans. Furthermore, they are frequently mounted against exquisite backgrounds to enhance their aesthetic effect.

Figure painting reached maturity during the Warring States Period (475–221 BCE). Landscape paintings and flower-and-bird paintings had already appeared by the Sui (581–618) and Tang (618–907) dynasties and flourished during the Song dynasty (960–1279). It was at this time that ink and wash paintings came into vogue. The Yuan dynasty (1279–1368) witnessed a gradual turn toward the freehand style, a trend which continued throughout the Ming (1368–1644) and Qing (1644–1911) dynasties

---

QING FANS

During the Qing dynasty (1644–1911), fans became popular in China in various styles with many kinds of covers, and made of various materials, such as paper, silk, feathers, or bamboo. The shapes of the fans have been in rectangular, round, pentagonal, hexagonal, and sunflower shapes. The folding fan is the most common in China today. Writing poems and drawing pictures on the cover of a fan was another characteristic of the Qing fans. From ancient times until now, many famous Chinese calligraphers and painters enjoyed themselves in doing so, leaving many excellent works.

---

up to the present day. Paintings on both modern and traditional themes are now permeated with the spirit of the age. Modern landscape painters, such as Huang Binhong (1865–1955), Pan Tianshou (1897–1971), Fu Baoshi (1904–1965), Guan Shanyue (1912–2000), and Li Keran (1907–1989), continue to study traditional techniques, but also immerse themselves in society and the world around them, opening new paths and creating their own individual styles. Modern bird-and-flower painters have carried on the tradition, and significant achievements have been made by Qi Baishi (1864–1957), Xu Beihong (1895–1953), and Chen Zhifo. The main question for painters of the traditional school today is how to advance traditional painting further, while keeping in step with the times.

See also: Chapter 2: Timeline. Chapter 11: Peking Opera; Tang-Song Poetry. Chapter 12: Chinese Silk and the Silk Road.

Further Reading

Dwight, Jane. *The Chinese Brush Painting Bible: Over 200 Motifs with Step by Step Illustrated Instructions.* New York: Chartwell, 2011.

Evans, Jane. *Chinese Brush Painting: A Complete Course in Traditional and Modern Techniques.* Mineola, NY: Dover, 2004.

He, Hanqiu, and Deng Jun. *An Introduction to Traditional Chinese Painting.* Beijing: Foreign Languages Press, 1995.

Yang, Guanghe, Guoqing Xu, and Qiubai Yan, eds. *A World in Art: Masterworks from the Last Five Centuries of Traditional Chinese Paintings.* Beijing: China Books, 1994.

CHAPTER 13

MUSIC AND DANCE

OVERVIEW

China has a long history of musical and dance culture. Documentary evidence and artifacts depict court music and dance as far back as the Shang (1766–1027 BCE) and Zhou (1066–221 BCE) dynasties. The sole function of many slaves at the time was to make musical instruments, as well as compose, sing, and dance. More than 80 kinds of musical instruments existed during the Zhou period. Dance had already reached and maintained a high level by that time, and full-length dances, portraying sacrificial ceremonies, were performed at court. Many Han (206 BCE–220 CE) figure paintings and pottery figurines that were excavated thereafter depict interesting and graceful dances such as the silk dance.

Traditional dance reached its peak in the Tang dynasty (618–907), a time when music also flourished. This was a golden age when native and foreign music combined to produce a new Chinese music. The chief musical achievement in this period was the development of *daqu,* a form of musical performance which combined singing, instrumental music, and dancing, melding into an integrated whole. The best-known work in this form is *Prince Qin Storms the Enemy Lines,* which consists of 52 stanzas, and has an intricate structure and complicated rhythm. The *daqu* orchestra usually consisted of several dozen kinds of musical instruments playing in unison, with attention to contrast and balance in tone, color, and volume. Later, with the rise of opera, the imposing *daqu,* suitable mainly for palace performances, was gradually replaced by simple but lively opera and ballad music which came from popular origins. From the 14th century on, music and singing gained an increasing importance in opera, and there gradually came into being a number of distinctive local opera forms.

The vocal and instrumental music for Chinese opera does not consist of fixed melodies, as in the West, but of "tune families" or systems. This music, which was not written down, was based on a set of tunes, usually of folk origin, which were open to considerable variation by the performer in pitch, melody, and rhythm. Each form of opera is primarily identified by its "tune family," which varies from region to region or even from one locality to another. There were also major advances in music for folk songs and dances, and small ensembles of folk instruments were very active. The lion dance, for example, became popular after the Tang period, and developed into large-scale singing and dancing performed by hundreds of people during the major festivals, traditional weddings, and other celebrations.

Modern Western dance was introduced to China at the turn of the century. Pioneers of Chinese modern dance worked under difficult conditions, devoting themselves to the study and exploration of a native Chinese dance theater, creating many new dances that exposed the dark side of the old society.

In the 20th century, music and dances created at different times display different forms and themes. In the 1920s through 1940s, a large-scale campaign to develop modern opera was launched. Many musicians enthusiastically went to the front line of the Anti-Japanese War in 1937–1945 and worked with soldiers, peasants, and workers to create many new modern operas.

After the founding of the People's Republic of China (PRC) in 1949, popular music and songs carried a strong political signal. In 1949–1966, music praising the Chinese Communist Party (CCP) and the motherland was promoted. The Cultural Revolution which began in 1966 targeted the old tradition and intended to build a new world, and this principle applied to music and dance. In 1966–1976, traditional Chinese music was trashed as one of the Four Olds (old ideas, old culture, old customs, and old habits). Previously popular folk music and dances were banned, and many new songs were created, laden with the radical political ideology of the time. After the end of the Cultural Revolution, people began to again give recognition to their homeland and acknowledge the value of Chinese music and dance. The theme shifted from class struggle to glorification, patriotism, and devotion to the motherland. The reform movement in the 1980s through 2000s has opened new ground for Chinese songs, operas, and performing art, and has laid a solid foundation to prepare waves of musicians for the development of fine arts in the 21st century.

There is great diversity in China's folk music and dance, which carry different local characteristics and unique graces of the 55 ethnic groups. They are different in form, style, and performance according to different geographic regions, social background, and local customs. In folk music and dance, dialects and minority languages are commonly used, in addition to Modern Standard Chinese. Although one may not always understand all the lyrics, one can clearly tell the differences among them from their melodies and other musical characteristics. At the beginning of the new millennium, there has been a trend to return to Chinese folk music and songs from a moment of passion for China's Western music. Thus, folk music and dance have recently regained the appreciation of Chinese mass audiences, and folk musicians and singers are becoming increasingly popular on the stage.

Further Reading

Baranovitch, Nimrod. *China's New Voices: Popular Music, Ethnicity, Gender, and Politics, 1978–1997*. Berkeley: University of California Press, 2003.

Jin, Jie. *Chinese Music: Introduction to Chinese Culture*. 3rd ed. Cambridge, UK: Cambridge University Press, 2011.

Jones, Stephen. *Folk Music of China: Living Instrumental Traditions*. Oxford, UK: Oxford University Press, 1999.

Kwan, San San. *Kinesthetic City: Dance and Movement in Chinese Urban Spaces*. Oxford, UK: Oxford University Press, 2013.

Lau, Frederick. *Music in China: Experiencing Music, Expressing Culture*. Oxford, UK: Oxford University Press, 2007.

Li, Beida. *Dances of the Chinese Minorities*. Beijing: China Intercontinental, 2006.

Liu, C. *A Critical History of New Music in China*. Hong Kong: Chinese University Press, 2010.

Qiang, Xi. *Chinese Music and Musical Instruments*. Shanghai: Shanghai Press, 2011.

Folk Dance

Chinese folk dance has a long and brilliant history. It is an age-old custom for people in China to watch or even to take part in folk dancing in the streets on traditional holidays. Such open performances do not need stages or a large number of professional dancers. The free and easy atmosphere encourages mass participation. One of the Han

The Dragon Dance, performed in celebration of the Chinese New Year, ensures good weather and bountiful harvests for Wuhan City in Hubei Province, China, on February 17, 2011. As a popular folk dance in Chinese culture, the Dragon Dance involves at least a dozen dancers who hold poles overhead to support a long figure of a dragon, usually made of silk or other light fabrics. Two dancers hold up the dragon's head, six to eight move the body, and one guides the tail. A couple of female dancers hold a lantern or a colorful ball to lead the dragon up and down, right and left as it "chases the pearl." Additional performers join the team by playing the drums and other instruments for the dancing music. (Gan Hui/Dreamstime.com)

folk dances, *Yangge* (or "Rice Sprout Song") originated from the Song dynasty (960–1279), varies greatly from region to region, and is very popular in the northeastern and northwestern regions. In the Haicheng region of Liaoning, for example, there are more than 300 *Yangge* groups that dance in the streets, involving 50 percent of the adult population. During the Chinese New Year's celebrations in northwestern Shaanxi Province, dozens of villages usually perform combined *Yangge* performances involving thousands of peasants dancing together. Other popular Han folk dances include the lion dance and dragon dance.

Folk dancing is even more popular and lively in the ethnic minority regions, where men and women, old and young, sing and dance throughout day and night on holidays and festivals. Each of the 55 ethnic groups in China has their own rich and distinctive dance traditions. There are more than 120 different types of folk dance among the 23 ethnic groups in Yunnan. Because of differences in customs and habits between north and south China, these folk dances tend to be rather bold and robust in the north and more delicate and subject to variation in the south. The development of amateur folk dancing among the masses has enriched people's cultural and recreational life, and has also provided abundant material for stage presentations of folk dancing by professional dancers.

Professional ethnic song and dance troupes have been founded, and national and local performances of folk music and dances have been organized across the country. More than 2,000 dancing shows were staged and revised between 1949 and 1966. Among the many popular ethnic dances, *Ordos and Herdsmen's Dance* (Mongolian), *Country Joys Dance and Long Drum Dance* (Korean), *Song of the Grasslands* (Tibetan), *Grape-Picking Dance and Tambourine Dance* (Uyghur), and *Peacock Dance* (Dai) have won praise from audiences in China and abroad. After the reform movement began in 1978, there was a new wave of interest in folk dance. Cultural festivals and performances were held annually in provinces, municipalities, and autonomous regions. A large number of outstanding folk dancers performed from 55 ethnic groups in 18 provinces and autonomous regions, and national minority theatrical awards were given to 300 shows

LION DANCE

As a traditional art and traditional sport in China, people can enjoy seeing lion dances across the country during all celebrations, especially on holidays such as the Chinese New Year, weddings, and other major events. Local folks believe that the lion dance expresses people's feelings of joy, and it can also influence the lively atmosphere. The Chinese people have a totemistic worship of the lion and have many legends about lions. The lion's position is next only to the dragon which brings a sense of mystery to the lion dance. The lion dance as an accomplishment is passed down from generation to generation, based on an ancient traditional entertainment activity to an athletic sport. The lion dance and dragon dance often appear in Chinese films.

including 1,400 dancers. New forms and styles of folk dance also flourished in the 1980s, such as the native dance-dramas, which have a strong element of traditional folk dances and opera and have reached a new level of artistry. Excellent shows in the 1990s included *Along the Silk Road*, created by northwestern Gansu Song and Dance Troupe; *Zhaoshu-tun and Nanmunuona*, by the Yunnan Song and Dance Troupe, a popular legend from the Dai people; *Going Out to Battle*, by the Qinghai Song and Dance Troupe and based on a Tibetan folk epic about a legendary hero; *Princess Wencheng*, by the Chinese Modern Opera and Dance-Drama Theatre; and *Cleft Mountain* and *Fight to the Moon*, two fairy tales by the Shanghai Modern Opera and Dance-Drama Theatre.

See also: Chapter 6: Major Ethnic Groups; Mongols; Uyghur. Chapter 10: Symbols of Auspice in Tradition. Chapter 13: Overview; Modern Chinese Dance.

Further Reading

Li, Beida. *Dances of the Chinese Minorities*. Beijing: China Intercontinental, 2006.

Pearlman, Ellen. *Tibetan Sacred Dance: A Journey into the Religious and Folk Traditions.* Rochester, NY: Inner Traditions, 2002.

Pegg, Carole. *Mongolian Music, Dance, and Oral Narrative: Performing Diverse Identities.* Seattle: University of Washington Press, 2001.

Thrasher, Alan R. *La-Li-Luo Dance-Dongs of the Yunnan Province*. Wauwatosa, WI: World Music, 1990.

Wang, Yunyu, and Stephanie Burridge, eds. *Identity and Diversity: Celebrating Dance in Taiwan*. London: Routledge, 2013.

Modern Chinese Dance

Modern dance became popular in China after modern Western dance was introduced during the 1920s. Pioneers like Wu Xiaobang and Dai Ailian, working under difficult conditions through the Anti-Japanese War of 1937–1945, devoted themselves to the study and exploration of a native modern Chinese dance theater, creating many new dances exposing social realities and reflecting the people's struggle. Among their early works are *By the Huangpu River*, *Shameless Bragging*, *Air Raid*, *Song of the Guerrilla*, and *Child for Sale*.

After the founding of the People's Republic of China (PRC) in 1949, modern dancers attempted to plunge into people's lives and to integrate with the social changes, thus opening up a new realm for dance choreography. A great number of dances on historical and contemporary themes were created, such as *A Thousand Miles of Lovely Land* and *Song of the Volunteers* based on the events of the Korean War of 1950–1953, and *The Five Heroes of Mt. Langya*, about the Chinese soldiers who fought and died in the Anti-Japanese War. The dance *Laundry Song*, about life in the People's Liberation Army (PLA) and relations between the army and the people, became popular. Beijing Academy of Dancing invited Western ballet instructors to teach ballet classes in the 1950s.

The first ballet company was formed in 1959. Within a few years, the ballet company performed famous European classical ballets such as *Swan Lake*, *The Fountain of Bakhchisaray*, and *The Corsair*. None of them, however, survived the Cultural Revolution of 1966–1976, and many of the directors, choreographers, and dancers were purged or attacked during the Cultural Revolution. Jiang Qing, the wife of Mao Zedong and one of the radical leaders of the Cultural Revolution, along with her associates, completely banned traditional dance and classical ballet. They organized the creation of "revolutionary ballets" such as *The Red Detachment of Women* and *The White-Haired Girl* in the late 1960s.

After the reform movement began in 1978, innovations were encouraged in theme, genre, form, and style. Many artists and performers took up the challenge, enlarging the range of subjects and techniques for expressing modern life in dance. At the 1998 national dance contest for solo, *pas de deux*, and trio performances, great breakthroughs were made in regard to theme and style. Among the 485 entries at the national contest, 320 were on modern themes; not only was this a comparatively high proportion, but the artistic quality was also deemed high. The same event saw an increase in the number of dances using flowers, birds, fish, insects, and other natural phenomena to express thoughts and feelings and to praise lofty sentiments, such as *Spring Silkworm*, about people who devote their whole lives to serving the masses; *Little Golden Deer*, which celebrates youthful vigor; *War Drum on Gold Mountain* and *The Drunken Sword*, both on historical themes, and *The Surprising Transformation* based on a famous legend. In all of these modern dances, the emphasis is on character portrayal and the depiction of the characters' inner world. A wide range of modern Chinese and foreign techniques were drawn on and amalgamated to form original new styles of dance.

See also: Chapter 2: Timeline; Mao Zedong. Chapter 3: People's Liberation Army. Chapter 13: Overview.

Further Reading

Kwan, San San. *Kinesthetic City: Dance and Movement in Chinese Urban Spaces*. Oxford, UK: Oxford University Press, 2013.

Li, Beida. *Dances of the Chinese Minorities*. Beijing: China Intercontinental, 2006.

Li, Cunxin. *Mao's Last Dancer*. New York: Berkley, 2005.

Riley, Jo. *Chinese Theatre and the Actor in Performance*. Cambridge, UK: Cambridge University Press, 2006.

Traditional Instruments

Instruments of traditional Chinese music have a long history and have experienced tremendous changes. As early as the Zhou dynasty (1066–221 BCE), more than 80 types of musical instruments existed. The excavation of an early Warring States (475–221 BCE) tomb in Sui County, Hubei, revealed a set of 124 musical instruments, among

A terra-cotta painted statue of a *qin* player from a province in Northern China, in the late Western Han dynasty, first century. *Qin*, a traditional Chinese string instrument, has a history of 3,000 years, including various shapes with different numbers of strings. Many varieties of this instrument, like the *guqin* and *yangqin*, are still popular in today's China. (De Agostini/Getty Images)

them a stand of bells (consisting of 32 sonorous stones of different sizes and tones), two *guqin* (a kind of lute or zither), one with 5 strings and one with 10 strings, 12 *se* (a kind of zither with 25 strings), one large and one small *chi* (a traverse bamboo flute), two *paixiao* (pan-pipes with 16 pipes), five *sheng* (a set of bamboo pipes), and four drums. This find indicates the enormous range of orchestras at aristocratic feasts during that time. The neatly arranged and exquisitely made set of bells is particularly remarkable. Tests have shown that each bell can produce a range of more than five octaves, divided into over 90 musical tones.

Through a 3,000-year history, traditional Chinese instruments have evolved into different types of wind, string, and percussion instruments. The wind instruments include *xiao*, *di*, *suona*, and *sheng*. The string instruments include *urhu*, *jinghu*, and *guzheng*. *Guqin*, also called *qixianqin* (seven-stringed *qin*), is the oldest traditional string instrument in China, with a history of over 3,000 years. Its long narrow body is made of two pieces of board at the top and with the bottom glued together. *Guqin* can be played in many forms and can produce a deep, restrained sound. The fourth type is also a string instrument, played by striking the strings with slips, such as *yangqin* (a dulcimer with metal strings, played with two light slips of bamboo). The fifth type is a percussion instrument, seen usually as a gong or drum.

In recent decades, Chinese musicians and instrument manufacturers have improved these traditional instruments and invented new functions by enlarging their range, improving their tonal color, and enriching their sound. Special, but rather weak, efforts have been made to improve and trial-produce bass instruments. Many ensembles for performing traditional music have been formed. Almost every region, province, city, county, university and college, Buddhist and Daoist temple, and the unit of the People's Liberation Army (PLA) has its own traditional music troupes. Many folk music troupes are self-organized by traditional music fans similar to neighborhood or garage bands in America.

Although many traditional songs were lost during the past centuries, some of the songs composed in the early dynasties and sung with the traditional instruments have survived. The extant melodies include "The Ambush on All Sides" (*Simian maifu*), "Spring Snow" (*Chunxue*), "Hundred Birds Worshipping the Phoenix" (*Bainiao chao meng*), "Spring River Moon Night" (*Chunjiang yueye*), and "Higher Step by Step" (*Bubu gao*). These well-known melodies are often performed by the traditional instruments at home and abroad, and some have won international awards.

See also: Chapter 2: Timeline. Chapter 3: People's Liberation Army. Chapter 5: Buddhism; Daoism. Chapter 13: Overview.

Further Reading

Furniss, Ingrid Maren. *Music in Ancient China: An Archaeological and Art Historical Study of Strings, Winds, and Drums During the Zhou and Han Period.* New York: Cambria, 2008.

Jones, Stephen. *Folk Music of China: Living Instrumental Traditions.* Oxford, UK: Oxford University Press, 1999.

Myers, John. *The Way of the Pipa: Structure and Imagery in Chinese Lute Music.* Kent, OH: Kent University Press, 1992.

Qiang, Xi. *Chinese Music and Musical Instruments.* Shanghai: Shanghai Press, 2011.

Witzleben, Lawrence. *Silk and Bamboo Music in Shanghai: The Jiangnan Sizhu Instrumental Ensemble Tradition.* Kent, OH: Kent University Press, 2013.

CHAPTER 14

FOOD

OVERVIEW

The traditional Chinese saying goes, "The masses regard food as their heaven" (*Min yi shi wei tian*), which indicates that food is people's primal want. Chinese cuisine enjoys a unique reputation for its colors, scents, tastes, and presentations, as well as its variety. There is perhaps no other place in the world that has as great a variety of delicious fare as in China. Among the precious delicacies on the menus of those seeking the unique are bears' paws, swallows' nests, sharks' fins, sea cucumbers, elephant trunks, deer tails, and monkey brains. But eating trends have changed in China, and Chinese cooking style is now healthier and has more variety.

The Chinese have created and exported various kinds of regional food cultures far across the seas. Regional dishes, together with distinctive local climate, geography, history, food products, and eating customs, have gradually developed through a long history into many unique cuisines with various cooking techniques and flavors. The people of China generalize the different regional tastes with the saying, "South is sweet, north is salty; east is spicy, and west is sour." Chinese dishes can be roughly divided into eight regional cuisines: Lu, Chuan, Su, Yue, Min, Zhe, Xiang, and Hui cuisines. Each of the eight regional cuisines has distinctive characteristics and delicious tastes. Among the eight cuisines, Lu, Chuan, Su, and Yue cuisines are called the "Grand Four Categories of Chinese Cuisine."

Lu cuisine (*Lu Cai*), or Shandong cuisine, representing the northern region, is the most influential and popular cuisine in China. Located in the lower reaches of the Huanghe (Yellow) River, Shandong Province is surrounded by seas on three sides, with hills and plains in the center. It is rich in all sorts of food products, such as seafood, grain, oil, animals, insects, fruits, and vegetables, which provide abundant cooking resources for Lu cuisine. During the Spring and Autumn Period (770–476 BCE), Shandong, the state of Lu and of the great philosopher Confucius, developed Lu cuisine into maturity with all-around cooking skills, specializing in quick-frying, stir-frying, braising, and deep frying. With shallots, ginger, and garlic frequently used as seasonings, Lu cuisine is characterized by its emphasis on fragrance, freshness, crispiness, and tenderness, with soy sauce or brown sauce available. This food style is a true embodiment of Confucian teachings: "No such thing as too much refinement." It can be further divided into three cuisines. The first is coastal Jiaodong cuisine, focusing on seafood with famous dishes like braised sea cucumber with soy sauce and roasted prawns. The second

AMERICAN-CHINESE FOOD

Chinese restaurants in the United States offer many dishes that satisfy the taste of American customers, such as sweet and sour pork, lemon chicken, pepper steak, fried shrimp, egg rolls, and fortune cookies. Many of these menu items became popular in America after World War II, but were not available in China, Taiwan, or Hong Kong.

is inland Ji'nan cuisine, having a comparatively stronger taste such as dezhou stewed chicken, braised intestines in brown sauce, fried carp with sweet and sour sauce, deep-fried pig tripe with chicken gizzard, and braised pork in crock. The third is Confucian cuisine with imperial dishes having delicate and elegant characteristics such as "eight immortals surrounding arhat" and hot pot.

Chuan cuisine (*Chuan Cai*), or Sichuan cuisine, popular in south China, has world-wide fame for its special spicy, fresh, and fragrant flavor. Sichuan Province is located in the upper reaches of the Yangzi (Yangtze) River surrounded by hills and mountains, as well as many rivers within. It is a place with plenty of rainfalls and is rich in products. Originating in the Qin dynasty (221–206 BCE), Chuan cuisine took its initial shape in the Han dynasty (206 BCE–220 CE), developed in the Tang (618–907) and Song (960–1279) dynasties, and finally moved into maturity in the late Qing dynasty (1644–1911). It consists of regional dishes in Chongqing, Chengdu, and other parts of Sichuan. Chongqing Chafing Dish is considered the representative of Chuan cuisine for its unique and special spicy flavor. Combining various cooking techniques, such as frying, stewing, pickling, sautéing, and grilling, Chuan cuisine is skillful at using hot peppers, black pepper, Chinese prickly ash, and broad-bean sauce as seasonings. Based on Qizi, which is seven flavors of sour, sweet, bitter, hot, spicy, fragrant, and salty, Chuan cuisine creates Bawei with different proportions of seasonings, which is eight tastes of special-spicy, sour-hot, chili-spicy, chili-oil, grilled, spicy, ocean-flavor, and special hot season-ing. The famous Chuan cuisine includes *mapo* (pockmarked woman) tofu (*dofu*), ocean-flavored shredded pork, *kongbao* (*kung pao*) chicken, boiled beef, and fish with pickled cabbage.

Su cuisine (*Huaiyang Cai*), or Jiangsu cuisine, consists of Yangzhou, Suzhou, and Nanjing cuisines. Laying stress on soup taste, Su cuisine is well known for its freshness, light flavor, and elegance. Jiangsu Province is located along the East China Sea and in the lower reaches of the Yangzi River. In Jiangsu the climate is pleasant and the land is fertile with numerous rivers and lakes, which are abundant with fishes, shrimps, crabs, water chestnuts, and lotus roots. Dating from the pre-Qin, Su cuisine developed its regional flavor from the Han to Tang dynasties. During the Yuan (1279–1386) and Ming (1386–1644) dynasties, convenient transportation led to frequent commercial trading, and Su cuisine expanded its fame north and south along the Beijing-Hangzhou Grand Canal as well as east and west along the Yangzi River. It has a large variety of ingredients and features river food and vegetables. Specializing in cooking techniques of stewing, braising, roasting, and simmering, Su cuisine creates a mild taste of freshness, fragrance, crispiness, and tenderness. The famous Su cuisine includes Hangzhou's roast chicken (commonly known as beggar's chicken), Nanjing salted duck, steamed shad herring, and shredded bean curd in chicken soup.

Yue cuisine (*Yue Cai*), or Guangdong (Cantonese) cuisine, consisting of Guangzhou cuisine, Chaozhou cuisine, and Dongjiang cuisine, with Guangzhou cuisine as its representative, represents the unique flavors of south China. Located in the subtropical and coastal region of the South China Sea, Guangdong Province has delicacies of every kind as well as vegetables and fruits of all seasons. Since the Han, Guangdong has always been the opening gate to the south, and while overseas commerce brings about the exchange of cooking culture among countries, Yue cuisine has gradually succeeded in integrating both Chinese and Western features well. It has a wide ingredient selection, lays emphasis upon cooking techniques, and creates a fresh, tender, and crispy flavor. With its special dish design, it enjoys a worldwide reputation for perfection in all colors, smells, tastes, and appearance. The famous Yue cuisine includes steamed fish, sautéed shrimp, crispy chicken, roast suckling pig, and white gourd soup.

Min cuisine (*Min Cai*), or Fujian cuisine, originating from regional dishes in Fuzhou, Quanzhou, and Xiamen, is best represented by Fuzhou cuisine. Located in southeast China, facing the East China Sea and backing on mountains, Fujian Province has plenty of rainfall and a mild climate, which makes it seem to enjoy spring all year round. Min cuisine focuses on cutting and heating ingredients together, creating a diversity of soups. It specializes in stir-frying, steaming, and simmering. In this cuisine, red wine dregs, shrimp oil, satay sauce, and chili sauce are widely used. Min dishes often have a sweet, sour, and light flavor—sweet but not greasy, sour but not choking, light but not thin. Fuzhou cuisine, the mainstream of Min cuisine, stresses creating soup with a sweet and sour flavor. The famous Fuzhou cuisine includes Buddha-jumping-over-the-wall, which is steamed abalone with shark's fin and fish maw in broth, chicken pickled in wine, and *tai-chi* prawn. Southern Min cuisine has a hot spicy flavor. Its famous dishes include stewed chicken with satay sauce, shredded chicken with mustard, quick-fried hamster with pork, and fried horseshoe crab.

Zhe cuisine (*Zhe Cai*), or Zhejiang cuisine, consists of Hangzhou, Ningbo, Shaoxing, and Wenzhou cuisines. Fine and exquisite, it focuses on cooking techniques of stir-frying, deep-frying, stewing, quick-frying, steaming, and braising. Located on the east coast of China, Zhejiang Province is beautiful, with green mountains and clean water, known as a land of honey and milk. Hangzhou cuisine has a long history dating back to the Southern Song dynasty (1127–1279), when Hangzhou became the capital city of the Song dynasty. Restaurants from different regions sprang up in Hangzhou. As the saying goes, "Up above there is heaven, down below there are Suzhou and Hangzhou." Hangzhou cuisine features freshness, crispiness, delicacy, and elegance. The famous cuisine includes west lake carp in vinegar sauce, *dongpo* pork, fried shrimps with *longjing* tea, braised bamboo shoots, and west lake water shield soup. The famous Ningbo cuisine includes croaker with pickled vegetables soup, fried eel shreds, steamed turtle in crystal sugar soup, and croaker fried with seaweed. The famous Shaoxing cuisine includes Shao-style fried prawn ball and fish braised with bean curd. Wenzhou cuisine, mainly based on seafood, has a fresh light but thick flavor. It focuses on "two lights and one heavy," which is light oil, light thickening, and heavy cutting. The famous Wenzhou cuisine includes chopping fish with three shreds, garlic fish skin, and quick-fried cuttlefish.

Xiang cuisine (*Xiang Cai*), or Hunan cuisine, consists of regional flavor in the reaches of the Xiang River, the Dongting Lake, and mountain regions of western Hunan Province. Focusing on hot pepper, Xiang cuisine features a countryside flavor which is fragrant, spicy, and tender. Using delicate processes and various cooking resources, it stresses thick oil, dark color, and diverse taste, with cooking techniques of simmering, stewing, steaming, and stir-frying. The most famous dishes are steamed multiple preserved hams and peppery chicken. Cuisine in the reaches of the Dongting Lake, specializing in stewing and braising river food and poultry, features a salty spicy fragrance, and a tender flavor with thick sauce and heavy oil. Cuisine in the mountain regions focuses on cooking mountain delicacies. Charcoal is often used as fuel to smoke cured and pickled meat of various kinds, creating a salty fragrant sour with a spicy flavor. The famous dishes are western Xiang fried meat and duck fried with blood.

Hui cuisine (*Hui Cai*), or Anhui cuisine, has three major characteristics; that is, thick oil, emphasis on color, and different heating degrees based on different ingredients. Despite the dried ingredients, original flavor is kept through the cooking process. Hui cuisine uses shallots and ginger to absorb strange smells, soup stock to enlighten the taste, ham and crystal sugar to enhance the taste, and homemade sauces to enrich both color and smell. Hui cuisine, focusing on control of the heating temperature, is featured by cooking, braising, stewing, simmering, and steaming. Many dishes are served in cooking pots after being braised individually over a charcoal fire in order to keep the original flavor. Hui cuisine can be divided into three cuisines: the Wannan region, the Yangzi River region, and the Huai River region. Its famous cuisine includes turtle stewed with ham, strong-smelling preserved fish, smoked shad herring with maofeng tea, and bamboo shoots stewed with ham.

Besides the eight major cuisines, there are other distinctive dishes across the country. Beijing is well known for its Peking roast duck, which has a history over a hundred years and is served in many Chinese restaurants all over the world. Tianjin, a neighboring city of Beijing, offers its famous "Dog-Won't-Eat stuffed bun," a thick-tasting, symmetrically formed, wrinkled bun, a result of kneading the dough and sealing in the stuffing. Traveling a little bit southwest of Tianjin, one arrives at Xi'an, ancient capital city of the Qin, Han, and Tang dynasties. Its soaked buns in mutton soup and *tang* dumpling feasts still attract millions of tourists each year for a unique eating experience.

Further Reading

Anderson, Eugene. *The Food of China*. New Haven, CT: Yale University Press, 1990.

Chen, Yong. *Chop Suey, USA: The Story of Chinese Food in America*. New York: Columbia University Press, 2014.

Hollmann, Thomas. *The Land of the Five Flavors: A Cultural History of Chinese Cuisine*. New York: Columbia University Press, 2013.

Lee, Jennifer. *The Fortune Cookie Chronicles: Adventures in the World of Chinese Food*. New York: Twelve Publishing, 2009.

Liu, Junru. *Chinese Food*. 3rd ed. Cambridge, UK: Cambridge University Press, 2011.

Lu, Henry. *Chinese System of Food Cures: Prevention and Remedies*. New York: Sterling, 1986.

Young, Grace. *The Wisdom of the Chinese Kitchen*. New York: Simon & Schuster, 1999.

Cantonese Dim Sum

Dim Sum are also called *Dim-sim* or "*yum cha*" (tea tasting) in Cantonese, and "*zao cha*" (morning tea) or *dian-xin* (pastry) in Mandarin. Dim sum is the Cantonese name for a traditional and popular brunch serving pastry-style food from morning to afternoon hours in southern Guangdong (Canton) Province, Hong Kong, Macao, and overseas Chinese communities. As part of Yue cuisine (*Yue Cai*), or Guangdong cuisine, dim sum cooking provides small, bite-sized, or individual portions of a variety of food from poultry, meat, seafood, vegetables, and fruits, served for both breakfast and lunch. Dim sum has gradually succeeded in developing its well-integrated features of both Chinese and Western cooking with a wide ingredient selection, emphasizing cooking techniques and creating a fresh, tender, and crispy flavor. With its broad offerings, it enjoys a worldwide reputation for its perfection in color, smell, taste, and appearance. It is always served with hot teas such as green tea, wulong (oolong) tea, black (red) tea, and scented (such as jasmine and chrysanthemum) teas.

One can see dim sum food sold at nearly every street corner in Hong Kong. You will find a good choice of 120–280 dishes from any menu of the restaurants or teahouses which serve dim sum during breakfast and lunch hours. The customers can view most of the food items when the serving crew comes to the table with a steam-heated cart carrying 20–30 dim sum items each time. You can easily choose your favorite dishes when these serving carts move from table to table. Although each restaurant has its own specialties, the popular dishes of dim sum include rolls, dumplings, noodles, buns, poultry, meat, seafood, and vegetables.

There are many different rolls on a dim sum menu. Spring rolls, smaller than egg rolls, but more crisp, have bamboo shoots, bean sprouts, roast pork, shrimp, and water chestnuts. Summer rolls, a cold dish, that are not deep fried, contain preboiled pork and fresh lettuce in parchment-like rice paper made of cooked rice starch. There are regular egg rolls, filled with either pork or beef. Other popular rolls include tofu (Dofu) skin rolls; rice noodle rolls with popular fillings such as beef, dough fritter, shrimp, and barbecued pork; "dust roll" (or "Mandarin Dust Roll"), which is wrapped around sweet red or green bean paste with sesame seeds and brown sugar; and banana rolls, which are rolled, flavored, glutinous rice, not cooked any further after preparation. The last two kinds of the rolls are most often served as dessert during the dim sum hours.

The dumplings include steamed, pan-fried (also called pot stickers, or *Guo-tie* in Mandarin), and deep-fried dumplings with pork, beef, or shrimp. Delicate and tiny shrimp dumplings (or *Har-gow* in Cantonese) are the most popular dumplings, steamed

Several bamboo steamers and plates of dim sum sit ready to serve, including steamed baby buns, shrimp dumplings, pork shaomai, and fried cream puffs. Dim sum are also available in the frozen food section in some local supermarkets. (Shoutforhumanity/Dreamstime.com)

in a bamboo steamer and served with a choice of soy sauce or vinegar. *Teochew* (Chaozhou)-style dumplings, with thicker glutinous rice flour or *Tang* flour wrappers, contain pork, dried shrimp, peanuts, and Chinese mushrooms. Taro dumplings are made with smashed taro, stuffed with diced Chinese mushrooms and shrimp, and deep-fried in a crispy batter. The most popular dumplings are also called *Shao-mai*, steamed and filled with pork or shrimp. The smaller dumplings, or *Wonton*, are cooked either in soup or in deep-fried style.

Pasta has a wide variety, including deep-fried crispy noodles, stir-fried *Lou-mian* noodles with different meats and vegetables, boiled egg noodles, cold noodle dishes with spicy sauce, and hot rice noodle soup with beef or shrimp (or *Pho* in both Cantonese and Vietnamese). The popular pan-fried flat rice noodle is similar to *Pad Thai*. Rice soup, or congee (*Zhou* in Mandarin), is also a popular item for dim sum when it is served with preserved egg and barbequed pork.

Buns, a popular dim sum food, include the good-sized *Baozi* (*Da-bao* in Cantonese), a generic term for a steamed or baked yeast bun, which has fluffy skin filled with various types of fillings; *Char-sui-baau* (*Cha-shao-bao* in Mandarin), the most popular bun with barbecued pork and sweet onion filling; *Xiaolong-bao*, steamed tiny dumplings filled with meat or seafood and famous for their flavor and rich broth inside; beef buns, filled with ground beef, sometimes flavored with curry; chicken buns; and steam buns (*mantou* in Mandarin).

Popular meat and poultry dishes of dim sum include lotus leaf rice (or pearl chicken), sweet rice wrapped with pork or chicken in a lotus leaf and steamed with various vegetables; phoenix claws, chicken feet steamed with a black bean sauce; steamed meatballs, finely ground beef steamed with preserved orange peel; steamed spare ribs; crispy fried squid (or calamari); and smoked duck.

See also: Chapter 1: Hong Kong. Chapter 10: Table Manners. Chapter 14: Overview; Holiday Feasts. Chapter 15: Chinese Tea.

Further Reading

Blonder, Ellen. *Dim Sum: The Art of Chinese Tea Lunch.* New York: Clarkson Potter, 2002.

Mabbott, Lizzie. *Chinatown Kitchen: From Noodles to Nuoc Cham.* Chicago: Mitchell Beazley, 2015.

Wong, Janice. *Dim Sum: A Flour-Forward Approach to Traditional Favorites and Contemporary Creations.* Singapore: Gatehouse, 2014.

Yee, Rhoda. *Dim Sum.* New York: Random, 1978.

Holiday Feasts

The Chinese celebrate their holidays with a sumptuous family feast, just like every other country in the world. Food traditions attach to the important national holidays, including both "official" and traditional. The official "big four" celebrations are New Year's Day on January 1; Labor Day on May 1; Children's Day on June 1; the National Day of the People's Republic on October 1; the Dragon Boat Festival on the fifth day of the fifth month in the lunar calendar; and the Mid-Autumn Festival, or the Moon Festival, on the 15th day of the eighth lunar month. Typical food is served for the different traditional holidays.

The Chinese Lunar New Year (Spring Festival) is the most important and popular of all Chinese holidays, similar to Christmas in America. Although officially everyone has three days off from work, family members begin preparing the New Year's Eve meal up to a week in advance. From that point on, people are busy shopping, getting ready to cook, and inviting relatives and friends. Certain types of food are commonly served at the New Year's Eve dinner, including whole fish, roast suckling pig, pigeon, chicken cooked with lobster in red oil, and dumplings. The pronunciation of fish "*yu*" in Chinese is the same as "abundance," meaning the family will have a plentitude of wealth in the New Year. The serving of pigeon implies a peaceful future for the family. Chicken means phoenix, while lobster is literally called "dragon" in Chinese. Having lobster and chicken together at the New Year's feast indicates that harmony, and a balance of Yin and Yang elements, have been achieved. At the New Year's feast, the most important dish for all families across the country is the dumpling (*jiaozi*), a classic Chinese delicacy and a holiday must-have food with a long history. Dumplings may be steamed, pan-fried (also called pot stickers, or *Guo-tie*), or deep-fried, stuffed with pork, beef, or shrimp. Making dumplings is considered teamwork, or a family effort to prepare. Everyone in the family, including the guests, gather around the table and together make several hundred dumplings while catching up with news about their careers and lives and talking about the New Year.

Fifteen days after the Chinese New Year comes the Lantern Festival, another important holiday for the Chinese, when the first full moon of the year appears. Beautiful lanterns are displayed everywhere at night, and lantern shows and contests in various forms are organized. The typical food for this holiday is *yuanxiao*, which the southerners call *tangyuan*, round dumplings made of glutinous rice flour and stuffed with a variety of sweet fillings, including sweet red or green bean paste, sesame seeds, lotus seeds, jujube (Chinese date) paste, nuts, and brown sugar. The type of *yuanxiao* and ways of eating them are numerous. They are most often served in soup, although they are sometimes pan-fried or deep-fried.

The Dragon Boat Festival emphasizes the significance of curing diseases and dispelling evil spirits. In many parts of the country, it is a customary practice for people to tread grass in the morning, and hang Chinese mugwort on the door. In the afternoon, the dragon boat rowing races are held along the rivers and canals. It has become a traditional holiday in commemoration of Qu Yuan (340–278 BCE), a statesman and poet of the Warring States Period (475–221 BCE). *Zongzi*, a glutinous rice cake wrapped in lotus or bamboo leaves, is the festival food. They are wrapped into a triangular shape and filled with different ingredients. The southern fillings are more copious, including eggs, meats, and vegetables. Sweet or salty flavors, each with their own satisfying taste, are available.

The Mid-Autumn Festival (Moon Festival) celebrates the harvest and the family, like the Thanksgiving holiday in the United States. All families have a big reunion while

Mooncakes, a traditional Chinese mid-autumn festival food, on a table setting. The Chinese words on the mooncakes mean assorted fruits and nuts, not a logo or trademark. Other popular fillings inside the cakes include red and green beans, coconut, sesame seeds, brown sugar, duck eggs, roast beef, Cantonese sausage, and barbecued pork. (Szefei/Dreamstime.com)

enjoying a view of the bright, full autumn moon. On this holiday, the Chinese people eat round mooncakes. There are over 100 kinds of mooncakes in many flavors and with various fillings, such as nuts, lotus seed paste, egg yolk, bean paste, crystal sugar, sesame seed, ham, shrimp, vegetables, and more. They may taste sweet, salty, spicy, or salty and sweet. Traditional Beijing-style mooncakes are similar to the sesame seed cake, with an outer crust that is crispy and delicious. The Cantonese-style mooncake's skin is similar to Western cakes, but its inner filling makes it the most famous.

See also: Chapter 2: Timeline. Chapter 5: Daoism. Chapter 14: Overview; Cantonese Dim Sum.

Further Reading

Anderson, Eugene. *The Food of China*. New Haven, CT: Yale University Press, 1990.

Chai, May-lee, and Winberg Chai. *China A to Z: Everything You Need to Know to Understand Chinese Customs and Culture*. New York: Plume, 2007.

Moey, S. *Chinese Feasts and Festivals*. Hong Kong: Periplus, 2014.

Zhou, Yiqun. *Festivals, Feasts, and Gender Relations in Ancient China and Greece*. Cambridge, UK: Cambridge University Press, 2013.

Hunan and Sichuan Cooking Styles

In recent decades, Hunan and Sichuan (Szechuan) cuisines have become popular in America and the West when local Chinese restaurants began adding more dishes from the Xiang and Chuan cuisines to their menus. Xiang cuisine (*Xiang Cai*), or Hunan cuisine, consists of regional flavors from the reaches of the Xiang River, the Dongting Lake, and mountain regions of Hunan. Chuan cuisine (*Chuan Cai*), or Sichuan cuisine, is popular in Sichuan, around the upper reaches of the Yangzi (Yangtze) River, and South China.

Focusing on hot peppers, both cuisines have a worldwide fame for their special spicy, fresh, and fragrant flavor. With delicate processes and various cooking resources, they stress thick oil, dark color, and diverse taste with cooking techniques of simmering, stewing, steaming, and stir-frying. The most commonly used technique is to "*chao*," or stir-fry, in Hunan or Sichuan cooking. Before the 1970s, most Chinese restaurants in America offered Cantonese cuisine (or Yue cuisine), with roasted and deep-fried traditional dishes such as egg foo yung, sweet and sour chicken, and chop suey. In 1972, when U.S. President Richard Nixon made his historic trip to Beijing, Chinese leader Mao Zedong (Mao Tse-tung) (1893–1976) treated him to a Hunan banquet, Mao's hometown cuisine. After Nixon's return, the Hunan cooking style became popular in America as an authentic Chinese food. Hunan cuisine features a salty and spicy fragrance with a tender flavor, and with a thick sauce and heavy oil. The famous dishes are General Zuo's (Tsou) chicken, double cooked pork, ocean-flavored beef, orange beef, steamed multiple preserved hams, and peppery chicken.

In the 1980s, when President Ronald Reagan visited Beijing, the Chinese leader at the time, Deng Xiaoping (Deng Hsiao-ping, 1904–1997), offered him a Sichuan banquet, Deng's hometown cuisine. After Reagan's return, the Sichuan cuisine then became popular in America's Chinese restaurants. Combining various cooking techniques, such as frying, stewing, pickling, sautéing, and grilling, Sichuan cuisine is skillful at using hot peppers, black pepper, Chinese prickly ash, and broad-bean sauce as seasonings. Based on *Qizi*, which is seven flavors of sour, sweet, bitter, hot, spicy, fragrant, and salty, it creates *Bawei* with different proportions of seasonings, which is eight tastes of special-spicy, sour-hot, chili-spicy, chili-oil, grilled, spicy, ocean-flavor, and special hot. The famous Sichuan cuisine includes *mapo* (Pockmarked Woman) Tofu (Dofu), *Kongbao* (Kung Pao) chicken, boiled beef, *dandan* noodle, and fish with pickled cabbage.

See also: Chapter 1: Yangzi River. Chapter 2: Deng Xiaoping; Mao Zedong. Chapter 14: Overview; Holiday Feasts.

Further Reading

Chang, K. C. *Food in Chinese Culture: Anthropological and Historical Perspectives*. New Haven, CT: Yale University Press, 1977.

Dunlop, Fuchsia. *Shark's Fin and Sichuan Pepper: A Sweet-Sour Memoir of Eating in China*. New York: Norton, 2009.

Lu, Yi, and Li Du. *China's Sichuan Cuisine*. Chengdu: Sichuan Science, 2010.

CHAPTER 15

LEISURE AND SPORTS

OVERVIEW

Although living conditions and lifestyle in China have undergone tremendous changes from the ancient age to modern times, Chinese people have maintained some traditional practices and unique customs to keep themselves and their families happy and healthy. One of the traditional practices of Chinese daily life is to preserve balance throughout one's body and mind by obtaining physical harmony with nature through care of the self. Chinese culture views the individual body as a small cosmos. Hence, consideration of the concept of spatial harmony starts with the ideas of Yin and Yang, and then moves along the five elements and the eight characters.

For example, the basic concept of harmony between hot and cold or weak and strong extends into some aspects of the culinary world, where objects as well as movements are attributed to the properties of either hot or cold and soft or hard. This is done in order to strive for either an active workout or a relaxation exercise that preserves the internal harmonious balance of the small cosmos of the individual subject, in order to bring about or preserve one's health. The Yin and Yang or hot-cold conceptualization has a long lineage and is vastly influential, not only in relation to leisure and sports, but also to traditional medicine.

Having leisure time for fun constitutes one of the most significant features of Chinese daily life. Eating and drinking are perhaps the most popular leisure activities for the majority of Chinese families every day. When it comes to food, the Chinese have a common saying: "The masses regard food as their heaven" (*Min yi shi wei tian*), indicating that eating is people's primal desire. This clearly demonstrates the importance of eating in Chinese people's lives. Chinese cuisine enjoys a unique reputation for its colors, scents, tastes, and presentations, as well as its wide variety.

The Chinese do not have alcohol with every family meal when eating at home. But on other occasions, such as reunion dinners, business meals, holiday banquets, and birthday parties, alcoholic drinks are essential. Chinese liquors (*baijiu*) are served at dinners. These are strong distilled spirits, most of them approximately 40 to 65 percent alcohol by volume (ABV). Some Chinese grape wines, or red wines (*hongjiu*), are also renowned abroad as well as at home. The most common alcoholic drink is beer (*pijiu*), served at both dinner and lunch. If you wish to express respect to the elders or superiors, you may make a toast. Before drinking, however, you must use your cup to touch the elders' or superiors' cups (*pengbei*) to show your affection. When you begin to drink, your cup should be lower than the elders and superiors to show respect. It is customary to empty your cup of wine first (*ganbei*) to demonstrate sincerity.

The most common drink in China is tea (*cha* or *chai*), an important part of the Chinese people's social life, and drinking tea has become a daily leisure practice. It is believed that drinking tea regularly can dispel fatigue, help digestion, prevent some diseases, and generally benefit health. In comparison with Western tea consumption, the Chinese make a cup of tea from tea leaves, rather than from a tea bag or tea powder. Some have tea in place of alcohol. The method of offering tea is very simple. The standard set for tea making includes a water cooker, teapot, filter, and cup. Before preparing tea, the guest is asked for his or her preference, whether green tea, red tea, oolong, or scented tea. The host may then put some tea leaves into the teapot and then pour boiled water into it. Most Chinese do not drink the tea immediately, but cover the pot and wait for a while until the tea leaves fall down to the bottom of the teapot (it may take five to eight minutes). When the tea is ready, the host should evenly distribute the tea into each cup.

Many Chinese like to drink tea together as a social meeting, such as morning tea at a veteran center; afternoon tea in a company lobby or school faculty lounge; or evening tea with friends at a teahouse or tea-garden. Teahouses are like coffee shops in America and are very popular in China, Taiwan, and Hong Kong. One can see a teahouse on nearly every corner of the street, whether in a small town or large city. Many teahouses also serve food and alcohol, thereby combining features of cafes and bars. Some offer live entertainment, including traditional music, dance, and Peking Opera. Many customers also play a game of Go or Chinese chess at a teahouse as they drink tea. Go (*Weiqi* or *Wei-ch'i*) is the world's earliest form of chess, which originated in China. Chinese chess (*Xiangqi*) is also a traditional Chinese game. Playing these games in a teahouse often attracts a large number of people who watch the proceedings. Some teahouses even hold neighborhood tournaments for both the game of Go and of Chinese chess.

Other leisure activities include shopping, folk temple fairs, family trips, and international traveling. Both the world's largest and second largest shopping malls are in China. The world's largest is the New South China Mall. It was built in Dongguan, southern Guangdong Province, in 2005, with 9.6 million square feet as total area and 7.1 million square feet of leasable space for 2,350 retail stores. The world's second largest shopping mall is the Golden Resources Shopping Mall in Beijing. It was completed in 2004 with a total area of 6 million square feet for 1,200 retail stores, more than 150 restaurants, and 230 escalators. The Beijing Mall, built in 2005, is ranked the 19th largest mall in the world with 3.4 million square feet and 600 retail shops. The Zhengjia Plaza (Grandview Mall) in Guangzhou, Guangdong Province, built in 2005, is ranked the 20th largest mall in the world with a total of 3 million square feet. (The two largest malls in the United States are King of Prussia Mall built in 1963 in Pennsylvania, with 2.79 million square feet and 327 shops, and the Mall of America built in 1992 in Minnesota, with 2.78 million square feet and 520 shops; they are ranked the 25th and 26th largest in the world, respectively.)

Besides shopping, many Chinese take family trips during holidays and weekends. China's tourism is one of the fastest-growing businesses in the national economy.

According to the World Travel & Tourism Council, travel and tourism directly contribute $216 billion annually to the Chinese economy, about 3 percent of GDP. During the National Day in October 2012, for example, approximately 740 million Chinese holiday-makers traveled within the country. China's overseas tourists reached 20 million in 2003, overtaking Japan for the first time.

The local temple fair is a kind of cultural and social event in China, transformed from religious ceremonies and sacrifices in ancient times to market exchanges and entertainments in the present day. The open ground in or near a temple hosts a temple fair like a village fair, town fair, or city fair on traditional holidays such as the Spring Festival or specified days for the local people. Farmers and merchants sell their fresh farm produce, homemade snacks, local specialties, and antiques on the market. Artisans set up booths to show and sell their paintings, handcrafts, and outfits. Local musicians put together a performing stage for singing, dancing, and *quyi* (Chinese folk performing arts, including ballad singing, storytelling, comedies, and clapper talks). Villagers and their children sample snacks, exchange recipes, ride on a horse or a camel, enjoy the shows, and watch some local sport events such as a martial arts (*Wushu*) tournament. It has also become a tradition for young men and women to set up their first date or to look for a new girlfriend or boyfriend at the local temple fairs. Some of the large cities continue to hold traditional temple fairs. For example, Beijing hosts many temple fairs during the Spring Festival, including famous ones at the White Cloud Temple, the Altar of Earth, the Dragon Pool, and the Temple of Intense Happiness.

The best way to obtain and maintain a healthy and happy lifestyle in China is to work out on a regular basis or participate in some of the popular sports activities. Although China has long been associated with the martial arts, its sports consist of a variety of popular and competitive sports. The 2008 Beijing Olympics further promoted popular sports such as soccer, or *zuqiu* (football) in Chinese, table tennis (Ping-Pong), basketball, badminton, and volleyball. Some Chinese athletes have become world-class players in these sports.

Soccer is the most popular spectator sport in China since it was introduced to the country in the 1900s. After the founding of the People's Republic of China (PRC) in 1949, the National Chinese Soccer Association (or Chinese Football Association, CFA) was organized. Each middle school, high school, and college has its own boys' and girls' soccer teams. These schools use or rent their soccer fields on weekends to local amateur teams to organize matches. Most counties, towns, cities, and provinces have their own men's and women's professional soccer teams as well as local soccer associations. In 1994, CFA created a national professional soccer league. In 2004, CFA renamed the "Jia A" teams as the Chinese Super League, the premier soccer teams in the country. While the men's teams are still struggling to win matches in Asia, the Chinese Women's Soccer Team has finished second at both the World Championships and the Olympic Games.

Table tennis is the second most popular sport in China with over 300 million people across the country playing it. Its popularity has led some foreigners to call table tennis China's "national sport." Each middle school, high school, and college has its own boys' and girls' table tennis teams. Most counties, towns, cities, and provinces have their own men's and women's professional teams and local table tennis associations. The National

Chinese Table Tennis Association was founded in 1951 and held the first National Table Tennis Championships in Beijing in 1952. In 1959, Rong Guotuan became the first Chinese citizen to win a world championship. Since then, Chinese players have won over 200 world titles. In the 36th World Championships in 1981, for example, Chinese teams won first place and second place in all seven events. In the 37th World Championships in 1983, the Chinese teams won first place in all seven events and second place in five events.

Volleyball and basketball have also become popular in China during recent decades. In the 1980s, the Women's National Volleyball Team won the "Big Threes," the Olympic title in 1984 and 2004, Volleyball World Cup in 1981 and 1985, and World Championship in 1982 and 1986. Their consecutive victories have made volleyball one of the most popular sports in the country. Basketball gained popularity after the Chinese player Yao Ming joined the NBA in the United States and became a Houston Rockets player in 2002. Thereafter, more Chinese players like Yi Jianlian and Sun Yue joined the NBA, and Sun signed a contract with the Los Angeles Lakers in 2008. The Chinese Basketball Association (CBA) was founded in 1995 and had 21 teams by 2012. Millions of Chinese fans watched and closely followed the NBA and CBA games.

It is estimated that more than 400 million Chinese people play basketball regularly for exercise and leisure. Certainly, traditional sports such as *wushu* (martial arts), *tai-chi quan*, and *qi-gong* retain their popularity in China. One can see millions of Chinese exercising and practicing these sports with their own groups each morning in the parks, along the rivers and lakes, at community centers, or on public track fields. Schools, companies, military units, and government offices also organize these sports into morning exercises. Before class begins in the morning, for example, each school assembles all its students, faculty, and staff at the track field for morning exercise by playing music through the loud speakers and having physical education teachers and coaches lead the movements. Some moves are from traditional shadow boxing, or *tai-chi quan*, and are included in the 10- to 20-minute period. Some companies and factories organize their group exercises in the afternoon.

Further Reading

Brownell, Susan. *Training the Body for China: Sports in the Moral Order of the People's Republic*. Chicago: University of Chicago Press, 1995.

Dong, Jinxia. *Women, Sport and Society in Modern China: Holding Up More than Half the Sky*. London: Routledge, 2002.

Hollmann, Thomas. *The Land of the Five Flavors: A Cultural History of Chinese Cuisine*. New York: Columbia University Press, 2013.

Larmer, Brook. *Operation Yao Ming: The Chinese Sports Empire, American Big Business, and the Making of a NBA Superstar*. New York: Gotham, 2005.

Lu, Henry. *Chinese System of Food Cures: Prevention and Remedies*. New York: Sterling, 1986.

Morris, Andrew. *Marrow of the Nation: A History of Sport and Physical Culture in Republican China*. Berkeley: University of California Press, 2004.

Rolandsen, Unn. *Leisure and Power in Urban China: Everyday Life in a Chinese City*. London: Routledge, 2011.

Washburn, Dan. *The Forbidden Game: Golf and the Chinese Dream*. London: Oneworld, 2014.

Xu, Guoqi. *Olympic Dreams: China and Sports, 1895–2008*. Cambridge, MA: Harvard University Press, 2008.

Acupuncture, Moxibustion, and Narcotherapy

In traditional Chinese medicine, acupuncture, moxibustion therapy, and narcotherapy are the most unique and widely used treatment methods among other practices in China to relieve people of their pains and diseases. They have numerous applications in internal medicine, surgery, ophthalmology, otolaryngology, gynecology, and pediatrics. Acupuncture and moxibustion therapies produce rapid results, and are rarely accompanied by undesirable side effects. Narcotherapy, which disables the body or one part temporarily, is most often used in surgical operations (without anesthesia). They are very popular in Taiwan, Hong Kong, Singapore, and other Asian countries.

In ancient China, some well-known doctors used acupuncture and moxibustion therapy to treat difficult and complicated cases, including Bian Que (?–310 BCE) of the Zhou dynasty (1066–221 BCE) and Hua Tuo (140–208) of the Han (206 BCE–220 CE). Wang Weiyi, a Song (960–1279) medical official, designed and created two bronze human figures carved with 12 channels of vessels and marked with 354 acupuncture points for doctors to use when learning the acupuncture therapy. It was the earliest bronze human figure for medical use in China. Acupuncture and moxibustion therapy spread from China to Korea in 600, to Japan in 700, to Southeast and Central Asia in about 1000, and to Europe in the 17th century. They have been practiced in ever-increasing numbers of countries in today's world.

According to the theory, the human body is traversed by a network of main and collateral channels through which blood and energy (*Qi*) circulate. The main channels are called *Jing* and the collateral ones are called *luo*. Each channel has a definite circulatory route, along which the acupuncture points are distributed. A blockage at any given point along one of these passages is manifested by some particular symptom. Based on evidence produced by these symptoms, a doctor makes a diagnosis and then conducts therapeutic treatment. The doctor places a certain number of very tiny needles at these acupunctural points, and then gently and gradually twists them into the body through the skin. These needles are round, smaller than sewing needles, and between three and six inches in length. The acupuncture needles commonly used abroad are made of gold or silver, which were widely in use in China through Ming (1368–1644) and Qing (1644–1911). But the most therapeutically effective are perforated square needles. In recent decades, the scope of acupunctural treatments has expanded to many areas, some of which have become standard treatments such as acute bacteria dysentery, certain kinds of paralysis, coronary heart disease, and gallstones. Acupuncture is applicable to obstetrics, where it can be used to correct an abnormal fetal position and to induce labor.

Moxibustion is a type of thermotherapy. In ancient times, accidental burns eased some pain, resulting in fire or high temperature applications in dealing with certain revelations. Then, *Ai* (moxa) was gradually chosen as the main fuel material since it grows everywhere on China's vast land, has a unique fragrance, burns warmly, and provides firepower to cure. The traditional moxibustion therapy process was to burn a few pieces of dried moxa plant, contain its smoke and heat into a small jar or bottle, and then place the jar at an acupunctural point of the body. Usually one moxibustion treatment involves applications at several points at the same time. According to the literature of the Sui (581–618) and Tang (618–907) dynasties, moxibustion therapy became popular in treating the common cold, diarrhea, and body pain. Its explanation points out an imbalance of the body system between the *Yin* (cold) and *Yang* (hot), causing the sickness or discomfort. Moxibustion therapy provides additional warm temperature to the body to restore the balance.

Narcotherapy is a traditional clinical experience in the practice of acupuncture analgesia. The unique feature of operations carried out this way, using needles at certain neurotic points, is that the patient remains fully awake during surgery. Because little or no anesthetic is used, any potential danger arising from its use can be avoided, and the patient experiences no unpleasant after effects. After undergoing an operation in which acupuncture anesthesia is used, the patient generally experiences only slight post-operational pains and rarely experiences such reactions as nausea and vomiting. Generally speaking, the use of acupuncture as an anesthetic technique promotes quick recovery of the post-operative patient. Although this form of anesthesia is now used in many types of operations, it has proved particularly suitable for those in the area of the neck, head, and chest. Nevertheless, some Western medical experts question the scientific evidence and safety of acupuncture and narcotherapy, and they are only used as a supplementary approach in the West.

See also: Chapter 1: Hong Kong; Taiwan. Chapter 2: Timeline. Chapter 6: Health Care. Chapter 15: Overview; Chinese Herbs and Alternative Medicine; Qi-Gong.

Further Reading

Maciocia, Giovanni. *The Foundations of Chinese Medicine: A Comprehensive Text for Acupuncturists and Herbalists.* 2nd ed. London: Churchill Livingstone, 2005.

McCann, Henry, and Hans-Georg Ross. *Practical Atlas of Tung's Acupuncture.* Saarbrucken, Germany: Verlag Muller and Steinicke, 2014.

Zhao, Ji-ping, and Yan-ping Wang. *Acupuncture and Moxibustion: Chinese Medicine Study Guide Series.* Beijing: People's Medical Publishing House, 2008.

Alcoholic Beverages

Chinese alcoholic beverages not only have an age-old history, but are also extremely rich in variety. An important process of Chinese winemaking is the ancient use of yeast.

Early farmers learned they could transform molded crops into distiller's yeast. Different varieties of yeasts are adopted in different regions, creating different varieties of wine. By the Sui dynasty (581–618), winemaking techniques had already reached an elevated level. White or clear spirits, usually distilled from sorghum or maize, also have a history that dates back more than a thousand years in China. The technique of making white spirits appears to have first originated in western Shanxi Province, then spreading farther into northwestern Shaanxi, southwestern Sichuan, and the Guizhou Provinces.

Guizhou and Sichuan retain their superiority in white winemaking in China. Guizhou Maotai is perhaps today's best known Chinese liquor. Among the popular white wines (*baijiu*) from Sichuan are Laojiao Daqu and Luzhou Laojiao. Shanxi and Shaanxi continue to offer their celebrated labels such as Shanxi Fenjiu and Zhuyeqing, and Shaanxi Xifengjiu. Every province produces its own white wine by using local materials and matching local taste. There are more than 50 different white wines in China, including some internationally known labels like Jiangsu's Yanghe Daqu (major yeast), Anhui's Gujingong, and Beijing Erguotou. These are strong distilled spirits; most of them are approximately 40 to 65 percent alcohol by volume (ABV).

Some Chinese grape wines, or red wines (*hongjiu*), are also renowned abroad as well as at home, such as Beijing's Great Wall Wines, Changyu's Pioneer Wine, Tonghua's Grape Wines, and Yantai's Red Wines. Yantai of the eastern Shandong Province has become the largest wine-producing region in the country with over 140 wineries and producing 40 percent of China's wine. The total production of wine in 2004 was 370,000 tons, an increase of 15 percent from the previous year. The total domestic market grew 68 percent between 2001 and 2006. Some international statistics have shown that China is now the world's largest market for red wine. China's consumption of red wine has grown by 136 percent, whereas it has declined by 18 percent in France, the second-largest red wine consumer in the world.

The Chinese began their beer (*pijiu*) production in 1900 when they learned brewing technology from Russians and Germans who had established beer breweries in Harbin, Heilongjiang, and Qingdao (Tsingtao), Shandong. Although beer brewing is a relatively young industry, beer has become the top selling alcoholic beverage in China. In 2010, China's beer consumption totaled 450 million hectoliters (or 45 billion liters), about twice that of the United States. Snow Beer has recently overtaken Tsingtao Beer and become the best selling beer in the country, having 21.7 percent of China's market. Tsingtao is still the brand most widely exported to the international market.

Wine and beers are offered and served at dinner tables, and people celebrate their birthdays, holidays, and important events with alcoholic beverages. If you like to express your respect to the elders or superiors, you may make a toast. Before your drinking, you must use your cup to touch the elders' or superiors' cups (*pengbei*) to show your affection. When you begin to drink, your cup should be lower than the elders and superiors to show respect. It is customary to empty your cup of wine first (*ganbei*) to show sincerity.

See also: Chapter 2: Timeline. Chapter 4: Agriculture. Chapter 10: Overview; Table Manners. Chapter 14: Holiday Feasts. Chapter 15: Overview.

Further Reading

Flaws, Bob. *Chinese Medicinal Wines and Elixirs*. Boulder, CO: Blue Poppy, 1994.

Li, Zhengping. *Chinese Wine: Introduction to Chinese Culture*. 3rd ed. Cambridge, UK: Cambridge University Press, 2011.

Smith, Norman. *Intoxicating Manchuria: Alcohol, Opium, and Culture in China's Northeast*. Seattle: University of Washington Press, 2013.

Chinese Chess

Traditional Chinese chess (*Xiangqi*) is not the same game as Western chess. It originated from the Warring States Period (475–221 BCE) and became popular in the Tang (618–907). Its rules have undergone many changes before taking their present-day form toward the mid-Song dynasty (960–1279).

Like Western chess, Chinese chess is a game for two players, and each has 16 pieces (usually painted in red and black, or red and blue) for a total of 32 pieces These include a Marshal (*Jiang* or King), two Mandarins (*Shi* or Assistants), two Elephants (*Xiang*), two Chariots (*Jue*), two Horses (*Ma*), two Cannons (*Pao*), and five Soldiers (called *Bing* on one side and *Zu* on the other). Characters are engraved in the chessmen, and each has its own designated pattern of movement. At the start of play, all chessmen must be placed in fixed positions. The red side moves first, and the players take alternate turns.

The chessboard is a grid formed by the intersections of 9 vertical and 10 horizontal lines, forming 90 intersections, where pieces are placed. The players move their pieces from intersection to intersection, rather than in the squares they form, as in Western chess. The board is further subdivided by a "Chuhe River" which runs through the center, demarcating each player's territory.

The object of the game is to capture the opponent's Marshal. When the Marshal is checked and there is no way to save him, or he is unmovable, that side has lost. In the event that neither player attains this objective, the game is called a draw.

In China, it is estimated that there are roughly over 100 million chess enthusiasts. Many of them are so devoted to the game that they play it whenever they can find a stretch of free time. They set up their chessboard at the street corners, and play Chinese chess while they wait for their flights or trains at airports and train stations. Many schools have their own teams and participate in district tournaments, each city and province holds its own annual competitions, and a national championship game has been organized regularly. Since 1949, Chinese chess has been included among sports events in athletic competitions. The top national players are divided into the ranks of grand master and master. Among the several grant masters are Hu Ronghua from Shanghai and Yang Guanlin from Guangdong. The best woman player in China is Xie Siming from Beijing.

Two men play Chinese chess in Beijing, China, on March 14, 2009. As a popular game in Chinese tradition, Chinese chess is played by more than 100 million chess enthusiasts in the country. It has also been included among sporting events in national athletic competitions in the People's Republic of China (PRC) since 1949. (Lucidwaters/Dreamstime.com)

Chinese chess has also become popular in many countries and regions throughout Asia, including Taiwan, Hong Kong, Japan, Singapore, Malaysia, Philippines, and Thailand. More than 40 countries have established Chinese chess clubs and national associations. In 1979, the Asian Chinese Chess Association was established, and each year it sponsors an annual International Chinese Chess Tournament.

See also: Chapter 1: Hong Kong; Taiwan. Chapter 2: Timeline. Chapter 15: Overview; The Game of Go.

Further Reading

Cheng, Ah. *The Chess Master*. Trans. W. Jenner. Hong Kong: Chinese University Press, 2005.

Lau, H. *Chinese Chess: An Introduction to China's Ancient Game of Strategy*. North Clarendon, VT: Tuttle, 2003.

Rea, Tyler. *A Beginners Guide to Xiangqi: Chinese Elephant Chess*. Las Vegas, NV: CreateSpace Independent, 2014.

Sloan, Sam. *Chinese Chess for Beginners*. Tokyo, Japan: Ishi, 2006.

Chinese Herbs and Alternative Medicine

Traditional medicine is an important part of China's cultural heritage with a long history, and it has played a crucial role in the struggle, survival, and success of the Chinese race. Before Western medicine entered China on a large scale in the 1840s and 1850s, the Chinese people relied solely on their traditional medicines. China's earliest existing medical book, *Huangdi Neijing* (Canon of Medicine of the Yellow Emperor), systematically summarized medical experience before the Spring and Autumn Period (770–476 BCE) of the Zhou dynasty (1066–221 BCE). It lays a theoretical foundation for traditional Chinese medical science. There are numerous famous Chinese medical doctors in history, such as Bian Que (?–310 BCE) of the Warring States Period (475–221 BCE), Hua Tuo (140–208) of the Han (206 BCE–220 CE), Zhang Zhongjing (150–219) of Han, Sun Simiao (?–682) of the Sui (581–618) and Tang (618–907), and Li Shizhen (1518–1593) of the Ming (1368–1644). These doctors had relieved patients of pains and illness with their consummate medical skills. Chinese herbal medicines and diagnostic therapy spread from China to Korea in 600, to Japan in 700, to Southeast and Central Asia in about 1000, and to Europe in the 17th century.

Traditional Chinese medicine comprises a complete and independent system, the theory and practice of which have been continuously enriched over the course of the past 2,000 years. Its practice includes herb medicines and medical diagnosis and treatments.

Traditional Chinese medicine is mainly derived from plants, some animals, and minerals. Each of China's regions has its own distinctive climatic and geological conditions, which give rise to certain native medicinal materials and tonic substances. Among the most well-known and widely used herbal medicines are the northeastern *ginseng* and *pilose antler* and the *tianma* (*gastrodia clota*), bezoar, and musk of Sichuan. After being specially prepared, these are made into oral or external medicines. The famous medical book of the Han, *Shennong Bencao Jing* (Shennong's Material Medicines) recorded 365 herbs. The Ming doctor Li Shizhen finished his book, *The Compendium of Material Medicine*, in 1578. It was composed of 52 volumes, including 1,892 medicines with 1,109 pictures of medicine and 11,096 prescriptions. He also knew and recorded the anesthesia function of some herbs. This masterpiece is one of the representative works of Chinese medical science. More than 87 types of medicinal plants and herbs collected in the wild are now under cultivation in China, *tianma*, *banxia* (*pinellia ternata*), and balloon-flower being but three examples. In 1977, there were over 400,000 acres of medicinal plants under cultivation. By 2010, the herbal medicinal plant fields had exceeded 1.2 million acres. Chinese herbal medicines have been exported to many countries in the world, and traditional Chinese medicines are also very popular in Taiwan, Hong Kong, Singapore, and other Asian countries.

Diagnostic methods of traditional Chinese medicine are observation, auscultation, and olfaction, interrogation, and palpation. A Chinese doctor observes the patient's appearance and mental status first; then listens to the patient's breathing; inquires about the onset of the problems and the patient's feelings, diet, and daily life; and feels the patient's pulse. After the diagnosis, the doctor treats the patient with acupuncture, moxibustion, or other therapies according to the health diagnosis. The doctor sometimes prescribes herbal medicines. In recent decades, there has been much progress in the setting of bones, and now such disorders as slipped disks, disorders of the lower back, joint disorders, and injuries of the soft tissues can be diagnosed and treated. In 1965, there were approximately 280,000 doctors of Chinese medicine working in 43 Chinese medical hospitals and nearly 4,000 clinics. By 2010, there were more than 600,000 doctors of Chinese traditional medicine, working in 112 hospitals, 232 health agencies, 67 institutes, and approximately 9,700 clinics.

New research efforts in China have combined traditional Chinese medicine with Western medical science. A new development in orthopedics is the application of traditional Chinese and Western methods of treatment for fractures and joint injuries. This involves immobilizing the injured limb with small light mobile splints, applying a poultice and prescribing light exercises at an early stage to hasten healing. This combined treatment not only speeds the healing, but also stops pain, reduces swelling, and stimulates circulation. In 1979, the First National Conference on Traditional Chinese Medicine was held in Beijing and founded the All-China Society of Traditional Medicine. Currently there are 38 colleges of traditional Chinese medicine that graduate about 20,000 students annually. Nevertheless, some Western medical experts have questioned the scientific evidence, safety, cost effectiveness, and drug research of the traditional Chinese medicine, which is still used as a complementary alternative medicine approach in the West.

See also: Chapter 1: Hong Kong; Taiwan. Chapter 2: Timeline. Chapter 6: Health Care. Chapter 15: Overview; Acupuncture, Moxibustion, and Narcotherapy; Qi-Gong.

Further Reading

Beinfield, Harriet, and Efrem Korngold. *Between Heaven and Earth: A Guide to Chinese Medicine*. New York: Ballantine Books, 1992.

Gao, Duo, ed. *Traditional Chinese Medicine: The Complete Guide to Acupressure, Acupuncture, Chinese Herbal Medicine, Food Cures, and Qi Gong*. London: Carlton, 2013.

Maciocia, Giovanni. *The Foundations of Chinese Medicine: A Comprehensive Text for Acupuncturists and Herbalists*. 2nd ed. London: Churchill Livingstone, 2005.

Ody, Penelope. *The Chinese Medicine Bible: The Definitive Guide to Holistic Healing*. New York: Sterling, 2011.

Yi, Qiao, and Al Stone. *Traditional Chinese Medicine Diagnosis Study Guide*. Seattle, WA: Eastland Press, 2008.

Zhou, Xue-sheng. *Fundamentals: Chinese Medicine Study Guide Series*. Beijing: People's Medical Publishing, 2007.

Chinese Tea

China is the homeland of tea, first cultivated some 4,700 years ago. Tea drinking is deeply rooted in Chinese culture. In ancient China, tea, or *cha* and *chai* (in different dialects), was used not only as a beverage, but also as a medicinal drug, a garnish for cooking, and a sacrificial offering in spiritual ceremonies. Tea cultivation first took place in Sichuan during the early period, and by the Tang dynasty (618–907) had expanded to the Yangzi (Yangtze), Zhu (Pearl), and Minjiang river basins, forming the basis of what are today's three main Chinese tea-growing regions. During the Tang period, tea and tea-drinking customs were brought to Japan by Buddhist monks. Chinese teas are famous throughout the world for their unique color, fragrance, flavor, and finely shaped leaves. In the 16th century, the Chinese shipped large quantities of tea abroad. In 1773, the revolutionary Boston Tea Party threw 342 chests of Chinese tea into Boston Harbor against the tea tax enforced by the British government on its American colonies. Chinese tea has been referred to as "green gold" in the international trade with China.

China has 16 provinces and regions that produce tea. Their different processing produces different kinds of tea. Green tea is not fermented, using fresh tea-leave tops without a process called "withering." When brewed, green tea is verdurous in color or has a touch of yellow within. Famous green tea includes the Longjing (Lungching) tea from the region of the West Lake in Hangzhou and the Biluochun (or Pilochun) tea from Jiangsu. Red tea (known as black tea) is completely fermented and becomes a brilliant red since it goes through the withering, in which the tea leaves are placed under sunlight. Famous Chinese red tea is the Qimen (Keemun) Red Tea, Ninghong *Gongfu* tea, and Fujian Minhong tea. Oolong tea is half fermented as a unique Chinese specialty. It can be divided into three levels: light, medium, and heavy fermentation.

Scented tea or *hua cha* is distinctive to China and is made by smoking tea leaves with fragrant flowers, such as jasmine and chrysanthemum. A famous scented tea is jasmine tea, produced in southeastern Fujian Province. Other varieties of tea include white tea from Fujian; yellow tea from Hunan; dark black tea, including the famous Pu-erh (Pu'er) Tea, from Yunnan Province; tuo tea of Sichuan, and brick tea from Tibet and Inner Mongolia.

See also: Chapter 1: Overview; Yangzi River. Chapter 4: Agriculture. Chapter 5: Buddhism. Chapter 14: Cantonese Dim Sum.

Further Reading

Fong, Roy. *Great Tea of China*. Layton, UT: Gibbs Smith, 2013.

Peltier, Warren. *The Ancient Art of Tea: Wisdom from the Old Chinese Tea Master*. North Clarendon, VT: Tuttle, 2011.

Reid, Daniel. *The Art and Alchemy of Chinese Tea*. London: Singing Dragon, 2011.

Rose, Sarah. *For All the Tea in China: How England Stole the World's Favorite Drink and Changed History*. New York: Penguin Books, 2011.

Wang, Jian. *All the Tea in China: History, Methods, and Musings*. Shanghai: Shanghai Press, 2012.

The Game of Go

Go (*Weiqi* or *Wei-ch'i*) is the world's earliest form of chess, and it originated in China. Written accounts from as early as the Spring and Autumn and Warring States Periods (770–221 BCE) testify to the game having been played. It was introduced to Japan during the Sui (581–618) and Tang (618–907) dynasties and to Europe in the 19th century. Today the game is played in more than 40 countries and has become popular in Japan and Korea as an important international contest.

Go is played with 181 black and 180 white pieces (generally flat round stones or marbles) on a square board, which consists of a grid 19 by 19 resulting in 361 intersecting points. Each player takes a turn to place one of his/her stones at one intersection. Players compete to occupy and conquer territory by surrounding vacant points with their stones. A single stone, or a group of stones, can be captured and removed from the board if they are completely encircled by the opponent's stones. Each player's final score is her/his number of occupied and surrounded points less the number of stones lost by capture. Since the strategy and tactics in Go are profound, Western scholars point out that some Chinese leaders and generals applied them to their policy-making and war-fighting.

The game of Go is very popular, especially among young people in China. Many schools have their own teams and participate in district tournaments; each city and province holds its own annual competitions and a national championship game is organized regularly. In 1979, the first World Amateur Go Championship was held in Tokyo, Japan. The participants came from 15 countries of Europe, Asia, and America. Chinese contestants captured both first and second place in the competition with Nie Weiping winning the championship and Chen Zude coming in second.

Go players in China are divided by a nine-rank system, which was borrowed from Japan. Players above the fifth rank are designated as "high-ranking" (*gaoshou*, meaning master). China has a total of six players of the ninth rank. Among them are Nie, Chen, Wu Songsheng, and Ma Xiaochun. China's highest ranking woman Go player is Kong Xiangming, a sixth-ranking player from southwestern Sichuan Province.

See also: Chapter 2: Timeline; Mao Zedong. Chapter 15: Overview; Chinese Chess.

Further Reading

Craig, Steve. *Sports and Games of the Ancients*. Westport, CT: Greenwood, 2002.

Moskowitz, Marc L. *Go Nation: Chinese Masculinities and the Game of Weiqi in China*. Berkeley: University of California Press, 2013.

Shotwell, Peter. *Go! More Than a Game*. North Clarendon, VT: Tuttle, 2011.

Smith, Arthur. *The Game of Go*. New York: Evergreen, 2014.

Qi-Gong

As a form of traditional Chinese breathing exercises, Qi-gong (or Qi Gong, Ch'i-kung) increases vitality, improves health, and regulates the body by regulating the breath. The Chinese term *Qi*, meaning air, breath, energy, or spirit, has a very wide range of reference in everyday language. Classic Daoist (Taoist) scholars simply described it as a force of nature, which derives from the interaction of Yin and Yang, and in turn can push, slow down, or even change the course of the transition between Yin and Yang. It is thought that capacity, and the art of utilizing Qi, may improve one's physical, mental, and social conditions. Daoist scholar Xu Sun (Hsu Sun) (239–374) wrote about Qi-gong in a chapter, "*Qigong Puchi*" (An Additional Treatise on Qi-gong), in his book, *Record of Pure and Bright Ancestral Teachings*. The Ming (1368–1644) medical expert Li Shizhen (1518–1593) also includes Qi-gong in his works. Thus, herbal medicine and Qi-gong have become integral parts of China's ancient heritage which, because of their importance, have been passed down to the present day.

Qi-gong itself can be divided into three forms, a martial form known as "hard Qi-gong," a therapeutic form known as "soft Qi-gong," and a popular Qi-gong fitness exercise. Martial arts professionals who have fully mastered the art of breath control (sometimes referred to as "vital energy training") can concentrate their vital energy (*Qi*) in various points of their body and render these areas enormously strong and relatively insensitive to pain. Such persons can break wood, brick, or even stones with their bare hands or feet. Many martial arts schools offer Qi-gong classes and certificates.

The therapeutic Qi-gong is also called *waiQi* (outflowing energy). Specially trained Qi-gong healers learn to release a form of energy through their fingertips. When this energy is directed toward a patient's acupunctural point, it stimulates the body's self-regulating system and can correct a variety of physical imbalances, thereby helping to restore health. Some Chinese traditional medical hospitals offer Qi-gong therapies as alternative medication. More Qi-gong clinics, Qi-gong treatment centers, and Qi-gong rehabilitation offices are now open for patients with special needs in mental health, cancer treatment, and injury recovery, as well as alcohol and drug addictions.

Qi-gong has become a popular physical fitness exercises in China, Hong Kong, and Taiwan. The essential three major techniques are "calming the mind," "concentrating the attention," and "regulating the breath." They may induce inhibitory activity in the areas of the cerebral cortex which controls the brain and the rest of the body, stimulate the nervous system in a concentrated area, and increase the flow of endocrines in the organs located there, and promote circulation in the portal veins as well as in the systemic and pulmonary circulatory systems. Qi-gong exercise may increase the vital capacity of the lungs, improve functioning of the heart, and stimulate metabolism. If practiced over a period of time, Qi-gong may possibly strengthen the physique and prevent illness. Some people believe that it may be also effective in certain chronic ill-nesses which commonly afflict middle-aged and elderly people, such as high blood pressure, coronary heart disease, ulcers, neurasthenia, pains in the lower back and limbs, and certain soft tissue injuries.

Since the reform movement began in the People's Republic of China (PRC) in 1978, Qi-gong has become more popular than ever and has been given a new face and placed squarely on a par with mainstream modern science. With active official support, na-tional research committees have been set up to investigate Qi-gong's scientific, medical, sporting, defense, and other applications. There are also local Qi-gong organizations throughout the country, and explicit regulations on the assessment and certification of Qi-gong masters, clinics, academies, and the like. Academic institutions such as Peking University, Qinghua (Tsing-hua) University, and the Beijing Institute of Chinese Medi-cine in particular, vie with one another in conducting research as well as publishing papers and reports. Nevertheless, people should be cautious about Qi-gong beauty shops, Qi-gong massage, and Qi-gong fortune-telling on the streets.

See also: Chapter 2: Timeline. Chapter 5: Daoism; Feng-Shui. Chapter 15: Overview; Acupuncture, Moxibustion, and Narcotherapy; Chinese Herbs and Alternative Medi-cine; *Wushu*: Martial Arts.

Further Reading

Brown, Barbara, and Gunter Knoferl. *Qi Gong*. Emeryville, CA: Thorsons, 2001.

Holland, Alex. *Voices of Qi: An Introduction Guide to Traditional Chinese Medicine*. Berke-ley, CA: North Atlantic Books, 2000.

Liu, Hong, and Paul Perry. *The Healing Art of Qi Gong: Ancient Wisdom from a Modern Master*. New York: Grand Central, 2008.

Wu, Baolin, and Jessica Eckstein. *Qi Gong for Total Wellness: Increase Your Energy, Vitality, and Longevity with the Ancient Nine Palaces System from the White Cloud Monastery*. New York: St. Martin's Griffin, 2006.

Wu, Zhongxian. *Chinese Shamanic Cosmic Orbit Qi-gong: Esoteric Talismans, Mantras, and Mudras in Healing and Inner Cultivation*. London: Singing Dragon, 2011.

Tai-Chi Quan

As the most popular style of *wushu* or martial arts, as well as one of the rich cultural heritages of China, Tai-chi (or Taiji) and Quan (or Chuan) originated during the late Ming dynasty (1368–1644). Chen Wangting, army garrison commander at Wen County, Henan, made great contributions to the creation of Tai-chi Quan through his troop-training exercises. While previous martial arts emphasized quick movements, vigorous punches, and hard strikes, this newer style follows the principles of "subduing the vigorous by the soft" and "adapting oneself to the style of others." Some of its move-ments are energetic while others are gentle, some rapid while others slow, and one

A Chinese man practices Tai-chi (or Taiji) at a Shanghai park. Tai-chi is a form of meditation characterized by flowing movements. As part of the Chinese martial arts, it strengthens muscles, improves body circulation, and builds flexibility. Because of its slow and gentle movements, Tai-chi has become a popular workout among Chinese women, children, and senior citizens. Many martial art schools, fitness clubs, and senior centers offer Tai-chi classes. (Corel)

movement follows another in uninterrupted rhythmic harmony similar to a flowing stream.

Since this new style of boxing consisted of eight primary hand gestures and five major body movements, it was originally called the "Thirteen Forms." It rapidly spread throughout the countryside since many of the elderly, as well as women and children, who had previously been rejected by the martial arts schools, could practice this soft and slow style. In the late 18th century, Wang Zongyue, a great martial arts master, wrote a systematical account of this new *quan-shu* (boxing style), and formally named it "Tai-chi Quan," relating it to the classic Daoist (Taoist) philosophy of Yin and Yang. Some translated it as "supreme ultimate fist," or "great extremes boxing."

Over the past 200 years, Tai-chi Quan has undergone a variety of changes, with increasing emphasis on the health-building and therapeutic value, while many movements involving explosive thrusts are being eliminated Having evolved, its movements have tended to become more relaxed, smooth, and graceful, making it a form of exercise suitable for people of all ages regardless of their physical condition.

Among its five major styles, the Yang School is the most widely practiced and best known. Founded by Yang Chengfu (1883–1936), its features and postures are slow with smooth motions, light with steady movements, and flowing lines of performance. The second most well-known school is the Wu School founded by Wu Jianquan (1870–1942). It is characterized by tightly orchestrated movements executed in a circular pattern. The third is the Sun School, founded by Sun Lutang (1861–1932). He created a style with nimble movements performed at quick tempo and accompanied by lively footwork. The fourth is the Chen School, founded by Chen Faxie (1887–1957), with the longest history and most traditional style. Retaining many elements of the ancient style of Chinese shadow boxing, it is featured by a combination of vigorous and gentle movements performed in a circular pattern. The fifth is the Wu style, also referred to as the

Hao style, which was established by Wu Xiang (1812–1880). This style has clearly articulated movements.

After the founding of the People's Republic of China (PRC) in 1949, the National Association of Wushu issued a simplified set of Tai-chi Quan practices in 1956, based on the most representative sequences of the Yang School. The series consists of 24 forms which progress from the simplest to the most difficult movements. The creation of a national standard form has done much to bring about a resurgence of interest and practice in *wushu*, both in China and abroad. In recent decades, China has standardized three other forms of Tai-chi Quan, involving cycles of 42, 68, and 88 forms respectively, to meet the needs of advanced students and martial arts professionals. More demanding and varied in contents, these styles combine traditional Tai-chi Quan with other *wushu* movements. In the Eleventh Asian Games of 1990, the 42-form Tai-chi Quan was chosen as an item for competition for the first time.

See also: Chapter 5: Daoism; Feng-Shui. Chapter 6: Health Care. Chapter 15: Overview; *Wushu*: Martial Arts.

Further Reading

Marshall, Prescott. *Tai Chi: A Beginners Guide to Achieving Physical, Mental, and Spiritual Balance*. Las Vegas, NV: CreateSpace Independent, 2014.

Rosenfeld, Arthur. *Tai Chi—The Perfect Exercise: Finding Health, Happiness, Balance, and Strength*. Jackson, TN: Da Capo, 2013.

Wayne, Peter. *The Harvard Medical School Guide to Tai Chi*. Boston, MA: Shambhala, 2013.

Yang, Jwing-Ming. *Tai Chi Chuan Classical Yang Style: The Complete Form*. Wolfeboro, NH: Ymaa, 2010.

2008 Beijing Olympics

From August 8 through August 24, 2008, the Games of the XXIX Olympiad (or the 2008 Summer Olympic Games) were held in Beijing, the capital city of the People's Republic of China (PRC). Beijing won the bid at the International Olympics Committee (IOC) meeting in Moscow in July 2001, winning over other applicants on the final list, which included Toronto, Paris, Istanbul, and Osaka. It was the first time for China to host the Olympics and the third time for Asian countries to hold the Summer Olympics; Japan held it at Tokyo in 1964, and Korea at Seoul in 1988. China became the 18th nation to host a Summer Olympic Games, and 22nd to hold the Olympic Games.

More than 11,400 athletes, including 4,637 women and 6,305 men, from 204 countries and regions which had National Olympic Committees (NOCs), traveled to Beijing and competed in 28 sports and 302 events, more than those for the 2004 Games. China had the largest participating team with a total of 639 athletes; the United States was second with 596; Russia 467; Germany 463; Australia 433; Japan 351; Italy 344; Canada 332; France 323; and Great Britain 311. The participating athletes broke 43 world records and set 132 Olympic records during these 17 days. For the first time, Chinese athletes won the most gold medals and had a total of 100 medals, including 51 gold, 21 silver, and 28 bronze. The United States was second in gold, but first in total, with 110 medals, including 36 gold, 38 silver, and 36 bronze. They were followed by Russia with 23 gold, 21 silver, and 29 bronze medals; Great Britain won 19 gold, 13 silver, and 15 bronze medals; Germany 16 gold, 10 silver, and 15 bronze medals; Australia 14 gold, 15 silver, and 17 bronze medals; South Korea 13 gold, 10 silver, and 8 bronze medals; Japan 9 gold, 6 silver, and 10 bronze medals; Italy 8 gold, 9 silver, and 10 bronze medals; and France 7 gold, 16 silver, and 18 bronze medals. Another record that was broken was an unprecedented 87 countries that won at least one medal during the Beijing Games.

The 2008 Beijing Olympics was the most-watched international event in sports history, with 4.7 billion viewers, about 70 percent of the total world population, compared to more than the 3.9 billion viewers of the 2004 Olympics in Athens. More than 100 heads of states from all over the world attended the Opening Ceremony and the Games in Beijing, including former U.S. President George W. Bush and his wife. The Opening Ceremony, presenting the official motto for the 2008 Olympics, "One World, One Dream," lasted for more than four hours and cost over $100 million to produce. The reported total costs of the 2008 Olympics were between $40 billion and $44 billion, vastly more than the total costs of $15 billion for the 2004 Olympics at Athens. Other critiques included limited access for the international media, air and water pollution in Beijing, as well as human and civil rights conditions, which had not been improved upon in China, as the Chinese government had promised.

See also: Chapter 1: Major Cities. Chapter 3: Civil Rights; Human Rights. Chapter 15: Overview.

Further Reading

Jarvie, Grant, Dong-Jhy Hwang, and Mel Brennan. *Sport, Revolution and the Beijing Olympics*. London: Bloomsbury Academic, 2008.

Li, Lillian, Alison Dray-Novery, and Haili Kong. *Beijing: From Imperial Capital to Olympic City*. London: Palgrave Macmillan, 2008.

Xu, Guoqi. *Olympic Dreams: China and Sports, 1895–2008*. Cambridge, MA: Harvard University Press, 2008.

Worden, Minky, ed. *China's Great Leap: The Beijing Games and Olympian Human Rights*. New York: Seven Stories, 2008.

Wushu: Martial Arts

Also known as *kongfu*, or *kung fu* (*gong fu*), *wushu* has been practiced for several thousand years by the Chinese people as a mass fitness exercise as well as in public health care, military training, civil self-defense, and competitive sports. As early as the Zhou dynasty (1066–221 BCE), *wushu* and archery were included among sports events.

During the Ming (1368–1644) and Qing (1644–1911) dynasties, the increasing complexity of Chinese martial arts began with a quantitative increase of styles, techniques, and information. Complex systems of martial arts, such as Shaolin Quan, Tai-chi (Taiji) Quan, and Bagua Quan, emerged in ways that exceeded the former styles, which were often connected with special techniques and individuals. The Chinese law enforcement and military practice of martial arts differed from other forms. The famous Ming general Qi Jiguang (Ch'i Ji-guang) (1528–1588) described martial arts as the way for the solider to defend his life, to kill his enemies, and to establish his merit.

Wushu can be divided into four main categories: bare-hand boxing (*quan-shu*), weapon plays, and group exercise. There are many types of bare-hand (quan) boxing, and as the Chinese saying goes, "there are 18 fighting skills" (*ban wuyi*), including long, short, southern, eastern, Shaolin, Eight Diagram, Xingyi or Xiangxing, and Tai-chi Quans. Each type has many different schools of styles, tradition, and location. Southern boxing (*Nan Quan*), for example, is the collective name of the many schools of boxing widely practiced in southern China, which are based on stylized movements of the dragon, tiger, leopard, snake, and crane. Eight Diagram boxing is based on varied combinations of eight different hand positions or boxing movements derived from the Eight Diagrams (eight combinations of whole or broken lines arranged around a circle formerly used for divination). *Xingyi Quan* or *Xiangxing Quan* (imitation or simulation boxing) is based on the movements of 12 different birds and beasts, including monkey, horse, turtle, snake, chicken, swallow, sparrow, hawk, and eagle, and develops certain forms such as monkey boxing, preying mantis boxing, eagle talon boxing, and snake boxing. There is another form which imitates postures and movements of a drunken person, which is called the "Eight Drunken Immortals" school.

Many weapons are used in *wushu*, and a Chinese saying goes: "There are 17 types of weapons" (*yang bingqi*), such as the longbow, crossbow, sword, spear, sabre, pike, shield, hatchet, club, battle-axe, halberd, mace, cudgel, trident, nine-sectioned chain, and plummet, to name a few, in many styles with different schools. The most commonly used weapons also differed by area. In the north, horses were widely used for transport, and warriors would mount their steeds by digging the points of their spears into the ground and using them to vault up onto their horses' backs before galloping away. Thus, the spear was the preferred weapon of the north. Although Chinese martial arts provide an extensive repertoire of weapons, only a few have been used in police and military training and tests.

Not only did choice of weapons differ according to local topography, the various major *wushu* styles also took their names from places and locations such as Shaolin style from the Shaolin Temple and Wudang School based at the Wudang Mountain. Each school has developed its popular legend, traditional ritual, practical rules, hierarchy institution, and national or worldwide system. Martial arts are also very popular in Hong Kong, Taiwan, Japan, Korea, Vietnam, Thailand, and Cambodia.

See also: Chapter 1: Hong Kong; Taiwan. Chapter 2: Timeline. Chapter 3: Law Enforcement; People's Armed Police; People's Liberation Army. Chapter 15: Overview; Qi-Gong; Tai-Chi Quan.

Further Reading

Dupont, Chantal. *Wushu: The Basics of Chinese Exercises for the Whole Family.* Tempe, AZ: Astrology Publishing, 2005.

Lorge, Peter. *Chinese Martial Arts: From Antiquity to the Twenty-first Century.* Cambridge, UK: Cambridge University Press, 2011.

Wong, Kiew. *The Art of Shaolin Kung Fu: The Secrets of Kung Fu for Self-defense, Health, and Enlightenment.* North Clarendon, VT: Tuttle, 2002.

Wu, Bin. *Essentials of Chinese Wushu.* Beijing: Foreign Languages Press, 1995.

CHAPTER 16

MEDIA AND POPULAR CULTURE

OVERVIEW

In China, the mass media is regarded as the voice of the Chinese Communist Party (CCP) and its government. In the 1950s, the Party Center began using domestic media outlets as a mouthpiece for their propaganda machine. This was both to mobilize the masses as well as to manage impressions of the country to both its own citizens and to the outside world. Since the 1960s, a censorship system has been adopted for news of great importance, which must be issued by appointed authoritative bodies and not by private media outlets. Controversial political topics may be discussed individually, or in small groups, but if a speech that includes controversial material is made public, or disseminated to overseas audiences, those involved may be, and often are, punished. During the Cultural Revolution of 1966–1976, the media was used as a tool in political struggles. In the People's Republic of China (PRC), the number of daily newspapers was reduced from 200 in the 1950s to 40 in the late 1960s.

State control of the news has been successful in China because of government ownership of all media, in whole or in part, and especially control of newspapers and magazines. Also, the government manages all media outlets, with powers that include production, the hiring of journalists, and restriction of access to information. All reporters, editors, producers, and administrators are employed or closely monitored by the central government. In addition, local governments at the provincial, county, and city levels also set up guidelines for the restriction of media activities. Many places where records are kept, such as court houses, police stations, and city and provincial government offices, remain closed to reporters. The government controls all information concerning the Tibetan areas, as well as access to the region. In many cases, reporters must have permission before they begin interviews or investigations. The fourth measure of state control is government censorship of sensitive stories from the bottom up, focusing on the news reporting system. Each reporter must know the line between what is permitted or forbidden. Each is expected to practice self-censorship, since their jobs are on the line. Their editors must then use the same rules to approve or unapprove news reports. They can reject an article or reassign a reporter with the use of overt intimidation. Their producers and directors act as further instruments of control.

Mass media has experienced tremendous change during the past 30 years. Market reforms, which began in 1978, have forced Chinese media providers to consider income provided by advertisements, subscribers, and viewership. The bureaucratic nature of the

Chinese media has begun to accept these economic pressures and to embrace commercialization and business strategies. Local governments have shifted their control mechanisms to include elaborate censorship and licensing procedures. More and more often, journalists enjoy relatively broad discretion in their ability to report on topics such as sports, entertainment, and consumer lifestyles, as well as local news that has no extensive political implications.

Chinese media enjoyed rapid growth in the past 30 years in terms of circulation, utilization, commercialization, consumption, and globalization. In 1982, only one-third of Chinese people had access to TV through 44 stations, mostly supplying black and white television screens. From the 1980s to the 1990s, television underwent swift development in China. In 1985, consumers purchased 15 million new TV sets, including 4 million color sets. By the early 1990s, television was reaching two-thirds of the population through more than 104 stations, including provincial and municipal stations. By 2000, there were 651 program-generating TV stations, 42,228 TV transmitting and relaying stations, and 368,553 satellite-TV receiving and relaying stations. At that time, the penetration rate of television had reached 92.5 percent, covering a population of 1 billion, making China the largest television-watching country in the world. Although no private-ownership or foreign-ownership television is permitted, about 30 overseas television networks entered China, with certain limitations, in 2003. By 2015, China had more than 840 program-generating TV stations with 3,000 channels available.

China's radio broadcasting developed rapidly in the 1980s and 1990s. In 1982, China had 118 radio stations and 328 relaying stations. By 1998, the number of radio stations increased to 673. Overseas broadcasting includes International Broadcasting Station, China Radio International (CRI), and Radio Beijing, responsible for China's overseas broadcasts. Radio Beijing broadcasts for 300 hours a day in 46 foreign languages, and also reaches, with broadcasts in Mandarin Chinese and four dialects, overseas Chinese. In 2003, China had 1,026 radio stations and shortwave radio transmitting and relaying stations. By 2015, there were more than 3,000 radio stations in the country. Nevertheless, without government permission, receiving or listening to a foreign radio program such as the Voice of America (VOA) is still prohibited. China continues to jam program signals from several dozen foreign radio broadcasts, including the U.S.-based Free Asia Station.

The PRC published only 382 daily newspapers and 930 magazines and periodicals in 1980. By 2001, the country circulated 2,000 newspapers and more than 8,000 magazines and periodicals. By 2015, the number of newspapers had increased to more than 2,200, including national, provincial, regional, and metropolitan daily papers. Daily newspaper sales increased from 80 million copies in 2004 to 97 million in 2006. By that time, China had become the largest newspaper market in the world, followed by India with 78 million copies daily, Japan with 69 million, and the United States with 53 million.

In China, the Internet has become popular for communication, education, and business operations. In 2003, more than 80 million households logged in to the Internet. According to official statistics, the country had a total of 103 million users by June 2005, with particularly high numbers among youths between the ages of 18 and 24. The number grew to 144 million users at the end of 2006 and increased to 162 million in 2007. According to research completed by Qinghua (Tsing-hua) University, the country had 100 million bloggers in 2007. The China Internet Network Information Center reported that the number of Internet users increased to 298 million in 2008 and jumped to 618 million in 2014.

China has become one of the leading countries in terms of telecommunications development. About 100 million cell phones were sold in 2006, and 190 million were sold in 2007, increasing by 74 percent. In 2007, more than 600 million mobile phones were manufactured in China, over 50 percent of the world's total production. China's telecom market has been shared by many companies such as China Telecom, CNC, China Mobile, China Unicom, and China Satcom. The tremendous changes in communications technology, particularly the transition from printed media to more rapid digital formats, are challenging the authority of official Chinese political and social institutions.

The popular culture of China has also experienced unprecedented transformation from an official, one-standard, and fixed culture to an "unofficial," chaotic mixed, and diversified culture. These changes come in the form of music, arts, films, books, and performances. All are constantly changing in the cacophony of popular conversation, and many have contradictory ideas and practices in their theories and methods. Nevertheless, they have been chosen by ordinary Chinese people, rather than the government, as a popular movie in the cinemas or a bestseller book in the stores.

Among the popular movies in the 1980s were *One and Eight* (1983), *Yellow Earth* (1984), and *Red Sorghum* (1987). Film directors Zhang Yimou, Tian Zhuangzhuang, Zhang Junzhao, and Chen Kaige made giant steps in transforming Chinese film from praising the CCP revolution to an objective attitude in displaying human nature. They revolutionized Chinese film both in content and in technique by embracing the "art-for-art" ideal and to be more creative in making new films that differed from the old ones. Among other popular movies, *Let the Bullets Fly* (2010) has become China's highest grossing domestic film, earning 730 million yuan *renminbi* (RMB) (about $111 million); *Aftershock* (2009) came in second, earning 670 million yuan RMB ($105 million). In 2005, the number of cinema admissions totaled 157.2 million from 4,425 screens, with a gross sale of 2 billion yuan RMB (about $322.5 million). In 2009, total admissions increased to 263.8 million from 6,323 screens with a box office sale of 6.21 billion yuan RMB ($1 billion). In 2012, China became the second-largest market in the world according to box office receipts. In 2013, the number of cinema admissions totaled 612 million from 18,195 screens, with a gross sale of 21.77 billion yuan RMB (about $3.51 billion). In January 2014, 6 of the top 10 highest-grossing films in China were domestic productions, with *Lost in Thailand* (2012) reaching sales of 1 billion yuan RMB (about $161 million) in domestic theaters. In 2014, the number of cinema admissions totaled 830 million in 23,600 screens nationwide, and its gross box office totaled 29.6 billion yuan RMB (about $4.76 billion), with domestic films having a share of 54.5 percent (16 billion yuan RMB or $2.6 billion). China is expected to have the largest film market in the world by 2018.

Further Reading

Bandurski, David. *Investigative Journalism in China: Eight Cases in Chinese Watchdog Journalism*. Hong Kong: Hong Kong University Press, 2010.

Chin, Yik-Chan. *Television Regulation and Media Policy in China*. London: Routledge, 2015.

Curtin, Michael. *Playing to the World's Biggest Audience: The Globalization of Chinese Film and TV*. Berkeley: University of California Press, 2007.

Herold, David Kurt, and Peter Marolt, eds. *Online Society in China: Creating, Celebrating, and Instrumentalizing the Online Carnival*. London: Routledge, 2013.

Hockx, Michel. *Internet Literature in China*. New York: Columbia University Press, 2015.

Lu, Sheldon. *Chinese-Language Film: Historiography, Poetics, Politics*. Honolulu: University of Hawaii Press, 2004.

Marolt, Peter, and David Kurt Herold, eds. *China Online: Locating Society in Online Spaces*. London, UK: Routledge, 2014.

Pickowicz, Paul. *China on Film: A Century of Exploration, Confrontation, and Controversy*. Boulder, CO: Rowman & Littlefield, 2011.

Shen, Yipeng. *Public Discourses of Contemporary China: The Narration of the Nation in Popular Literatures, Film, and Television*. London: Palgrave Macmillan, 2015.

Shirt, Susan. *Changing Media, Changing China*. Oxford, UK: Oxford University Press, 2010.

Sun, Helen. *Internet Policy in China: A Field Study of Internet Cafes*. Lanham, MD: Lexington, 2011.

Tai, Zixue. *The Internet in China: Cyberspace and Civil Society*. London: Routledge, 2006.

Zhu, Ying. *Two Billion Eyes: The Story of China Central Television*. The New Press, 2012.

Censor System

In China, most newspapers, magazines, book publishers and sellers are managed by the state, under the belief that these outlets must follow the Chinese Communist Party (CCP) and support its government. In the 1950s, the Party Center began using domestic media outlets as a mouthpiece for their propaganda machine, both to mobilize the masses as well as to manage the impressions it gave of the country to both its own citizens and to the outside world. Since the 1960s, a censorship system has been adopted for news of great importance, which must be issued by appointed authoritative bodies and not private media outlets. Controversial political topics may be discussed individually or in small groups, but if a speech that includes controversial material is made publicly, or disseminated to overseas audiences, those involved may be, and often are, punished.

In Beijing, the Department of Propaganda in the CCP Central Committee currently sets up guidelines as well as issues the party's instructions on a regular basis to the media, instructing them on what news to report and how to state it. The Xinhua (New

Journalists from China's official news agency, Xinhua, report directly to their Web site from the National People's Congress (NPC) in 2001. As the mouthpiece of the Chinese Communist Party (CCP), Xinhua News Agency in Beijing releases the official version of the news for the other news agencies, newspapers, TV, radio, and magazines. As a ministry-level government agency, it also has 170 news bureaus overseas. (AFP/Getty Images)

China) News Agency, acting as the party's mouthpiece, releases the official version of the news for the other news agencies, newspapers, TV, radio, and magazines to follow. The General Administration of Press and Publications (GAPP) in the State Council has the authority to screen, censor, and ban any print or electronic publication in China. It does so by controlling publishing licenses and quotas, such as ISBN and ISSN numbers. The GAPP can also recall books, destroy printed journals, or shut down an entire publishing house. What is especially crucial is to ensure that voices critical of the state will not be heard, and the authorities have organized huge institutions and related networks charged with key duties, such as monitoring speeches, to reach this end. In January 1997, the State Council placed restrictions on publications, and particularly on their scope, while at the same time granting the freedom to publish. Books and articles that address sensitive areas of the party and government are frequently suppressed. In late 2004, a wave of detentions reflected a new campaign targeting writers, journalists, and political commentators.

State control of the news has been successful in China for the following reasons. First, the government manages all media outlets, with powers that include the hiring of journalists, production, and restriction of access to information. Moreover, the government continues to monitor, harass, detain, arrest, and imprison journalists, writers, editors, and their families, if there is a violation of official reporting guidelines. The SARS outbreak in 2002–2003 is a major example of the government controlling access to information. It began in southern Guangdong Province in November 2002, and, despite taking some measures to control it, government officials did not inform the World Health Organization (WHO) of the outbreak until February 2003. During the critical early months, the government restricted media coverage and did not allow reporters to interview concerned families or medical personnel. The Chinese authorities attempted to preserve public confidence and assure foreign investors and tourists that everything was business as usual. In early April, Chinese health officials insisted that the epidemic was under "effective control." In Beijing, they reported only 37 cases and continued to delay reporting or to give false figures. In May, Chinese censors blocked the airing of an American-based CNN (Cable News Network) program that criticized Beijing's handling of the SARS epidemic. This lack of openness resulted in delayed efforts to control the disease, and the censorship process predated the worst of the outbreak. By July 31, there were 5,328 cases in the country and 349 fatalities. In the interim, the disease spread from China, rapidly infecting individuals in approximately 38 countries around the world. Following the rapid spread of the disease, the government acknowledged it had underreported the number of SARS cases, and, as a result, both the mayor of Beijing and the health minister were fired, but only after the outbreak had killed more than 700 people in nine countries.

Second, local governments at the provincial, county, and city levels also set up their own guidelines for the restriction of media activities. In August 2002, the Public Security Bureau of Lanzhou City in northwestern Gansu Province sent an official letter to all news media in the city naming 16 journalists who had published "inaccurate" reports concerning law enforcement personnel breaking the law. The journalists on this blacklist were banned from future interviews and investigations with police and public security officers.

The third measure of state control is government censorship of sensitive stories from the bottom up, focusing on the news reporting system. Each reporter must know the line between what is permitted and forbidden. They are expected to practice self-censorship since their jobs are on the line. Their editors must then use the same rules to approve or unapprove news reports. They can reject an article or reassign a reporter with the use of often overt intimidation. Their producers and directors act as further instruments of control. If a reporter or editor is perceived to have crossed the line, his or her employer can kill the product and relocate, demote, or even fire the individuals responsible as punishment. On important issues, the upper management must report to party officials and the CEOs of their outlet for final approval. These latter two groups of officials receive the party's instructions, reporting guidelines, and official news releases on a daily basis from the central government's agencies, including the official Xinhua News Agency, or from local organizations such as city and provincial party committees. In the occasional instance in which a newspaper or television station made a mistake by releasing a piece that differed from the official party line, the CEOs either lost their jobs or faced criminal charges.

In 2004, Shi Tao, an editor with the *Dangdai Shangbao* (*Contemporary Business News*) in Changsha, southern Hunan Province, was arrested for "leaking state secrets." His actual offense was divulging the Propaganda Department's instructions to his paper. In April 2005, Shi received a 10-year prison sentence from the Changsha's Court. In 2005, Chinese authorities held 32 journalists in jail, more than any other country. In 2007, 29 were imprisoned. For the ninth consecutive year, China has been one of the leading nations in the incarceration of journalists. According to the Committee to Protect Journalists, some of those prosecuted have served long sentences. Two of those, Chen Renjie and Lin Youping, were jailed in 1983 for publishing a pamphlet titled *Ziyou Bao* (*Freedom Report*), and reporter Chen Biling was executed.

The Chinese government also limits the access of foreign reporters and journalists to information. Beijing continues to jam Radio Free Asia (RFA), the British Broadcasting Corporation (BBC), and the Voice of America (VOA). Broadcasting to China in Chinese, Tibetan, and Uyghur languages, they have a large audience that includes activists, ordinary citizens, and even government officials. Some of these institutions' reporters, researchers, and assistants are not allowed to conduct interviews, visit sites, or take pictures. According to the FCCC (Foreign Correspondents' Club of China), in 2008 there were 178 incidents of harassment of foreign journalists while they conducted interviews. The number increased from 160 cases for all of 2007. In their annual report on world media freedom, American-based organization Freedom House ranked China on the same level as Iran, 181, with only communist countries and dictatorships such as Cuba, North Korea, and Myanmar (Burma) lower on the list in 2013.

See also: Chapter 3: Chinese Communist Party; Civil Rights; Death Penalty; Human Rights; Law Enforcement; Political Dissents. Chapter 16: Overview; Freedom of Speech; Internet and Social Media.

Further Reading

Bandurski, David. *Investigative Journalism in China: Eight Cases in Chinese Watchdog Journalism*. Hong Kong: Hong Kong University Press, 2010.

Tang, Wenfang, and Shanto Iyengar, eds. *Political Communication in China: Convergence or Divergence between the Media and Political System?* London: Routledge, 2012.

U.S.-China Economic and Security Review Commission. *Access to Information and Media Control in the People's Republic of China*. Las Vegas, NV: CreateSpace Independent, 2008.

Xu, Youyu, and Hua Ze, eds. *In the Shadow of the Rising Dragon: Stories of Repression in the New China*. London: Palgrave Macmillan, 2013.

Cyber Policing

The digital revolution has had a strong and positive impact in the public arena, as well as in civil society. As the Chinese people become better informed and connected, both the impact of the digital transformation on the evolution of democratic and civil rights, as well as the influence on the flexibility of government policy in the context of this major social and political transition, are uncertain. In the past, the Chinese Communist Party (CCP) used the media as an instrument to articulate and build support for its policies. In recent years, however, the Party Center has adjusted its approach while maintaining its control of mass media and public opinion.

Government censorship and surveillance have increased in cyberspace in response to the Internet's growing popularity and its use as a medium for activism throughout China. More than a dozen regulations relating to the Internet have been implemented by the Party Central Committee's Department of Propaganda, the Ministry of Public Security, the Ministry of Information Industry (MII), the Ministry of Culture, and relevant departments of ministries at various levels. By August 2005, the government had already spent at least $800 million on state-of-the-art equipment in an attempt to control its citizens online. In May 2007, China's Internet authorities issued new rules in the Regulations for the Management of Internet Publishing. These new guidelines brought online magazines, or webzines, under the same control as print publications. Webzines must now obtain prior agreement from the General Administration of Press and Publications (GAPP) in the State Council before seeking approval to set up a telecommunications business from MII. In September 2007, MII issued a new set of rules aimed at curbing the spread of "interactive" Internet sites such as bulletin boards, chat rooms, blogs, and discussion forums. According to these guidelines, all providers that were currently offering the aforementioned services must reapply for a license in order to operate, and, if denied, would be closed down. Tens of thousands of police monitor the Internet around the clock, and the government has heavily invested in a network infrastructure that boosts efficiency, aiding in the monitoring of web content.

Westerners call China's elaborate system of censorship the "Great Firewall of China." American and other foreign information-technology companies' contributions to official censorship raise serious issues concerning socially responsible corporate practices and policies.

New advances in technology have greatly enabled the government, through several different measures, to tighten its grip on cyberspace. The first is instant control over the content of online information exchanges. Officials have developed lists of sensitive key words, or "bad words," that are used to facilitate censorship. Major search engines, service providers, and technology companies such as U.S.-based Yahoo, Cisco, and Microsoft, have been cooperating with the Chinese government to restrict information that includes words such as "1989 Tiananmen Incident," the outlawed Falun Gong "evil cult," "separatist" elements in Tibet and Xinjiang, "Taiwan independence," and "democracy." Whenever these words occur in search results, or whenever content appears that the government does not approve, Web sites are blocked by servers. According to a recent report by the Harvard University–backed Open Net Initiative (ONI), China's Internet filtering capabilities are the most sophisticated of its kind in the world, involving multiple levels of technical control. The government also censors pornography and online religious materials. This instant "bad word" system of control is expected to increase self-censorship by netizens who realize the problem and will then stop writing about these sensitive topics. Officials continue to censor, ban, and sanction reporting and writing about labor, health, environmental crises, and industrial accidents.

A second measure used to control Internet communication is enhanced identification procedures, including online registration that identifies users by their real name, and password verification. These measures are performed by public security departments, police, or Internet service providers acting on behalf of the authorities. Chinese bloggers who use their own domain name are required to register, a process that requires the relinquishing of the names and addresses of all site administrators, who are in turn responsible for monitoring site content. Thus, organizers must personally scrutinize speech themselves, for fear of getting into trouble. Residents in Shenzhen, Guangdong Province, for example, are required to have their real identities verified by the IM Company of Tencent in Shenzhen if they wish to use instant messaging software to engage in group discussions. Through this procedure, a person's actual identity is connected with the opinion expressed online. This provides authorities with increased control in cyberspace and greater surveillance capabilities of public opinion. Because of the loss of privacy, however, many users are not comfortable with the real-name registration.

The third measure the government uses to exercise control over the Internet is to have its own "bloggers" and commentators. The Propaganda Department and public security departments have trained a network of online commentators to manipulate public opinion expressed in Internet forums and message groups. They are either employees of the government or are paid by the departments as a part-time job. They hide their real identities to facilitate government ideas or to fabricate false public opinion through multiple levels, such as web pages, web logs, online discussion forums, university bulletin board systems, and e-mail messages. Even though the government has these multiple control mechanisms, they can always shut down Web sites or individual blogs if officials think it necessary.

This well-developed network is, in fact, aided by extensive corporate and private sector interests, including some of the world's major international technological and Internet-based companies, such as Google, Yahoo, and Microsoft. In the spring of 2005, Yahoo China merged with Chinese-owned Alibaba. After this $1 billion merger, Yahoo, as an international partner and 40 percent stakeholder, was required to follow Beijing on issues of censorship and to devolve all related decisions to the local management teams. In 2006, Google cooperated with China by fracturing the Internet and creating Google.cn. This local Chinese-language search engine soon became very popular, but it is run there with Chinese censorship laws. Chinese authorities use the Web site to spy on Chinese political dissidents by reading their e-mails and checking on their search results. In 2010, Google announced that the company would no longer cooperate with China's censorship laws and would stop censoring Google.cn, even if the Internet giant would have to pull out of China. The Internet giant was forced out of China by the shutting down of its Chinese-language search engine, and negotiations failed. The international rights organizations praised Google's cyber war against China's violation of human and civil rights. It is significant that Google set up a principled stand on free speech and human rights. It is also important that Google publicly challenged China's censorship, since the Chinese government recently claimed that constraints on free speech on the Internet are crucial to China's political stability and economic prosperity.

See also: Chapter 1: Taiwan; Xinjiang. Chapter 3: Chinese Communist Party; Civil Rights; Law Enforcement; Political Dissents; Xi Jinping. Chapter 5: Falun Gong. Chapter 16: Overview; Censor System; Internet and Social Media.

Further Reading

Sun, Helen. *Internet Policy in China: A Field Study of Internet Cafes*. Lanham, MD: Lexington, 2011.

Tai, Zixue. *The Internet in China: Cyberspace and Civil Society*. London: Routledge, 2006.

U.S. Congressional-Executive Commission on China. *China's Censorship of the Internet and Social Media: The Human Toll and Trade Impact*. Las Vegas, NV: CreateSpace Independent Publishing, 2012.

Yang, Guobin. *The Power of the Internet in China: Citizen Activism Online*. New York: Columbia University Press, 2011.

Freedom of Speech

Despite provisions in the Chinese Constitution that protect the freedoms of speech, a clear gap exists between law and reality. On one side are the citizens, lawyers, and reporters who are trying to protect civil rights, while those in charge of the Chinese Communist Party (CCP), the government, the army, and the police trample on the aforementioned legal protections. The government has little tolerance for criticism or calls for greater transparency and accountability, and emphasizes the need for a harmonious society and political stability during the economic recession.

The limits and problems of China's civil liberties protection can be identified in the legislative, executive, and judicial procedures. First, the Constitution stresses in its preamble that any expression of rights or freedoms was unlawful if it violated the "Four Basic Fundamental Principles": to keep the country on the socialist road, uphold the people's democratic dictatorship, promote the leadership of the CCP, and follow Marxism-Leninism and Mao Zedong's (Mao Tse-tung) (1893–1976) thought. Moreover, a citizen's exercise of his or her rights and freedoms may not infringe upon the interests of the state, society, the collective, or the lawful freedoms and rights of other citizens.

In the existing laws, the restrictions on freedom of speech primarily include, first, Article 51 of the Constitution, which stipulates that the "Citizens of the People's Republic of China, in exercising their freedom and rights, may not infringe upon the interests of the State, of society or of the collective, or upon the lawful freedoms and rights of other citizens." Second, speeches may be judged according to the provisions of "Criminal Law," such as for crimes of anti-revolutionary propaganda, insults, slander, and false witness. Third, similar restrictions on speech can be found in civil and administrative law. Thus, the Chinese government can easily restrict the freedom of speech and press wherever it wants to link them to the jeopardy of national, social, and collective interests.

The Chinese judicial procedure also allows the legislature and legal system to restrain freedom of speech and freedom of press. The legal system of the People's Republic of China (PRC) is different from other civil law systems. The PRC Constitution does not systematically outline general principles that all administrative regulations and rules must follow. Instead, each governmental branch is capable of setting up its own guidelines, while the principles of legislation are listed in the basic laws enacted by the National People's Congress (NPC) and its standing committee. The provincial governments also create their local ordinary laws. Local laws and regulations are issued by the provincial, city and county governments, even though all of these ordinary laws are in theory incorporated with those at the national level.

The way in which civil liberties can be compromised by ordinary laws is illustrated by examining the laws relating to freedom of speech. The "Criminal Law," for instance, was adopted by the NPC's Standing Committee in 1979, and amended in 1997, due to an increase in crime throughout the country. This body of legal provisions provides the Principal Punishments, including criminal detention, fixed term imprisonment, life imprisonment, and the death penalty. Under some criticism, it provides for counter-revolutionary offences, such as anti-government propaganda, or other acts that "endanger the PRC" and is "committed to the goal of overthrowing the political power of the dictatorship of the proletariat and the socialist system."

Beijing continues to restrict some of its citizens' fundamental rights by targeting unwanted opinion and policy criticism. From May to June 2007, for example, authorities arrested some members of the "Pan-Blue Alliance," which recognized the Chinese Nationalist Party in Taiwan, and promoted the Three Principles of the People. Most of its leaders were arrested or sent to labor camps or mental hospitals, while its Web sites and newsletters were shut down by the government. Liu Xiaobo (1955–), professor of Beijing Normal University with a PhD in literature, served as president (2003–2007) of the Independent Chinese Pen Society. In 2008, he coauthored the *Charter 08* manifesto and posted it online, calling for increased political freedoms and human rights in China. He was arrested in 2009 and on December 23, 2009, was sentenced to 11 years of imprisonment for "the crime of inciting subversion of state power." In October 2010, Liu was awarded the Nobel Peace Prize for his "long and nonviolent struggle for fundamental human rights in China." Liu, however, will likely remain in jail until 2020. According to the annual reports released by the U.S. Department of State, the U.S. Congressional Executive Commission on China, and Amnesty International, the condition of civil liberties in China remained poor in 2015.

See also: Chapter 3: Chinese Communist Party; Civil Rights; Constitution; Criminal Law; Liu Xiaobo; National People's Congress; Political Dissents. Chapter 16: Overview; Censor System; Cyber Policing; Internet and Social Media; Netizen and Online Guerrilla.

Further Reading

Garrett, Daniel. *Counter-Hegemonic Resistance in China's Hong Kong: Visualizing Protest in the City*. New York: Springer, 2015.

Goldman, Merle. *From Comrade to Citizen: The Struggle for Political Rights in China*. Cambridge, MA: Harvard University Press, 2007.

Mühlhahn, Klaus. *Criminal Justice in China: A History*. Cambridge, MA: Harvard University Press, 2009.

Sun, Xupei. *An Orchestra of Voices: Making the Argument for Greater Speech and Press Freedom in the People's Republic of China*. New York: Praeger, 2000.

Xu, Youyu, and Hua Ze, eds. *In the Shadow of the Rising Dragon: Stories of Repression in the New China*. London: Palgrave Macmillan, 2013.

Internet and Social Media

In China, the Internet has become popular for communication, education, and business operations. In 2003, more than 80 million households logged in to the Internet. According to official statistics, the country had a total of 103 million users by June 2005, with particularly high numbers among youths between the ages of 18 and 24. The number grew to 144 million users at the end of 2006 and increased to 162 million in 2007. According to research completed by Qinghua (Tsing-hua) University, the country had 100 million bloggers in 2007. By 2009, the number of domestic Web sites grew to 3.23 million, an annual increase rate of 12.3 percent. The China Internet Network Information Center reported that the number of Internet users increased to 298 million in 2008 and jumped to 618 million in 2014.

China has become a leading country in telecommunications development. About 100 million cell phones were sold in 2006, and 190 million were sold in 2007, increasing by 74 percent. In 2007, more than 600 million mobile phones were manufactured in China, over 50 percent of the world's total production. China's telecom market has been shared by many companies such as China Telecom, CNC, China Mobile, China Unicom, and China Satcom. The tremendous changes in communications technology, particularly the transition from printed media to more rapid digital formats, are challenging the authority of official Chinese political and social institutions.

While encouraging Internet use for business and educational purposes, the government has kept tight controls on its use for political discussion. The authorities fear that critics could organize "netizens" into an effective source of opposition, disseminating their views to China's fast-growing population of cyber-surfers. The Center Committee of the Chinese Communist Party (CCP) has strengthened control of the Internet by setting up new regulations and establishing a new central governmental agency. At a Politburo meeting in January 2007, Hu Jintao (1942–), China's president from 2002 to 2012, said that the Internet was related to the country's safety, security, and source of sensitive information. As a result, the State Council established the Bureau of Internet within the State Council's Media Department, while a mirror organization, the Bureau of Internet

Propaganda, was formed in the office of External Propaganda in the CCP Central Committee. In 2014, Xi Jinping (1953–), China's president from 2012 to 2022, established the Central Network Security and Informationization Leading Group for Xi and other senior officials to prioritize network security in national security considerations.

New advances in technology have greatly enabled the government, through several different measures, to tighten its grip on cyberspace. Furthermore, state control over the content of online information exchanges has been strengthened. In January 2010, U.S.-based Google announced that the company would no longer cooperate with China's censorship laws and would discontinue censoring Google.cn. The Internet giant felt compelled to pull out of China by shutting down its Chinese-language search engine, and negotiations failed. Other popular Web sites in the West and United States such as Facebook and Godaddy.com also have problems with China's censorship laws.

See also: Chapter 2: Hu Jintao. Chapter 3: Chinese Communist Party; Civil Rights; Xi Jinping. Chapter 8: Qinhua University. Chapter 16: Overview; Cyber Policing; Netizen and Online Guerrilla.

Further Reading

Herold, David Kurt, and Peter Marolt, eds. *Online Society in China: Creating, Celebrating, and Instrumentalizing the Online Carnival*. London: Routledge, 2013.

Hockx, Michel. *Internet Literature in China*. New York: Columbia University Press, 2015.

Marolt, Peter, and David Herold, eds. *China Online: Locating Society in Online Spaces*. London: Routledge, 2014.

Sun, Helen. *Internet Policy in China: A Field Study of Internet Cafes*. Lanham, MD: Lexington, 2011.

Tai, Zixue. *The Internet in China: Cyberspace and Civil Society*. London: Routledge, 2006.

Yang, Guobin. *The Power of the Internet in China: Citizen Activism Online*. New York: Columbia University Press, 2011.

Movies and Film Industry

In 1896 motion pictures were introduced to China, and the first Chinese film, *The Battle of Dingjunshan*, a recording of the Peking Opera, was made in Beijing in 1905. The Chinese film industry was first established in Shanghai in 1913. The first movie with sound, *Sing-Song Girl Red Peony*, was produced in 1931. However, this early development was cut short by the invasion of Japan in 1937 when some of the film makers moved to Hong Kong and Chongqing during the Pacific War (1937–1945). The first Chinese animated feature film, *Princess Iron Fan*, was made in 1941. After the war, the film industry returned to Shanghai and began the second golden period in film production. The first Chinese color film, *Remorse at Death*, was produced in 1948.

After the founding of the People's Republic of China (PRC), the film industry on the mainland was under the shadow of the politics of the Chinese Communist Party (CCP).

Under the control of the Ministry of Culture, it was relentlessly molded, both in art expression and in content, by the ideological framework of Mao Zedong. Nevertheless, the number of annual movie viewers increased from 47 million in 1949 to 415 million in 1959. The PRC made 603 feature films between 1949 and 1966. During the Cultural Revolution of 1966–1976, the entire film industry was nearly shut down, and most previous films were banned. Most actors, actresses, directors, and screenwriters were criticized and purged; and some were jailed, tortured, or even killed. A few films were made to serve the political agenda of the CCP and its government.

After Deng Xiaoping launched the reform movement in 1978, films became more and more geared toward reflecting and exploring reality. The year of 1980 saw the production of 82 feature movies, 32 animation films, 365 documentaries, and 337 scientific and educational films. Some are described as "scar dramas," which depicted the emotional traumas left by the Cultural Revolution. The number of the film companies increased from 10 in 1953 to 20 in 1980. With the ever-increasing output of the Chinese film industry and with growing interest of the nation's audiences, the question of improving the quality of the films came to the fore. It was with a view to raising the overall quality of Chinese films as well as the professional level of people engaged in film production, that in 1981 the Chinese Film Artists' Association established the Golden Rooster Film Award (similar to the Oscar Award in America). The Golden Rooster Award is comprised of 20 prizes, including best picture, best director, best actress, best actor, and so on. The winners are decided by the Award Assessment Committee, a panel composed of China's most prominent film critics and specialists. Among the winners in the 1980s were *One and Eight* (1983), *Yellow Earth* (1984), and *Red Sorghum* (1987). The film directors, headed by Zhang Yimou, Tian Zhuangzhuang, Zhang Junzhao, and Chen Kaige, made giant steps in transforming Chinese film that praised the CCP revolution to an objective attitude in displaying human nature. They revolutionized Chinese film both in content and in technique by insisting on embracing the "art-for-art" ideal and being more creative in making new films differing from the early ones.

In the 1990s, the new generation of film makers had matured and was focused on modern social and cultural issues. *Raise the Red Lantern* (1991) and *To Live* (1993), both directed by Zhang Yimou, were powerful productions that explored cultural tradition as well as the fate of man. Both won major international film awards and *Raise the Red Lantern* was twice an Oscar nominee in foreign-language films. The number of film companies increased from 20 in 1980 to 31 in 1998.

This generation also introduced some of their films to the Western movie-goers, such as *The Story of Qiu Ju* (1992) and *Farewell My Concubine* (1993), in addition to Zhang's films. Political films, however, made their return to cinema in the 1990s since the government provided an abundance of financial sponsorship and strengthened its control. The political films get an easy pass while the others are under "stricter control and management" to "strengthen supervision over production." Among the popular productions were *Zhou Enlai* (1991), *Mao Zedong and His Sons* (1991), *The Story of Mao Zedong* (1992), and *The Forty-four Days of Liu Shaoqi* (1992). There is a significant difference from the political films of the past, which lies in the touch of personality and objectivity.

The 2000s embraced major waves of commercialization, nationalism, and globalization of the Chinese film industry. *The Dream Factory* illustrated the viability of the commercial model at the end of the 1990s. Among the popular themes have been *Wushu* (martial arts), comedies, and translated foreign films. Some of the Mandarin-language films are dubbed into Cantonese when exported to Hong Kong. *Let the Bullets Fly* (2010) has become China's highest grossing domestic film, earning 730 million *renminbi* or RMB (about $111 million), and *Aftershock* (2009) in second earning 670 million yuan RMB ($105 million). While the entertainment films generate both box office revenues and some adversary effect, a number of film-goers are longing to see films with an uplifting effect. Some recent films have carried a strong patriotic and sometimes nationalistic tendency, such as *Trilogy: The Grand Final Battles* and *The Chongqing Negotiation*. Chinese film makers also began looking for foreign investors and Hollywood partners through joint ventures in their film making in the 2000s. Films such as *Crouching Tiger, Hidden Dragon* (2000), *Hero* (2002), and *House of Flying Daggers* (2004) became models for the international commercial class. In 2005, the number of cinema admissions totaled 157.2 million from 4,425 screens with a gross sale of 2 billion yuan (about $322.5 million). In 2009, total admissions increased to 263.8 million stemming from 6,323 screens with a box office sale of 6.21 billion yuan ($1 billion).

The 2010s reflect the continuing growth of the Chinese film industry on an unprecedented scale. By 2010, China had become the third largest film industry in the world by number of feature films produced annually. China made 618 feature films in 2014. Its Hengdian World Studios (Hollywood in China) is the largest studio in the world, with a total area of 900 acres and 13 shooting bases. In 2012, China became the second largest market in the world by box office receipts. In 2013, the number of cinema admissions totaled 612 million from 18,195 screens with a gross sale of 21.77 billion yuan (about $3.51 billion). In January 2014, 6 of the top 10 highest-grossing films in China were domestic productions, with *Lost in Thailand* (2012) reaching 1 billion yuan (about $161 million) in sales in domestic theaters. In 2014, the number of cinema admissions totaled 830 million on 23,600 screens nationwide and its gross box office totaled 29.6 billion yuan (about $4.76 billion), with domestic films having a share of 54.5 percent (16 billion yuan or $2.6 billion). China is expected to have the largest film market in the world by 2018.

See also: Chapter 2: Deng Xiaoping; Mao Zedong. Chapter 3: Chinese Communist Party. Chapter 4: Foreign Investment; Joint Ventures. Chapter 9: Local Dialects; Mandarin. Chapter 15: *Wushu*: Martial Arts. Chapter 16: Overview; Censor System.

Further Reading

Curtin, Michael. *Playing to the World's Biggest Audience: The Globalization of Chinese Film and TV*. Berkeley: University of California Press, 2007.

Fu, Poshek. *China Forever: The Shaw Brothers and Diasporic Cinema*. Champaign: University of Illinois Press, 2008.

Lu, Sheldon. *Chinese-Language Film: Historiography, Poetics, Politics*. Honolulu: University of Hawaii Press, 2004.

Meyers, Ric. *Films of Fury: The Kung Fu Movie Book.* Emeryville, CA: Emery, 2011.

Pickowicz, Paul. *China on Film: A Century of Exploration, Confrontation, and Controversy.* Boulder, CO: Rowman & Littlefield, 2011.

National Broadcasting Networks

National broadcasts including both television and radio stations in the People's Republic of China (PRC) are under state control because of government ownership of all networks. This concentrated control protects the authorities, provides political supervision of the Chinese Communist Party (CCP), and ensures that the companies are run by handpicked executives and staff. All reporters, editors, producers, and administrators are employed by either central or local governments, and are closely monitored. However, after the 1990s, market reforms have forced Chinese media providers to consider income provided by advertisements, subscribers, and the viewership. The bureaucratic nature of the Chinese media has begun to give in to these economic pressures and to embrace commercialization and business strategies. The government has shifted its control mechanisms to include elaborate censorship and licensing procedures. More and more, journalists can enjoy relatively broad discretion in their ability to report on topics such as sports, entertainment, consumer lifestyles, and local news, without extensive political implications.

In 1978, CCTV (China Central Television) began broadcasting as the country's only national network with only three sets of programs on two channels. By 1982, one-third of Chinese people had access to TV through 44 stations, mostly supplying black and white televisions. In 1985, consumers purchased 15 million new TV sets, including 4 million color sets. By the early 1990s, television was reaching a large population. The national TV stations, as well as provincial and municipal stations, all under the supervision of the Ministry of Radio and Television Broadcasting (changed to the Ministry of Radio, Film, and Television in 2001), were located in Beijing and administrated directly by provincial and city governments.

By 2000, there were 651 program-generating TV stations, 42,228 TV transmitting and relaying stations, and 368,553 satellite-TV receiving and relaying stations. The penetration rate of television had reached 92.5 percent, covering a population of 1 billion, making China the largest television-watching country in the world. Although no private-ownership or foreign-ownership television is permitted, about 30 overseas television networks, including Phoenix TV (Hong Kong), Bloomberg TV, CNN, BBC World, CNBC, STAR TV, and Eurosport, entered China, with certain limitations, in 2003. At the same time, CCTV English-language channel entered the United States. CCTV is still the largest and most powerful national TV station in China, with multiple channels introduced in 2004–2005 such as CCTV-News, CCTV-Sports, CCTV-Music, and CCTV-Children. By 2015, China had more than 840 program-generating TV stations with 3,000 channels available.

China's radio broadcasting developed rapidly in the 1950s and 1960s. By 1979, the country had a radio system that included both domestic and overseas radio broadcasts, as well as a rural wire-broadcasting network. The domestic broadcasting includes the Central People's Broadcasting Station (CPBS) in Beijing, as well as local broadcasting stations run by provincial, municipal, and city governments. CPBS, responsible for promulgating the agenda of the CCP and central government to the entire country, has eight channels and broadcasts over 200 hours a day via satellite. By 1982, China had 118 radio stations and 328 relaying stations. The overseas broadcasting includes International Broadcasting Station, China Radio International (CRI), and Radio Beijing, responsible for China's overseas broadcasts. Radio Beijing broadcasts for 300 hours a day in 46 foreign languages, and also reaches overseas Chinese, with broadcasts in Mandarin Chinese and four dialects. In 2003, China had 282 radio stations, as well as 744 medium and shortwave radio transmitting and relaying stations. By 2015, there were more than 3,000 radio stations in the country. Nevertheless, without government permission, receiving or listening to a foreign radio program such as the Voice of America (VOA) is still prohibited. China continues to jam the program signals from several dozen foreign radio broadcasts, including the U.S.-based Free Asia Station.

See also: Chapter 1: Hong Kong. Chapter 3: Chinese Communist Party; Civil Rights; Provincial and County Governments. Chapter 9: Local Dialects; Mandarin. Chapter 16: Censor System; Freedom of Speech.

Further Reading

Chin, Yik-Chan. *Television Regulation and Media Policy in China*. London: Routledge, 2015.

Schneider, Florian. *Visual Political Communication in Popular Chinese Television Series*. Leiden, Netherlands: Brill, 2012.

Shen, Yipeng. *Public Discourses of Contemporary China: The Narration of the Nation in Popular Literatures, Film, and Television*. London: Palgrave Macmillan, 2015.

Shirt, Susan L. *Changing Media, Changing China*. Oxford, UK: Oxford University Press, 2010.

Young, Doug. *The Party Line: How the Media Dictates Public Opinion in Modern China*. Hoboken, NJ: Wiley, 2013.

Zhu, Ying. *Two Billion Eyes: The Story of China Central Television*. New York: The New Press, 2012.

Netizen and Online Guerrilla

The new vigor of the Internet and social media has had a significant impact on the development of democracy in China, especially since citizens can now, for the most part, speak privately about the government. Government censorship and surveillance have increased in cyberspace in response to the Internet's growing popularity and its use as a medium for activism throughout China. More than a dozen regulations relating to the Internet have been implemented by the Department of Propaganda of the Central

Committee of the Chinese Communist Party (CCP), the Ministry of Public Security, the Ministry of Information Industry (MII), the Ministry of Culture, and relevant departments of ministries at various levels. In 2004, MII issued a new set of rules aimed at curbing the spread of "interactive" Internet sites such as bulletin boards, chat rooms, blogs, and discussion forums. According to these guidelines, all providers offering the aforementioned services must reapply for a license in order to operate, and, if denied, are to be closed down. Tens of thousands of police monitor the Internet around the clock, and the government has heavily invested in a network infrastructure that boosts efficiency, aiding in the monitoring of web content. By 2005, the government had already spent at least $800 million on state-of-the-art equipment to control its online citizens.

In the 2000s, officials reported that the government frequently shut down the "illegal Web sites" and even cut off Internet connection for political reasons. After the "July 5th riots" in Xinjiang, for example, the Chinese government cut off almost all Internet access to the entire region of 19 million people from July 2009 to February 2010. The online blackout was temporarily lifted only before the Chinese New Year Eve.

Writers, bloggers, and journalists risk punishments ranging from immediate dismissal from positions and jobs, to prosecution and lengthy jail terms for offenses such as sending news via e-mail to those outside the country or posting articles critical of the political system. Authorities enforce official regulations and punish those who violate them, especially political dissidents. In April 2005, Shi Tao, the editor arrested for divulging the Propaganda Department's instructions to his paper, was sentenced to 10 years imprisonment for sending an e-mail to an overseas rights group detailing the activities of the same CCP Central Committee organization. Reportedly, Yahoo provided evidence for activities that did not threaten China's national security, which contributed to Shi's arrest and conviction The company's representative in Hong Kong, however, stated that the company must comply with the laws of the country in which it operates. Online author Li Hong (the pen name of Zhang Jianhong) was one of those punished for expressing political opinions on the Internet. Li Hong created a Web site, "Aegean Sea," that published news, articles, and comments. Some of her discussions were critical of government policies, and she was considered an online political dissident. Before the end of 2006, Li Hong was arrested, and in March 2007, she was sentenced to six years' imprisonment under the charge of "inciting subversion of the government."

The government's measures, however, are not universally effective. An increasing number of Chinese rights activists are also taking their battle for the freedom of expression to the Internet. The activists engage in guerrilla-style tactics of posting dissenting opinions and critiques on bulletin boards, chat rooms, and YouTube. They set up quickly, moving Web sites and linking them together. These numerous "hacktivists" seek out or create ways to circumvent government controls. Because of developments such as these, many are stating that the battle for the rights of the Chinese people is now online. Surveillance programs established by the Chinese police are not always capable of completely suppressing online political debates and dissenting opinions. Internet police cannot monitor all online traffic from the numerous Internet cafes. Web activist

Wu Wei set up a site in June 2010, but it was quickly shut down. After this incident, Wu and two students started a new Web site, Democracy and Freedom Forum. During their cat and mouse game, Wu and his colleagues have already been harassed by officials. Not all of the "mice" were so lucky. Liu Di, a student Internet activist known as the "Stainless Steel Mouse," was arrested in 2011.

Many rights groups are demanding better protection of netizens, especially in the area of freedom of speech and the press. Chinese activists fear that a long, hard road may be ahead before individuals are able to truly express their views and achieve civil liberties online. Many prominent Chinese academics and journalists have spoken out against new restrictive rules issued in 2014. They believe the government should open more channels in which civic groups and the mass media may engage freely in public discourse with the party and state, especially on important issues such as the environment, corruption, and welfare.

See also: Chapter 1: Hong Kong; Xinjiang. Chapter 3: Chinese Communist Party; Civil Rights; Criminal Law; Law Enforcement; Political Dissents. Chapter 16: Overview; Censor System; Cyber Policing; Freedom of Speech; Internet and Social Media.

Further Reading

Sun, Helen. *Internet Policy in China: A Field Study of Internet Cafes.* Lanham, MD: Lexington, 2011.

Tai, Zixue. *The Internet in China: Cyberspace and Civil Society.* London: Routledge, 2006.

Xu, Youyu, and Hua Ze, eds. *In the Shadow of the Rising Dragon: Stories of Repression in the New China.* London: Palgrave Macmillan, 2013.

Yang, Guobin. *The Power of the Internet in China: Citizen Activism Online.* New York: Columbia University Press, 2011.

State-Owned Newspapers

In the People's Republic of China (PRC), government ownership of all media, in whole or in part, is an effective measure of state control, especially control of the newspapers. The number of Chinese newspapers has increased from 382 in 1980 to more than 2,200 in 2015, including the national, province, regional, and metropolitan daily papers. The national newspapers include *People's Daily* (*Renmin Ribao*), mouthpiece of the Central Committee of the Chinese Communist Party (CCP); *China Daily*, English version of the *People's Daily*; *China Youth Daily* (*Zhongguo Qingnian Bao*), voice of the CCYL (Chinese Communist Youth League) with a daily circulation of 2.9 million in the 1980s; *PLA Daily* (*Jiefangjun Bao*), official daily of the People's Liberation Army (PLA) and controlled directly by the PLA General Department of Political Tasks with a total daily circulation of 1.5 million; *Enlightenment Daily* (*Guangming Ribao*), a conservative daily, close to the CCP, with an average daily circulation in 1981, was approximately 1.06 million; *China Education Daily* (*Zhongguo Jiaoyu Bao*), official paper of the PRC

Ministry of Education; *China Public Security Daily* (*Zhongguo Gong'an Bao*), official newspaper of the PRC Ministry of Public Security; and *Reference News* (*Cankao Xiaoxi*), published by the official Xinhua (New China) News Agency and having the largest circulation, totaling 4 million in 1985.

Daily newspaper sales increased from 80 million copies in 2004 to 97 million in 2006. China had become the largest newspaper market in the world by that time, followed by India with 78 million copies daily, Japan with 69 million, and the United States with 53 million in 2006.

Total control of these national newspapers protects CCP authorities, provides political supervision, and ensures that the companies are run by handpicked executives and staff. All reporters, editors, producers, and administrators are employed or closely monitored by the central government. The next measure is the government's control of access to information. Many records of places such as court houses, police stations, and city and provincial government offices remain closed to reporters. The government controls all information concerning the Tibetan areas, as well as access to the region. In many cases, reporters must have permission before they begin interviews or investigations. It is even more difficult for foreign reporters to apply for these types of access. The only available information is provided by the two official news agencies: Xinhua News Agency and the Chinese News Service, which are the major sources of news and photos for all central and local newspapers.

Regional, provincial, and metro newspapers are under the control of local governments by the same measures: government ownership, hiring process, and information access. For example, Shanghai has 16 daily newspapers, all of which are owned by four governmental newspaper groups. *Liberation Daily* (*Jiefang Ribao*) was first published in 1949 as the official daily of Shanghai Party Committee of the CCP. *Shanghai Morning Post* (*Shanghai Chenbao*) and *Shanghai Daily Post* belong to the *Jiefang Ribao* Newspaper Group. *Shanghai Daily* (*Shanghai Ribao*) is the voice of the Shanghai Municipal Government that owns the Wenhui-Xinmin United Press Group. *Wenhui Newspaper* (*Wenhui Bao*), *Xinmin Evening News* (*Xinmin Wanbao*), and *Wenhui Book Review* belong to the Wenhui-Xinmin United Press Group. *Wenhui Bao* enjoys a large circulation in Hong Kong. *Shanghai Star* and other newspapers are owned and operated by *China Daily* in Beijing.

Local control of the news is successful because the government manages all media outlets, with powers that include the hiring of journalists, production, and restriction of access to information. Moreover, the journalists, writers, and editors, as well as their families, are monitored by the local governments, in case of a violation of official reporting guidelines.

However, market reforms have forced Chinese media providers to consider income provided by advertisements, subscribers, and viewership. The bureaucratic nature of the Chinese media has begun to accept these economic pressures and to embrace commercialization and business strategies. Local governments have shifted their control mechanisms to include elaborate censorship and licensing procedures. More and more often, journalists enjoy relatively broad discretion in their ability to report on topics such as sports, entertainment, consumer lifestyles, and local news that has no extensive political implications.

See also: Chapter 1: Hong Kong. Chapter 3: Chinese Communist Party; Civil Rights; People's Liberation Army; Provincial and County Governments. Chapter 16: Overview; Censor System; Freedom of Speech.

Further Reading

He, Qinglian. *The Fog of Censorship: Media Control in China*. New York: Human Rights in China Publishing, 2008.

Mittler, Barbara. *A Newspaper for China? Power, Identity, and Change in Shanghai's News Media, 1872–1912*. Cambridge, MA: Harvard University Press, 2004.

Plate, Tom. *In the Middle of China's Future: What Two Decades of Worldwide Newspaper Columns Prefigure about the Future of China*. Singapore: Marshall Cavendish, 2015.

U.S.-China Economic and Security Review Commission. *Access to Information and Media Control in the People's Republic of China*. Las Vegas, NV: CreateSpace Independent, 2008.

A DAY IN THE LIFE

*Note: The following accounts have been fictionalized, but are based on the lives of real people.

A DAY IN THE LIFE OF A FACTORY WORKER

A female factory worker works as a seamstress for a mattress manufacturing company, which is a joint venture with a Taiwanese investor, located in Shenyang, capital city of Liaoning Province. Young and single, she does not mind working from 12:00 midnight to 8:00 a.m. in the morning, which is considered the worst of the three-shift schedule. She even tried working two shifts in a row (16 hours) with an entire day off until one of her friends lost two of her fingers, cut off by a machine during her second consecutive shift. Doctors refused to treat her friend for nearly two days, since she, like many of the other 169 million migrant workers who had left the country in 2014 and moved into cities for manufacturing jobs, had no health care, insurance, or money in the bank. Moreover, there is usually no friend, relative, union, or organization that can help. She sent her friend off at the train station, since they came from the same village. After that, she has never worked a double-shift again.

Working conditions are tough in her factory, with rooms that are crowded and poorly lit. The atmosphere is dusty and noisy, and she must stand and move around for eight hours, since her sewing machine is huge, and the mattresses are large— 4×6 feet if full sized, 5×7 if queen size, and 6×7 if king size. She sews the silk cover to each mattress with large needles and colorful threads. It is considered one of the better or easier positions in this manufacturing factory, in comparison with other heavy labor work and the dangerous processing needed to make box-springs and bed frames with little protection.

She likes working here as a "machine operator" after she quit three manual labor jobs in two years at Shenyang. She learned some sewing skills, understood the machine manuals, and made some friends in the factory. Her salary also increased gradually, from 800 yuan *renminbi* or RMB ($130) to 2,000 yuan ($320) a month. Although she never complains about workplace safety, she wore gloves during the time she visited her parents' home during the Chinese New Year, since she did not want her parents and relatives to see the injuries and cuts on both of her hands. She is never heard to complain about the unequal pay and unfairness, when the Shenyang workers make twice as much as migrant workers, who consist of 46 percent of all urban employment in the

2000s, on the same job; and city workers have no pay-cut when a silk cover or a mattress gets a little dirty or damaged during sewing. In such a case, she is required to pay for it.

In order to send money home as well as save a little for herself, she lives with seven other factory girls in one small bedroom. She shares a "bed" with another girl when they work on different shifts. They have to press together and hold each other when they sleep at the same time on this small, old futon sofa on the floor. Several of the new arrivals that live in the basement are very young, about 15–17 years old. Two girls next door were just fired by their factory because of pregnancies. Females comprise more than 30 percent of all migrant workers in China. The "migrant towns," as these villages in the city are called, are overcrowded, unsanitary, and encourage rampant graft without police protection, fire protection, or any city public service, since the migrant workers do not have urban ID (*hukou*).

She enjoys her day off, having learned how to apply makeup and how to order a dish in a restaurant. She enjoys window shopping in the mall with her friends. Her hope is to meet a nice city boy with a college degree, showing him off in her village, getting married, and buying a king-size bed with a mattress made by her company.

See also: Chapter 1: Taiwan. Chapter 4: Cost Production; Joint Ventures; Manufacturing; Migrant Laborers; Trade Union and Labor Movement; Workplace Safety. Chapter 6: Urban Poor. Chapter 7: All-China Women's Federation; Child Labor; Gender Inequality.

Further Reading

Chang, Leslie. *Factory Girls: From Village to City in a Changing China*. New York: Spiegel & Grau, 2009.

Hurst, William. *The Chinese Workers after Socialism*. Cambridge, UK: Cambridge University Press, 2012.

Loyalka, Michelle. *Eating Bitterness: Stories from the Front Lines of China's Great Urban Migration*. Berkeley: University of California Press, 2013.

Miller, Tom. *China's Urban Billion: The Story Behind the Biggest Migration in Human History*. London: Zed Books, 2012.

A DAY IN THE LIFE OF A FARMER

A member of a family who has farmed for generations in the southeast Yangzi (Yangtze) River Delta, a male farmer starts his daily routine early by cleaning a hogcote first; letting the chickens, ducks, and dogs out; and watering his vegetable garden. Since there is no running water in the village, he totes a bamboo carrying pole with two water buckets attached, one at each end, on his back, running back and forth between the community water well and his own backyard. The distance is about 300 yards each way, and he makes 8–12 round-trips. During the dry season, his vegetables require even more water, often about 20–28 trips each morning. He usually has everything done before 7:00 a.m. when he has breakfast, typically rice soup and steamed buns with pickled vegetables. During the busy season, his wife scrambles a couple of eggs or even warms up a few pieces of home-preserved meat (like bacon or ham) for his breakfast.

At around 7:30 a.m. he rides a bicycle to the rice paddy, and works there for most of the day. Rice production, the backbone of Chinese farmers' life everywhere in the south, demands intensive care and manual labor. The Lower Yangzi Valley Plain, known as China's "rice bowl," sustains highly productive rice cultivation with at least two harvests a year. He prepares the rice seedbeds in both January and July, while subsidiary crops are raised in the dry fields. In March and September, he transplants the rice seedlings from seedbeds to the rice field, using his hands. He bends from the waist as he moves backward step by step through the ankle-high muddy water of each terrace. He irrigates, fertilizes, and weeds the wet rice paddy in April and October. Finally the plant is mature, the field is drained, and the crop is harvested, again by hand, in May and November. After each harvest, in June and December he plows the field and prepares for the next season.

Transplanting and harvest are obviously the busiest seasons in the year, not only labor intensive with the greatest expenditure of muscular energy, but also time critical. He gets used to the back-breaking labor of rice cultivation, accepting traditional farming as the norm without machines. During the harvest, the village-run toy factory allows his wife and her co-workers time off to provide supplementary labor to the rice fields. His son is also given extra time off from the middle school in the nearby town and provides some help. His aging parents always bring his lunch, fresh tea, and a dry shirt to the rice field for him near noon. The annual income from the family farm has increased from about 8,000 yuan *renminbi* or RMB ($1,290) in the 1990s to 12,000 yuan ($1,940) in the 2000s.

He gets back home about 5:00 or 6:00 p.m., depending on the daylight. His evening is the most enjoyable time of the day, smelling his wife's stir-frying in the kitchen, watching his son doing his homework, and talking to his parents while listening to the news from CCTV. He has no complaint at the monthly village meetings and has no intent to leave for the city as some of the younger villagers have. His departure would terminate his land contract with the government, and he does not want to lose his rice farm. His hope is that his son can enter the county high school, pass the National College Entrance Examination (NCEE) in his senior year, and enroll in a college. It depends on whether he can save enough by that time. In that case, his son and his grandchild will not be a farmer like him.

See also: Chapter 1: Overview; Yangzi River. Chapter 4: Agriculture; Migrant Laborers. Chapter 6: Rural-Urban Conflicts. Chapter 8: Elementary and Secondary Education; National College Entrance Examination.

Further Reading

Chen, Jean Jinghan, and David Wills, eds. *The Impact of China's Economic Reforms upon Land, Property and Construction*. London: Ashgate, 1999.

Hinton, William. *Fanshen: A Documentary of Revolution in a Chinese Village*. Berkeley: University of California Press, 1997.

Oi, Jean. *State and Peasant in Contemporary China: The Political Economy of Village Government*. Berkeley: University of California Press, 1991.

Zweig, David. *Freeing China's Farmers: Rural Restructuring in the Reform Era*. Armonk, NY: M. E. Sharpe, 1997.

A DAY IN THE LIFE OF A HIGH SCHOOL STUDENT

A typical male student studies hard and has made it to the top 10 percent of his junior class of more than 800 students in this suburban public high school in central China. He gets up at 5:30 a.m. every morning, including weekends, rushing to school by bicycle to attend an early morning study session from 6:30 to 7:30 a.m. before classes begin. Except on rainy days, all students, teachers, and staff members, about 3,000 people, assembly at 7:40 a.m. at the school track field for limbering exercises performed to radio music. His classes begin at 8:10 a.m. with algebra, chemistry, classic Chinese literature, and English in the morning, and physics, geometry, political study, and European history in the afternoon, totaling eight hours of classes every day. The spring semester starts after the Chinese New Year, around late January, and lasts to the end of June; the fall semester starts on September 1 and ends before the Chinese New Year. In China's high schools, 40 weeks per year are devoted to studying, with a summer vacation of eight weeks and a winter vacation of four weeks.

His favorite subjects are math and the sciences, but he does not like political education, studying the history of the Chinese Communist Party (CCP), or current government policy. He once made a few low grades on his exams and his parents received a letter from the political education teacher, since he did other homework during the class. His parents warn him that as their only child, he must keep a perfect grade (all As) on his high school transcript if he wants to get into a national key university, and that political study is part of the National College Entrance Examination (NCEE) that he will take by the end of his senior year. In June 2008, among the 10.5 million high school seniors who took the NCEE, about 5.9 million, or 57 percent of the total, passed the examination and were eligible to enroll in the colleges; and only 1 million, less than 10 percent of the total, got into the national key universities. Many of the college candidates are required to retake the NCEE two or three times, meaning two or three years, before they are able to begin a college education.

He tries to work harder and make it to the top 5 percent of his class during the last one and an half years in high school. He has no time for a girlfriend or for weekend parties. He surprised his coach and teammates when he said that he was leaving the school soccer team, his favorite sport for years, the following semester. He has promised his cousin all of his video games. He talks to one of his father's colleagues in the hospital to get him some fake sick-leave notes to avoid one-week military training and two-week manual labor in a nearby village each semester. He thinks his father, as a medical doctor, should understand that he tries to focus on his school work and NCEE preparation. His father met his mother in America during his medical training as a visiting scholar and her graduate study for her PhD degree in the 1990s. Both of them then returned to China and were married. His mother now teaches at a city college.

Sometimes he wonders why his parents did not remain in America, and he believes that one day he will go to the United States.

See also: Chapter 3: Chinese Communist Party. Chapter 7: One-Child Policy. Chapter 8: Elementary and Secondary Education; National College Entrance Examination; Project 211 and Key Universities; Returning Students.

Further Reading

Goh, Esther. *China's One-Child Policy and Multiple Care-Giving: Raising Little Suns in Xiamen*. London: Routledge, 2011.

Yang, Ming. *Educational System in China*. Paramus, NJ: Homa & Sekey, 2009.

Zhao, Yong. *Who's Afraid of the Big Bad Dragon: Why China Has the Best (and Worst) Education System in the World?* San Francisco, CA: Jossey-Bass, 2014.

A DAY IN THE LIFE OF A HOUSEWIFE

An early riser, this typical housewife gets breakfast ready before waking her husband. Seeing him off to work at 6:30, she takes their daughter to kindergarten before 7:15 a.m. On her way back, she stops at the farmers' market and gets some early bird specials or discounted vegetables from the night before. They have lived on a tight budget for almost four years in order to save enough for a small car down payment next summer. With a car, she would not have to get up so early to take three buses for one and a half hours. She would not have to ride her bicycle in the cold, rainy, or snowy weather. Instead, she would wait for her daughter in the car after school, while many parents and grandparents would stand there, looking at her new car. Recently she had convinced her husband to quit smoking. "It's not good for you," she said. But in fact, it saves money.

They met in college and married after he secured a government job in the city, a provincial capital in northwest China. Her happiest moments include their wedding reception, giving birth to their daughter, hearing her first word, and watching her first step. Her problems include being unemployed after childbirth, urban inflation and high living costs, and a lack of social connections. In fact social connections, or *guanxi*, are crucial for an urban family's survival because of rapid urbanization and limited resources. It seems to her that urbanization is nothing but population explosion. Their city almost doubled its population from 4.5 million in 2004 to 8.7 million by 2014, with few new highways, slow housing development, and no new public services. Her husband had to fight for two years to get permission to allow a pregnancy for their only child. They have to get a quota before they can purchase a car because of traffic and pollution problems. Nearly 1 million car buyers in the city are on the license plate waiting list.

The rest of the morning is the best time of weekdays, as she can read a book, go to the gym, or cook a Muslim lunch. She is from an Islamic family and belongs to the Hui minority, and they do not eat pork. She sometimes almost forgot this when she was in college, and she tries to ignore it when she cooks for her family. She behaves well when she visits her parents in the countryside. Her husband and daughter also follow the Muslim tradition for several days to please the in-laws. She sometimes thinks about having her parents come to live with them. But she does not know what to do about their strict religious practices and ethnic traditions, or where they would sleep, since their small apartment has only two bedrooms.

After picking up her daughter, her own busy schedule resumes with three or four private violin lessons every afternoon; practicing in a quartet with her college friends to play at restaurants, weddings, and other events; and subbing for extracurricular music instructors at a nearby junior high in late afternoons. In between, she takes her daughter to a math tutor for one hour every day and an English conversation class twice a week. She wants her daughter to be ahead of her class, and she tries to make sure that she can get into a good elementary school next fall.

Today she is too hungry and too tired to wait for her husband to come home for dinner. Sometimes she worries about his working late and returning home around 9:00 or 10:00 p.m., or taking out-of-town business trips. She has never missed any of his office parties or staff potluck dinners. His boss and his colleagues know that he has a "beautiful wife," as he has said many times.

She manages to stay awake until she hears him calling. "Honey, I'm home!"

See also: Chapter 1: Major Cities. Chapter 5: Islam. Chapter 6: Major Ethnic Groups; Muslims; Rural-Urban Conflicts. Chapter 7: Gender Inequality; One-Child Policy. Chapter 8: Elementary and Secondary Education.

Further Reading

Barlow, Tani. *The Question of Women in Chinese Feminism*. Durham, NC: Duke University Press, 2004.

Davis, Deborah, and Sara Friedman, eds. *Wives, Husbands, and Lovers: Marriage and Sexuality in Hong Kong, Taiwan, and Urban China*. Stanford, CA: Stanford University Press, 2014.

Farquhar, Judith. *Appetites: Food and Sex in Post-Socialist China*. Durham, NC: Duke University Press, 2002.

Fong, Vanessa. *Only Hope: Coming of Age under China's One-Child Policy*. Stanford, CA: Stanford University Press, 2006.

A DAY IN THE LIFE OF A PLA SOLDIER

After his high school graduation, this young man twice failed the National College Entrance Examination (NCEE) and could not find a full-time job for three years. He then decided to serve in the People's Liberation Army (PLA, the official name for China's armed forces, which includes the army, navy, air force, and strategic force, totaling 2.3 million troops) against the wishes of his parents, who provided him with everything when he lived with them at home as the "only child." He joined the PLA, which has become the "only child" army since 2006 when 52.4 percent of the PLA were only-child soldiers like him. After a brief orientation, he was assigned to an artillery regiment of an infantry army in a remote mountainous area in southwestern China. He was given the rank of private second class, according to the PLA conscription.

Young and fit, he becomes accustomed to early morning physicals, including jogging with weights up and down hills, doing push-ups and sit-ups on the rocks, and practicing hand-to-hand combat fighting (or martial arts, the civilian term). The daily drill of the howitzer guns includes combat ready practice, artillery barrage, bracket, speed firing, curved and high-angle firing, break out, air defense, and artillery maneuvers. As a gun layer, his training focuses on aiming exercises, adjustment methods, angle of position, sight line angle of elevation, and air spotting. It is necessary for him to know every position of the crew, including recognizing the different kinds and models of shells. After the lunch break, the battery commander analyzes some combat cases in the 1979 offensive campaign in Vietnam and the 1984–1987 artillery defense campaigns along the Sino-Vietnamese border. He is not interested in the political study session in the late afternoon, when the company political instructor lectures about the current policies of the Chinese Communist Party (CCP) and why PLA soldiers must be loyal to the party. The gunners always have more questions than the instructor can handle, such as why an army commander would commit suicide, might it be caused by a power struggle, or by corruption? How many PLA generals were dismissed and jailed last month? While joining in the laughter with other men, he stays busy finishing his daily battery survey chart and training report. Hard working and technology-oriented, he is promoted to private first class after completion of his first year of service.

He does not like battery maneuvers and relocations, since it takes a lot of hard manual labor for battery emplacement and rebuilding the gun foundation for their 152 mm howitzer, about 3.6 tons (8,000 lbs.). He hates the heat and forest as much as he hates the bugs, rats, and snakes on the mountain. The battery often operates in temperatures of 100–110 degrees, and the men are perspiring all day long. After dinner, they play basketball, ping pong (table tennis), or volleyball outdoors when the weather is nice; or Chinese chess, Go, or card games indoors during rainy days. There is only one satellite TV and two laptops in the company, for use primarily by the officers. The men have only limited time and access to watch news or get online, and there is no cell phone signal or public phone. The men still depend upon the postal service to keep in touch with their families across the country. Very little social or cultural activity exists on or off the army base, which is near a small town. He joins other men during the weekends, walking down the streets and talking to the girls in the tea house, a social place for the local people.

Nevertheless, he somehow likes this quiet and simple life of a serviceman. He has not told his parents yet about a possible service extension after his completion of a standard two years. His reasons may include that there are still few jobs in the market, and that he may be able to learn more and build a career in the military, actually building his life. After the second year, he will be up for promotion as a noncommissioned officer; he will be sent to one of the PLA Artillery Academies to study high-tech gunnery, such as gun-directing radar; and he might work in the battery observation post of the company or even in a battalion as a gunnery liaison officer. He first needs to prove that he would be successful, and that he is not a loser. But he knows that all these plans will not prevent his mother's tears.

See also: Chapter 1: Disputed Islands and Territories. Chapter 3: Chinese Communist Party; Corruption and Punishment; People's Liberation Army. Chapter 7: One-Child Policy. Chapter 8: National College Entrance Examination. Chapter 15: Overview; Chinese Chess; The Game of Go; *Wushu*: Martial Arts.

Further Reading

Mulvenon, James. *The People's Liberation Army in the Information Age*. Santa Monica, CA: RAND, 1999.

Ryan, Mark, David Finkelstein, and Michael McDevitt, eds. *Chinese Warfighting; the PLA Experience since 1949*. Armonk, NY: M. E. Sharpe, 2003.

Shambaugh, David. *Modernizing China's Military: Progress, Problems, and Prospects*. Berkeley: University of California Press, 2002.

GLOSSARY OF KEY TERMS

ACFTU: The All-China Federation of Trade Unions is a CCP (Chinese Communist Party)-controlled national labor organization. The only national union in the country, it has 1.8 million primary trade union organizations with 134 million union members in China and is the largest trade union in the world.

Anti-Rightist Movement: A political mass movement launched by Mao Zedong in 1957 targeting nonparty members and those intellectuals who were not interested in CCP politics. More than 550,000 journalists, educators, and writers were labeled as "rightists" and dismissed from their jobs. A large number were exiled to labor camps, jailed, or executed. A whole generation of artists, scientists, and college students were penalized.

Calligraphy: A traditional way to write Chinese characters with writing brush, black ink, and thin papers made from rice. It has become one of the national artistic forms using different styles by many professional calligraphers, and is a national association. All elementary students in China are required to practice calligraphy at least one hour each day.

CCYL: The Chinese Communist Youth League, founded in 1920, is a youth organization under the leadership of the Chinese Communist Party (CCP). The league recruits young members between 14 and 28, training them with Communist doctrine, involving them in revolutionary activities, and preparing them for future membership in the CCP. It has 74 million members, 49 percent of whom are students.

China Threat: An ongoing debate based on the assumption that China's dramatic economic development will inevitably result in the strengthening of its military power and its desire for expansion and control of energy resources, global markets, and international politics. No country that has risen to power in modern history has done so in a peaceful manner. This includes Great Britain in the 18th century, Germany at the end of the 19th century, Japan during the first half of the 20th century, and the Soviet Union after end of World War II.

Cloisonné: A kind of enamelware introduced to China in the 14th or 15th century. The enamel is poured into *cloisonné*, or compartments formed by copper wire welded on to an object made of red copper. The enamel is baked on to the object in several firings, then polished and gilded. The finished article is splendid, with gleaming gilded copper wire separating each segment of brilliant enamel color.

CMC: The Central Military Commission of the Chinese Communist Party's (CCP) Central Committee is the highest command of China's armed forces with Xi Jinping, commander in chief of the People's Liberation Army (PLA), as its chairman from 2012 to 2022 and with defense minister and joint chiefs as its vice chairmen.

CPG: The Central People's Government was established by the Chinese Communist Party (CCP) in October 1949 after the CCP won the civil war (1946–1949) on mainland China. It served as the national government with Mao Zedong, the CCP chairman, as its president until 1954 when the First National People's Congress (NPC) passed the Constitution and elected Mao as the president of the People's Republic of China (PRC).

Cultural Revolution: A political movement launched by Mao Zedong, lasting from 1966 to 1976. Mao used mass organizations such as the millions involved in the Red Guards to publicly attack his political rivalries in the party, government, and army such as Liu Shaoqi and Deng Xiaoping in 1966–1968 and then Lin Biao in 1970–1972. It became an extensive purge, in which an estimated 100 million people were killed, injured, or persecuted and victimized.

Defense Budget: China's sustained economic growth from a GDP of $1.95 trillion in 2000 to $4.19 trillion in 2008 has enabled the country to ensure its ability to modernize its military. In past years, China has annually increased its defense budget by double digits. In 2000, China's defense spending was $20.9 billion. It rose to about $30 billion in 2003 and over $40 billion in 2006. In 2007 China's defense spending rose 17.6 percent from 2006 to $57.2 billion, and in 2008 it increased to $61 billion.

Embroidery: A traditional occupation of Chinese women from all ethnic groups and areas of the country. There are many different kinds of hand embroidery and countless unique stitches which produce different effects in texture, tone, shading, bulk, and perspective. Much embroidery is now created with modern sewing machines, though hand-sewn embroidery is still important.

Five Antis Movement: A massive campaign launched by the Chinese Communist Party (CCP) in 1952 targeted the capitalist class in urban areas. The CCP-controlled government mobilized workers and employees to report their owners' and managements' bribery, theft of state property, tax evasion, cheating on government contracts, and stealing state economic information. The criteria for punishable crimes and their accompanying sentences became noticeably harsher against business owners and more than 200,000 of these individuals and their families died from 1952 to 1954, resulting in the virtual elimination of the bourgeoisie as a class.

Five-Year Plan: The national economic plan designed by the Chinese Communist Party (CCP) and passed by the National People's Congress (NPC) every five years as the central strategy, principles, development programs, government budget, and production goals of the People's Republic of China (PRC). Following the Soviet model, Mao Zedong started the first Five-Year Plan (1953–1957). The government of the PRC now carries out its 13th Five-Year Plan (2016–2020).

Gang of Four: The Maoist leaders who tried to carry on Mao's Cultural Revolution after his death on September 9, 1976, including Jiang Qing, Mao's widow; Zhang Chunqiao; Yao Wenyuan; and Wang Hongwen. After losing the power struggle, they were arrested and sentenced to long jail terms by a special court within the Supreme Court in 1980–1981.

GMD: Guomindang (or Kuomintang, KMT), the Chinese Nationalist Party, established in August 1912 by Sun Yat-sen in Nanjing, becoming the dominant political party from 1927 to 1949 on mainland China and from 1950 to 2000 and 2008 to the present in Taiwan (Republic of China).

Great Leap Forward: A mass industrial movement launched by Mao Zedong in 1958 aimed at transforming China's agricultural economy to a manufacturing one through government policy. In 1958–1959, tens of millions of peasants were mobilized in this nationwide movement of steelmaking. The movement failed and led to widespread famine for the next three years (1960–1963).

***Guanxi*, Social Connections:** The Chinese government controls the country through a highly centralized bureaucratic system, in which individual officials, most appointed by the Chinese Communist Party, have personal power to make decisions, prove or reject plans, and run their offices through his or her own personal network. To know inside people or have some connections to the administrative bureaucracy has become crucial for many Chinese citizens in terms of business, education, jobs, family, or even daily life.

Limbering Exercises: From the 1950s to 1980s, limbering exercises performed to radio music were one of the most popular forms of mass workout activities in China. The government promulgated the first series of exercises for adults in 1951, then created a series for children in 1954, and introduced the last revised series in 1981. Each morning, except on rainy days and weekends, most offices, companies, army units, schools, and neighborhood associations assemble employees, workers, soldiers, students, housewives, and senior citizens to participate in this nationwide physical workout for 15 to 30 minutes before work and school.

National Rejuvenation: One of the Chinese arguments to explain the country's recent economic achievements as an attempt to recover the greatness of its past and to resume its big-power status in the world prior to the invasion by European powers in the 19th century. The term views China's rise as regaining its lost international status rather than obtaining something new.

Nuclear Arsenal: The Second Artillery Corps (SAC), China's strategic force, responsible for establishing a "minimal nuclear deterrent." It has more than 300 nuclear warheads with 20 intercontinental ballistic missiles (ICBMs) and one ballistic missile submarine (SSBN). It has now developed a new solid-fuel and road-mobile Dong Feng 31A ICBM system in order to increase the survivability of its nuclear deterrent.

Poetry: Chinese poetry written today falls into two groups: "new" poetry which is based on new forms introduced in the early 20th century and is written in the modern spoken language, and "old" poetry based on traditional Chinese poetic forms and written in the old literary language.

"Princelings": Or "Prince Party." Children of the first generation of the Chinese Communist Party's (CCP) leaders, who have become new leaders in China, such as Xi Jinping, president of the People's Republic of China (PRC) in 2012–2022, whose father Xi Zhongxun (1913–2002) served as vice premier and vice chairman of the National People's Congress (NPC).

Red Envelopes: Traditionally used by parents to enclose cash for their children's birthday, graduation, and holiday celebrations such as the Chinese New Year. Recently, the term has been used for bribery, kickbacks, and illegal transactions, since a red envelope means cash in hand.

Red Guard: Mostly college and high school students who were mobilized and empowered by Mao Zedong to criticize his political rivalries such as Liu Shaoqi and Deng Xiaoping. An estimated 30 million young people joined the Red Guards in 1966–1968, and they became the driving force for the Cultural Revolution.

ROC: The Republic of China founded by Sun Yat-sen in January 1, 1912, established its national government in Nanjing under the leadership of Chiang Kai-shek in 1927. After Chiang lost the civil war to the Chinese Communist Army, he removed the seat of the ROC government from the mainland China to Taiwan in 1949.

Role Ethics: Confucianism emphasizes a social order that includes a moral government and good family relations: father and son, husband and wife, brothers, and so on. It also includes individual observance of traditional ideas, ethnical codes, suitable relations, and certain obligations according to his or her role in the family as well as in the society. Role ethics provides family unity and social harmony.

RTL: The Reeducation Through Labor system was adopted in 1957 as a unique jail system practiced in China. RTL allowed authorities to arrest and detain someone for a minor offense and, without trial, send that person to a prison labor camp for up to four years. The annual average number of prisoners sent to RTL camps in the 1980s was 870,000.

SARS: An outbreak of Severe Acute Respiratory Syndrome occurred in the fall of 2002. By July 2003, there were 5,328 cases and 349 fatalities in China. In the interim, the disease spread from China and rapidly infected individuals in at least 37 countries around the world. The government underreported the statistics, and the outbreak took the lives of more than 700 people in nine countries.

Security Concerns: Since China has entered a global security environment, it faces new security challenges, such as international struggles for strategic resources, strategic locations, and strategic dominance. While traditional hegemonism and power politics still exist, regional turmoil continues to spill over, and hot-spot issues are increasing. China is prepared for local conflicts over territorial disputes with its neighboring countries.

Stone Carving: Part of traditional Chinese architecture. The massive ornamental platforms, terraces, balustrades, arches, columns, lions, and so on, seen in old palaces, temples, and pagodas, are evidence of the skill of the Chinese people.

"Technocrats": Leaders of the Chinese Communist Party (CCP) and employees in the government in the 1990s to 2010s, who have a college education and advanced degrees. Many have a professional background and working experience in engineering and technology, such as Jiang Zemin, president of the People's Republic of China (PRC) in 1990–2002.

Three Antis Movement: A mass urban movement that targeted corruption, waste, and obstructionist bureaucracy during 1951–1953. The government mobilized employees in private enterprises and businesses against illegal activities of their employers or the industrial owners. The campaign created an unprecedented political storm against the bourgeoisie.

United Front: A political and military coalition established between the Chinese Communist Party (CCP) and the Nationalist Party (Guomindang, GMD) during World War II against Japanese invasion of China in 1937–1945. The United Front received Allied support, but collapsed in 1946.

Wood Carving: Used as decoration in buildings and furniture, often shown on chests, cabinets, and screens. Their use is mainly ornamental, but may also have religious themes. The main woods used are boxwood, camphorwood, Long'an-wood, lacquer, and tree stump carvings.

FACTS AND FIGURES

Table 1: GEOGRAPHY

Location	Covering a large part of eastern Asia, China is bordered by Mongolia and Russia to the north; Vietnam, Laos, Thailand, Myanmar, Bhutan, Nepal, and India to the south; Pakistan and Afghanistan to the west; and Tajikistan, Kyrgyzstan, and Kazakhstan to the northwest. China borders the Democratic People's Republic of Korea to the northeast and has a long Pacific coastline.
Time Zone	13 hours ahead of U.S. Eastern Standard
Land Borders	13,760 miles
Coastline	9,010 miles
Capital	Beijing
Area	3,695,500 sq. miles
Climate	China's climate varies widely across its diverse geographic regions, ranging from subtropical in the far south to cold and rainy in the east. While the average annual temperature in the north is below 50°F, the northwestern regions are characterized by hot, arid weather.
Land Use	15.1% arable land; 1.3% permanent crops; 42.9% permanent meadows and pastures; 22.0% forest land; 18.7% other.
Arable Land	15% (2007)
Arable Land Per Capita	0.2 acres per person (2012)

Sources: ABC-CLIO World Geography database; CIA World Factbook. http://www.cia.gov; FAO (FAOSTAT database). http://www.fao.org; World Bank. http://www.worldbank.org.

Table 2: POPULATION

Population	1,361,512,535 (estimate) (2015)
World Population Rank	1st (2010)
Population Density	363.8 people per sq. mile (estimate) (2011)
Population Distribution	47% urban (2011)
Age Distribution (2009 est.)	
0–14:	17.90%
15–64:	73.40%
65+:	8.60%
Median Age	36.7 years (estimate) (2014)
Population Growth Rate	0.4% per year (estimate) (2015)
Net Migration Rate	−0.3 (estimate) (2015)

Sources: ABC-CLIO World Geography database; CIA World Factbook. http://www.cia.gov; U.S. Census Bureau (International Data Base). http://www.census.gov.

Table 3: HEALTH

Average Life Expectancy	75.2 years (2014)
Average Life Expectancy, Male	73.1 years (2014)
Average Life Expectancy, Female	77.4 years (2014)
Crude Birth Rate	12.1 (estimate) (2015)
Crude Death Rate	7.6 (estimate) (2015)
Maternal Mortality	56 per 100,000 live births (2005–2012 projection)
Infant Mortality	12 per 1,000 live births (2012)
Doctors	1.9 per 1,000 people (2012)

Sources: ABC-CLIO World Geography Database; U.S. Census Bureau (International Data Base). http://www.census.gov; World Bank. http://www.worldbank.org; World Health Organization. http://www.who.int.

Table 4: ENVIRONMENT

CO_2 Emissions	5.8 metric tons per capita (2009)
Alternative and Nuclear Energy	4.0% of total energy use (2010)
Threatened Species	917 (2010)
Protected Areas	1,562,718 (estimate) (2010)

Sources: ABC-CLIO World Geography database; UN Statistical Database. http://unstats.un.org/unsd/databases.htm; United Nations Statistical Yearbook http://unstats.un.org/unsd/syb/; World Bank. http://www.worldbank.org

Table 5: ENERGY AND NATURAL RESOURCES

Electric Power Generation	5,398,000,000,000 kilowatt hours per year (estimate) (2013)
Electric Power Consumption	5,322,000,000,000 kilowatt hours per year (estimate) (2013)
Nuclear Power Plants	21 (2014)
Crude Oil Production	4,459,400 barrels per day (2013)
Crude Oil Consumption	10,276,800 barrels per day (2012)
Natural Gas Production	117,100,000,000 cubic meters per year (estimate) (2013)
Natural Gas Consumption	150,000,000,000 cubic meters per year (estimate) (2013)
Natural Resources	Coal, iron ore, petroleum, natural gas, mercury, tin, tungsten, antimony, manganese, molybdenum, vanadium, magnetite, aluminum, lead, zinc, rare earth elements, uranium, hydropower potential (world's largest)

Sources: ABC-CLIO World Geography database; CIA World Factbook. http://www.cia.gov; U.S. Energy Information Administration. http://www.eia.gov.

Table 6: NATIONAL FINANCES

Currency	Yuan
Total Government Revenues	$2,118,000,000,000 (estimate) (2013)
Total Government Expenditures	$2,292,000,000,000 (estimate) (2013)
Budget Deficit	−2.1 (estimate) (2013)
GDP Contribution by Sector	agriculture: 10.1% industry: 45.3% services: 44.6% (2012 est.)
External Debt	$863,200,000,000 (estimate) (2013)
Economic Aid Extended	$0 (2011)
Economic Aid Received	$−796,000,000 (2011)

Sources: ABC-CLIO World Geography database; CIA World Factbook, http://www.cia.gov; IMF (World Economic Outlook), http://www.imf.org; OECD (Organization for Economic Cooperation and Development), http://www.oecd.org/dac/stats/idsonline.htm.

Table 7: INDUSTRY AND LABOR

Gross Domestic Product (GDP) - official exchange rate	$10,940,377,000,000 (estimate) (2015)
GDP per Capita	$7,961 (estimate) (2015)
GDP - Purchasing Power Parity (PPP)	$13,623,255,000,000 (estimate) (2013)
GDP (PPP) per Capita	$10,011 (estimate) (2013)
Industry Products	Textiles, iron, coal, cement, machinery, steel, fertilizer, processed foods, wood, armaments, petroleum, automobiles, consumer electronics.
Agriculture Products	Rice, vegetables, sweet potatoes, sorghum, maize, wheat, peanuts, sugarcane, potatoes, pigs, sheep, cattle, soy beans, cotton, opium (illicit).
Unemployment	4.5% (2012)
Labor Profile	Agriculture: 34.8% industry: 29.5% services: 35.7% (estimate) (2011)

Sources: ABC-CLIO World Geography database; CIA World Factbook, http://www.cia.gov; ILO (LABORSTA database), http://www.ilo.org; IMF (World Economic Outlook), http://www.imf.org; World Bank, http://www.worldbank.org.

Table 8: TRADE

Imported Goods	Machinery and transportation equipment, petroleum and petroleum products, telecommunications equipment, plastics, chemicals, fertilizer, steel, iron, foodstuffs.
Total Value of Imports	$353,300,800,000 (2009)
Exported Goods	Clothing, footwear, fabric, machinery and transportation equipment, chemicals, petroleum and petroleum products, fertilizer, minerals, toys, textiles.
Total Value of Exports	$2,021,000,000,000 (estimate) (2012)
Import Partners	Japan - 4.1%; Taiwan - 3.1%; South Korea - 2.9%; United States - 2.7%; Germany - 1.8% (2009)
Export Partners	United States - 8.0%; Japan - 3.5%; Germany - 1.9%; South Korea - 1.8%; Netherlands - 1.3% (2009)
Current Account Balance	$182,800,000,000 (estimate) (2013)
Weights and Measures	The metric system is in force, although traditional Chinese measurement units are also widely used.

Sources: ABC-CLIO World Geography database; CIA World Factbook, http://www.cia.gov; Europa World Year Book; IMF Direction of Trade Statistics.

Table 9: EDUCATION

School System	Chinese students begin school at the age of six. After six years of primary school, they continue to three years of early secondary education and three years of upper secondary education.
Mandatory Education	9 years, from ages 6 to 15.
Average Years Spent in School for Current Students	13 (2012)
Average Years Spent in School for Current Students, Male	13 (2012)
Average Years Spent in School for Current Students, Female	13 (estimate) (2012)
Primary School-age Children Enrolled in Primary School	99,540,477 (2012)
Primary School-age Males Enrolled in Primary School	98,814,166 (2012)
Primary School-age Females Enrolled in Primary School	726,311 (2012)
Secondary School-age Children Enrolled in Secondary School	95,004,209 (2012)
Secondary School-age Males Enrolled in Secondary School	50,174,443 (2012)
Secondary School-age Females Enrolled in Secondary School	44,829,766 (2012)
Students Per Teacher, Primary School	18.2 (2012)
Students Per Teacher, Secondary School	14.5 (2012)
Enrollment in Tertiary Education	32,385,961 (2012)
Enrollment in Tertiary Education, Male	15,969,145 (2012)
Enrollment in Tertiary Education, Female	16,416,816 (2012)
Literacy	95% (2010)

Sources: ABC-CLIO World Geography database; Country government; UNESCO, http://www.unesco.org; World Bank, http://www.worldbank.org.

Table 10: MILITARY

Total Active Armed Forces	2,285,000 (estimate) (2010)
Active Armed Forces	0% (2010)
Annual Military Expenditures	$70,300,000,000 (2009)
Military Service	Service in China's military is by selective conscription, with two-year terms.

Sources: ABC-CLIO World Geography database; Military Balance.

Table 11: TRANSPORTATION

Airports	497 (2012)
Paved Roads	53.5% (2008)
Roads, Unpaved	Not Available
Passenger Cars per 1,000 People	44 (2010)
Number of Trucks, Buses, and Commercial Vehicles	9,555,500 (2005)
Railroads	48,364 (2008)
Ports	Major: 12 (including Dalian, Qinhuangdao, Tianjin, Qingdao, Shanghai, Huangpu, Yantai, and Ningbo).

Sources: ABC-CLIO World Geography database; CIA World Factbook, http://www.cia.gov; World Bank, http://www.worldbank.org.

Table 12: COMMUNICATIONS

Facebook Users	560,000 (estimate) (2013)
Internet Users	389,000,000 (2009)
Internet Users (% of Population)	45.8% (2013)
Television	38 sets per 100 population (2006)
Land-based Telephones in Use	278,860,000 (2012)
Mobile Telephone Subscribers	1,100,000,000 (2012)
Major Daily Newspapers	1,021 (2004)
Average Circulation of Daily Newspapers	96,762,558 (2004)

Sources: ABC-CLIO World Geography database; CIA World Factbook, http://www.cia.gov; Facebook, https://www.facebook.com/.

Table 13: POPULATIONS OF MAJOR CITIES IN 2013–2014

Four municipalities directly under the central government	
City	**Population**
Beijing	19,612,368
Shanghai	23,019,148
Tianjin	12,937,954
Chongqing	28,846,170

167 cities with a population over 1 million		
City	**Location**	**Population**
Chengdu	Sichuan Provincial Capital	14,297,600
Guangzhou	Guangdong Provincial Capital	12,700,800
Baoding	Hebei Province	11,194,379
Harbin	Heilongjiang Provincial Capital	10,635,971
Suzhou	Jiangsu Province	10,578,700
Shenzhen	Guangdong Province	10,357,938
Nanyang	Henan Province	10,263,006
Shijiazhuang	Hebei Provincial Capital	10,163,788
Wuhan	Hubei Provincial Capital	10,120,000
Linyi	Shandong Province	10,039,400
Handan	Hebei Province	9,174,679
Wenzhou	Zhejiang Province	9,122,100
Weifang	Shandong Province	9,086,200
Qingdao	Shandong Province	8,964,000
Zhoukou	Henan Province	8,953,172
Hangzhou	Zhejiang Provincial Capital	8,844,000
Zhengzhou	Henan Provincial Capital	8,626,505
Xuzhou	Jiangsu Province	8,580,500
Xi'an	Shaanxi Provincial Capital	8,552,900
Ganzhou	Jiangxi Province	8,368,440
Dongguan	Guangdong Province	8,316,600
Heze	Shandong Province	8,287,800
Shenyang	Liaoning Provincial Capital	8,257,000
Nanjing	Jiangsu Provincial Capital	8,187,800
Quanzhou	Fujian Province	8,128,530
Ji'ning	Shandong Province	8,081,900
Changchun	Jilin Provincial Capital	7,677,089
Ningbo	Zhejiang Province	7,605,700
Fuyang	Anhui Province	7,599,918
Tangshan	Hebei Province	7,577,284

Nantong	Jiangsu Province	7,282,835
Yancheng	Jiangsu Province	7,262,200
Fushan	Guangdong Province	7,194,300
Hengyang	Hunan Province	7,141,462
Cangzhou	Hebei Province	7,134,053
Fuzhou	Fujian Province	7,115,370
Xingtai	Hebei Province	7,104,114
Shaoyang	Hunan Province	7,071,741
Hong Kong	Special Administrative Region	7,055,071
Changsha	Hunan Provincial Capital	7,044,118
Ji'nan	Shandong Provincial Capital	6,999,000
Yantai	Shandong Province	6,968,200
Dalian	Liaoning Province	6,690,432
Nanning	Guangxi Zhuang Autonomous Region's Capital	6,661,600
Luoyang	Henan Province	6,549,486
Kunming	Yunnan Provincial Capital	6,432,212
Wuxi	Jiangsu Province	6,372,624
Nanchong	Sichuan Province	6,278,622
Zunyi	Guizhou Province	6,127,009
Xinyang	Henan Province	6,108,683
Taizhou	Zhejiang Province	5,968,800
Quqing	Yunnan Province	5,855,055
Maiming	Guangdong Province	5,817,753
Liaocheng	Shandong Province	5,789,900
Changde	Hunan Province	5,717,218
Xinxiang	Henan Province	5,707,801
Hefei	Anhui Provincial Capital	5,702,466
Jingzhou	Hubei Province	5,691,707
Liuan	Anhui Province	5,612,000
Qiqihar	Heilongjiang Province	5,611,000
Dezhou	Shandong Province	5,568,200
Xiangyang	Hubei Province	5,500,307
Taian	Shandong Province	5,494,200
Yueyang	Hunan Province	5,477,911
Suihua	Heilongjiang Province	5,416,339
Shantou	Guangdong Province	5,391,028
Jinhua	Zhejiang Province	5,361,600
Suozhou	Anhui Province	5,352,924
Anqing	Anhui Province	5,311,000
Anyang	Henan Province	5,172,834
Nanchang	Jiangxi Provincial Capital	5,042,565

Shaoxing	Zhejiang Province	4,912,200
Pingdingshan	Henan Province	4,903,367
Huizhou	Anhui Province	4,851,000
Zhangzhou	Fujian Province	4,809,983
Huai'an	Jiangsu Province	4,799,899
Guilin	Guangxi Zhuang Autonomous Region	4,748,000
Jiujiang	Jiangxi Province	4,728,764
Suqian	Jiangsu Province	4,715,553
Kaifeng	Henan Province	4,676,159
Taizhou	Jiangsu Province	4,618,558
Mianyang	Sichuan Province	4,613,862
Huizhou	Guangdong Province	4,597,002
Changzhou	Jiangsu Province	4,591,972
Zibo	Shandong Province	4,530,600
Jiaxing	Zhejiang Province	4,501,600
Yibin	Sichuan Province	4,472,001
Yangzhou	Jiangsu Province	4,459,760
Jiangmen	Guangdong Province	4,448,871
Jilin	Jilin Province	4,414,681
Lianyungang	Jiangsu Province	4,393,914
Langfang	Hebei Province	4,358,839
Chifeng	Inner Mongolian Autonomous Region	4,341,245
Guiyang	Guizhou Provincial Capital	4,324,561
Linfen	Shanxi Province	4,316,612
Xuchang	Henan Province	4,307,199
Taiyuan	Shanxi Provincial Capital	4,201,591
Guigang	Guangxi Zhuang Autonomous Region	4,118,808
Yichang	Hubei Province	4,059,686
Keshi	Xinjiang Uyghur Autonomous Region	3,979,321
Shezhou	Anhui Province	3,937,868
Zhaoqing	Guangdong Province	3,918,085
Zhuzhou	Hunan Province	3,855,609
Liuzhou	Guangxi Zhuang Autonomous Region	3,758,704
Binzhou	Shandong Province	3,748,500
Zaozhuang	Shandong Province	3,729,300
Baoji	Shaanxi Province	3,716,731
Neijiang	Sichuan Province	3,702,847
Anshan	Liaoning Province	3,654,884
Lanzhou	Gansu Provincial Capital	3,616,163
Puyang	Henan Province	3,598,494
Jiaozuo	Henan Province	3,539,860

Xiamen	Fujian Province	3,531,147
Wuhu	Anhui Province	3,443,192
Yulin	Shaanxi Province	3,351,437
Datong	Shanxi Province	3,318,057
Bazhong	Sichuan Province	3,283,771
Tianshui	Gansu Province	3,262,548
Bangpu	Anhui Province	3,164,467
Jinzhou	Liaoning Province	3,126,463
Zhenjiang	Jiangsu Province	3,113,384
Urumqi	Xinjiang Uyghur Autonomous Region's Capital	3,110,280
Qinhuangdao	Hebei Province	2,987,605
Daqing	Heilongjiang Province	2,904,532
Huhehot	Inner Mongolian Autonomous Region	2,866,615
Weihai	Shandong Province	2,804,800
Rizhao	Shandong Province	2,801,100
Mudanjiang	Heilongjiang Province	2,798,723
Putian	Fujian Province	2,778,508
Xiangtan	Hunan Province	2,748,552
Tieling	Liaoning Province	2,717,732
Zhigong	Sichuan Province	2,678,898
Chaozhou	Guangdong Province	2,669,844
Baotou	Inner Mongolian Autonomous Region	2,650,364
Nanping	Fujian Province	2,645,549
Huludao	Liaoning Province	2,623,541
Jiamusi	Heilongjiang Province	2,552,097
Dandong	Liaoning Province	2,444,697
Huangshi	Hubei Province	2,429,318
Yingkou	Liaoning Province	2,428,000
Yangjiang	Guangdong Province	2,421,812
Akesu	Xinjiang Uyghur Autonomous Region	2,370,887
Huinan	Anhui Province	2,334,000
Xi'ning	Qinghai Provincial Capital	2,208,708
Fushun	Liaoning Province	2,138,090
Lishui	Zhejiang Province	2,117,000
Huibei	Anhui Province	2,114,276
Haikou	Hainan Provincial Capital	2,046,189
Dongying	Shandong Province	2,035,300
Yinchuan	Ningxia Hui Autonomous Region's Capital	1,993,088
Hezhou	Guangxi Zhuang Autonomous Region	1,954,100
Liaoyang	Liaoning Province	1,859,768
Fuxin	Liaoning Province	1,819,339

Wuwei	Gansu Province	1,815,054
Benxi	Liaoning Province	1,709,538
Zhuhai	including Macao, Guangdong Province	1,560,229
Beihai	Guangxi Zhuang Autonomous Region	1,539,300
Zhanjiang	Guangdong Province	1,392,493
Panjin	Liaoning Province	1,392,400
Ma'anshan	Anhui Province	1,366,302
Laiwu	Shandong Province	1,298,500
Lijiang	Yunnan Province	1,244,769
Panzhihua	Sichuan Province	1,214,121
Danshan	Zhejiang Province	1,121,300
Hegang	Heilongjiang Province	1,058,665
Ezhou	Hubei Province	1,048,627

Source: National Census Office of the PRC State Council, Zhongguo renko pucha ziliao [National Census Documents], 1982, 1990, 2000, and 2010 (Beijing: Zhongguo tongji chubanshe, 1985, 1993, 2002, and 2012).

Table 14:   POPULATIONS OF THE 56 ETHNIC GROUPS OF CHINA

Group	1982	2000	2010
Han	936,703,824	1,139,773,008	1,220,844,520
Zhuang	13,378,162	16,187,163	16,926,381
Manchu	4,299,159	10,708,464	10,387,958
Hui	7,219,352	9,828,126	10,586,087
Miao	5,030,897	8,945,538	9,426,007
Uyghur	5,957,112	8,405,416	10,069,346
Yi	5,453,448	7,765,858	8,714,393
Tujia	2,832,743	8,037,014	8,353,912
Mongolian	3,411,657	5,827,808	5,981,840
Tibetan	3,870,068	5,422,954	6,282,187
Bouyei	2,120,469	2,973,217	2,870,034
Dong	1,425,100	2,962,911	2,879,974
Yao	1,402,676	2,638,878	2,796,003
Korean	1,763,870	1,929,696	1,830,929
Bai	1,131,124	1,861,895	1,933,510
Hani	1,058,836	1,440,029	1,660,932
Kazak	907,582	1,251,023	1,462,588
Li	817,562	1,248,022	1,463,064
Dai	839,797	1,159,231	1,261,311
She	368,832	710,039	708,651
Lisu	480,960	635,101	702,839

Dongxiang	279,397	513,826	621,500
Lahu	304,174	453,765	485,966
Shui	286,487	407,000	411,847
Va	298,591	396,709	429,709
Naxi	245,154	309,477	326,295
Qiang	102,768	306,476	309,576
Tu	159,426	241,593	289,565
Mulam	90,426	207,464	216,257
Xibe	83,629	189,357	190,481
Kirgiz	113,999	160,875	186,708
Daur	94,014	132,747	131,992
Jingpo	93,008	132,158	147,828
Maonan	38,135	107,184	101,192
Salar	69,102	104,521	130,607
Blang	58,476	91,891	119,639
Gelo	53,802	75,635	86,443
Tajik	26,503	41,056	51,069
Achang	20,411	33,954	39,555
Pumi	20,441	33,628	42,861
Ewenki	19,343	30,545	30,875
Nu	23,166	28,770	37,523
Jing	11,995	22,584	28,199
Jino	11,974	20,899	23,143
Benglong	12,292	17,935	20,556
Bonan	9,027	16,505	20,074
Russian	2,935	15,631	15,393
Yugur	10,569	13,747	14,378
Ozbek	12,453	12,423	10,569
Moinba	6,248	8,928	10,561
Oroqen	4,132	8,216	8,659
Drung	4,682	7,431	6,930
Tatar	4,127	4,895	3,556
Hezhen	1,476	4,664	5,354
Gaoshan	1,549	4,488	4,009
Luoba	2,065	2,970	3,682
Unclassified Ethnic Minorities	879,201	734,438	640,101

Source: National Census Office of the PRC State Council, Zhongguo renko pucha ziliao [National Census Documents], 1982, 1990, 2000, and 2010 (Beijing: Zhongguo tongji chubanshe, 1985, 1993, 2002, and 2012).

Table 15:   Chinese Dynasties and Governments

Three Sovereigns and Five–Emperor Period (3000–2200 BCE)

    Yellow Emperor (Huang-di) (2300–2250 BCE)

    Emperor Yao (2250–2230 BCE)

    Shun (2230–2205 BCE)

Xia Dynasty (2205–1766 BCE)

    Yu (Dayu, Yu the Great) (2205–)

Shang Dynasty (1766–1027 BCE)

Zhou Dynasty (1066–221 BCE)

    Western Zhou Dynasty (1066–771 BCE)

        Wen Wang (reigned 1099–1050 BCE)

        Zhao Wang (Ch'ao Wang) (996–977 BCE)

        Mu Wang (977–922 BCE)

        Gong Wang (922–900 BCE)

        Yi Wang (900–891 BCE)

        Yi Wang (the second, 885–878 BCE)

        Li Wang (877–841 BCE)

        Xuan Wang (Hsuan Wang) (827–782 BCE)

        You Wang (781–771 BCE)

        Ping Wang (771–720 BCE)

    Eastern Zhou Dynasty (770–221 BCE)

    Spring and Autumn Period (770–476 BCE)

        Ping Wang (771–720 BCE)

        Huan Wang (720–697 BCE)

        Zhuang Wang (Ch'uang Wang) (697–682 BCE)

        Xi Wang (Hsi Wang) (682–677 BCE)

        Hui Wang (677–652 BCE)

        Xiang Wang (Hsiang Wang) (651–619 BCE)

        Qing Wang (Ch'ing Wang) (618–613 BCE)

        Kuang Wang (612–607 BCE)

        Ding Wang (Ting Wang) (606–586 BCE)

        Jian Wang (Kian Wang) (585–572 BCE)

        Ling Wang (571–545 BCE)

        Jing Wang (King Wang) (544–520 BCE)

        Dao Wang (Tao Wang) (520 BCE)

        Jing Wang (the second, 520–476 BCE)

    Warring States Period (475–221 BCE)

        Yuan Wang (475–469 BCE)

        Zhending Wang (Ch'en-ting Wang) (468–441 BCE)

        Kao Wang (440–426 BCE)

Weilie Wang (Wei-lie Wang) (425–402 BCE)

An Wang (401–376 BCE)

Lie Wang (375–369 BCE)

Xian Wang (Hsian Wang) (368–321 BCE)

Shenjing Wang (Shen–king Wang) (320–315 BCE)

Nan Wang (314–256 BCE)

Seven Warring States:

Zhao (Ch'ao)

Yan

Qin (Ch'in)

Chu

Lu

Wei

Han

Qin Dynasty (221–206 BCE)

Qin Shi Huangdi (Ch'in Shih Huang-ti) (221–210 BCE)

Qin Er Shi (Ying Huhai) (209–207 BCE)

Qin San Shi (Ying Ziying) (207–206 BCE)

Han Dynasty (206 BCE–220 CE)

Western Han Dynasty (206 BCE–8 CE)

Han Gaozu (Kao-tsu) (206–195 BCE)

Han Huidi (Hui-ti) (194–188 BCE)

Han Gaohou (Kao-hou) (187–180 BCE)

Han Wendi (Wen-ti) (179–157 BCE)

Han Jingdi (Ching-ti) (156–141 BCE)

Han Wudi (Wu-ti) (140–87 BCE)

Han Zhaodi (Chao-ti) (86–74 BCE)

Han Xuandi (Hsüan-ti) (73–49 BCE)

Han Yuandi (Yüan-ti) (48–33BCE)

Han Chengdi (Ch'eng-ti) (32–7 BCE)

Han Aidi (Ai-ti) (6–1 BCE)

Han Pingdi (P'ing-ti) (1 BCE–5 CE)

Han Ruzi (Ju-tzu) (6–8)

Wang Mang (9–23)

Eastern Han Dynasty (25–220)

Han Guangwudi (Kuang-wu-ti) (25–57)

Han Mingdi (Ming-ti) (58–75)

Han Zhangdi (Chang-ti) (75–88)

Han Hedi (Ho-ti) (89–105)

Han Shangdi (Shang-ti) (106)

Han Andi (An-ti) (107–125)

Han Shaodi (Shao-ti) (125)

Han Shundi (Shun-ti) (126–144)

Han Chongdi (Ch'ung-ti) (145)

Han Zhidi (Chih-ti) (146)

Han Huandi (Huan-ti) (147–167)

Han Lingdi (Ling-ti) (168–189)

Han Shaodi (Shao-ti) (189)

Han Xiandi (Hsian-ti) (189–220)

Three Kingdoms (220–280)

Wei (220–265)

Wendi (Wen-ti) (220–226)

Mingdi (Ming-ti) (226–239)

Shaodi (Shao-ti) (239–254)

Gao Gui Xianggong (Gao Gui Hsiang-kong) (254–260)

Yuandi (Yuan-ti) (260–265)

Shu (221–263)

Zhaoliedi (Ch'ao-lie-ti) (221–223)

Xiaohuaidi (Hsiao-huai-ti) (223–263)

Wu (229–280)

Sun Quan (Sun Ch'uan) (229–252)

Sun Liang (252–258)

Sun Xiu (Sun Hsiu) (258–264)

Sun Hao (264–280)

Jin Dynasty (265–420)

Western Jin Dynasty (265–316)

Wudi (Wu-ti) (265–290)

Huidi (Hui-ti) (290–307)

Huaidi (Huai-ti) (307–311)

Mindi (Min-ti) (313–316)

Eastern Jin Dynasty (317–420)

Yuandi (Yuan-ti) (317–323)

Mingdi (Ming-ti) (323–326)

Chengdi (Cheng-ti) (326–342)

Kangdi (Kang-ti) (342–344)

Mudi (Mu-ti) (344–361)

Aidi (Ai-ti) (362–365)

Feidi (Fei-ti) (366–371)

Wendi (Wen-ti) (371–372)

Xiao Wudi (Hsiao-wu-ti) (373–396)

Andi (An-ti) (397–418)

Gongdi (Kung-ti) (419–420)

Northern–Southern Dynasties (386–582)

Northern Dynasties (386–581)

Northern Wei Dynasty (386–535)

Dao Wudi (Tao Wu-ti) (386–409)

Ming Yuandi (Ming Yuan-ti) (409–423)

Tai Wudi (Tai Wu-ti) (424–452)

Wen Chengdi (Wen Cheng-ti) (452–465)

Xian Wendi (Hsian Wen-ti) (466–471)

Xiao Wendi (Hsiao Wen-ti) (471–499)

Xuan Wudi (Hsuan Wu-ti) (499–515)

Xiao Mingdi (Hsiao Ming-ti) (516–528)

Xiao Zhuangdi (Hsiao Ch'uang-ti) (528–530)

Chang Guang Wang (530–531)

Jie Mindi (Kie Min-ti) (531–532)

Xiao Wudi (Hsiao Wu-ti) (532–535)

Eastern Wei Dynasty (534–550)

Xiao Jingdi (Hsiao King-ti) (534–550)

Northern Qi (Ch'i) Dynasty (550–577)

Wen Xuandi (Wen Hsuan-ti) (550–559)

Feidi (Fei-ti) (559–560)

Xiao Zhaodi (Hsiao Ch'ao-ti) (560–561)

Wu Chengdi (Wu Cheng-ti) (561–565)

Hou Zhu (Hou Ch'u) (565–577)

Western Wei Dynasty (535–556)

Wendi (Wen-ti) (535–551)

Feidi (Fei-ti) (552–554)

Gongdi (Gong-ti) (554–556)

Northern Zhou Dynasty (557–581)

Xiao Mindi (Hsiao Min-ti) (557)

Mingdi (Ming-ti) (557–560)

Wudi (Wu-ti) (561–578)

Xuandi (Hsuan-ti) (578–579)

Jingdi (King-ti) (579–581)

Southern Dynasties (420–589)

Song Dynasty (420–479)

Wudi (Wu-ti) (420–422)

Shaodi (Shao-ti) (423–424)

Wendi (Wen-ti) (424–453)

Xiaowudi (Hsiao-wu-ti) (454–464)

Qianfeidi (Ch'ian-fei-ti) (465)

        Mingdi (Ming-ti) (465–472)

        Houfeidi (Hou-fei-ti) (473–477)

        Shundi (Shun-ti) 477–479)

    Qi (Ch'i) Dynasty (479–502)

        Gaodi (Gao-ti) (479–482)

        Wudi (Wu-ti) (482–493)

        Yulin Wang (493–494)

        Hailing Wang (494)

        Mingdi (Ming-ti) (494–498)

        Dong Hun Hou (499–501)

        Hedi (He-ti) (501–502)

    Liang Dynasty (502–557)

        Wudi (Wu-ti) (502–549)

        Jianwendi (Kian-wen-ti) (549–551)

        Yu Zhang Wang (Yu Chang Wang) (551–552)

        Yuandi (Yuan-ti) (552–555)

        Zhen Yang Hou (Ch'en Yang Hou) (555)

        Jingdi (King-ti) (555–557)

    Chen Dynasty (557–589)

        Wudi (Wu-ti) (557–559)

        Wendi (Wen-ti) (559–556)

        Feidi (Fei-ti) (566–568)

        Xuandi (Hsuan-ti) (569–582)

        Houzhu (Hou-chu) (583–589)

    Southern Liang Dynasty (555–587)

    Xuandi (Hsuan-ti) (555–562)

        Xiao Mingdi (Hsiao Ming-ti) (562–585)

        Xiao Jingdi (Hsiao King-ti) (585–587)

Sui Dynasty (581–618)

    Sui Wendi (Wen-ti) (581–604)

    Sui Yangdi (Yang-ti) (605–617)

    Sui Gongdi (Kung-ti) (617–618)

Tang Dynasty (618–907)

    Tang Gaozu (Kao-Tsu) (618–626)

    Tang Taizong (T'ai-Tsung) (627–649)

    Tang Gaozong (Kao-Tsung) (650–683)

    Tang Zhongzong (Chung-Tsung) (683–684)

    Tang Ruizong (Jui-Tsung) (684)

    Wu Zetian (Wu Tse-tien) (684–704)

    Tang Zhongzong (Chung-Tsung) (705–710)

    Tang Ruizong (Jui-Tsung) (710–712)

Tang Xuanzong (Hsuan-Tsung) (712–756)

Tang Suzong (Su-tsung) (756–761)

Tang Daizong (Tai-tsung) (762–779)

Tang Dezong (Te-tsung) (780–805)

Tang Shunzong (Shun-tsung) (805)

Tang Xianzong (Hsian-tsung) (806–820)

Tang Muzong (Mu-tsung) (821–824)

Tang Jingzong (Ching-tsung) (825–827)

Tang Wenzong (Wen-tsung) (827–840)

Tang Wuzong (Wu-tsung) (841–846)

Tang Xuanzong (Hsüan-tsung) (847–859)

Tang Yizong (I-tsung) (859–874)

Tang Xizong (Hsi-tsung) (874–888)

Tang Zhaozong (Chao-tsung) (889–904)

Zhao Xuandi (Hsüan-ti) (905–907)

Song Dynasty (960–1279)

Northern Song (960–1127)

Song Taizu (T'ai-tsu) (960–976)

Song Taizong (T'ai-tsung) (976–997)

Song Zhenzong (Chen-tsung) (998–1022)

Song Renzong (Jen-tsung) (1023–1063)

Song Yingzong (Ying-tsung) (1064–1067)

Song Shenzong (Shen-tsung) (1068–1085)

Song Zhezong (Che-tsung) (1086–1100)

Song Huizong (Hui-tsung) (1101–1125)

Song Qinzong (Chin-tsung) (1126–1127)

Southern Song (1127–1279)

Song Gaozong (Kao-tsung) (1127–1162)

Song Xiaozong (Hsiao-tsung) (1163–1189)

Song Guangzong (Kwang-tsung) (1190–1194)

Song Ningzong (Ning-tsung) (1195–1224)

Song Lizong (Li-tsung) (1225–1264)

Song Duzong (Tu-tsung) (1265–1274)

Song Gongdi (Kung-ti) (1275–1276)

Song Duanzong (Tuan-tsung) (1276–1278)

Song Dibing (Ti-ping) (1278–1279)

Yuan Dynasty (1271–1368)

Yuan Shizu (Shih-tsu) (1260–1270)

Yuan Chengzong (Ch'eng-tsung) (1295–1307)

Yuan Wuzong (Wu-tsung) (1308–1311)

Yuan Renzong (Jen-tsung) (1312–1320)

Yuan Yingzong (Ying-tsung) (1321–1323)

Taiding (Thai-ting) (1324–1328)

Tianshun (T'ien-shun) (1328)

Yuan Wenzong (Wen-tsung) (1328–1332)

Yuan Ninzong (Nin-tsung) (1332–1333)

Yuan Shundi (Shun-ti) (1333–1370)

Ming Dynasty (1368–1644)

Hongwu (Hung-wu Ti) (1368–1398)

Jianwen (Chien-wen) (1399–1402)

Yongle (Yung-lo) (1403–1424)

Hongxi (Hung-hsi) (1425)

Xuande (Hsuan-te) (1426–1435)

Zhengtong (Cheng-t'ung) (1436–1449)

Jingtai (Ching-t'ai) (1450–1456)

Tianshun (T'ien-shun) (1457–1464)

Chenghua (Ch'eng-hua) (1465–1487)

Hongzhi (Hung-chih) (1488–1505)

Zhengde (Cheng-te) (1506–1521)

Jiajing (Chia-ching) (1522–1566)

Longqing (Lung-ch'ing) (1567–1572)

Wanli (Wan-li) (1573–1620)

Taichang (T'ai-ch'ang) (1620)

Tianqi (T'ien-ch'i) (1621–1627)

Chongzhen (Ch'ung-cheng) (1628–1644)

Qing Dynasty (1644–1912)

Shunzhi (Shun-chih) (1644–1661)

Kangxi (K'ang-hsi) (1662–1722)

Yongzheng (Yung-cheng) (1723–1735)

Qianlong (Ch'ien-lung) (1736–1795)

Jiaqing (Chia-ch'ing) (1796–1820)

Daoguang (Tao-kuang) (1821–1850)

Xianfeng (Hsian-feng) (1851–1863)

Tongzhi (T'ung-chih) (1862–1874)

Guangxu (Kwang Hsu) (1875–1908)

Xuantong (Hsüan-t'ung) (1909–1912)

Republic of China (1912–)

Sun Yat-sen (1912)

Yuan Shikai (Yuan Shih-k'ai) (1912–1916)

Li Yuanhong (1916–1917)

Feng Guozhang (Feng Kuo-chang) (1917–1918)

Xu Shichang (Hsu Shih-chang) (1918–1922)

Zhou Ziqi (Chou Tzu-chi) (1922)

Li Yuanhong (1922–1923)

Gao Lingwei (Kao Ling-wei) (1923)

Can Kun (1923–1924)

Huang Fu (1924)

Duan Qirui (Tuan Chi-jui) (1924–1926)

Hu Weide (Hu Wei-te) (1926)

Yan Huiqing (Yen Hui-Ching) (1926)

Du Xigui (Tu Hsi-Kuei) (1926)

Gu Weijun (Koo Vi-kyuin) (1926–1927)

Zhang Zuolin (Chang Tso-lin) (1927–1928)

Jiang Jieshi (Chiang Kai-shek) (1928–1931)

Lin Sen (1931–1943)

Jiang Jieshi (Chiang Kai-shek) (1943–1949)

Li Zongren (Li Tsung-jen)(1949–1950)

Jiang Jieshi (Chiang Kai-shek) (1950–1975)

Yen Jiagan (Yan Chia-kan) (1975–1978)

Jiang Jingguo (Chiang Ching-kuo) (1978–1988)

Li Denghui (Lee Teng-hui) (1988–2000)

Chen Shuibian (Chen Shui-bian) (2000–2008)

Ma Yingjiu (Ma Ying-jeou) (2008–2016)

People's Republic of China (1949–)

Mao Zedong (Mao Tse-tung) (1949–1959)

Liu Shaoqi (Liu Shao-ch'i) (1959–1968)

Song Qingling (Sung Ch'ing-ling) (1968–1972)

Dong Biwu (Tung Pi-wu) (1972–1975)

(During this interval, the Presidency was abolished in 1975–1982)

Li Xiannian (1983–1988)

Yang Shangkun (Yang Shang-kun) (1988–1993)

Jiang Zemin (Chiang Tse-min) (1993–2003)

Hu Jintao (2003–2012)

Xi Jinping (2013–2022)

Sources: John Fairbank and Merle Goldman, *China: A New History*, 2nd ed. (Cambridge, MA: Harvard University Press, 2006); and Xiaobing Li, *China at War: An Encyclopedia of the Chinese Military History* (ABC–CLIO, 2013).

HOLIDAYS

Date/Day	Holiday
January 1	New Year Day (official solar calendar; national holiday)
Late January or early February	Chinese Lunar New Year (or Spring Festival; from the first to the fifth day of the first month in the lunar calendar; national holiday)
Late February	Lantern Festival (15th of the first lunar month)
March 8	International Women's Day (National women's holiday)
April 4	*Qing Ming* (The Pure Brightness Day, or Tomb Sweeping Day)
April 8	April 8th Festival (Miao minority annual celebration)
Early April	Three-Three Festival (Li minority holiday on Hainan)
Mid-April	Song Fair (Zhuang minority bi-annual music and dance carnival, 8th of the third lunar month)
May 1	International Labor Day (National holiday)
May 4	National Youth Day
Early May	Goddess of Mercy Festival (Third Moon Fair of the Bai minority; 15th–20th of the third lunar month)
May 25	Buddha's Birthday
Late May	Nadam Festival (Traditional Mongolian annual fair; 20th–26th of the fourth lunar month)
June 1	International Children's Day (National holiday)
Mid-June	Dragon Boat Festival (5th of the fifth lunar month)
Late June	Song Fair (Zhuang minority bi-annual music and dance carnival; 12th of the fifth lunar month)
Late June	Danu Festival (Yao minority annual harvest celebration; 29th of the fifth lunar month)
July 1	Chinese Communist Party Day (National holiday)
August 1	National Army's Day (PLA); Tibetan Festival (or Tibetan Fruit-Expecting Festival)
Early August	Torch Festival (Yi and Bai minorities annual holiday; 24th of the sixth lunar month)
September 15	Mid-Autumn Festival (Harvest Moon Festival; 15th day of the eighth lunar month)

October 1	National Day of the PRC (National holiday)
October 10	National Day of the ROC (National holiday in Taiwan)
November 17	Student Day
December 1	AIDS Day
Late December	*Laba* (Shakyamuni's Buddhahood Day; 8th of the twelfth lunar month)

SELECTED BIBLIOGRAPHY

Andrews, Julia, and Kuiyi Shen. *The Art of Modern China*. Berkeley: University of California Press, 2012.

Angle, Stephen. *Human Rights in Chinese Thought: A Cross-Cultural Inquiry*. Cambridge, UK: Cambridge University Press, 2002.

Bakken, Borge, ed. *Crime, Punishment, and Policing in China*. Boulder, CO: Rowman & Littlefield, 2007.

Baranovitch, Nimrod. *China's New Voices: Popular Music, Ethnicity, Gender, and Politics, 1978–1997*. Berkeley: University of California Press, 2003.

Barlow, Tani. *The Question of Women in Chinese Feminism*. Durham, NC: Duke University Press, 2004.

Bays, Daniel. *Christianity in China: From the Eighteenth Century to the Present*. Stanford, CA: Stanford University Press, 1999.

Bell, Stephen, and Hui Feng. *The Rise of the People's Bank of China: The Politics of Institutional Change*. Cambridge, MA: Harvard University Press, 2013.

Biddulph, Sarah. *Legal Reform and Administrative Detention Powers in China*. Cambridge, UK: Cambridge University Press, 2008.

Birrell, Anne. *Chinese Mythology: An Introduction*. Baltimore, MD: Johns Hopkins University Press, 1999.

Bovingdon, Gardner. *The Uyghurs: Strangers in Their Own Land*. New York: Columbia University Press, 2010.

Brownell, Susan. *Training the Body for China: Sports in the Moral Order of the People's Republic*. Chicago: University of Chicago Press, 1995.

Cai, Yanxin. *Chinese Architecture: Introduction to Chinese Culture*. Cambridge, UK: Cambridge University Press, 2011.

Cai, Zong-qi, ed. *How to Read Chinese Poetry: A Guided Anthology*. New York: Columbia University Press, 2007. Cambridge, MA: Harvard University Press, 2007.

Campanella, Thomas. *The Concrete Dragon: China's Urban Revolution and What It Means for the World*. Princeton, NJ: Princeton University Press, 2011.

Chang, Maria Hsia. *Falun Gong: The End of Days*. New Haven, CT: Yale University Press, 2004.

Chen, Jie. *A Middle Class without Democracy: Economic Growth and the Prospects for Democratization in China*. Oxford, UK: Oxford University Press, 2014.

Chen, Nancy et al., eds. *China Urban: Ethnographies of Contemporary Culture.* Durham, NC: Duke University Press, 2001.

Chen, Yulu. *Chinese Currency and the Global Economy: The Rise of the Renminbi.* New York: McGraw, 2014.

Cheung, Gordon. *Intellectual Property Rights in China: Politics of Piracy, Trade and Protection.* London: Routledge, 2011.

Chin, Yik-Chan. *Television Regulation and Media Policy in China.* London: Routledge, 2015.

Cho, Mun Young. *The Specter of "the People": Urban Poverty in Northeast China.* Ithaca, NY: Cornell University Press, 2013.

Clunas, Craig. *Art in China: Oxford History of Art.* 2nd ed. Oxford, UK: Oxford University Press, 2009.

Cody, Jeffrey, Nancy Steinhardt, and Tony Atkin, eds. *Chinese Architecture and the Beaux-Arts.* Honolulu: University of Hawaii Press, 2011.

Collins, Gabriel et al., eds. *China's Energy Strategy: The Impact on Beijing's Maritime Policies.* Annapolis, MD: Naval Institute Press, 2008.

Curtin, Michael. *Playing to the World's Biggest Audience: The Globalization of Chinese Film and TV.* Berkeley: University of California Press, 2007.

Dautcher, Jay. *Down a Narrow Road: Identity and Masculinity in a Uyghur Community in Xinjiang China.* Cambridge, MA: Harvard University Press, 2009.

Davis, Deborah, and Sara Friedman, eds. *Wives, Husbands, and Lovers: Marriage and Sexuality in Hong Kong, Taiwan, and Urban China.* Stanford, CA: Stanford University Press, 2014.

Davis, Deborah, and Feng Wang, eds. *Creating Wealth and Poverty in Post-socialist China.* Stanford, CA: Stanford University Press, 2008.

De Mente, Boye. *Etiquette Guide to China: Know the Rules that Make the Difference.* North Clarendon, VT: Tuttle, 2008.

Dimitrov, Martin. *Piracy and the State: The Politics of Intellectual Property Rights in China.* New York: Cambridge University Press, 2012.

Dong, Hongyuan. *A History of the Chinese Language.* London: Routledge, 2014.

Dreyer, June. *China's Political System.* New York: Pearson, 2011.

Economy, Elizabeth. *By All Means Necessary: How China's Resource Quest Is Changing the World.* Oxford, UK: Oxford University Press, 2014.

Elvin, Mark. *The Retreat of the Elephants: An Environmental History of China.* Ithaca, NY: Yale University Press, 2006.

England, Robert. *Aging China: The Demographic Challenge to China' Economic Prospects.* New York: Praeger, 2005.

Farquhar, Judith. *Appetites: Food and Sex in Post-Socialist China.* Durham, NC: Duke University Press, 2002.

Flower, Kathy. *China—Culture Smart! The Essential Guide to Customs and Culture.* London: Kuperard, 2010.

Fong, Vanessa. *Only Hope: Coming of Age under China's One-Child Policy.* Stanford, CA: Stanford University Press, 2006.

Foot, Rosemary. *Rights beyond Borders: The Global Community and the Struggle over Human Rights in China.* Oxford, UK: Oxford University Press, 2001.

Frazier, Mark. *Socialist Insecurity: Pensions and the Politics of Uneven Development in China.* Ithaca, NY: Cornell University Press, 2010.

Gallagher, Kelly. *China Shifts Gears: Automakers, Oil, Pollution, and Development.* Cambridge, MA: MIT Press, 2006.

Gallagher, Mary. *Contagious Capitalism: Globalization and the Politics of Labor in China.* Princeton, NJ: Princeton University Press, 2007.

Gardner, Daniel. *Confucianism: A Very Short Introduction.* Oxford, UK: Oxford University Press, 2014.

Gladney, Dru. *Dislocating China: Muslims, Minorities, and Other Subaltern Subjects.* Chicago: University of Chicago Press, 2004.

Goldman, Merle. *From Comrade to Citizen: The Struggle for Political Rights in China.* Cambridge, MA: Harvard University Press, 2007.

Graff, Kristen, and Rio Ramadhana. *Chinese Dining Etiquette.* Austin, TX: Magnolia, 2011.

Greenhalgh, Susan, and Edwin Winckler. *Governing China's Population: From Leninist to Neoliberal Bio-politics.* Stanford, CA: Stanford University Press, 2005.

Greenhalgh, Susan. *Just One Child: Science and Policy in Deng's China.* Berkeley: University of California Press, 2008.

Gries, Peter, and Stanley Rosen, eds. *Chinese Politics: State, Society and the Market.* London: Routledge, 2010.

Guo, Sujian. *Chinese Politics and Government: Power, Ideology, and Organization.* London: Routledge, 2013.

Haley, Usha, and George Haley. *Subsidies to Chinese Industry: State Capitalism, Business Strategy, and Trade Policy.* Oxford, UK: Oxford University Press, 2013.

Hannas, William, James Mulvenon, and Anna Puglisi. *Chinese Industrial Espionage: Technology Acquisition and Military Modernization.* London: Routledge, 2013.

Harney, Alexandra. *The China Price: The True Cost of Chinese Competitive Advantage.* New York: Penguin, 2009.

Heisig, James, and Timothy Richardson. *Remembering Traditional Hanzi: How Not to Forget the Meaning and Writing of Chinese Characters.* Honolulu: University of Hawaii Press, 2008.

Ho, Loretta Wing Wah. *Gay and Lesbian Subculture in Urban China.* London: Routledge, 2011.

Hockx, Michel. *Internet Literature in China.* New York: Columbia University Press, 2015.

Hollmann, Thomas. *The Land of the Five Flavors: A Cultural History of Chinese Cuisine.* New York: Columbia University Press, 2013.

Hsu, Stephen, ed. *Understanding China's Legal System.* New York: New York University Press, 2003.

Hsueh, Roselyn. *China's Regulatory State: A New Strategy for Globalization.* Ithaca, NY: Cornell University Press, 2011.

Huang, Hua-lun. *The Missing Girls and Women of China, Hong Kong and Taiwan, 1900–2000s.* Jefferson, NC: McFarland, 2012.

Huang, Yanzhong. *Governing Health in Contemporary China.* London: Routledge, 2014.

Huang, Yasheng. *Selling China: Foreign Direct Investment during the Reform Era.* Cambridge, UK: Cambridge University Press, 2005.

Hurst, William. *The Chinese Workers after Socialism*. Cambridge, UK: Cambridge University Press, 2012.

Jacka, Tamara, Andrew Kipnis, and Sally Sargeson. *Contemporary China: Society and Social Change*. Cambridge, UK: Cambridge University Press, 2013.

Jeffreys, Elaine. *China, Sex and Prostitution*. London: Routledge, 2004.

Jin, Jie. *Chinese Music: Introduction to Chinese Culture*. Cambridge, UK: Cambridge University Press, 2011.

Jones, Stephen. *Folk Music of China: Living Instrumental Traditions*. Oxford, UK: Oxford University Press, 1999.

Joseph, William, ed. *Politics in China: An Introduction*. New York: Oxford University Press, 2010.

Keith, Ronald, Zhiqiu Lin, and Shumei Hou. *China's Supreme Court*. London: Routledge, 2013.

Kieschnick, John. *The Impact of Buddhism on Chinese Material Culture*. Princeton, NJ: Princeton University Press, 2003.

Knapp, Ronald, Jonathan Spence, and Chester Ong. *Chinese Houses: The Architectural Heritage of a Nation*. North Clarendon, VT: Tuttle, 2006.

Kong, Bo. *China's International Petroleum Policy*. Santa Barbara, CA: ABC-CLIO, 2010.

Kong, Travis. *Chinese Male Homosexualities: Memba, Tongzhi and Golden Boy*. London: Routledge, 2012.

Kuhn, Dieter. *Chinese Silk: The Culture and Civilization of China*. New Haven, CT: Yale University Press, 2012.

Kurlantzick, Joshua. *Charm Offensive: How China's Soft Power Is Transforming the World*. New Haven, CT: Yale University Press, 2007.

Kynge, James. *China Shakes the World: A Titan's Rise and Troubled Future—and the Challenge for America*. New York: Houghton, 2006.

Lampton, David. *Following the Leader: Ruling China, from Deng Xiaoping to Xi Jinping*. Berkeley: University of California Press, 2014.

Larmer, Brook. *Operation Yao Ming: The Chinese Sports Empire, American Big Business, and the Making of a NBA Superstar*. New York: Gotham, 2005.

Lau, Frederick. *Music in China: Experiencing Music, Expressing Culture*. Oxford, UK: Oxford University Press, 2007.

Lau, H. *Chinese Chess: An Introduction to China's Ancient Game of Strategy*. North Clarendon, VT: Tuttle, 2003.

Lau, Joseph, and Howard Goldblatt. *The Columbia Anthology of Modern Chinese Literature*. New York: Columbia University Press, 2007.

Li, Nan, ed. *Chinese Civil-Military Relations: The Transformation of the People's Liberation Army*. London, UK: Routledge, 2006.

Li, Ruru. *The Soul of Beijing Opera: Theatrical Creativity and Continuity in the Changing World*. Hong Kong: Hong Kong University Press, 2010.

Li, Xiaobing. *Civil Liberties in China*. Santa Barbara, CA: ABC-CLIO, 2010.

Li, Xiaobing. *A History of the Modern Chinese Army*. Lexington: University of Kentucky Press, 2007.

Li, Xiaobing, and Xiansheng Tian, eds. *Evolution of Power: China's Struggle, Survival, and Success*. Lanham, MD: Lexington, 2014.

Li, Zhengping. *Chinese Wine: Introduction to Chinese Culture.* Cambridge, UK: Cambridge University Press, 2011.

Lian, Xi. *Redeemed by Fire: The Rise of Popular Christianity in Modern China.* New Haven, CT: Yale University Press, 2010.

Lieberthal, Kenneth. *Governing China: From Revolution to Reform.* New York: Norton, 2003.

Lin, Justin Yifu. *Demystifying the Chinese Economy.* Cambridge, UK: Cambridge University Press, 2011.

Liu, C. *A Critical History of New Music in China.* Hong Kong: Chinese University Press, 2010.

Liu, Junru. *Chinese Food.* 3rd ed. Cambridge, UK: Cambridge University Press, 2011.

Lorge, Peter. *Chinese Martial Arts: From Antiquity to the Twenty-first Century.* Cambridge, UK: Cambridge University Press, 2011.

Loyalka, Michelle. *Eating Bitterness: Stories from the Front Lines of China's Great Urban Migration.* Berkeley: University of California Press, 2013.

Lu, Hong, and Terance Miethe. *China's Death Penalty: History, Law and Contemporary Practices.* London: Routledge, 2007.

Lubman, Stanley. *Bird in a Cage: Legal Reform in China after Mao.* Stanford, CA: Stanford University Press, 2002.

Maciocia, Giovanni. *The Foundations of Chinese Medicine: A Comprehensive Text for Acupuncturists and Herbalists.* London: Churchill Livingstone, 2005.

Mann, Susan. *Gender and Sexuality in Modern Chinese History.* Cambridge, UK: Cambridge University Press, 2011.

Marolt, Peter, and David Herold, eds. *China Online: Locating Society in Online Spaces.* London: Routledge, 2014.

McGregor, Richard. *The Party: The Secret World of China's Communist Rulers.* New York: Harper, 2012.

Meng, Jinmei. *On the Decriminalization of Sex Work in China: HIV and Patients' Rights.* London: Palgrave, 2013.

Midler, Paul. *Poorly Made in China: An Insider's Account of the China Production Game.* Hoboken, NJ: Wiley, 2011.

Miller, Tom. *China's Urban Billion: The Story behind the Biggest Migration in Human History.* London: Zed, 2012.

Mittler, Barbara. *A Newspaper for China? Power, Identity, and Change in Shanghai's News Media, 1872–1912.* Cambridge, MA: Harvard University Press, 2004.

Morgan, John, and Bin Wu, eds. *Higher Education Reform in China: Beyond the Expansion.* London: Routledge, 2011.

Moskowitz, Marc. *Go Nation: Chinese Masculinities and the Game of Weiqi in China.* Berkeley: University of California Press, 2013.

Moyo, Dambisa. *Winner Take All: China's Race for Resources and What It Means for the World.* New York: Basic Books, 2012.

Mühlhahn, Klaus. *Criminal Justice in China: A History.* Cambridge, MA: Harvard University Press, 2009.

Mullaney, Thomas. *Coming to Terms with the Nation: Ethnic Classification in Modern China.* Berkeley: University of California Press, 2011.

Nie, Jing-Bao. *Behind the Silence: Chinese Voices on Abortion.* Boulder, CO: Rowman & Littlefield, 2005.

Ody, Penelope. *The Chinese Medicine Bible: The Definitive Guide to Holistic Healing.* New York: Sterling, 2011.

Osburg, John. *Anxious Wealth: Money and Morality Among China's New Rich.* Stanford, CA: Stanford University Press, 2013.

Otis, Eileen. *Markets and Bodies: Women, Service Work, and the Making of Inequality in China.* Stanford, CA: Stanford University Press, 2011.

Ownby, David. *Falun Gong and the Future of China.* Oxford, UK: Oxford University Press, 2008.

Pegg, Carole. *Mongolian Music, Dance, and Oral Narrative: Performing Diverse Identities.* Seattle: University of Washington Press, 2001.

Penny, Benjamin. *The Religion of Falun Gong.* Chicago: University of Chicago Press, 2012.

Pickowicz, Paul. *China on Film: A Century of Exploration, Confrontation, and Controversy.* Boulder, CO: Rowman & Littlefield, 2011.

Potter, Pitman. *The Chinese Legal System: Globalization and Local Legal Culture.* London: Routledge, 2001.

Pringle, Tim. *Trade Unions in China: The Challenge of Labor Unrest.* London: Routledge, 2011.

Rein, Shaun. *The End of Cheap China: Economic and Cultural Trends That Will Disrupt the World.* Hoboken, NJ: Wiley, 2014.

Riley, Jo. *Chinese Theatre and the Actor in Performance.* Cambridge, UK: Cambridge University Press, 2006.

Roach, Stephen. *Unbalanced: The Codependency of America and China.* New Haven, CT: Yale University Press, 2014.

Rolandsen, Unn. *Leisure and Power in Urban China: Everyday Life in a Chinese City.* London: Routledge, 2011.

Rossabi, Morris. *Governing China's Multiethnic Frontiers.* Seattle: University of Washington Press, 2004.

Saich, Tony. *Governance and Politics of China.* London: Palgrave, 2011.

Sang, Tze-Lan. *The Emerging Lesbian: Female Same-Sex Desire in Modern China.* Chicago: University of Chicago Press, 2003.

Santoro, Michael. *China 2020: How Western Business Can—and Should—Influence Social and Political Change in the Coming Decade.* Ithaca, NY: Cornell University Press, 2009.

Schell, Orville, and John Delury. *Wealth and Power: China's Long March to the Twenty-First Century.* New York: Random, 2013.

Searle, Mike. *Colliding Continents: A Geological Exploration of the Himalaya, Karakoram, and Tibet.* New York: Oxford University Press, 2013.

Seligman, Scott. *Chinese Business Etiquette: A Guide to Protocol, Manners, and Culture in the People's Republic of China.* New York: Grand Central, 1999.

Shakya, Tsering. *The Dragon in the Land of Snows: A History of Modern Tibet since 1947.* New York: Penguin, 2000.

Shambaugh, David. *Modernizing China's Military: Progress, Problems, and Prospects.* Berkeley: University of California Press, 2002.

Shen, Helen. *Introduction to Standard Chinese Pinyin System*. Beijing: Language and Culture University Press, 2007.

Shen, Yipeng. *Public Discourses of Contemporary China: The Narration of the Nation in Popular Literatures, Film, and Television*. London: Palgrave, 2015.

Shirk, Susan. *Changing Media, Changing China*. Oxford, UK: Oxford University Press, 2010.

Spence, Jonathan. *The Search for Modern China*. New York: Norton, 2012.

Steinberg, James, and Michael O'Hanlon. *Strategic Reassurance and Resolve: U.S.-China Relations in the Twenty-first Century*. Princeton, NJ: Princeton University Press, 2014.

Stern, Rachel. *Environmental Litigation in China: A Study in Political Ambivalence*. New York: Cambridge University Press, 2013.

Sun, Chaofen. *Chinese: A Linguistic Introduction*. Cambridge, UK: Cambridge University Press, 2006.

Temple, Robert, and Joseph Needham. *The Genius of China: 3,000 Years of Science, Discovery, and Invention*. Rochester, NY: Inner Traditions, 2007.

Thompson, Gerry. *The Guide to Chinese Horoscopes: The Twelve Animal Signs—Personality and Aptitude Relationships*. London: Watkins, 2012.

Tsang, Eileen Yuk-Ha. *The New Middle Class in China: Consumption, Politics and the Market Economy*. London: Palgrave, 2014.

Unschuld, Paul. *Medicine in China: A History of Ideas*. Berkeley: University of California Press, 2010.

Vainker, Shelagh. *Chinese Silk: A Cultural History*. New Brunswick, NJ: Rutgers University Press, 2004.

Veeck, Gregory et al. *China's Geography: Globalization and the Dynamics of Political, Economic, and Social Change*. Boulder, CO: Rowman & Littlefield, 2011.

Walter, Carl, and Howie Fraser. *Red Capitalism: The Fragile Financial Foundation of China's Extraordinary Rise*. Hoboken, NJ: Wiley, 2012.

Wang, Xiaolin, Limin Wang, and Yan Wang. *The Quality of Growth and Poverty Reduction in China*. New York: Springer, 2014.

Wasserstrom, Jeffrey. *China in the 21st Century: What Everyone Needs to Know*. New York: Oxford University Press, 2010.

Watts, Franklin. *Population 1.3 Billion: China Becomes a Super Superpower*. New York: Scholastic, 2009.

Wedeman, Andrew. *Double Paradox: Rapid Growth and Rising Corruption in China*. Ithaca, NY: Cornell University Press, 2012.

White, Tyrene. *China's Longest Campaign: Birth Planning in the People's Republic, 1949–2005*. Ithaca, NY: Cornell University Press, 2006.

Whiting, Susan. *Power and Wealth in Rural China: The Political Economy of Institutional Change*. Cambridge, UK: Cambridge University Press, 2006.

Xu, Chengbei. *Peking Opera: Introduction to Chinese Culture*. New York: Columbia University Press, 2012.

Yan, Xuetong. *Ancient Chinese Thought, Modern Chinese Power*. Princeton, NJ: Princeton University Press, 2013.

Yang, Fenggang. *Religion in China: Survival and Revival under Communist Rule*. Oxford, UK: Oxford University Press, 2011.

Yang, Guobin. *The Power of the Internet in China: Citizen Activism Online*. New York: Columbia University Press, 2011.

Yang, Huilin. *China, Christianity, and the Question of Culture*. Waco, TX: Baylor University Press, 2014.

Yang, Lihui, and Deming An. *Handbook of Chinese Mythology*. Oxford, UK: Oxford University Press, 2008.

Zhang, Dainian, and Edmund Ryden. *Key Concepts in Chinese Philosophy*. New Haven, CT: Yale University Press, 2000.

Zhang, Li. *In Search of Paradise: Middle-class Living in a Chinese Metropolis*. Ithaca, NY: Cornell University Press, 2010.

Zhang, Li. *Strangers in the City: Reconfigurations of Space, Power, and Social Networks within China's Floating Population*. Stanford, CA: Stanford University Press, 2002.

Zheng, Tiantian. *Red Lights: The Lives of Sex Workers in Post-socialist China*. Minneapolis: University of Minnesota Press, 2009.

Zhu, Ying. *Two Billion Eyes: The Story of China Central Television*. New York: New Press, 2012.

INDEX

ABOUT THE AUTHOR

Xiaobing Li is a professor and chair of the Department of History and Geography and director of the Western Pacific Institute at the University of Central Oklahoma. Dr. Li is the author or coauthor of several recent books, including *China's Battle for Korea* (2014), *Evolution of Power* (2013), *Modern Chinese Legal Reform* (2013), *China at War* (2012), *Civil Liberties in China* (2010), *Voices from the Vietnam War* (2010), *A History of the Modern Chinese Army* (2009), *Taiwan in the 21st Century* (2005), *Voices from the Korean War* (2004), and *Mao's Generals Remember Korea* (2000).